CONSTANTINE
AND THE CITIES

EMPIRE AND AFTER

Series Editor: Clifford Ando

A complete list of books in the series
is available from the publisher.

CONSTANTINE
AND THE CITIES

IMPERIAL AUTHORITY
AND CIVIC POLITICS

NOEL LENSKI

PENN

UNIVERSITY OF PENNSYLVANIA PRESS

PHILADELPHIA

Published by
University of Pennsylvania Press
Philadelphia, Pennsylvania 19104–4112
www.upenn.edu/pennpress

Printed in the United States of America on acid-free paper
1 3 5 7 9 10 8 6 4 2

Library of Congress Cataloging-in-Publication Data
Lenski, Noel, author.
Constantine and the cities : imperial authority and civic politics / Noel Lenski.
    pages : maps ; cm. — (Empire and after)
    ISBN 978-0-8122-4777-0 (alk. paper)
    1. Constantine I, Emperor of Rome, –337.   2. Constantine I, Emperor of Rome, –337—
Influence.   3. Rome—History—Constantine I, the Great, 306–337.   4. Rome—Politics
and government—284–476.   5. Rome—Religion.   6. Power (Social sciences)—Rome—
History.   7. Social change—Rome—History.   8. Christianity and politics—Rome—
History.   I. Title. II. Series: Empire and after.
    DG315.L46 2016
    937′.08—dc23
                                                                    2015022966

For Paul
From whom I have learned much

CONTENTS

~

LIST OF MAPS

Many Faces of Constantine

Constantine's Past

Within two years of Constantine's death in 337, Eusebius of Caesarea put the finishing touches on his *Life of the Blessed Emperor Constantine*, the single best source we have for understanding this pivotal ruler.[1] Eusebius was perhaps Constantine's greatest admirer and was unstinting in his praise. He portrays his subject as a latter-day Moses: born to nobility but raised among tyrants, he led his holy people out of the darkness of persecution and into the brilliant light of cosmic victory. Not only had Constantine defeated his every rival with the help of God, he had gone on to wrest concord from the incipient chaos of doctrinal bickering and had begun to point the way toward the final triumph of Christian truth over pagan and Jewish falsehood throughout the *oikoumene*. Half history, half panegyric, the *Life of Constantine* leaves unsaid anything that would have compromised Constantine's reputation—his ruthless land grab of his colleague Licinius's territory in 316, his murder of his own son and wife, his baptism at the hands of the Arianizing bishop Eusebius of Nicomedia. Instead it leaves to posterity not so much a biography as a hagiography of the first Christian emperor.[2]

If the story had stopped here, we might have had no clear idea of just how complex and difficult a subject Constantine is. But, fortunate for us if not Eusebius himself, the *Life* was used by few readers in the years to come, and even those who encountered it—especially Socrates and Sozomen—were so keenly aware of its shortcomings that they spent a good deal of effort critiquing and correcting it. Meanwhile, within a generation, a very different Constantine began to emerge from an altogether different set of authors.[3] The first and most important of these was Constantine's nephew—and imperial successor—Julian, who took great pleasure in assaulting his uncle's reputation throughout his oeuvre, and particularly in his satire *The Caesars*. He takes Constantine to task as a braggart whose defeats of rival emperors were insignificant and whose barbarian victories were far surpassed by those of his more illustrious predecessors.[4] He was given to primping and vanity and was obsessed primarily with greed and luxury (*truphē*), the goddess Julian claims he most favored.[5] Above all, he and his sons were savage toward their own kindred, whom they murdered ruthlessly, necessitating Constantine's conversion to Jesus, who alone among the gods forgave him his unthinkable crimes.[6]

This storyline was in turn picked up and elaborated by the pagan Eunapius of Sardis, whose *Histories* are now lost, although their content is largely preserved in the *New History* of the early sixth-century historian Zosimus. Zosimus offers a complete but tendentious account of Constantine's reign in his second book, which charges the emperor with illegitimate birth, diminishes his military accomplishments, mocks his administrative reforms, and attacks him for lavishing wealth on Constantinople, a city seething with wasteful luxury (*truphē*).[7] He is even more caustic than Julian against Constantine's religious policies, and specifically his refusal to perform sacrifice to Jupiter Capitolinus and his failure to continue the tradition of offering Rome's age-old Secular Games.[8] Above all, Zosimus further develops Julian's attack on Constantine's murder of his son and wife and its effects on his decision to seek reconciliation with the Christian god.[9] Within a generation of his death, then, a tradition of what some have termed "anti-Constantinianism" had arisen, and this came to be elaborated in the decades to come, offering us a portrait of Constantine that stood in direct opposition to that of Eusebius.[10]

A related stream of negative press can be found in a different source tradition, originally dating to the now lost "Enmannsche Kaisergeschichte," which was used by Eutropius, also a pagan, although he wrote for the Christian emperor Valens. For Eutropius, Constantine was of questionable birth; he cruelly and unjustly murdered his own relatives; and he issued laws that were excessive and severe.[11] The same tradition was followed by the scrupulously Christian Jerome in his continuation of Eusebius's *Chronicle*, where Constantine is criticized roundly for illegitimate birth, for murdering his brother-in-law Licinius, his nephew Licinianus, his son Crispus, and his wife Fausta, for robbing the empire of its wealth to build Constantinople, and above all for submitting to baptism at the hands of an Arian.[12] It is also picked up by the early fifth-century Christian historian Orosius, who criticizes Constantine for murdering his kin and initiating wars.[13] Coming as they do from authors with no overtly religious motivation for attacking the first Christian emperor, these accounts offer a third perspective on Constantine and thus begin to reveal just how multifarious were the reactions to this complex figure.

By the mid-fifth century these conflicting viewpoints were brought into dialogue when Sozomen used chronological arguments to refute Eunapius's charges that Constantine had converted after killing his son in hopes of expiating his crime: Crispus was executed in the twentieth year of Constantine's reign, long after his conversion; moreover, Crispus himself was listed in the headings of a number of pro-Christian laws to which Sozomen had access.[14] Sozomen also touched on the question of Constantine's baptism by the Arianizing bishop Eusebius of Nicomedia by blaming the emperor's half-sister Constantia for effecting this ill-fated association and thus dissociating Constantine from his theology.[15]

Around the same period, further engagements with the negative tradition were launched from less scientific quarters. No later than the early sixth century, and likely a half-century or more before that, a legend arose that Constantine had converted not after his famous vision of the cross, but thanks to the good offices of the Roman Pope Sylvester, who had miraculously cured him of a debilitating skin disease: still a heathen, Constantine had been counseled by pagan priests to bathe in the blood of infants to remedy his malady but refused; after experiencing a vision of the apostles Peter and Paul, he made contact with Sylvester, who convinced him to receive Christian baptism; this rid him of his illness and convinced him to dedicate himself to Christianity.[16] This story simultaneously detached Constantine's conversion from connections with the murder of his son, relocated his baptism to a context where it could be carried out by the very touchstone of orthodoxy (the Pope), and elevated the stature of the western church by making Rome the wellspring of imperial support for Christianity. In the eighth century the legend spawned another story that Constantine had offered Sylvester exclusive control over the city of Rome, its Italian territories, the eastern provinces, and even Judaea, a legend now known as the "Donation of Constantine." A pious invention of the papacy, this legend was clearly introduced to confirm the supremacy of the Roman see both over the Lombards of northern Italy and over the eastern church.[17] Constantine's legend had thus taken on a life of its own. The emperor had metamorphosed from a site of contention between pagans and Christians—or alternatively between rival groups of Christians—into an archetypal symbol of religious authority whose narrative could be rewritten and supplemented to suit the shifting valences of historical circumstance.[18]

In a renowned essay of 1440 Lorenzo Valla put paid to the "Donation" legend and opened a new era in Constantinian studies that has brought us considerably closer to understanding the emperor and his policies in their own context.[19] It is thus surprising to learn that, despite considerable advances in source criticism, chronology, and critical method, we are in many ways no closer to arriving at a "definitive" picture of Constantine than we ever were. To understand how this is so, it is worth examining, even if only briefly, the perspectives of at least some of Constantine's most important interpreters from the mid-nineteenth century up to the present. Superficial though it must be, such a survey will give an impression both of the development of approaches to Constantine in modern scholarship and also of the sheer breadth of opinion that continues to prevail.

Modern Constantines

Such a survey must begin with the Swiss scholar J. Burckhardt, who offered the first truly critical look at the full range of evidence available. From this vantage point Burckhardt conceived of Constantine as a sly and cynical impresario who exploited the power of the church in order to promote his own political program without ever convincing himself of the validity of Christian religion.[20] This image stands in open contrast with the Constantine of Burckhardt's younger contemporary, O. Seeck, according to whom Constantine was a sincere war hero whose trust in his own good fortune was ultimately transformed into a belief that he had been sent as the earthly agent of the heavenly god.[21] Similarly sober Constantines prevail in the works of mid-twentieth-century scholars like A. H. M. Jones and R. MacMullen, who accepted the earnestness of Constantine's religious convictions, but depicted him as a credulous and often bumbling bully, lacking in discipline and often heedless of the consequences of his impulsive actions.[22] From yet another perspective, H. Grégoire raised objections to Constantine's story of conversion altogether. He argued that it was rather Licinius who initiated philo-Christian imperial politics in the 310s and that Constantine converted only after taking control of Licinius's domains in the East, where the power of the Christian movement could be exploited to political advantage.[23] This understanding continued to form the core of arguments made by J. Bleicken as recently as 1992.[24] From the mid-nineteenth to the mid-twentieth century, then, most scholars put little credence in a genuinely Christian Constantine, preferring instead to hold political motives or simple fatuousness responsible for what proved almost by accident to have been the emperor's momentous decision to convert.

Opposition to this viewpoint was, however, expressed by N. H. Baynes already by 1929. His Constantine experienced a sincere conversion and became a deeply religious Christian who strove to reenact his personal convictions at the global level by tirelessly working to Christianize his subjects.[25] Based as it was on the wealth of Constantinian documents preserved in Christian sources, this viewpoint exercised tremendous influence by the mid-twentieth century and came to enjoy widespread support from scholars like A. Alföldi, S. Calderone, and above all T. D. Barnes.[26] Indeed, Barnes, who is surely the most important scholar of Constantine still publishing, has been on something of a crusade to use the tools of scientific history to prove the decisiveness of Constantine's conversion in 312 and to argue that the emperor became rigidly intransigent against non-Christians from 324 onward.[27] In recent years this unquestionably Christian Constantine has been presented in even more mannered fashion in the studies of C. Odahl and T. Elliott, the latter of whom holds that the emperor had no need for conversion since he had been raised a Christian from childhood.[28]

In the past fifteen years, work has appeared with dizzying rapidity, and in it the trend has been to accept a Christian Constantine but to add shading to his broader outlines by focusing on motifs other than Christianity that served as guideposts for the emperor's life and rule.[29] H. A. Drake, whose work first moved studies on Constantine into a twenty-first-century analytical framework, conceives of a Christian emperor, to be sure, but one ready to seek compromise and concessions in his pursuit of consensus and harmony.[30] K. M. Girardet's Constantine is deeply spiritual, a convert already by 311, who from this point forward became ever more concerned with his role not just as a politician, but above all as a religious leader.[31] Similar is the Constantine of H. Brandt, whose Constantine made a clear "qualitative leap" toward Christianity after his conversion, even if the roots of that conversion—like the roots of most of Constantine's policies—lay in ground well prepared by his tetrarchic predecessors.[32] P. Stephenson outlines an emperor who was riding a rising wave of conversion when he turned to Christianity, and who hoped to use his new religion as a guarantor of military victory.[33] P. Veyne, by contrast, sees Constantine's conversion as a radical but ingenious maneuver that exploited the inherent brilliance of this new religion to set the church on a path toward world dominance.[34]

Nevertheless, these Christian Constantines are by no means the only actors on the stage. Many contemporary scholars cleave to a more spiritually neutral figure, much more interested in politics and rulership than faith or religion. A. Marcone's Constantine is Christian, to be sure, but became so entangled in obsessions with sexual morality, family intrigue, and dynastic politics that he diminished his impact as a standard-bearer for the faith.[35] R. Van Dam conceives of a Constantine who revolutionizes the empire on a number of other fronts without expressing any pronounced concern for Christianity. Standing as a sort of living embodiment of the late Roman Zeitgeist, this Constantine finds his way almost by accident toward a Christian empire that is constructed around him by bishops and biographers.[36] D. Potter's Constantine is a highly sensible ruler with more important matters on his mind than an obsession with religion.[37] The Constantine of J. Harries is by all means Christian but is cautious in his reforms and always willing to compromise in order to maintain tradition and keep the peace.[38] Without denying conversion on some level, these scholars thus refocus attention on aspects of Constantine that pull our gaze away from the classic Constantinian question.

Others view Constantine as a transitional figure whose understanding of Christianity was far from monolithic and who drew just as freely from traditions of ruler cult and sun worship as from Christian theology. M. Wallraff views the abundant evidence for Constantine's attachment to the Sun God as confirmation that he had no firm notion of a clear line between pagan and Christian practice and no strong idea what would distinguish a Christian ruler from his pagan predecessors.[39] According to E. Herrmann-Otto, Constantine's turn toward Christianity was rooted in the failure of the Great Persecution, not his heavenly vision, and his involvement in church politics reflected more the dutiful performance of his traditional role as *pontifex maximus* than his commitment to the faith.[40] O. Schmitt's Constantine hearkens back to that of Seeck in his ignorance of anything but warfare and his astonishing obtuseness about the new religion that apologists like Eusebius and Lactantius ascribe to him.[41] Most recently, J. Bardill's Constantine builds on traditions of divine rulership and solar monotheism in order to reconstruct himself into a new type of leader that could stand as the earthly representative of a new but hardly unique god named Christ.[42] These ambiguous Constantines prove that the early twentieth-century tradition of an emperor only incompletely aware of what it might mean to be a Christian ruler is far from moribund.

This survey, incomplete though it is, gives some fleeting impression of the sheer variety of interpretations that prevail right up to the present. Not surprisingly, most of them focus in one way or another on the question of Christian religion, Constantine's understanding of it, and his commitment to its furtherance. This is true even of those studies by scholars who are by no means convinced that religion was of paramount concern to Constantine. Indeed, struggle though scholars might to escape an eternal return to the problem of Constantine qua *homo religiosus*, for any number of reasons such efforts almost always prove elusive.[43] Nor is this obsession with Constantine's conversion and his efforts to instantiate it at the level of the Roman Empire necessarily a problem, for given the nature of our sources and the magnitude of his conversion (regardless of how we feel about its timing or sincerity), Christianity will likely always remain the central "Constantinian question." Yet on precisely this issue, as this survey has revealed, there remains little accord. The variety of Constantines that came into being in the immediate aftermath of his death and then proliferated into the Middle Ages and beyond shows no signs of diminishing, qualitatively or quantitatively. Constantine simply does not present a single face, a single clear impression.

Composite Constantine

Despite the wide variety of approaches to Constantine just outlined, it is ironically the case that the majority of those who study him conceive of a coherent and unified subject: focusing narrowly on his Christian religiosity, his covert paganism, his ruthless militarism, his administrative scrupulosity, his naive impetuousness, or his political realism, they see in Constantine a figure capable of authoritative definition, provided the proper interpretive strategy is deployed. It is this fundamental assumption, the assumption that an essential Constantine exists and that, once uncovered, its framework can be used as the key to unlock this perennial hermeneutic mystery, that this monograph draws into question.

In the chapters that follow, and particularly Chapters 1–3, I undertake an investigation of Constantine that avoids the pursuit of fixity. In so doing, I build on the interpretive framework of reception theory. This method of analysis, associated in particular with H. R. Jauss, assumes that "the historical consciousness of a given period never exists as a set of openly stated or recorded propositions [but] as a horizon of expectations."[44] Reception theory conceives of art—and by extension all forms of cultural production—not so much as the representation of reality but rather as itself constitutive of reality. The interplay between a work—a poem, a portrait, a panegyric—and the audience that receives it generates meaning that is not merely reflexive of existing social and aesthetic assumptions, but also creates new meanings that arise in the very dialectic between creator and audience. Jauss's theory is particularly useful for explaining the process of aesthetic and cultural *change*, for it focuses attention on the way in which old assumptions and realities are negated as new forms are brought to consciousness.[45]

Jauss's hermeneutic was developed as a tool for literary interpretation, but its methods can also be applied to sociological investigations. In a study entitled "Encoding/Decoding," S. Hall readapted reception theory for the analysis of systems of mass communication.[46] He pointed out that all such systems take their start in subjects whose own horizons are circumscribed both by limitations in their field of knowledge and by assumptions based on their position within the relations of production. In trying to communicate with mass audiences, a subject or authority will encode messages using conventional signs transmitted through existing channels of media. Such signs—words, images, sounds—necessarily flatten, elide, and distort meaning as it was initially conceived by the subject. These signs are then received by mass audiences who are never homogenous and whose knowledge and assumptions never map perfectly onto those of the subject. Because of the ineluctable slippage between signifier and signified as well as the essential disparity between subject and audience, the decoding of these messages *never* follows inevitably from encodings. The recipients of a communication are therefore assigned an active role in its interpretation and in the construction of meaning from the messages they receive.

Readings by mass audiences are of course always multiform and complex. While it would be impossible to account for this heterogeneity fully with a schematic approach, Hall attempts to aggregate the interpretative power of mass audiences into groupings by stressing the role of social positioning. In terms that necessarily oversimplify a complex set of variables, he identifies three types of collective readings:

- The dominant "hegemonic" reading arises when the viewer or reader "takes the connoted meaning . . . and decodes the message in terms of the reference code in which it has been encoded." This reading appears coterminous with what is "natural" and "inevitable" in the context of the hegemonic discourse prevalent in a society.
- The negotiated reading "contains a mixture of adaptive and opposi-tional elements. It acknowledges the legitimacy of the hegemonic defi-nitions to make the grand significations while, at a more restricted, situational level, it makes its own ground rules."
- The oppositional reading "detotalises the message in the preferred code in order to retotalise it within some alternative framework of reference." Here the reader finds him- or herself in a social position opposed to that of the hegemonic discourse and in response to this dissonance interprets messages—consciously or subconsciously—in terms contrary to those used to encode them.

Hall also emphasizes that a number of assumptions and parameters are built into the process at the *professional* level—that is, by those who do the encoding. These are not the subject or authority issuing the communication as such, but rather those responsible for disseminating messages for them—in antiquity these were imperial panegyrists, poets, legal sec-retaries, moneyers, sculptors, artists, and so forth. These too engage in an interpretive process in dialectic with the rulers and policy makers on whose orders they operate. Even in the process of encoding, then, the subject or authority is at least one stage—often several—removed from the professionals whom they charge with transmit-ting their messages.

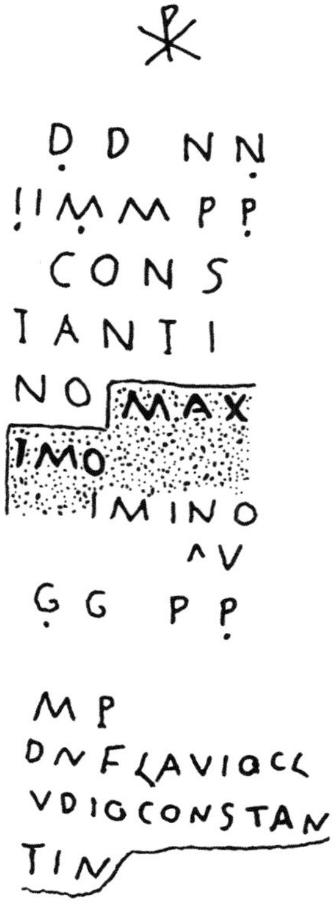

FIGURE 1. Milestone inscription of Beni Fouda, twenty-five kilometers southwest of Djemila. [chi-rho symbol] *DD(ominis) nn(ostris)* / *IImmpp(eratoribus)*/*Cons*/*tanti*/*no* [[*et Gal(erio)*]]/ [[*Val(erio)*]]/[*Max*]*imino*/ [[*PP(iis) FF(elicibus)*]] *Au*/*gg(ustis) PP(erpetuis) m(ille) p(assuum)* [I]/*D(omino) N(ostro) Flavio Cl*/*audio Constan*/*tin[o]* [II], datable between January 1, 313, when Constantine and Maximinus Daia began serving as co-Consuls, and April 30, 313, when Maximinus was defeated by Licinius—who took his place as Consul—and his name was hammered out and replaced with Constantine's new title, *Maximus. AE* 2000: 1801. Drawing by P. Lenski, after Salama, "Les provinces d'Afrique," p. 156, Fig. 13.

A single example from the Constantinian world might serve to bring this abstract schema into the realm of the concrete. The consummate Constantinian symbol, the labarum, was hardly subject to simple or monolithic interpretation when it was first produced.[47] Our earliest account of it, from the well-connected court apologist Lactantius, writing in 315, describes its original form not as that of a chi-rho/"Christogram" (☧)—a schematic representation of the first two letters of the name "Christos" in Greek—but as a "staurogram" (⳨)—a tau cross surmounted by a half circle.[48] J. Bardill has made the case that the staurogram was indeed the symbolic form Constantine first adopted in response to his vision and dream (however these are interpreted), and that it was only later reshaped into the chi-rho, which is first described in detail by Eusebius in his *Life of Constantine*, written after the emperor's death.[49] In support of his argument, Bardill has even identified iconographic representations of the staurogram that appear to date to a Constantinian context. Nevertheless, the first datable appearance of the labarum in an epigraphic context—on two inscriptions from North African milestones dated to early 313—represents not the staurogram but the Christogram (Fig. 1).[50] So too with the coinage, for a Christogram is also depicted on the front roundel of Constantine's helmet in the famous Ticinum medallion, which is usually dated to 315—the same year that Lactantius was writing (Fig. 2).[51] This means that this much heralded symbol, so inextricably tied to Constantine, was from its beginnings encoded in dimorphic form and thus susceptible to variant interpretations.[52]

To add to this ambiguity, as we shall see in Chapter 1, while the labarum occasionally appears in prominent positions on Constantinian coins (above all on military standards), for the most part throughout Constantine's reign it remains

FIGURE 2. Obverse of the Ticinum Medallion: IMP CONSTANT–INVS PF AVG. Constantine facing, holding the bridle of a horse in his right hand and a shield with the *lupa Romana* in his left. The frontal medallion on his helmet features a chi-rho. *RIC* 7: Ticinum 36. Hirmer Verlag Munich, reproduced with permission.

FIGURE 3. Obverse: IMP CONSTANT-INVS AVG. Constantine helmeted, facing left with spear in right hand and shield in left. Note the chi-rho on the side of his high-crested helmet. Reverse: VICTORIAE LAETAE PRINC PERP. Two victories facing one another holding a shield inscribed VOT/PR. *RIC* 7: Siscia 61. Kunsthistorisches Museum Vienna.

FIGURE 4. Obverse: VRBS–ROMA. Rome helmeted, facing left. Reverse: She-wolf suckling twins with starbursts and chi-rho in the field above. *RIC* 6: Arles 385. Photo by Victor Clark, reproduced with permission.

FIGURE 5. Bronze coin similar to Figure 3, but Constantine's helmet features starbursts and no chi-rho. *RIC* 7: Siscia 61. Kunsthistorisches Museum Vienna.

discreetly tucked away on the emperor's helmet (Fig. 3) or even in the coin "field," the space beside the primary figure or figures represented on the reverse (Fig. 4). Given that Constantine's coins regularly display a variety of ornaments on his helmet—starbursts are much more common than the chi-rho (Fig. 5)—and that Constantinian coin fields are regularly populated with a variety of symbols other than the Christogram (symbols generally interpreted as minters marks with little further referential value), it has been hotly debated just how much significance Constantine's moneyers attached to the Christogram.[53] It is unclear, in other words, whether the moneyers believed this was *the* consummate Constantinian symbol, or simply one of many symbols of varying import. Already at the stage of encoding, then, this sign was imbued with ambiguities—regarding both its form and its significance—by the *professionals* who were responsible for transmitting Constantine's message to the broader public.

The labarum's interpretive horizons then expanded considerably in the face of the various audiences that encountered it. Lactantius and Eusebius, who were Christian and favorable toward Constantine and were thus inclined to offer a *dominant* reading, connect the labarum with the name of Christ. Both also associate it with Constantine's military successes. Here again, however, we witness another interpretive dichotomy that creates slippage between the sign and its interpretation: in addition to its possible religious meanings, the chi-rho was from its beginnings also a military symbol, and although these two valences can be connected, as they were by Eusebius and Lactantius, they could also be separated. In other words, some will have seen the labarum as simply another in a long line of military ensigns.[54] Nor were these the only possible readings of this undeniably ambiguous sign. Indeed, the staurogram and to a lesser degree the Christogram bear an obvious resemblance to the Egyptian ankh (☥), a symbol of life associated with the Sun God Ra for centuries before the arrival of Constantine.[55] Constantine's Egyptian subjects and those familiar with Egyptian iconography were thus likely to have seen in the labarum a further confirmation of Constantine's well-documented attachment to the divine Sun.[56]

From this complex of possible meanings, his subjects were free to choose some while rejecting others and thus to offer their own *negotiated* readings of the sign. Pagan and Jewish soldiers, while likely willing to acknowledge the military power of the labarum, did not necessarily assume its potency derived from the Christian or even the Egyptian pantheon. Meanwhile, those who opposed Constantine altogether might have seen the labarum as nothing less than an abomination: an abuse of an ancient Egyptian religious sign; the threatening and decentering encroachment of a Christian symbol into the world of imperial iconography; or even a meaningless assemblage of markings with no power whatsoever. These *oppositional* readings were surely present among some readers, even if we have no strong trace of them in our source record, which is obviously biased toward Christian texts.

Over time, of course, the interpretive horizons of the labarum narrowed, so that by the late fourth century few would have challenged the Christian or military signification of the symbol. But even this late, not all would have accepted it as an indicator of imperial legitimacy. This is true a fortiori in the context of Constantine's reign, when the labarum and its interpretation were very much up for grabs and depended as much on historical contingencies—the success or failure of Constantine's armies; the durability or transience of his conversion; the acceptance or rejection of that conversion by his subjects—as on the varied and competing readings of its ineluctable dimorphism and its undeniable polyvalence. In the chapters that follow, I hope to unfold similarly multifarious and competing interpretations of a variety of Constantinian signs and pronouncements. In so doing, I hope to map out a contingent and therefore less stable, but also more genuine reading of the emperor.

Law as Communicative Action

This book will thus attempt to investigate Constantine as a composite of readings both by the message makers who created signs, symbols, speeches, and laws for the court, and also by those subjects of Constantine who received them. It will thus proceed from two interrelated assumptions that will affect every reading that follows:

1. *The narrative of Constantine's life was very much a collective affair,* constructed not just from his own self-assertion and self-description but also from the interpretations of his many subjects who wished to exert their own influence over the unfolding discourse that was the emperor. When we view a statue or coin or read an inscription or panegyric, we cannot assume that these offer unfiltered windows onto Constantine's own narrative as he would have told it. Even laws, the most manifest evidence of imperial power crystalized as written discourse, involved complex processes of negotiation between the ruler and his subjects, and at times involved very little input from the emperor himself, who was deluged with business and entrusted much of the process of legal production to bureaucrats.[57]
2. No emperor was ever a static and essential agent, a sort of unmoved mover. Rather, for emperors as for all rulers, *power derived from intersubjective processes* that entailed input and reaction from the ruler himself, but also and in turn counter-input from his many relatives, administrators, soldiers, subjects, opponents, and enemies. In other words, power must be treated as a complex equation with multiple variables that cannot be resolved with reference to the ruler alone. This is not to deny that the emperor's power was vast, but any discussion of that power must factor in the fundamental reality that it was a matter of negotiation and mutual agreement—of consent, but also of dispute.

Although this study attempts to present Constantine from a variety of perspectives, it does not sidestep the fact that Constantine was himself an active agent—the best-documented and certainly the single most important player—in this process. In other words, while accepting the basic premise that our understanding of Constantine is necessarily conditioned by third-party interpretation and by his dialogic engagement with his subjects, the book also builds on the abundant writings left by Constantine himself in order to explore his agency in the discursive process of governing the empire. In examining Constantine's pronouncements and above all the legal regulations and normative utterances he issued, it relies especially on the sociological theory of J. Habermas. In his *Theory of Communicative Action,* Habermas develops an explanation of collective social practice that can be used to explain how Constantine participated in the vast intersubjective enterprise that was the Roman Empire.[58]

Habermas's theory is broad ranging, and much of it stretches beyond the purview of this book, but that part of most use here examines the way in which social activity is structured through discourse. In the third chapter of his work, Habermas builds on speech act theory as expounded by J. L. Austin and J. R. Searle.[59] Austin and Searle developed their theory to explain how words mediate, constitute, and affect lived realities. They build on the notion that all speech acts have an illocutionary force—the power to communicate based in their syntactical structure and its formal relation to the rules of language—and that some also have a perlocutionary intent—a purposive object, which can be achieved only if the speech act is successful. The aim of purposive speech acts is not only to communicate a message, but also to accomplish some end. This could be everything from affirming a constative understanding ("Constantine is emperor") to compelling or prohibiting a particular behavior ("Stop all sacrifice!"). Nevertheless, not every speech act is successful, for speech acts ultimately constitute an offer from a speaker to a hearer that can be either accepted or rejected.[60] The hearer determines his or her reaction to the offer based on assumptions about the validity both of the speaker and of his utterance. The hearer may reject the speaker's offer:

- Because he or she does not accept the *authority* of the speaker as valid: "You have no *right* to tell me to stop sacrificing."
- Because he or she does not accept the *existential preconditions* that would permit him to act on the speaker's utterance: "If I stop sacrificing, the gods will punish me."
- Because he or she does not accept the *sincerity* of the speaker's intent: "Surely you don't really expect me to stop sacrificing."[61]

Habermas integrates Austin's theory of "how to do things with words" into a broader sociological framework through the notion of what he calls the "lifeworld."[62] For an individual, this consists of: (1) objective experience of the external world; (2) intersubjective social experience of other individuals; and (3) inner-subjective personal experience. Societies succeed in integrating individual members into a collective whole only to the extent that the lifeworlds of these individuals overlap and coalesce around shared background convictions commonly regarded as unproblematic—what anthropologists would call pre-reflective knowledge. The successful social collective then reproduces itself through a continuation and renewal of traditions based on this pre-reflective knowledge, which, however, develops constantly along an ever shifting horizon of evolving preconceptions. In the process, the integration of the collective lifeworld coordinates actions by way of interpersonal relations that are regulated through both social and systemic structures. The latter include nonlinguistic modes of interchange like economic exchange. The former, by contrast, is always linguistically mediated and numbers among its fundamental manifestations religion—especially in premodern societies.

The world of Late Antiquity was, of course, an epoch in which commonly shared religious truths had become sites of public contention. Pre-reflective knowledge about the nature of the divine had, in other words, been problematized and was no longer taken for granted by some groups, most notably the Christians. The empire-wide persecutory regimes that began in the mid-third century and culminated in the Great Persecution of the early fourth had striven to compel conformity with traditions of shared knowledge about the divine.[63] As a reflection of this dysfunction in the collective lifeworld, the growing Christian community bore the brunt of social outrage over shifts in the horizons of what was known to be true. With his conversion, Constantine took sides with the Christian minority and thus found himself at odds with the traditional collective conviction of most of his subjects. The fact that an emperor began enacting through his own lifeworld the rift that had opened up in the collective lifeworld of the broader society presented obvious challenges. Constantine's efforts to resolve this dilemma constitute the primary subject of much of this book beyond the first section.

The peculiarity of Constantine's situation was that, on the political plane, most of his subjects do not appear to have rejected the validity of his claim to rule over them as sovereign. Throughout his reign, his position went largely unchallenged by those over whom he ruled—even if not by those co-rulers with whom he fought civil wars. This meant that his regulatory speech acts as lawgiver were generally fated to be successful, for they were redeemable against the commonly accepted truth that, as emperor, he had every right to direct civic action. Nevertheless, in the period following his conversion, he was operating in a theological space that was noticeably at odds with the horizons of understanding of the majority of the social collective. Where in previous centuries a common set of assumptions about the nature of the divine had been shared between emperor and subjects, Constantine's conversion put his religious worldview at odds with collective truths shared by most of his subjects—truths about cosmology (Olympian versus Judeo-Christian), ritual (the value of sacrifice and idolatry), and theology (above all, polytheism). Thus, although his authority to issue normative regulations was accepted as valid, his claims regarding the divine authority that undergirded his imperial authority became open to challenge.

In the face of this disconnect, Constantine could have attempted to assert the validity claims of his religious ideas with imperative speech acts cast in the language of legal obligations that used the threat of sanctions to motivate conformity. Unsurprisingly, in some instances he did just this—at places like Heliopolis, Aphaca, or Aegeae, he actively intervened using legal imperatives prohibiting specific forms of worship and even ordering the destruction of pagan holy sites. More commonly, however, Constantine engaged his subjects in a dialogue that invited them to use those validity claims that they accepted—his right to rule and to establish a legal framework for civic interaction—in order to test the validity of other claims his subjects may not, initially, have been willing to redeem—that the Christian god was the one true god.

In enacting this process, he was particularly adroit at employing the traditional and fundamental tool of Roman governance, the petition. As we shall see, in instance after instance, he exploited the space opened up for dialogue by his own subjects when they lodged petitions in order to shift the horizons of their expectations in a direction that naturalized Christianity and subsumed it within the sphere of their pre-reflective knowledge. In other words, he built on the universal recognition of his validity claim to be the source for normative authority in order to transform his subjects' viewpoint about the validity of his religious truth claims. Using petition and response, he sought to talk his subjects into talking themselves into becoming Christian.

Constantine and the Cities

The ancient historian perennially faces the problem of sources. The records remaining are so scanty that they resist the sort of study usually undertaken by contemporary social theorists. This is certainly true of Constantine, for while the documentation for his reign is relatively abundant when compared with that for many other Roman rulers, we have very little remaining that would allow us to gauge the contemporary reactions of the vast majority of his subjects. Even the few contemporary responses we do have tend to have been composed by people so closely connected to the emperor that they are more easily identified with what we have called the *professional code* than with the reactions of independent individuals. One thinks, for example, of Eusebius, the Latin panegyrists, or even the poet Optatianus Porphyrius, most of whom had the opportunity to meet Constantine personally and all of whom wrote from a perspective informed by messages emanating from the emperor with the object of disseminating those messages to a wider audience. We do, however, still have some localized, independent responses, not from individuals but rather from cities and their councils. With this in mind, much of this book will examine the interactions between Constantine and the cities of his empire.

The approach taken is related to that of several studies that have used the abundant evidence of communications between cities and rulers recorded on inscriptions or monumentalized in built structures as a medium with which to explore the articulation of power relations. Among the most important of these is the groundbreaking work of J. Ma, *Antiochus III and the Cities of Western Asia Minor*.[64] In this book, Ma demonstrates how power is constructed in the space between monarch and polity in a dynamic process involving the exchange of words. Ma shows how the power of the Hellenistic ruler was not absolute but was negotiated in exchanges mediated by letters, petitions, and decrees. The intersubjective process of communication, which followed a fixed and formal grammar, and which was predicated upon historicizing discourse, literally created the power dynamic we term the Seleucid Empire. That is to say, the formal expression of requests, of claims, and of rights—from both ruler and ruled— were ipso facto constitutive of political reality. This resulted from the fact that power was always a reciprocal dynamic wherein both sides—ruler and subject, king and polity— accepted the limitations of their position, and both therefore assumed that the perpetuation and renewal of power could be maintained only through mutual recognition and ongoing interchange.

So it was with Constantine, whose power was also constituted of reciprocal relationships with the people and polities over whom he claimed authority. Because these latter were key players in the process, he could not impose his will free of negotiation. Thus, although Constantine's reign represents a watershed moment in history due primarily to his choice to convert to Christianity, he alone was by no means responsible for the monumental changes that ensued: he was part of a revolution in which he was a—even the—major actor, but which he only partly controlled. In all that follows, we explore the process of power construction that developed from Constantine's efforts to enact his conversion at the level of empire. We will not essay a biography, a genre that is hardly underrepresented in scholarship and that scarcely needs to be reproduced here. Instead, we will focus on Constantine's efforts to build on existing power relations, existing assumptions about religious and civic ideology, and existing modes of discourse in order to nudge the empire in the direction he had taken by converting.

The book is divided into four parts. The first is focused on communications emanating from the emperor and his message makers. The second examines petitions used by Constantine's subjects to gain something from his court. The third looks at how emperor and subject colluded in the reconstruction of ancient cities into centers of Christian worship. The fourth covers those cities that read Constantine and his communiqués in mediated or even oppositional fashion. Each part consists of several chapters that, taken together, strive to reconstruct the dynamic of imperial power as a dialogue between ruler and ruled.

The book begins by examining the evidence for Constantine's own self-presentation as it can be reconstructed from the material created by those professional message makers whose works are still extant to us, as well as the extant public pronouncements of Constantine himself. The first section is divided into three chapters. In Chapter 1, I use the evidence of inscriptions, portraits, panegyrics, and coins to document the fact that Constantine's public image did not remain constant over time but was subject to significant change. Taking my cue from the four portrait styles commonly identified for the emperor and the four styles of titulature attested in his inscriptions and laws, I articulate four phases that are necessarily schematic and artificial, but which offer snapshots of the competing images Constantine projected of himself: the model tetrarch, the tyrannicide, the champion of the Christian faith, and the divine monarch. The very fact that Constantine can be shown to have made significant shifts in his public presentation helps to explain why his subjects reacted to him in such disparate and even contradictory ways, for once articulated, each persona had a lasting impact on the reception of Constantine as his subjects selected and emphasized those images that best fit their assumptions and desires for their ruler.

The next chapter in this section, Chapter 2, emphasizes instead various constants in Constantine's public self-presentation that counterbalance the picture of ongoing transformation. It begins with his obsession with light as both symbol and embodiment of divine power. This consuming and abiding interest allowed Constantine to bridge the gap between pagan and Christian religious imaginaries, for light was a sign and metaphor that resonated in both thought worlds. Similarly, Constantine's interest in victory, both its concrete achievement on the battlefield and its abstract expression as a representation of power, remained a bedrock value throughout his reign. Yet another Constantinian constant was his assumption that he enjoyed a singular and peculiarly intimate relationship with the divine. Finally, dynasty was a matter of ongoing importance, from the earliest days of Constantine's reign, when he focused on his dynastic pedigree, to the last, when he emphasized the authority afforded him by the extension of his dynastic authority to family successors. Interestingly, despite the constancy of these motifs, each was also transformed over time in keeping with the broader transformations manifest in his public image.

The third chapter takes advantage of the abundant material we have that was written by Constantine himself, almost all of it addressing Christian audiences. It begins in Constantine's earliest reign by exploring how his conversion involved the construction of a historical memory cum narrative mandate to defend the Christian religion and impose it upon the empire. This notion was initially adver-

tised in only indirect ways in media intended for broad audiences, but fairly
quickly, indications were given to Christians that the emperor favored their cause.
The argument then turns to the often vaguely defined "highest god" to whom
Constantine so regularly appeals in an effort to learn whether Christians were
given indications that this was in fact their god. Several Constantinian communications state this openly, others indirectly. Further examination of his writings
even shows that he conceived of his Christianity as a sort of pressing mandate, for
he assumed that his own safety and that of his empire depended on his success or
failure in imposing religious rectitude on his subjects. Even so, he clearly reserved
a space for failing to complete this project that allowed him regularly to back
away from the very real but always circumscribed violence he enacted against
pagans, schismatics, and heretics. His belief that God, and not the emperor, was
ultimately responsible for punishing recalcitrants opened opportunities for dialogue with those who refused to fall into line with his new religious agenda and
thereby permitted him to reconcile his zeal for religious conformity with the
messy practicalities of governing a pluralistic empire.

In the second section, the argument moves to the process of dialogue between
Constantine and his cities as mediated through the traditional communicative
form of the petition. The section opens with Chapter 4, which examines in depth
one of the single best pieces of evidence for this, the inscription of Orcistus. It
begins by outlining the system of petition and response that in many ways constituted the bedrock of imperial governance stretching back to the Hellenistic world.
Nevertheless, in the later empire we get evidence that the Roman government was
moving beyond this strictly reactive model and was attempting to direct policy
from the top down. A series of petitions from the reign of Maximinus Daia reveal
how the emperor himself could drive the petitioning process by actively encouraging polities to formulate requests to persecute Christians using a system of
rewards as a motivator. This reality serves as the background to a discussion of
the dossier of petitions to Constantine preserved from Orcistus. This community
had suffered the loss of its civic autonomy to its larger neighbor Nacoleia, a hub
of traditional religion, almost certainly because its populace was overwhelmingly
Christian. In response to Orcistus's request for the restoration of autonomy, Constantine simply turned Maximinus's formula on its head. Instead of encouraging
requests to promote persecution, he encouraged Orcistus to add its strongly pro-
Christian leanings to the list of attributes that had traditionally qualified a community for civic autonomy. By referencing the tiny polity's exclusivist devotion to
Christianity when granting its request for civic status, Constantine thus integrated his new religion into the repertoire of attributes expected of any city worthy of self-governance in the empire.

The fifth chapter continues the same dialogue using another important document in the Constantinian epigraphic dossier, the rescript to the city of Hispellum. This inscription has received intensive study in the scholarship, which has focused particularly on its date. Much more important, however, is the question of what precisely the Hispellates wished to gain by their petition. The rescript makes it clear that this Umbrian city hoped to modify the conduct of the annual religious festival it shared with the city of Volsinii by winning an opportunity to host the event at its own ceremonial precinct. In this instance, neither of the two communities was likely to turn its back on traditional religion in the way Orcistus had done. Indeed, a major request of the Hispellates was for permission to construct an imperial cult temple to Constantine's family. It has long puzzled historians that Constantine conceded to this demand, yet this seems less shocking if we keep in mind the intersubjective nature of power relations. Like any emperor, Constantine was compelled to operate within the horizons of the possible, but it was his genius to exploit the necessity of dialogue in order to promote his religious agenda even in areas like Hispellum that seemed less than receptive. He thus granted the city the right to host the provincial religious festival every other year and even allowed it to build a cult site to his family, but only on the condition that it abandon the practice of sacrifice.

We then turn to a series of cities that were renamed after Constantine or members of his family, which are surveyed in Chapters 6 and 7, covering, respectively, western and eastern cities. In light of the examples of Orcistus and Hispellum, patterns are sought of a relationship between grants of civic autonomy, imperial nomenclature, and favoritism for Constantine's religious program. In some instances few hints of interconnection can be found, as with the city of Autun, which came to be called Flavia Aeduorum before Constantine began advertising his conversion to Christianity. Other western cities, by contrast, offer more promising indications of efforts to reward Christian polities with privileges up to and including an imperial name. Arles, which was first endowed with the name Constantina in 328, had a long history of close relations with Constantine, but was particularly known for the ties Constantine cultivated with its Christian community. So too Numidian Cirta, which gained the name Constantina at least in part as a show of support for that city's staunchly resilient Christian community. Like Orcistus, the Italian city of Portus appears to have suffered religious repression at the hands of its more powerful neighbor, Ostia, until Constantine split it from Ostia's jurisdiction and gave it the name Flavia Constantiniana Portus. Perhaps the best example of this phenomenon comes in Palestinian Maiouma, for which we have solid testimony that this community's choice to proclaim exclusive adherence to Christianity resulted in its liberation from its powerful and religiously conservative neighbor Gaza and the receipt of a new name, Constantia. In similar fashion, Constantine granted the city of Antaradus independence from its meddlesome superior Aradus and renamed it Constantina or perhaps Constantia. Finally, two further hamlets were granted independence from their much larger neighbors and renamed Helenopolis. The first of these, Daburiyya, sought freedom from control not from a pagan but rather the exclusively Jewish city of Diocaesarea-Sepphoris, while Drepanum appears to have gained freedom from the more pluralistic, but equally oppressive Nicomedia. In many of these instances, Constantine fell back on the instrument of petition and response in order to actuate legal change through communicative action. Even in those cases where traces of this process are no longer visible, it is clear that Constantine was working with the traditional tools of civic governance in order to promote a pro-Christian politics on a city-by-city basis.

The third section turns to the ways in which Constantine also manipulated traditional financial arrangements between the imperial government and the cities in order to reconstruct urban centers into Christian centers. Examining both textual and archaeological sources, it explains how the emperor redeployed the traditional markers of civic distinction in order to promote both the prosperity of his subject polities and the relative position of Christian leaders within them. Chapter 8 explores the question of civic finance. It proceeds from the assumption that both cities and temples were, inter alia, massive financial undertakings that depended on the revenues of proprietary estates for the maintenance of public structures and the conduct of traditional cult. Knowing this, Constantine seems to have set out to starve pagan cults of financing by confiscating temple property—both real and movable—to his imperial purse. Moreover, it seems, in the instance of at least some cities, he also expropriated civic estates, at least in part because these too had been used to finance public cult. It is demonstrable that these seizures of property were never in practice systematic, and they were nowhere near complete before at least the mid-fifth century CE. Nevertheless, Constantine set the ball rolling in a process that then played itself out over the next century and eventually completely beggared the traditional cults. Constantine not only took over temple and civic estates, but also redirected at least some of the revenue this generated to support the clergy and indigent of Christian churches. Julian, for obvious reasons, attempted to reverse this process, but Jovian, Valentinian, and Valens soon restored, at least partially, Constantine's arrangements. In the end, this means that Constantine undertook a sizable wealth redistribution scheme within the cities that was at once costly and highly disruptive to civic finances.

In addition to redistributing the wealth of temples and cities, Constantine also began the process of outfitting cities with massive, sumptuously appointed, and well-endowed churches. Chapter 9 explores the evidence for this process and attempts to demonstrate how it reveals a consistent modus operandi. A law mentioned in Eusebius and evidenced in a letter he preserves indicates that the emperor informed bishops that they should petition his administration for funds with which to construct or enlarge Christian basilicas in their cities. A number of direct and indirect quotations from Constantinian correspondence show this process at work, with individual ecclesiastical leaders petitioning the emperor, who then instructs officials connected with his *res privata* to fund their projects. Details of the scale of this process, which was in fact massive, are well attested for Rome, at least, in the *Liber Pontificalis*, and its testimony is then confirmed by archaeological, textual, and epigraphic sources. The variety of architectural types that resulted is itself a testament to what we learn in the written sources: Constantine and his officials provided funding and supplies for this process through the petition and response system, but they left the design of churches up to the judgment of local authorities, who proceeded according to their own tastes. In the process, they began a trend that would soon result in the Christianization of the ancient cityscape through the imposition of church architecture all across the Mediterranean.

Chapter 10 offers a brief look at the privileges Constantine granted to bishops that allowed these to become central power brokers in the late antique city. Apart from the grants of land, buildings, revenues, and provisions he made to their benefit, Constantine also endowed bishops with powers that put them into a new category of civic grandee who outstripped the decurions alongside whom they operated. These new benefits included the power to offer judgments in civil cases that were backed up with the enforcement power of the imperial administration, and the power to manumit slaves with full Roman freedom. Both of these were privileges formerly reserved to provincial magistrates, which Constantine then devolved to church leaders who could now operate in the civic arena in ways that placed them above decurions. Constantine also granted bishops the right to use the public posting system for travel, again a privilege normally reserved for magistrates. Finally, he gave exemption to all Christian clergy from obligatory curial service. This last soon became a coveted privilege that attracted interest in ecclesiastical office for entirely selfish reasons. Here, as in so many instances, Constantine's successors felt compelled to rein in this benefit without, however, eliminating it entirely. The result was a net gain in the power of the bishop and clergy that helped spur their rise to dominance as civic leaders in the years to come.

The fourth and final section treats cities that read Constantine's message of Christianization in negotiated or even oppositional fashion. Chapter 11 explores a variety of largely pagan cities that engaged the emperor on their own terms and met with surprisingly receptive responses from the imperial leadership. These were communities by no means intent on resisting the new order but rather on offering alternate readings of the Constantinian message that could simultaneously promote their own interests and advance local causes in the eyes of the court. Several examples are explored, including Athens (to which Constantine granted a generous grain dole in no small part through the good offices of prominent pagan leaders), Termessus and Sagalassus (both of which folded Constantine into traditional cults already prominent in their cities), and Lepcis Magna (where Constantine was advertised late in his reign as a manifestation of the Sun God). The chapter then explores more closely the question of civic patrons. From epigraphic testimonia we learn that cities that had a decidedly pagan profile tended to gravitate to prominent pagan leaders to promote their interests before the court, and that the same pattern prevailed with largely Christian communities that sought support from Christian grandees. It closes with the examples of Puteoli and Naples, two neighbors in Campania that, to judge by the extant evidence, took rather different approaches to the rise of the state church, one by embracing traditional cults and the other by welcoming the new Christian faith. Both benefited greatly under Constantine, and both managed to work together to promote the imperial house while diverging sharply on questions of religious affiliation.

Despite Constantine's general efforts to meet cities on the terms on which they were willing to engage him, at times the dialogue devolved into resistance and open violence. The twelfth and thirteenth chapters explore these instances with an eye to explaining how this type of interaction was a normal and predictable part of imperial discourse. Constantine appears to have made only halting efforts to ban pagan religious praxis and particularly sacrifice. With some cities and holy sites, however, he proved willing to attack oppositional groups and even to destroy and confiscate their property. This was particularly true of those sites over which pagan and Christian religious communities came into direct conflict, like Jerusalem or Mamre, or those where ritual traditions overstepped the bounds of acceptable orthopraxy, like Aphaca or Baalbek, which were sites of ritual prostitution. These violent engagements should not be viewed as entirely foreclosing dialogue but merely moving it to the level of force and resistance, for the communities in question often continued to push back against imperial control with contrapuntal violence and ongoing resistance of their own. The thirteenth chapter shows how the same occurred with the Donatist communities of North Africa, whose group identity was formulated around resistance to state authority even before Constantine entered the scene. When Constantine and his imperial successors crossed into the realm of violence, they in many ways provided these dissident communities with the sort of discourse they most prized in their struggle for self-determination. Here too, Constantine did not achieve his end of compelling assent to his domination. He merely set the plate for ongoing confrontation, once again proving the limited and discursive nature of imperial power. To his credit, however, he did succeed in dialing back the pressure he initially applied to the Donatist community fairly quickly, and he seems never to have returned to an aggressive posture vis-à-vis this dissident group. This policy, we shall see, was undeniably rooted in Christian principles of long-suffering and trust in divine judgment that Constantine had learned from his adviser, the apologist Lactantius.

The fourteenth and final chapter looks at two megalopoleis of the eastern empire that do not fit the monolithic pattern witnessed in smaller communities like Orcistus and Hispellum. Of course, no ancient city was ever homogeneous in its religious makeup, and this was true a fortiori of Antioch and Alexandria, each of which had populations as large as 200,000 inhabitants, who were at once multi-ethnic and religiously pluralistic. Pagans, Jews, and Christians coexisted and established a modus vivendi with one another that generally permitted cooperation and mutual recognition. Tensions between these communities were, however, palpable and at times exploded into open violence. In dealing with these cities—and others like them—Constantine was thus compelled to operate gingerly and with the full awareness that his power was radically circumscribed. He appears to have taken only symbolic steps to challenge traditional cults in Alexandria, where he removed the Nilometer from the temple of Serapis but made no other moves against pagans, and in Antioch, where he may have converted a temple into a church and an idol into an imperial statue, but without provoking measurable unrest. His dealings with the Christian communities in both cities are much better attested and demonstrate clearly the very real limitations on his power to impose his will on the competing constituencies in each. In this tug of war, powerful ecclesiastical figures like Athanasius, Eustathius of Antioch, Eusebius of Nicomedia, and Eusebius of Caesarea maneuvered themselves into the role of leaders and representatives of their respective polities, and also maneuvered around the emperor in their power plays with one another. Using the instruments and protocols of imperial law, such bishops were able to monopolize control of civic and regional politics, while the emperor was relegated to the role of umpire in their squabbles.

PART I

~

CONSTANTINE'S SELF-PRESENTATION

CHAPTER 1

∿

Constantine Develops

A Sense of Transformation

We are fortunate to possess as many of Constantine's writings as we do. While all are highly mannered and each crafted to the exigencies of individual audiences, they offer at least some understanding of how the emperor constructed his own narrative. From these it is clear that an important part of that story was the notion of transformation.[1] This comes out most clearly in his *Oration to the Assembly of the Saints,* where Constantine laments: "I dismiss all that the awful sway of fortune imposed upon the random presence of ignorance and consider repentance to be the greatest salvation. I can only wish that long ago this revelation had been granted to me, if indeed that man is truly blessed who has been established in his knowledge of the divine ever since youth and has rejoiced in the beauty of virtue. . . . No human education ever helped me in this, but all the gifts that are sanctioned in one's morals and manners by the reasonable have come to me from God."[2] In his own words, then, Constantine's life story was one of conversion, effected directly by divine intervention, which transformed him from an unbeliever to a believer. This notion of error followed by personal reform is apparent already in the letter of 314 that Constantine addressed to the Catholic bishops following the Council of Arles.[3] It was also the story he told to Eusebius and other bishops at Nicaea in 325.[4] It would, of course, have differed slightly with each retelling, and it was no doubt rearranged and embellished over time, but at its heart was the notion of transformation.

Constantine's earliest commentators picked up on this idea and made transformation an important part of their own accounts. This is by all means the case with his earliest Christian narrators, including both Lactantius and Eusebius. Both were contemporaries, and both followed Constantine's lead in making his personal encounter with God and conversion to Christianity central to their stories.[5] But Constantine's pagan narrators also exploited the trope to paint their less flattering portraits of the same man. Working in the tradition of the Enmannsche

Kaisergeschichte, the author of the *Epitome de Caesaribus* claims that Constantine was "most outstanding for ten years, a brigand for the next twelve, and for the last ten he was called a 'spoiled child' because of his unbounded spending."[6] We find a similar assessment in the related account of Eutropius, who thought of Constantine as "a man comparable to the best emperors in the first part of his reign but only the mediocre in the last."[7] More dramatic still were the accounts of Julian and Zosimus, which, as we saw in the introduction, also focus on conversion, but in terms radically different from those of Lactantius and Eusebius: Constantine's turn to Christianity was, for them as well, the central event in his reign, but it was precipitated by his impious crimes against his family and resulted in a radical turn for the worse.[8] The narrative of conversion, so central to Constantine's own story, thus filtered its way well beyond the emperor and his supporters to become the very basis for judgment both for and against him. Transformation was, in other words, a crucial leitmotif in all Constantinian narratives, beginning with the one invented by the emperor himself and extending out to those radically opposed to him and his program.

The *Epitome de Caesaribus* had broken Constantine's reign not into two phases but three, each more or less equal in length: 306–315, 315–327, 327–337. This division shows the perceptiveness of its author, for although the analytical framework on which its schematization was based is not entirely convincing, the perception that Constantine's public persona could be periodized can be verified from the evidence. M. Grünewald has shown convincingly that Constantinian inscriptions shift themes and emphases in definable phases over time.[9] In similar fashion, art historians have also argued that Constantine's portrait styles can be broken into four discrete phases that can be measured chronologically using the datable evidence of the coins.[10] Building on these arguments, I would suggest that the entire scheme of Constantine's self-presentation to his broader public— including not just inscriptions but also coins, portraits, and panegyrics—can be broken into four phases. Thus the Constantine presented to the public through official channels in the years

- 306–310 fit himself within the existing structures of the Tetrarchy,
- 310–321 focused on his role as a conqueror of tyrants,
- 321–330 added the notion that in attacking tyrants he was championing the Christian faith,
- 330–337 explored the outlines of divine rulership as the first Christian emperor.

This scheme was surely not preconceived. On the contrary, it developed over time and in response to circumstances and changes in Constantine's own priorities and to limitations in his mental horizons and the bounds of his power. It can, however, be reconstructed from extant sources with some degree of precision and therefore remains a useful interpretive device. By describing how changes in Constantine's self-presentation occurred, we can begin to explain why Constantine's subjects derived such varying and at times contradictory interpretations of his motives and intentions. In other words, the kaleidoscope of self-presentations offered by Constantine over the course of his reign not only is traceable in the source record, but also helps in no small part to explain the many faces of this single emperor we find in interpretations ancient and modern.

Tetrarch

When Constantine was proclaimed emperor in the summer of 306, the tetrarchic system was still very much alive. From the beginning, he demonstrated that he was not entirely comfortable with its structures; both his readiness to assume the purple without prior approval from the other tetrarchs (especially Galerius) and also his eagerness to accept immediately the rank of Augustus went against earlier principles. Nevertheless, his efforts to seek ex post facto approval for his proclamation from Galerius and his willingness to accept a demotion to the rank of Caesar in order to secure a purchase in the system offer evidence that he presumed the importance—indeed the necessity—of inserting himself into the existing scheme of four-man rule.[11]

One of the key reflections of Constantine's public persona in this period can be found in his official portraiture, which must be reconstructed from the numismatic evidence because of the absence of identifiable sculptural images. In most of the earliest coins depicting Constantine, his facial characteristics are typical of the tetrarchs: his head is massive and its rendering schematic, his jaw strong and square, and his beard and hair closely cropped in the manner of a soldier (Fig. 6).[12] Constantine's official titulature also reflects a tetrarchic pose. In this early phase, he changed his titles rather often as he struggled to test the limits of his imperial self-identity, but the titles he adopted generally reflect the idea of cooperation inside the tetrarchic college: PIUS NOBILISSIMUS CAESAR, used in the years 306–307, represents the traditional title of junior emperors; IMPERATOR CAESAR PIUS FELIX AUGUSTUS, adopted in the period from 308 to 310, shows a readiness to advance within the college without displaying any particular ambition to operate above or outside it, for it combines—somewhat awkwardly—the lesser title Caesar with its superior counterpart Augustus.[13] The same can be seen on his coins in the use of the title "Prince of the Youth" (PRINCEPS IVVENTVTIS), an honorific for younger dynasts that stretched back to the grandsons of Augustus and

FIGURE 6. Obverse:
CONSTANTINVS NOB
CAES. Constantine
laureate, facing right, with
close-cropped beard and
square jaw. *RIC* 6: Roma
200. ANS 1944.100.2981.
Courtesy of the American
Numismatic Society.

had become synonymous with the junior status of Caesars under the Tetrarchy.[14]

A tetrarchic disposition can also be seen in the panegyric of 307 delivered on the occasion of Constantine's marriage to Fausta, daughter of the newly restored Augustus Maximianus Herculius. Such marriages were a standard element of tetrarchic relationship building, this one all the more so since it had been planned during the first Tetrarchy, when the bride and groom were still children.[15] The occasion was also used for Maximianus to restore to Constantine the title Augustus, which he had formerly surrendered at the insistence of Galerius in the fall of 306. By putting Constantine on a par with Maximianus and Galerius and thereby creating three concurrently reigning Augusti, this new dispensation at first appears to speak against tetrarchic norms. Nonetheless, the panegyrist who describes for us the occasion shows how it was in fact conceptualized very much within a tetrarchic framework: he represents the senior emperor as solely responsible for this increase in Constantine's power, and, in order to minimize any offense to Galerius and his Caesar, Maximinus, the panegyrist also avoids using Constantine's new title in favor of the more anodyne *Imperator*.[16] Falling back on tetrarchic themes, the panegyrist also describes Maximianus and Constantine as "father" and "son,"[17] and he unites the two under the title *Herculius*, long since the tetrarchic moniker of the more senior Maximianus.[18] Furthermore, the military achievements of the two emperors are described along tetrarchic lines, for the older emperor is praised for past victories, while the younger is said to win military kudos in the present.[19] Nowhere are the tetrarchic underpinnings of the relationship clearer than in the peroration, where the panegyrist describes a paternalistic relationship between senior and junior emperor in which the elder conceptualizes the good of the world while his younger subordinate actualizes it.[20] This same set of ideas is also reflected in the coin type minted under the legend CONCORDIA FELIX DD(ominorum) NN(ostrorum) (The happy concord of our Lords), featuring the two emperors standing, facing one another, and clasping right hands (Fig. 7).[21] Maximianus and Constantine were thus aware of their mutual dependence and chose to depict it within the framework of ideas and images familiar from a tetrarchic system that was now well established and widely accepted.

Of course, this relationship lasted only a year and a half before it was disturbed in late November 308, after the Council of Carnuntum ordered Maximianus to abdicate. Nevertheless, even following this setback, Constantine is

FIGURE 7. Obverse: IMP C VAL
MAXIMIANVS PF AVG. Maximianus
laureate and cuirassed, facing right,
with close-cropped beard and
square jaw. Reverse: CONCORDIA
FELIX DD NN. Two emperors
standing, facing each other, clasping
right hands, and leaning left on
scepter. *RIC* 6: Lugdunum 246. ANS
1984.146.353. Courtesy of the American Numismatic Society.

reported by Lactantius to have accorded honor and deference to Maximianus down to the moment of his father-in-law's uprising against him in 310.[22] Constantine's effort to maintain the pose of tetrarchic subordination is also underlined by the panegyrist of 313 and later by Eusebius when these attribute his reluctance to confront Maxentius any earlier than he did to his respect for more senior colleagues who had originally claimed responsibility for this task.[23] Regardless of how much credence we place in this claim, its appearance in contemporary sources makes it clear that Constantine wished to give the impression that he was striving to play the role of the dutiful junior ruler.

None of this is to deny that from the beginning Constantine also gave signs that he would soon overthrow the system he so skillfully manipulated in these early years. M. Grünewald has shown that Constantine disseminated his own name, titles, and portraits on coins issued and inscriptions carved from within his territories in markedly higher numbers than those of his imperial colleagues.[24] This same restless self-assertiveness is also attested by his refusal to accept the title FILIUS AUGUSTORUM, accorded him after the Council of Carnuntum in late 308 in recompense for Galerius's refusal to recognize his promotion to Augustus, and his choice instead to continue using AUGUSTUS on his own coins and inscriptions until it finally gained acknowledgment from Galerius in mid-310.[25] Beneath the mask of the tetrarch, then, one senses a more ambitious Constantine struggling to emerge almost from the beginning. Nevertheless, during these early years he never rebelled against Galerius or the other tetrarchs but instead chose to focus his military skills against foreign peoples, and he even refused the offer of a consulship in 309, a move well suited to an emperor still intent on showing deference to his senior colleagues.[26] Only with the death of Galerius in spring 311 did he move definitively away from the tetrarchic pose, a fact we witness first in the panegyric offered to him in summer 311, which makes no reference to his tetrarchic colleagues and even styles Constantine "emperor of the whole world."[27] The disappearance of the last tetrarchic strongman in the Diocletianic mold had thus left Constantine a free hand to realize loftier ambitions.

Tyrannicide

By 310 Constantine was well on his way to crafting a new public image to substitute for that of the junior tetrarch. That year his relationship with Maximianus Herculius had fallen victim to the latter's rebellion and forced suicide. In the period immediately following, as the panegyrist of 310 reveals, Constantine discovered for himself both a new ancestor—Claudius Gothicus—and a new divine protector—the Sun God.[28] This was the first indication that a radical shift was afoot in his public self-presentation. In the year and a half that followed, this political facelift would actualize itself on the military stage as Constantine put himself forward as the liberator of Rome from the clutches of a heinous tyrant.

As with the earliest period of Constantine's reign, this second phase in his public self-presentation was accompanied by the rise of its own portrait style and titles. Already in the earliest period, some numismatic images of Constantine differentiate him from his fellow tetrarchs as beardless and youthfully round-faced (Fig. 8),[29] but only in the context of his war against Maxentius do we get a consistent new portrait style. For this we have both numismatic and sculptural evidence, which reveals a much greater emphasis on individuality in the attention given to the emperor's aquiline nose and the careful rendering of his locks. The latter appear longer and are articulated into strands in the manner of the hairstyle worn by Trajan (Figs. 8 and 9).[30] His image in these years also features a new sense of gravitas and even spirituality with the introduction of more deeply-set eyes, most famously on the colossal statue now in the courtyard of the Palazzo dei Conservatori in Rome.

In this same period Constantine also changed his titulature by adding the designation INVICTUS.[31] This was of course directly connected with the sun god

FIGURE 8. Obverse: FL VAL CONSTANT-INVS NOB C. Constantine laureate, facing right. Mint of London. *RIC* 6: Londinium 79. ANS 1984.146.1196. Courtesy of the American Numismatic Society.

FIGURE 9. Obverse: CONSTANT–INVS PF AVG. Constantine laureate, facing right. Mint of Arles. *RIC* 7: Arles 6. ANS 1967.153.53. Courtesy of the American Numismatic Society.

FIGURE 10. Portrait of Constantine from the Arch of Constantine, north side, boar hunt tondo. Deutsches Archäologisches Institut, Rom, Neg. D-DAI-ROM-32.36.

Sol Invictus, who began to appear on his coins in 310 in the wake of his solar vision that year—a subject to be discussed in Chapter 2.[32] Sol Invictus's new prominence also represented a move away from traditional tetrarchic deities like Mars, who had appeared with some regularity on Constantine's earliest coins.[33] Shortly after defeating Maxentius, Constantine added yet another title that made him stand out quite noticeably from his fellow emperors. In 312 the Roman Senate accorded him the honor of primacy among the three remaining rulers, and in response he began using the title MAXIMUS, which became all but universal on his inscriptions by 315.[34] His victory over Maxentius thus opened the door wider to the expression of his ambitions toward supremacy.

At the same time Constantine was reinventing his portrait and titles, he was also engineering a linguistic revolution by introducing the notion of the rival ruler as "tyrant." This concept does not appear in extant propaganda before the Battle of the Milvian Bridge, a period during which the conflict with Maxentius was instead attributed to his rival's illegitimate usurpation of power, his destruction of Constantine's images, and his wanton craving for vengeance for the death of his father Maximianus.[35] In the period immediately following the battle, we get hints of alternative justifications as Constantine begins to be heralded as the "liberator of the city of Rome."[36] This same notion predominates in the panegyric delivered before Constantine in 313, which lambasts Maxentius for his greed and criminality but avoids the vocabulary of tyranny.[37] Nevertheless, at around this same time, several legal pronouncements, the earliest dating to early 313, show Constantine beginning to use the word "tyrant" as a label for Maxentius: these include two laws of January 6, 313, a letter of Constantine to Maximinus from the spring of that same year, and a third law of March 19, 314.[38] Thus, within months of overcoming Maxentius, Constantine had begun to present himself as the suppressor of tyranny.

Scholarship has long recognized the importance of this period in ushering in a change in the semantic range of the Latin and Greek words for tyrant—*tyrranus/ tyrannos*.[39] T. Barnes has argued further not only that Constantine began the shift, but also that he and his propagandists applied this slur quite specifically to persecutors of the Christian faith.[40] This is only partially true, for although Constantine obviously did brand Maxentius a tyrant beginning shortly after the battle, and although he did eventually come to connect the word "tyrant" with persecutors of Christianity, there is every indication that neither he nor his message makers accused Maxentius of attacking Christians in the first few years after 312. This is clear, for example, on the arch of Constantine, a monument dedicated in 315 by the Senate and People of Rome in thanks for Constantine's having avenged the republic, "both against the tyrant and against his entire faction" (*tam de tyranno quam de omni eius factione*).[41] This early witness to the use of "tyrant" is placed prominently on a monument famous for its emphasis on the role of the Sun God in effecting this victory and its total omission of any reference to Christianity.[42] An inscription dedicated around the same time to the pagan Urban Prefect of Rome, C. Vettius Cossinius Rufinus, shows the citizens of Atina also offering their thanks for preservation from harm under the reign of the "most savage tyrant" without the slightest hint of Maxentius's violence against Christians.[43] The same can be said of the panegyric of Nazarius, delivered in 321, which associates Maxentius's tyranny with avarice, cruelty, and lust—canonical characteristics of tyrannical behavior since the classical period—without mention of religious persecutions.[44] Above all, there is no evidence that "tyranny" was connected with persecution even in the overtly Christian portrait Eusebius says Constantine erected of himself in Rome. He reports that the statue bore a cross in its hand and was furnished with an inscription boasting that Constantine "freed your city, rescued from the yoke of the tyrant, by this salvific sign, the true proof of virtue."[45] To be sure, both statue and inscription offered early confirmation of Constantine's open acknowledgment of the power of the cross. But even if this symbol was clearly marked here as a victory talisman capable of bringing military success to the ruler against a tyrant, there is no obvious claim that Maxentius merited eviction and defeat because he had persecuted members of the faith.

In fact, this would have been a difficult case to make in the immediate aftermath of Maxentius's rule. To be sure, riots over food shortages had gripped Rome in the later years of his reign, and he had met these with open violence, slaughtering as many as six thousand citizens.[46] Moreover, he had indeed persecuted some senatorial aristocrats, including at least one Christian noblewoman, and had exiled three claimants to the episcopal see of Rome in response to rioting.[47] But Maxentius is also well known to have called a halt to Christian persecutions early in his reign—probably in 308—and even to have restored confiscated property to Christian churches.[48] It was likely this awareness that induced Lactantius in his *On the Deaths of Persecutors* to use *tyrannus* regularly of emperors whom he knew to have persecuted, but never of Maxentius.[49] Similarly, although Eusebius does call Maxentius a *tyrannos* in the eighth and ninth books of his *Ecclesiastical History* (completed by 314), he attributes generally violent and overbearing behavior to him without mentioning Christian persecutions.[50] This stands in contrast with his description of the "tyrant" Maximinus Daia, who is most definitely portrayed as a persecutor.[51] "Tyrant" and "persecutor" were thus separable concepts in the immediate aftermath of the Battle of the Milvian Bridge. Although the former could be used as a shorthand for the latter in Christian sources, the two were by no means synonymous. Thus, while the equation "tyrant = persecutor" had certainly been adduced by some Christians by around 314, Constantine and his supporters seem not to have made the connection in the instance of Maxentius in the years immediately following the battle. They remained content to designate this rival as a tyrant on the basis of a more generic understanding of the term.

This was to change, however, by the time Constantine undertook his second and final campaign against Licinius, in no small part because Licinius himself had turned to active persecution in the buildup to their war.[52] There is no use of the rhetoric of "tyranny" during Constantine's initial conflict with Licinius in 316. It was thus only after their alliance completely disintegrated[53] that Licinius was branded a tyrant, and by this point there is little doubt that this implied the persecution of Christians. Our first evidence for Constantine's use of the slur against Licinius comes from a set of laws dating to late 324 and thus after Constantine's victory over his eastern rival at Chrysopolis.[54] In this same year we find the word applied to Licinius in a letter from Constantine to Eusebius with clear implications that it connoted persecution; it recurs later that winter with the same connotations in Constantine's letter to the Nicomedians, and once again in spring 325 in a canon from the Council of Nicaea regarding Christians who had lapsed "in the reign of Licinius the tyrant."[55] Around this same time, we also first encounter the word "tyrant" of Maxentius with implications of Christian persecution in Constantine's *Oration to the Assembly of the Saints*, probably delivered in April 325.[56] And soon after this, the notion of both Maxentius and Licinius as tyrant-persecutors is picked up in the historiography. It is certainly found in Eusebius's portrayal of Licinius in the third and final edition of his *Ecclesiastical History,* published circa 325, and it also appears in his descriptions of Licinius and Maxentius in the *Life of Constantine*, written circa 338.[57] We thus witness a gradual development over the period between 312 and 324 in which the notion of "tyranny," first used as a generic slur against political rivals, comes to refer more specifically to persecutors of the Christian faith.[58] Concomitant with this process there arose a related homology that equated the welfare of the church with the welfare of the state: attacks on the Christian community could now be offered as a justification for the initiation of civil war against the "tyrants" who perpetrated them and thereby threatened the integrity of the *res publica*.

This same metamorphosis in Constantinian rhetoric can be seen in a related theme, the notion of the rival as monster. In the period immediately following the Battle of the Milvian Bridge, Maxentius is portrayed not just as a tyrant but also as a portentous beast. The pagan panegyrist of 313 calls him "that monster," "the filthiest of ogres," "that portent," and "such a deformed ogre."[59] In 321 Nazarius also emphasizes Maxentius's "beastly domination" and maligns him as "that monstrous ruination."[60] Picking up on this rhetoric, Eusebius calls Maxentius "some horrible beast" in his *Life of Constantine*.[61] By the time we arrive at Licinius, however, this rhetoric has gained in precision, for Licinius is described quite specifically as a "serpent" or "dragon."[62] This reference, with its scriptural allusion to Satan, pushes the analogy in a Christian direction. It is thus all the more interesting that Constantine's bureaucrats, artists, and moneyers also depicted Licinius as a snake or dragon. This we know from a rescript of Constantine to Eusebius that uses the trope, and from Eusebius's description of the portal to Constantine's new palace in Constantinople, over which the emperor had himself portrayed with his foot on a serpent pierced by a spear and cast out to sea.[63] Eusebius confidently connects this latter image, which clearly alluded to Constantine's defeat of Licinius on the waters of the Bosporus, with a passage in Isaiah that describes the prince of darkness in similarly serpentine terms (Is. 27.1; cf. Ez. 32.2). Thus for the Christian reader, at least, Constantine's iconography was interpretable within a Judeo-Christian framework. Recycling this same image, Constantine also introduced a bronze type in 326 on which a serpent is transfixed by a labarum—the emperor's Christian battle standard—under the legend "the hope of the state" (SPES PVBLICA: Fig. 11).[64] Thus, where Maxentius qua tyrant had been described as a beast in generic terms, Licinius came to be depicted as a serpent in what, to Christians at least, represented a clear allusion to Satan. The defeat of Licinius, Constantine's political rival but also an enemy of the faith, was assimilated to God's own defeat of the Prince of Darkness.

Constantinian public propaganda had thus developed over time. In the period immediately following the Battle of the Milvian Bridge, the emperor was heralded as a slayer of tyrants and monsters who threatened Rome and its citizens

FIGURE 11. Obverse: CONSTANTI-
NVS MAX AVG. Constantine laureate,
facing right. Reverse: SPES–PVBLICA.
Labarum surmounted by chi-rho
pierces serpent. *RIC 7*: Constantinople 19. Lars Ramskold collection,
reproduced with permission.

and by extension the state. By the time Constantine defeated Licinius, his victories were touted as the defeat of persecutors of Christians and even of the Devil
himself. The gradual development of this metaphor allowed Constantine to connect his unrelenting penchant for civil war with events of theological and even
cosmic significance. He had gone from being the defender of the Roman state
against the illegitimate rule of tyrants to becoming the defender of the Christian
church against the illicit attacks of persecutors.

Champion of the Faith

By the mid-320s, then, Constantine had begun openly to portray himself as a
champion of the Christian faith. He had grown increasingly comfortable disseminating public statements and images overtly connecting himself with Christianity. It is important to be aware that this transformation in public self-presentation
had been engineered in dialogue with the most important Christian thinkers of
the day. Chief among these in the years before his takeover of the East was Lactantius, who at some point toward the end of his life was asked to serve as a
teacher to Constantine's son Crispus.[65] The connection between Lactantius's and
Constantine's thought is especially clear from the former's masterwork, the *Divine
Institutes*, a seven-book treatise that was originally composed in the period
between 305 and 310, when Lactantius was operating in the East and had not yet
established contact with Constantine. At some point after taking up employment
in Constantine's court, Lactantius issued a second edition of the *Institutes* that
included two dedications—in books I and VII—to Constantine himself, probably
in the winter of 312/313. Among the main themes of this work were that the Christian god was the source of all true justice, and that those who attacked his religion
could expect his vengeance to be enacted upon them. The latter notion also constituted the backbone of Lactantius's work *On the Deaths of Persecutors*, published
circa 315. Picking up on both themes, Constantine began to show signs of con-
ceiving of the world in Lactantian terms already by 314, and by the mid-320s he

began publicly to slot himself into this cosmological framework by portraying himself as the agent of divine justice against the persecutors of the faith.[66]

As with the earlier shifts in Constantinian public propaganda, the move toward self-construction as a champion of the faith was accompanied by alterations in his portraiture and titles. With regard to the latter, beginning in late 324, Constantine exchanged his moniker *Invictus* for *Victor*.[67] This gave his claims to military authority a more definitive form: it was as if he wished to announce that he had overcome all earthly enemies and now ruled in a permanent state as the quintessence of "the champion." Equally important was the disappearance of *Invictus*, which signaled a retreat from his relationship with Sol Invictus, Constantine's protective deity since 310. It is thus no accident that the adoption of *Victor* occurred concurrently with the final disappearance of Sol Invictus from his coins after 325.[68] It has also been argued that, at the same time, Constantine began refusing to allow his Greek-speaking subjects to address him as *Sebastos*, a translation for the Latin title *Augustus*. Because *Sebastos* (Revered) retained strong religious connotations associated with the imperial cult, Constantine seems to have insisted that *Augustus* be rendered in Greek with a simple transliteration of the Latin—Αὔγουστος.[69]

Changes to Constantine's portrait during this third phase came in three forms. First, on his coins, he began to be depicted with his new Christian victory symbol, the Christogram, emblazoned on his helmet. This symbol appears on the frontal boss of a parade helmet in a limited number of silver medallions that some argue to have been produced in Ticinum as early as 313/315 (see Fig. 2). Nevertheless, these pieces were extremely rare, and both their date and place of minting are subject to question.[70] More secure are coins minted at Siscia in 319 with obverse portraits of Constantine wearing a high-crested helmet on the side of which flashes a Christogram (see Fig. 3).[71] This is especially significant because Siscia was Constantine's residence in precisely this period, making it likely that the portrait offers an accurate and contemporary picture of the ornamentation actually worn by the emperor.[72] Even so, the Christogram remained a relative rarity in Constantine's portraiture even down to his final days.

FIGURE 12. Obverse: Constantine facing right, wearing jeweled diadem. *RIC* 7: Constantinople 53. Nationalmuseet Denmark, reproduced with permission.

After the victory at Chrysopolis in late 324, Constantine added a second change to his portraiture by introducing an elaborate jeweled diadem that quickly became a standard symbol of imperial power (Fig. 12). From the coinage we can date its introduction fairly closely to the year 325—that is, one year after the defeat of Licinius—in the period when Constantine was beginning the celebrations of his vicennalia.[73] Numerous sources take note of this innovation, though only two describe the possible motivations behind it: a Byzantine *Life of Constantine* with connections to the fifth-century tradition of Philostorgius claims it was "the symbol of his monarchy and of his victory over his enemies," whereas Malalas holds that Constantine "wished to fulfill the prophetic words which said, 'You placed on his head a crown of precious stone.'" (Ps. 20.4).[74] These distinct but complementary interpretations were likely both at play, for Constantine's moneyers regularly made allusions to Hellenistic coinage and were surely intent on connecting the diadem with its ancient roots as a traditional symbol of eastern kingship. Nevertheless, the urge to elaborate a style of rulership imbued with Judeo-Christian symbolism was no doubt also on Con-

FIGURE 13. Obverse: Constantine facing right, gazing heavenward, wearing jeweled diadem. *RIC* 7: Nicomedia 176. ANS 1944.100.7973. Courtesy of the American Numismatic Society.

stantine's mind and would seem to be confirmed by his choice to embellish the simple band of cloth used by his Greek predecessors as a diadem with elaborate jewelwork in order to bring it into line with the passage from Psalms.

The same polyvalence can be seen in the third innovation in Constantinian portraiture from this period, the choice to depict the emperor with his eyes cast upward toward heaven (Fig. 13).[75] Here again, this had been commonplace among eastern Greek kings, but it could also be interpreted as a gesture of reverence for the Christian god. This was in fact the explanation arrived at by Eusebius, who saw in this portrait style an emperor looking upward, "in the manner of one reaching out to God in prayer."[76] Constantine was thus striving to communicate with multiple constituencies using signs that could be understood as affirmations of his sympathy for differing religious perspectives. At root, however, the message was unified around the notion that his rule was divinely ordained. As such both the diadem and the heavenly gaze permitted and even invited *negotiated* readings that affirmed the emperor's claims to power while allowing both pagans and Christians to decode his message as favorable to their viewpoint. These threads evident in titles and portraiture—the decisive defeat of all rivals, the empire's return to monarchy, and the link between the emperor and the divine—are woven together in an important passage of the *Life of Constantine* where Eusebius summarizes Constantine's achievement with the defeat of Licinius: "But he, conspicuous for every virtue of piety, Emperor Victor—for he himself invented this title as the most authoritative eponym for himself because of the victory God granted to him over all his enemies and foes—took control of the East and made the Roman Empire a unified whole as it had been long ago. He was thus the first to proclaim the sole rule [*monarchia*] of God to all, and he himself also governed all human life under Roman dominion through his own sole rule [*monarchia*]."[77] With the reconquest of the East, Constantine had thus simultaneously reintroduced the form of Roman government traditional since the reign of Augustus, recreated the monotheistic order of the cosmos on earth, and furnished the opportunity to reestablish concord between the two halves of the empire. Seizing this opportunity, he set about restructuring a variety of aspects of Roman administration.[78] As we shall see in subsequent chapters, he also used his new exclusive lock on power to reorient the focus of his dynastic politics and increase pressure on his subjects to abandon traditional religion and turn to Christianity. If any point in Constantine's reign can be seen as a turning point, then, it is surely the year 324.

In fact, Constantine himself made it clear in a variety of extant pronouncements that he regarded his victory over Licinius as a major watershed in his reign. We are fortunate that Eusebius has preserved six documents from the immediate aftermath of the defeat of Licinius that provide us with a direct window onto his conception of his rule at this period. The first five can all be dated to late 324, and the sixth to early 325:[79]

> 1. Letter to the provincials of Palestine (Eus. *V. Const.* 2.24–42)
> 2. Letter to Eusebius on the restoration of Christian churches (*V. Const.* 2.46)
> 3. Letter to the eastern provincials (*V. Const.* 2.48–60)
> 4. Letter to Alexander and Arius (*V. Const.* 2.64–72)
> 5. Letter to the Shahanshah Shapur II (*V. Const.* 4.9–13)
> 6. *Oration to the Assembly of the Saints*

Among all of these, the letter to the eastern provincials is perhaps most representative of Constantine's self-presentation to a broad segment of his subjects at this juncture. In it he lays out in detail his belief that divine power repays the faithful and punishes persecutors, which was, as we have seen, a characteristically Lactantian theme. As support for this, Constantine relates how he was present personally during the Christian persecutions of the tetrarchs and later witnessed the ruin of the persecuting emperors at God's hands. He then describes how he has transformed himself into the agent of the divine will who has carried the standard of God against its enemies.[80] He thus states explicitly his assumption that he has become the champion of the Christian faith. The same conceptions subtend his letter to the provincials of Palestine, which repeats the "punishment of persecutors" theme and once again paints Constantine as the enactor of God's justice.[81] They also recur in the letter to Eusebius on the restoration of churches, albeit quite briefly, and in the letter to Alexander and Arius, which represents Constantine's chief objective as the return of unity to both the church and the Empire now that he has destroyed "the common enemy of the whole world."[82] So too, the letter to Shapur II ascribes the capture of the emperor Valerian by Shapur I to the former's persecution of Christians and attributes Constantine's recent military victories to the divine favor of the Christian god.[83]

Finally, the much more elaborate *Oration to the Assembly of the Saints* takes as its starting point the concept that God imposes a just and perfect order on the world (again, a notion that permeates Lactantius)[84] before circling back to "the deaths of persecutors" topos: Constantine lists the divine punishments of Decius, Valerian, Aurelian, and Diocletian as examples of cosmic justice.[85] In keeping with his role as champion of the faith, he integrates himself into this scheme as the agent of divine vengeance against persecutors of the faith: "For my part I attribute my own good fortune and that of my entire family to your [God's] goodwill. This is attested by the outcome of all things that have turned out according to my prayers—acts of virtue, victories, triumphs over my enemies. Even the great city is aware of this and offers praise with reverence, and also the people of the beloved city wish it, even if it was deceived with false hopes and selected a defender unworthy of itself, who was suddenly captured fittingly and worthily in light of his misdeeds."[86] The "great city" to which Constantine refers has long been recognized as Rome, and B. Bleckmann has demonstrated that the "beloved city" must be Nicomedia, where Licinius had taken refuge during the final phase of his war with Constantine in 324 before suffering capture and punishment.[87] Constantine thus once again refers to himself here as the agent of the divine will, enacting God's justice in the secular world against those who had attacked the faith. This complex of ideas thus recurs repeatedly as a leitmotif in Constantinian public pronouncements in the immediate aftermath of the victory at Chrysopolis in November 324. As we might expect, it is picked up and repeated by other contemporary sources, and particularly Eusebius in the last book of his *Ecclesiastical History* (finished circa 325), his *Tricennalian Oration* (circa 336), and his *Life of Constantine* (circa 338).[88]

Constantine's public self-presentation in the years from circa 321 to 330 thus focused on his role as the sole ruler who had secured exclusive dominion over the Roman Empire by acting as the Christian god's agent. Bearing the Christogram as his new victory standard, he had championed the Christian faith by ridding the world of persecutors and spreading the justice of the Christian god. This notion is further reflected in Constantine's readiness to shed connections with the Sun God, including the title *Invictus*, to begin using the Christogram more openly in his visual propaganda, and above all to connect the "tyranny" of his rivals Licinius—and retroactively Maxentius—to the persecution of Christians. These messages converge in a variety of sources linked directly and indirectly to Constantine himself. They leave us with the clearest and most consistent self-portrait of the emperor found at any point in his reign. As such, the message of Constantine as champion of the faith would have offered the firmest basis for a *dominant* reading of any of the four Constantinian personae outlined in this chapter. It is therefore difficult not to have sympathy with those who read Constantine as a fundamentally Christian emperor. For all that he presented a variety of public personae over the course of his rule, Constantine the Christian victor stands out as perhaps the best attested and most fully articulated of them all.

Divine Ruler

Beginning around 330 and lasting until the end of his life, Constantine once again altered his public image, this time in ways that deemphasized his military accomplishments and gave greater weight to his role as a spiritual leader. Contemporary documents—other than laws—issued directly from the emperor in these final years are unfortunately less abundant than for Constantine's middle years, but what we have tells a consistent story: with no rivals for power and a clutch of successors coming of age, the wizened emperor turned away from direct involvement in the most burdensome aspects of military rulership and toward a more spiritually focused self-presentation.

FIGURE 14. Intaglio-cut amethyst with Constantine's portrait. Bpk, Berlin, Antikensammlung, Staatliche Museen, obj. inv. 30931, photo: Ingrid Geske-Heiden, Art Resource, NY.

As with the earlier periods, this new phase was marked by changes in Constantine's portrait and titles. His portrait in his last seven years is similar to that from the 320s insofar as it continues to emphasize his diadem and deep-set eyes, but the emperor appears heavier—and thus older—and is depicted in a manner more characteristic of earlier imperial portraiture than we find in the 320s (Fig. 14).[89] On the coins he appears almost exclusively in profile, togate, and with eyes fixed forward rather than raised toward heaven (Fig. 15).[90] Furthermore, his military role is deemphasized on the coins, which cease to portray the helmeted Constantine so popular during the 310s and 320s and focus instead on a more highly ornamented and spiritually serene ruler. The same can be said of Constantine's titulature, which adds the epithet *Triumphator* to *Victor* beginning around the year 330.[91] To be sure, *Victor ac Triumphator* continues to emphasize military achievements, but the combination points even more strongly to successes already achieved and by now celebrated. It thus fits well with the

fact that, in these last years, Constantine's role in the
conduct of wars became largely passive, making *Triumphator* the appropriate descriptor for a ruler whose battlefield accomplishments were a thing of the past.

Constantine's withdrawal from direct involvement
in military activity was in no small part a function of
his age. When he gained control of the East in 324, he
had likely reached his fifty-second year and was beginning to lose the physical vigor needed to continue the
exhausting pace of campaigning that had characterized his rule up to this point.[92] Nevertheless, the execution in 326 of his son Crispus—the only inheritor of
his military genius—had deprived him of the chance
to rest on his laurels immediately, for his next oldest
son, Constantine I, was likely only ten at the time.[93]
Thus as late as 328 Constantine went on campaign personally against Germanic tribes on the Rhine,[94] and he

FIGURE 15. Obverse:
CONSTANTI–NVS MAX
AVG. Constantine facing
right, wearing jeweled
diadem. *RIC* 7: Antioch 96.
ANS 1967.153.47. Courtesy
of the American Numis-
matic Society.

oversaw the construction of a bridge on the Danube at Oescus (Gigen) designed
to facilitate attacks against the Goths this same year.[95] Nevertheless, by 330, when
he was likely fifty-eight, he suffered a serious setback against the Taifali on the
Danube, and following this he seems to have withdrawn from military activities
and to have begun entrusting the conduct of wars to his sons and relatives.[96]

When in 332 the Goths invaded the territory of the Sarmatians, Constantine
left combat operations to Constantine II while he himself followed the war from
the frontier city of Marcianopolis.[97] When the brigand Calocaerus rose up on
Cyprus in 334, Constantine charged his stepbrother Dalmatius with the suppression of the revolt.[98] Again in 334, when the Sarmatians fled their territory in the
face of a rebellion by their slaves, Constantine's active involvement is reported,
but this was more a refugee crisis than a combat operation.[99] And by the time he
undertook his expedition against Persia in 337, he seems to have had little intention of actively engaging in field campaigns. By this point, his sixty-five-year-old
body was no longer up to the strains of campaigning, nor even travel, and he died
en route.[100] Even had he lived, Constantine does not seem to have had serious
plans to direct battle, for he entrusted military operations to his son Constantius
II while planning his own itinerary as a glorified pilgrimage that would culminate
in his baptism in the River Jordan.[101] Constantine was, in other words, now less
interested in playing the role of the soldier emperor and more intent on projecting the image of a divine monarch.

Aware of Constantine's growing devotion to religious interiority, Eusebius
associated this with the emperor's adoption of the titles *Victor* and *Triumphator* in

a way that showed how the military ruler of Constantine's past could be connected to the almost sacerdotal figure of these final years. In his *Tricennalian Oration*, pronounced for Constantine in the penultimate year of his life, he claims: "In the true sense, a 'Victor' is one who has achieved victory over the passions that overthrow the mortal human, who has modeled himself into the image of the archetype of the Supreme King, and who has been formed in his mind to reflect the rays of its virtues, and been perfected from these into one who is wise, good, just, virtuous, pious, and God-loving."[102] The earlier emphasis on triumphalism is thus embedded in a Christian symbolic framework in ways that deemphasize military glory in favor of divine rulership. Eusebius then expands upon this same theme in the last book of his *Life of Constantine*, which, as H. Drake has shown, represents something of a firsthand report of court activity as Eusebius witnessed it in the last three years of Constantine's reign.[103] He tells us Constantine spent long hours in the night praying and reading scripture, composed missives to his soldiers and subjects instructing them in how to glorify God, and pronounced didactic orations intended to push the *gens romana* to become a *populus christianus*.[104]

The very fact that the emperor offered the task of delivering the keynote oration on this quintessentially political occasion to a Christian bishop constitutes a powerful indicator of the image he was then striving to project.[105] Indeed, the passage of the oration that follows immediately after that just quoted gives even stronger testimony to the emperor's ostensible detachment from the conduct of government in favor of spiritual pursuits: "So he longs for the incorruptible and spiritual kingdom of God, and he prays to come into it. Through exalted contemplation he has raised his thoughts beyond the heavenly vault, and now he cherishes in his heart an indescribable longing for the lights there, by comparison with which he judges the honors of his present life to be no more than darkness. For he recognizes that rule over men is a small and fleeting authority over a mortal and temporary life, not much greater than the rule exercised by goatherds or shepherds or cowherds—in fact, he considers the job more troublesome and the creatures harder to satisfy."[106] This was truly a remarkable statement, coming as it does from a panegyrist of the ruler of the Roman world. It shows better than anything that we are now a universe away from the panegyric of 307 with its praise of the junior tetrarch for his unflagging commitment to battlefield success. We have entered a new era with a new style of leader whose very contempt for temporal authority is touted as his chief qualification for rule.[107]

Further evidence that Constantine had merged the traditions of imperial ceremonial with Christian ritualism can be found in the fact that he planned the dedication of the church he had constructed over the site of the Holy Sepulchre in Jerusalem to coincide with the opening celebrations of his tricennalia.[108] Similar constructions were proceeding apace back in Constantinople, where he was preparing his imperial mausoleum, the first such to house the remains of a Christian emperor. Not only did he outfit this new rotunda with cenotaphs (*thekai*) for the twelve apostles, but he also appears to have procured the relics of what he believed to be Saints Andrew and Luke for installation beside his own body.[109] The structure itself was similar enough to earlier imperial mausolea and the ceremonies associated with his burial close enough to previous deifications (*consecrationes*) that his interment there by no means precluded the worship of Constantine qua deified ruler from taking root. Nevertheless, Constantine's own self-projection in these final days was all but unprecedented in its patent gestures toward Christianity. Nowhere is this clearer than in his baptism immediately before his death, when he knelt in front of bishop Eusebius of Nicomedia and humbly subjected himself to a ceremony that would have been anathema to all previous Roman rulers.[110] After the ceremony, in the few days remaining to him, Constantine refused to don again the imperial purple but insisted instead on wearing a garment as white as divine light. More importantly, he is said to have promised solemnly that, if he survived his illness, he would commit himself wholly to a life of prayer.[111] All of this was unique in imperial tradition up to this point.

Constantine's final seven years thus represented yet another stage in his ongoing metamorphosis. In part compelled by the exigencies of age, in part by the desire to enact his conversion in a fashion more in keeping with the priestly and ascetic norms of the Christian church, Constantine began a process of withdrawal from active campaigning and underwent a transformation from military monarch to divine ruler. While continuing to exercise supreme power, he detached himself from direct involvement with army affairs and focused instead on the instruction of his ministers and subjects in Christian principles using both word and deed. By the time of his death, Constantine was willing to abdicate power, not in the manner of Diocletian, who had retired to the traditional Roman life of farming and leisure, but to the numinous lifestyle of a Christian zealot.

Conclusion

Constantine was thus a figure in a state of continuous self-transformation. Far from remaining static in his pursuits and self-presentation, he shifted his agenda at key moments in his reign in ways that are still perceptible in the source record. The most obvious example of this can be found in his titulature, which was gradually modified and adapted over time:

- He began with the acceptance of titles like CAESAR, NOBILISSIMUS, and PRINCEPS IUVENTUTIS, all marks of junior status used in varying combinations alongside the title AUGUSTUS—the mark of full imperial authority—in the first four years of his rule.
- These were abandoned in favor of INVICTUS in 310, which was supplemented with MAXIMUS AUGUSTUS by 315, the first a reflection of a purported special relationship with the Sun God, the second a claim to superiority vis-à-vis his fellow AUGUSTI.
- By late 324 Constantine abandoned INVICTUS in favor of VICTOR in the aftermath of the defeat of his last rival and his choice to distance himself publicly from previous claims to connections with the Sun God.
- Around 330 he again changed his titulature by adding the designation TRIUMPHATOR, which seemed to represent an admission that his fighting days were over, although he continued to rule as the embodiment of divine triumph.

This same gradual shift can be seen in his portraiture, which

- initially highlighted Constantine's connections with the tetrarchs (circa 307),
- then began to emphasize his individual physiognomy and hairstyle (circa 315),
- in turn drew attention to monarchy and his special relationship with the divine (circa 324),
- and finally laid weight on his gravitas as an inspired monarch (circa 330).

These same shifts can be seen in panegyrics and imperial communiqués. In the first panegyric delivered to Constantine in 307, his subordination to the senior Augustus Maximianus Herculius is foregrounded. By the time we reach the panegyric of 310, he has forged connections with a new dynasty, but also a new deity, the Sun God. In the years immediately following, Constantine gave himself the mission of suppressing "tyrants," a word he adopted as a designation for his rival Maxentius in order to emphasize his outrageous behavior and the illegitimacy of his claims to rule. By 324, the same notion was applied to Licinius, although by this date "tyrant" had taken on the added connotation of "persecutor of Christians." As part of this same shift, Constantine began quite openly to broadcast his conviction that he was the agent of divine vengeance against those who attacked the Christian church. He was, in other words, the champion of God's faith. These were terms conceptualized for him by his adviser and propagandist Lactantius, and they recur with remarkable regularity in Constantinian documents from precisely this period. By the early 330s, Constantine had pulled back from military commitments and transformed himself yet again into a sort of imperial bishop whose concerns were as much spiritual as administrative or military.

This gradual but radical transformation, mapped out here in stages, was surely more organic than the stepwise development I describe. Nevertheless, this schematism has relied on datable sources to re-create in the abstract an archaeology of Constantine's public personality. The advantage to this approach has been to permit us to isolate stages in the development of a complex emperor and thus to draw attention to the fact that he ended his reign in a very different place than it had begun. By examining these developmental phases diachronically, we have been able gradually to uncover—and thus to recover—the image of a man whose appearance changes as he emerges from the layers of the past. As noted at the beginning of the chapter, each of these has left its mark on subsequent interpretations, for in their variety, they have fostered the multiplicity of approaches to Constantine that make him appear to be so many things to so many people. Instead of a single Constantine with a thousand faces, however, I would propose instead that Constantine's gradual metamorphosis left variant marks and impressions depending on the social position and conceptual assumptions of each viewer, each interpreter, each reader. We thus return to the notion of a composite emperor, constructed from varied signals transmitted by the man himself and his professional image makers, but then reconstructed from selections and interpretations into the variety of Constantines that prevail even up to the present.

CHAPTER 2

Constantinian Constants

Pillars of Public Presentation

In the previous chapter, we examined Constantine as a figure in a continuous state of self-refashioning. He made and remade his image to suit changing circumstances, to adapt to chance occurrences, and to respond to political and military exigencies. We should not, however, lose sight of the fact that there are also many constants in Constantine's public persona that must be taken into account. Indeed, some aspects of his self-representation—as well as his self-construction—were remarkably long lived. In this chapter we will examine four of these: his unflagging obsession with the power of light, his enduring belief in his unimpeachable claims to victory, his deep-seated conviction that he was personally inspired by the divine, and his pervasive assumption that his rule was founded on rights of dynasty and strengthened by the extension of that dynasty into the future.

We shall see that in each instance these four pillars of Constantinian public presentation endured throughout his reign, yet they too were in their own ways subject to gradual transformation. As Constantine's assumptions and priorities changed, so too his presentation of the power of light, victory, divine inspiration, and dynasty. These foundational notions were adapted to take account of shifts brought about by past successes or failures and reformulated to conform to changing objectives for the future. Even these bedrocks of continuity thus offer evidence of unceasing adaptability and variability that help explain why they might have been treated as malleable symbols by the various audiences that received and interpreted them.

The Power of Light

It has long been accepted that Constantine developed an early attachment to the pagan god of the sun in his various guises: Apollo, Helios, and especially Sol Invictus. This deity formed a key component in Constantinian public propaganda from at least 310 until 325 and arguably both before and after these dates. This ongoing devotion to the Sun God in many ways reflected a much deeper obsession with the nature of light and, by extension, its power as a metaphor.[1] Indeed, Constantine's fascination with light appears to have been a constant that endured throughout his emperorship, from its beginnings, when he still adhered to a traditional religious framework, to its end, when his theological perspective was thoroughly Christian. Even as his worldview developed, the image of light provided a guiding principle around which he organized his conception of the universe and the divine.

Already in the first sentence of the first extant oration delivered to him, Constantine is portrayed as the "rising emperor" (*oriens imperator*), a reference not only to his standing as an up and coming junior tetrarch, but also to the image of the rising sun.[2] The sun god Sol Invictus, who had become popular under the Severans and was lionized by Aurelian in the 270s but then assigned a secondary role in the religious propaganda of the tetrarchs,[3] reappears on Constantine's coinage as early as 307 and comes to dominate imperial propaganda beginning in 310.[4] As we learn from the panegyric delivered to him in this year, Constantine believed he had witnessed an apparition from the Sun God while on a military expedition in southern Gaul, probably near the city of Grand with its famous temple to Apollo Grannus.[5] According to the theory of P. Weiss, whose interpretation takes best account of the full range of extant evidence, Constantine most likely experienced on that day the meteorological phenomenon known as a solar halo, in which ice crystals in the upper atmosphere create the image of a glowing cross surrounded by circles of light.[6] In this same year, Sol Invictus begins to appear regularly on Constantine's coins and medallions as the emperor's divine companion (*comes*), a phenomenon so well known that it requires little explication here.[7] It is worth stressing, however, the uncanny assimilation between Constantine and the divine Sun in the numismatic iconography of this period, with the best example being the famous nine-solidus gold medallion minted at Ticinum in 313 that portrays the emperor and Sol Invictus side by side in profile in such a way that the two seem veritable twins (Fig. 16).[8] Sol Invictus then endures as Constantine's divine Doppelgänger on the coinage for a decade and a half, down to 325, and thus well beyond the date when Constantine began openly to advertise his turn toward Christianity in late 312.[9] Even as late as 330, he erected atop the porphyry column in the forum of his new eastern capital an image of himself outfitted as the Sun God and established an annual festival there involving the procession of a statue of himself with the attributes of the sun.[10] Indeed, the resilience of the solar deity in Constantinian public propaganda has led to considerable debate about the extent, nature, and sincerity of Constantine's Christian "conversion" altogether.

In many ways, however, the transition between devotion to the pagan Sun God and the Christian sky god seemed both natural and unproblematic because of the

FIGURE 16. Obverse: INVICTVS CONSTANTINVS MA–X AVG. Constantine and Sol Comes jugate, 9 solidus gold medallion of Ticinum. Bibliothèque Nationale de France, Paris. Copyright Bibliothèque Nationale de France, Paris.

strong traditional associations of both with light. Scripture and iconography had connected the Judeo-Christian god with radiance and the sun stretching back to the Old Testament.[11] This made the emperor's transition from pagan solar henotheism to Christian solar monotheism relatively smooth. His move in this direction can be charted at the levels of politics, theology, and iconography. Immediately following his victory at the Milvian Bridge, Constantine's public propaganda began to bruit his achievement as the banishment of darkness in favor of revelatory light, and this same rhetoric was applied to the defeat of Licinius a dozen years later.[12] In his theological pronouncements on the Christian god, Constantine regularly describes the Father and above all Christ as the creator and restorer of light in the world.[13] In many of these same, Constantine portrays himself not just as a harbinger of divine light but also as an active agent in its spread, working to guarantee that the darkness of theological error should be banished by the light of truth.[14] At times this task involved organizing and shepherding church councils, at others enacting concrete legislation. It is arguable that, already in the immediate aftermath of the Battle of the Milvian Bridge, Constantine issued a law establishing Sunday as an official holiday. While this was by all means designed to impose Christian ritual praxis onto the rhythms of ancient calendrical time, the language used in the law—which referenced "the venerable day of the Sun" without any mention of Christ—opened a window onto ecumenical interpretations through the shared medium of light: by the rhetoric of the law, weekly rest was now to be taken not on the "Lord's Day" (*dies dominica*), as Christians would call it, but on the "Day of the Sun" (*dies solis*).[15]

Along these same lines, we find in art and literature produced by both pagans and Christians numerous connections between Constantine and divine light. A number of images draw direct comparisons between Constantine and the Sun riding in his fiery chariot above the firmament: this is present already in the words of the panegyrist of 310,[16] reappears on the eastern tondo of Constantine's arch in Rome dedicated in 315 (Fig. 17),[17] recurs on Constantine's shield in the gold medallion of Ticinum just mentioned (Fig. 16),[18] and even shows up as late as 336 when Eusebius compares the imperial college of Constantine and his Caesars to the solar quadriga in a passage quoted below from his *Tricennalian Oration*.[19] Without making direct reference to the solar quadriga, the panegyrical poet Optatianus Porphyrius also described the emperor as a manifestation of the divine Sun in his poetry composed in the mid-320s.[20] The power of the sun was thus persistent, reflecting both Constantine's own political and religious assumptions and the awareness of his subjects that this paradigm would resonate with the emperor.

More generic images of light and illumination also continued to play a crucial role in Constantine's imperial self-presentation in the final years of his reign. During the Council of Nicaea in 325, he is said to have appeared wearing garments of flaming color like the sun, and in his opening oration to have declared it God's intention to use him as his agent to lead those ignorant of the divine Sun "to the perfect splendor of the eternal light."[21] During the annual celebration of Easter in his new capital, he is said to have made the entire city shine with candles and torches.[22] After receiving baptism, he chose to dress only in dazzling clothes that gave the shining impression of the sun and proclaimed himself "blessed to receive a share of the divine light."[23]

Light was thus an image whose universal power worked just as well in the overtly Christian fora to which Constantine devoted himself at the end of his reign as it had in the traditional pagan religious circumstances of his earliest years as ruler. Far from shedding his initial fascination with the power of light, he maintained and even increased it from the beginning of his reign to the end. Not

FIGURE 17. The Sun God rides his four-horse chariot heavenward with the Genius Populi Romani above and Oceanus reclining below. Roundel on the eastern side of the Arch of Constantine, Rome. Photo by N. Lenski.

only did light allow him to unify his pagan and Christian subjects around a shared symbol of divine energy, it also served as a beacon of unwavering consistency in his public self-presentation even as he transformed himself from pagan to Christian ruler. The undeniable bivalency, or rather polyvalency, of this mysterious force opened a space for multiple and at times competing readings of Constantine's theological assumptions and his broader religious program. The messages his subjects decoded from this complex of ideas were thus bound to be fraught with ambivalence and at times contradiction.

Triumphalism and Victory

Second among the constants observable across Constantine's reign was an obsession with triumphalism and victory. To be sure, this was a quality expected of all late Roman emperors and indeed of Roman emperors *tout court*. Nevertheless, in Constantine's case, triumphalism was elevated to hyperbolic importance, in no small part because it fit so well with his skills as a military genius. The importance of martial valor is evident already in the stories he seems to have reported of his earliest achievements—successes fending off a wild lion in a contest forced upon him by Galerius, or victorious single combat with a Sarmatian chieftain.[24] In the second year of his reign, he is heralded by the panegyrist of 307 as the military enforcer of the elder Augustus Maximianus, and after the Battle of the Milvian Bridge, he began to assume the series of triumphalist epithets cataloged in Chapter 1: *Invictus*, *Victor*, and ultimately *Victor et Triumphator*. Throughout his reign, military imagery pervades the coinage, from the widely diffused VIRTVS MILITVM silver type of his earliest reign (Fig. 18), to the ubiquitous GLORIA EXERCITVS

FIGURE 18. Reverse: VIRTVS MILITVM. Four-turreted gateway. *RIC* 6: Treveri 200. ANS 1944.100.5964. Courtesy of the American Numismatic Society.

FIGURE 19. Reverse: GLOR-IA EXERC-{ITVS}. Two soldiers facing, holding spear and shield, between them a labarum. *RIC* 7: Arles 394. ANS 1944.100.11418. Courtesy of the American Numismatic Society.

bronzes that dominate its last decade (Fig. 19).[25] Even the labarum, read by Christian contemporaries as a decidedly Christian symbol, was first and foremost a military talisman. This is clear already in Lactantius's and Eusebius's accounts of its first appearance when the chi-rho was used to mark the shields and standards of Constantine's army in 312.[26] This remained the case in the 310s, when Constantine emblazoned his parade helmet with the symbol (see Figs. 2–3),[27] and still in 327 when the image appeared atop a cavalry *vexillum* in Constantinopolitan coin reverses with the legend SPES PVBLIC(a) (see Fig. 11).[28] In that same year it came to feature on the flags of standards in coins issued from Siscia under the legend GLORIA SECVLI (*sic*), and in 336 it recurred on coins from Arles under the legend GLORIA EXERCITVS.[29] Similar power is attributed by Constantine and his supporters to the cross, one of the most notable examples being the monumental statue of Constantine dedicated in Rome following the Battle of the Milvian Bridge that bore a cross in its right hand, an image discussed above in Chapter 1.[30] Late in his reign, the cross also appeared on coins atop or alongside military ensigns.[31]

By incorporating these new symbols into the broader palette of victory iconography, Constantine was able to capitalize on the idealization of victory shared by all his subjects in order to naturalize his adherence to the Christian community as an indispensable element in his successes as a martial leader. Turning a sign perceived by Christians as a reference to their own god into a standard—in both senses—for military success, Constantine could rally his subjects around the common good of victory while advertising a homology between that unquestioned good and his new god.

In the process, he made little effort to repress traditional victory imagery, not even when it verged into polytheism. While Sol Invictus has long been known as Constantine's favorite among the pagan gods, the scholarship has often ignored the central importance of the goddess Victoria as yet another divine figure that recurs repeatedly in Constantinian public propaganda. She features, for example, alongside the Sun God in Constantine's famous solar vision of 310— "For you saw, I believe, O Constantine, your Apollo accompanied by Victoria, offering you laurel wreaths."[32] Victoria had, of course, long been associated with imperial imagery in numismatic iconography in rather stereotyped representations, but for Constantine she represented something more than a simple personification of military achievement. On his arch in Rome, she is paired with Sol Invictus atop military standards in no fewer than four reliefs (Fig. 20), and she is also shown crowning Constantine across from Sol Invictus in the arch's eastern bay (Fig. 21).[33] She appears in the same aspect crowning Sol Invictus as he drives a chariot on a gold festival coin minted in Ticinum shortly after the Battle of the Milvian Bridge (Fig. 22),[34] and she remains a presence on the coinage down to Constantine's last days and indeed well into the fifth century.

FIGURE 20. Left: Two standard bearers with standards of Victoria (left) and Sol Invictus (right). Right: Victoria inscribes shield while kneeling on captive. Socle from north face of the Arch of Constantine, Rome. Photo by N. Lenski.

FIGURE 21. Victoria (badly damaged) flanks emperor (Constantine). Interior of eastern bay of the Arch of Constantine, Rome. Deutsches Archäologisches Institut, Rom. Neg. D-DAI-ROM 35.609.

Perhaps most striking of all, Victoria appears on the reverse of a series of large bronze medallions where she is depicted standing at the prow of a warship driven by the emperor himself under the legend VICTORIA AVG(usti) (Fig. 23).[35] These showpieces, bearing a personification of the city of Constantinople on their obverse, offer a clear reference to Constantine's naval victories over Licinius in 324 and the beginning of his efforts to transform Byzantium into a new imperial capital. Victoria also appears on a rare gold multiple of Heraclea from precisely this time period. She is shown crowning Constantine from behind even as a per-

FIGURE 22. Obverse: CONSTAN‐TINVS PF AVG. Constantine laureate, facing right. Reverse: SOLI INVICTO–AETERNO AVG. Sol radiate standing in quadriga, right hand raised; behind Victoria standing, right hand holding wreath. © The Trustees of the British Museum. All rights reserved, 1866,0721.14.

FIGURE 23. Obverse: CONSTANTI‐NOPOLIS. Constantinople facing left, with helmet, breastplate, and spear. Reverse: V‐IC–TORIA–AVG. Galley moving right with rowers and the emperor seated in the stern. Victoria stands at the prow and extends a crown. Bronze medallion of Constantinople. Ntantalia Gruppe 3, Rs.‐Typus a. Kunsthistorisches Museum Vienna.

FIGURE 24. Obverse: IMP CONSTANTINVS MAX PF AVG. Constantine diademed, victoriola on globe in right hand. Reverse: SALVS ET SPES REPVBLICAE. Emperor seated receiving victoriola on globe from turreted female (Constantinopolis) and crowned by Victoria standing behind. Gold Medallion. *RIC* 7: Heraclea 99. Kunsthistorisches Museum Vienna.

sonification of Constantinopolis herself hands Constantine a globe with a victoriola that itself bears a crown (Fig. 24).[36] Providing an oppositional reading of these and similar images, the pagan epigrammatist Palladas drew attention to the irony that they represented the goddess Victoria bringing trophies to the emperor's new "Christ-loving city."[37] The poet was commenting on and critiquing efforts to draw this traditional divinity into a new space thoroughly controlled by an emperor who was by now openly Christian.[38] He understood well that Constantine was rallying support around the shared value of military achievement but refused quietly to countenance the exportation of this traditional goddess onto more neutral ground and thereby to coopt her into the Christian pantheon as a part of Constantine's broader repertoire of victory symbology. With his epigram, Palladas chose to call Constantine out for this incongruity, or rather impiety, even as he was forced to acknowledge implicitly how successful Constantine had been at reorienting traditional victory imagery along Christian lines.

Divine Favor

A third constant in Constantine's self-presentation is the conviction that the divine favored him in his every undertaking. This idea first appears in extant sources in the panegyric of 310 with its report of a direct epiphany from the Sun God and the goddess Victoria cited above.[39] It becomes even more explicit in the Panegyric of 313, which regularly resorts to the notion that Constantine had direct and unique access to an unnamed divinity that instructed him in the proper timing and procedure for attacking Maxentius.[40] At one key point in the oration, the orator argues that Constantine was able to devise shackles to contain his surplus of captives because he had been "advised through divine instigation" (*divino monitus instinctu*).[41] This same idea is echoed in the same terms on Constantine's arch in Rome, dedicated in 315, where the victory over Maxentius is also attributed to the instigation of the divinity (*instinctu divinitatis*).[42] Iconographic confirmation of this notion from this same period came to light in 1981 in a new coin type from Ostia datable to 313 depicting a divine hand reaching down from heaven to defend the emperor in battle—surely the Milvian Bridge, given the timing and location of the coin's minting.[43] Once again in 321 the panegyrist Nazarius presents Constantine as the agent of justice who ruled through divine instigation (*divino instinctu*) and even claims that a celestial army was sent to assist him in his war of 312.[44] Building on this complex of ideas at precisely the same time, Lactantius presents a slightly different version of events that argues Constantine's inspiration derived from a miraculous dream vision sent by the Christian god in which the emperor was instructed to mark the shields of his soldiers with the staurogram before engaging in combat with Maxentius. Elaborating on this story two decades later, Eusebius appears to have connected Constantine's solar vision with this dream and to have attributed both to the Christian god.[45] Interpreters pagan and Christian thus accepted Constantine's publicly stated belief that he had direct contact with the divine and that this had been the key to his success against his rival Maxentius in 312.

Constantine and his message makers continued to advertise this same theme when the emperor turned his forces against Licinius for their final standoff in 324. From this context we have reports in the pagan tradition that he saw a pair of divine youths who fought back the enemy lines of Licinius at Adrianople and that he witnessed a divine light girding his encampment during the siege of Byzantium.[46] Describing these same events, the Christian Eusebius reports that rows of heavenly soldiers appeared in the eastern lands before the approach of Constantinian troops in order to herald his arrival.[47] Later, Eusebius also reports that before his engagements with Licinius, Constantine followed the practice of praying in his tent until he received a revelation from God, whereupon he would rush into battle and promptly achieve victory.[48] Such rhetoric of direct contact with the divine continues in public pronouncements down to the *Tricennalian Oration* of 336.[49] The conviction that Constantine was divinely inspired and was serving as the instrument of divine justice was thus shared by the full spectrum of his subjects, early and late, pagan and Christian. It was a truth all were willing to accept even if each conceived of its expression in slightly different terms, terms generally conditioned by the assumptions that underlay their own conceptions of the divine.

The readiness of Constantine's message makers to propagate the myth of his divine inspiration was in no small part governed by the fact that this was a story Constantine himself regularly broadcast. In his many extant communiqués, he consistently repeats his belief that his successes as ruler and conqueror were attributable directly to the will of the divine:

- 313: In his letter ordering the Council of Rome, he expresses concern that he manage religious affairs "in those provinces that Divine Providence has of its own accord entrusted to my devotedness [*tē emē kathosiōsei*]." (Eus. *HE* 10.5.18)
- 313: In the "Edict of Milan," Constantine and Licinius assert that they are granting freedom of worship "in order that the supreme divinity, whose religion we follow with free minds, may be able to offer us in all things its customary favor [*solitum favorem suum*] and benevolence," and they close the document, "Thus it will come about, just as we explained above, that the divine favor toward us [*divinus iuxta nos favor*], which we have experienced in such great matters, will continue to be beneficial to our successes with our public blessing." (Lact. *Mort. Pers.* 48.3, 11; cf. Eus. *V. Const.* 10.5.5, 13)
- 314: In his letter asking the vicar Aelafius to aid in organizing the Council of Arles, Constantine describes himself as the one "in whose care [the Highest God] committed for governance all earthly things through his heavenly approval." (Opt. *App.* 3 [*CSEL* 26: 206])
- 314: In his letter to the Catholic bishops of the Council of Arles, he speaks of his success as a gift granted "by the omnipotent God, who sits upon his watchtower in heaven." (Opt. *App.* 5 [*CSEL* 26: 208])
- 324: In his letter to the provincials of Palestine, he describes an end to the persecutions "through the power of almighty God, and both the encour-

agements and the benefits which he has so often seen fit to administer on my behalf [*hyper emou*]." (Eus. *V. Const.* 2.42.1)

- 324: In his letter to Eusebius on church construction, we read, "now that that dragon [Licinius] has been driven out from the management of the state through the providence of the supreme God and through our service [*hēmetera d'hypērēsia*], I believe that the divine power has been made manifest to all." (Eus. *V. Const.* 2.46.2)

- 324: In his letter to the eastern provincials, he implores the Christian god to "extend healing through me your servant [*di'emou tou sou ther-apontos*] . . . for by your guidance I have implemented deeds of salvation and brought them to completion. Carrying before me everywhere your seal [*sphragis*] as my protection, I have led a victorious army." (Eus. *V. Const.* 2.55.1)

- 324: In his letter to Alexander and Arius, he opens by invoking "God himself . . . the helper in my undertakings [*ton tōn emōn encheirēmatōn boēthon*] and Savior of the universe." (Eus. *V. Const.* 2.64.1)

- 325: In his *Oration to the Assembly of the Saints*, Constantine acknowledges that God has been the source of all his gifts (*hēmin . . . theou de estin hapanta dōrēmata*), and later he ascribes his good fortune and that of his followers to God's good will (*egō men tēs eutuxias tēs emaoutou kai tōn hemōn pantōn aitiōmai tēn sēn eumenian*); finally, he attributes his service to the inspiration of God and claims that victories were awarded to the people in response to his prayers (*hotan de tēn emēn hypēresian epainōsin ex epipnoias theou tēn arxēn exousan . . . tēs tou theou pronoias tēn nikēn tō dēmō brabeuousēs, kai eidon ton theon tais hēmeterais euxais sunairomenon*). (*Or. ad Sanct.* 11.2, 22.1, 26.1–2)

- 325: In Eusebius's reconstruction of Constantine's speech to the Council of Nicaea, he reports the emperor saying, "Thus when I achieved victories over enemies with the approval and support of the Supreme [*neumati kai sunergia tou kreittonos*], I considered that nothing remained but to acknowledge the thanks owed to God." (Eus. *V. Const.* 3.12.3)

- Late 330s: Eusebius claims Constantine would instruct his courtiers that "the God over all things had granted to him kingship over those on earth [*autō men gar ton epi pantōn theon tōn epi gēs tēn basileian paraschein*], and that he in imitation of the Supreme had turned over the districts of the empire piece by piece to them." (Eus. *V. Const.* 4.29.4)

- 335: In a letter summoning participants of the synod at Tyre to Constantinople, Constantine claims, "it is because of my religious service toward God that all the world is peaceful [*dia tēs emēs pros theon latreias ta pantaxou eirēneuetai*]." (Soc. 1.34.9)[50]

Constantine was thus consistent in his message to his various subjects: he had achieved and continued to achieve victory and political success through the direct support of the supreme divinity, which had ordained him personally to manage the affairs of state for the good of the world.

In a series of related pronouncements spread across the chronological span of his reign, Constantine adds a narrative strain to this notion by expressing the belief that he had been appointed by the divine to move from West to East across the *oikoumene* enacting God's justice. This is stated most explicitly in his letter to the Provincials of Palestine: "He [God] sought out my service [*tēn emēn hyperēsian*] and judged it fit for his own plan, and I, *beginning from that sea bordering the Britons and the lands where a more powerful force has ordered that the sun should set* [my italics], have driven away and scattered the horrors that held everything in subjection, in order that the human race, schooled by my obedience, might restore service to the most revered law, and at the same time that the most blessed faith might be made to grow through a more powerful guide."[51] Addressed as it was to a Christian audience, this letter cast Constantine's west-to-east procession in explicitly Christian terms. We find the same overtones in Constantine's use of this narrative trope in his letter to Shapur.[52] Nevertheless, we also find the notion expressed more ecumenically in an inscription of Thracian Beroe (Stara Zagora, Bulgaria), dated to the end of Constantine's reign, that honors him as "the one who has taken up bloodless victories, from the West to the East."[53] If we can believe a passage in Petrus Patricius, the idea was already floated in 316 when Constantine is reported to have offered it as justification for his refusal to relent to Licinius on the eve of their first civil war, and it is arguable that the Senate of Rome was aware of it as early as 315 when they dedicated Constantine's arch with a band of reliefs depicting a west-to-east journey as the guiding principle underlying their pictorial narrative of Constantine's crusade to liberate the city.[54] Picking up on this strain, Eusebius repeats it twice in his own words in the *Life of Constantine* and thus makes it clear that he was keenly aware of how Constantine conceived of his struggle for world rule as an eastward journey of cosmic significance.[55] More importantly, by proffering this dominant reading of Constantine's storyline, Eusebius demonstrates that he credits the narrative.

From the earliest period of his reign, then, Constantine was convinced that he had direct contact with the supreme divinity, which was using his service (*hypēsia*) in order to implement its providential plan on earth. To be sure, earlier emperors, including the tetrarchs, had also made claims to providentially inspired rule, but these were never as persistent nor their implications as personal and elaborate as Constantine's.[56] With Constantine's turn to Christianity, such claims became more rather than less common, even as he took on the role of crusader for the Christian god against those who persecuted his followers. At some point after the Battle of the Milvian Bridge, this overarching notion assumed a narrative aspect that presumed the force of destiny pulling Constantine from the western reaches of the *oikoumene* to its east. This conception justified his choice to gobble up the domains of his co-rulers Maxentius and in turn Licinius. Constantine's divine connection thus remained a constant throughout his reign, even if it too—just like his obsession with light and victory—was adapted gradually to suit shifts in his religious and political agenda.

Dynasticism

Finally, Constantine manifested a constant concern with dynasticism that endured from the beginning to the end of his reign. Early on, before the maturity of his son Crispus and the birth of his remaining children, this took the form of glorifying his ancestry. Thus already in his second year as emperor, the panegyrist of 307 praises Constantine for his royal birth, the heroic deeds of his father, and his physical resemblance to Constantius I.[57] These same themes are repeated by the panegyrists of 310 and 311.[58] In similar fashion, the coins and inscriptions from Constantine's early reign draw attention to the MEMORIA of the deified Constantius.[59] The desire to fortify his dynastic platform quickly pushed Constantine to expand his pedigree by arranging marriage with Maximianus's daughter Fausta in 307, a bond heralded in the panegyric of that year and further signaled in inscriptions that proclaim Constantine the "Descendant of Marcus Aurelius Valerius Maximianus Augustus."[60] Nevertheless, when Maximianus's star was eclipsed by his rebellion and forced suicide in 310, the propagandistic value of this link was severely damaged, compelling Constantine to condemn his father-in-law through a *damnatio memoriae* and to search for a new dynastic connection. This he achieved by inventing (or perhaps rediscovering) a relationship with the third-century emperor Claudius Gothicus, whose brief but glorious reign provided a perfect preamble to Constantine's growing sense of grandeur.[61] Moreover, with the death of Maximianus's son, Maxentius, in 312, Constantine rehabilitated his father-in-law so that by 318 he was able to boast a trifecta of imperial forebears in a numismatic series glorifying Constantius I (Fig. 25a), Maximianus (Fig. 25b), and Claudius Gothicus (Fig. 25c) as his deified ancestors.[62] It is of course striking that through much of this early period Constantine was operating within the bounds of official discourse established by the tetrarchy. The tetrarchs had, after all, deemphasized dynastic origins in their imperial self-presentation, a rhetorical strategy that contrasted starkly with Constantine's own obsession with his regal origins.[63] This disconnect illustrates well his unease with the limitations imposed on him by tetrarchic models and his desire to capitalize on his manifest—as well as manufactured—dynastic assets as a means to individuate his rulership.

FIGURE 25a. Obverse: DIVO CONSTANTIO PIO PRINCIPI. Constantius I laureate and veiled facing right. Reverse: REQVIES OPTIM−ORVM MERITORVM. Emperor seated left on curule chair raising right hand and holding scepter. *RIC* 7: Thessalonica 25. Kunsthistorisches Museum Vienna.

FIGURE 25b. Obverse: DIVO MAXIMIANO OPTIMO IMP. Maximianus laureate and veiled facing right. Reverse: Same as Figure 25a. *RIC* 7: Thessalonica 24. Kunsthistorisches Museum Vienna.

FIGURE 25c. Obverse: DIVO CLAVDIO OPTIMO IMP. Claudius II Gothicus laureate and veiled facing right. Reverse: Same as Figure 25a. *RIC* 7: Thessalonica 26. Kunsthistorisches Museum Vienna.

After his defeat of Maxentius in 312, Constantine began gradually to shift his dynastic politics from an emphasis on the past to a concentration on the present and future. This change is signaled already in the panegyric of 313, where he is not simply praised for having had an imperial father but also for having already surpassed his father's achievements.[64] When in this same year Constantine gave his half-sister Constantia as wife to Licinius, he began to broaden his dynastic interests to his own generation. This move also extended his dynastic claims outside his own territorial realm, a fact confirmed by a number of eastern inscriptions styling the first child of this marriage, named Licinius after his father, with the additional epithet "Constantinus."[65] Extraterritorial dynastic ambitions also underlay Constantine's attempts to foist his brother-in-law, Bassianus, as a Caesar upon Licinius in 315, a bungled effort that helped provoke the first civil war between these two

FIGURE 26. Obverse: FL HELENA–AVGVSTA. Helena facing right. Reverse: SECVRITAS–REIPVBLICE. Securitas standing lowering branch and raising robe. *RIC* 7: Arles 324. ANS 1984.146.1646. Courtesy of the American Numismatic Society.

Augusti.[66] As part of the treaty that ended that war, Constantine further advanced his dynastic agenda by having his sons Crispus and Constantine II proclaimed Caesars—along with Licinius the younger—on March 1, 317. The choice of date proves, once again, that Constantine was driving the agenda, for this was the same day on which his father Constantius I had been proclaimed Caesar in 293.[67] This synchrony allowed Constantine to bridge his imperial past to its future by highlighting the connections between the three generations of rulers in his family. The notion of dynastic continuity would later be reflected in claims by a number of sources—Eusebius, Libanius, and Julian—that Constantine's children received the empire by right of civil law, as if it were their inheritance.[68]

By the time we reach the next in the series of extant imperial panegyrics in 321, its author Nazarius—who spoke in celebration of the fifth anniversary of Crispus's and Constantine II's rule—has shifted the spotlight away from the glory of Constantine's predecessors and onto his exemplarity as a father.[69] Similarly, the anonymous author of the Gallic poem known as the *Laudes Domini,* composed between 317 and 323, dedicated his verses to Constantine as "a father through his piety" and wished "that his children may one day equal their father."[70] In this same vein, during the years following Constantine's defeat of Licinius in 324, Constantine's role as dynastic founder assumes even grander proportions. This was in no small part because the public profile of the next generation of his family

FIGURE 27. Obverse: FLAV MAX–FAVSTA AVG. Fausta facing right. Reverse: SALVS REI–PVBLICAE. Empress draped and veiled holding two children at her breasts. *RIC* 7: Ticinum 182. ANS 1967.153.50. Courtesy of the American Numismatic Society.

came into its own as he proclaimed no fewer than four male relatives Caesar between 324 and 335. On November 8, 324, he named his third son, Consantius II, Caesar in Constantinople in conjunction with the initiation of that city's reconstruction as an eastern capital.[71] Probably on that same occasion, he hailed as Augustae both his wife Fausta and his mother Helena—styled in inscriptions the "procreator" of Constantine and "grandmother of the Caesars."[72] Shortly thereafter, both Augustae began to appear with their new titles on the coinage in issues that emphasized their fertility and familial piety (Figs. 26–27).[73] In mid-326 Constantine ordered the execution of Crispus, briefly sidetracking his dynastic agenda, but by 333 he returned to a reserve of three heirs apparent by proclaiming Constans, his fourth son, Caesar on December 25—the *dies natalis* of Sol Invictus as well as the date of the incarnation of Christ.[74] Throughout this period Constantine's dynastic agenda was advertised widely on coins and medallions that regularly depicted not just Constantine Augustus but also his Caesars on obverses and portrayed Constantine flanked by his sons and heirs on reverses (Fig. 28).[75] Of special note in this regard is a group of bronze coins minted in 325 and often referred to as the "dynastic series" that depict Constantine and his three co-reigning Caesars on their anepigraphic obverses and then identify each with a plain inscription listing their titles on the reverse (e.g., Fig. 29a–b).[76]

Eventually, Constantine stretched his dynastic platform further by nominating his nephew Dalmatius as Caesar for Thrace, Macedonia, and Achaia on September 18, 335.[77] This may have represented an effort to recreate a tetrarchic system using members of his dynasty whereby the two most senior—Constantine II and Constantius II—would become Augusti upon his death, while the two more

FIGURE 28. Obverse: FL IVL CONSTANTIVS NOB CAES. Constantius II cuirassed with shield showing emperor on horseback. Reverse: GAVDIVM R–OMANORVM. Constantine in center being crowned by heavenly hand, between two Caesars, the one on the left being crowned by a soldier and the one on the right by Victoria. 30 solidus medallion. *RIC* 7: Constantinople 42. Kunsthistorisches Museum Vienna.

FIGURE 29a. Obverse: Anepigraphic. Crispus laureate facing left. Reverse: CRISPVS–CAESAR. Star in upper field, SMANTB (Antiochene) mint mark. *RIC* 7: Antioch 53. Lars Ramskold collection, reproduced with permission.

FIGURE 29b. Obverse: Anepigraphic. Constantius II laureate facing left. Reverse: CONSTAN–TIVS–CAESAR. Star in upper field, SMANTS (Antiochene) mint mark. *RIC* 7: Antioch 55. Lars Ramskold collection, reproduced with permission.

junior—Constans and Dalmatius—would serve as their Caesars.[78] Yet at the same time, Constantine also appointed a fifth ruler, Dalmatius's brother Hannibalianus, whom he married to his daughter Constantia and nominated King of Kings for Armenia and Pontica.[79] This appointment obviously cannot be slotted into a tetrarchic scheme, even if we discount for the fact that Hannibalianus's designated domain lay outside existing Roman territory and was likely slated for conquest only in Constantine's final eastern campaign. Furthermore, the theory that Constantine was creating a sort of dynastic tetrarchy has been built in no small part on arguments that Constantine assigned each of his Caesars a full imperial entourage, including a Praetorian Prefect, yet extant epigraphic evidence indicates that this assumption must be revised. An inscription dating to 331/332 and two more of 335/336 indicate instead that, in his final years, Constantine established a total of five Praetorian Prefects and that these had territorial jurisdiction rather than being assigned to individual emperors.[80] Constantine's plans for organizing the empire thus reflected more about his concerns with the promotion of dynasty than an orchestrated effort to recreate the tetrarchy he had so assiduously undermined by the end of the second decade of his reign.

This overriding sense of dynasty in his final years is further reflected by the fact that, around the same time he promoted his nephews, Constantine also entrusted a greater share in state affairs to their father, Dalmatius the Elder, as well as Dalmatius's brother, Julius Constantius, both Constantine's half-brothers.[81] This bloated extension of the family tree into the imperial apparatus can only be described as hypertrophic and must surely reflect as much Constantine's pretensions to grandeur as any coordinated attempt to craft a solid and enduring governmental scheme. Its fragility was all but guaranteed by its excess, and indeed, it collapsed in the well-known slaughter that followed Constantine's death on May 22, 337. Already by the end of June that year, the infamous "Great Massacre," an internecine slaughter engineered by Constantius II but carried out with the full complicity of army and officials, claimed the lives of Dalmatius *père et fils*, Hannibalianus, Julius Constantius, and most of the remaining offspring of Constantius I by his second wife Theodora—Constantine's stepmother.[82]

It is interesting that Constantine's mannered and unwieldy extension of this dynastic scheme coincides with the period when he was projecting the public image of a divine monarch. By this point his conviction that his rulership was the manifestation of some supernatural ordering of the cosmos had reached an all-time high. This same understanding seems to have subtended his desire to see to it that his entire extended family be given a share in the empire. Its grandiosity can also be found in Eusebius's *Triakontaiterikos,* which compares Constantine's dynasty to the very heavens above:

> As the light of the sun shines with rays sent forth over long distances upon those dwelling in the farthest reaches, so also does he grant to those of us who dwell in the East offspring worthy of himself, one of his sons to one nation of men and another to another, like lanterns or beacons of the light emanating from him. Then, having yoked the four valiant Caesars under one harness to his imperial quadriga, as if they were colts, and having united them with the reins of godly harmony and concord, he drives them holding the reins from high above, and he courses over the entire earth which the sun oversees, while he himself is present to all and oversees everything.[83]

With the white glare of this rhetoric, Eusebius blurs many boundaries here: that between emperor and god, between temporal rule and cosmic order, and between Christian and pagan solar theism. Through his dynasty, Constantine has become a god unto himself, guiding his empire even as he enlightens the world through the agency of his dynastic successors.[84] In this sense we return once again to the points made in the previous chapter: even the constants in Constantine's imperial self-presentation were transformed over time to reflect new agendas in keeping with developing conceptions of the nature of his rule. Constantine's unfaltering concern with dynasty had gradually shifted from an obsession with his regal ancestry to an overweening desire to populate the empire, and on a symbolic level the cosmos, with his offspring, like so many emanations from his divinely inspired rulership.

Conclusion

For all that Constantine's public self-presentation underwent changes in the course of his reign, it remained founded on certain principles that endured from beginning to end. Thus, throughout his lifetime we find an abiding fascination with light, a symbol of power shared across ancient religious and cosmological traditions. Even so, over the course of time, Constantine's public propaganda gradually deemphasized the role of the sun qua divine source of light in favor of a less focused understanding that conceived of light as a symbolic manifestation of the power of the Christian god. In keeping with long-standing Roman traditions, Constantine also assumed the importance of victory both as a representation of his own assertions of military authority and as a broader symbol for the power of the Roman state. Here too, however, while retaining the traditional iconography of the goddess Victoria in art and coinage up to his final years, Constantine displaced her from the realm of the divine and began to replace her with his new victory ensign—the labarum.

Constantine's repeated assertions to direct access to divine inspiration are perhaps the most forcefully and regularly attested constant of all. Yet these too shift depending not just on the passage of time but also on his audience, for while pagan observers as late as Nazarius and the Greek historiographic tradition depict Constantine's divine support in polytheist terms, Constantine's Christian supporters and indeed the emperor himself are more inclined to identify the Christian god as the source of his inspiration and success. And finally, dynasty recurs repeatedly as a bulwark underpinning Constantine's claims to legitimacy. Here too, however, he gradually moved away from an emphasis on his ancestry and toward a reliance on his own offspring as the manifestation of his dynastic prowess. This was of course the direction in which time carried the development of his family, but it also reflected a growing sense of grandiosity as he filled out the empire and its frontiers with his sons and nephews as rulers, but also extensions of himself into the next generation.

The enduring symbols of Constantine's rule were thus subject to change over time, and their gradual metamorphosis opened the door to his subjects to interpret their significance as polyvalent and at times even self-contradictory. In subsequent sections of this book, we shall see how the various Constantines presented to the empire were received and reflected back, but for now we must close this section with a final chapter that will offer a closer look at the single largest body of sources attesting to Constantine's self-presentation, the extensive series of communications he directed to Christian audiences.

CHAPTER 3

∾

Constantine and the Christians
Controlling the Message

Emperor and Audience

An emperor modulated his message not only to suit the advance of time and shifts in circumstance, but also with an eye to his audience. Many of the changes we witnessed in Constantine's self-presentation in Chapter 1 were traced using that group of sources intended for the widest and most general pool of his subjects: coins, portraits, inscriptions, and panegyrics. There were also media for communicating with more restricted audiences, especially letters and laws, both of which could pinpoint narrower constituencies. Because of the imperfect preservation of our sources, we have very few testimonia to Constantine's dealings with certain groups that we know to have existed as collectivities but to whom we have few if any imperial communications. In terms of religious groups, these include the Jews, who were a relatively unified if hardly monolithic collectivity and concerning whom we have precisely four Constantinian laws.[1] More frustrating still, we have only scanty evidence with which to reconstruct Constantine's dealings with pagans, a word we use as shorthand to characterize the largest religious class of his subjects, even if these were anything but a homogeneous or centrally organized collective unit.[2]

The one religious group for whom we do still possess a sizable number of communiqués is Christians. Here too, we would be mistaken to assume that Christians constituted anything like a uniform and cohesive body in Constantine's day, or for that matter in any period before or afterward. Nevertheless, we do have the advantage when speaking of Christians that these themselves generally bracketed the messy realities of doctrinal and organizational factionalism that always divided their movement and ideated their collective identity as a cohesive whole. This was also Constantine's perspective, for although he was fully aware of the multiplicity of conflicts dividing the Christians of his empire, he always maintained the belief that, with God's help, these were striving toward a unity that he himself was in no small part responsible for instantiating.

In this chapter we will focus on these communications in an effort to map out how Christians might have read their emperor by examining how his messages to them appear to have shaped their interpretations of the first emperor also to be their coreligionist. It is divided into four parts, the first of which examines the meager evidence for Constantine's earliest dealings with Christians and his conversion. Here we will see that Constantine's conversion story was by all means a narrative construction, but that it came into being fairly early in his reign and that it entailed real consequences for his dealings with the church. In the second it turns to the question of the identity of the god Constantine insisted was his comrade and helper. For all that Constantine and his message makers were publicizing reports that the Sun God was his "companion" (*comes*) on coins and in other visual media, from as early as 314 his communications with Christians indicated instead that he identified his helper god as Christ. In the third part, we will look at the relationship he cultivated with bishops, in whose councils he participated and in whose numbers he wished to rank himself. Finally, in the fourth we will see that Constantine came to imagine connections with the church as coterminous with his responsibilities to the empire. High on his list of priorities was thus the obligation to push his subjects, and by extension his empire, toward adherence to the church and compliance with what he believed to be its rules.

Early Constantine

Constantine initiated his relationship with the Christian church already at the opening of his reign. If we can believe Lactantius, "Once he took up power, Constantine Augustus did nothing before restoring Christians to their worship and god. This was his first legal measure for the restoration of the holy religion."[3] Some have seen in this brief statement a mythologizing retrojection of pro-Christian politics back to the beginnings of Constantine's reign. T. Barnes, by contrast, has strongly defended Lactantius's veracity.[4] Although Lactantius is likely right to imply that Constantine relaxed persecutions against Christians shortly after his accession, we have almost no idea precisely what this entailed. Did he simply revoke Diocletian's persecuting edicts (only the first of which had been enforced systematically in the West), or did he go further by granting the restoration of confiscated property, or even the conferral of privileges on Christian leaders? Given the present state of the evidence, there is no way to know. It does seem that this early expression of toleration reflected a sentiment Constantine himself describes in his *Oration to the Assembly of the Saints* when he explains that his personal experience of the Great Persecution under Diocletian and Galerius had convinced him that further attacks on the Christian community were at once futile and wrongheaded.[5] Apart from this, however, we have very little idea about the nature of his earliest moves in favor of Christians.

At some point, in these early years, Constantine is likely to have established contact with a number of western bishops, including Ossius of Corduba, who would serve as a close adviser to him until the end of his reign,[6] as well as Reticius of Autun, Marinus of Arles, and Maternus of Cologne, all of whom were invited to travel from north of the Alps in order to attend the church council he sponsored in Rome in October 313. As W. Eck has argued, these latter had almost certainly come to know the emperor during his years in Gaul.[7] Moreover, as discussed in the Chapter 1, Constantine also had at his side the learned Christian apologist Lactantius, who was serving as tutor to his son Crispus in Gaul from around 310 until 313, and whose work directly influenced Constantine's own writings beginning as early as the winter of 312/313.[8] Nevertheless, it was only after his conversion experience that we begin to get clearer signs of Constantine's favor for the broader Christian community.

Constantine's conversion has, of course, been the subject of repeated interpretive forays and cannot detain us at length here. It must, however, be touched upon, for it bears heavily on the manner in which he presented himself to the broader public. As noted earlier, I hold with the theory of P. Weiss that the sequence of events related to Constantine's conversion unfolded thus:[9]

- In 310 Constantine witnessed an atmospheric phenomenon known as a "solar halo," consisting of an X or cross inside a circle of light, which at the time he interpreted as a vision from Apollo.
- In the buildup to the Battle of the Milvian Bridge he then had (or claimed to have had) a dream in which he believed a divinity told him to reproduce the sign he had seen in the sky on his battle standards.
- In consultation with Christian advisers, Constantine associated this divinity with the Christian god and understood the symbol as a staurogram or chi-rho (Christogram).
- He ordered this symbol (or symbols) to be reproduced on his shields and perhaps also his battle standards and marched at the Milvian Bridge under this sign.
- Constantine's subsequent victory cemented his credence in the interpretation of the sign he had adopted.

In making this argument, Weiss operated on the assumption that Constantine's dream and consultation with Christian advisers occurred in 312, the year in which the Battle of the Milvian Bridge occurred and the traditional date for Constantine's conversion. K. M. Girardet subsequently made a strong case that it may have occurred as early as late 311.[10] I am inclined to agree with Girardet's arguments, although the precise date affects the case presented here very little.

The first written account to narrate all of these events in sequence—but with no mention of Apollo in its description of the original vision—comes in Eusebius's *Life of Constantine* written circa 338. According to Eusebius, Constantine himself had reported this story at a personal meeting the bishop had with the emperor during which he was shown what was purported to be the original labarum that Constantine ordered to be fashioned in response to his dream.[11] R. Van Dam has argued that the sequence of events stitched together by Eusebius here was actually an invention of the author himself, who was attempting to defend his subordinationist theology by portraying Constantine as a Christlike subordinate to God the Father.[12] As we shall see, this argument is vitiated by inattention to sources outside Eusebius, but it does have the virtue of emphasizing the constructed nature of Constantine's conversion account. The conversion was, in other words, a story created out of a series of experiences, interpreted and refashioned into a continuous and teleological narrative—what we might call a historical memory.

Our first written document from the pen of Constantine confirming that he believed the labarum to be a Christian symbol that had guaranteed him victory in battle dates to 324, when Constantine wrote in his letter to the eastern provincials: "And in fact, I ask these things of you quite fittingly, O Lord of All, Holy God. For by your guidance I have implemented deeds of salvation and brought them to completion. *Carrying before me everywhere your seal* [sphragis] *as my protection, I have led a victorious army* [my italics]. And if ever public need called for it anywhere, following the same symbols [*synthēmata*] of your virtue I have gone forth against the enemy."[13] This full-throated interpretation of the labarum as a Christian sign and as a metonym for Constantine's military mission on behalf of the church fits perfectly with the sequence of development of Constantine's public personality laid out in Chapter 1. There we saw that Constantine only came to portray himself openly as a champion of the faith in the period straddling his war with Licinius in 324. Indeed, in the years immediately following the Battle of the Milvian Bridge, his story of vision, dream, consultation, creation of the labarum, and conquest was not apparently in wide circulation. Lactantius, in his *On the Deaths of Persecutors* written circa 315, describes the Battle of the Milvian Bridge in some detail, but mentions only the dream and creation of the standard while omitting the vision and consultation with Christian advisers.[14] Moreover, his description of the dream and labarum are hardly given center stage in his broader narrative, for Lactantius in no way signposts them as pivotal to his story nor to the story of Constantine's development. Meanwhile Eusebius, whose original account of the Battle of the Milvian Bridge was written into his *Ecclesiastical History*, first published circa 313/314 and revised in 315/316, makes no mention of the vision or dream whatsoever.[15] We must thus conclude either that Constantine had not yet fully developed the story he would tell in 324 in his own mind, or that he was as yet reluctant to broadcast it in the period immediately following the battle.

This is, however, a far cry from saying that the sequence Eusebius would describe in the *Life of Constantine* or its interpretation as evidence of Constantine's connection with the Christian god were an invention of Eusebius some quarter-century after the fact. Indeed, we have good material evidence for Constantine's official use of the labarum before 320, and we also have strong indications that he showed great favor to the Christian church beginning already in 312. As to the first, we have already seen in the Introduction and Chapter 2 that the chi-rho was first depicted on coins minted perhaps as early as 313/315 but certainly by 319, when it appears on the emperor's helmet in coins minted at Siscia (see Figs. 2–3). It also appears on the shield borne by his son Crispus in coins from Trier dated to 322 (Fig. 30).[16] Moreover, we have two milestones from North Africa attesting to the official use of the chi-rho in imperial inscriptions from the period immediately following the Battle of the Milvian Bridge: one from Mauretania Caesariensis (near modern Beni Fouda—see Fig. 1) and the other from Cuicul (Djémila) in Numidia, both datable to the first four months of 313.[17] Constantine was thus broadcasting the Christogram as his special sign almost immediately following his defeat of Maxentius. Finally, although Eusebius seems not to have heard the narrative of Constantine's conversion as recounted in the *Life* when he was writing the *Ecclesiastical History* in 313/316, he definitely believed Constantine was already advertising his adherence to Christianity by the earlier date, for he describes there a statue Constantine erected in Rome bearing a cross with an inscription claiming he had saved the city "by this salvific sign" (*toutō tō sōtēriōdei sēmeiō*).[18]

As to Constantine's favor for the church, a host of textual sources from the years between 312 and 324 confirm that Constantine's turn toward Christianity was remarkably sudden and dramatic. In the first two years after the battle he began funding the construction of Christian churches in Rome, organized two church

FIGURE 30. Obverse: IVL CRISPVS NOB CAES. Crispus right with spear across right shoulder and shield with chi-rho on left arm. Reverse: BEATA TRANQVILLITAS. Globe set on altar inscribed VOTIS XX. *RIC* 5: 224 Crispus 17 = *RIC* 7: Trier 372. © The Hunterian, University of Glasgow 2014.

councils, granted immunity to Christian clerics from curial service, and initiated government subsidies to Christian congregations.[19] With the so-called Edict of Milan from early 313, he began imposing his pro-Christian program in the eastern domains of his ally Licinius,[20] and in that same year he issued a letter to Maximinus Daia threatening attacks if the latter did not cease persecuting in the East.[21] He also issued a number of extant laws in this period that openly advertise his Christianity: shortly after 312 he instituted Sunday as a legal holiday across his domains;[22] between 312 and 316 he granted Christian priests or bishops the power to manumit slaves in churches during prayer services;[23] in 316 he forbade the tattooing of criminals on the face, "because it is formed in the likeness of heavenly beauty" (a reference to Gen. 1:26);[24] in 318 he permitted bishops to act in place of judges in civil suits;[25] around 320, he issued a law forbidding crucifixion, a measure that took its roots in his veneration for the cross;[26] in 321 he granted churches the right to receive inheritances as corporate bodies.[27] There is thus ample evidence that Constantine made public indications of his growing favoritism for the Christian church beginning shortly after the Battle of the Milvian Bridge.

None of this is to deny, however, that it took time for the story of his conversion as recounted in Eusebius to develop. Indeed, this is precisely the argument Weiss has made, for his understanding is that Constantine gradually connected the solar vision he had experienced in 310 with the dream he claims to have experienced—in either 311 or 312—and to have reinterpreted both as inspired communications from the Christian god. The fact, however, that he so quickly deployed his new symbols, the chi-rho and cross, in public contexts and that he so promptly began taking concrete measures, in terms of laws, finance, and public architecture, in favor of the church make it much more likely that Constantine *himself* rather than Eusebius was the originator of the historical memory recounted in Eusebius's *Life of Constantine*. The absence of overt expressions of this fully developed narrative as late as 315 may therefore say more about Constantine's reluctance to broadcast his narrative widely than about his failure to connect the dots.

Which God Was Constantine's God?

We have seen in Chapter 2 that Constantine advertised himself consistently as the agent of the divine will, on a mission from "the highest god" to conquer and then rule the *oikoumene*. Nevertheless, we also saw there that in many instances non-Christian subjects could have been forgiven if they could not pinpoint with precision the identity of the god to whom he was referring. In the period between 312 and 321, Constantine's panegyrists make no mention of his conversion, and in this same period the emperor and his propagandists made very sparing use of the chi-rho and other Christian symbols on coins and public inscriptions. Indeed, those coins where the chi-rho does appear are quite rare even to the end of Constantine's reign.[28] And although the chi-rho does appear on inscriptions as early as 313, it only becomes common after 326 and still remains relatively scarce in official epigraphic contexts throughout the remainder of the reign.[29]

The message might have seemed less ambiguous, however, to Constantine's Christian subjects. In every instance but one of his references to divine support listed in Chapter 2, the testimonia derive from documents originally directed at Christian audiences. These will surely have assumed that it was their god to whom the emperor was referring, and this was likely the dominant reading intended by Constantine. Indeed, he states quite openly in one of the earliest of these documents, his letter to the Catholic bishops of Arles from 314, "The omnipotent God, who sits upon his watchtower in heaven, has granted to me that which I did not deserve: in fact, the things that he has conceded to me, his servant [*in me famulum suum*], through his heavenly benevolence could no longer be recounted nor enumerated, most reverend bishops of Christ our Savior [*antistites Christi Salvatoris*], beloved brethren [*fratres carissimi*]."[30] The letter goes on to refer directly to Christ three more times, leaving no room for doubt in the minds of its recipients about the identity of Constantine's god. The passage quoted is in fact crucial for bearing witness so early in Constantine's reign and so soon after 312 to three salient ideas: first, Constantine's readiness to confess Christianity openly before Christian audiences; second, his conceptualization of himself as "the servant of God," and third, his desire to be associated with Christian bishops as his "beloved brethren." As we shall see, all three strategies of self-presentation became crucial in his rhetorical self-construction before Christian audiences in the years that followed.

As to the first, throughout his extant writings Constantine is inclined to refer to his guiding divinity as the "highest God" (*summus deus/ ho megistos theos*), a designation that was generic, even ambiguous.[31] As such, it could be and often was interpreted by non-Christian subjects as coincident with their own cosmology. Firmicus Maternus, for example, used *summus deus* throughout his work on astrology composed late in Constantine's reign to designate the pagan deity he worshipped.[32] The same broad-brush theological framework also underlies the description of the divinity offered by the panegyrists of 313 and 321. The anonymous author of the first, who was clearly a polytheist, speaks directly of Constantine's divine inspiration from some single supreme deity but remains vague about its identity, calling it "whatever that god may be," "the divine mind," "the divine spirit," "that creator and lord of the world," or "the highest progenitor of the universe, whose names number as many as the languages of the nations."[33] Nazarius, the author of the 321 panegyric, is equally cagey in his circumlocutions: "god, the judge of the universe," "that power, that majesty of the speakable and unspeakable," "that highest majesty," "the beneficent majesty," or simply "god" with no modifiers.[34] Pagan religion had, of course, been tending in a monotheistic (or henotheistic) direction since the early third century. This left ample room for Constantine's "highest god" to dovetail with contemporary pagan religious thought and thus to seem like an expression of ecumenism in a religiously pluralistic environment.[35] Their reading of Constantine's god was thus negotiated but—in a world that was coming to see all divinities as one—surely not antipathetic to the emperor's own understanding.

It is thus significant that, in the letter to the Catholic bishops quoted above, Constantine is quite explicit and emphatic about his devotion to *Christ*. Nor is this the only such reference we have, for in at least three other letters—all directed at Christian bishops—as well as his *Oration to the Saints*, Constantine was quite open in specifying the Christian savior as the object of his veneration.[36] Eusebius understood the importance of this when he praised Constantine, "for he continually proclaimed to all the Christ of God quite openly, in no way hiding the savior's name, but rather being proud of the practice."[37] It is hard to judge the accuracy of his statement given that Eusebius was himself a bishop and as such will have seen Constantine at his most pious and unabashed toward the faith. Given the bifurcation in our source tradition, it seems safer to assume that Constantine's open profession of Christianity came out most strongly before Christian audiences, while his unconverted subjects tended instead to hear the generic designations or circumlocutions for the divine we find in so many other sources. This was certainly the case, for example, with his non-Christian soldiers, who were expected to recite an imperially dictated prayer weekly that, although it was meant to be pronounced on Sundays, was entirely devoid of overt or even covert references to Christianity.[38] His open profession of Christ, as opposed to god, was thus first and foremost reserved for Christians, who will consequently have read into their Constantine a more zealous supporter of their religion than pagan subjects.

As to Constantine's self-conception as the servant (*famulus*) of God, this notion formed a crucial leitmotif in his rhetoric that is traceable from its first mention in the letter to the Catholic bishops of Arles from 314 down to the end of his reign. Most of our extant documents from the pen of Constantine have, of course, been translated by Eusebius or Athanasius into Greek; thus, in most instances this formula is found as *ho therapōn tou theou*. As such it occurs seven times in extant sources:[39]

- Eus. *V. Const.* 2.29.3 (a. 324): Letter to the Provincials of Palestine
- Eus. *V. Const.* 2.55.1 (a. 324): Letter to the eastern Provincials
- Eus. *V. Const.* 2.71.2 and 4 (a. 324): Letter to Alexander and Arius

- Gel. Cyz. *HE* 2.7.38 (a. 325): Address to the Council of Nicaea
- Athan. *Apol. Sec.* 86.1 (a. 335) (twice): Letter to the Council of Tyre

In addition, Constantine also frequently refers to himself as the "fellow servant" (*suntherapōn*) of bishops, combining the theme of service to God with the desire to conceptualize himself as another bishop. This terminology is used nine times in extant sources:

- Eus. *V. Const.* 2.69.2 and 72.1 (a. 324): Letter to Alexander and Arius
- Eus. *V. Const.* 3.12.5 (a. 325): Address to the Council of Nicaea
- Eus. *V. Const.* 3.17.2 (a. 325): The report on the Council of Nicaea
- Gel. Cyz. *HE* 2.7.13 (a. 325): Address to the Council of Nicaea
- Opitz *Urkunde* 25.3 pp. 52–53 = Brennecke *Dokument* 29.3 p. 115: Letter to the Alexandrian community
- Opitz *Urkunde* 27.6 p. 59 = Brennecke *Dokument* 31.6 p. 118 (a. 325): Letter to the Nicomedians
- Opitz *Urkunde* 32.2–3 p. 66 = Brennecke *Dokument* 37.2–3 p. 136 (a. 328) (twice): Letter to Alexander of Alexandria (cf. Eus. *V. Const.* 3.24.1)

Paul had, of course, identified himself as the "slave of god" (*doulos theou/ servus dei*), but this is not precisely what Constantine calls himself.[40] The notion of God's *servant* (*famulus/ therapōn*) seems to trace its biblical origins to the figure of Moses, who is designated thus throughout scripture.[41] Playing on this typology, Eusebius compares Constantine's victory over Maxentius, who drowned in the Tiber, to Moses's defeat of the army of Pharaoh, which drowned in the Red Sea, already in the ninth book of his *Ecclesiastical History*, first composed circa 313/314. When he added the tenth book in 325, Eusebius carried the comparison even further by using the designation "servant of God" (*therapōn tou theou*) for the emperor.[42] By this point, of course, Eusebius had already been exposed to Constantine's own use of this term in the letter to the Provincials of Palestine as well as the letter to the eastern provincials. This synchrony makes it difficult to determine whether it was Constantine himself who first drew the comparison with Moses and thus chose for himself the title "servant of God," or perhaps Eusebius who derived the comparison with Moses from his awareness that Constantine was now employing the name "servant of god," or even whether the two might have developed the notion in written or verbal dialogue with one another. Whatever the case, by the time he came to write his *Life of Constantine*, Eusebius had bought into the parallel wholeheartedly and thus quite consciously wrote the emperor into a scriptural framework that canonized him as a latter-day Moses and devoted "servant of God."[43]

Constantine as Bishop

As to Constantine's desire to be associated with bishops, this is evident in no small part from his choice to become increasingly involved in their deliberations over the course of his reign. Although he cannot have been present for the Council of Rome in 313, when he is known to have been in Gaul, some believe he may have attended the Council of Arles in 314 (possible, but not likely),[44] and it is beyond doubt that he organized and participated in the Council of Nicaea in 325.[45] Indeed, he advertised his attendance there quite proudly in extant correspondence and even played a leading role in the deliberations by insisting on the use of the term *homoousios* (one in being) to characterize the Son's relationship to the Father, a move that has affected Christian theology ever since.[46] In the years to come, he also participated in the council held at Nicomedia in early 328 and that at Constantinople in the summer of 336.[47] In his letter to Macarius of Jerusalem and the bishops of Palestine, he goes so far as to presume to instruct these ecclesiastics on the history of scripture, and his *Oration to the Assembly of the Saints*, which situates his reign at the pinnacle of Judeo-Christian history, could fairly be classed a veritable sermon.[48] On some level, then, Constantine regarded himself as a sort of ersatz bishop, a fact further reflected in a special form of salutation he uses for bishops and bishops alone in his correspondence: "May the almighty God grant you perpetual security."[49] For Constantine, then, bishops amounted to a specially favored constituency in whose presence he wished to operate as a fellow religious leader.

In fact, Constantine's engagement with the Catholic bishops of Arles in his letter of 314 as "beloved brethren" signaled his belief that, on some level, he considered himself to *be* a bishop. Eusebius had the same impression, for early in his *Life of Constantine* he claims that Constantine assembled church councils "as if he were a sort of universal bishop [*tis koinos episkopos*] appointed by God."[50] In an even more telling passage, he reports that he once heard Constantine address a group of bishops he was entertaining as dinner guests: "You are bishops of those within the church, but I am perhaps a bishop appointed by God over those outside [*tōn ektos episkopos*]."[51] This vague and curious phrasing has attracted much scholarly attention, with no definitive resolution as to its precise meaning.[52]

At a minimum, we know that Eusebius takes "those outside" to refer to those of Constantine's subjects who were not members of the church and thus assumes that the emperor's declaration expressed a compulsion to press all his subjects—especially pagans—toward "the godly life." Paul had used "those outside" [*hoi exō(then)*] to refer to nonbelievers—those outside the Christian community—on five occasions in his epistles.[53] Indeed, Al. Cameron has argued that the word *paganus* itself was adopted by Latin speakers in the fourth century to characterize non-Christian polytheists precisely because this word was the closest equivalent to the "outsider" [*hoi exō(then)*] so commonly used in Greek to designate non-Christians.[54] It is thus no surprise that the desire to act as bishop to nonbelievers can be detected in documents written by Constantine himself. In his letter to the eastern provincials, a document directed to all eastern subjects regardless of their beliefs, he invokes the "greatest God" (*ton megiston theon*) in a prayer expressing the desire that "those in error" will be convinced by the peace he has introduced to live according to God's holy laws.[55] In a similar vein, in his letter to the Nicomedians from 325, he expresses his marvel that he had been able "to lead so many nations [*ethnē*—a word that could mean both 'provinces' and 'pagans'] to concord who had formerly not known God at all."[56] In the same passage, however, he also voices his concern that these would return to their error if they saw the present bickering of church leaders.

As this implies, there is reason to think that Constantine felt his pastoral duties also extended to those who had converted but had then been led astray by heresy or schism. In one of his earliest extant letters (early 314), written to the vicar Aelafius on the Donatist controversy, he argues that his personal success as a ruler depended on his ability to see to it that "all men worship the most holy God by the due rites of the Catholic religion in harmonious and brotherly observance."[57] He expressed similar sentiments two and a half years later when, following the refusal of the Donatists to accept the decision of the Council of Arles, he promised to journey to Africa to judge the matter in person: "What could be more important for me to do, in keeping with my own purpose and the bounty of the sovereign himself, than to shatter all errors and amputate all rashness and then bring it about that all people manifest true religion and concordant unanimity and the worship owed to the almighty God."[58] The pastoral and the political were thus interlinked. Constantine saw himself as called to a cosmic role to battle against those in erroneous relationships with the church and to bring them violently—or at least with violent rhetoric—back into the fold.

Finally, there is also a sense that Constantine conceived of his duties as "bishop of those outside" as extending to peoples beyond the frontiers who had either converted but were being persecuted or those heathen barbarians for whose conversion he believed himself to be responsible. As to the former, his letter to Shapur II from 324 constitutes an extended deed of guardianship whereby he commends the Christians of Persia to the Shahanshah's care with the imprecation—not to say threat—that Shapur "will do an unbounded favor both to yourself and to us by keeping faith."[59] Constantine then acted on this warning in 337 by initiating a final expedition, cut short by his death, against Shapur after the latter deposed the Christian king of Armenia and began persecuting Christians within his realm.[60] With regard to converting barbarians outside his territory, in summoning the bishops from the synod of Tyre to Constantinople in 335, he holds: "Even the barbarians, on account of me, who am a genuine servant of God, have acknowledged and learned to worship him, whom they have perceived in very deed protecting and caring for me everywhere. So that from dread of us, they have been thus brought to the knowledge of the true God whom they now worship."[61] Precisely which barbarians Constantine references we no longer know, but at least two possibilities suggest themselves. We hear from Rufinus that Constantine was instrumental in coordinating the conversion of the Georgians, whose king explicitly requested his support in this process.[62] It is also possible that Constantine consecrated the Goth Ulfilas to serve as missionary bishop to his people in 336, although some would date the beginning of Ulfilas's episcopacy to 340.[63] Regardless, we learn from Socrates that a different Gothic bishop named Theophilus was present at the Council of Nicaea, which could just as easily have induced Constantine's triumphalist claim in 335.[64] Constantine thus seems to have had a sense that he was somehow responsible for the conversion and well-being of those Christians who dwelled outside Roman territory.[65] He thought of himself, in other words, as "bishop of those outside" on three counts: to those outside the church through lack of faith (above all pagans), to those separated from it by wrong belief (heretics and schismatics), and to those beyond the frontiers of the empire (barbarians).

Christianity and Empire

Indeed, several of the statements quoted give the sense that Constantine believed in a sort of causal link between his ability to steer others to right religion and his success as a ruler. Internalizing the traditional sense of the *pax deorum* that had driven Roman religious thinking since the early Republic, Constantine assumed that the continuation of his felicitous rule and indeed the restoration of cosmic harmony hung upon his ability to guarantee concord and prosperity in the church. For this reason, he felt a calling to rid the church both of external persecution and of internal dissension. This connection appears in his letter to the governor of Africa Anullinus, whom he instructed in 313 to grant curial immunity to clerics: "Because it appears from many circumstances that, when we neglect completely that religion in which the chief reverence for the most holy and celestial power is observed, great dangers are brought upon the commonweal, but that when it is instead rightfully restored and observed, it offers the greatest good fortune to the Roman name and remarkable well-being to all human affairs, with divine benefactions being the cause."[66] The same idea recurs in his letter to the vicar Aelafius a year later, where he asks for aid in quelling the

Donatist dispute, lest "it arouse the highest deity not only against the human race but also against myself."[67] His letter to the Catholic bishops of Arles from that same year orders the rounding up of schismatics, "in order that, under the shining light of our god, nothing further be done by these which might incite the greatest anger of divine providence,"[68] and the letter of 315 to the Vicar Celsus expresses the belief that the Donatist controversy should be settled by him in person, "for in no other way at all do I believe I shall be able to escape the greatest guilt."[69] Constantine returns to this circle of ideas in confronting the Arian controversy when he expresses his hope to Alexander and Arius that, "if I should be able to establish a common harmony among all the servants of God through my prayers, the needs of public affairs will also benefit from the transformation consonant with the pious wishes of all."[70] Similar notions are expressed in Constantine's letter to the Nicomedians, which lists the restoration of concord as his chief desire, and in Eusebius's recreation of Constantine's speech before the Council of Nicaea, which expresses the longing personally to resolve the crisis not just for the good of the church but also for the security of the world.[71]

Given his conviction that the world's safety depended not just on his skills as a general and ruler but also on his ability to guide his subjects and indeed all peoples toward right religion, it should come as no great surprise that Constantine felt a sense of nagging urgency about this mission. As we have seen, this surfaces in his extant writings already in his dealings with the Donatist controversy and continues to the end of his reign. One of the clearest manifestations of this attitude can be found in the blustery and exasperated letter he addressed to Arius and his partisans in 333.[72] This searing reprimand, which was clearly intended for distribution to a wider audience across the empire, seethes with rage as Constantine pummels Arius with an oratorical fusillade: "Turn the Devil's sword toward your own destruction! Behold, all of you, behold the lamentable cries [Arius] emits now that he is held fast by the bite of the serpent, how his arteries and flesh have been seized by the poison and he shudders in horrific pain, how his body grows weak as it wastes away! He is filled with want, with filth, with lamentations and paleness, with tremors and countless evils, and he wastes away woefully."[73] The rhetoric here and throughout is clearly steeped in Christian notions of theodicy, but also in the idea that Arius suffers some malady that may be curable. In this spirit, the document does not stop with rebuke but aims therapeutically to shock Arius out of his afflicted way of thinking. At its close, Constantine offers Arius the chance to prove the worthiness of his theology during an imperial audience and projects himself as capable of judging—or, rather, diagnosing—Arius and thus helping to restore health to his relationship with God: "Come to me, I say, come to the man of God. Trust that through my own inquiries I can discover the secrets of your heart. And if there seems to be anything maniacal in there, I will call down divine grace and heal you more beautifully than any demonstration. But if you are manifestly healthy in your soul, I will recognize the light of truth in you and will see grace toward God, and I will rejoice in myself at your piety."[74] Constantine thus conceived of himself as the final arbiter of holiness. As the "man of God," he would be able to discern Arius's inner relationship with the divine and to remedy the unholy contagion with which Arius was afflicted. More important, Constantine extrapolated this role outward to the entire empire, making himself responsible for the religious rectitude of all his subjects and in the process for the ongoing stability of the commonweal.

At times this zeal manifested itself in forceful and even violent action. Having wearied of the Donatists' refusal to abide by the decision of three councils—Rome 313, Arles 314, and Milan 316—Constantine issued an order in late 316 commanding union in the church of Africa and ordering its enforcement at the hands of military commanders. When the Donatists of Carthage hardened in their refusal to surrender their churches, violence ensued in which many were wounded and some even killed, including Honoratus, the bishop of Sicilibba, and a number of Carthaginian congregants.[75] As we shall see in the sections to come, similar strong-arm tactics were ordered against certain pagan temples at Aegeae in Cilicia, Aphaca in Syria, and Mamre and Jerusalem in Palestine.[76] He ordered the public burning of the writings of the pagan philosopher Porphyry circa 325, and circa 333 the burning of writings by Arius and his followers, whom he lumped with the pagans under the label "Porphyriani."[77] And in a letter likely datable between mid-325 and mid-326, Constantine railed against the schismatic Novatians and heretical Valentinians, Marcionites, Paulians, and Cataphrygians (Montanists) as "opponents of truth, enemies of life, and counselors of ruin." Red with rage, he ordered them to be expelled from their churches, their property confiscated, and their meetings banned.[78] Finally, Constantine chose to exile bishops who refused to subscribe to the decisions of the Council of Nicaea and to abide by the decisions of subsequent councils, including such powerful figures as Eusebius of Nicomedia and Athanasius of Alexandria.[79] He was thus ready to bring the full force of imperial power to bear on those whom he felt threatened the religious harmony he so eagerly desired to implement.

In most instances, however, Constantine backed away from his initial violent reactions and eventually exercised considerable forbearance toward religious dissidents. In the instance of the Donatists, when they refused to accept the judgment of the Council of Arles, he showed remarkable patience with their intransigence, famously claiming, "They demand my judgment when I myself await the judgment of Christ."[80] Following his failed effort to compel compliance with his order of 316 that they turn over their churches, he issued a letter in 321 that forbade further violent action against the schismatics, even when they provoked it with violence of their own.[81] In a similar letter dated 330, Constantine refused to allow the Catholics of Cirta to reclaim the church he had built for them, which had recently been forcibly taken over by Donatists, and instead assured them that "God promises to be the avenger of all, and thus when vengeance is left to God, a harsher penalty is exacted from one's enemies."[82] As we shall see below, these statements of tolerance, for all that they display disgust and exasperation toward the Donatists, are based in theological principles advocated by Lactantius that counseled the truly just ruler—that is, the Christian emperor—to remand the punishment of religious dissenters to divine judgment. Constantine was thus actively enacting Christian ethical norms into Roman law.[83]

He expressed much the same sentiment toward pagans in his letter to the eastern provincials, which on the one hand rails against the wrong belief of his pagan subjects, but on the other insists, "Let no one molest another, but let everyone do as his soul desires."[84] The letter closes with similarly cautious resignation: "We understand there are some who say that the rites of the heathen temples, and the power of darkness, have been entirely removed. We should have wholeheartedly made this recommendation to all men, except that the violent urge of wicked error remains immoderately fixed in the souls of some with the aim of doing harm to the common salvation."[85] Thus, although he did seize some limited opportunities to enact his violent wishes on certain pagan shrines, Constantine was more commonly willing to tolerate the ongoing existence of pagans in the hope that God would do his part—spurred on by Constantine's example—to bring all to right worship.

Finally, with regard to his order of 325/326 against heretics and schismatics, Constantine also backed away from his initial harshness. Two of the initial five groups singled out in this missive were later given some form of reprieve: the Novatians were allowed to keep their property unmolested and maintain their separate ecclesiastical hierarchy, and exemption from confiscation was also granted to Montanists in Phrygia and neighboring regions, "because here they had, since the time of Montanus, existed in great numbers."[86] Even as to exiled dissidents, he eventually recalled Eusebius of Nicomedia and Arius himself, and he appeared eager to avoid exiling other bishops whenever agreements could be reached.[87] He thus continually vacillated between rabidly intolerant rhetoric and sometimes even violent action, and a practical—but also theologically motivated—concern for peace and concord. Ultimately, his impatient desire to enforce right religion among his subjects was tempered with an almost puckish relish in leaving the punishment of error to God, whose judgment would ultimately be much more severe.

Conclusion

We have thus seen that there remains very little evidence for Constantine's deal-ings with the church in the first five years of his reign. The material becomes more abundant in the period of his conversion, but its interpretation is clouded by variant versions of events in the sources and by the lack of a coherent early narra-tive of the canonical story of vision–dream–labarum–battle told by Eusebius in his *Life of Constantine*. This narrative took time to develop, but not so very much time, for Constantine begins proffering unmistakable signs in his inscriptions, coins, laws, financial and tax subventions, and building constructions that he was granting previously unheard-of favors to the Christians and their churches. In this same period—the decade after 312—Constantine's communiqués to Chris-tians give open proof that, to this audience at least, he was willing to identify his "supreme deity" unequivocally as the Christian god. This message appears, how-ever, to have been more muted for non-Christian audiences, who could therefore continue to identify his favored deity in more generic terms or even quite specif-ically as pagan deities like the Sun God, whose presence never fully vanished from his propaganda. Other rhetorical strategies deployed for Christian audiences included self-identification as the "servant of God" and the effort to portray him-self as some near approximation to a bishop. This last entailed a conviction that he was personally responsible for actuating right religion among heretics, pagans, and even barbarians outside the empire. Indeed, Constantine seems to have felt an almost neurotic urgency about the necessity of prodding the world into con-formity with the principles of the orthodox church. This stemmed in no small part from a traditional Roman conviction that the safety of the empire hung on a properly equilibrated relationship between the subjects of the Roman state and the divine. In Constantine's instance, however, the religious principles he was enforcing were undoubtedly Christian. Counterbalancing this urgency, however, was an equally powerful conviction that God himself was more than capable of punishing those who failed to comply. This consolation gave Constantine the space he needed to tolerate considerable resistance to his program of religious unification, even as it validated his subjects' assumptions that he was ready to countenance their ongoing attachment to their own beliefs and practices.

This investigation into the Christian Constantine has thus afforded a surpris-ingly consistent picture of a certain "face of Constantine." In fact, the impression left by Constantine's engagements with Christians seems so coherent that it is tempting to believe that they mirror perfectly the "true Constantine," a glimpse into the soul of this complex man. This was surely the understanding of many of Constantine's most influential Christian subjects, not least among them his apol-ogist Lactantius and biographer Eusebius. We must be careful, however, about assuming that this same Constantine was available for viewing to all audiences or even that this was the only self-portrait Constantine wished to disseminate. We must, in other words, be careful to read Constantine's messages to Christians against the background of other material presented earlier in Chapters 1 and 2, a background that offers widely divergent impressions of Constantine that vary over time and according to audience and circumstance. Even when consistent across time, these situate their message in neutral territory that could serve as common ground for all subjects regardless of their religious convictions or affiliations. We must above all keep in mind that qua emperor Constantine was an institution, a figure shaped by the history and sheer momentum of a three-centuries-long tradition of rulership and by a vast and variegated empire filled with complex congeries of subjects and interest groups. Constantine the Christian was thus real, and Constantine's writings to fellow Christians no doubt reflect a strain of thought and an approach to rulership that was of paramount concern to Constantine the man. But they also represent only one approach to a ruler caught up in webs of power and signification that he controlled only by being willing to mobilize the full range of constituencies and symbols available to him.

PART II

~

THE POWER
OF PETITIONS

CHAPTER 4

Approaching Constantine
The Orcistus Dossier

Knowing What to Expect

It has long been agreed that Roman government tended to implement policy in response to problems and petitions rather than working in preplanned and proactive ways. With his foundational work on the Roman emperor, F. Millar demonstrated this brilliantly, and his ongoing study of documents from Late Antiquity proves that this approach to rule continued to prevail down through the fifth century.[1] Emperors governed above all through a system of petition and response in which their subjects brought problems to their attention, and the ruler—or his charges—then devised solutions in answer to these pleas. Well over a thousand private petitions to the emperor survive in the law codes, and the papyri reveal that imperial governors as well were deluged with hundreds of petitions in a single day to which they did their best to respond.[2] Petitions were used not just by individuals but also cities, villages, and other communities, for these regularly approached the emperor and his officials for privileges or the redress of grievances. We know this above all from the couple dozen extant petitions lodged with the emperor and his officials by polities throughout the empire that are still preserved in inscriptions.[3] Indeed, epigraphic registration was surely the most desirable method for recording an imperial response, for it locked pronouncements in stone or bronze at the site of their implementation in a way that fixed permanently in space the privileges granted by the emperor and guaranteed across time their symbolic efficacy.[4]

Further work on the voluminous legal evidence from Late Antiquity has shown that, despite the fundamental soundness of the petition and response model, the later empire offers good evidence for a noticeable, if also limited, degree of central planning and proactive governance.[5] Petitions remained the standard format for communication between subject and emperor, but late Roman government underwent a massive expansion in its bureaucratic apparatus that increased the possibilities for super-regional initiatives and facilitated the imposition of uniform rules. The tetrarchs and in turn Constantine promoted the rise of new super-regional administrative districts like dioceses and regional prefectures across which enactments could be propagated with heightened efficiency.[6] Moreover, the central bureaucracy was also expanded, permitting an increase in the government's ability to handle a greater number of petitions.[7] And the extension of citizenship to most of the empire's subjects from 212 CE onward occasioned an increase in communication between subject and emperor as normative questions formerly solved at the local level were now subject to a system of Roman civil law whose ultimate arbiter was the emperor.[8] The late fourth-century *Notitia Dignitatum* reports no less than three high-level bureaucrats charged with answering petitions—the *magister memoriae*, the *magister epistolarum,* and the *magister libellorum*—each with slightly different remits, and each with bureaus of assistants numbering around thirty.[9] S. Connolly's study of the petitioning process administered by these has demonstrated that one of their offices, the *scrinium a libellis*, whose activities are particularly well recorded in the texts preserved through the *Codex Hermogenianus*, issued more than 350 official responses (*rescripta*) in a single year and as many as 90 in a busy month.[10]

The system was not, however, a simple matter of "ask and you shall receive." The respondent, whether a bureaucrat or the emperor himself, always dealt with requests according to predictable norms and expectations. Above all, every effort was made to ensure that responses were constructed in accordance with the principles of established law: Roman civil and administrative law, or, when this did not apply, the received laws and customs of local communities.[11] In addition, responses usually reflected prevailing moral codes and shared ideals—such as the promotion of freedom or the protection of the family—and could thus fall back on a series of symbolic systems shared among the citizens of the empire and communicated through the vehicles of rhetoric, art, literature, spectacle, public display, and above all the collective inertia of social practice.

High among the priorities in this shared value system was the advancement of cities. Urban centers represented the nodes of civil life around which the empire constructed its networks of power. It is thus unsurprising that we have a number of petitions from cities that survive in both the epigraphic and papyrological record, and that both the petitions and the responses to them follow predictable principles. Indeed, in most extant epigraphic copies of civic petitions, the emperor and petitioning polity express openly their shared assumption that cities should be made to thrive and that an ideal city should display a specific set of qualities: populousness, good governance by a city council, and a standard repertoire of built structures and public amenities.[12] Interestingly, almost all extant civic petitions on stone also share a common complaint, for most were lodged by communities that claimed to have suffered abuse by a particular constituency—imperial soldiers and officials, or a powerful neighboring city—and most ask the emperor to respond by offering patronly protection against such threats.[13] In every one of these cases, as we might expect and indeed as the petitioners surely also expected, the emperor rallies to the polity's defense with stern warnings that abuses must cease.

Constantine was himself well aware of the way the system worked and more than ready to comply with its protocols. Indeed, the *Epitome de Caesaribus* reports that he personally took an interest in listening to embassies and petitions from the provinces.[14] In a law preserved in the *Theodosian Code,* we catch a glimpse of him actively responding to a petition lodged by a group of veterans of his war against Licinius who sought exemption from curial service.[15] On a similar note, Optatus preserves a letter of his to the Catholic bishops of Numidian Cirta in which the emperor boasts, "This petition, according to my customary policy, I have gladly embraced."[16] In other words, Constantine understood well the tradition of petition and response and its importance as a tool of governance.

We also have evidence for his narrower concern with the welfare of cities as modules of local governance. Nazarius's panegyric of 321 praises him for fostering an atmosphere of prosperity in which "the cities have been adorned in marvelous fashion and are practically refounded entirely."[17] At the local level, the same concern is reflected in an oration delivered by a rhetor from Augustodunum (Autun), the central focus of which is Constantine's favorable response to that city's petition for a remission of its taxes.[18] Constantine was thus highly attuned to the manner in which an emperor was expected to behave vis-à-vis the petitions of cities, towns, and villages. Both he and the inhabitants of the empire had been programmed through ancient and oft-repeated rituals to follow a well-patterned dialogue in which protection and favor were offered by the emperor in exchange for deference and support from the polity in a conversation structured through the shared intermediation of the petition.

Tymandus and Heraclea Sintica: Striving for City Status Under the Tetrarchs

Among the most coveted privileges sought by civic communities was promotion to the status of *civitas,* or in Greek, *polis.* With this came the right to be free of control by a neighboring city, to have an assembly and magistrates, to pass decrees and judge cases in local courts, and to have control over local religious practice. The counterpoint was status as a village—in Latin *vicus* or *pagus,* in Greek *kōmē.* Regarding this distinction, Isidore of Seville writes, "Villages and castles and cantons are communities that are not honored with the rank of a city, but are inhabited by a common assemblage of people and are subject to larger cities because of their lowliness."[19]

The distinction is also evident from what was long the only extant inscription explicitly to record the grant of civic privileges to a village, a stone from the Pisidian city of Tymandus (Yassiören: see Map 1).[20] The beginning of the inscription is missing, which means that we can no longer say with certainty which emperor or emperors issued the rescript, but the most extensive study of the text yet published has reaffirmed the long-held view that the stone is tetrarchic.[21] Where the text picks up, we learn that Tymandus itself had petitioned the emperor for the "right and rank of city status" (ll. 5–6: *ius et dignitatem civita/tis*). Later in the petition a similar duality—name and office—is repeated (ll. 11–12: *civitatis/ nomen honestatemque*). The importance of this binary rested in the fact that the honorific "title of city" (*nomen civitatis*) was separable from the right of self–governance that went with "city status" (*ius civitatis*), a reality that will become clear in what follows.

As the inscription continues, we learn that the emperor was willing to grant the Tymandeans' demand in part because of his general concern that "the honor and number of cities grow throughout our entire world."[22] Just as important, however, was the emperor's concern that Tymandus be able to field an adequate number of curials and that these form themselves into structures of civic governance recognized under the empire as normative: executives termed *Magistratus* (elsewhere often *Duumviri*), *Aediles*, and *Quaestores*, who were then to be supported by a council of *decuriones* that, in Tymandus's case, had to number at least fifty (ll. 26–33). For the privilege of local autonomy, Tymandus thus had to show that it had a flourishing populace and was willing to constitute itself around structures of governmentality that were acceptable to the emperor. Finally, the inscription closes with a subjunctive clause praying that the favor of the immortal gods (*deorum inmortalium favor*) might help Tymandus flourish and achieve this greater number of curials (ll. 33–37). In addition to strictly civic criteria, then, religious concerns also enter into the city's petition and the emperors' response to it. Although we have only the emperors' words, these assume both that Tymandus and its leaders shared the religious convictions of their rulers and that they agreed that the traditional gods would be responsible for the success of their civic enterprise.

In 2002 a new stone was discovered at Rupite (Bulgaria) that records a similar grant of city status to the community of Heraclea Sintica.[23] Its heading survives, demonstrating that it was issued by emperors Galerius and Maximinus Daia. The heading also permits us to date the inscription quite precisely to the eleven months between October 307 and September 308.[24] Following the heading, the text reads: "Although your city [*civitas vestra*] never previously had the rights of

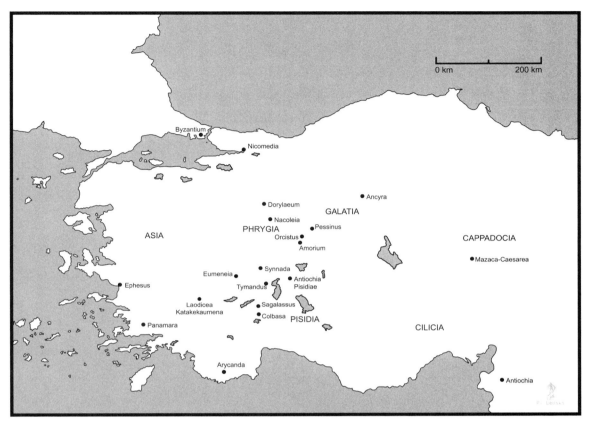

MAP 1. Anatolia

city status [*iura civitatis*], nevertheless, in accord with the zeal native to us toward our state and the favoritism for growth of our new foresight and goodwill, we wish to ennoble your homeland with the ornaments and with the right of city status [*ornamentis et iure civitatis*]. Wherefore, because you say this same place was [called] the City of the Herculeans [*Civitas Heracleotarum*] already in the past [*etiam de praeterito*], and now you ask that the rights of city status [*iura civitatis*] be granted to it through our favor, we offer support for your petition quite willingly."[25] Interestingly, in the Heraclea Sintica inscription, we find once again the distinction between "the name of city" and "the right of city status" seen already at Tymandus. In this instance, Heraclea appears to have claimed the title *Civitas Heracleotarum* previously without having enjoyed the rights of local self-governance appertaining to the legal status of *civitas*. The distinction was clearly significant. In a world where Caracalla's grant of universal citizenship after 212 had largely erased the importance of maintaining fine-tuned gradations in legal designations for polities (*colonia, municipium, oppidum, civitas*), these titles had taken on an honorific air but had lost most of their legal ramifications.[26] *Civitas* had thus begun to serve as a generic name for a civic community regardless of its legal standing. Nevertheless, the *ius civitatis* was still operative as a normative category and clearly still mattered, for with it came the right to self-governance and autonomy from the dictates of a neighboring city regarding tax collection, the extraction of mandatory services, the conduct of local courts, and the maintenance of religious shrines and festivals.[27]

The inscription continues with further assertions that this grant of civic status reflected a larger program aimed at benefiting cities (ll. 15–19) which, as noted, constituted a standard expectation of both emperors and subjects already present in the Tymandus rescript. It then proceeds to the legal disposition at the heart of the text, which is unfortunately damaged. As with the Tymandus rescript, then, we have a petition lodged by the citizens themselves that has been approved by the reigning emperors based on commonly accepted criteria, particularly the broader imperial desire to promote cities throughout the empire.

Religion was, as we have seen, certainly a concern in the Tymandus rescript. It is less overt in the instance of Heraclea Sintica, but not entirely muted. A religious connection with the ruling tetrarchs is at least hinted at by the name the petitioners employed of themselves. By styling themselves "Heracleans," they were surely drawing attention to their attachment to a god openly favored by the tetrarchs. The same strategy had won considerable privileges for the nearby city of Perinthus, which parlayed its own long-standing claims to have been founded by Heracles into a variety of privileges in precisely this period, among them the new name of Heraclea.[28] Thus, even if religion was not a paramount concern expressed in the petition of Tymandus, devotion to the god Hercules probably ranked among the attributes the polity used to curry imperial favor.

This pair of inscriptions—both likely tetrarchic—thus illustrate well the broader process of petition and response as well as the more specific nature of petitions for status as a *civitas*. Emperor and subject approached the matter with a fixed set of assumptions that dictated the terms of their dialogue. In the instance of requests for civic status, these included demands that a city's size and infrastructure be robust, that its governmental machinery comply with norms of representative democracy under the control of local aristocrats, and that it comply with the religious standards fostered by the emperor and the broader majority of his subjects. As Constantine secured control of an ever-growing share of the empire, his dealings with cities were governed by these same assumptions and circumscribed by the practices of governance that had preceded him. Nevertheless, as we shall see, he managed subtly to manipulate the standards maintained by his predecessors so as to favor his own program of narrowing the horizons of traditional religious practices and promoting the Christian cult he had come to favor.

Hidden Agendas: Petitions, Patronage, Punishment

The emperor's commonly expressed desire to promote the welfare of cities was more than mere window dressing. Flourishing cities collected more taxes, did better at keeping the peace, contributed more labor to the imperial road system, and better promoted the imperial cult, which was run at the local level by civic office holders. With this in mind, the tetrarchs had deployed civic elites when they undertook to eradicate the Christian cult during the Great Persecution beginning in 303. Civic officials and their subordinates were enlisted to post edicts, enforce orders to sacrifice, collect and destroy ecclesiastical property, round up Christians, and turn them over to imperial officials for trial and execution. This was true until Galerius issued his Edict of Toleration on April 30, 311.[29] His death shortly thereafter left the eastern empire in a state of flux as two Augusti remained to vie for the territories he had once controlled. In the month immediately following Galerius's death, Maximinus Daia, who had been resident in Syria, stole a move on his rival Licinius, stationed in the Balkans, and successfully gained control of all of Anatolia. Licinius was outraged but avoided open war by making a tense agreement with Maximinus on the Bosporus to refrain from further hostilities.[30] In his newly expanded jurisdiction, Maximinus soon turned his attention to undoing the effects of Galerius's Edict of Toleration and reinstituting harsh measures against the Christians.

Maximinus had always been a convinced persecutor and was determined to continue what he thought to be sound religious policy.[31] He was thus overjoyed when embassies from city councils approached him with petitions asking for help in their efforts to rid themselves of their Christian inhabitants. First among these were community leaders from Nicomedia, who presented themselves before Maximinus in autumn of 311 carrying images of their gods and requesting that all Christians be expelled from their city.[32] In his generosity, Maximinus consented: "I considered it necessary to give a friendly answer to the inhabitants of Nicomedia . . . and to confirm the petition [aitēsin] they presented on behalf of the worship of their deity."[33] In the last days of 311 another embassy arrived from Antioch led by Theotecnus, a civic magistrate holding the office of Curator. The Antiochene delegation also requested a rescript permitting the expulsion of its Christians.[34] They too were granted their request, and Theotecnus was even rewarded with the governorship of Galatia Prima.[35] Other cities soon followed suit with delegations of their own.

In response to these petitions, Maximinus began issuing a flurry of rescripts, three of which are recorded in our sources: one to Tyre (in a Greek copy preserved by Eusebius from May or June 312),[36] one to Arycanda (in a very fragmentary inscription),[37] and one to Colbasa (in an inscription recording a rescript issued on April 6, 312, and first published in 1988).[38] The kernel of dispositive text reported in the Colbasa inscription reads: "But as for those who have persisted in the abominable cult, let them be separated, just as you ask, far from your city and territory, and be removed, whereby, in accord with the praiseworthy zeal of your petition, your city, separated from the stain of every impiety, may respond, as it has been accustomed, to the sacred rites of the immortal gods with the worship that is owed to them."[39] While not openly granting the right to do harm to Christians, these rescripts offered their recipients permission to expel them from the community and treat them as outsiders. Although Maximinus insisted that his subjects should be brought to the worship of the gods by "flatteries and exhortations" rather than by open violence,[40] the inevitable effect of the privilege he permitted was that Christians were once again tortured and killed, this time without recourse to the municipal juridical systems, whose protections Christians had now lost. This is precisely what occurred at Ancyra (Ankara), where seven virgins were executed by drowning and a local shopkeeper named Theodotus, who had fled into the neighboring countryside, was martyred upon returning.[41] More spectacularly, the bishop of Alexandria, Peter, was seized along with a number of his subordinates and executed in November 311.[42]

Interesting in all three of the extant rescripts from Maximinus Daia is the strong emphasis on the fact that the initiative came from individual cities: the emperor was merely responding to locally generated petitions.[43] Nevertheless, this assumption is drawn directly into question by both Lactantius and Eusebius, who report that in fact Maximinus had put the word out encouraging cities to make precisely the same request and confirming in advance that he would gladly honor it.[44] Some commentators have impugned their credibility on this point, but the verbatim parallels between the three extant versions of the rescript—parallels whose import came into full relief only with the publication of the Colbasa rescript in 1988—leave no doubt that Lactantius and Eusebius were correct.[45] Maximinus was not tailoring rescripts to meet the individual demands of cities but rather churning out virtual photocopies of a prescripted response to any city answering his clarion call for petitions to persecute.

It must surely have been the case that many of the citizens of Nicomedia, Antioch, Colbasa, Tyre, Arycanda, Alexandria, Ancyra, and the various other polities that requested such a rescript actually shared Maximinus's desire to expel Christians from their cities. As was just noted, these same citizens, particularly those who represented the elites most closely connected with the control of local—and imperial—cult, had cooperated all along with the Great Persecution. But Maximinus now offered new and supplemental incentives for cooperation. This we know from the clause in his rescripts that promises: "We grant permission to your devotion to request, in return for your religious resolution of that sort, whatsoever bounty you want. And may you do and request this now in the knowledge that you will obtain without any postponement something which, when granted to your city for all time, may as much bear witness to our own religious piety toward the immortal gods as it may show to your sons and grandsons that you have achieved rewards worthy of your traditions from Our Clemency."[46] We know that, in an effort to generate additional revenue, Galerius had extended the poll tax (*capitatio*), formerly restricted to the empire's rural citizens, to the inhabitants of cities.[47] This was of course deeply unpopular among urban dwellers, and Mitchell has argued that, with this clause of the rescript, Maximinus was offering an advance promise to remit this new burden.[48] The call for petitions from the cities to expel their Christians thus came with a built-in reward that must have been difficult to overlook.

Nor does our evidence for such quid pro quo gamesmanship end with these petitions. M. Christol and T. Drew-Bear have reconstructed a dossier from fragmentary inscriptions of Pisidia to demonstrate that Galerius and Maximinus showed extraordinary favor toward M. Valerius Diogenes, governor of that newly created province, by offering him support to implement an extensive building program in Antioch of Pisidia in 311.[49] We know from another inscription that Diogenes was a convinced and militant persecutor of Christians, in keeping with imperial mandates in this period. As Christol and Drew-Bear have rightly argued, the connection between funding and fundamentalism can hardly have been accidental.[50] Furthermore, we know that circa 312, Maximinus granted a select number of cities the right to mint their own coinage. Civic coining had of course thrived in the High Empire but had slowed in the third century and ground to a halt by the 290s.[51] Maximinus revived it briefly by granting minting rights to three select cities: Nicomedia, Antioch, and Alexandria. The first two, as we have seen, were the first to have requested permission from Maximinus to renew persecutions following the death of Galerius, and the last is the only city known to have executed its Christian bishop under Maximinus's overlordship.[52] The new civic coins of all three cities focus entirely on the pagan deities each most favored.[53] Again one senses a connection between the grant of civic privileges and the readiness to promote the emperor's religious program.

The traditional system of petition and response had, as we have discussed, always been underpinned by a series of unstated assumptions and expectations. Taking advantage of this fact, Maximinus had shown that it could be mobilized toward proactive ends. By making it known that privileges would be accorded through rescripts to cities that actively sought permission to enact his centrally conceived program of persecution, he was able to promote a hidden agenda that represents a step well beyond the norms of reactive governance. Although Maximinus is the first attested late Roman emperor to have made this move, we have good evidence that he was not the last. Sozomen tells us that, once he attained sole power, Julian "wrote frequently to the council of those cities if he knew they had turned to paganism, and urged them to ask what gifts they might desire. Toward those that were Christian, on the contrary, he openly manifested his aversion, not suffering to visit them nor receiving their ambassadors delegated to report about grievances."[54] Maximinus had thus reworked the practice of petition and response in ways that would continue to affect policy formation for years to come.

Although it is possible that Constantine and his Christian successors refrained from using this new tool, it would have been more natural for them too to take advantage of it, albeit toward different ends. Indeed, in what follows Constantine will be shown to have understood fully the value of foregrounding his own expectations in ways that would invite petitions to implement religious policies that actively supported Christianity while chipping away at traditional paganism. In other words, like his predecessor, Maximinus Daia, as well as his successor, Julian, Constantine sought to redirect the traditional system of reactive governance in order to promote a proactive, centrally devised religious policy.

Orcistus: Reading an Epigraphic Dossier

Orcistus (Alikân/Doganay) was an insignificant town in northeastern Phrygia situated along a tributary of the Sangarius River.[55] Little remains of this tiny community with which to reconstruct its history apart from some scanty aboveground remains and a handful of inscriptions. One of these has been recognized since its discovery as one of the most important documents not only for the city and region but also for the history of imperial relations with civic polities altogether. The inscription was recorded on three sides of a square pillar standing one and a half meters high and measuring half a meter on each side. It was first rediscovered in 1740 and published in 1752 by R. Pococke, who was able to view only its front and left side. It was found again by W. J. Hamilton in 1839 and in turn by W. M. Ramsay and J. R. S. Sterret in 1883 and again in 1886. Ramsay and Sterret were able to view the entire monument, and their transcription of its epigraph formed the basis for the edition published by Mommsen in 1902 as *CIL* 3: 7000, which in turn forms the basis for most modern editions. Nevertheless, a far better transcription, also based on autopsy, was published by W. M. Calder in 1956 as *MAMA* 7: 305.[56] Sadly, the stone was destroyed by locals in subsequent years, and only its fragments remain in the Afyonkarahisar Museum. Even so, further convincing emendations were able to be offered to its opening by D. Feissel in 1999.[57] (See Table 1 at the end of this chapter for a text and translation of the inscription.)

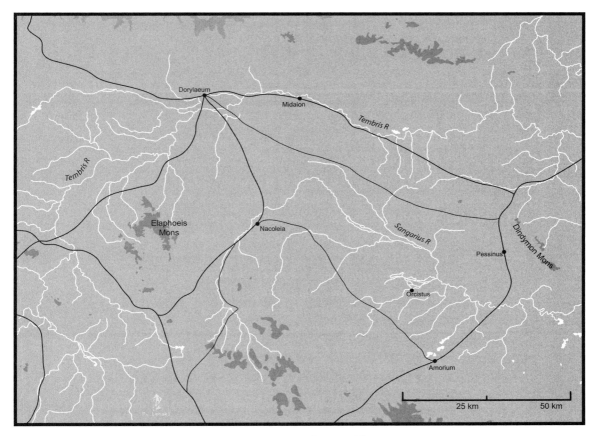

Map 2. Orcistus and Its Neighbors

Feissel was also able to explain the order in which to read the various documents the inscription records. These number four and were issued in two, rather than three phases, as had been previously assumed. The first phase dates between November 8, 324, and summer 326 and comprises:

1. Constantine's *adnotatio* to the people of Orcistus,
2. His rescript to Ablabius, who was then serving as *Vicarius Asiae*, laying out the reasons for his order and the protocols for its execution,[58]
3. A copy of the original request of the Orcistans, which is now truncated.

The second phase, datable precisely to June 30, 331, comprises only one document:

4. A second imperial rescript reconfirming the privileges Constantine had already granted.

This last was necessitated by the fact that these were being ignored by Orcistus's neighbor and rival, the city of Nacoleia (Seyit Gazi).

The substance of the dossier can best be understood by beginning with the first rescript. This opens with a greeting to Ablabius, which instantly makes clear that the Orcistans have now been granted their request for civic status (Panel 1, ll. 9–10: *iam nu(n)c oppidi et/ civitatis*). There follows a more sweeping statement outlining Constantine's broader concern with the promotion of cities (Panel 1, ll. 13–16), precisely the sort of language we have seen describing Constantine's civic politics in the panegyrics of Nazarius and the anonymous rhetor of Autun, but also familiar from the tetrarchic inscriptions from Tymandus and Heraclea Sintica. As noted earlier, this was not mere rhetoric, but represented the emperor and his subjects uniting around a common discourse of civic promotion. The Orcistans had capitalized on this shared repertory of values to win approval for their request.

The rescript goes on to indicate that Orcistus was not seeking civic status for the first time but rather attempting to reclaim a right now lost (Panel 1, ll. 16–20). Some scholars have called into question the veracity of this assertion, but their case is based strictly on inferences drawn from the relative insignificance of Orcistus.[59] In support of the Orcistans' claim, an inscription of the 170s lists various magistrates of Orcistus (including *epimelētai* and *archontes*),[60] another records a dedication to Commodus by Orcistus's *dēmos* and *gerousia*,[61] and a third from 237 records the establishment of an annual grain distribution scheme, managed by Orcistus's *archontes,* that was ratified in a decree (*psephisma*) passed by its *ecclesia* and *gerousia*.[62] The existence of these civic functions and functionaries does not of itself guarantee that the community was a *polis*, for even if these offices were requisite components of *poleis*, ambitious villages (*kōmai*) regularly adopted the same structures and titles for organizational and self-promotional purposes.[63] Nevertheless, the regular recurrence of references to civic offices in Orcistus's epigraphic dossier over a period of seventy years points strongly in the direction of civic status. An even stronger claim can be made based on the Constantinian dossier's sheer repetition of the assertion that Orcistus had once enjoyed the status of a city, which recurs no less than eight times.[64] Some have assumed that the Orcistans were protesting so very much precisely because they were lying, but this argument is entirely circular. It seems safer to accept that they were simply stating a fact: their polity had been promoted to civic status, probably in the second century, and had then lost this privilege at some subsequent date between the mid-third and early fourth.

The inscription goes on to justify the grant of *civitas* in very much the same terms used in the instances of Tymandus and Heraclea Sintica. The rescript emphasizes attributes of the city's populace (its size, organization, and promotion of the imperial agenda), and its topographical advantages (both natural and manmade).[65] Constantine's first line of reasoning in granting their request thus stresses Orcistus's report that "it was adorned with magistrates in annual offices and was abundant with curials and filled with a populace of citizens" (Panel 1, ll. 18–20). Later he notes that its populace was "so abundant that the seats [of the forum] are easily filled" (Panel 1, ll. 27–29). The city's thriving population is thus linked to its organization as a polity of the sort promoted by the emperor. As such, the emperor interpellates its inhabitants into subjects worthy of assuming an identity ideated for them by his regime and the empire he represents. The second line of justification was based on Orcistus's advantages as a *locus opportunus* (Panel 1, ll. 21 and 35–36). It could boast the intersection of four major roadways along which it served as a posting station, an abundant water supply that fed public and private baths and even watermills,[66] and a forum bedecked with the statues of revered emperors of the past (Panel 1, ll. 20–31; cf. ll. 38–39). In this sense, the city qua spatial entity was rhetorically reconstructed in accordance with idealized norms that prevailed across the empire and represented constitutive grounds for obtaining the status of a city as well.[67]

The community's claims to city status thus look remarkably traditional when set against the examples examined earlier in this chapter. Moreover, as with these earlier petitioners, the Orcistans also emphasize the importance of attaining not just the *name*, but also the *rights* of civic status. In their dossier this distinction is repeated six times in various formulations, making it clear that this was a fundamental issue.[68] The Orcistans were fighting not just to be *called* a city but to enjoy the *rights of self-governance* attached to a city.

The rescript departs from the commonplaces of the two earlier inscriptions only when it turns to the reasons offered for Orcistus's loss of status: "Although the aforementioned place is said to abound in all these things, they assert that the citizens of Nacoleia happened to demand that they be joined to their city at some previous time. It is unworthy of our times that so favorable a place should lose the name of city, and it is harmful to the inhabitants that they are deprived of all their advantages and benefits through the depredation of those who are more powerful" (Panel 1, ll. 31–39). A rivalry between cities, like the one alluded to here, was not an issue raised in the earlier rescripts to Tymandus and Heraclea Sintica. All the same, struggles between neighboring polities over autonomy and self-governance were a standard feature of provincial politics. In many ways such conflicts mirrored on a civil level the military brinkmanship that had once characterized peer polity relations in the region prior to the arrival of the Romans. But Orcistus offers our first epigraphically attested example of a polity "at war" with its neighbor over its own autonomy in the Roman imperial period.

The precise development of the dispute between Orcistus and Nacoleia can probably never again be recovered, but the line that follows the passage just quoted must surely shed light on at least one of the issues at stake: "To all of these things could be added, like a sort of crowning achievement, that all who live there are said to be followers of the most holy religion [*sectatores sanctissimae religionis*]" (Panel 1 ll. 39–42). This brief but important reference makes clear that, in addition to concerns over populace and physical attributes, Constantine also took account of religious criteria in making his decision about whether to grant Orcistus civic status. Religion was, as we have seen, mentioned in the rescript from Tymandus and hinted at in that from Heraclea Sintica, but it played at best a secondary role among the rationales for granting these cities' requests. The decrees from Tyre, Arycanda, and Colbasa, however, have alerted us to the fact that religious compliance could and did play a key role in struggles for civic privileges and in an emperor's choice to grant the petitions of his cities.

Scholars have traditionally taken the phrase "followers of the most holy religion" (*sanctissima religio*) to mean Christianity.[69] Nevertheless, in his groundbreaking book on *The Roman Revolution of Constantine,* R. Van Dam has questioned this assumption and argued that this indirect formulation may instead reflect the language of a cautious populace cultivating deliberate vagueness about the nature of its religion in the face of an emperor whose own cultic affiliation still seemed to them unclear.[70] On two counts, this interpretation cannot stand. First, the Orcistan petition was crafted shortly after Constantine's defeat of Licinius in a battle tinged with pro-Christian politics, and Constantine's professed crusade on behalf of Christianity then surfaced almost immediately in the iconographic and textual propaganda that followed. Among many examples that could be cited, his letter to the eastern provincials, which was widely circulated to cities (perhaps even Orcistus) at precisely this time, could not have made any clearer to the emperor's new subjects his public profession of the Christian faith.[71]

Second, Van Dam's argument that the Orcistans are hedging their bets by using the phrasing *sanctissima religio* also misses the mark because this phrase is not nearly as indeterminate as he believes. On the contrary, *sanctissima religio* is used to denote Christianity in the early fourth-century text known as the *Acts of the Martyrs of Abitina,* and in a later fourth-century letter of Gratian to the vicar of North Africa, Aquilinus.[72] More importantly, it also occurs in a Latin letter composed by Constantine himself, where it unmistakably refers to Christianity. In the same letter, preserved as Appendix 3 of Optatus, Constantine also speaks of Christianity as the *sanctissima observantia* and the *sanctissima lex.*[73] Constantine also uses *sanctissima lex* to refer to Christianity in a letter of 314 and a law of 326 and *sacrosanctae religio* to refer to it in a law of 333.[74] Most telling of all, in Eusebius's Greek translations of Constantine's letters, the emperor refers directly to Christianity as "the most holy religion" on four occasions, the earliest dating to 313.[75] So too, Athanasius's Greek translation of the letter Constantine sent to Theodotus of Laodicea in late 325 uses the exact same designation for Christianity.[76] *Sanctissima religio* was thus a thoroughly Constantinian construction that clearly referred to Christianity, as the Orcistans must have known.

If we can assume with Van Dam that Constantine is referencing claims made by the Orcistans themselves to be universal followers of the *sanctissima religio*— and the nature of petition and response make this a good assumption—we are thus witnessing a near perfect coincidence between the lifeworlds of Constantine and the subjects of this tiny Anatolian town. By positioning themselves as entirely consonant with Constantine's radical new assumptions about the ideal political community and offering him a dominant reading of his own rhetoric in the form of an official petition, they are presenting him an opportunity to advance his religious agenda through the efficacious medium of legal discourse. Constantine's favorable response to Orcistus was thus founded in part on demographic, political, and architectural concerns—the size of its populace, its governmental structures, its location and amenities—but in no small part also on religious grounds— its adherence to Constantine's favored cult.

The rescript continues on the second panel at the right side of the pillar, where Constantine describes his positive response to the petition and alludes to the fact that this has already been communicated to the Orcistans directly in an *adnotatio*. In his study of *adnotationes*, W. Turpin has demonstrated that this form of legal response came into existence in the later empire as a way for the emperor to communicate his *personal* answer to private petitions.[77] In a world where a growing bureaucracy, coupled with a burgeoning number of petitions, had permitted the imperial government to respond to queries largely in isolation from the emperor himself,[78] the *adnotatio* was used to signal an emperor's personal involvement and interest in a particular issue. R. Mathisen has shown further that *adnotationes* signal that they are granting special favors from the emperor by using words such as *beneficium* (favor) and *indulgentia* (indulgence).[79] Thus in the Orcistus dossier, the emperor's second rescript refers to the original *adnotatio* with the term *indulgentia* three times.[80] The significance of the emperor's personal concern with their situation was by no means lost on the Orcistans themselves, for they placed this text prominently on the front of the capital at the top of the pillar on which they inscribed the dossier, above all other texts inscribed there.[81]

The *adnotatio*'s wording is repeated more or less verbatim in the dispositive part of the rescript to Ablabius, whose beginning is signaled, as usual, by a word equivalent to "therefore" (*proinde*: Panel 1, l. 3 = Panel 2, l. 2). In the *adnotatio* and the rescript's disposition, Constantine draws attention to the fact that he was not innovating but merely restoring to wholeness an honor that had been "mutilated" by the Nacoleians (Panel 1, ll. 3–4 = Panel 2, l. 4). His word choice would have been as striking to ancient readers as it is to moderns for its connotations of violence. This same notion was already present earlier in the rescript with the mention of "the depredations of those who are more powerful" (Panel 1, ll. 37–38: *depraedatione potiorum*), and it recurs in the second rescript, which mentions the "effrontery of the Nacoleians" (Panel 3, ll. 14–15: *Nacolensium iniuriam*). The reader cannot help but think of the Christian persecutions and wonder if perhaps Nacoleia had taken advantage both of its superior power and of the climate of vindictiveness fostered by the tetrarchs and Maximinus in order to receive permission to subsume Orcistus as a dependent *kōmē* with the promise that it would compel its smaller neighbor to participate in the traditional cults.

The second panel continues with the fragmentary copy of the original petition. In it the Orcistans themselves supply Constantine and his officials with the rhetoric they will deploy in their own rescript and *adnotatio*. The citizens open with their claim to have obtained the rank of city long ago and then launch into an elaborate description of their geographical setting at the nexus of four roadways leading to the powerful cities of Pessinus (Sivrihisar), Midaion, Amorium, and (one assumes) Nacoleia (Panel 2, ll. 27–34; see Map 2).[82] The name of the last of the four cities is uncertain because the inscription breaks off,[83] but enough remains to offer the sense that the petition's description was much more elaborate than the summary we find in Constantine's rescript. Even so, the mirroring of the two texts offers a strong sense of the functioning of the system, for the emperor and his bureaucrats worked in counterpoint with the petitioners, whose rhetoric and rationale they build into their response.

This does not mean, however, that the rhetoric and ideals they shared were closed to question and dispute. Indeed, tensions over ideological and particularly religious norms are patently confirmed by the last document in the dossier, which appears on the left side of the pillar and consists of a second rescript. Its heading survives and is datable to June 30, 331, some five to seven years after the first response. At this point, we learn, the Nacoleians were continuing to assert their claims over Orcistus, a violation that the second rescript strives to halt. It is a recurring feature of inscriptions recording civic petitions that they catalogue multiple documents designed to stamp out ingrained or recurring problems.[84] The Orcistus dossier stands out, however, in that it not only reaffirms what was stated earlier but also fills out our understanding of the basis for the dispute. This is intimated already at Panel 3, lines 11–13, where Constantine states that his original response was designed to safeguard Orcistus's civic status not merely through honor but also through the privilege of liberty (*libertatis etiam privilegium*). As I have argued elsewhere, *libertas* was a concept closely linked with religious freedom in Constantinian rhetoric.[85] That the root of the problem here was religious as well is confirmed in what follows: "Therefore through this present rescript, we eliminate the effrontery of the citizens of Nacoleia, which has persisted even after the favors of our indulgence [*indulgentia*—that is, the first rescript with its *adnotatio*], and we grant to your requests and to your petition that the money which you were accustomed to paying previously for religious rites, you need in no way spend from now onward."[86] Thus, in as far as the problem persisted, the disputes revolved around religious differences and their expression in financial compulsion. Lurking behind the question of civic status was, in other words, a feud over cultic practice.

Redressing Grievances, Reestablishing Cities

How, we might ask, might this feud have arisen? This question is obviously connected with the circumstances under which Orcistus was annexed by Nacoleia, circumstances that are no longer known. Orcistus was by no means the first city to have lost its independence to a neighbor. In fact, depriving cities of their civic status had long been a tactic used by emperors, and indeed Hellenistic monarchs before them, to punish disobedient polities.[87] By the same token, the transfer of control over such cities to their neighboring polities was sometimes used to reward the neighbor for loyalty and compliance. Surely the most famous instance of this phenomenon occurred in 194 CE when Septimius Severus punished both Byzantium and Syrian Antioch for supporting his rival Pescennius Niger by depriving both of their civic status and subjecting the one to its neighbor Perinthus and the other to its neighbor and rival Syrian Laodicea.[88] Lucullus had done the same when he reduced Tigranocerta to a *kōmē* for resisting him in the first century BCE, and Augustus assigned the Messenian city of Thouria as a dependency to its neighbor Sparta for having supported Mark Antony in the civil war of 31 BCE.[89] In the first century CE, Tiberius deprived Cyzicus of its liberty and reduced it to provincial status for having violently imprisoned some Roman citizens and for neglecting to complete a promised shrine to Augustus; and Vespasian deprived a number of provinces and cities—including Byzantium—of freedom in part to restore tax revenues lost to Nero's freehandedness, but also to punish some for opposition.[90] Although the import of civic autonomy and freedom declined with the introduction of universal Roman citizenship in 212 CE, cities continued to guard their claims to civic liberty in the years to come, as attested by Aphrodisias's successful petition for acknowledgment of its freedom in late 250.[91] And the question of civic status and liberty remained an issue well beyond the reign of Constantine. In the mid-fourth century Julian deprived Cappadocian Caesarea and Palestinian Maiouma of their civic status and reduced them to *kōmai* as punishment because, like Orcistus, both claimed exclusively Christian populations that refused to implement his program of reviving traditional paganism.[92]

A. Chastagnol has suggested that Orcistus might have lost its civic status under Maximinus Daia or Licinius, who objected to its exclusivist Christian populace.[93] This cannot be proven, but we do know that the tetrarchs operated on this sort of logic from an incident reported in Eusebius and alluded to in Lactantius: "At this time some soldiers surrounded in a ring a tiny city entirely of Christians [*holēn xristianōn polichnēn*] in Phrygia together with its inhabitants, set it on fire, and burned it, including small children and women who were beseeching the God of the universe. They did this because all the inhabitants of the city and the Curator himself and the Duumvirs and all those in offices together with the entire people had declared themselves to be Christians [*xristianous sphās homologountes*] and did not obey those who ordered them to worship idols."[94] Unfortunately, neither Eusebius nor Lactantius attests the name of the city in question, but we can at least infer that it was not Orcistus, which obviously survived the Great Persecution.[95] Regardless, the story makes clear that the tetrarchs were anxious to punish any community that self-identified as "wholly Christian," which of course brings to mind the Orcistans' own assertion to this effect.

The strict accuracy of this claim to religious homogeneity must of course remain in doubt. For some it may seem implausible that the populace of an entire city—even a small one—could adhere to a single religion. Nevertheless, the repetition of similar claims in the instances of Eusebius's anonymous Phrygian *polichnē*, as well as Cappadocian Caesarea and Maiouma just mentioned, is balanced by assertions of similarly exclusivist pagan populations in towns like Tainia, Petra, Carrhae, Gaza, and Heliopolis-Baalbek.[96] Libanius claims that Julian took delight in cities with temples still standing but considered those that had destroyed all their temples to be polluted, obviously implying religious homogeneity; and Sozomen informs us that, on his journey to the eastern frontier, Julian refused to stop at Edessa even though it was directly on his path because its population was entirely (*pandēmei*) Christian.[97] S. Mitchell has made strong arguments that the thick record of funerary and dedicatory epigraphy in central Anatolia reflects a pattern in which "areas where virtually the entire population had been converted contrasted, sometimes starkly, with others where pagans still prevailed."[98] We should not, therefore, underestimate the ability of small communities to dictate with stark efficiency the religious norms of their people. As Lucian of Antioch is said to have proclaimed during the trial that preceded his execution in 312, Christianity was no false religion, but rather: "Practically the majority of the world bears witness to this truth, including entire cities, or if this somehow seems suspicious, even the rustic folk ignorant of idols offers similar testament to these things."[99] For Lucian, at least, the comprehensive conversion of entire cities or rural communities represented the most obvious witness to the religious truth he proclaimed. Thus, even if some minority of the inhabitants of Orcistus, or for that matter any other city, lived in defiance of local norms, this need not derogate from the generalizing claim of a city to have been "Christian" from its highest to its lowest ranks.

Such cities would have represented incredibly hard nuts for emperors with opposing religious views to crack. In previous centuries the rapprochement between locally defined and imperially imposed religious practice had been facilitated in large part through the assimilation of both sides to the norms of the other through the intermediacy of the imperial cult. The tremendous success of emperor cult was based largely on the fact that it offered local communities an opportunity to invite the numinosity of the emperor into their presence and to use his symbolic power to bridge the gap between local and transregional systems of belief and practice. This created a variety of hybrid cults that could satisfy both local and imperial needs.[100] But the exclusivism and monolatry so staunchly insisted upon by Christians left little room for such dialogue, which meant that, in a city like Orcistus, compliance with traditional and imperial religious norms may have been achievable only by subjecting the smaller city to a larger neighboring polis.

Nacoleia would indeed have been an ideal candidate for the task of religious overlord to a Christian Orcistus. It sat at the foot of the Elaphoeis Mons (Türkmen Dağı), home to at least six cult shrines to Zeus the Thunderer (*Zeus Brontōn*), including the important temple of Zeus Brontōn Megas.[101] Devotion to Zeus-Jupiter must have seemed especially appealing to the eastern tetrarchs, who touted their Jovian connections, and particularly to Maximinus Daia, who is known to have participated personally in celebrations at Zeus's shrine in Panamara in 312.[102] The city's elite was closely involved with the maintenance and operation of the Zeus Brontōn cult along with the worship of other typically Phrygian deities like Zeus Bennios, Papias, Mēn, and of course Cybēlē.[103] The nearly watertight nature of its pagan populace has been observed in the city's epigraphy, about which W. Cox and A. Cameron observed, "only one pre-Constantinian monument has been found in this whole area which is certainly Christian."[104] Even after Constantine, pagans seem to have continued to dominate Nacoleia's civic horizons, for they dedicated a large altar to Julian in 362.[105]

Indeed, Orcistus sat along a sort of a pagan corridor, for not only Nacoleia, fifty kilometers to its west, but also Pessinus, thirty kilometers to its east, was notorious as a center of traditional worship. The Nacoleians made their dedication to Julian in no small part because he had taken a detour on his journey to Antioch that year in order to visit Pessinus and its storied shrine of Cybēlē. There the apostate emperor slept in the temple and was inspired to compose his oration

On the Mother of the Gods, and from there he also issued his letter to Callixeine, whom he appointed high priestess of the Great Mother of the Phrygians.[106] Orcistus was thus enveloped by larger and more powerful polities dominated by pagan cult sites and pagan ruling elites. With its petition to Constantine, this tiny Christian rival wished to exploit the power of an emperor who at long last shared their religious views in order to free itself of the influence of its neighbors and above all of their attempts to impose upon it the implementation of their religious norms.

Given that imperial policies were necessarily promulgated and enforced at the civic level, this sort of jockeying for local control should come as no surprise. When we consider the fundamental role played by civic political structures in carrying out the Great Persecution, it seems entirely natural that the tetrarchs felt particularly threatened by those communities where Christian uniformity offered not the slightest chink for the imposition of their boldly universalizing and highly traditionalist religious program. To overcome this obstacle, they resolved either to subordinate such Christian strongholds to another city whose pagan elite could enforce compliance (as with Orcistus), or, where this seemed impracticable, to eradicate the Christian town altogether (as happened with the Phrygian *polichnē* described in Eusebius). With his rescripts, Constantine strove to reverse this process, rupturing the uncomfortable union of Orcistus with Nacoleia and thereby permitting the smaller Christian community to flourish on its own terms. In the bargain, he surely calculated that precisely such communities would become his steadfast allies, for not only were they now beholden to him for their civic privileges and immunities, but their exclusivist Christian populations could also offer an unbreachable base for the spread of his new faith in the region.

By using the petition and response system as the vehicle to accomplish this goal, Constantine also achieved yet another coup, which he may not have predicted but which would have an even greater impact over the long run. The process of dialogue inherent in petition and response allowed Constantine more successfully to connect previously recognized civic criteria to his new agenda and thus to build the traditional strengths of civic governance into Christian polities. By juxtaposing traditional attributes—like the presence of a flourishing population, the organization of councils and magistrates, the abundance of public architecture, and the favorable topography of the city—alongside the value he now attached to a Christianized populace, Constantine reoriented the definition of the polis in ways that built new requirements onto the solid base of inherited civic values. The ideal polis was no longer simply a collectivity of people unified around a pre-established system of governance within a pre-established organization of space. It was now also a community of Christians, a microcosmic reflection of the ecclesiastical *oikoumene*.

Conclusion

The Roman Empire has often been characterized as a network of cities, and indeed this modern understanding has ancient roots. Aware of the importance of civic polities, emperors had long worked to promote the welfare and growth of urban centers throughout the realm. Often this involved privileging the claims of one polity over another, for the network operated only through systems of comparison and subordination. Prior to the fourth century, the playing field within which cities structured this dialogue was laid out around the clearly identifiable markers of civic attributes: population size, structures of self-governance, geographical advantage, and urban embellishments. A significant role, however, had always been assigned to religion, which remained a major channel through which power relations between the emperor and his subjects were mediated.

During the High Empire this meant especially the promotion of the imperial cult. In the late third and early fourth centuries, cities had emphasized their religious adherence to the tetrarchs not just by celebrating the imperial cult, but also by promoting the brutal anti-Christian program implemented by the tetrarchs in no small part through the civic apparatus used to enact traditional religion at the local level. In this environment, opposition to Christianity offered a tool with which to leverage imperial favor. At no time was this truer than in the final years of the reign of Maximinus Daia, who openly exploited the rescript system to promote pagan communities within cities even while using these to hammer local Christians.

As Constantine moved onto the scene, he put this same tool to work toward quite different ends. While keeping alive the old criteria for civic promotion, he began to privilege Christianity as a trump card in the high-stakes game for civic rights. This was certainly true with Orcistus, whose petition differs from earlier extant requests for civic status primarily in its emphasis on the religious adherence of its populace, which the petition claims was exclusively Christian. Orcistus used this attribute to achieve independence from the neighboring city of Nacoleia, a city that had once punished the tiny polity for its people's unwillingness to support the traditional cults. Orcistus was able, in other words, to use a dominant reading of the pro-Christian messages emanating from Constantine's chancery and indeed from the emperor's own pen in order to advance its political agenda vis-à-vis this powerful neighbor. Taking advantage of this local rivalry and rewarding Orcistus for its readiness to reflect back to him the message he was most strongly pushing, Constantine was himself able to begin a process of redefining the ancient city as a political and geographical structure organized around the worship of the Christian god, a Christian polity. As we shall see in Chapters 6 and 7, Orcistus was by no means unique in this regard. Indeed, Constantine cleverly exploited inter-polis rivalries—common since the classical period—in order to advance his religious agenda all across the empire. First, however, we must turn to the second major epigraphic attestation to Constantine's relationship with his cities, the Hispellum rescript.

Table 1. Orcistus Dossier: Text and Translation

The text presented here follows *MAMA* 7: 305 as emended by Feissel, "L'adnotatio de Constantin" = *AE* 1999: 1577. Earlier editions include: *CIL* 3: 352, greatly improved at *CIL* 3: 7000 = *ILS* 6091 = Bruns *FIRA*⁷ no. 35 = Riccobono *FIRA* 1: 95 = Abbott and Johnson, *Municipal Administration*, no. 154 = *ILCV* 3; cf. Chastagnol, "L'inscription Constantinienne," pp. 384–88.

Previous translations include: Johnson, Coleman-Norton, and Bourne, pp. 240–41; Lee, *Pagans and Christians*, pp. 90–93 no. 4.9; Van Dam, *Roman Revolution*, p. 371 (English); Chastagnol, "L'inscription Constantinienne," pp. 389–91 (French); Kolb, "Bemerkungen," pp. 328–31 (German).

Orcistus Panel 1: Front of Pillar
Document 1: Adnotatio

[S]ac(rae) li[tte]r(ae?). Hae(c) quae in precem con[tu]lis[tis et nominis] et dignitatis reparationem iure qua[erunt obtine-]re. Proinde vicari intercessione qua[e fuerant mu-][t]ilata ad integrum prisgi(*sic*) honoris r[educi san-]5. cimus ut et vos oppidumque dilig[entia tui-]tum expetito legum adque appellationis s[plendore] (*vacat*) perfruamini. Infra: scrib<s>i(?) (*vacat*)	Imperial letter. The things that you assembled in your petition rightly require that you obtain the restoration of both name and rank. Therefore we decree that, through the intercession of the *vicarius*, those things that had been mutilated should be restored to the wholeness of the old honor so that you and your township, safeguarded by diligence, may fully enjoy the radiance of the laws and title for which you petitioned. Below: I have written.

(*continued*)

Table 1. Orcistus Dossier: Text and Translation (*continued*)

Orcistus Panel 1: Front of Pillar
Document 2: Rescript

Have Ablabi carissime nobis.	Greetings Ablabius, Our dearest.
Incole Orcisti iam nu(n)c oppidi et	The inhabitants of Orcistus, from now on
10. civitatis iucundam munificien-	a township and city, have offered to Our
tiae nostrae materiem praebue-	Munificence a favorable opportunity,
runt Ablabi carissime et iucundiss[i-]	Oh dearest and most favorable Ablabius.
me. Quibus enim studium est urbes vel n[o-]	Indeed, we who are zealous either to found new
vas condere vel longaevas erudire vel in-	cities or to improve ancient ones or repair
15. termortuas reparare id quod petebatur acc[e-]	those that are imperiled found their petition
ptissimum fuit. Adseruerunt enim vicum suum	thoroughly welcome. Indeed, they have asserted
spatiis prioris aetatis oppidi splendore floru-	that their village used to flourish with the splendor
isse ut et annuis magistratum fascibus orn[a-]	of a township for a considerable period in times past, so
retur essetque curialibus celebre et popul[o]	that it was adorned with magistrates in annual offices
20. civium plenum. Ita enim ei situ ad[q]ue ingenio	and was abundant with curials and filled with a
locus opportunus esse perhib[e]tur ut ex qu-	populace of citizens. Indeed, the place is reported to
attuor partibu[s e]o totidem in sese confluan[t]	be so favored by its location and nature that from
viae quibus omnibus publicis mansio tamen [u-]	four different directions four roads converge upon it,
tilis adque accomo[da] esse dicat[u]r, aquaru[m]	for all of which it is said to be a way-station that is
25. ibi abundantem aflu[en]tiam, labacra quoqu[e]	both useful and suitable for imperial (transports); and
publica priva[taqu]e, forum istatui(*sic*) veterum	that there is an abundant supply of water, and public
principum ornatum, populum comm[a]nentium	as well as private baths, and a forum adorned with
adeo celebrem [ut se]dilia [qu]ae ibidem sunt [fa-]	statues of former emperors, and a populace of
cile conpleantur, pr[aeter]ea ex decursibus	inhabitants so abundant that the seats there are easily
30. praeterfluentium [a]quarum aquim(o)lin[a-]	filled; furthermore, from the water channels running
rum numerum copiosum. Quibus cum omni-	past, there is an abundant number of water-
bus memoratus locus abundare dicatur c[on-]	mills. Although the aforementioned place is said to
[t]igisse adseruerunt ut eos Nacolenses si[bi]	abound in all these things, they assert the citizens of
[a]dnecti ante id temporis postularent. Quo[d]	Nacoleia happened to demand that they be
35. [es]t indignum temporibus nostr(i)s ut tam o[p-]	joined to their city at some previous time. It
[p]ortunus locus civitatis nomen amittat	is unworthy of our times, that so favorable a place

should lose the name of city, and it is harmful
to the inhabitants that they are deprived of all their
advantages and benefits through the depredation of
those who are more powerful. To all of these things
could be added, like a sort of crowning achievement,
that all who live there are said to be followers of the
most holy religion. Since they have petitioned Our
Clemency to grant them the former right and name of
city, we have given them a judgment to this effect,
just as the copy of our *adnotatio* appended with their
petition testifies. For the things which they assembled
in their petition rightly require that they obtain the . . .

restoration of both name and rank.
Therefore we decree that, through
the intercession of Your Gravity,
those things that had been mutilated
should be restored to the
wholeness of their old honor
so that they themselves and their town,
safeguarded by their diligence, may fully
enjoy the radiance of the laws and
title for which they petitioned. It is thus
right that Your Sincerity swiftly fulfill
what we have most readily
conceded to these petitioners in accord
with the dignity of our times.
Farewell Ablabius,
Our dearest and most favorable.

et inutile commanentibus ut depraeda-
[t]ione potiorum omnia sua commoda utilit[a-]
[tes]que deperdant. Quibus omnibus quasi
40. quidam cumulus accedit quod omnes
[i]bidem sectatores sanctissimae religionis habitare dicantur. Qui cum praeca-
rentur ut sibi ius antiquum nomenque
civitatis concederet nostra clementia
45. sicuti adnotationis nostrae subiec[t]a
cum precibus exempla testantur huius mo-
di sententiam dedimus. Nam haec quae in pre-
cem contulerunt et nominis et dignitatis . . .

Orcistus Panel 2. Right Side of Pillar
Document 2: Rescript (continued)

1. reparation[em iure quae-]
runt obtinere. P[roinde gra-]
vitatis tuae inte[rcessione]
quae fuerant mu[tilata]
5. [a]d integrum prisgi(!) [honoris]
[re]duci sancimus ut et [ipsi]
[o]ppidumque diligent[ia sua]
[t]uitum expetito legum [ad]
[q]ue appellationis splen-
10. [d]ore perfruantur. Par es[t]
[i]gitur sinceritatem tuam i[d]
[q]uod promptissime pro tem[po-]
[ri]s nostri dignitate conces-
[si]mus erga supplicantes fes-
15. [ti]nanter implere. Vale Abla[bi]
[ca]rissime ac iucundissime n[obis]
(leaf)   (leaf)

Table 1. Orcistus Dossier: Text and Translation (*continued*)

Document 3: Copy of Orcistus's Petition
(*Nov. 8, 324 / July 326*)

Exemplum precum.	Copy of the Petition.
[A]d auxilium pietatis vestrae	We have fled to the aid of Your Piety,
[conf]lugimus domini Impp(eratores) Constantine	Oh Lord Emperors Constantinus
20. [maxi]me Victor semper Aug(uste) et Crispe et	Greatest, Victorious, Augustus forever, and Crispus
[Con]stantine et Constanti nobb(ilissimi) Caess(ares).	and Constantinus and Constantius, Most Noble Caesars.
[Patri]a nostra Orcistos vetusti[s-]	Our homeland of Orcistus was a very old township and from times
[sim]um oppidum fuit et ex antiquis[si]	long
[m]is temporibus ab origine etiam	past since its origin it also obtained the rank of city;
25. [civ]itatis dignitatem obtinuit	and it is located in the midst of the borderland of
[e]t in medio confinio Gal[a]tiae P(h)ri[g-]	Galatia and Phrygia, for it furnishes the
iae situm est, nam quattuor viar[um]	crossing points of four roads, namely that from
[t]ransitus exhibet id est civita[tis	the city of Pessinus, which city is
[P]essinunte(n)sium quae civita[s dis-]	at about the thirtieth mile marker from
30. [ta]t a patria nostra tricensim[o fe-]	our homeland, as well as the city of Midaion,
[re]lapide necnon etiam civitat[is Mi-]	which is also at the thirtieth
[d]aitanorum, quae et ipsa est a [patria]	mile marker from our homeland,
[n]ostra in tricensimo miliario e[t civi-]/	and the city of Amorium, which is located . . .
[t]atis Amorianorum quae posita (*vacat*)	

Panel 3. Left Side of Pillar
Document 4: June 30, 331

[S]cr(iptum) prid(ie)	Written on the day
Kal(endas) Iulias	before the Kalends of July
[C]onstantinopoli	at Constantinople.
Imp(erator) Caes(ar) Consta[n]tinus	Emperor Caesar Constantinus
5. Maximus Guth(icus)(*sic*) Victor ac trium-	Maximus Gothicus Victorious and
fator Aug(ustus) et Fl(avius) Clau(dius) Constantinus	Triumphant, Augustus, and Flavius Claudius Constantinus

Alaman(nicus) et Fl(avius) Iul(ius) Const(ant)ius nn(o)bb(ilissimi)
Caess(ares) s[al]utem dicunt
ordini civit(atis) Orcistanorum.
10. Actum est indulgentiae nostrae munere ius vobis civitatis tributum non honore modo
verum libertatis etiam privilegi[[o]]^a custodire. Itaque Na-
15. colensium iniuriam ultra indulgentiae nostrae beneficia
perdurantem praesenti re-
scribtione removemus idque
oratis vestris petitionique
20. deferimus ut pecuniam quam
pro cultis ante solebatis in-
ferre minime deinceps dependa-
tis. Hoc igitur ad virum perfe
[c]tissimum rationalem Asia-
25. nae dioeceseos lenitas nostra
perscribsit qui secutus for-
[mam] indulgentiae concessae
vobis pecuniam deinceps pr[o]
supra dicta specie expeti a vo-
30. bis postularique prohibeb[it.]
Bene valere vos cupim[us]
Basso et Ablabio cons(ulibus)

Alamannicus and Flavius Julius Constantius, Most Noble
Caesars send greetings to
the Order of the City of the Orcistans.
It was decided through the gift of our
indulgence to safeguard the right of civic status
attributed to you not merely as an honor,
but also through the privilege of liberty.
Therefore through this present rescript,
we eliminate the effrontery of the citizens of
Nacoleia, which has persisted even after
the favors of our indulgence,
and we grant to your requests
and to your petition that the money
which you were accustomed to paying
previously for religious rites, you need in no way
spend from now onward. Our Mildness has
written this to the Vir Perfectissimus,
Accountant for the Diocese of Asiana,
who, in following the protocol of this
indulgence as it has been granted
to you, will from now on prohibit the money
for the above mentioned pretext to be sought
or demanded from you.
May you fare well.
In the consulship of Bassus and Ablabius

^a Calder: privilegium.

CHAPTER 5

The Exigencies of Dialogue
Hispellum

The Limits of the Possible

In contrast with Phrygia, where a patchwork of exclusive religious communities—some Christian, others pagan—coexisted alongside, but also in tension with one another, central Italy in the early fourth century was much more religiously homogeneous and much less open to Christian interpenetration. The territories of Umbria and Tuscia, immediately north of Rome and Latium, had long-standing traditions of cultic practice that predated Roman control of the region and that continued to influence Roman cult-ways down into Late Antiquity.[1] We have very little testimony of active Christian worship in either region before the fourth century, and even with the rise of Constantine, it was some time before the Christian cult took firm root. This would not, in other words, have been fertile ground for the promotion of Constantine's new religion, for the wooded hills and rich valleys of Tuscia and Umbria clung quite tenaciously to the gods who had rendered these territories so prosperous for centuries previous.

The town of Hispellum (modern Spello) is located in the heart of Umbria. Perched at the foot of the steep southwestern slopes of Monte Subasio, a mass of pink limestone shrouded in forests, it overlooks the rich valley created by the stream called the Tinea (Topino) about thirty kilometers southeast of Perusia (Perugia).[2] Archaeological remains confirm that the city had an Umbrian prehistory, and we know from a variety of sources that it enjoyed a period of particular favor under Octavian, who established it as a colony (Colonia Iulia Hispellum) and endowed it with walls and with control of the famous spring of Clitumnus, formerly managed by neighboring Spoletium (Spoleto).[3] By the High Empire it had a thriving population in the tens of thousands and was equipped with formidable walls outfitted with six gates, the principal one of which still stands largely intact on the southern edge of the city. Hispellum also boasted baths, a theater and amphitheater, and a massive religious complex just outside its northern walls. There, worship of Venus, Minerva, and Jupiter continued into the fourth century. There are no attestations of Christian cult at Hispellum before the year 487. It was not, in other words, a city that would have accepted a dominant reading of Constantine's new devotion to the Christian god without question and even resistance.[4]

The best Constantine could hope for in his relations with this city was thus a negotiated reading of his religious program. Dialogue would be necessary, and with it compromise on both sides was inevitable. To his good fortune, the Hispellates opened the door to just such an exchange when they petitioned Constantine for support in overturning what they regarded as a lopsided arrangement in the celebration of the region's annual religious festival. In the decades before they lodged their petition, this event had been dominated by the powerful city of Volsinii in the neighboring region of Tuscia. Tuscia and Umbria had been joined into a single province under the tetrarchs, who had given the former the exclusive right to host the annual festival. When the Hispellates begged Constantine for a greater role, he seized on their request as a chance to explore the limits of the possible. As we shall see in what follows, he made no effort to turn traditional religious practice on its head. Instead, he granted the Hispellates' petition to establish an imperial cult temple to his family, the *gens Flavia*, and even allowed the colony to rename itself Flavia Constans, after his son. This was, in every way, good politics, for it built allegiance to himself and his family on a symbolic level even while enhancing the strength of a powerful city in the region that had formerly been upstaged by its local rival. In recompense for these privileges, Constantine insisted that Hispellum call a halt to the practice of blood sacrifice at this new cultic center. Through the rescript system, the Hispellates had thus gained their demand, but they had done so only by accepting the emperor's counterdemand that they curb a revered and sacred pagan rite that was as central to traditional religious practice as it was abhorrent to Constantine.[5]

The Hispellum Rescript: Questions
of Date and Attribution

The Constantinian inscription of Hispellum was first found in 1733 and was almost instantly regarded as a forgery. This remained the prevailing opinion until 1850, when Mommsen published a commentary that definitively demonstrated its authenticity.[6] Although the inscription itself is now widely regarded as genuine, the details of the rescript it records and especially its date remain a matter of debate. K. Tabata, for example, proposed that it may have been composed as early as 326, when Constantine is known to have visited the region; at the other extreme, T. Barnes has argued for summer 337, a dating so late that it calls into question authorship by Constantine, who died on May 22 of that year.[7] In fact, based on his dating, Barnes would attribute the rescript not to Constantine himself but to his youngest son Constans.

It has long been recognized that the heading of the inscription is peculiar.[8] Constantine himself is given his full titulature, including the titles *Victor* and *Triumphator*, which he took after his defeat of Licinius in 324. It also lists three Caesars: Fl. Constantinus (II), Fl. Iul. Constantius (II), and Fl. Constans, the last of whom was appointed on December 25, 333. Not listed are Flavius Iulius Dalmatius and Flavius Hannibalianus, both of whom were associated with the imperial college from September 18, 335. The most common conclusion has therefore been that the rescript was issued between these two dates.[9] Nevertheless, a further detail complicates the matter: the inscription does not list the title "Most Noble Caesars" (*Nobilissimi Caesares*) normally given to Constantine's sons while they reigned jointly with their father. It is this anomaly, above all, that has occasioned debate about the rescript's dating.

Reviving earlier arguments laid out by R. Andreotti and J. Gascou, Barnes has asserted that the rescript was issued after Constantine's death but before his sons had been promoted to full Augusti on September 9.[10] This argument is certainly plausible in light of a passage from the final pages of Eusebius's *Life of Constantine,* which claims that Constantine "reigned even after death, and the customs were maintained just as if he were alive."[11] This has been taken to indicate a period of interregnum in which the fiction was maintained that Constantine continued to rule in the months between his death and the proclamation of his sons as Augusti. From the Theodosian Code we have only one law extant from summer 337 that might prove this, but its heading provides only ambiguous evidence. *CTh* 13.4.2, dated August 2, 337, opens: *Idem A ad Maximum PP*, wherein the *Idem A(ugustus)* references *Imperator Constantinus Augustus* in the heading of the constitution immediately preceding in the *Codex.* This would seem to confirm the notion of an interregnum, but provides no support for the use of a hybrid imperial titulature in which Constantine was listed (posthumously) as Augustus alongside the three Caesars, now named without their title *Nobilissimus.* Gascou made the further argument that the name Flavia Constans given to Hispellum in the rescript may allude to the fact that Constans had already been granted provisional control of Italy by the time the rescript was issued, perhaps as early as 335. Barnes carries this one step further by contending that the city's new name confirms that Constans *himself* must have issued the rescript after Constantine's death, a deduction he characterizes as "inexorable in logic."[12]

In fact the deduction is flawed, for Constantine and other emperors before and after him regularly renamed cities, forts, and provinces after various members of their household, male and female, at all points in their reign.[13] This was also pointed out in a refutation of Barnes's proposed reattribution of the rescript to Constans by K. M. Girardet. Girardet offers a series of hypothetical dating scenarios that could just as easily account for the irregular heading of the inscription, and he himself settles for one whereby its rescript was issued by Constantine late in his reign but then inscribed only after Constantine's death had been announced; the engraver might thus have omitted the titles of Constantine's sons, who were not yet Augusti but no longer properly Caesares.[14] This was in fact the same position adopted by Gascou in his landmark study on which Barnes's argument draws.

Although propositions for a date during the interregnum of summer 337 merit attention, their conclusions are by no means definitive. In fact, the only strong reason for rejecting a date between December 25, 333, and September 18, 335, is the absence of the title *Nobilissimi Caesares*. The title was indeed standard in inscriptions listing the imperial college of Constantine and his sons, but not universal.[15] Its omission could simply represent an oversight on the part of the stonecutter, especially given that the title was usually abbreviated NCAES or simply NC.[16] Furthermore, Barnes in particular offers no good reason why, if Constans were aware of his father's death and willing to permit the construction of a new imperial cult temple to the *gens Flavia* (as the rescript in fact allows), he would not have ordered that it be dedicated to his deified father, who had after all been enshrined among the *divi Augusti* earlier that summer in a ceremony that combined elements of a traditional pagan *consecratio* with a Christian funeral.[17]

In light of these ambiguities, I prefer to abide by the traditional dating of 333/335, which represents a reading of the criteria available on the stone itself without the need for recourse to hypothetical explanations for its silences—explanations which could go on ad infinitum. I do this while admitting that no definitive argument for the dating has yet been advanced and that, in the absence of further evidence, none is likely to be. At the very least, however, I abide by the conviction—shared by all who have written on the question except Barnes—that the rescript is accurate in listing Constantine himself as the issuing authority.

Managing Divisions: Hispellum and Volsinii

The Hispellum inscription (see Table 2) begins, much like those of Tymandus, Heraclea Sintica, and Orcistus, with a general statement about the emperor's concern for the promotion of cities (ll. 11–15) "whose beauty and form distinguishes them in the eyes of all the provinces and regions." Such expressions were, as we have seen in our discussion in Chapter 4, generic, yet they also reflected the perpetuation of ideals that directly affected the way in which emperors interacted

Table 2. The Hispellum Rescript: Text and Translation

The text presented here follows *CIL* 11: 5265 = *ILS* 705 = *ILCV* 5 = Abbot and Johnson, *Municipal Administration*, no. 155; Gascou, "Rescrit d'Hispellum," pp. 610–12 = *AE* 1967: 112; Amann, "Reskript von Hispellum," pp. 1–3 = *AE* 2002: 442.

Earlier translations of the Hispellum rescript can be found at Gascou, "Rescrit d'Hispellum," pp. 615–16 (French); Lewis and Reinhold, *Roman Civilization*, pp. 579–60 no. 174; Tabata, "Date and Setting," pp. 404–5; Lee, *Pagans and Christians*, pp. 92–93 no. 4.10; Van Dam, *Roman Revolution of Constantine*, pp. 366–67 (English).

E(xemplum) s(acri) r(escripti)	Copy of the Imperial Rescript.
Imp(erator) Caes(ar) Fl(avius) Constantinus	Emperor Caesar Flavius Constantinus
Max(imus) Germ(anicus) Sarm(aticus) Got(icus) Victor	Greatest, Germanicus, Sarmaticus, Gothicus, Victorious
triump(hator) Aug(ustus) et Fl(avius) Constantinus	Triumphant Augustus and Flavius Constantinus
5. et Fl(avius) Iul(ius) Constantius et Fl(avius)	and Flavius Julius Constantius and Flavius
Constans.	Constans.
Omnia quidem, quae humani gene-	We embrace everything that safeguards the fellowship
ris societate(m) tuentur, pervigili{um} cu-	of the human race with watchful thoughts of
rae cogitatione conplectimur, sed pro-	concern, but the greatest object of our foresight is
10. visionum nostrarum opus maximum[a]	that all cities, whose beauty and form
est ut universae urbes quas in luminibus provin-	distinguishes them in the eyes of all the provinces and
ciarum {h}ac regionum omnium species et forma dis-	regions, not only retain their former rank but also are
tinguit{ur} non modo dignitate(m) pristinam teneant	advanced to a better status through the gift of Our
sed etiam ad meliorem statum beneficentiae nos-	Beneficence. Therefore, since you have asserted that you
15. trae munere provehantur.[b] Cum igitur ita vos Tusci-	were joined to Tuscia in such a way that,
ae adsereretis esse coniunctos ut in{i}stituto	according to the arrangement of the old custom,
consuetudinis priscae per singulas annorum vi-	each year in alternating turns priests are
ces a vobis [a]dque praedictis sacerdotes creentur	created by you and the aforementioned [Tuscians]
qui aput [sic] Vulsinios Tusciae civitate(m) ludos	who offer theatrical shows and a gladiatorial
20. sc{h}{a}enicos et gladiatorum munus exhibeant,	contest at/near Volsinii, a city in Tuscia,
sed propter ardua montium et difficultates iti-	but because of the steepness of the mountains and the difficulties
nerum saltuosa(s) inpendio posceretis, ut indulto	of the wooded routes you have urgently demanded
remedio sacerdoti vestro ob editiones cele-	that through the grant of a remedy your priest may
brandas Vulsinios pergere necesse non esset,	not be required to travel to Volsinii in order to celebrate
25. scilicet ut civitati cui nunc Hispellum nomen	games; and specifically that we grant to your city,
est quamque Flaminiae viae confinem adque con-	which is now called Hispellum and which you report borders
tinuam esse memoratis de nostro cognomine	immediately on the via Flaminia, a name taken from our

family name, and that in it a temple of the Flavian family name be built in very grand fashion in accord with the greatness of its appellation; and that in that same place that priest whom Umbria had provided in alternate years should offer a spectacle of both theater shows and a gladiatorial contest, even while the same custom remains for Tuscia, that the priest created in that place should attend the spectacles of the aforementioned games at Volsinii, as was customary:

Our consent has readily been added to your petition and request. For we have conceded to the city of Hispellum the eternal designation and venerable name from our own appellation, and specifically that in future the aforementioned city be called Flavia Constans, in whose embrace we wish to be completed in grand fashion a temple also of the Flavian family, that is of Ours, as you desire, with the following restriction being prescribed, that the temple dedicated to our name not be polluted with the deceits of any contagious superstition. Consequently, we also grant you permission to host games in the aforementioned city on the specific condition that, as was stated, the annual tradition of giving games in alternate periods not depart from Volsinii either, where the aforementioned festival should be celebrated by priests created from Tuscia. In this way not much will seem to be diminished from previous customs and you, who come to us as suppliants because of the aforementioned case, will enjoy the pleasure of having obtained that which you so urgently demanded.

---

nomen daremus in qua templum Flaviae gentis
opere magnifico nimirum pro amplitudine{m}
30. nuncupationis exsurgere(t) ibidemque {h}is
sacerdos quem anniversaria vice Umbria de-
disset spectaculum tam sc(a)enicorum ludorum
quam gladiatorii muneris exhibere(t) manente
per Tuscia(m) ea consuetudine ut indidem cre-
35. atus sacerdos aput[sic] Vulsinios ut solebat
editionum antedictarum spectacula fre-
quentare(t), pr{a}ecationi {h}ac desiderio vestro
facilis accessit noster adsensus. Nam civitati Hispello aeternum vocabulum nomenq(ue)
40. venerandum de nostra nuncupatione conces-
simus scilicet ut in posterum praedicta urbs
Flavia Constans vocetur in cuius gremio
aedem quoque Flaviae hoc est nostrae gentis ut desideratis magnifico opere perfici
45. volumus, ea observatione perscripta ne aedis nostro nomini dedicata cuiusquam con-
tagios(a)e superstitionis fraudibus polluatur.
Consequenter etiam editionum in praedicta civitate exhibendorum(sic)c vobis
50. licentiam dedimus, scilicet ut, sicuti
dictum est per vices temporis sollemnitas editionum Vulsinios quoque non de-
serat ubi creati(s) e Tuscia sacerdotibus memo-
rata celebritas exhibenda est. Ita quippe nec
55. veteribus institutis plurimum videbitur
derogatum et vos, qui ob praedictas causas
nobis supplices extitistis, ea quae inpen-
dio postulastis impetrata esse gaude-
bitis.

ainsc: maximus
binsc: probeantur
cread: exhibendarum

with polities. As the text continues, we get the sense that the Hispellates have sup-plied Constantine with rhetoric similar to that proffered by the Orcistans about the favorable location and amenities of their city. At lines 25–28 the emperor repeats a fact he learned from their petition, that the city "borders immediately on the Via Flaminia." This was, of course, the most important road heading northeast out of Rome, a road with which Constantine was familiar from his journey through Italy on the way to fight Maxentius in late 312, and from his more recent visit to Rome on the occasion of his vicennalia in 326. In that year he issued a law from the neighboring city of Spoletium (Spoleto) just thirty kilometers to the south and also on the Flaminia.[18] The Hispellates have thus introduced their location in part to valorize their city's position along a major artery of the imperial road system— much as the Orcistans had done—but also in no small part to orient Constantine in a geography with which he was familiar from recent experience.

Constantine's response asserts at several points that he wished to uphold long-established traditions.[19] This same claim is also found in the Orcistus dos-sier, as indeed in a number of other extant petitions. From these parallels, we might be led to assume that the Hispellum rescript is nothing more than a typical response to a civic petition with little that could be called distinctive. Fairly quickly, however, we become aware that, although Constantine always keeps one eye on precedent, he is also ever searching for ways to innovate. This we see most clearly at lines 15–24, which reproduce the nub of the Hispellates' request: "since then you asserted that you had been joined to Tuscia in such a way that, accord-ing to the arrangement of the old custom [in{i}stituto consuetudinis priscae], each year in alternating turns, priests are created by you and by the aforementioned [Tuscians] who offer theatrical shows and a gladiatorial contest at/ near Volsinii, a city in Tuscia, but because of the steepness of the mountains and the difficulties of the wooded routes you have urgently demanded that through the grant of a remedy your priest may not be required to travel to Volsinii in order to celebrate games." In 2001, F. Coarelli argued that "the arrangment of the old custom" must refer to a long-standing religious festival, which he would trace all the way back to the federation of twelve Etruscan peoples known to have met since early Republican times at the cultic site of Fanum Voltumnae. Coarelli contends fur-ther that Etruscan religious forms had come to influence religious practice in Umbria, which he believes was accepted into the celebrations at Fanum Voltum-nae or Volsinii by the late Republic or early empire.[20] In point of fact, however, the purported connection he adduces between these Etruscan holy sites and His-pellum is entirely circumstantial and highly speculative.[21] Indeed, the very fact that Hispellum was attempting to use an imperial rescript to break away from the religious festival of Volsinii is a priori evidence that cultic ties between the two were hardly rock solid.

In a 2012 study, G. Cecconi has shown that the Latin expression for "old custom" (*prisca consuetudo*) used in the rescript is generally employed in extant legal sources to characterize norms that prevailed in circumstances *immediately preceding* the current order. By this reading, *prisca consuetudo* need not point to remote antiquity but may simply mean "the previous way of doing things" or "the earlier protocol."[22] In favor of this less grandiose interpretation, Cecconi lays emphasis on the rescript's insistence that problems have arisen because Hispellum and its Umbrians "have been joined to Tuscia," a merger believed to have occurred during the tetrarchic reorganization of Italy.[23] The existence of a joint province of *Tuscia et Umbria* is attested only in texts and inscriptions of the fourth century, which show that this new hybrid unit was managed under a single governor and hosted a single provincial council.[24] By Cecconi's reading, only this relatively recent merger occasioned the establishment of a joint festival between the two regions, which would not, therefore, have dated back any further than the late third century. Within this new administrative district, the Tuscian city of Volsinii held the upper hand as capital, at least originally, although sources from later in the fourth century attest to the presence of the governor of Tuscia et Umbria at Florentia (Florence) and Pistoriae (Pistoia).[25] According to Cecconi's thesis, then, tensions arose after the creation of the combined province and its new joint council and festival, and the Hispellum rescript shows merely Constantine's attempts to relieve these by splitting the festival from direct connections with the council—without dissecting the new joint province—in such a way as to give Hispellum, and by extension Umbria, a larger profile in the conduct of affairs in the region.

Cultic Competition

Quite apart from its administrative role, Volsinii was an obvious choice to be the seat of an annual religious festival. It had been a traditional locus of sacred authority for the Etruscans already in archaic times. The site of the original city of Volsinii, Etruscan Velzna, was probably on or near the citadel of modern Orvieto, but its location is no longer known definitively, for the Romans destroyed it in 264 BCE and moved Volsinii's inhabitants to a new locale, on the shores of the Lacus Volsiniensis (Lago di Bolsena).[26] The new Volsinii (modern Bolsena) continued to uphold Etruscan religious traditions, particularly at its temple to the regional goddess Nortia.[27] Meanwhile, however, traditional cultic practice probably continued near the original site of Velzna at the shrine of Fanum Voltumnae, a joint religious center for the Etruscan federation since the seventh century BCE.[28] Through excavations begun in the 2000s, archaeologist S. Stopponi appears to have discovered this shrine in excavations near Orvieto at Campo della Fiera,

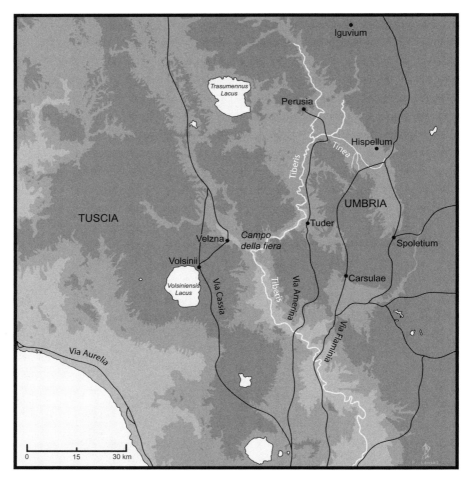

MAP 3. Hispellum and Its Neighbors

just southwest of Orvieto on the road to Bolsena.[29] The site preserves as many as five temples arranged into a festival precinct at which cultic activity is attested from the sixth century BCE to the fourth century CE, and over which a church was built in the sixth century CE that played host to annual celebrations lasting until the fourteenth century. We can no longer say whether the festival "at/near Volsinii" (*aput Vulsinios*) attested in the Hispellum rescript was in fact celebrated at this newly discovered site or, rather, at the site of modern Bolsena, or perhaps both. We do know, however, that in attempting to upend the protocols of the annual provincial festival of Tuscia et Umbria, Hispellum was competing with a neighbor that had extremely powerful claims to archaic and authentic religious authority.

Nevertheless, Hispellum had important traditions of its own. We have only fragmentary intimations of religious activity in the city from the Republican

FIGURE 31. Sixteenth-century Villa Fidelia (left) in Spello beside the terrace wall for the imperial temple complex, with early imperial stone courses surmounted by modern. Photo by N. Lenski.

period: a stone statue base with an Umbrian inscription to *iu[v]ip* (Iovis Pater);[30] and the remains of what appear to be a Republican-era temple of Venus.[31] Nevertheless, these finds from a hillside five hundred meters northeast of the city are significant, for in the late first century BCE, the notables of Hispellum constructed a massive terrace system in precisely this area to serve as the substructure for a sizable ceremonial and festival complex. These retaining walls continue to stand today as the substructure of the impressive gardens of the sixteenth-century Villa Fidelia.[32] Into and onto these terraces the Hispellates built impressive temples dedicated to Venus, Minerva, and, apparently, Jupiter as well (Fig. 31).[33] This sacred precinct overlooked a theater, now almost totally destroyed, as well as an amphitheater, whose standing ruins reveal its considerable dimensions (60 × 35 m).[34] Taken together, this remarkable display of public architecture constitutes one of the largest festival complexes in central Italy. Constantine's famous inscription was found on the site of the theater and was thus clearly meant to advertise and regulate the conduct of celebrations held at this impressive installation (Fig. 32).[35] Although the rescript mentions nothing of these constructions—a surprising omission—Hispellum was nevertheless able to make a good case that it was well equipped to compete for a larger role in the annual celebrations of

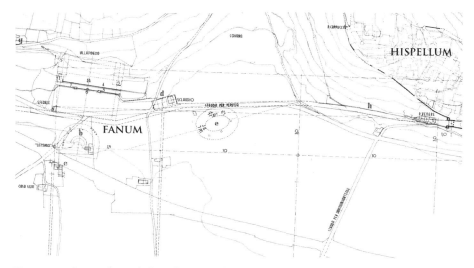

FIGURE 32. Cropped aerial plan of Spello and its surroundings, including the sanctuary at the Villa Fidelia (a), the theater (b), and amphitheater (e), after Camerieri, "Il catasto antico di Mevania," tav. 8.

the combined province of Tuscia et Umbria. Indeed, through its history of self-embellishment, it had set itself up as an ideal site for the conduct of religious festivals as they were enacted in imperial times. With the rise of the imperial cult as the axis of religious activity empire-wide, religious praxis had coalesced around the personality of the emperor and the celebration of the major events that punctuated his life and reign.[36] In this context, festivals and public benefactions in the form of theatrical and gladiatorial shows became staples of religious ceremonies in both West and East.[37] By creating the hybrid province of Tuscia et Umbria and assigning its annual provincial festival to Volsinii alone, the tetrarchs had thus shunned a serious contender for the conduct of imperial cult celebrations and had thereby set the plate for a dispute.[38]

In addition to granting Hispellum a share in the provincial festival, Constantine's rescript also permitted the city to rename itself Flavia Constans and, far more striking, to establish an imperial cult temple (*aedem*) to his family, the *gens Flavia*.[39] This fact is beyond dispute and cannot be emphasized strongly enough, for it shows that the first Christian emperor was anything but intransigent in his approach to traditional religion. Indeed, given his provisions to promote imperial worship not just here, but also in Constantinople and other cities of the empire, any assumptions that Constantine became unbending toward all forms of traditional worship in the last years of his reign must be reexamined.[40] It is less clear from the inscription, however, precisely how these celebrations were to be organized. Many have assumed that Umbria would host its own annual celebrations separate from those of Tuscia, but already in 1929, A. Piganiol pointed to the importance of the word *vices* (turns), used three times in the rescript,[41] as an indication that a festival once held exclusively at Volsinii with priests chosen *in turn* annually from Volsinii and Hispellum, would now be held at Volsinii and *in turn* Hispellum in alternating years. Cecconi has reinforced Piganiol's case with reference to a striking parallel from Asia, where in 371 CE the emperor Valens permitted each of the four metropoleis of this province to host the provincial celebrations once every four years by taking turns (*servatis vicibus*), a pattern Valens claims was already common in Illyricum and Italy.[42] The Umbrians had thus won permission to host the religious festival of Tuscia et Umbria in Hispellum at their own temple of the *gens Flavia* every other year, while Volsinii retained the right to play host in the alternate year. This was not, then, a radical departure from received custom but rather a minor alteration, as Constantine himself emphasizes (ll. 54–56).

Negotiating Religious Change

Nevertheless, we must still ask why the Hispellates might have requested this change and, more importantly, why Constantine might have permitted it. The sole reason reported in the rescript turns on the difficulty of travel between the two cities on existing roadways: "because of the steepness of the mountains and the difficulties of the wooded routes." The Via Flaminia south of Hispellum split into two branches, both of which did indeed move through mountainous and wooded terrain (Fig. 33). But a far easier route would have circumvented this ridge altogether and simply followed the Tinea north to Perugia and then returned south along the valley of the Tiber on the Via Amerina to Tuder (Todi), then west still following the Tiber Valley to Velzna (Orvieto—where the festival may have occurred), and from there over a small hill on to Volsinii (if this was in fact the site of the celebrations). By car along modern roads both routes clock in at approximately one hundred kilometers.[43] Given that the much smoother route on the Via Amerina was equidistant with the hilly approach, Hispellum's complaint about the mountain road seems rather disingenuous.[44] This is not to say that the distance between the two cities was of no concern, but only that its impact seems to have been exaggerated for effect.

A scholarly consensus has come to prevail that the deeper motivation for the request must have been rooted in the Hispellates' resentment over the need to fund and attend a festival some three days' journey from their own city.[45] Such festivals—particularly those involving theatrical and gladiatorial spectacles— were extremely costly for local elites to sponsor; they chose to host them above all

FIGURE 33. View of Rocca Prodo in the hills between Spello and Orvieto. Photo by N. Lenski.

in order to garner favor from their fellow citizens. By forcing the curial leaders of Hispellum to fund a festival that was held exclusively at or near Volsinii, the tetrarchs had thus created a source of tension with the elites of Hispellum that, with his rescript, Constantine was attempting to alleviate.[46]

The manner in which he did so shows well his skill at exploiting rivalries between peer polities in order to push his religious agenda, even in areas less than favorable to the immediate and wholesale adoption of Christianity. In their request, the Hispellates were hardly offering to abandon traditional worship in favor of Christianity. On the contrary, as mentioned, they were seeking to establish a locus for the practice of the imperial cult to the *gens Flavia*. In so doing, they were following a well-established model of using the imperial cult as a medium with which to forge bonds of patronage between themselves, the emperor, and his dynasty. They were, in other words, offering to appease Constantine on traditional terms. These may not have been optimal, but they were accepted by Constantine so that he could use the give and take of the petition system to win concessions of his own.

While granting the Hispellates' request, Constantine insisted on a condition that satisfied his broader religious agenda. From lines 42–47, we learn that he demanded that the new temple be kept free of sacrifice: "in whose embrace we wish to be completed in grand fashion a temple also of the Flavian family, that is of Ours, as you desire, with the following restriction being prescribed, that the temple dedicated to our name not be polluted with the deceits of any contagious superstition [con/tagios[a]e superstitionis fraudibus]." Superstitio is a notoriously difficult word to translate, but in the context of the Christian fourth century, it has a semantic range covering certain aspects of pagan practice considered unacceptable, particularly sacrifice.[47] This is certainly how the word is used in the extant legislation of Constantine and his successors.[48] Contagio is also a favorite word of Christian authors, who assign to it a broader range of meanings covering all deviations from acceptable social and religious practice, including fornication, heresy, and even Judaism. Nevertheless, among its most common uses in authors of the second through fourth centuries is as a brandmark with which to stigmatize idolatry and sacrifice.[49] Regardless of what one thinks about whether Constantine issued a general edict forbidding blood sacrifice (a subject treated in Chapter 12), it is abundantly clear from extant sources that he harbored great distaste for the practice.[50] The restriction against contagiosa superstitio is thus a blanket ban on sacrifice and perhaps also idolatry at this new imperial cult site in Umbria.

This ban on the fundamental ritual activity of pagan worship represents a major coup at the level of local cultic practice. For Hispellum to gain the privileges and status it desired, it had to sacrifice the practice of sacrifice, as it were, and to record this concession in stone.[51] Moreover, the inscription also exempted the imperial cult priests elected by the Hispellates from the need to travel to Volsinii for their semiannual celebrations, which almost certainly continued to involve sacrifice.[52] By splitting Hispellum from Volsinii for purposes of the annual provincial festival, Constantine was thus methodically and quite skillfully carving away at traditional practices in a region where these were too well rooted to be eliminated root and branch at one stroke. If he could not convert the Hispellates to Christianity, he could at least inoculate them from the malign influence of sacrifice.

It is thus important not to downplay the religious elements in the inscription in favor of the administrative aspects of the dispute, as many scholars have often done.[53] Read on its own terms, the inscription does not change the administrative organization of the new province in any appreciable way but rather calls only for a reorganization of its festival: the province's boundaries are not redrawn, its capital not shifted, nor its council restructured.[54] Even J. Gascou and K. Tabata, who do see the festival itself as Constantine's primary concern, insist that this consisted merely in games and entertainments, which they would distinguish from religious worship.[55] Here again, this underestimates the central role of religion in the rescript and the festival itself. The work of S. Price, J. Rives, and P. Van Nuffelen has alerted us to the fact that imperial religion always interwove the ludic with the cultic.[56] Both were integral parts of ritual patterns that were at once well rooted and religiously efficacious. Such religio-ludic festivals proved remarkably effective at integrating the emperor into the sacral worldview of his subjects, making it unacceptable to draw a firm line between the celebration of games and theater shows and the practice of imperial cult.

The interconnection of religion and spectacle are well attested in the inscription itself, which seamlessly joins the two in ways that should not be overlooked. At four points the rescript states directly that it was the job of local imperial cult priests (*sacredotes*) to host theatrical and gladiatorial shows.[57] Furthermore, an inscription from Hispellum's amphitheater dated between 337 and 340 shows the new arrangement in operation and leaves no room for doubt that the festival continued to serve as an occasion for the performance of imperial cult ritual.[58] In it, the Hispellates open by duly referring to themselves with their new name, "the urban plebs of Flavia Constans," a name that continued to affect local toponymy down to the early eighth century.[59] They then offer heartfelt thanks to C. Matrinius Aurelius Antoninus: "crown-bearing officiant [*coronatus*][60] of Tuscia et Umbria and priest [*pontifex*] of the cult of the Flavian family, sponsor of a lavish gladiatorial show [*munus*] and a top theater spectacle [*laetitia theatralis*]."[61] The Matrinius inscription confirms that the games and shows were organized and conducted by a priest of the imperial cult. It also proves that these included gladiatorial combats, yet another practice that grated on Constantine's Christian sensibilities but that he was willing to permit in exchange for the concessions he received from the Hispellates.[62] Indeed, pace Barnes, it was Constantine himself who had granted the city the right to host such combats explicitly in his rescript.[63]

Thus our lone piece of evidence for the new festival in action at Hispellum shows that it involved a priest of Constantine's family cult, celebrating in Constantine's family temple, at a city now named after Constantine's son, according to prescriptions laid out by Constantine himself. Nor should any of this come as a surprise, for we also know that at some point in his reign, likely still in the 310s, Constantine granted the province of Africa the right to establish a priesthood to the *gens Flavia*. Reaffirming this privilege, he later rewarded priests of the imperial cult in Africa with immunity from civic burdens in two laws dated to 334 and 337— that is, right around the time the Hispellum rescript was issued.[64] Down to the end of his reign, then, Constantine continued to promote the imperial cult to his own family in Italy and Africa, and he is likely to have done so elsewhere as well.

As with the Orcistus rescript, Constantine's approach to the Hispellates was all the savvier precisely because it used a grassroots request as the basis for its alterations to received custom. This is made clear in the rescript with what seems like an excessive number of references to the petition of the Hispellates and their demands.[65] The rapprochement afforded by the system of petition and response brought the emperor into dialogue with the Hispellates, enabling him to gain ground in the imposition of his new religious program through the quid pro quo inherent in rescript praxis. Whether or not Constantine, like Maximinus, spread the word through back channels that he would be receptive to petitions that excluded sacrifice from imperial cult sites and festivals, we can no longer say. But the Hispellates could surely have seen which way the emperor was moving and taken advantage of the situation by offering up concessions to their emperor in order to forge independence from neighboring Volsinii. Nevertheless, as a manifestation of the system of petition and response, the rescript was also bounded by the limitations of its protocols. By maintaining the fiction that he was merely responding to the Hispellates' request, Constantine was forced into a dialogue that compelled compromise on his part as well: Hispellum would continue with its festival at its new pagan shrine, even if it was required to do so without the performance of sacrifice. This interactive process pulled the emperor and his subjects into a space where both could explore the limits of the possible while remaining within its bounds, neither eliminating traditional practice nor leaving it unaltered.[66]

Conclusion

If Orcistus had offered Constantine fertile ground on which to cultivate an ideal Christian polity, Hispellum presented, by contrast, only stony soil in which to grow the Christian cult. Its religious past and civic apparatus were structured around traditions developed in the high empire that offered little purchase for Christianity. Constantine could thus never have expected to dismantle the edifice of traditional religion there at one go. Instead, he used the careful allotment of civic privileges to whittle away at the pagan practice of an individual city by granting it certain religious privileges fully in line with traditional cultic norms while revoking others. Hispellum could gain a measure of independence from its neighbor Volsinii along with the privilege of housing an imperial cult shrine, but only on the condition that it refrain from performing sacrifice there. The dialogic nature of the rescript system was thus employed to extract concessions even as it was granting honors. In the instances of both Orcistus and Hispellum, Constantine cleverly exploited inter-polis rivalries—between Orcistus and Nacoleia on the one hand, and Hispellum and Volsinii on the other—in order to advance his religious goals.

Emperors had long worked to mediate disputes between cities, even while striving to promote the growth and prosperity of urban centers as engines of imperial control at the local level. Constantine's rescripts to cities, fixed as they were in publicly displayed inscriptions, will have cemented his new dispensations into place at the local level with effects on social and religious praxis lasting into the future. To be sure, his call for a ban on sacrifice at the new imperial shrine in Hispellum did not spell the end of the traditional cults here any more than any of his normative regulations put a stop to pagan practices in the cities of the empire. He did, however, pioneer a peaceful and quite effective way for bringing the network of diverse cities in the empire into line with his new order. By deploying the tradition of petition and response to open dialogues between himself as ruler and his cities as subjects, he also opened the door to compromise—from both sides—as part of the process of exchange inherent in the economy of imperial power. As we shall see in the chapter to come, while Orcistus and Hispellum constitute our two best documented examples of this modus operandi, it can be traced in numerous other cities where Constantine's active dialogues using the traditional apparatus of normative regulation allowed him to leverage Christianity into cities and regions in ways that would help it gain a firm footing all across the empire.

CHAPTER 6

~

Constantine's Cities in the West
Nomen Venerandum

Breaking Bonds, Building Allies: Turning Faith
into Action at Maiouma

In the fourth chapter we saw that a politics of civic favoritism was operative under Constantine. He split tiny Orcistus from its much larger neighbor Nacoleia and endowed it with civic status in no small part because of its adherence to Christianity. In the fifth, we learned that he also promoted the fortunes of Hispellum vis-à-vis its neighbor Volsinii by permitting it to establish a temple and cult to his family and endowing it with his family's "eternal designation and venerable name" (*aeternum vocabulum nomenq(ue) venerandum*). In this and the next chapter, we shall examine other cities to which Constantine accorded similar privileges, focusing in particular on those—like Hispellum—granted the use of his name or that of his family members. In the process, we shall see that Constantine exploited traditional strategies for courting civic favor by exploiting long-standing rivalries between polities in order to gain not just clients for his broader administration, but also adherents to his faith.

We shall focus in this chapter on western cities, but it is worth beginning with the single most compelling example of the phenomenon, the Palestinian city of Maiouma, which can be taken as exemplary of a pattern I will argue was repeated all across the empire in varying degrees. Maiouma served as the port to its much larger neighbor Gaza, situated about three and a half kilometers up from the coast. Gaza was, notoriously, a city whose identity was entirely wrapped up with its revered temple to the god Marnas (Aramaic *Marnā*: the Lord). The worship of this deity and maintenance of his temple was crucial to the civic life of this city, the majority of whose inhabitants were staunchly devoted to his cult. Indeed, Gaza and its Marneion have been immortalized in the colorful *Life of Porphyry of Gaza*, a hagiographical biography of the bishop appointed to preside over Gaza in the early fifth century, when its inhabitants were still strongly opposed to the

introduction of Christian cult. The Gazaeans resistance to the imposition of this
outsider as a religious leader of their community was so strong that Porphyry was
eventually driven to take refuge in Constantinople, where he succeeded in obtaining an imperial rescript permitting him to eradicate the Marneion altogether.[1]

This is not to say that there were no Christians in the city prior to the fifth
century, for already during the Great Persecution we encounter a group presided
over by a certain Silvanus, a bishop not from Gaza itself but from its surrounding
chōra. Nevertheless, this exception would seem to prove the rule, for their story
arrives to us through Eusebius, who reports that some thirty-nine members of
this community, including Silvanus, were arrested, tortured, and executed or sent
to the mines of Phaeno.[2] Gaza appears not to have had a bishop of its own before
Asclepas, who held the see under Constantine, but even he was deposed and sent
into exile around 328.[3] If we can believe the *Life of Porphyry of Gaza,* even as late
as 395, its only Christian church was located outside the city's walls, and its populace was so hostile to Christian penetration that Porphyry had to be consecrated
at a synod held at Caesarea.[4] When he first entered the city as its newly appointed
prelate, he was greeted with a hail of verbal and physical abuse. According to the
life, he found only 280 believers among the residents, an exiguous congregation
for a city with an estimated population of 25,000 to 30,000.[5]

Maiouma had long been a village (*kōmē*) dependent on Gaza, although with a
population as high as 9,000 inhabitants it was a community of no small importance. By the early fourth century, Maiouma seems to have been home to a pre-
dominantly Christian population, which naturally chafed under the control of its
more powerful neighbor.[6] Our first report on its fate in the Constantinian period
comes from Eusebius, who reveals that the emperor endowed it with civic privileges and a name from his own family: "For now in the province of Palestine,
Constantia inscribed itself [*epigrapsamenē*] on the rolls of the saving religion and
was deemed worthy of a greater reward by both God and the emperor, for on the
one hand it was proclaimed a city, which it had not been formerly, and on the
other it changed its name to the greater appellation of the pious sister of the
emperor."[7] Maiouma thus chose to make some public declaration of its Christianity, whereupon Constantine endowed it with civic status—and thus independence from Gaza—and permitted it to take the name of his sister Constantia.[8]

Subsequent reports reveal even more about the history of the dispute between
the port town and her mother city. Our best source is Sozomen, whose family was
from the village of Bethelia in the Gazaean *chōra*.[9] In his discussion of Constantine's reign, Sozomen reaffirms the testimony of Eusebius by asserting that
Maiouma had "turned unitedly with all its inhabitants to Christianity" and that it
was rewarded with civic status and the name Constantia.[10] Later in his narrative,
when discussing events under Julian in the 360s, Sozomen continues:

[Julian] likewise accused the inhabitants of Constantia in Palestine [of attachment to Christianity] and allotted their city to the Gazaeans. Constantia, as we stated before, was the harbor of the Gazaeans and used to be called Maiouma. But when Constantine learned that a majority of them preferred the Christian religion, he rewarded them with the honor of city status and renamed them after his son Constantius, and he permitted them to conduct their own civic government, for he thought it was unjust that they should be tributary to the Gazaeans, who were extremely devoted to paganism [*telein hypo Gazaiois eisagan hellēnizousin*]. But when Julian became emperor, the Gazaeans brought suit against the citizens of Constantia. Sitting as judge himself, Julian reassigned Constantia to Gaza, even though almost twenty stades separate the two. And from that point forward it was deprived of its earlier designation and has been called the Maritime Portion of the City of Gaza [*parathalattion meros tēs Gazaiōn poleōs*]. They share civic archons and strategoi and public government. Only with regard to the church are they still considered to be two separate cities up to the present.[11]

Once again, we find confirmation that Constantine had awarded Maiouma its independence because of its claim to having a majority Christian populace, although Sozomen argues that it received its name not from Constantine's sister but from his son Constantius.[12] Furthermore, Sozomen reports, Gaza petitioned Julian to regain control of its neighbor by convincing the emperor to reconsider the case and to reverse Constantine's division, revoking both Maiouma's civic status and its new name. He goes on to say that Julian's successors refused to overturn his decision, even if Maiouma was allowed to maintain an independent bishopric.[13]

The dispute between the two communities was clearly not just a matter of local pride and autonomy but also of religious difference. Of particular concern was the celebration of civic festivals, which demanded large outlays of cash as well as common adherence to collective expressions of local religion. Festivals enacted a community's cultic identity, which is precisely what the Christian Maioumans did not wish to be dictated by their pagan neighbors. Indeed, Sozomen goes on to report, the dispute continued to fester into his own day when it was brought before a provincial council, which we know to have taken place at Diospolis in 415. By this point Gaza's Marneion had been destroyed and the city was firmly in Christian hands, but Maiouma continued to strive for independence from Gaza's bishop as well as its religious festivals and saints' cults.[14] The council found in Maiouma's favor, and despite the irregularity of maintaining a see in a village that was subordinate to another city, the smaller port was allowed to keep its bishop, shrines, and festivals: "for those who had been deemed worthy of the honors of a city on account of their piety should not be deprived of the privilege conferred upon the priesthood and rank of their churches through the decision of a pagan emperor."[15] Thus nearly a century after parlaying its profession of Christianity into civic independence, and half a century after losing this political autonomy, Maiouma capitalized on its grant of privileges under Constantine to win the next move in its battle with Gaza for self-determination.

It is little wonder that the tension between these two polities continued for over a century, for Constantine's decision to separate port from metropolis had stoked a conflagration that flared into open hostility already within a generation of his death. Sometime in the mid-fourth century, Sozomen's grandfather and much of his extended family were expelled from their native village of Bethelia—a populous community famous for its pagan temples—for having converted to Christianity.[16] Around the same time, we learn from Ambrose, the pagans of Gaza took advantage of Julian's restoration of favor to their city by burning local churches.[17] And the contemporary Gregory Nazianzen reports that under Julian the people of Gaza and nearby Ascalon disemboweled Christian priests and virgins and then filled their abdomens with barley so that their bodies would be eaten by swine.[18] Such spectacular acts of violence were surely provoked, at least in part, by Christians themselves eager to win salvation through martyrdom. This was probably the case with Eusebius, Nestabus, Zeno, and Nestor, Christians whose brutal martyrdoms under Julian are also related by Sozomen. Despite the Gazaeans' efforts to obliterate their remains, gobbets of their flesh and bones were collected in jars and stored—unsurprisingly—in Maiouma until the reign of Theodosius. When confronted with reports of the original incident, Julian ordered the dismissal of the governor of Palestine, not for losing control of public order but for having arrested the perpetrators in the first place: "For what right had he to arrest the citizens merely for retaliating on a few Galileans the injuries that had been inflicted on them and their gods?"[19] Antagonism was thus common on both sides, and both sought cover from the emperor for the enactment of violence against their religious rivals.

Another local religious provocateur was Hilarion, a Christian from the village of Tabatha five miles south of Gaza, who turned to a life of asceticism in the early 300s and was eventually forced to flee the area in the reign of Julian.[20] Prior to this, his zeal had manifested itself on a number of occasions, one of which suffices for purposes of illustration. A Christian notable named Italicus wished to enter a chariot team in the upcoming races connected with Gaza's civic festival. Fearing, however, that a certain duumvir of Gaza, "a devotee to the idol of Marnas," would hamstring his team with curses, Italicus approached Hilarion for help. Hilarion blessed a jar of water that Italicus then sprinkled on his stable, his horses, his chariots, their wheels, and the starting gates. With this protection in place, his entry easily rode to victory, causing the crowds to cheer, "Marnas has been defeated by Christ," and even leading to a number of conversions, but also to charges of magic against Hilarion.[21] Here we see in crystalline fashion the manner in which civic and religious politics coalesced around public festivals in moments that brought latent tensions to a flash point by enacting them in the symbolic arena of the circus.

This charged atmosphere formed the background to Constantine's civic politics at Gaza and Maiouma. It is instantly striking how closely it reproduces what we can know of the rivalry between Orcistus and Nacoleia. In both instances, Constantine deployed the classic tool, used by kings and emperors since Hellenistic times, of honoring petitions to promote one polity's status at the expense of its neighbor. This allowed Constantine to break down old structures of patronage and control and to reformulate new constituencies favorable to his agenda. As we saw in Chapter 4, Constantine may have further modified this instrument by circulating in advance news that he would look especially favorably on petitions from cities that professed to have a population that was "exclusively" Christian. This may explain Eusebius's choice to credit the success of Maiouma's appeal to its claim to have "inscribed itself on the rolls of the saving religion." With Maiouma, Constantine also sweetened his offer by conferring not just civic status but also an imperial name on the lesser of the two rival cities. In the process he was able to cultivate a seedling Christian community in the territory of a staunchly pagan polity, a community that, like Orcistus, could be relied on aggressively to propagate his new faith in the hostile ground surrounding it. This community took advantage of his largesse and the power it afforded to assert its autonomy not just in Constantine's lifetime, but for a century to come.

Constantine's Cities in the West: A Cautionary Note

If Constantine promoted Orcistus and Maiouma to civic status on the strength of their populace's profession of Christianity, and if he assigned a name from his family to Maiouma and Hispellum in exchange for cooperation with his religious agenda, we are surely right to wonder if he did not engage in similar gambits with other cities. In the remainder of this chapter and the next, we will examine this question with regard to those cities known to have been given the "eternal designation and venerable name" of Constantine or other members of his family, beginning with cities in the West and moving in Chapter 7 to those in the East.[22]

We should clarify at the outset that the practice of assigning an imperial name to a locale was hardly unique to Constantine. This tradition had been followed by Hellenistic monarchs since Alexander, and it had already been taken up by Roman generals in the first century BCE and practiced repeatedly by emperors

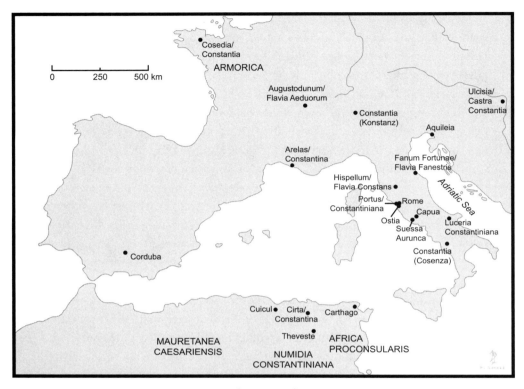

MAP 4. Constantine's Cities in the Western Empire

from Augustus onward.[23] In every instance, the assignment of a royal or imperial name to a place or polity indicated some special relationship, but this need not have involved the promotion of shared religious values. Most eponymous cities won their names because of their foundation or re-foundation by a ruler; some because of some accomplishment achieved by that ruler in or near their city; others still because of a special benefaction conveyed during a visit by the ruler or in response to a petition, often in the aftermath of a crisis or natural disaster.

In the instance of entirely new foundations, particularly military camps, the name of the reigning emperor or a member of his family was regularly assigned to locales that had no previous history of cooperation or special relations with the emperor. This tradition continued into the reign of Constantine, when we know of eight frontier settlements and one frontier province that bear a version of the name of Constantine or a member of his family.[24] Given how little we know about the history of these locales, it is impossible to say whether they were established under Constantine rather than one of his sons, or perhaps even founded earlier and simply renamed by Constantine or his successors. Such difficulties are well illustrated in the eastern cities of Amida and Antoninopolis-Tella, both of which are attested in variant sources under the names Constantina and Constantia, and both of which are reported in those sources to have received their new names at the end of Constantine's reign or, alternatively, early in the reign of Constantius II. Sorting through these contradictions is nearly impossible and would, at any rate, yield little of use for the study of their religious leanings.[25] As cities of the Syrian East with long previous histories, they are likely to have had sizable Christian populations by the 330s, but this may have had little to do with their renaming given their strategic locations and the long-standing tradition of assigning imperial names to frontier cities at the point when they were fortified or refortified. In the case of western forts with Constantinian names, it is likely that none had displayed any particularly strong devotion to Christianity up to the 330s. As military emperors, the neo-Flavians saw the defense of the state as their primary responsibility and would have lent their names readily to frontier cities whose fortifications they built or strengthened, regardless of the confessional status of their populations.

Indeed, it is by no means necessary to assume that even non-military foundations were given a Constantinian name from religious motives. The city of Fanum Fortunae (Fano), along the Via Flaminia on the Adriatic coast of Umbria, is attested in a law of 365 with the name "Flavia Fanestris," apparently deriving from Constantine's family.[26] After his death, Constantine was honored—alongside Augustus—on the city's triumphal arch, but otherwise we have no idea what sort of relationship existed between Constantine, his family, and this city.[27] This makes it unwise to speculate about the motives for this conferral upon it of a Constantinian name. Similarly, Luceria (Lucera), in Apulia, is attested in a single late antique inscription with the name Constantiniana, but once again, we can no longer determine why.[28] Nor can the Calabrian city of Constantia (Cosenza), whose name is attested in several Byzantine regionary catalogs, be made to reveal anything about the broader context in which it gained its name.[29] Given the absence of fuller testimony, it is best to admit that the origin of these Constantinian names remains unknown.

Augustodunum-Flavia Aeduorum

Even in some instances where we have more extensive evidence for Constantine's relationship with such cities, this does not necessarily indicate that religion played a significant role. Such is the case with Augustodunum (Autun) in eastern Gaul. In the summer of 311, an orator of Autun delivered a panegyric thanking Constantine for rescuing his city from suffocating debt by drastically cutting its tax assessment.[30] In keeping with its genre, the speech is unstinting in its praise, so much so that by the peroration its orator must beg a preemptory indulgence if, when the emperor next visits the city, his fellow citizens refuse to let him depart: "For you will pardon us, and put up with the insubordination which springs from our love. Although you may be the master of all cities, of all nations, yet we have even taken your name: no longer ancient Bibracte, which has up to now been called Iulia Polia Florentia, but the city is now Flavia Aeduorum."[31] The city had thus been given Constantine's gentilician name in the very recent past. Although this is only stated explicitly at the close of the speech, it is also alluded to in the opening and in its second paragraph.[32] The new name is thus used twice to bracket the whole speech, making this not simply a *gratiarum actio* for Constantine's fiscal generosity, but also a public proclamation of the city's newly cemented ties with the Constantinian household.

This was, of course, still a year or so before Constantine claimed to have converted. As we would expect, therefore, the orator engages him very much as a fellow pagan. He twice addresses Constantine as "your divinity" (*numen tuum*), describes lavishly the pagan ceremonials organized to celebrate the emperor's *adventus* to the city the year before, and even reports that Constantine's benefactions led to an increase in offerings at the city's temples.[33] Insofar as this orator can be assumed to represent the collective will of the city, Christian religion does not, therefore, seem to have played a role in influencing Constantine's choice to offer Autun his family name. Instead, as the panegyrist makes clear, the city's special relationship with the emperor was based primarily on two things: his clement remission of taxes, and the long-standing relationship between Autun and Constantine's imperial ancestors, Claudius II and Constantius I, the former of whom Autun had invoked for help during a siege, and the latter who then repopulated it and restored its infrastructure damaged in this attack.[34] Indeed, Latin Panegyric 9 of circa 298, delivered to Constantius I himself, confirms that he took a special interest in Autun and invested considerable resources in its reconstruction.[35] Constantine's ties to Autun were thus a family affair, and his choice to grant his gentilician—rather than his personal—name is as strong a proof as any that his concerns were with dynasty more than cult.

That said, Constantine's favoritism did bear some fruit on the level of promoting Christian religion in Autun after his conversion, for when he called the council at Rome in October 313 to decide the fate of bishop Caecilianus of Carthage, he selected the bishop of Autun, Reticius, as one of just three top advisers to join Rome's bishop as an overseer of the proceedings.[36] Furthermore, a Christian author of Autun whose name is no longer preserved wrote a brief poem called the *Laudes Domini* that he dedicated to Constantine, probably in the years between 317 and 323.[37] In it the author recounts briefly a recent miracle witnessed in the city, which he follows with a long lyrical passage on the beauty of God's creation and its relation to the incarnation. He closes with words of high praise for Constantine as father, lawgiver, and victor.[38] The dialogue Constantine had initiated with Autun by granting the city tax remissions and even the right to use his name in 311 had thus opened channels of communication through which he could foster the Christian leadership of the city and thereby win both cooperation and praise from this constituency.[39] Even if Christian religion played no clear role in Constantine's choice to rename Autun "Flavia Aeduorum," the city's new name and the imperial bond it represented signaled Christian denizens of the city that they could expect a favorable reception from an emperor who began professing openly to share in their beliefs shortly after adopting their city as his own.[40]

Arelate-Constantina

Autun's bishop Reticius was joined at the Council of Rome in 313 by Marinus, bishop of Arelas (Arles), another "Constantinian city." Arles's relationship with Constantine went back to the earliest years of his reign. The emperor's presence there is firmly attested by two laws of August 316,[41] and his son Constantine II is known to have been born there, perhaps at this time.[42] It has been argued that Constantine used the city as a capital in the first years of his reign, and that it may have been the venue for his wedding to the princess Fausta in the summer of 307.[43] Constantine thus had good reason to lavish rewards upon the city, and his readiness to do so is in fact confirmed by a variety of archaeological testimonia. A concentration of milestones in Viennensis from the early years of his reign indicates that he coordinated the rebuilding of the road system around the city between 307 and 310,[44] and the city also rededicated an arch originally dating back to the Augustan period in Constantine's name around the same time.[45] In addition, he transferred the personnel and equipment of the mint Maxentius established at Ostia to Arles and thus founded a new imperial mint there in 313.[46] A fragmentary inscription from the monumental entryway to the city's porticoed market square indicates that he had it built or rebuilt.[47] Then too, he appears to have had the city's circus remodeled and to have furnished it with the obelisk that still stands in Arles's main square today.[48] He may also have been responsible for the construction of a palace complex, including baths and a basilical hall, although the dating of these structures is far from certain.[49]

Constantine's concentrated personal involvement with Arles in the early years of his reign might lead to the suspicion that he endowed it with all of these embellishments early on, but much of the evidence for his benefactions dates later. The inscription recording his restoration of the market gate dates between November 324 and late 326, and the obelisk was probably also erected after Constantine gained control of Licinius's eastern domains in 324, for it was carved of granite from a quarry in the Troad. Constantine thus cultivated his relationship with the city throughout the duration of his reign and, if anything, increased the level of his benefactions with the passing of time.

At some point in the course of this history he chose to endow Arles with the name Constantina. This we learn most explicitly in a letter from the city to Leo the Great dated to 450: "This city was especially honored by Constantine of most glorious memory so greatly that from his designation [*vocabulo*] the city received the name Constantina in addition to its own name, which is called Arelas."[50] Leo's testimony is confirmed by an imperial epistle dated to 418 in which Honorius refers to Arles as Constantina Urbs.[51] More decisively still, already in the reign of Constantine the moneyers of Arles began using the name CONST(antina) and variants in their mint mark, and they continued this practice into the mid-fifth century.[52] The careful numismatic study of P. Bruun has pinpointed the initiation of this usage to the year 328,[53] making it appear that, despite his intensive contact with Arles early in his reign, Constantine waited until his later years to reward the city with an imperial moniker. Our knowledge of Constantine's itinerary in this period indicates that he came west from the Bosporus to campaign on the Rhine in late 328 and early 329. It was perhaps on the occasion of this visit to the region that he conferred his name on a city to which he had already begun to show favor in the years preceding.[54]

In their study of Constantine's obelisk in the circus of Arles, A. Charron and M. Heijmans have argued that it may have been intended to symbolize the emperor's ongoing devotion to the Sun God and may therefore have represented a gesture toward the city's pagan community.[55] This surely stretches the evidence too far. Indeed, we have much stronger indications that the emperor was more closely allied with Arles's Christian leadership. The city had a long-established Christian community by the time Constantine came to power. Its prelate Marcianus, attested already in 254, is one of the earliest confirmed bishops from Gaul.[56] It is thus little wonder that Constantine selected Marinus of Arles as one of the three Gallic bishops designated to help oversee the Council of Rome.[57] The emperor then organized a Council at Arles itself beginning on August 1 the following year, and at its head he placed, once again, Marinus.[58] Shortly after its opening, the new Arelatensian mint took on a distinctly Christian cast, as evidenced by the unusually high number of Christian symbols it placed on its reverses.[59] Constantine thus treated the city not just as an alternative western capital, but very much as a hub of Christian authority.

A Christian sarcophagus discovered at Arles in 1974 indicates that Constantine also had close contact with the Christian aristocracy of the city. The imposing tomb, bedecked with reliefs of Old and New Testament scenes, is identified by its inscription as the final resting place of Marcia Romania Celsa, wife of Flavius

Ianuarinus, who was a *vir clarissimus* and ex–*Consul Ordinarius*.[60] Consular fasti confirm that Ianuarinus was Consul Prior in 328, and should likely be identified with the Ianuarinus known from the *Theodosian Code* to have served as a Vicar to Constantine in 319–320.[61] Although we cannot be certain that he and Celsa hailed from Arles, the likelihood is high given the investment they made in her tomb there. The inference may be strengthened by the fact that Ianuarinus was granted the ordinary consulship in precisely the year that Arles received its Constantinian name. Obviously, these local aristocrats will have further cemented Constantine's relationship with the city's thriving Christian community. Thus, although we have no direct testimony that the emperor chose to grant Arles his name because of his relationship with its Christian leaders, we do know that he regarded it as a reliable stronghold of Christianity in southern Gaul, and this surely factored in his decision.

Cirta-Constantina

Constantine's sensitivity to religious circumstances at the regional and local levels and his willingness to reward communities that took decisive moves in the direction of his new religion is also attested in North Africa. A passage from Aurelius Victor informs us of policies that at first sight seem to point in a quite different direction, but on closer analysis reveal the same combination of favoritism toward Christianity and tolerance toward traditional religion exercised in the interests of maintaining a hand in affairs at the provincial and civic levels: "at that time a priesthood was decreed to the *gens Flavia* throughout Africa; and the town of Cirta, because it had been destroyed by the siege under Alexander [308/310], was restored and embellished and endowed with the name Constantina."[62] The establishment of a provincial cult to the Flavian family in Africa, by which Aurelius Victor apparently means Africa Proconsularis,[63] has already been set in relation to Constantine's readiness to permit a similar cult to his family at Hispellum. The latter, as we have seen, was established only in the final years of his reign, yet Africa's cult is most likely to have arisen earlier, when Constantine was still regularly resident in the West. With its strong connections to senatorial Rome, Proconsularis had an extremely conservative population of prosperous taxpayers. Constantine was surely eager to cultivate their allegiance by permitting this cult. An inscription published in 2003 offers a new dedication to Constantine at the imperial cult temple in Thugga from the governor of Proconsularis Anullinus, who is known to have held office in 313.[64] In 320 another dedication was offered to the deities Asclepius and Hygeia at Lambaesis in Numidia by the pagan *Proconsul Africae*, Zenophilus.[65] Moreover, two laws confirm that Constantine continued to promote the interests of priests of the imperial cult of Proconsularis down to the end of his reign. The first, issued in 334, responds to complaints from African curials (*Afri curiales*) that those who had held the honor of *flamen* (civic priest of the imperial cult), *sacerdos* (provincial priest of the imperial cult), or magistrate (city president) were being compelled to serve as heads of public posting stations. The second, written in 337 to the Council of Africa, reports that these same three groups had also been compelled to collect taxes.[66] In both instances, Constantine reaffirms that priests and magistrates were entitled to immunity from such burdens. The emperor's interest in cultivating curial support through the promotion of the councils and the imperial cult thus remained strong down to the end of his reign.

The city of Cirta in central Numidia was, by contrast, much more robustly Christian. Already prior to the Great Persecution, its Christians were so wealthy and powerful that they controlled more than one ecclesial structure grand enough to be referred to as a *basilica*.[67] Even so, Cirta was far from religiously homogeneous, for we know that during the Great Persecution those who served as its town councilors and priests of its imperial cult (*flamines*) were willing to facilitate in the confiscation and destruction of ecclesiastical property, including one of the city's churches.[68] Cirta's infrastructure had suffered further due to a siege during Maxentius's campaigns against the usurper Domitius Alexander, as revealed in the passage from Aurelius Victor just quoted.[69] Thus, when Constantine gained control of the region in 312, the Cirtans were so overjoyed that they promptly honored him with a pair of inscriptions praising him for "restoring liberty [*libertas*], long oppressed with the shadows of servitude, and illuminating it with new light through his fortunate victory."[70] I have shown elsewhere that *libertas* was a word encoded with Christian meaning by Constantine and his administration from 312 onward.[71] With these inscriptions, the Cirtans were thus borrowing Constantine's phraseology even as they praised him for restoring freedom—religious and otherwise—to their city.

It was in the aftermath of this period of jubilation that Cirta won the title Constantina. Our first firmly dated testimony comes in 320 when, during an inquest before the consular governor Zenophilus, the Christian grammarian Victor claimed that his father had been a "Decurion of the citizens of Constantina."[72] The notice is doubly important, for not only does it confirm early acceptance of this new name by a native son, but it also indicates that Christian families had by this point penetrated the ranks of Cirta's curial order. Around the same time the Cirtans offered a dedication to Crispus in honor of a recent victory, likely that over the Franks in 319, under their new name, the *Constantinianenses*.[73] We have further testimony in a letter written by Constantine himself in 330 that informs us that the Donatist community of "Constantina" had taken over the church that the emperor had constructed for the city's Christians and refused to surrender it. This led Constantine to authorize the transfer of fiscal land into the hands of Cirta's Catholics and to order the consular *officialis* of Numidia to aid them in constructing a second imperially funded basilica for themselves.[74] An inscription of 362 confirms that a *basilica [Cons]tantiniana*—likely this same building—was finally brought to completion in this year, replete with porticoes and a tetrapylon, the last of which still survives.[75] And evidence for the new name continues to appear in the source record after Constantine's death. A law of 340 authorizes the "curial order of the city of Cirta Constantina" to recall those fleeing service, and inscriptions attesting the name Constantina continue to be found throughout the fourth century.[76] Once it had received its Constantinian name, then, Cirta paraded it proudly ever thereafter. Indeed, the impact of its new identity can still be felt today, thirteen centuries after the Muslim conquests, in the modern Algerian city, which is still named Constantine.

The Cirtans' gratitude toward Constantine and their special relationship with the emperor are also well evidenced in their civic inscriptions with dedications to Constantine and his family, no less than nine of which have been identified.[77] The latest two, carved in the 340s, were set up by the "Civic Order of the Fortunate Colony of Constantina."[78] In addition to his basilica, Constantine constructed another public structure, likely baths, in his own name at Cirta.[79] And there is evidence that as early as 314 he elevated Cirta to the status of primary residence of the consular governor of Numidia, a single province he had reunited from the two into which this territory had been split by the tetrarchs.[80] Certainly by the 370s inscriptions from Cuicul (Djemila), Theveste (Tebessa), and Cirta itself confirm that the entire province was referred to as Numidia Constantiniana.[81] There can thus be little doubt that Constantine singled out Cirta as a community to be rewarded with imperial benefaction and that this had an impact that lasted well after his death. Moreover, we can also be certain that Constantine regarded Cirta as a stronghold of Christianity, given his attention to ecclesiastical order and church buildings there. It represents no great leap of logic to conclude that the emperor's choice to endow Cirta with benefactions and with his own name stemmed at least in part from his sympathy with its powerful and well-attested Christian populace.

This can be set in contrast with neighboring Africa Proconsularis, where the population was much more heterogeneous and the provincial elite still very much dominated by adherents of traditional religion. Constantine's choice to respond to both communities' interests in honoring his imperial persona along different lines demonstrates his flexibility toward those who made an effort to cooperate with his broader agenda, be they pagan or Christian. Nevertheless, even if his willingness to allow Proconsularis to establish an imperial cult to the *gens Flavia* revealed an eagerness to maintain relations with traditional constituencies, his particular favor for Constantina would have left no doubt which community he preferred.

Flavia Constantiniana Portus

Turning to Italy, the rival cities of Ostia and Portus offer another interesting case that appears to bear remarkable resemblances to the situations at Nacoleia/ Orcistus and Gaza/ Maiouma. Ostia was of course on the south bank of the Tiber and had served as the port of Rome since the early republican period. Under the emperors Claudius and Nero, a manmade port, named simply Portus, was constructed north of the river's bend, and under Trajan this was supplemented with an artificial lagoon and connected directly to the Tiber with a canal that bypassed Ostia. Ostia thus ceased to serve as a docking place for incoming ships, but in many ways only grew in status as a haven for wealthy aristocrats, who by Late Antiquity had colonized it with their opulent mansions.[82]

In this same period Ostia was known for retaining a particularly strong attachment to the traditional cults, particularly those of Mithras, Magna Mater, Vulcan, Hercules, and above all Castor and Pollux—the Dioscouri. As the protectors of sailors and sea-lanes, these last were of obvious importance to a city under tremendous pressure to ensure the steady flow of grain to the world's capital across an unpredictable Mediterranean Sea. For this reason, the temple of the Castores, as they were called in Latin, was built above the docking complex at the mouth of Ostia's original harbor, where it could welcome incoming freighters.[83] When Maxentius endowed Ostia with an imperial mint in 308, the Castores featured as the most common deities on its bronze types, indicating the ongoing centrality of their cult to the city's identity.[84] Still in 359, the Castores were propitiated in Ostia with blood offerings by the urban prefect of Rome, Tertullus, who defied the imperial ban on sacrifice in an effort to calm choppy seas and thus avert a food shortage.[85] Worship of the Castores continued in the fifth century, as reported in the *Cosmographia* of Pseudo-Aethicus: "The Tiber forms an island between the Portus of the City and the city of Ostia, where the Roman people with the Urban Prefect or Consul proceed in a delightful annual ritual for the purpose of celebrating the festival of the Castores."[86] Even as late as the 490s, Pope Gelasius claimed, the Dioscouri continued to receive worship at Ostia as part of the massive collective human and divine effort marshalled to guarantee Rome's supply of food.[87] In addition to this steady stream of late Roman evidence for ongoing worship of these twin gods, we have ample testimony to the active use and maintenance of Ostia's sacred precinct of Magna Mater and its temples of Isis and Hercules in inscriptions of 360/390, 375/376, and 393/394, respectively.[88] Ostia thus maintained a very active—one could even say defiantly traditional— attachment to its pagan cults stretching deep into Late Antiquity.

This is not to say that it lacked a Christian community. Already at the Council of Rome held in 313 a bishop of Ostia was present.[89] Furthermore, the *Liber Pontificalis* reports that beginning in 336 Ostia's bishop was charged with consecrating the bishop of Rome, and that Constantine actually constructed and endowed a basilica for the city's Christians.[90] This last notice had been doubted until the archaeological remains of the church were partially excavated in 1996–1999.[91] Even this church, however, gives the impression that Christianity was being imposed on the city from the outside, for the building was collocated at the edge of Ostia's walls near its southern gate and was endowed not by locals but by the emperor himself and a private benefactor named Gallicanus. Gallicanus was not from Ostia but from Suessa Aurunca in Campania. He had won his way into the highest echelons of power under Constantine and was appointed Urban Prefect in 316/317 and Consul in 330.[92] Ostia's new church was not, therefore, the product of local initiative but of the emperor and a trusted confidant with no known connections to the city.

Studies of the martyrological accounts for Ostia and Portus as well as the epigraphy and archaeology of Ostia point in the same direction. These indicate that Ostia's Christian community came into its own only in the late 300s.[93] Indeed, the sculptural appointment of numerous luxury houses in the city indicates rather that the leadership classes, at least, remained strongly aligned with paganism deep into the fourth century.[94] We might conclude, then, that the population of Ostia was Christianizing only gradually, and under pressure from the emperor and his associates.

Portus, by contrast, already had a strong Christian community at the start of the Great Persecution. The early fourth century *Depositio martyrum* names five martyrs of Portus, and these are supplemented by the testimony of a pair of fourth-century inscriptions that catalog four more.[95] Portus's basilica to Saints Peter and Paul has been known of from martyrological accounts for some time, and excavations have uncovered the original structure, revealing that it was built in two phases, the first in the late third or early fourth century, and the second later in the 300s.[96] At this later time Pammachius, a Roman senator and confidant of St. Jerome's, selected Portus rather than its neighbor as the site at which to erect a Christian guesthouse (*xenodochium*).[97] Portus has also yielded a considerably larger number of paleo-Christian inscriptions than its neighbor, which, when combined with the testimony of martyr acts—albeit of dubious quality—points to a significant Christian populace there that arose by the early third century and suffered greatly in the early fourth at the hands of neighboring pagans.[98]

With this background in mind, we approach an inscription discovered in 1926 on a statue base from near the harbors in Portus: "To Lucius Crepereius Madalianus, *Vir Clarissimus*, powerful in his fidelity, energy, and beneficence, who was Prefect of the Grain Supply with the right of the sword, *comes flavialis*, Governor of Flaminia et Picenum, Propraetorian Legate of the Province of Asia, Legate of the Province of Africa, Consular for Sacred Temples, Consular of the Piers, Lighthouse, and Dredging, Quaestor Candidatus, Praetor, and Consul, the Order and People of Flavia Constantiniana Portus decided to erect a statue publicly on account of his many testimonials on their behalf."[99] The inscription can be dated between 337 and 341 and clearly indicates that, by this date, Portus was using the name Flavia Constantiniana.[100] Given the freedom of its "order and people" to decree a public statue to their benefactor, the inscription also indicates that Portus had been split from Ostia's administrative control and granted the right of civic status. Such a bifurcation is widely assumed in the scholarship and is confirmed in sources from the fifth century onward, including Philostorgius, Cassiodorus, the *Liber Pontificalis*, and Procopius, which identify Ostia and Portus as two separate *civitates*.[101] Indeed, Procopius indicates that by his day Portus had overtaken Ostia in importance and was still very much thriving even as Ostia had fallen into disrepair.[102]

The inscription's recipient, Lucius Crepereius Madalianus, is interesting on several counts. His status as a *comes flavialis* indicates that he was a close confidant of the emperor's, a personal adviser to Constantine in what would later come to be called the *consistorium*.[103] His gentilician name, Crepereius, is well attested in North Africa,[104] an excellent starting point for a man much of whose career would revolve around the oversight of the grain supply.[105] Up until the fourth century, the Creperei had been a family of only tertiary importance in the Senate.[106] Indeed, the relative insignificance of Madalianus's background is confirmed by the broad range of low-level positions he held early in his career—like the administrative office of Consular of the Piers, Lighthouse, and Dredging.[107] These then gave way to the exalted position of Consul, which he held as suffect at some unknown date circa 335.[108] Madalianus's career was thus a product of Constantine's restructuring of the government, which injected a growing stream of administrators into the traditional ranks of the Senate using the apparatus of the imperial bureaucracy.

Madalianus's meteoric rise must also have been influenced by the new religious order. While serving as vicar, he was the recipient of the first extant constitution banning animal sacrifice in the *Theodosian Code*, Constantius II's famous *cesset superstitio* of 341.[109] It is highly unlikely that such a drastic prohibition on pagan practice would have been issued to a pagan officeholder. The only piece of evidence that at first blush seems to speak to the contrary is Madalianus's tenure in the office of Consular for Sacred Temples. But even this exception proves the rule, for Chastagnol argued convincingly that Madalianus was in fact appointed the last holder of this office before Constantine abolished it circa 331 in order that Madalianus should enact in Rome Constantine's empire-wide program of confiscating temple treasuries, which was under way at this time.[110] If this is correct, Madalianus's assignment to this post combined with his receipt of *cesset superstitio* would make him into something of a hit-man for Constantine and his family against traditional cult. Madalianus's "many testimonials" on behalf of Portus and its citizens mentioned in the inscription may thus represent the advocacy of a Christian ally of Constantine's on behalf of a strongly Christian community celebrating its newfound freedom from its largely pagan neighbor.[111]

We can no longer say for certain when Portus gained its Constantinian name and independence from Ostia, but a good indication can be found in the list of bishops from the Councils of Rome in 313 and Arles in 314. No bishop of Portus is attested at the former, but by August 1, 314, a Gregorius is attested at the Council of Arles as "the bishop from the place that is at the Portus Romae."[112] Traditionally, Portus had been termed Portus Ostiensis, making this new name evidence of a change in status. The title Portus Romae—along with variants like Portus Urbis Sacrae—remained in use in legal and literary sources from 324 through the sixth century.[113] Portus thus appears to have gained its autonomy in the year following Constantine's conquest of Rome, quite soon after the close of the Great Persecution.[114]

We also know that at precisely the same time, Constantine punished Ostia by depriving it of its imperial mint and transferring its personnel and operations to the city of Arles—as we have just seen, another city with a Constantinian name.[115] Given the large number of martyrs attested at Portus during the Great Persecution and the absence of martyrs from Ostia, it is not difficult to imagine a scenario in which the traditional Ostian aristocracy lorded it over the Christians of neighboring Portus, only to watch as their overzealous imposition of the imperial will of the tetrarchs backfired under Constantine. This may explain why the guild of grain measurers (*codicarii navicularii*), who were stationed at Portus in the fourth century, enthusiastically dedicated a statue to Constantine as "Restorer of public liberty, defender of the city of Rome, and author of the common salvation of all" in the period immediately following the Battle of the Milvian Bridge.[116] Although the precise motivations for their gift can no longer be recovered, they had at a minimum assimilated Constantine's rhetoric and, one can assume, the Christian overtones of phrases like "restorer of public liberty" and "author of the common salvation of all."[117] There is thus good reason, if not absolute proof, for thinking that the new city of Portus can be added to Orcistus and Maiouma as a community that was able to parlay its own attachment to Christianity into independence from a more powerful pagan neighbor and promotion to the status of *civitas*.

Conclusion: Civic Benefaction, Christian Promotion

Apart from Maiouma, none of the cities discussed in this chapter can be proven to have received a Constantinian name because of its attachment to Christianity. Although the circumstantial case is strong in the instances of Arelas-Constantina, Cirta-Constantina, and Flavia Constantiniana Portus, we have seen that Augustodunum was renamed Flavia Aeduorum before Constantine converted, and many other western cities and towns leave us no evidence with which to argue the case one way or another. To be sure, emperors and kings had endowed cities with their names long before Constantine's conversion, and Constantine was in many ways simply following his predecessors in maintaining this tradition. It made sense to promote civic communities in this and other ways since these offered nodes through which to concentrate and project imperial power at the local and regional levels. For this reason, renaming a city was only one of many benefactions available to ancient rulers for promoting urban prosperity.

Indeed, apart from whole cities, we also have ample testimony of Constantine lending his name to various structures in other western polities. Aquileia, for example, saw the construction of Thermae Constantinianae in conjunction with a larger imperial building program.[118] Rome too received Thermae Constantinianae, as did the tiny city of Trebula Balliensis (Treglia) in Campania.[119] At times these Constantinian structures were Christian, as, for example, in Capua, where the emperor constructed a Basilica Constantiniana and endowed it with vessels and rent-paying real estate.[120] This sort of patronage was of course typical of imperial interactions with civic communities dating back to the days of Augustus and cannot be shown to have reflected any of the particulars of local civic politics reconstructed in the foregoing examples. Constantine's cities and structures need not then have been uniformly pressed into the service of propagating the Christian faith. Indeed, Constantine's dealings with the contrasting situations in Africa Proconsularis and Numidian Cirta offer proof that his underlying goal was first and foremost to lubricate relations with urban centers rather than pushing them unyieldingly in the direction of Christianity.

Nevertheless, at times Constantine clearly did choose to lend a city the distinction of using his name in recompense for its demonstrated support for his Christian agenda. We should not carry the argument too far, but given explicit testimony in instances like Orcistus and Maiouma, it is entirely reasonable to seek examples elsewhere. The fact that Arles in Viennensis and Cirta in Numidia had strong and active Christian communities early in the fourth century and that Constantine's close relationship with these cities is well attested indicates that their early and powerful support for Christian religion factored in the emperor's choice to lend them his name. In the instance of Portus, whose Christian community is also well attested and stands in contrast with the pagan leanings of neighboring Ostia, the parallel with the clear-cut case of Maiouma is even stronger. In both cases, a smaller port city seems to have used its attachment to Christianity to secure not just a Constantinian name but also independence from its more powerful and much more religiously conservative neighbor. As we shall see in the chapter that follows, the same argument can be made for other cities in the East, even if civic politics there differed in significant ways that in many respects rendered eastern polities even more fertile ground for the sort of pro-Christian civic politics we have glimpsed in the West.

CHAPTER 7

Constantine's Cities in the East

Peer Polity Interaction

Peer Polity Interaction/Rivalry

Civic politics in the East operated according to slightly different norms than in the West. To be sure, rivalries between neighboring polities arose in both places, and these were often mediated through the emperor. But in contrast with most western cities, the polities of Rome's eastern domains had been formed centuries before the arrival of Roman authority in the region and had developed their own traditions of self-governance and interurban engagement that remained remarkably resilient down to the fourth century. Archaeologists D. Cherry and C. Renfrew coined the phrase "peer polity interaction" to describe the sorts of horizontal relationships that prevailed among Greek cities in the archaic period. The interactions between the community of archaic *poleis*—at times collegial and friendly, at times tense or even hostile—fostered the growth and flourish of homologous urban cultures across an expansive landscape without interference from a central authority.[1] J. Ma applied this same hermeneutic to the Greek cities of the Hellenistic world, a period when centralized powers ultimately did come to prevail and significantly changed, without in any way obliterating, long-standing patterns of positive and negative association.[2] Ma's analysis showed that, with the arrival of supra-poliadic hyper-powers, Greek cities continued to cultivate interurban cooperation through shared interactions in the symbolic sphere. These included the use of "international" panels of arbitrators to resolve internal disputes; the production and recording of parallel decrees; the exploitation of shared assumptions about common myth-historical ancestry (*syngeneia*) for political ends; and the settlement of interurban conflicts through the intermediacy of multi-city delegations.[3] Unsurprisingly, this same dynamic continued in the Roman imperial period, although it came increasingly to be mediated through powerful individuals, who served as metonyms for communities formerly represented by aristocratic or democratic bodies of governance.[4] Peer polity interaction thus remained

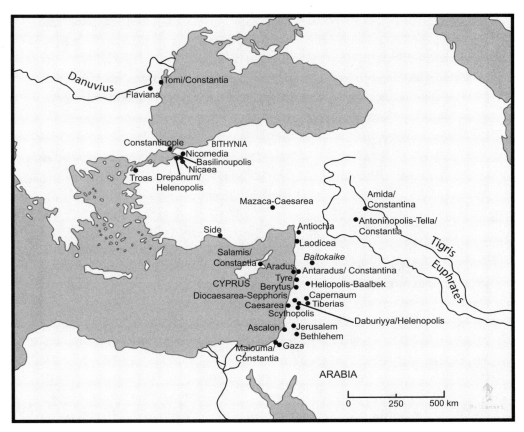

MAP 5. Constantine's Cities in the Eastern Empire

a centuries-long way-of-being for Greek-speaking cities that knitted them into a network of structurally homologous units operating as largely autonomous, horizontally equal agents.

A necessary corollary of peer polity interaction was peer polity rivalry, which was always attendant upon interurban dialogue. Imitation and emulation, after all, go hand in hand. Such rivalry manifested itself in the sponsorship of athletic and artistic competitions; the struggle to outpace peers in the construction of civic and sacral architecture; the pursuit of scarcely rationed honors and titles from central rulers; and at times pitched battle over boundaries and resources.[5] Although the occurrence of open combat disappeared by the dawn of the Christian era, rivalries continued in all of the remaining arenas well into Late Antiquity. Ephesus and Pergamum, for example, were deadlocked in a long-term struggle for claims to superiority in the province of Asia Minor. Caracalla tipped the balance in favor of Pergamum by granting it the right to a third imperial cult temple and thus to the title *tris neōkoros*, an honor he denied Ephesus. Following

Caracalla's murder and precipitous replacement by Macrinus, the Ephesians fired back by convincing the new emperor to strip Pergamum of these recent honors, with the result that its populace broke into rioting. This eventually led to the removal of all of Pergamum's honorary titles and the imposition on the city of formal dishonor (*atimia*)—a misfortune that was short-lived thanks to the brevity of Macrinus's reign.[6]

Often, these sorts of peer polity conflicts continued long past the Hellenistic and high imperial age. At the same time Septimius Severus was punishing Antioch while rewarding its neighbor Laodicea (as we saw in Chapter 4), he was also honoring the Phoenician city of Tyre and punishing its neighbor Berytus, which, like Antioch, had supported Pescennius Niger. Severus honored Tyre and its citizens with the title "Septimians" even as he avenged himself on Berytus by splitting its dependency, Heliopolis-Baalbek, from its control and elevating its status to that of an independent colony.[7] Here again, the dispute continued into Late Antiquity when Theodosius II, for reasons no longer known to us, showed favor to Berytus in 449 by granting it the title of *mētropolis*, although "Tyre's rights should not be compromised in any way," as the lone rescript attesting this privilege asserts.[8] Notwithstanding this admonition, Berytus promptly usurped the right to consecrate bishops for a wide range of Phoenician cities, with the result that Photius, bishop of Tyre, lodged a formal petition for redress of this shift in the balance of power. The Council of Chalcedon ultimately dedicated a session to the matter, held on October 20, 451, where it was decided to restore to Photius and Tyre the right to consecrate all bishops in Phoenicia I without, however, depriving Berytus of its metropolitan title.[9]

A similar contretemps roiled between the Bithynian cities of Nicaea and Nicomedia over their competing claims to be the "first city" (*prōtē polis*) of their shared province of Bithynia Pontus. In a speech of the late first century dedicated to the issue, Dio Chrysostom lays out the conflict as a sort of battle (*maxē*) or civil war (*stasis*) over titles and proposes as a solution that both cities share the honor. This suggestion was implemented under the Flavians, but it hardly solved the dispute, and Nicaea's choice to support Pescennius Niger in the civil war with Septimius Severus in 194 led to its temporary loss of the title "first city" (*prōtē polis*)—yet another instance of Severan civic vengefulness.[10] The flames of conflict were whipped up once again in the fourth century when Nicaea played host to Valentinian I on the occasion of his proclamation as Augustus in 364 and then capitalized on this good fortune in order to win from the new emperor the title of *mētropolis*, an honor formerly reserved only for Nicomedia. This gambit occasioned a successful countermove from Nicomedia in 451, when yet another session was devoted to the question at the Council of Chalcedon. There it was decided that Nicaea could retain the title of *mētropolis* but not the attendant privilege of overseeing other bishops in the province.[11] The Acts of Chalcedon also reveal that the dispute had come to a head because Nicomedia had been pressing Nicaea for the right to elect the bishop of the neighboring city of Basilinoupolis. As Anastasius, the bishop of Nicaea, explains, Basilinoupolis was a new foundation formed from two former territories (*regeōnes*) of Nicaea by Julian the Apostate, who then populated it with citizens of Nicaea and named it after his mother, Basilina.[12] Julian harbored deep affection for Nicomedia, where he had been sent by Constantius after the murder of his father and where he had received his earliest schooling under his dear tutor Mardonius. Nicaea, on the other hand, had by now fallen much more squarely into the hands of Christian leaders and was, at any rate, tainted with the reputation of hosting Constantine's famous ecumenical council. Ammianus relates how, when Julian journeyed eastward in 362, he came to Nicomedia and wept for the destruction caused by the earthquake and fire that had ravaged the city in 358. In an outpouring of generosity, he opened the imperial purse strings to fund Nicomedia's lavish reconstruction, then passed through Nicaea briefly on his way eastward—probably stopping just long enough to oversee the fragmentation of the city and foundation of Basilinoupolis.[13] One cannot help but wonder if we are witnessing here an example of the urban politics of Constantine in reverse: Julian punishing a strongly Christian city made famous by Constantine by detaching a sizable portion of its territory and assigning this for the foundation of a new polis named after his mother to a select group of Nicene citizens—perhaps its pagan leadership.[14]

Far from eliminating peer polity rivalry, then, the imposition of Roman imperial rule in the East merely sublimated it to the symbolic sphere, where conflicts were waged over titles, honors, and privileges. In some ways this complicated the business of ruling eastern cities: navigating these complex networks of power and mediating these centuries-long disputes could cost precious time and energy, and the net result was often little more than further bickering and frustration. At the same time, however, peer polity interactions offered the emperor the chance to enhance his power in local and regional contexts by positioning him to serve as the final arbiter for the mediation of such disputes. From this position of supreme authority, the ruler could perform and implement his power in ways that helped regenerate and increase it. Such interactions were also generally good for the cities themselves, for they encouraged these to compete for imperial favors and rewards. More importantly, such privileges and titles came with real dispositive force: independence from the control of neighbors; influence over neighboring territories, villages, towns, and estates; control over religious autonomy and ritual practice.

After gaining control of the East in 324, Constantine was thus forced to negotiate this rather different environment of civic politics. We have already seen in

Chapters 4 and 6 that, in the instances of Orcistus and Maiouma, he managed to do so successfully. In this chapter we shall find that these two cases are not unique, for in multiple instances he was able to exploit the rich history of peer polity inter-action and rivalry between eastern cities in order to further his agenda of pro-moting Christian religion at the level of the polis.

Joseph of Tiberias and the Cities of Palestine

Before turning to a continuation of our investigation of cities named after Con-stantine or members of his family, it is worthwhile to examine the case of an individual who helped Constantine promote his program of Christian civic poli-tics in the cities of Palestine. Joseph of Tiberias was the scion of Jewish leaders from this region. We learn of his story from a single source, Epiphanius of Sala-mis, who claims to have met the aging Joseph personally when he lodged with him in Palestinian Scythopolis.[15] Joseph and his family were members of the priestly elite who attended upon the Jewish Patriarch, who resided in Tiberias in the fourth century.[16] Joseph, however, began exploring Christianity in ways that provoked anger and even violence from his fellow Jews, and, after receiving bap-tism, he sought to fortify himself against further attacks by obtaining an audience with Constantine. Taken with his story, the emperor offered Joseph the honorific title of *Comes* and permitted him to ask for whatever favor he might wish. To this, Epiphanius reports: "[Joseph] asked only the great favor of being entrusted by the emperor, by imperial order, with building churches of Christ in the cities and villages of the Jews, where no one had ever been able to put up churches, since there were no pagans, Samaritans, or Christians in them. Especially in Tiberias, Diocaesarea, also called Sepphoris, Nazareth, and Capernaum they take care to have no foreigners living among them [*phylassetai to par'autois mē einai alloeth-non*]."[17] This statement is invaluable for what it tells us about the fortress mental-ity that prevailed in some smaller cities—cities we have already witnessed in the instances of Gaza and Nacoleia, as well as their tiny dependencies Maiouma and Orcistus—and it thereby gives strong support for earlier arguments that ancient polities made self-conscious efforts to police their religious boundaries unbend-ingly. The predicament this created gave Constantine a strong motivation to take advantage of the opportunity offered by Joseph in order to wedge his way into these tightly knit, locally controlled Jewish strongholds.

Epiphanius goes on to say that Joseph received letters from the emperor authorizing construction and even granting access to funds from the imperial fisc with which to cover supplies and expenditures.[18] He then proceeded to his native Tiberias, where he first attempted to rebuild a half-finished "Hadrianeum" into a

Christian basilica, but, after meeting with local resistance, settled for completing a small church. Still unwelcome in Tiberias, Joseph relocated to Scythopolis—by all accounts a more religiously pluralistic city[19]—and there he resided until the day he met Epiphanius. Epiphanius claims Joseph also completed projects in Diocaesarea-Sepphoris and elsewhere, but his lack of specifics gives the distinct impression that none succeeded in blossoming into self-sustaining Christian churches. Joseph's quixotic project and the struggles he faced give us some idea how tough it must have been to break into such airtight enclaves. They also tell us much about the type of politics Constantine practiced in his efforts to convert just such places. He did not send in troops but attempted to work from the ground up, using a local agent who approached him with admirable zeal, and naiveté.

Antaradus-Constanti(n)a

Turning back to our investigation of those cities to which Constantine granted his own name or that of one of his family members, we light first on the Phoenician coastal city of Antaradus. Immediately after his mention of the split between Gaza and Maiouma, Eusebius reports:

> Very many other territories [chōrai] accomplished the same thing, as for example the one that is named after the emperor himself in the province of Phoenicia, whose citizens handed over to the flames innumerable sacred idols and exchanged them for the salvific law. Furthermore, in other provinces innumerable people fled to the salvific understanding in territories and cities [kata chōras kai kata poleis] and obliterated the things that they formerly considered holy but were really just a bunch of wooden idols, as if they were worthless, and they destroyed their once exalted temples and sacred precincts without even being ordered to do so, and erecting churches from the foundations up they exchanged their earlier error for these.[20]

The latter part of Eusebius's statement is generalizing and, while evocative, cannot be verified. The opening sentence, however, clearly refers to a specific locale, albeit only in allusive terms. Sozomen, offering only a bit more specificity, informs us that this Phoenician city was renamed Constantina.[21]

Despite this vagueness, we can say with some certainty that the city in question can be connected with the bishopric of Antaradus-Constantina listed alongside the Phoenician city of Aradus in the early sixth-century episcopal list of Hierocles.[22] A related notice in the tradition R. Burgess has identified as the

Anonymous Antiochene Continuation of Eusebius specifies that, in *anno mundi* 5838 (345/346 CE): "Constantius founded a city in Phoenicia which he named Constantia; it had previously been known as Antaradus."[23] The name Constantia is also repeated for Antaradus in the subscriptions to a letter of Dorotheus bishop of Tyre to Emperor Leo preserved in the *Collectio Sangermanesis*.[24] Neither Burgess nor J.-P. Rey-Coquais, who wrote a monographic study of Aradus, noticed the obvious connection between the chronicle tradition and the reports in Eusebius and Sozomen.[25] The most evident reason for this oversight is the clear divergence between the two traditions: Eusebius and Sozomen place the refoundation in the reign of Constantine, and Sozomen as well as Hierocles call the city Constantina; the Antiochene chronicle tradition, by contrast, dates the city's creation nine years later, attributes it to Constantius II, and, along with the Acts of Chalcedon, dubs the city Constantia. One could speculate that Antaradus was perhaps refounded twice, or that the sources are speaking of two different cities in the vicinity of Aradus, but the most economical solution is to assume that the Antiochene chronicle is guilty of slight inaccuracies. Indeed, the early reference to the city in Phoenicia renamed after Constantine in Eusebius's *Life of Constantine* (written circa 338) precludes the later dating and attribution to Constantius found in the Antiochene tradition.

Both source traditions indicate that the city that was renamed was within the ambit of Aradus. This was an island city (modern Ruad), just three kilometers off the coast of Phoenicia, which had traditionally controlled a constellation of less powerful polities along the coastline opposite. These included Antaradus (Tuad) but also Marathos, Enydra, Iammura, Maraccas, and Carne.[26] We have evidence for this constellation going back to Seleucid times that indicates Aradus was unusually aggressive in pursuing dominance over these neighbors, with its vehemence likely exacerbated because its insular geography required a lock hold over territory on the neighboring mainland in order to ensure its food supply.[27]

Perhaps the best evidence for Aradus's aggressive intervention in regional affairs can be found in its struggle for control over the important shrine of Zeus at Baitokaikē, some thirty kilometers inland from the coast, perched atop Mount Emblonos (Jebel Ansariye). A third-century CE inscription from the shrine records a dossier of five documents stretching back five centuries that cast a bright light on Aradus's campaign for regional dominion.[28] The two oldest were a letter and accompanying memorandum (*hypomnēmatismos*) issued by "King Antiochus" (probably one of the early Seleucids) that permitted the village (*kōmē*) of Baitokaikē to enjoy, among other things, the right to control revenue from its local territories, to host a bimonthly fair free from taxation, and not to be subject to the quartering of troops and grandees; the third document was a resolution (*psēphisma*) sent by "the city" (*polis*—that is, Aradus)[29] to Augustus conceding that it would assist with the sale and transport of goods at Baitokaikē's bimonthly fair without interfering or claiming free quartering, taxation, or fees for its officials. The engraver has sandwiched these three earlier documents between two more recent texts, both parts of a rescript of Valerian dated 258/259 CE, that offers ongoing imperial support against "the violence of the opposing party" (*violentia partis adversae*) in order to guarantee that the "ancient benefits of kings" (*regum antiqua beneficia*) would remain undisturbed for the Baitokaikē shrine. Aradus had thus been pressing its suit for control over the temple and its lucrative trade fair for half a millennium, right up to the eve of Constantine's birth. It was surely precisely this sort of power politics from which the Antaradians sought refuge with their appeal for independence under Constantine.

If we can believe Eusebius and Sozomen, religion was at the center of Antaradus's conflict with its more powerful neighbor. Like Orcistus and Maiouma, it deployed claims to mass conversion and the destruction of its temples as a wedge with which to leverage imperial support. The fact that Antaradus was located between the powerful religious poles of Zeus Baitokaikēnē and Aradus—which had its own powerful cults, particularly to Aphrodite[30]—must have caught the emperor's attention and increased his motivation to grant the new city independence as well as his name. Moreover, the petition must have reached Constantine fairly soon after he gained control of the East in 324, for a bishop named Zenodorus is attested for Antaradus in two versions of the lists of fathers alleged to have participated at the Council of Nicaea in 325, and—more reliably—Athanasius attests a bishop of Antaradus named Carterius in 328.[31] By 415, Antaradus's bishop was prestigious enough to have played a key role in the translation of the relics of Joseph, the son of Jacob, and Zachariah, the father of John the Baptist, to Constantinople, and Antaradus is known to have continued to assert its independence down to the sixth century.[32] Nevertheless, struggles with its neighbor remained fierce, and their attestation in the sources reinforces the assumption that this was both a civic as well as religious rivalry. At the Council of Ephesus in 431, Musaeus is recorded as bishop of both cities.[33] By contrast, at the Council of Chalcedon in 451, however, each city fielded a bishop—Paul of Aradus, who appears seven times in the documents, and Alexander of Antaradus, who appears just once.[34] We learn in the Syriac acts of the second "robber" council of Ephesus in 449 that Alexander had been appointed bishop of Antaradus by supporters of Cyril of Alexandria but was then deposed by Cyril's opponent, Domnus, the metropolitan bishop of Antioch in 445. When Domnus was himself deposed in 449, Alexander was reinstated by Eustathius of Berytus, only to be demoted once again in the wake of Chalcedon to a titular bishop subordinate to Paul.[35] Far from extinguishing the smoldering embers of this regional rivalry, then, Constantine had merely added fuel to the fire. In so doing, however, he had clearly pushed both communities in the direction of Christianizing their leadership in order to keep up with the shifting horizons of imperial religious preference. Instead of fighting for control of a neighboring pagan shrine, Aradus was now battling its nearer neighbor for episcopal supremacy, a process that Constantine had jump-started with his grant of independent civic status to Antaradus for its headlong rush toward Christianity.

Salamis-Constantia

Whether it was renamed after Constantia or Constantius, Antaradus took its name not from Constantine himself but from a member of his family. The same can be said, as we have seen, of Maiouma (also renamed after either Constantius or Constantia) and Hispellum (named after Constans). This is also true of the city of Salamis in eastern Cyprus, which was renamed Constantia at some point in the early fourth century, although the circumstances behind this change are maddeningly obscured by contradictions in our sources.[36] John Malalas reports that Salamis was destroyed by earthquake under the emperor "Constantius Chlorus," who then rebuilt it and granted it a four-year remission of taxes.[37] This cannot be accurate, for Constantius I Chlorus never exercised imperial authority in the eastern empire. Historians have thus assumed that Malalas has confused the tetrarchic emperor for his grandson, Constantius II. Nevertheless, Theophanes reports that Salamis was badly damaged by earthquakes in both 332 and 342,[38] opening the possibility that it was renamed already under Constantine and that rebuilding began in the 330s, only to reach completion after a second earthquake. Indeed, we know that Constantine was forced to suppress a revolt that began on Cyprus in 334, and this may have been connected with the consequences of this natural disaster.[39] There is, however, no source that connects all these events—earthquake, revolt, rebuilding—and Theophanes' twin notices of Salaminian earthquakes may just as easily represent a doublet.[40]

On balance, it is safer to assume that Salamis first collapsed in 342 and was renamed and rebuilt by Constantius II alone. Supporting this argument are two Salaminian inscriptions, one attesting rebuilding of the collapsed baths under Constantius and Constans, and a second the dedication of bronze statues in honor of these same.[41] Like the fortress cities listed in Chapter 6, then, Salamis-Constantia cautions against associating every "Constantinian" city with Constantine and his religious agenda. Religion may, however, have played a role in its renaming, as indeed may interurban rivalry. In the Byzantine episcopal *notitiae* Salamis-Constantia is consistently named as the ecclesiastical metropolis of the island.[42] Other sources, however, make it clear that the city was locked in a long-term struggle over claims it made to independence from its more powerful neighbor, Syrian Antioch, almost 250 kilometers seaward to its northeast. In the mid-410s, the Roman primate Innocent I wrote to Alexander, bishop of Antioch, charging: "You claim the Cypriots, who were dogged long ago by the power of Arian impiety (*Arianae impietatis potentia fatigatos*), did not hold to the canons of Nicaea in ordaining their bishops, and even to this day they presume to make ordinations according to their own judgments without consulting others."[43] In response, Innocent upholds Alexander's request that the Cypriots be compelled to yield to the authority of the broader church. This was not, however the end of the story, for in a letter preserved in the Acts of the Council of Ephesus dated May 21, 431, the *Magister Utriusque Militiae* Flavius Dionysius reports to the consular governor of Cyprus that, upon the death of the bishop of Constantia, the Cypriots had once again attempted to appoint a successor without recourse to Antioch, forcing Dionysius to order this appointee to report to the council for resolution of the dispute.[44] Jumping back to the 340s, could it be that Constantius II seized on the chaos in Cyprus—one or more earthquakes and a revolt—as an opportunity to rebuild Salamis, rename it after himself, *and* co-opt it to his Arianizing cause? This cannot, of course, be proven, but at a minimum, we know Salamis to have been a city with cause to seek support from the Constantinian household not just to solve problems created by earthquake damage, but also to assert its independence vis-à-vis Antioch. If it sought to fold its request into a petition asking for the honor of a Constantinian name, there were clearly earlier models to which it could look to bolster its hopes of success.

Daburiyya-Helenopolis

Two other eastern cities that took their name from members of the Constantinian family almost certainly won this right as a result of the Christianization of their populace. Both were named after Constantine's mother Helena. Here too Constantine was following a long tradition of assigning the name of a reigning queen or empress to an urban foundation—one thinks of the Apameas, Berenikes, Laodiceas, and Stratoniceas of the Hellenistic world, or of Marcianopolis and Faustinopolis in the Roman.[45] In the instance of the two eastern Helenopoleis, however, both follow a pattern that has by now become familiar: smaller cities exploiting claims to Christian adherence in order to win civic status and independence from more powerful neighbors.

In his obituary of Helena, Sozomen reports that the empress lives on in eternal memory, for there are two cities named after her, one in Bithynia and the second in Palestine.[46] Palestinian Helenopolis has been plausibly identified with Daburiyya (modern Kafr Kama), at the foot of Mount Tabor in southern Galilee.[47]

In his *Onomastikon,* written at the turn of the fourth century, Eusebius tells us that Daburiyya was a village dependency in the territory of Diocaesarea-Sepphoris.[48] This latter was of course one of the watertight Jewish cities of Palestine in which the Jewish apostate Joseph of Tiberias was permitted by Constantine to attempt construction of a Christian church. Diocaesarea-Sepphoris's strong Jewish identity is confirmed by Eusebius, who claims its populace was entirely Jewish during the persecutions in 309 when ninety-seven Christian confessors were transported there from the Thebaid for public torture by the notoriously savage governor Firmilianus.[49] Pointing in this same direction, rabbinic sources indicate that in the third and fourth centuries, the city was home to a variety of priestly schools and was also the residence of the Jewish patriarch.[50] A passage in the Jerusalem Talmud indicates that it boasted eighteen synagogues,[51] at least one of which has been excavated. Its fifth-century mosaics express a conservatism in their iconography that responds to and appears to resist growing pressures from Hellenism and Christianity.[52] This same spirit of religious independence manifested itself quite openly in a full-scale revolt launched from Diocaesarea-Sepphoris in 352 that, one source claims, strove to establish an independent Jewish kingdom. The uprising quickly spread to other strongholds of Judaism, including Joseph's native Tiberias.[53] The rebels were violently suppressed by imperial forces, and reports in the Greek sources state that Diocaesarea-Sepphoris was obliterated, which is surely an exaggeration, even if recent excavations do confirm considerable destruction in the mid-fourth century.[54] Talmudic sources imply only a brief period of Roman occupation, and a letter of Peter of Alexandria proves that the city continued to thrive as home to a sizable, exclusivist Jewish population in the 370s when the emperor Valens chose it as a place of exile for recalcitrant monks because of its known antipathy to Christians.[55] Indeed, Diocaesarea-Sepphoris appears from archaeological sources to have continued as a Jewish stronghold even down to the late fifth century.[56]

Daburiyya's request for independence from Diocaesarea-Sepphoris and for the imperial name of Constantine's mother must be set in relief against the background of this powerful and conservative Jewish neighbor. Until the advent of Constantine, Diocaesarea-Sepphoris had exercised political and religious control over the tiny dependency, but Daburiyya apparently tapped into Constantine's program of promoting Christian cities to turn the tables. From later Byzantine sources, we even learn the possible circumstances of these events, for the *Guidi Life of Constantine* reports that, on her journey to Palestine, Helena visited not only Jerusalem and Bethlehem but also the area of Mount Tabor and the towns of southern Galilee.[57] This is likely the point at which Daburiyya came to Helena's, and Constantine's, attention and was able to petition successfully for its independence and new name. Despite its exiguous size, Helenopolis-Daburiyya retained its episcopate and its name into the sixth century, when the catalog of Hierocles lists it under the name Helenopolis in the province of Palestina II.[58] It thus seems to constitute a clear-cut example of yet another small polity that used the power of the petition to win extraordinary favors from the first Christian emperor on the basis of its willingness to self-represent as a Christian town in the midst of a staunchly non-Christian landscape.

Drepanum-Helenopolis

The second and more famous Helenopolis, also referenced by Sozomen, was located in Bithynia, on the Gulf of Astaca, not far from Nicomedia, at the site of modern Hersek.[59] Because of the sickle-shaped promontory on which it was located, the village was originally named Drepanum (or perhaps Drepana).[60] Its change of name to Helenopolis is first attested in Eusebius's *Life of Constantine*, which says nothing of the circumstances of its promotion but only reports in passing that Constantine stopped to take healing waters at "the city named after his mother" in his final days on earth.[61] At a minimum, then, the city had been renamed by May 337. Philostorgius reports more fully: "The mother of the emperor Constantine built a city on the mouth of the bay of Nicomedia and called it Helenopolis. The place meant so much to her simply because it was there that the martyr Lucian had been borne [to his burial] by a dolphin after his death by martyrdom."[62] Helenopolis may thus have been established not just in Helena's honor but also at her initiative. Jerome and the *Chronicon Paschale* both date this refounding to 327,[63] when the empress dowager was indeed still alive.[64] If their dating is accurate, it would place the city's promotion around the same time the imperial name was being conferred on several other cities, including Arles, Maiouma, Daburiyya, and of course Orcistus. Furthermore, if the Byzantine *Life of Lucian*—embedded in the ninth- to eleventh-century *Opitz Life of Constantine*—is to be believed, Helena and Constantine also endowed the city with major architectural embellishments, including walls and a martyrion.[65]

The sources make it quite explicit that Drepanum-Helenopolis had been promoted from a *kōmē* to an independent *polis*,[66] and at least one source testifies that it was also favored with tax immunity.[67] In this sense, it would appear to fit into the category of cities like Maiouma, Antaradus, Portus, and Daburiyya that won independence from a more powerful neighbor along with their imperial name. The question remains, what might that neighboring overlord have been? L. Robert has shown that, in the High Empire, the territory where Drepanum was located had been under the control of Byzantium.[68] It is odd, however, that Constantine would have detached this dependency from a city so firmly in his favor. But there is reason to argue that at this late date Drepanum may instead have been connected with Nicomedia, which at only forty kilometers to its east was much closer geographically. The reorganization of the provinces into dioceses (under either Diocletian or, as more recently argued, Licinius)[69] placed Drepanum in the dioceses of Pontica, while Byzantium was assigned to Thracia. It is only from the twelfth-century chronographer Cedrenus that we hear explicitly that Drepanum had been "in the territory of Nicomedia," but given the reshuffling of boundaries known to have taken place in the early fourth century and the favoritism shown to Nicomedia by the tetrarchs, it seems likely that his report is accurate and that Drepanum had been removed from the control of Byzantium and placed under that of its most powerful neighbor.[70]

Nicomedia had of course served as the launching place of the Great Persecution, and its curials later provoked Maximinus Daia to revive the slaughter in 312.[71] It was to Nicomedia that Lucian of Antioch was transported for trial and execution, a fact that would have made it awkward for the city to exercise control over the site of his martyrion.[72] Nicomedia also provided the last place of refuge to Licinius before his capture by Constantine in 324 and thus earned rebuke from Constantine in a letter to the church there in 325.[73] Although it was outfitted with an elaborate palace that had housed emperors for decades, and although Constantine did reside there in the first years of his residency in the East, he pointedly rejected Nicomedia as the location for his eastern capital and ceased to dwell there after 328. To be sure, Nicomedia had a powerful Christian community of its own that Constantine supported by rebuilding the church it had lost during the Great Persecution, and Constantine later showed favor to Nicomedia's bishop Eusebius.[74] Nevertheless, in 327, when he granted Drepanum its independence, the emperor was on distinctly chilly terms with Eusebius, whose deposition and exile he had approved in 325 and would not revoke until 328. Indeed, in his letter to the Nicomedians from late 325, Constantine even accused Eusebius of Nicomedia of conspiring with Licinius and had some of his priests and deacons arrested.[75] One would not wish to push the point too far, but it may well have been the case that Constantine was simultaneously rewarding Drepanum for its piety and punishing Nicomedia for its involvement in the recent persecution of Christians by granting Helenopolis its independence and imperial name.

Conclusion

Reconstructing local and regional politics for most any ancient city is extremely precarious given the state of the source record. Although we can often gain a fairly clear picture of broader contexts, arriving at the specific circumstances of any given time period and unraveling the complex relationships that influenced both civic petitions and imperial responses necessarily involves a degree of speculation. Moreover, in any one instance, religious affiliations alone cannot have sufficed to move the emperor to action. The inscription of Orcistus makes clear that other criteria had to be met before the emperor was willing to grant a petition for civic status, let alone the use of the imperial name. As noted in Chapter 6, some cities certainly received a Constantinian name for reasons unrelated to their religious self-construction. These included Autun, which was renamed Flavia Aeduorum before Constantine's conversion, as well as the various fortress cities of East and West about whose civic histories we know next to nothing. Other cities, like Cypriot Salamis, likely received their Constantinian names only after Constantine's death, even if this may well have occurred in response to a petition requesting independence from the control of an oppressive metropolis.

Nevertheless, enough confirmed instances have been cataloged in this and the previous chapter that the case is strong for a link between the imperial name, the grant of civic privileges, and the willingness of a city to promote Constantine's religious program. With Maiouma the evidence is solid and explicit: Constantine freed this Christian port from the control of its pagan neighbor and distinguished it with the name Constantia, taken from either his daughter or his son, and he did so—on the explicit testimony of Eusebius and Sozomen—because its populace had "inscribed itself on the rolls of the saving religion."[76] A case has been made for a parallel situation in the West with Portus and its neighbor Ostia. Slightly different situations obtained at Arles and Cirta, where Christian self-construction does seem to have played a role in earning these cities a Constantinian name even if they were not confronted with opposition from rival pagan neighbors. In the East, Antaradus used its profession of Christianity to win independence from neighboring Aradus, a city with a long tradition of lording it over subordinate towns. Renamed either Constantina or Constantia, it came to rival its former master as a dominant polity in the region. Daburiyya, the tiniest notion of a town, caught the attention of Empress Helena during her visit to Palestine and used the Christianity of its populace to break free from the Jewish stronghold of Diocaesarea-Sepphoris. So too Drepanum on the Gulf of Astaca won Helena's favor because it housed the relics of Lucian of Antioch and was granted freedom as well as tax immunity by Constantine. As part of these arrangements, both cities were renamed Helenopolis.

There is clearly a pattern here: those cities willing to promote Constantine's religion could expect freedom from meddlesome relationships of dependency and often an imperial name. This politics of favoritism in exchange for religious adherence has already been witnessed in the case of Orcistus, which did not gain a Constantinian name despite its Christian populace, and Hispellum, which did despite its ongoing attachment to traditional religion. The contrast between the two cities makes it clear that religious cooperation could be variously defined depending on local traditions and variously rewarded depending on the willingness of both sides to compromise. Both cities should also warn us against easy assumptions that, with the examples discussed in these two chapters, we know the full story of how this pattern of civic favoritism was implemented. Were it not for the chance discovery of the Orcistus and Hispellum inscriptions, we would have no idea from the textual sources about these crucial case studies in Constantinian civic politics. Far from assuming that the few cities treated in this chapter were the only ones to receive independence or even a Constantinian name, we must acknowledge that the pattern outlined here likely obtained in other polities for which we simply lack further testimony.

Surely the most important of the cities named after Constantine was Constantinople. Its history is so complex and the circumstances of its foundation so important that I intend to devote a separate book to it and its triangular relationship with the city of Rome and the emperor. Here it suffices to say that, as with Hispellum or the fortress cities outlined at the beginning of Chapter 6, Constantinople gives pause to anyone wishing to see in Constantine's urban politics a stark adherence to an inflexible and intolerant Christianity. On the contrary, Constantine proved there as elsewhere that he was eager to open a dialogue with the civic community of the ancient city of Byzantium in order to push his new religious agenda without entirely pushing aside indigenous cult. This same approach, as we shall see in Chapter 11, was also evident in other cities of the East, for although Constantine certainly showed favor for civic communities that worked to reconstitute themselves as "Christian" cities, he always did so in ways that respected age-old traditions of interaction and compromise encapsulated in the system of petition and response.

PART III

~

RECONSTRUCTING
THE ANCIENT CITY

CHAPTER 8

Redistributing Wealth

Civic Wealth, Temple Wealth

The ancient city was a complicated financial undertaking. Cities were at once property owners and revenue-producing entities. In the former capacity they owned both real and movable wealth, including considerable amounts of land in their neighboring territories and at times much farther afield. These properties were usually leased out to contractors or tenants in exchange for rents, which were in turn deployed to cover the expenses of city services, the maintenance of public slaves, the cost of civic festivals, and the upkeep and repair of publicly owned buildings. Such buildings included both secular and sacred architecture and could be extensive and at times quite expensive. It was thus important that the financial formulas of individual cities, worked out over centuries of careful property management, be respected by emperors if the cities they hoped to foster were to succeed in managing their affairs.

Constantine was, as we have seen in earlier chapters, just as concerned as any previous emperor with the welfare of his cities. We have also seen, however, that he had novel and ambitious goals for the transformation of his empire through the establishment of Christianity as its dominant religion, and that he regularly worked to actuate these goals at the level of civic politics. Often, of course, the objective of promoting Christianity in the cities did not coincide with local desires, and where this was the case, he was at times willing to override the wishes of subject cities using force. Although, as we shall see in Chapters 12 and 13, he was not beyond the use of physical violence, he preferred to use the power of law and preexisting channels of communication to coax or even coerce reluctant constituencies into cooperation. Among the most effective instruments at his disposal was of course the control of finances, for not only was he the most powerful economic player in the empire, but he also had at his disposal legal instruments with which to outmaneuver local communities in the game of property ownership and management as well as revenue generation and distribution.

Temples had formed part of the patrimony of local communities since the classical period. Temples within a city often occupied prime real estate, and most were granted ownership of lands in the city's *chōra,* whose revenues could be used to maintain the cult. Those outside of cities and beyond their administrative control enjoyed even greater opportunities to become centers for the collection and redistribution of wealth. The temples at Delphi, Delos, and Didyma—Greek cult sites that in the empire maintained a political identity of their own—exercised powerful influence over trade and banking and controlled sizable revenue-producing estates. Like any property, temple property was owned, but its masters were the gods rather than human agents. To maintain this distinction, the ancients classified temple property into a special category that generally rendered it less accessible to expropriation and redistribution, *ta hiera* in Greek law—*res sacrae* in Roman. The real estate controlled by the gods was administered by priests or sometimes civic officials, and the revenues it generated were used to meet the costs of festivals, the salaries of officiants and acolytes, and the maintenance and expansion of temple infrastructure. Even with the arrival of Hellenistic kings and in turn Roman magistrates and emperors, this distinction was maintained.[1] Although individual monarchs and generals did at times tap into temple treasuries and confiscate property, unless this was at some later point repaid, it was considered bad form, and their actions were usually reversed or at least regretted by successors.

The Confiscation of Temple Wealth

At some point after gaining control of the East in 324, Constantine appears to have infringed on the long-standing immunity of temples from random confiscations. This is described in rather stylized terms in the *Life of Constantine*.[2] Eusebius begins by telling us that he stripped the temples of their doors and the cladding of their roofs—which constituted massive depositories of metallic wealth because of their bronze construction and gold covering. He then explains the fate of gold and silver idols in much the same terms: avoiding the use of military force, Constantine simply sent out "one or two of his nobles alone" to proceed through the provinces and order pagan idols in gold and silver to be brought forth from temples and melted down into bullion in public view. Some bronze statues were also brought forth, but rather than being destroyed, they were confiscated and transported to his new city of Constantinople for public exhibition.[3] If we can believe the catalog in the Byzantine *Patria Constantinopoleos*, objects expropriated in this way for display in the city's Hippodrome alone came from shrines at Rome, Nicomedia, Athens, Cyzicus, Caesarea, Tralles, Sardis, Mocissus, Sebasteia,

Satala, Antioch, Cyprus, Crete, Rhodes, Chios, Attaleia, Smyrna, Seleucia, Tyana, Iconium, Nicaea, Sicily, and other unnamed eastern and western cities.[4] In essence, then, Constantine engineered a widespread program of iconoclasm that simultaneously removed pagan idols and liquid wealth from temples and converted these into bullion or movable art works.

This confiscation of chattel property from pagan temples did not go unnoticed in other sources. Jerome reports the removal of artworks to Constantinople as well as the "subversion" of temples under entries for the years 330 and 331 in his *Chronicle*,[5] and Julian criticizes Constantine's sons for destroying temples whose votive offerings Constantine himself had already seized.[6] The same is hinted in an epigram of Palladas, whose work has now been re-dated to the Constantinian period by K. Wilkinson,[7] and the anonymous author of the *De rebus bellicis* implies a broader confiscation of precious metals and jewels from temple treasuries.[8] Libanius would seem to indicate the same in his *Oration on the Temples* from the 380s when he writes that Constantine "employed the sacred treasures [*tois hierois chrēmasi*] for the building of the city upon which his heart was set," and that he was punished for his policy concerning "temple treasures" (*ta hiera chrēmata*) by the strife into which his family descended upon his death.[9] Again in his *Oration Against the Critics of His Educational System* (circa 382), Libanius criticizes Constantine for having "stripped the gods of their wealth," further implying a broad confiscation of movable property.[10] The conclusion is thus unavoidable that Constantine expropriated temple treasures both in the form of sacred statues, which were either melted into bullion (if made of precious metals) or ported away to Constantinople, and in the form of liquid wealth formerly stored in treasuries or as building decorations but now converted into coin.

His actions were certainly a tremendous blow to the shrines, for they represented an unprecedented loss of accumulated movable property. It did not, however, result in the immediate confiscation of all accumulated treasure and images, for Constantine's sweep of temples was neither systematic nor thorough enough to have wiped them clean. At a minimum, we know that many sacred statues remained in place, whether because they did not attract the attention of Constantine's inspectors, or because they were safely hidden away, or even because their removal would have been too dangerous in the face of local opposition. Thus the statue of Athena Promachos remained in the Parthenon into the fifth century despite its considerable value in raw materials.[11] So too, the famous statue of Serapis at his shrine in Alexandria, which only fell prey to Christian zealots in 392.[12] These were of course massive images from major shrines, but much smaller idols survived as well. When Julian toured Troas in 362, its bishop Pegasius, a sympathizer with the traditional cults, guided him around the temples showing him various bronze statues locked away and lovingly preserved in perfect condition.[13] Indeed, many sacred images are attested not just as remaining in place but as continuing to attract worship in urban contexts around the Mediterranean well into the fifth century.[14]

The Fate of Temple Property

Larger questions arise with regard to the real estate attached to temples. Constantine was willing in some limited instances to countenance and even command the destruction of temples. This is likely to have resulted in the confiscation of attendant property holdings to the imperial treasury. When the emperor condemned an individual or institution, he laid legal claim to its residual property as *bona damnatorum*.[15] The building materials as well as the land accrued to his purse—in Late Antiquity the *res privata*—which could then keep the property or redistribute it through sale or as gifts. This had occurred, for example, during the Great Persecution, when huge numbers of church properties were confiscated and many of them sold or otherwise redistributed to private individuals. Indeed, this situation lies at the heart of the "Edict of Milan," which reversed this process by restoring to the church those properties still held by the *res privata* or purchased from it by private interests.[16] Constantine used the same process against heretical Christian sects, a fact we know from a letter preserved in Eusebius that orders the confiscation of buildings controlled by such groups and their appropriation by the *res privata* or transfer to the Catholic Church.[17]

Constantine's readiness to use confiscation and redistribution in order to promote Christianity at the expense of paganism is a matter of some debate. We have direct testimony to this occurring in only one city: Aegeae, where the architectural elements left over from the destruction of the temple of Asclepius were turned over to the city's bishop for use in the construction of the town's church.[18] Nevertheless, more general use of the same tactic is certainly indicated in other sources. Eunapius, for example, claimed that when Constantine ruled, he destroyed the most magnificent temples while constructing new Christian churches, implying the two were interrelated.[19] Similarly, Eusebius compared the tetrarchs, who honored the demons with dedications, to Constantine, who denuded these false gods and distributed the resultant materials to those able to use them properly.[20] The most striking source on the question is a passage of Theophanes that derives from the fourth-century historian Philostorgius: "In this year [330] the pious Constantine intensified the destruction of idols and their temples, and they were demolished in various places. The revenues (*hai prosodoi*) from these were bestowed upon the churches of God."[21] The passage is also related to the same chronographic tradition from which we get a lemma in Jerome's *Chronicle* for the year 331: "By an edict of Constantine the temples of the pagans were subverted."[22] There is thus reason to believe that a direct transfer of property from pagan cults to Christian churches occurred, and that this process intensified in the wake of a general law of 330 or 331.[23]

This process of reappropriation apparently gained momentum over the course of the early fourth century as temple destructions became more common. Libanius claims that Constantius "presented his courtiers with gifts of temples as though it were a present of a horse, a slave, a dog, or a golden goblet," and Ammianus speaks in much the same terms.[24] Julian, Libanius claims, was later to reverse this by ordering the restoration of temple property to its rightful owners, the gods.[25] Strikingly, however, during Julian's reign Libanius more than once found himself in the position of defending friends in possession of temple property acquired on the open market, a powerful testimony to how banal this process had become by the mid-fourth century.[26] The systematic nature of Julian's effort to undo the damage Constantine and Constantius had done is apparent not just from the quantity of Libanius's letters on the subject, but also from an edict of Julian's, published February 4, 362, whereby "it was ordered that all property be restored to idols, neokoric temples, and the public treasury that was taken away from these in previous times."[27] How this played out at a local level can be seen in a letter of Julian's to Hecebolius, who was probably acting as governor in Osrhoene when the citizens of Edessa broke into riots over sectarian squabbles within their Christian community. Julian seized on the opportunity to confiscate all of the liquid wealth (*chrēmata*) of their church for distribution to his army and all of its real property (*ktēmata*) to his *res privata*.[28] Building materials were thus confiscated and redistributed by Constantine and his sons, and in turn reappropriated and returned to the temples—or deployed for other needs—by Julian.

The Seizure of Temple Estates

The most puzzling question, however, remains whether Constantine and/or Constantius II also confiscated temple lands, and above all revenue-producing estates.[29] We have no direct evidence in extant sources, but one hint that they did comes in a law of 405 stating: "By the sanction of the renowned emperor Constantine, which we too reaffirm by this law, in the case of those estates (*in his possessionibus*) that have been removed from the jurisdiction of our patrimony, or of a city, or of temples, or of any title of this sort, and are sought from our beneficence, let the wicked name of informants not be involved and let all refrain from this nefarious sort of petition."[30] The Constantinian law referenced is no longer extant, and furthermore this 405 law is principally aimed at curbing delation, not regulating the confiscation of temple property. It clearly implies, however, that by the terms of Constantine's law, temple estates were indeed open to expropriation and redistribution through the *res privata*. Whether the original enactment referenced was also aimed principally at delation or instead included broader provisions outlining property confiscations, we can no longer know. At a minimum, Constantine's original law envisioned the *res privata* as a vehicle through which temple property could be reassigned to private individuals, a new departure in the imperial regulation of pagan cult. The only other vague intimation of the confiscation of temple estates comes in a passage of Libanius's *Oration on the Temples* claiming that, under Constantine, "poverty reigned in the temples," an allusion that is suggestive but far too terse to carry much weight.[31]

To this can be added the more decisive—but also indirect—testimony that Julian made a concerted effort to move sacred lands off the accounts of the *res privata* and back into the ownership of the temples. This we know from a constitution of Jovian dated to February 364 and another from December of that same year issued by Valentinian. Both order that all landed estates (*universa loca vel praedia*) that Julian had transferred from the *res privata* into the ownership of the temples were to be restored immediately to the imperial patrimony.[32] The fact that one of the two laws was directed to the eastern *Comes Rerum Privatarum* and the other to the western Praetorian Prefect makes it clear that Julian's reassignment affected both halves of the empire and was thus systematic in its sweep. We also know from a passage in Sozomen that Julian not only ordered the restoration of temples, festivals, and public sacrifices, but also reassigned considerable money to pay for these and restored publicly financed provisions to those who served as temple guardians.[33] It seems likely that some, even most, of these revenues and supplies derived from the restoration of landed estates to the control of the temples.

Combined with the law of 405, this evidence strongly implies that Constantine had indeed confiscated temple estates, then redistributed either the land or its revenues to private individuals or Christian churches. Julian in turn attempted to reverse his uncle's policy by returning the lands to temples and restoring to their operations the revenues these could generate. Finally, Jovian and in turn Valentinian restored the *status quo Constantinianus*. Here again, however, Constantine's confiscations were never systematic, for the seizure of temple property by the *res privata* continued into the 380s, when Gratian seems to have issued a law authorizing universal expropriation, and it was still happening as late as 415, when it is again prescribed in a law of the *Theodosian Code*.[34] Constantine had thus started a process that continued to work itself out over the course of the next century.

The Confiscation of Civic Estates

The law of 405 indicates that Constantine not only expropriated temple properties and revenues but also confiscated some of the estates of cities or their revenues. Previous scholarship had long assumed the same, but G. Bransbourg has denied this altogether. Bransbourg argues that Constantine instead simply recalibrated the formula for the emperor's share of civic *vectigalia,* and that there is no direct attestation for the confiscation of civic estates in the sources.[35] This first assertion is entirely speculative; the second is incorrect. In fact, Bransbourg is not the only one not to have noticed that such confiscations are directly described in a passage of Sozomen: "He [Constantine] confiscated the fixed revenue of the civic treasury from the tributary land of each city and reappropriated it to the churches and clergy in each respective place, and he legislated that this gift should remain valid for all time."[36] We also have an inscription of Valens from circa 370, *IKEph* 42, informing us that, at this point at least, bursars of the imperial estates (ll. 5–6: *acto[ri]bus/ [pr]ibatae*(sic) *rei nostrae;* cf. ll. 7, 18, 22) in Asia were managing landed properties with civic legal status (l. 2: *fundorum iuris re[i publicae];* ll. 12–13: *rei publicae/ iuga;* cf. l. 19: *rationibus civitatum*).[37] From this it is evident that at least some civic estates were, in the 370s, managed as part of the landholdings of the emperor's purse. This can only have been the case if such civic properties had at some point been seized. In the inscription, it is not at all clear that the revenues of these estates were flowing directly to churches, as the passage in Sozomen would imply. As we shall see in what follows, however, the fate of these confiscated territories was by no means uncomplicated. But before we turn to the question of whether they were used by Constantine to fund local churches, we must first inquire into the nature of their expropriation: was it universal in scope or more limited? And was it aimed not just at benefiting the church but also at starving pagan cult of revenue?

As to the first question, a number of sources confirm that cities continued to control revenues from their own civic estates up to the reign of Julian at least.[38] This makes it all but certain that, as with the confiscation of temple properties, the imperial appropriation of civic revenues likely affected only certain cities and probably only certain territories of any given city.[39] As to the consequences for traditional cults, it should be remembered that cities often used a portion of the money derived from their estates to cover the expenses of their temples—festivals, public meals, sacrificial animals, and above all building maintenance.[40] Constantine's re-diversion of civic estate revenue may thus have been intended at least in part to disadvantage public cult.[41] This was indeed the reading of Julian, who ordered the restoration of civic estates to the cities in order to generate revenue for the maintenance of public structures—which would have included temples.[42]

Libanius certainly made the connection between the revenues of civic estates and the maintenance of civic temples when he marveled that Julian's restoration of the former was having a very positive impact on the latter.[43] The link was also made by the dedicants of a statue to Julian in northern Palestine, who praised the Apostate as both "the re-creator of the *curiae* and the city" and "the restorer of temples."[44] The same can be deduced from a cryptic passage in Eunapius reporting how the Christian sophist Prohaeresius was able to learn whether Julian's law against Christian teachers of the classics would endure: rather than ask the Eleusinian hierophant for an oracle predicting how long Julian would live, he inquired about the longevity of the Apostate's new law whereby "the emperor had surveyed the land for the purpose of rent payments to the benefit of the pagans (*hellēsin*) so that they would not be oppressed."[45] Whatever the economic impact of Constantine's confiscation of civic revenues, their symbolic value was thus highly significant: Constantine had upended the traditional funding structures for the maintenance of civic cult, and only Julian's restoration had set the cities and their temples back on proper footing.

Unsurprisingly, Jovian is reported to have reconfiscated the civic revenues the moment he came to power.[46] In the inscription mentioned above, *IKEph* 42, Valens partially reversed this, allowing cities in Asia—which had been devastated by earthquake in 365—to regain possession of some estates for the reconstruction of public buildings, but insisting that a large portion of their revenues still be transferred to the *res privata*.[47] Later laws indicate that this quota system was shortly thereafter implemented more broadly and the proportions fixed such that one-third of the revenues flowed to the cities, while the remaining two-thirds went to the imperial treasury.[48] As noted above, the scanty sources do not permit a firm understanding of the precise nature of this jockeying for control over the civic estates and the money they generated. From the evidence presented here, however, it appears that Constantine set about exploring options for redirecting civic revenues from pagan to imperial coffers; Julian reversed this in a decision that was itself reversed by Jovian; and Valentinian and Valens then worked out a compromise in which cities and the *res privata* shared the revenues on a one-third to two-thirds basis.

This is thus very close to the pattern witnessed above in the instance of temple properties. With the cities, as with the temples, Constantine's original plan did not remain in place past the mid-fourth century, but his experimentation with the confiscation of civic estates succeeded in drawing into question the age-old systems of civic financing. By directing civic revenues away from city treasuries, he broke down received preconceptions about the connection between a city's revenues and the maintenance of its buildings, particularly its pagan shrines. This allowed him to begin a realignment of urban fiscal structures to the detriment of traditional cult.[49]

In the broadest sense, then, Constantine put the imperial *res privata* to work as a massive organ for the consumption and digestion of property—chattel and landed—formerly used for the maintenance of civic structures and public temples, and its redistribution for his own use or—as we shall see in what follows—the use of Christian churches. Because of the emperor's extraordinary powers over property and his unique position as the receiver of last resort of abandoned, ownerless, and confiscated estates, there was both a precedent and a mechanism for his expropriation of sacred wealth. This does not mean that every transfer of wealth from the temples and cities into the *res privata* was then redirected to churches in a one-to-one swap—from temple to basilica, as it were. This was certainly an option, one we know he exercised in the case of Aegeae and one that sources like the chronicle tradition reported in Theophanes imply was deployed more generally in 330/331. Just as commonly, however, the process was surely indirect and followed roundabout channels. What mattered was that Constantine used an old tool in the emperor's kit in order to begin dispossessing temples and cities of their property and, after absorbing these into his treasury, using it to enrich the church.

Enriching the Churches

At the same time the *res privata* was growing wealthier at the expense of the temples and their estates, Christian churches and their members were winning tremendous financial advantages from the *res privata*. We have just seen Sozomen's report that Constantine diverted revenues from civic estates to local churches and members of their clergy.[50] Theodoret makes similar claims in a passage he places immediately after his report on the Council of Nicaea in 325: "Once the banquet had ended, he proffered still further gifts on them. More specifically, he gave letters to the governors in charge of the provinces and ordered that in each city annual grain rations [*etēsia sitēresia*] were to be provided for the perpetual virgins and widows and those consecrated to divine service. He fixed the amount according to his desire to display generosity rather than according to need."[51] Athanasius provides similar testimony to imperially sponsored grain doles for widows and orphans in Alexandria in a passage quoted below, and the *Chronicon Paschale* and Theophanes attest to the same in Constantinople and Antioch.[52] Eusebius writes along similar lines in more generic terms: "His liberality, however, was most especially exercised on behalf of the churches of God. In some cases he granted lands, in others he issued supplies of food for the support of the poor, of orphan children, and widows."[53] Eusebius would seem to distinguish between two methods for channeling wealth to the churches and their indigent: (1) direct grants of land,

and (2) the transfer of revenues or provisions from estates held by the emperor or even a third-party contractor. As mentioned, Sozomen and Theodoret describe schemes designed to benefit local churches and their needy by transferring revenue or rations to these from civic estates. This seems to fit the latter category. But we also have evidence that the *res privata* was tapped directly for these doles, for this is confirmed explicitly in a document preserved in Eusebius's *Ecclesiastical History*. A letter of Constantine's from 313 informs the Bishop of Carthage, Caecilianus, that the emperor had directed his account manager Ursus in a separate missive to transfer three thousand *folles* to Caecilianus for distribution among his clergy. Constantine also invites Caecilianus to write Heracleides, a procurator of the *res privata,* to request further funds if that should seem necessary.[54] Thus already in the year following his conversion, Constantine was authorizing western bishops to draw directly from the *res privata* in order to provision their clergy, and the passage cited from Theodoret indicates that he initiated the same program in the East beginning in 325. Nor were these insignificant sums: careful calculation indicates that Constantine's subvention to Caecilianus and the clergy of Carthage alone could have purchased enough wheat to feed almost 7,300 people per year![55] The grant of such *beneficia*, including grain rations to cities, was of course nothing new for Roman emperors, but by channeling his largesse through the bishops and by targeting underserved communities that had long constituted a focal point for Christian euergetism, Constantine was turning the church into a crucial structure in the complex fabric of cities.[56]

Athanasius's experience with the system helps clarify further both how it was structured and what sorts of problems it could generate. In the first part of his *Apology Against the Arians*, composed shortly after Constantine's death, he complains: "A grain allowance [*sitos*] had been given by the father of the Emperors for the support of the widows, partly to the Libyas [*sic*] and partly for some from Egypt. They have all received it up to this time, Athanasius getting nothing from it except the trouble of assisting them. But now, although they receive it and have made no complaint but acknowledge that they have received it, Athanasius has been accused of selling all the grain and appropriating the profits to his own use."[57] Whether or not the charges against Athanasius were true, the passage throws into relief the wealth and corresponding power associated with this grant of grain rations, as well as the possibilities it opened for corruption. Later, in his *History of the Arians,* Athanasius indicates that these same food rations were withdrawn from his control in 356, when he was deposed, and transferred to the oversight of his replacement as bishop of Alexandria, George of Cappadocia.[58] Grain subventions to clergy, widows, and orphans were thus a source of tremendous power, flowing in the form of food rations from the emperor to local Christian communities, but channeled through the intermediacy of the bishop. This obviously gave bishops tremendous influence but also tremendous leeway, leeway that could nevertheless backfire if a person like Athanasius asserted his independence from imperial control too aggressively.

Unsurprisingly, Julian revoked Constantine's transfer of these revenues as well. He did not, however, keep the income regained from this for his privy purse. Rather, following Constantine's lead, he set up in their stead a scheme whereby monies from civic estates and the *res privata* were transferred to pagan worshippers through the intermediacy of provincial priests.[59] Naturally, this did not outlive his reign, which nevertheless acted as a watershed beyond which the direct endowment of Christian churches from the *res privata* or from civic estates was greatly curbed. Indeed, the same passage of Theodoret cited above continues by reporting that, after Julian's moratorium on subventions to Christians, his successors restored only one-third the amount Constantine had initially granted, interestingly the same mathematical ratio used in sharing civic estate revenues between cities and the emperor.[60] Constantine can thus be argued to have started out of the gates rather too quickly in his zeal to promote local churches with direct grants of revenue from civic and imperial estates and thus to have forced his Christian successors to use Julian's reversal of these benefactions as cover for their own diminution of his excessive largesse.[61]

Conclusion

Ancient rulers had long enjoyed the option of confiscating the property of their subjects for their own benefit, but only few had exercised this power against the property of temples, which was regarded as a hallmark of tyranny. These compunctions do not seem to have bothered Constantine when, around 330, he ordered officials to fan out through the empire and collect gold and silver statues as well as liquid wealth for reduction to bullion and bronzes for transport to Constantinople. The amount of the accumulated precious metals at play was so great that the author of the later fourth-century *De rebus bellicis* could argue that it essentially funded a shift in the fourth-century economy from a bronze-based to a gold-based monetary system.[62] Constantine also appears to have called for the confiscation of estate lands formerly controlled by pagan temples and their absorption into the imperial *res privata*. So too with the estates controlled by cities. In all of these instances—the confiscation of precious metals, temple estates, and civic properties—Constantine's expropriations were clearly never complete or systematic. Temples and cities held onto some of their liquid and real property beyond his reign, and some of it even until the early fifth century. They were also not irreversible, for Julian the Apostate attempted to undo the damage done to temples and cities by his uncle only to have his rulings reversed by his successors. Interestingly, however, at least in the case of civic estates, the return to Constantinian standards was only partial, for the more pragmatic Valentinian and Valens saw that the first Christian emperor had gone too far in depriving cities of the revenues needed for the maintenance of their public structures.

At the same time Constantine was dispossessing temples and cities, he was diverting considerable wealth to the Christian church. For one thing, he used the *res privata* as a supplier for free grain rations to be distributed through local bishops to the poor, to widows, and to Christian clergy in the cities. Here again, Julian sought to reverse this by redirecting these supply schemes into the control of pagan priests, but Valentinian and Valens once more restored Constantine's scheme at a reduced scale. We shall see in the next chapter that Constantine also opened imperial coffers for the construction of churches. There is evidence for this process from all across the empire but particularly from Rome and the Holy Land. Local bishops were invited to petition regional governors for land, building materials, manpower, and provisions, all of which were supplied by the imperial fisc. The line of investigation begun here will thus continue into Chapter 9, which should reinforce the argument that Constantine used his *res privata* as an instrument through which to actuate his plan to turn the cities from pagan into Christian religious centers.

CHAPTER 9

Building Churches

Christianizing the Cityscape

Ancient cities took great pride in their temples, not just as cultic centers but also as architectural showpieces. In this sense, the identity of any given polity was intimately intertwined with the size and beauty of its sanctuaries. It is thus difficult to conceive of eastern cities like Athens without the Parthenon or Ephesus without its temple of Artemis, or in the West to think of Rome without the Pantheon or temple of Venus and Roma or Dougga without its temple of Tanit-Juno Caelestis. Major religious shrines were, in other words, an essential part of the urban fabric of an antique city. They conditioned reactions to a place not just as sites of worship but also as statements of power, guarantors of status, and symbols of self-definition.

Christian sacred buildings were not, before the reign of Constantine, considered a significant component of any city's architectural repertoire. They were often simply private houses that had been turned over to local Christian communities and reappointed as meeting places for congregants. Even the few purpose-built churches known from the pre-Constantinian period were unprepossessing and unlikely to have added to a city's architectural luster.[1] Almost immediately after advertising his conversion, Constantine set about remedying this. First in Rome, but soon in other major cities across the empire, he undertook to impose a Christian architectural footprint on the urban landscape. This he did not by forcing upon cities a preplanned scheme for state-designed constructions, but by opening the coffers of his *res privata*—now enriched with wealth from temple confiscations—to local clergymen for projects of their own. In instance after instance, he made it clear that if these clergy asked for financing, he would provide it directly through his officers from funds in his own purse.

In the realm of sacred architecture, we see once again, then, Constantine deploying the classic instrument of petition and response to push cities into actualizing his own conversion at the local level. He solicited grassroots requests for imperial finances and then converted these into action on the ground by granting capital in order to enable church leaders to invent a Christian architecture for their own towns and cities. The resulting efflorescence of ecclesiastical buildings profoundly altered the landscape not just of the cities that received these funds, but of the Mediterranean city for the rest of history. Thanks to this ingenious undertaking, Christian church structures became a sine qua non of the urban fabric of any town.

Petitioning for Funding

Already before the Great Persecution, Christians had built churches or converted existing structures into meeting places in numerous cities across the empire. Indeed, the Great Persecution opened with the destruction of the Church of Nicomedia on February 23, 303, and its first edict called for the destruction of ecclesiastical property, including churches, all across the empire.[2] With the cessation of persecution in 311, Galerius permitted Christians to rebuild church structures, and some communities certainly did, as is well attested by Eusebius's lengthy oration delivered circa 315 at the rededication of the Church of Tyre, a victim of the Great Persecution.[3] Nevertheless, prior to Constantine, emperors had never supported the construction of churches, nor had they donated land or estates to them. This was to change radically when Constantine began enriching Christian communities in the empire's cities with financial support for the construction of ecclesiastical buildings.[4]

In a crucial passage Eusebius reports that, shortly after gaining control of the East in 324, Constantine issued two laws: the first (to be discussed in Chapter 12) banned sacrifice and other forms of pagan worship, and "another ordered buildings to be erected as places of worship and churches of God to be increased in breadth and length, as if almost everybody would be associated with God in the future, once the obstacle of polytheistic madness had been removed."[5] Eusebius mentions the same ordinance in much the same terms, both in his *Oration on Christ's Sepulcher* delivered in Jerusalem in 335, and in his *Tricennalian Oration* delivered to Constantine himself the following summer.[6] The evidence is thus emphatic that Constantine issued some sort of law ordering the construction or expansion of Christian basilicas across the cities of his newly unified empire.

In the *Life of Constantine* Eusebius goes on to provide direct and circumstantial evidence for the workings of this process in a letter he received from Constantine in 324 in which the emperor orders: "Whatever churches you yourself are in charge of or if you know other bishops, presbyters, or deacons in charge of other locales, be mindful to attend to these church structures, whether by restoring existing buildings or enlarging them or, where need arises, constructing new ones. You yourself and through you any others should petition for the necessary resources from the governors and the imperial office of the Prefect. For I have written to these that they should obey whatever your Holiness proposes with the utmost zeal."[7] It would be difficult to conceive of a more patent statement of pre-planned imperial initiative. With no apparent external prompting, the emperor had already corresponded with his officials conveying orders that they should provide financing for the repair, enlargement, or erection of church buildings, and with this letter he was now prompting bishops and other members of the clergy to petition said governors and prefects directly to put these resources to work for the benefit of local churches.

We have irrefutable confirmation that this order to Eusebius was not unique to Palestine, but rather the letter just quoted must have represented only a single exemplar of a type circulated throughout East and West. This we know because precisely this sort of transfer of imperial wealth for the construction of churches is attested in patterned fashion in a broad array of sources stemming directly or indirectly from the pen of Constantine:

- Joseph of Tiberias was issued letters (*epistolai*) authorizing him to spend from the imperial estates (*apo tōn basilikōn*) and had also been granted the honor of receiving supplies from the emperor (*opsōnia para tou basileōs*) for the construction of churches in Palestine (Epiph. *Pan.* 30.12.1).
- The Catholics of Cirta were informed that an imperial accountant (*rationalis*) was given letters (*litterae*) authorizing him to transfer a house from the imperial estates (*domus bonorum nostrorum*) with all its rights to their ownership where a church (*basilica*) was ordered to be built at the expense of the fisc (*sumptu fiscali*); a separate letter was sent to the governor of Numidia authorizing him to aid in its construction (Opt. *App.* 10.36b [*CSEL* 26: 215]).
- Macarius of Jerusalem was informed that the Prefect Dracilianus and the governor of Palestine had been charged with oversight (*egkecheiristhai tēn phrontida*) of the construction of the Church (*basilikē*) of the Holy Sepulchre; they were ordered to supply craftsmen and workers and whatever else Macarius thought necessary, although Macarius was allowed to dictate the design and furnishings (Eus. *V. Const.* 3.31.2–32.2).[8]
- Macarius was informed that the Count Acacius was given a letter (*gramma*) instructing him to destroy all idols at Mamre and directing

that the place be adorned with a new church (*basilikē*) whose design was to be determined by a council of bishops from Palestine and Phoenicia (Eus. *V. Const.* 3.53.2).

- In a personal letter (*di'oikeiou grammatos*), Constantine ordered that the foundations be laid for a massive prayer-house church (*oikos euktērios ekklēsias megas*) among the Heliopolitans (Eus. *V. Const.* 3.58.2–3; cf. Soz. 1.18.7–9).

- Athanasius preserves a letter from Flavius Himerius, the *rationalis* (*katholikos*) of Egypt, to the tax receiver (*exaktor*) of the Maereotis authorizing him to transfer the expenses for the construction of a church (*ekklēsia*) to imperial accounts upon receipt of a letter of confirmation (*gramma*) (Athan. *Apol. c. Ar.* 85.7).[9]

Collectively, this testimony resoundingly communicates a pattern of coordinated imperial correspondence, driven in response to petitions, which had themselves been solicited from local bishops, that authorized the construction of church buildings through direct transfers of funds from the *res privata* to a particular local Christian community.

Scales of Wealth

We also have another witness to this process that helps fill out our understanding of the massive scale on which it must have been undertaken. Some of our most detailed testimony on the matter comes from the *Liber Pontificalis*, which records not only the churches Constantine built in Rome and southern Italy, but also the liquid wealth with which he enriched them and the estates with which he endowed them. Chief among these was the *Basilica Constantiniana*, the church now called San Giovanni in Laterano.[10] This structure, on the Caelian Hill just inside the Aurelian walls, is widely known to have been built over the barracks of Maxentius's former horse guard, the *Equites singulares*. It was also adjoined to two former imperial palaces—the *Domus Lateranorum* and the *Domus Faustae*—the latter of which was used already in 313 by the bishop of Rome to host the council he headed that year concerning the Donatists.[11] This fact combined with numismatic evidence from the building's foundations indicates that work on the church was begun late in 312, within weeks of Constantine's victory over Maxentius.[12] Thus, even at this very early date Constantine was lavishing the Roman church with a direct and massive grant of prime imperial real estate and with funds to build a church there.

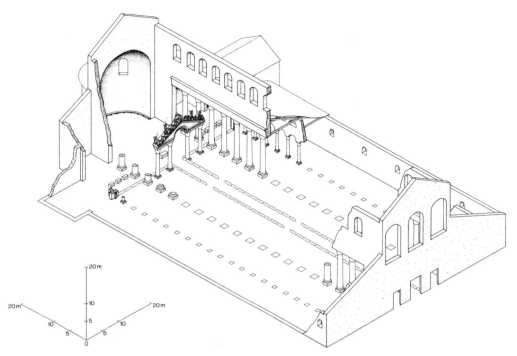

FIGURE 34. Basilica Constantiniana of the Lateran in Rome, isometric reconstruction. Drawing by S. L. de Blaauw, from De Blaauw, *Cultus et decor* (1994), reproduced with permission.

The structure that resulted was a colossal five-aisled building, one hundred meters in length, whose infrastructure remains largely intact under the baroque veneer added to it by Borromini in the 1600s (Fig. 34). It was outfitted with an octagonal baptistery and embellished with decorations and liturgical implements in worked precious metals amounting to 1,232 pounds of gold and 11,525 pounds of silver. Management of the structure—its upkeep, lighting, and ceremonial costs—was then funded by revenues generated through the award of imperial estates in Italy, Africa, and Greece that yielded 202 pounds of gold per year. This massive architectural imposition on Roman topography—a blatant reorientation of what had formerly been imperially controlled space—stood as a monumental symbol of the shift in religious priorities Constantine was setting into motion. Even while civic temples were being stripped of their stores of gold and silver and deprived of their estates and revenues, this flashy new religious complex was being outfitted with wealth, at least some of which must have derived directly from the spoils of Constantine's encroachments on civic and temple finances.

Nor did Constantine's very public endowment of the Christian church in Rome and Italy stop here. In addition to this showpiece of imperial might, the

Liber Pontificalis records the construction and endowment of a further seven basilicas in and around the city and four in Latium and Campania. Although the reliability of this catalog has been questioned by some, many scholars agree that most of its material regarding Constantine's constructions derives from the reign of Constantius II and merits credence.[13] Moreover, excavations in the 1990s turned up the remains of Constantinian churches mentioned in the *Liber Pontificalis* as being located at Ostia and on the Via Ardeatina even though the absence of material evidence for these had once been used to argue against this source's credibility.[14] Similarly, although T. Barnes has argued—on scant evidence, all textual—against Constantine's construction of a church to Saint Paul on the Via Ostiense, a more careful reading of the archaeological work would have shown that a small apsidal structure discovered under the present Theodosian church was almost certainly the original church of Constantine.[15] So too, G. Bowersock has attempted to prove that the original basilica of Saint Peter at the Vatican was begun not by Constantine but his son Constantius II, but P. Liverani has shown that records of

FIGURE 35. Constantinian Basilica of Saint Peter, seventeenth-century fresco by Giovanni Battista Ricci da Novara depicting the nave with the dividing wall erected by Paul III Farnese. Cappella della Madonna della Bocciata, Grotte Vaticane of Saint Peter's. Reproduced with kind permission from the Fabbrica di San Pietro in Vaticano.

the mosaic inscription from the original structure's archway confirm Constantine as the initiator of the structure (Fig. 35).[16] The evidence from the physical remains has thus vindicated the value of the *Liber Pontificalis* against its critics.

Its data can best be presented in tabular form (see Table 3). This was obviously a massive commitment of imperial resources to Roman and south Italian churches. If we take the early fourth-century gold to silver ratio to have been 1 to 14.4, a well-attested figure, the total amount given in worked precious metals amounted to 4,342 pounds of gold or gold equivalent.[17] This was then supplemented by almost 450 pounds of gold in annual revenue for the maintenance of these structures. These figures should be compared with the 153 pounds of gold generated annually from the civic estates of Asia Minor, as recorded in the

Table 3. Constantinian Church Foundations in the *Liber Pontificalis*

Basilica	*Liber Pontificalis*	Gold dedications (lbs.)	Silver dedications (lbs.)	Primary locus of endowment	Revenue: gold / annum (lbs.)
Constantiniana	34.9–15	1,232	11,525	Western	202
S. Pietro	34.16–20	126	1,685	Eastern	62
Sessorian	34.22	25	1,374	Western	15
S. Agnese[1]	34.23	45	330	Western	9.6
S. Lorenzo	34.25	55	1,990	Western	12
SS. Marcellino e Pietro	34.26–27	155	1,900	Western	52
Via Ardeatina	35.3	—	—	Western	0.55
Pallacinae (St. Mark)[2]	35.2–4	—	96	Western	1.74
Ostia	34.28–29	—	266	Western	10
Albanum	34.30	—	112	Western	20
Capua	34.31	—	264	Western	10
Naples[3]	34.32	—	290	Western	9
S. Paolo	34.21	150	—	Eastern	45
[Titulus of Silvester/ Aequitius][4]	34.3, 33	—	[106]	Western	[7]
Totals		2,965	19,832 [19,938]		448.89 [455.89]

[1] On this church, see Rasch and Arbeiter, *Das Mausoleum der Constantina*, and below n. 23.
[2] Cecchelli.
[3] On the Constantinian churches of Capua and Naples, see M. J. Johnson, "Constantinian Churches in Campania."
[4] This entry is almost certainly a later addition; cf. Duchesne, vol. 3, p. 77.

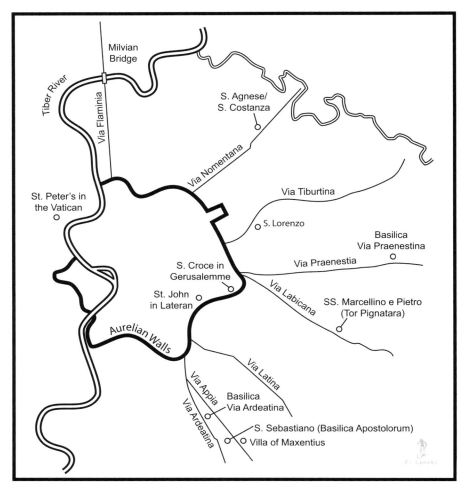

MAP 6. Ecclesiastical Foundations of Rome

inscription from circa 370 discussed in Chapter 8 in the context of civic finances (*IKEph.* 42). There Valens had permitted the Asian cities to retain some of the revenue from their old civic estates—likely one-third of it, or 51 pounds annually—for the restoration of public buildings (*moenia*).[18] The Christian churches of Rome and Italy were thus allotted nine times the amount granted to the cities of Asia annually, with the *Basilica Constantiniana* alone receiving four times the combined revenues for the Asian cities. Although we cannot prove that former civic or temple lands paid for these endowments, at a minimum we do know that, along with the *Basilica Constantiniana*, several of these structures were built on land formerly controlled by the *res privata*: the church of San Lorenzo was built on a plot known to have been in the ownership of the imperial treasury for a cen-

tury previous,[19] and that of Santi Marcellino e Pietro was located over the burial
ground of Maxentius's horse guard and endowed with estates formerly controlled
by the Augusta Helena.[20] It is thus not unreasonable to assume that at least some
of the estates used to enrich the Italian churches had been transferred to them by
the emperor from former temple or civic estates that he had confiscated.

The evidence of the *Liber Pontificalis* should not be taken to mean that Constantine himself ordered the construction of each of these churches individually
or oversaw their design and creation. On the contrary, at several points the text
indicates that construction was undertaken at the request of the bishop of Rome.[21]
With regard to the church of Saint Agnes, it indicates that the structure was built
"at the request of his daughter."[22] This is confirmed by the original building
inscription, which is no longer extant but has been preserved by copyists. Its text,
an acrostic epigram in hexameters, directly attributes the structure to Constantine's eldest daughter, Constantina.[23] The evidence of the *Liber Pontificalis* thus
offers a remarkably consistent picture: the emperor directly supported Christian
civic communities with the construction of churches, which he paid for with
imperial funds, enriched with liquid wealth, and endowed with landed estates for
their ongoing management.

An Empire-wide Program

The evidence from Constantine's correspondence of the use of petition and
response presented in the second section of this chapter, as also the evidence of the
Liber Pontificalis just covered, fit with other sources that indicate Constantine did
not dictate the specifics of new ecclesiastical foundations but rather advertised
among Christian leaders his readiness to respond positively to their requests for
financial and logistical support with their own projects.[24] We have only much
scantier evidence for how this process played itself out in other cities across the
empire, but what little we have points in the same direction. The data is especially
sketchy because of the drop-off in the epigraphic habit by the early fourth century.
This, combined with the fact that churches are often living monuments with histories lasting at times up to the present, has erased much of the direct testimony for
the scale of Constantine's church-building program at the local level. Nevertheless,
for some idea of the impact of Constantine's efforts, it is worthwhile focusing on
those cities treated since the early days of the Tetrarchy as regional capitals—Trier,
Milan, Aquileia, Sirmium, Serdica, Thessalonica, Nicomedia, and Antioch. These
larger, more prestigious polities would have seemed obvious magnets for Constantine's attention, and there is indeed evidence that they played this role.[25]

FIGURE 36. Possible depiction of the Octagonal Church of Antioch (right) next to the imperial palace, from the border of the fifth-century Megalopsychia mosaic of Daphne (Yakto), near Antioch. Photo by N. Lenski.

Eusebius reports that Diocletian had ordered the destruction of the basilica at Nicomedia in 303, but that Constantine rebuilt the church there "from his personal funds" (*ex oikeiōn thēsaurōn*). He claims this new church represented a sort of victory monument over the emperor's enemies and the foes of God, a predictable interpretation in light of the building's recent history, and one that Constantine may well have encouraged.[26] Eusebius also tells us that Constantine initiated construction on the famous Great Church at Antioch (Antakya), a unique and profoundly original octagon constructed to great heights and adorned with gold and bronze revetment.[27] Later textual sources on this structure—which has yet to be located archaeologically—as well as a possible depiction of it in a mosaic from nearby Daphne indicate that it was built alongside the imperial palace on the island in the River Orontes (Fig. 36).[28] Its collocation and construction would thus have represented a bold statement of the emperor's new religious priorities in this eastern capital. At Serdica (Sofia), excavations under the present church of Sveta Sofia have uncovered four late antique phases of building, the earliest of which dates to the first third of the fourth century. Although there is no secure connection with Constantine, the timing strongly suggest that he was involved.[29]

In the West, the same could be said of the imperial capital of Trier, where Constantine based his operations for most of the first decade of his reign. In these early years, he began the building of new baths and lavished the city with an elaborate palace whose gargantuan audience hall (*aula palatina*) still stands.[30] Sometime after 330, he appears to have torn down part of this palace complex in order to adjoin a new church whose remains have been partially excavated beneath the city's present basilica. Thus, as at Antioch, the emperor was not only embellishing the city with a new church, but he was also grafting this onto his own palace. Trier's new Christian basilica consisted of a double-halled structure (with two flanking naves), a type that then became common in this region in the fourth and fifth centuries (Fig. 37).[31] The date of the complex, whose dimensions rivaled those of the Lateran (73 × 68 meters), can be pinpointed to the late Constantinian period by numismatic finds from foundation trenches and by a passage of Athanasius recounting how he worshipped in the—still unfinished—basilica during his exile in Trier in the years 336 and 337.[32] In the same passage, Athanasius mentions that he also prayed in the newly built church of the regional capital of Aquileia, whose foundations have also been recovered archaeologically (Fig. 38). Its

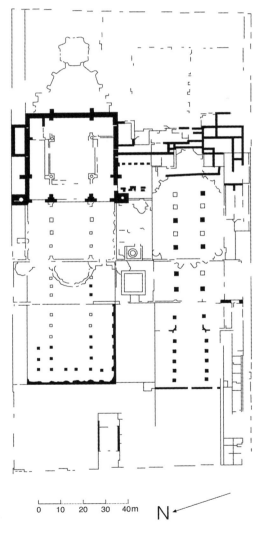

FIGURE 37. Plan of the fourth-century double basilica of Trier (outlines in bold). Drawing by D. Underwood, after Kuhnen, *Das römische Trier,* fig. 118, reproduced with permission.

FIGURE 38. Plan of the fourth-century double basilica of Aquileia, from Pelizzari, *Il Pastore ad Aquileia*, fig. 1, reproduced with permission.

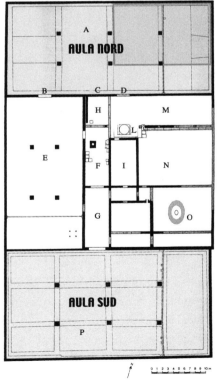

FIGURE 39. Dedicatory inscription of the Basilica Theodoriana of Aquileia (*ILCV* 1863 = *AE* 1986: 243), from Pelizzari, *Il Pastore ad Aquileia,* fig. 24, reproduced with permission.

Constantinian date is further secured by a roundel in the center of the structure's floor mosaic dedicated to the church's founder, Theodorus (Fig. 39).[33] Theodorus is known to have attended the Council of Arles as bishop of Aquileia in 314, and his bishopric is thought to have ended already in 319; thus the church is likely to have been built in the later 310s.[34] Interestingly, Aquileia's was also a double-halled basilica, although it was smaller than the complex at Trier (37 × 67 meters).[35] It has been argued that the dual naves at Aquileia and Trier, adjoined in the middle with what appear to have been baptisteries, were designed for liturgical purposes: one hall for catechumens and the second for the celebration of the Eucharist.[36] Whether or not this is true, the form clearly did not win wide acceptance in other regions of the empire, nor did it prevail over the longue durée.

Evidence for Constantinian ecclesial structures in Milan, Thessalonica, and Sirmium is, by contrast, lacking, but these are cities with a continuous habitation history up to the present, and consequently all have only fragmentary archaeological records. But the evidence for Nicomedia, Antioch, Trier, Serdica, and Aquileia—only two of which have similar habitation histories—offers ample proof that Constantine's church-building program was implemented quite actively in regional imperial capitals. Furthermore, in at least three instances—Antioch, Trier, and Aquileia—we find a pattern of experimentation in design that appears to have resulted from the situation described in the written sources: the emperor opened his purse for church construction but left architectural planning to the judgment of local authorities.

The same might be determined from the architecture of the churches of Rome. The Lateran church and St. Peter's were both laid out as *basilicae*, audience halls with a central nave and four aisles. Of course, this architectural form had been common across the city since the second century BCE, and although it would spread widely across the West as a standard for ecclesial structures in the years to come, it remains important to bear in mind that these earliest expressions of "imperial" church construction sprang up in Rome using a strikingly Roman form. Yet even this can be contrasted with most of the remaining churches of Rome from the period—that is, the martyr shrines built outside the Aurelian walls. These number six: San Lorenzo, San Agnese, Santi Marcellino e Pietro, San Sebastiano (the *Basilica Apostolorum*),[37] the church on the Via Ardeatina, and a church on the Via Praenestina. All follow a floor plan termed "circiform": a U-shaped structure with long sides capped at one end by a slightly oblique entry; in other words, following the shape of an ancient circus course (Fig. 40).[38] This peculiar plan, unheard of in other times and places, also represents a local invention of the era. Although the circiform martyrium did not catch on elsewhere, as the basilica was destined to do, its sudden and prolific abundance in Rome of the Constantinian era proves all the more emphatically that the emperor was working in dialogue with regional ecclesiastical leaders, providing them with an impetus and funding to build, but entrusting design and artistic details to local creativity.

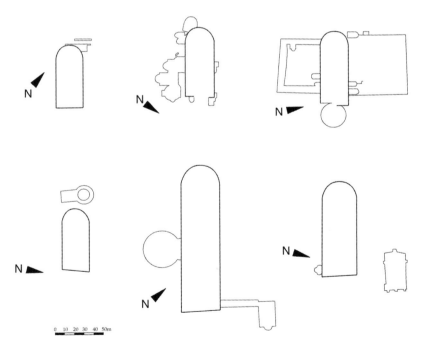

FIGURE 40. Schematic plans of six cemetery churches in Rome and its vicinity (top, left to right: San Lorenzo, Basilica Apostolorum, Santi Marcellino e Pietro; bottom, left to right: Via Praenestina, Sant'Agnese, Via Ardeatina). Drawing by D. Underwood, based on the plan at Fiocchi Nicolai, *Strutture funerarie,* fig. 29, reproduced with permission.

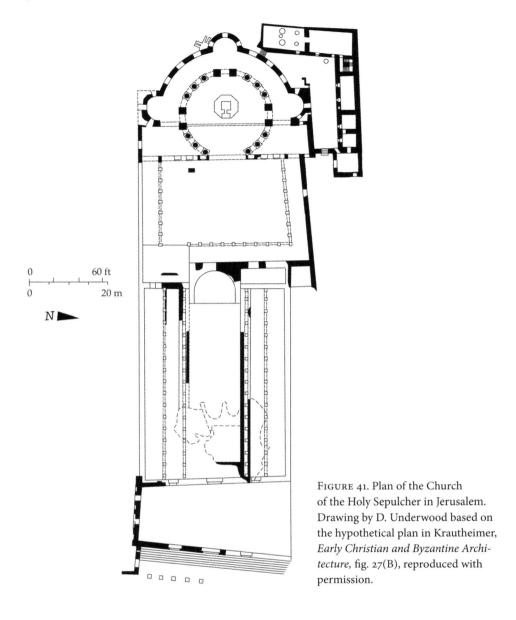

FIGURE 41. Plan of the Church
of the Holy Sepulcher in Jerusalem.
Drawing by D. Underwood based on
the hypothetical plan in Krautheimer,
*Early Christian and Byzantine Archi-
tecture,* fig. 27(B), reproduced with
permission.

In Palestine more than anywhere, this system was brought to its fullest realization, as Eusebius himself acknowledged both in the *Life of Constantine* and in
the oration he delivered at the dedication of the Church of the Holy Sepulchre in
335 (Fig. 41).[39] In addition to this massive complex and the new church at the site
of Mamre—the latter begun on the initiative of the queen mother Eutropia and
discussed in more detail in Chapter 12, Constantine also oversaw the construction of a church on the Mount of Olives and over the cave of Christ's birth in
Bethlehem (Fig. 42). In these latter two instances, we witness once again projects

whose original conception is reported to have come from someone other than the emperor himself, for Eusebius states explicitly that it was Helena who began work on the Eleona Church (on the Mount of Olives) and the Church of the Nativity.[40] This is not to say that Constantine would have been unhappy with these projects, but here as elsewhere he seems to have followed the principle of inviting Christian leaders—in this instance his own mother—to petition for help with projects that they themselves had first conceptualized. The churches of the Nativity, the Holy Sepulchre, and the Mount of Olives all display interrelated ground plans which combined a porticoed open atrium, a multi-aisled basilica, and a circular or polygonal structure at the rear of the complex that covered the sacred site each memorialized—the places of the incarnation, resurrection, and ascension. The Church of the Nativity, whose outlines are best known of the three, was also peculiar for being relatively wide and short, proportions that were unusual elsewhere but became common in Palestine—once again evidence for local control over design.[41] Moreover, as with the Roman churches, we learn something of the liquid wealth with which Constantine endowed these from Eusebius's report that the

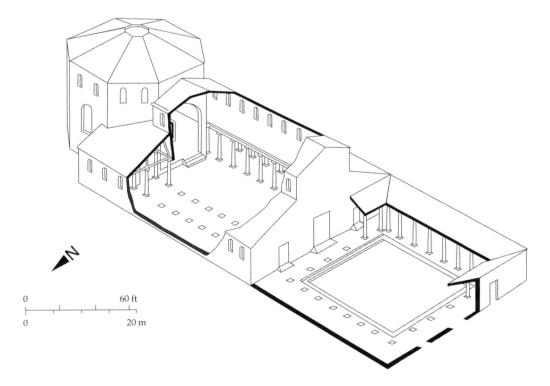

FIGURE 42. Isometric plan of the Church of the Nativity in Bethlehem. Drawing by D. Underwood based on the isometric reconstruction in Krautheimer, *Early Christian and Byzantine Architecture,* fig. 26, reproduced with permission.

emperor gave to the Church of the Holy Sepulchre, "a large number of offerings made of gold, silver, and precious stones."[42]

Epigraphic Evidence

It is a pity that the abundant testimonia to this church construction process include almost no inscriptions. Even the mosaic inscription of Theodorus's basilica at Aquileia, mentioned above, provides a Constantinian date but says nothing of the precise terms of the church's construction. A similar instance occurs in the Basilica of Stobi (Gradsko), whose earliest phase is also datable to the Constantinian period by a floor mosaic identifying its patron as bishop Budios—attested as having attended the Council of Nicaea.[43] Two further epigraphic attestations of churches built under Constantine can be found in Numidia and Phrygia. The former comes from the remains of a sizable basilica (26 × 16 meters) partially unearthed in 1843 at the tiny town of Castellum Tingitanum (el Asnam / Chlef, formerly Orléansville). Inlaid into its floor is a mosaic roundel inscribed with a now fragmentary text reporting that the foundations of the church were laid on November 22 in the 285th year of the province—that is, 324.[44] The date is striking, for it pinpoints the initiation of construction to just two months after the surrender of Licinius and thus to *precisely* the time when Eusebius tells us Constantine issued his empire-wide order for "buildings to be erected as places of worship and churches of God to be increased in breadth and length."[45] The end of the inscription makes it clear that this was a memorial church for a male martyr, perhaps a victim of the Great Persecution, although the name and further details of his death are now lost.[46] Although we cannot say with certainty that this edifice was built in response to Constantine's order, the evidence is highly suggestive.

The only Greek inscription firmly attesting the construction of a church in the Constantinian period has formerly been taken to reflect traditional patterns of civic euergetism rather than connections with this larger imperial program.[47] In light of the pattern of imperial impetus and funding coordinated with local design and implementation established above, this assumption surely bears reexamination. The epitaph of Marcus Julius Eugenius, bishop of Laodicea Katakekaumenē (about 250 kilometers east of Orcistus in eastern Phrygia) recounts the heroic story of this individual, who had once served in the office of Valerius Diogenes, governor of Pisidia, a notorious persecutor whom we met in Chapter 4. When Maximinus Daia ordered all of his officials to perform sacrifice, Eugenius chose instead to endure torture, but he eventually won release from office and moved to Laodicea, a city whose Christian population is well attested epigraphically from the early third century.[48] Shortly after his arrival, Eugenius was appointed bishop, an office he claims to have held for twenty-five years. Given that Diogenes's governorship dates to 311–312, Eugenius's death must have occurred around 337, making him a contemporary of Constantine's. Apart from his manful confession, Eugenius also records: "He rebuilt (*anoikodo[m]ēsas*) from its foundations the entire church and all the adornment around it, consisting of *stoai* and *tetrastoa* and paintings and mosaics and a fountain and outer gateway and furnished (*kataskeua[sas]*) it with all the construction in masonry and, in a word, with everything."[49]

Eugenius's inscription says nothing about where he obtained funding for all this work. It may well have come from his own pocket. Interestingly, however, he uses none of the phrases so common in building inscriptions that credit a dedicant with covering the costs of his or her own constructions.[50] Although Eugenius's silence on the role played by his personal wealth should not be overinterpreted, it remains possible, perhaps even likely, that he too tapped into the *res privata* to fund the construction of his church, even if he was able to take credit for its actual design and construction. If we had the building inscription from Macarius's Church of the Holy Sepulchre, where precisely this arrangement is well attested in the letter preserved by Eusebius, it may well tell a similar story. Under Constantine, bishops would not have been wrong to claim they had "built" churches and "furnished" them with embellishments, even if full disclosure would have required that they specify the money had come from the emperor's *res privata*.[51]

Conclusion

It is thus difficult to escape the impression that Constantine's was a well-defined program that provided imperial support in the form of liquid wealth, real estate, building materials, and manpower, supplied upon petition, derived from imperial estates, and managed through the intermediacy of imperial officials, which allowed Christian leaders to outfit their cities with impressive new structures built to suit their own tastes and demands. The impact of this program can hardly be overstated. On the broadest level, Constantine was jumpstarting a process of Christianizing ancient cities by inscribing their landscape all across his empire with massive Christian prayer houses.[52] Where the first four centuries of Roman rule in the West—and even in the East—had seen the introduction of *fora* and *capitolia* as standard "Roman" elements in the ground plan of cities, Constantine's program brought a new architectural cornerstone to urban infrastructure that moved Christianity firmly into the center of late antique civic life.[53] In this sense, his building program is to be understood alongside the inscription of Orcistus, which, as we have seen, made collective adherence to the Christian faith a new criterion for promotion to civic status. The church-building program also had effects at the regional level. In certain cities—certainly Trier and Antioch, but perhaps also others—church and palace were adjoined as one, giving locals a strong signal that Christianity was now the religion of empire. At Rome, the emphasis on the construction of martyr shrines brought the cult of the saints to local prominence in ways that affect the Roman church up to the present. In Palestine, Constantine's building program had far and away the greatest impact of all. Prior to the early fourth century, the region had been of only minor importance to the functioning of the church and its ritual and hierarchical ontology, but Constantine's construction of a Christian Holy Land pulled Christianity into an involvement with the Palestinian landscape that remains crucial to world religion and politics into the modern world.

CHAPTER 10

Empowering Bishops

Redistributing Power

At the same time that Constantine was redirecting landed and movable property from cities and temples to Christian churches and building Christian architecture into the urban infrastructure of cities, he was also working to transfer power from traditional civic magistrates to the officers of the church. Once again his steps in this direction were neither comprehensive nor decisive, but they pointed the way toward a shift in civic power that would, over the course of the next two centuries, become complete. In this chapter, we briefly examine this process in four primary arenas: Constantine's grant to bishops of the right to adjudicate civil cases with full reliance on imperial authorities for the enforcement of their decisions (*episcopale iudicium*); his institution of a new manumission process whereby Christian clergy could offer full and formal freedom to slaves in their places of worship; his opening of the use of the public posting system (*cursus publicus*) to Christian clergy; and his grant of curial immunity to Christian clerics. Each of these new privileges represented a significant departure from earlier precedent, and they quickly began to be overused and abused by individuals eager to seize on these new opportunities for personal gain. As with the grants of public subsidies, these new rights were thus repealed by Julian and later restored only with some reluctance—and considerable restrictions—by his Christian successors. Nevertheless, with this redistribution of power at the local level from civic aristocrats and members of the old curial elite to a new class of civic grandee, the bishop, Constantine was initiating a trend that would eventually result in the radical transformation of power structures at the local level in all ancient cities.[1]

The Power to Judge

The most obvious example of this is the attribution to local bishops of the right to judge civil cases. Already Matthew's gospel (18:15–17) and Paul's First Epistle to the Corinthians (6:1–6) admonish Christians to avoid bringing suit against one another in the courts of unbelievers and advise instead that they settle disputes among themselves. Following this same principle, the third-century *Didascalia Apostolorum* and its fourth-century descendant the *Constitutiones Apostolorum* set out procedures for Christians to settle conflicts before bishops.[2] Within six years of the Battle of the Milvian Bridge, Constantine issued legislation that formalized this process and integrated it into the state judicial apparatus by creating what he called *episcopale iudicium* (the bishop's jurisdiction), later referred to as *audientia episcopalis*.

Previous work on *audientia episcopalis* has been abundant, yet many questions remain, in large part because of difficulties in the source record.[3] C. Humfress has even gone so far as to suggest that the extant laws on the matter do not indicate the creation of a new judicial procedure but represent instead responses to petitions about a system of informal arbitration, long permitted in Roman law, that simply extended this authority to bishops.[4] This surely underestimates the scope of Constantine's innovation.

Extant Constantinian laws on the question number just two: *Theodosian Code* 1.27.1 of June 23, 318,[5] and *Sirmondian Constitution* 1 of May 5, 333. Although they constitute meager evidence, both offer clear signs that these were only part of what was originally a larger dossier of legislation on the matter. The former is transmitted through the *Theodosian Code*, whose compilers heavily abbreviated original laws as part of their process of excerption. Furthermore, it derives from that part of the *Code* that was not transmitted to modern times in the manuscript tradition and which must therefore be reconstructed—with major gaps—from the *Justinian Code* and the *Breviarium of Alaric*.[6] It is thus possible that *CTh* 1.27.1 was not Constantine's only law on *episcopale iudicium* in the *Code* as originally published. Moreover, it is certain that this constitution lacks a considerable amount of its original verbiage, which would have recorded the details surrounding its issuance and possibly more specifics on the provisions of the law itself. Nevertheless, as transmitted, 1.27.1 shows no obvious evidence that it responds to a specific case at law. On the contrary, at first face it would appear to be a general law stating that any suit may be brought for resolution to the bishop's jurisdiction, even if it had already been initiated before a civil judge. Moreover, the law states that the decisions of bishops should be considered "as sacred" (*pro sanctis*), an unusual expression that, as J. N. Dillon has explained, surely means that—like the decisions of the emperor and those entitled to issue judgments in his stead (*vice sacra*)—the bishop's decision was not subject to appeal.[7] The only restriction stated in the law was that the decision to transfer legal venue had to be formally announced to the judge from whose jurisdiction the case had been removed.

The second law, *Sirmondian* 1, is preserved in its entirety and makes clear reference to an earlier Constantinian law, whether this means *CTh* 1.27.1 or—more likely—an even earlier enactment that is no longer extant.[8] It twice calls this earlier law "our edict," a specific type of constitution that explicitly does *not* respond to an individual query but lays out general dispositions.[9] That said, *Sirm.* 1 *is* itself clearly a response to a specific query about whether a bishop's decision might be appealed if it had been issued in a case involving minors, whose appeals were normally governed by special rules. Constantine's answer affirms the inviolability of the bishop's decision, which—once again—is to be considered "as sacred" (*pro sanctis*) even in this instance.[10] In the process, the constitution informs us further of the nature of the original enactment: it permits the transfer of a case to a bishop's court even if only one party in the suit requests this,[11] and it permits the bishop to use officers of the state for the execution of his judgment.[12] The former point represents a remarkable show of favoritism for Christian litigants. Even more strikingly, the latter demonstrates that this was much more than just the formalization of arbitration processes conducted by bishops: it was rather a grant of authority to bishops to undergird their judgments with the full force of the imperial administration—the bishop's judgments were to be enforced by the emperor's officers.[13] This represents a significant departure from other forms of arbitration attested for earlier periods,[14] for Constantine's *episcopale iudicium* integrates the bishop into the larger scheme of imperial jurisdiction, making his decisions not only equivalent to those of secular magistrates, but even superior to those of any official other than Urban and Praetorian Prefects, whose decisions were also unappealable.[15]

In granting this broad leeway, Constantine had by all means gone too far.[16] Though some bishops had a background in Roman law, most did not, leaving them ill equipped to adjudicate imperial law on the bewildering variety of questions they now faced.[17] Furthermore, bishops often resented this additional demand on their time, and even when they did grant a judicial audience, they regularly attempted to resolve cases in ways that emphasized mediation and compromise rather than adherence to the norms and procedures of Roman law.[18] It is for this reason that we find only limited evidence for the law's implementation in the early fourth century, and by the 360s Julian appears to have repealed it—in keeping with his tendency, already witnessed in Chapter 8, to nullify Constantine's efforts to transfer civic power to the church and its officials.[19] The evidence for its reimplementation later in the fourth century is spotty, but by the fifth, a lengthy constitution issued by Valentinian III imposes serious restrictions on episcopal jurisdiction and alludes to further limitations already in place but no longer traceable in extant sources.[20] In this sense, Constantine's initial efforts to create episcopal jurisdiction were something of a failure, for they aimed to establish a structure that was poorly delimited, overly grandiose in its conception, and too reliant on idealistic assumptions about the pious intentions of bishops and the reliability of their divinely inspired legal reasoning.[21] Even so, by attributing to bishops the authority to adjudge civil cases, Constantine opened a new avenue to power that would eventually widen considerably. Indeed, although the bishop did not immediately replace the city councilor or governor as the primary arbiter of legal disputes, the expectations created by Constantine's laws led to the rise of a new forum at the local and regional levels that would only grow in importance over time.[22] The first Christian emperor thus set a bold new course that, although it had to be corrected significantly, made a lasting impact on the bishop's rise to dominance.

Manumission in Churches

Around the same time Constantine was turning bishops into judges of first resort, he also empowered them with the related authority to manumit slaves in their churches in such a way as to bestow on them full Roman citizenship. Our first testimony to this comes with a law preserved only in the *Justinian Code* and dated June 8, 316.[23] This law is clearly a rescript to a cleric named Protogenes that was meant to confirm the right of clerics to manumit their own slaves in whatever form they wished. Nevertheless, it mentions an earlier ruling by which, "in a Catholic church, masters may grant freedom to their own slaves, if they do this in the presence of the people with Christian priests attending."[24] We do in fact have one further extant law on the manumission of slaves by bishops from Constantine's pen, but it dates later than *CJ* 1.13.1 and clearly represents a further extension of the rights of clerics to manumit their own slaves without formalities.[25] Fortunately, however, we also have the testimony of the church historian Sozomen, himself a lawyer, that Constantine in fact issued three laws on the question that were still in circulation in his day.[26] The original grant of this privilege must, therefore, predate the June 316 law and is thus likely to fall close in time to Constantine's grant to bishops of the right to adjudicate civil suits. Formerly, grants of full manumission had been attainable only when freedom was either offered in a will or ratified in front of a Roman magistrate. By extending the authority to endow freed slaves with full citizenship to bishops, Constantine was thus taking further steps in assimilating these church leaders to magistrates and thus establishing them as the supreme power brokers at the civic level. Furthermore, because these manumissions had to take place inside churches, he was showcasing these new structures, some built at his own expense and with his encouragement, as seats of civic administration.

The Public Posting System

Yet another extraordinary privilege granted by Constantine to clerics was the right to use the imperial post system (*cursus publicus*) for ecclesiastical business. The post service, which not only transported missives and grain rations across the empire but also provided livery stables with horses and wagons for use by imperial officials, had always been strictly regulated.[27] Constantine himself felt compelled to issue a series of rules limiting its employment because of the ease with which this privilege could be abused.[28] Nevertheless, by 314 he began granting Christian clerics the right to use the *cursus publicus* for transport to church councils, as attested in a letter preserved by Eusebius permitting Chrestus, bishop of Syracuse, to travel to Arles on a public wagon along with two of his clergymen and three servants for the council to be held there.[29] Two documents preserved in Optatus confirm that the same privilege was granted to a number of African bishops who attended the council as well.[30]

The same privilege is also attested for the Council of Nicaea in 325 when, Eusebius says, many bishops were granted the right to a post wagon and others the use of pack animals.[31] Bishops traveled to the Council of Jerusalem in the summer of 335 with the imperial post, and Constantine also allowed Eusebius to use the post system for transporting to Constantinople copies of the scriptures he was preparing.[32] Even the heretic Arius and the schismatic bishop John Arkaph were given a post warrant to travel to Constantinople for meetings with the emperor.[33] As with the grant of *episcopalis audientia*, this new right elevated bishops within their civic communities but also created a host of unintended expenses and problems. Ammianus roundly criticized Constantius II for "splitting the sinews of the public post" by transporting bishops back and forth to councils, and the privilege was greatly restricted by Julian, whose reign was a watershed beyond which warrants were granted much more sparingly.[34] Here again, the familiar pattern: an overzealous Constantine opens the floodgates of imperial benefaction to the church and its officials, thereby creating problems for his successors to solve, but also precedents that forever increased the authority of the bishop.

Exemption from Curial Service

A similar redistribution of power at the civic level was also enacted with Constantine's grant of exemption from curial service to bishops. One of our best pieces of evidence on the matter is preserved in Eusebius's *Ecclesiastical History*. It is a Greek translation of a letter to the Proconsul of Africa Anullinus from 313[35] in which Constantine reports that he wishes to reward the servants of the church by

exempting them from all public duties in order that they may pay proper attention to God and thus benefit the state. The dispositive part of the letter states:

> Wherefore those persons who . . . bestow their service on this holy reli-
> gion, that is those whom they are accustomed to call clerics, should, I
> declare, be kept free from all public offices [*apo pantōn tōn leitourgiōn*]
> altogether, lest by any error or sacrilegious negligence they be drawn away
> from the service due to the Deity, but rather that they may serve to the
> utmost their own law without any hindrance.[36]

The *Theodosian Code* preserves the same law, although it is addressed not to the
Proconsul of Africa but rather to the governor (*corrector*) of Lucania and Brut-
tium, Octavianus:

> Those persons who devote the services of their reverence to the divine
> religion, that is, those who are called clerics, are to be excused from all
> public offices [*ab omnibus muneribus*] altogether, lest through the sacrile-
> gious envy of others they be called away from divine obedience.[37]

As is entirely normal, the *Code* version is somewhat abbreviated, but its similari-
ties in wording and structure make it certain that what we have here are two
exemplars of a single imperial law, an edict issued in the form of an epistle.[38]
Thus, within a year of openly professing his conversion, Constantine was issuing
a law valid throughout his western territories granting curial exemption to Christian clergy.[39]

There can be no doubt that this privilege was designed as a reward to church
leaders, a benefit intended to relieve them of the financial and administrative
responsibilities of curial service.[40] But Constantine's language reveals that another
issue was also at stake. The last clause ("lest by any error or sacrilegious negli-
gence they be drawn away from the service due to the Deity") is almost certainly
a reference to public sacrifice. The heads of curial and provincial councils were
also chief priests in the local chapters of the imperial cult, holding titles like
flamen (city priest) or *sacerdos coronatus* (provincial priest). This was because, up
through the early fourth century, curial service necessarily entailed the performance of sacrifice, making it extremely problematic for Christians. For this reason, the church council that met at Elvira (Illiberis) circa 300 ordered the permanent excommunication of any Christian who had been appointed *flamen* and
performed sacrifice after receiving baptism, and it demanded extensive penance
even from those who had declined to perform sacrifice but nevertheless remained
in office as *flamines*.[41] The council also laid out provisions for any imperial cult

priests (*sacerdotes*) who wished to convert: those who had only worn priestly crowns but not performed sacrifices or paid for offerings to idols could communicate after a two-year waiting period.[42] Even those who had merely assumed the civic magistracy of *duumvir* were forbidden to enter the church during their year in office.[43] In granting exemption from curial service to clergy, then, Constantine was in no small part shielding this elite class of Christians from the need to sully themselves with the rites that went hand in glove with civic office holding.[44] Nor did the association between curial service and pagan worship disappear once Constantine gained power. In some regions the titles *flamen* and *sacerdos* continued to be used of curial and provincial magistrates deep into the fifth century, and it has even been argued that some councils persevered in coordinating ritual veneration of the emperor and his statues into the 430s, albeit without the practice of sacrifice.[45] This was obviously an important concern of Constantine's when he granted exemption to the clergy from curial service, a point that is clear already in the two copies of the 313 law making the initial grant.

This same concern is also evident from a law of December 323 that threatens with clubbing any who, the emperor has learned, have compelled ecclesiastics and clerics to perform lustral sacrifices in conjunction with curial celebrations.[46] The law was issued from Sirmium—near the border with Licinius's territory— even as tensions between Constantine and Licinius were reaching their apex, in no small part over Licinius's increasing harshness against Christian clergy, some of whom he forcibly enrolled into *curiae* in contravention of Constantine's grant of exemption. O. Seeck first saw that the December 323 law must have been issued against councilors in those Balkan cities still controlled by Licinius who had compelled Christian clergymen to perform cult sacrifices for Licinius's *quindecennalia*, celebrated on November 11, 323.[47] In this specific instance, therefore, we see Constantine's main concern to be the protection of bishops and clergy from the need to make the sacrifices associated with traditional civic ceremonial.[48] Constantine's grant to Christian clergy of exemption from curial obligations was thus designed in no small part to free the Christian priestly class from connections with a type of service that would have required their participation in traditional pagan ceremonies. In the bargain, however, it represented yet another privilege that would have attracted potential candidates to the episcopacy with the promise of release from mandatory services that, by the fourth century, had become an unwelcome burden for local middling aristocrats.

With this exemption, Constantine appears once again to have overlooked possible unintended consequences. These began to emerge within a few months of the initial grant. First the question arose of which clerics were eligible for this privilege: did these include clergy from sects regarded as schismatic or heretical? This issue was raised in a letter to Constantine written shortly after his initial legislation on the matter by the same Anullinus to whom the first letter granting immunity in Africa had been sent. In it the governor explains that the followers of Maiorinus, who refused to acknowledge Caecilianus as bishop of Carthage, were hoping for immunity for their own claimant to the Carthaginian see.[49] With a law of October 31, 313, preserved not in Eusebius but in the *Theodosian Code*, Constantine answered in terms that would have brought the schismatics little comfort. In it he reports, "clerics of the Catholic church" (*ecclesiae catholicae clericos*) were being forced by the "faction of the heretics" (*haereticorum factione*) to perform municipal services contrary to his new grant of immunity. The law orders its recipient—whose name is no longer preserved but who is likely once again to have been Anullinus—to prevent this from happening.[50] This is also the tenor of a constitution of September 1, 326, to the Vicar of Oriens denying curial immunity to heretical or schismatic clergymen.[51] The same refusal was repeated in yet another law of 330 to the governor of Numidia, a law to which Constantine himself refers in a separate letter of that same year written to the church at Cirta in which the emperor insists that those Catholic churchmen forced into curial service by the "heretics" should be immediately released.[52]

These issues may have come to a head in the West in response to another law of June 1, 329, preserved in a copy to the eastern Praetorian Prefect Ablabius. In it Constantine set out comprehensive and strict regulations on eligibility for curial immunity: (1) the number of clerical positions available was to be limited; (2) posts were to be filled only on the death of a sitting cleric; (3) those chosen for the clergy were not to be of curial descent nor to be allowed to have fortunes large enough to require curial service; and (4) city councils were permitted to recall into service any curials who had evaded these provisions and won appointment to the clergy.[53] Later that same summer, Constantine qualified this final provision in another enactment permitting exemptions to those who had entered the clergy prior to the issuance of the June 1 law.[54] His grant of curial exemption to clerics had thus opened yet another set of floodgates, this time to those eager to escape the burdens imposed by service on a local city council: what started off as a boon and a shield from polluting ritual had become a boondoggle and a weapon for punishing sectarian opponents. Not having anticipated these consequences, Constantine had to impose restrictions on service in the clergy, which he had suddenly transformed into a coveted tax shelter and refuge from mandatory obligations. In this sense, curial immunity became at once a tool of empowerment for a new group of civic elites but also a site of contention around which various sects and creeds fought.

Constantine's exemptions were soon extended by Constantius II, who went so far as to grant tax immunity to clerics as well as their wives, children, and even slaves.[55] Constantine's concerns about rewarding the clergy and assisting them in the avoidance of polluting civic ritual had thus opened the door for this group to separate themselves from the traditional organs of civic governance even as he greatly expanded their wealth and power through new immunities, privileges, and subventions. Seeing the consequences of this, Julian revoked curial exemption, as he had done with grants to clergy of revenues from imperial properties.[56] His efforts to undo what Constantine had set in motion are mirrored at the local level by a lengthy inscription from Timgad cataloging the city's entire curial order in 361. It lists eleven members of the clergy (*clerici*) in such a way that it is clear these continued to be exempted from curial service but were nevertheless obliged to fulfill the financial obligations (*munera*) associated with curial office.[57] Once again, however, Julian's reversal was itself reversed and the exemption restored under Valentinian and Valens, albeit with considerable restrictions. This more limited immunity then continued throughout the remainder of Late Antiquity.[58] Here too, then, we see Constantine almost stumbling his way into effecting a shift in local power relations. Originally intended as a religious gesture, clerical immunity created additional and unexpected complications that demanded a serious course correction, but ultimately led to the rise of a new tax-exempt class of local leaders who operated independently of the city councils that had formerly controlled local politics.

Conclusion

Constantine thus created a number of privileges for members of the Christian clergy, particularly bishops, that transformed Christian religious office into a desirable career choice and a significant new locus of power at the civic level. Chief among these was the invention of episcopal jurisdiction whereby Constantine endowed bishops with the right to adjudicate civil suits with unappealable decisions enforced by imperial administrative authority. Far from constituting a mere institutionalization of traditional arbitration procedures, *episcopale iudicium* turned bishops' courts into the venue of first resort for civil law adjudication at the local level. He also granted bishops the right to manumit slaves formally in their churches and thus to privilege freedmen with Roman citizenship. Both of these powers had formerly been reserved for magistrates operating under the authority of the emperor himself. By sharing these powers with bishops, he was establishing them as a sort of vice-magistrate and as such vaulting them above the power of the decurions with whom they shared civic power at the local level. Bishops were also regularly permitted the use of the *cursus publicus*, a right formerly guarded jealously by the imperial administration and, once again, generally reserved for imperial officials and close friends of the emperor. Finally, Constantine granted clerics exemption from the need to serve as curials in their local city councils. This measure was designed both to reward Christian clergy for their service to God and to prevent them from performing the pagan ceremonials traditionally associated with service in the curia.

In all of these instances, Constantine had taken a giant step down the road to converting the bishop and his clergy into a new class of civic leader separate from and much more powerful than the traditional curial order. Although civic curiae had been losing power and membership well before Constantine, his establishment of the bishop as a counterpoint to these surely contributed greatly to the precipitous decline experienced by city councils as the fourth century progressed.[59] Knowing this, Julian the Apostate reversed Constantine's policy and attempted to restore traditional religious and political power structures in the cities.[60] In many ways his about-face proved useful to subsequent rulers, for in every instance Constantine's grants of power to the clergy had gone too far, and Julian's efforts to reset the standards allowed his successors to place limitations on Constantine's excessive liberality. Nevertheless, the Christian rulers of the later fourth century were essentially obliged to return these privileges to the church and its leaders, albeit in curtailed form, for Constantine had set in motion a process of transforming the bishops into major power brokers in civic politics who could not be disempowered.[61]

PART IV

~

ALTERNATIVE
RESPONSES
TO CONSTANTINE

CHAPTER 11

Engaging Cities

Accessing Alternative Constantines

An emperor's relationship with his people was always discursive. To be sure, he generally had the upper hand in any dialogue, for by virtue of his vast administrative, military, and symbolic power, he could control access to governmental authority, to the enforcement of his writ, and to the downward flow of publicly generated information. Nevertheless, he could never firmly control reactions to his efforts to govern, nor predict public readings of the image of his imperial persona he strove to project. The slippage between his exertions and their efficacy as speech acts generated the need to adjust his actions to the responses of his people, just as his people constantly shifted their reactions to take account of his evolving expressions of power.

This dynamic played itself out not just at the level of subject citizens but also at that of polities. Cities and towns had a sort of personality of their own that was defined by the traditions, the leadership, and the infrastructure each inherited and passed on from one generation to the next. To be sure, each community was complex and multiform, and all shifted and adapted their collective identity over time. But just as one personality differs from the next, so a city like Rome differed from Alexandria, or Athens, and a town like Orcistus from Nacoleia, or Aquileia, in ways that set each apart as a unique and definable space of collective identity. As a corollary to this principle, each city and town was bound to have its own reactions to the emperor, who, in his turn, was obliged to modulate his approach to any given polity in ways that, at least ideally, would foster harmony between ruler and subject along the horizons of their mutual expectations.[1]

In the sixth and seventh chapters we examined a group of cities whose expectations aligned well with the dominant reading of Constantine's public message in the period after he began advertising his conversion to Christianity. In the twelfth, we will look at those places that self-consciously opposed Constantine's message in ways that provoked violent reactions from the emperor. In this present chapter we focus instead on those polities whose dealings with Constantine reflect a negotiated reading, neither entirely in line with what the emperor may have wished nor entirely in opposition to key messages he transmitted. As we reflect on their reactions, we will witness a dialogue with a ruler who could be engaged in ways much more reflexive of traditional religious norms than we might be led to expect by, for example, Constantine's correspondence with ecclesiastics. We will see, in other words, a cluster of pagan Constantines, each conceptualized along locally conditioned parameters that reflect in part images projected by the emperor himself and in part the expectations and desires of the cities engaging with him. Theirs was neither the right reading of Constantine nor the wrong one, but simply an alternative Constantine, a Constantine that could be accommodated into the context of their own locally delimited understanding of proper rulership.

Naturalizing the Emperor

No city better epitomizes a general adherence to traditional religious principles in Late Antiquity than Athens.[2] With its alluring reputation as a religious and cultural center, and its unprecedented status as a magnet for those seeking a traditional education, Athens stood for all that was great in the classical past, from its literature to its gods. Constantine gained control of Athens in the aftermath of his defeat of Licinius at Cibalae in 316 and thus in the period when his readiness to hem in pagan cult and practice had only begun to quicken. Yet far from punishing the city, he lavished it with emoluments. This we learn from no less jaundiced a critic than Constantine's nephew Julian:

> Here it might be proper to mention Athens, the illustrious, seeing that during his whole life he honored her in word and deed. He who was emperor and lord of all did not disdain the title of General [*stratēgos*] of the Athenians, and when they gave him a statue with an inscription to that effect he felt more pride than if he had been awarded the highest honors. To repay Athens for this compliment, he bestowed on her annually a gift of many tens of thousands of bushels of wheat to enjoy, so that while she experienced plenty, he won applause and reverence from the best of men [*para tōn beltistōn*].[3]

For Julian, "the best of men" can only have meant fellow pagans, and indeed, we know two specific examples of pagan Athenians who supported Constantine in this period. The first, Praxagoras, wrote a two-book panegyrical history of the

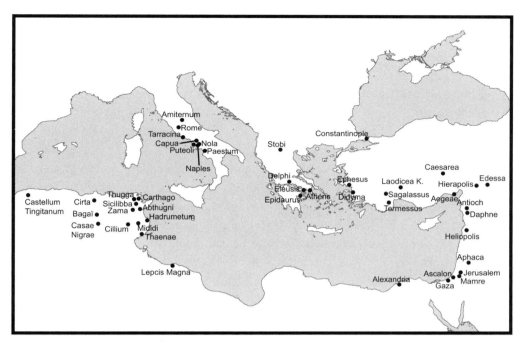

Map 7. Engaging Cities/Resisting Cities

emperor, only a small fragment of which survives.[4] Praxagoras came from an extremely prominent Athenian family, with ancestors, many of whom served as archons, that can be traced back to the first century CE from extant epigraphy, and that seems even to have boasted connections stretching back to Pericles and Alexander the Great. He was also a prominent pagan, coming as he did from a family of *dadouchoi*, torch-bearers for the cult of Demeter at Eleusis.[5] The second, Nicagoras, son of Minucianus, was sent by Constantine in 326 on an embassy to the Valley of the Kings in Egypt and there left two graffiti on the Colossi of Memnon at Thebes, a hallowed site of pilgrimage for pagans.[6] Nicagoras was himself a *daduchos,* and he has also been identified as a priest of the cult of Asclepius Sōtēr from a series of inscriptions at Epidaurus.[7] Praxagoras and Nicagoras were thus committed, open, and quite influential adherents of the ancient cults of Attica who both befriended and served Constantine. In one of Nicagoras's Theban inscriptions from the later 320s, the Athenian gives "thanks to the gods and to the Most Pious Constantine," a juxtaposition that reveals much about the manner in which this subject approached his emperor. Both figures will surely have played a role in convincing Constantine to lavish grandiose favors on their city and especially the annual grant of "many tens of thousands of bushels of wheat."[8]

For his part, Constantine benefited from this relationship as well, not only gaining the support and praise of these prominent rhetoricians but also winning his way into the good graces of the Athenian elite, which, as Julian reveals, granted him the title General of the Athenians and an honorific statue. Nor was this the only such image in the city, for the recent re-publication of a series of fragmentary inscriptions from Athens's Roman Agora has shown that the city in fact dedicated a group of five statues to Constantine and his Caesars during the final years of his reign.[9] The economy of power and praise was thus well primed with ongoing exchanges between the emperor and this quintessentially pagan metropolis. By channeling contact between the ruler and their city through pagan members of their elite and by according Constantine the indigenous office of *stratēgos*[10] and a prominently placed statuary group, the Athenians exercised great influence in this dialogic relationship. They formulated their discourse along lines that they themselves defined and thereby succeeded in imagining an Athenian Constantine who could represent their values and benefit them with material and symbolic favors.

Several other cities also used aspects of Constantine's self-presentation that coincided with their own interests and preconceptions in order to access an emperor with whom they felt comfortable communicating.[11] Sagalassus in Pisidia, for example, dedicated an honorific inscription to the Augustus and his three Caesars, Constantine II, Constantius II, and Constans, on the stone marking the *caput viae* for roads leading out from its lower agora. The inscription is in Latin but is recorded above an epigraph in Greek reading:

> The sacred and splendid
> and glorious, twice *neōkoros*,
> city of the Sagalassans,
> first city of Pisidia,
> friend and ally
> of the Romans.[12]

This Greek text may or may not have been contemporaneous with the dedication to Constantine that precedes it. Regardless, the dedication was carefully and consciously collocated above it in a fashion that indicates a deliberate juxtaposition of the two texts. Constantine and his sons were thus embedded in the larger narrative of a city that openly boasted of its status as twice *neōkoros*—that is, host to two imperial cult temples.[13] This is striking in light of the fact that the Latin dedication can be dated after the proclamation of Constans as Caesar in 333, and thus in the final years of Constantine's reign. Yet in precisely these halcyon days, when Constantine was most unabashed about the public promotion of Christianity, the Sagalassans approached him, even as the Hispellates had done, through the medium of the imperial cult. For centuries imperial cult had served as a site of mediation that could bridge the distance between subject and emperor through the exchange of honor in return for local authority.[14] Not wishing to part with this mode of discourse, the Sagalassans cleverly joined ruler (Constantine and sons), civic privilege (first city of Pisidia), and imperial cult (twice *neōkoros*) in their inscription and thus reaffirmed the relationship between the two in a mode of discourse they expected would endure.

Another Pisidian city, Termessus, was also concerned to engage with Constantine as a ruler who shared their reverence for traditional religion. There we find a brief but monumental inscription on a large statue base (1.04m high × 1.84m wide × 0.81m deep) still visible in the city's agora:

> To Constantine Aug(ustus),
> the Sun
> All-Seeing [*pantepoptē*],
> the *dēmos*.[15]

The top of the base is furnished with fittings for a larger-than-life-sized equestrian statue in bronze. In a superb study, I. Tantillo has shown that the first line of the inscription was carved at a later date than the three following, which originally honored a local god named "The All-Seeing Sun" (*Hēlios Pantepoptēs*). This deity is known from inscriptions to have had a temple at Termessus since the second century CE.[16] A coin of the city depicts the same Hēlios Pantepoptēs with a radiate crown riding on a horse, probably a reproduction of the statue as it appeared on this same base (Fig. 43).[17] When confronted with an emperor whose propaganda so widely advertised his attachment to the solar god, the Termessans apparently chose to honor him by assimilating Constantine to their local solar divinity (Fig. 44). By converting their emperor into a manifestation of this indigenous god, they naturalized him in ways that allowed them to legitimate their own religious practice under imperial auspices.

This sort of homology will have been facilitated by imperial rhetoric that continued up to Constantine's final years in power. Eusebius's *Tricennalian Oration*,

FIGURE 43. Obverse: TEPM–HCCEΩ–N. Bearded bust of Zeus(?) right. Reverse: Legend illegible. Radiate rider on horseback right, cape trailing. Bronze coin of Termessus. *SNG Deutschland, Sammlung von Aulock* 12: 5355 pl. 117. Yale University Art Gallery, Ruth Elizabeth White Fund 2004.6.3281. Open access.

FIGURE 44. Hypothetical reconstruction of the Termessus monument featuring Constantine as Helios Pantepoptēs, after Tantillo, "Costantino e Helios Pantepoptēs," fig. 5. Drawing by Francesca Bigi, reproduced with permission.

for example, flatters Constantine with similar comparisons: "riding across the totality of the earth as far as the Sun watches, he is present in all places and looks out over all."[18] Similar conclusions could be drawn from Constantine's *Oration to the Saints*, which says that god "is always present, a seer of our actions," and calls for Constantine's subjects to offer praise to "the seer of all things."[19] The letter Constantine sent to cities reporting the findings of the Council of Nicaea in 325 similarly asserts that inquiry was held "until a judgment pleasing to the all-seeing god . . . was brought to light."[20] So too, in a letter of Constantine's preserved in Athanasius's *Apology Against the Arians* and dating to 335, Constantine speaks of "the god who sees over all things."[21] Encountering such language and symbols from the court, the Termessans knew perfectly well who Constantine and his divine spirit were, for he had lived among them for centuries. When they chose to recognize Constantine by rededicating their statue of Hēlios Pantepoptēs to him, they were thus assimilating his message on their own locally conditioned terms.

Cultivating a Pagan Constantine

The famous shrine at Delphi, which had its own independent council that oper-ated alongside that of the neighboring city, offers another example of a local pol-ity struggling to invent a Constantine consonant with its peculiar conceptions of the emperor and its own religious interests. The sacred precinct had enjoyed a run of prosperity in the half century before Constantine's takeover of Greece in 316. In the late third and early fourth centuries, it had witnessed the construction of a new market space, the "Roman Agora," as well as a new set of baths (the so-called East Baths) below its terrace of Attalos.[22] An inscription of 319 records a decree of the shrine's councillors (*damiourgoi*) reporting that one of their own, Lucius Gellius Mēnogenēs, together with his wife, Aurelia Iulia Sōtia, had just given an endowment of one million denarii for the rebuilding and provisioning of the East Baths.[23] Mēnogenēs, who was a holder of priesthoods in both Delphi and Athens, was thus operating according to traditional euergetic norms, follow-ing traditional protocols in support of this ever so traditional temple. Here in these earliest years of Constantine's rule over Delphi, the shrine had every reason to expect happy days ahead.

This was surely reaffirmed by first impressions from Constantine. The new emperor had, of course, been an openly professed devotee of the shrine's imma-nent god Apollo since the beginning of his reign, and coins featuring his divine companion, Sol Invictus, no doubt circulated in the hands of Delphians down to the emperor's death. Nevertheless, following his rise to sole rule in 324, Constan-tine had grown increasingly harsh in his rhetoric against pagan practice in gen-eral, but also against Apolline prophecy more particularly. In his letter to the eastern provincials of 324, he rails against the oracles that helped launch the Great Persecution,[24] oracles given from Apollo's shrines in Didyma in Asia and Daphne in Syria—nevertheless, not, to our knowledge, from Delphi.[25] In 313 Licinius had seen to the execution of the individuals whose interpretation of these oracles had provoked the tetrarchs to open violence against Christians.[26] Yet, after gaining control of Achaia in 316 and the remainder of the East in 324, Constantine appears to have done little if anything to punish the shrines themselves.[27] Indeed, in the *Oration to the Saints*, he made no bones about citing Apollo's priestess, the Eryth-raean Sibyl, as an accurate prophet of the coming of Christ, and he turned to her once again in 333 to argue that she had also foretold the coming of Arius and his heresy.[28] As we explored in Chapter 2, Constantine even gave signs in his new eastern capital that he favored the Sun God until the time of his death.[29] In light of these mixed signals, Delphi must surely have hoped that Constantine's ongoing attachment to Apollo could serve as a point of common contact with the emperor.

These expectations proved illusory when, in order to embellish his new capital of Constantinople, Constantine did irreparable damage to the patrimony of the shrine by confiscating a number of its most prized dedications—its famous serpent column, its statues of the Heliconian Muses, and above all its tripod—for display in the city's public spaces.[30] Given that he then grouped these cultic objects into a sort of Apolline precinct in Constantinople's hippodrome, however, even this was by no means an unambiguous gesture of irreverence.[31] Furthermore, there is every indication that oracular prophecy continued to issue from Delphi's shrine—as indeed from that of Didyma—into the reign of Julian, and from Daphne's up to the mid-350s.[32] Insofar as any of the three oracular sites saw encroachment from Christians—and Delphi did not—this resulted from neighboring Christian believers moving their dwellings and even relics of their martyrs into the temple precinct to take advantage of the protection of its walls.[33] Christian intrusion into Apolline shrines in the late third and early fourth centuries was not, therefore, the result of active interference by the emperors. Constantine had thus nudged Delphi with the removal of its hallowed art treasures but by no means threatened its survival nor even the continuation of its sacred rites.

Only in 341 and thus early in Constantius II's reign did worship at Delphi come under threat. This is revealed in an inscription that has yet to be properly edited, but a translation of which was published by P. Athanassiadi in 1991. It records a letter from the Praetorian Prefects Leontius, Titianus, and Placidus to Count Flavius Felicianus, "who has merited the priesthood of Pythian Apollo" and "who has been raised to every single honor by our deified [*en theois*] emperor"—that is, Constantine.[34] The letter laments that Felicianus had been disturbed in his exercise of the priesthood and guarantees that any further assaults would lead to exile for the troublemaker(s). The affronts it mentions may well have arisen from overzealous enforcement of the edict *cesset superstitio* issued against sacrifice in this same year.[35] Regardless, this response from the college of prefects makes it clear that worship at Delphi was to continue unmolested.

The inscription sheds light on Delphi's relationship with Constantine on two levels. First, the Delphians' choice to enlist Count Felicianus as one of their priests clearly betrays an effort to cultivate favor from a patron with strong Constantinian ties. Felicianus had been appointed *comes orientis* in 335 by Constantine himself and stationed in Antioch to calm the city as it witnessed the transformation of its landscape through the introduction of Christian monuments.[36] From numerous sources, we also know that Felicianus was appointed Ordinary Consul by Constantine for 337, although this appointment was not—as we shall see—without problems of its own.[37] The Delphians were thus quite shrewd in choosing this prominent pagan to reward with so lofty an honor, for his connections with the highest levels of the Constantinian administration clearly insulated them from the need to make radical compromises to their religious practices. Second, the decree's reference to Constantine as "our deified emperor" illustrates the city's preference for engaging the deceased ruler along lines laid out by the traditions of imperial cult. Indeed, we have two further inscriptions of Delphi, both marking statue bases and both apparently posthumous, one of which refers to Constantine as "our deified lord," as if the Delphians wished to validate their adherence to traditional practice by coopting the apotheosized emperor as a local divinity.[38] There can be little doubt that the Delphians would have resented Constantine's removal of sacred—and precious—dedications from their shrine, yet this epigraphic testimony implies that they reconciled themselves to this affront at least to the extent of posthumously reconceptualizing the first Christian emperor as yet another in the long line of deified rulers to have benefited their city. This shrewd recasting of Constantine during the reign of his successors helped insulate them from attacks on their modes of worship even as Constantius II was ratcheting up his assault on paganism elsewhere.

The city of Lepcis Magna in Libya Tripolitania moved in similar directions. It dedicated two inscriptions to Maxentius as "the restorer of liberty" in the aftermath of Domitius Alexander's usurpation,[39] but then shifted allegiance to Constantine after his arrival on the scene with four further inscriptions to the emperor and his sons.[40] The residents of Lepcis had good reason to be grateful to Constantine, who had eliminated a grain and oil surtax superimposed upon their province in the time of the Severans. Once freed of this burden circa 324, they were in a position to initiate a building boom that has left traces in the archaeological record.[41] The most important of the projects undertaken was the rebuilding of their *basilica vetus*, which had collapsed but was restored with the addition of a tripartite portico constructed with new columns of stone imported from the Troad. As we learn from an inscription commemorating this project, the work was completed by the curator of Lepcis and its curials but was funded through the provincial governor Laenatius Romulus.[42] Ultimately, then, the money may well have come from Constantine. The inscription also reports that the rebuilders offered in thanksgiving "a marble statue radiant with his divine spirit as an everlasting memorial to Our Lord Constantine the Greatest, Victor, forever Augustus."[43] Although some might be tempted to assume that the term "radiant" (*radiantem*) refers to gilding, it is preferable to read it in conjunction with the term "his divine spirit" (*suo numine*) and thus to assign to it a religious significance. I. Tantillo has made this very case in an article where he also argues that the statue commemorated by the inscription—no longer extant—likely bore a now badly damaged imperial head found nearby that was outfitted with seven holes in its forehead for the insertion of metal rays (Fig. 45). This head, it would seem, served to depict Constantine with a radiate crown, in his role as representative of the Sun

FIGURE 45. Head of Julio-Claudian emperor, recarved as Constantine(?) with seven holes on browline for the insertion of metal rods. Lepcis Magna. Photo by I. Tantillo, reproduced with permission.

God, much as he was depicted on Constantinian coins and monuments in the middle years of the emperor's reign.[44] As Tantillo argues, the Lepcitani need not have worked hard to arrive at such a conception of the emperor, for Constantinian rhetoric had long emphasized the power of the emperor's *numen*, and the panegyric of 310, where this notion receives particular weight, connects that sacred power directly with the solar divinity Apollo.[45] What is striking, however, is the relatively late date at which this image was dedicated. The combination of Constantine's titulature in the inscription and our knowledge of the career of the dedicant, Laenatius Romulus, allow us to fix it to the years between 324 and 326.[46] This overtly Apolline image of the emperor was thus erected in the full flower of his sole rule, a period when he is generally argued to have been most active in his promotion of Christianity. The changes in Constantinian self-presentation that followed his victory over Licinius in 324 thus appear to have had little impact on his Lepcitanian subjects—and their governor—when they chose to continue cultivating Constantine as a manifestation of the solar godhead.[47]

Seeking Patrons in Times of Uncertainty

Inscriptions recording the public recognition of local patrons (*tabulae patronatus*) survive in unusually high numbers from the Constantinian years.[48] These figures often played a key role in representing the interests of civic and village communities before the emperor. The process by which cities selected patrons is no longer easy to determine given the sources, but what testimony remains indicates this was generally a bottom-up affair: cities were not assigned a *patronus* by the emperor but chose one on their own based on a variety of factors, including thanks for the receipt of benefactions, the cultivation of preexisting relationships, and the exploitation of contacts with super-regional grandees when these owned estates in their territory or served as administrators there.[49] Obviously, in the world of rapid religious and political change ushered in by Constantine, these choices became fraught with potential pitfalls. Without strong and sympathetic patrons, polities had little chance of attaining the sorts of privileges that might allow them either to profit from their conversion to the Christian faith or help them maintain traditional religious practices in the face of growing imperial resistance. The cities of the early fourth century must therefore have been extremely careful about seeking patrons, paying attention not just to their access to wealth and power, but also to their shared adherence to systems of religious belief. Already in Chapter 6 we have seen one instance of this in the Consul L. Crepereius Madalianus, a *comes flavialis* and long-serving bureaucrat under Constantine, who—it was argued—promoted the interests of Portus by helping it win civic status and independence for this largely Christian city from its neighbor Ostia. As we shall see, however, Madalianus is far from the only example we can cite.

This process could, of course, cut both ways, for those polities whose leaders preferred to identify with traditional religions were just as anxious to find likeminded patrons that could defend their interests in the face of the new tastes and regulations of the Constantinian regime. One such city was Amiternum (Poggio San Vittorino), in eastern Italy, which preserves two *tabulae patronatus* from the reign of Constantine, rediscovered in the remains of its amphitheater. The first, dated December 7, 325, honors C. Sallius Sofronius Pompeianus as patron of the city and region and extends thanks for his restoration of an aqueduct, a water tower, and the baths of Aveia Vestinorum.[50] Pompeianus had outfitted the baths with a new portico and statues and reopened them in honor of the first anniversary of the proclamation of Constantius Caesar, after whom they were renamed. The second inscription, dated December 18, 335, records a public decree naming Pompeianus's young son, C. Sallius Sofronius, as patron both of Amiternum and of its neighbor Vicus Foruli.[51] Pompeianus was himself the son and grandson of patrons of Amiternum, a fact we learn from the first inscription. So the adoption of his son as patron in 335 extended the family's tenure in this position to a fourth generation.[52] The shifts in civic and religious politics introduced by Constantine had not, in other words, disrupted long-standing local networks of power, which remained remarkably resilient over the course of time.

The political and religious changes of Constantine's reign had, however, altered the way in which patrons and their communities expressed their honor and loyalty to the emperor, a fact made clear by a careful reading of both texts. In the first inscription Pompeianus's new bath complex was opened with two days of theatrical shows followed by ten days of "youth games" (*iuvenalia*) and a public feast hosted in the presence of the provincial governor.[53] The second was decreed in the course of another public feast laid out in honor of the emperor (*[e]pulo Aug(usteo)*).[54] These were clearly civic events with broad appeal, events of the sort long associated in particular with the celebration of the imperial cult. In a brilliant study of both inscriptions, C. Goddard has demonstrated the fundamentally traditional nature of Amiternum's celebrations and has also connected one of the civic notables who presided over the dedication of the first inscription, the *principalis* Atrius Arrentianus, with a votive offering found nearby to Jupiter Optimus Maximus.[55] The Sofronii and their fellow notables were thus working to uphold religious custom as it had been practiced in the decades and even centuries past.

Yet they did so in a distinctly newfangled way, for Goddard has also pointed out that neither inscription mentions public sacrifices or gladiatorial contests, both of which had long been staples of similar celebrations. As we shall see at the beginning of Chapter 12, sacrifice had fallen under increasing scrutiny beginning in the 310s, and Constantine may even have made halting efforts to ban it outright circa 325. Similarly, gladiatorial shows had come under severe restrictions with a law of October 1, 325, just two months before the first of these two decrees was issued.[56] It would appear, then, that this family of long-standing patrons, as well as the broader city council, had sensed the shifts in the religious winds and trimmed their sails accordingly. Their flexibility was in turn met with accommodation on the part of the imperial administration, for Constantine's governor Claudius Uranius indicated his support for the city's festival by choosing to attend the first set of celebrations. In this sense, the Sofronii were valuable patrons not just because of their long-standing ties with Amiternum and their freehanded beneficence, but also because of their ability to adapt to the contemporary religious climate without entirely cashiering the traditional festivals so beloved by their community.

Along similar lines, we have a series of inscriptions dating to 321–322 in which six separate cities in the North African province of Byzacena sent embassies to Rome recognizing as their patron Q. Aradius Rufinus Valerius Proculus, who was then serving as their governor.[57] These included Hadrumetum (Sousse), Thaenae (Henchir Thina), Zama Regia (Jama), Mididi (Henchir Medid), the Municipium Chullitanum (Cululis-Aïn Jelloula), and Civitas Faustianensis.[58] The inscription from Zama is the most revealing of the lot, for it records the names and offices of the ten local ambassadors who had traveled to Rome to make their dedication.

Strikingly, all served as *flamines* or *flamines perpetui* (current or former imperial cult priests), and of these four were also *pontifices*, two others *augures*, and one a priest of Saturn (*sacerdos Saturni*).[59] Religious concerns were thus of some importance to these ambassadors, who quite openly advertised their adherence to traditional cults and traditional modes of worship. Religion may also explain the timing of this and the other embassies, for five resulted from local decrees passed in the year 321[60] and thus at the close of a period in which Constantine had issued a flurry of legislation limiting pagan religious practice.[61]

If it was indeed the pagan leadership of these communities that organized these embassies in the interests of defending their religious traditions, we would surely expect them to have looked to a patron who was not only influential with the Constantinian court but also shared their religious sentiments. Proculus was indeed such a fellow. First off, his family enjoyed particularly close ties with the new Flavian dynasty. His father was almost certainly Aradius Rufinus, who had been Urban Prefect of Rome in 313, the first year after Constantine gained control of the city.[62] His brother would thus have been L. Aradius Valerius Proculus Populonius, who served as Praetorian Prefect circa 330 and Urban Prefect in early 337 and was named Count of the First Rank within the Imperial Palace by Constantine.[63] Indeed, we possess a fragmentary inscription recording a letter of Constantine, written to the senate of Rome, in which he asks for special privileges—likely a gilded statue—for Populonius.[64] This was thus a family with extremely close ties to the emperor.

It was also a family of devoted pagans. Aradius Rufinus *père* is known to have made dedications to pagan deities, including Constantine's favorite, the Sun God.[65] Populonius is attested as *augur, pontifex maior, quindecimvir sacris faciundis,* and, most strikingly, *pontifex flavialis*—that is, priest of the cult of the imperial family of Constantine.[66] Populonius's pull with the emperor was great enough that he appears to have felt little compunction about funding the restoration of the temple of Magna Mater at Carthage while serving as Proconsul of Africa in the early 330s.[67] These were aristocratic Romans who had managed to hold onto their traditional system of beliefs even while tailoring their public self-expression to suit the tastes and interests of the new regime. Q. Aradius Rufinus Valerius Proculus was thus chosen by these six African cities as a patron who could promote their cause before a court that was moving in new directions but remained willing to accept traditional forms of religious worship, despite recent legislation intimating otherwise. Proculus was well positioned not only to defend their interests but also to interpret the new religious ukase promulgated in 321 with leniency for his client cities.

As we might expect, such patronage relationships were never irrevocable nor their consequences irreversible. The south Italian city of Paestum, whose archaic

Greek temples to Poseidon, Hera, and Athena still stand as testaments to the enduring force of pagan religion on the ancient landscape, offers a case in point. From this city we possess an epigraphic dossier of four documents inscribed within a decade of each other, the first in the final year of Constantine's reign:

1. On April 30, 337, less than a month before Constantine's death, the decurions of Paestum dedicated a bronze *tabula patronatus* to Aurelius Gentianus, a man of equestrian rank, in the belief that he would "willingly support and foster us and our *patria* in all things."[68] For reasons now lost to us, sometime before 347 Gentianus's name was quite purposefully hammered out on the tablet, as were the names of one of the Consuls of 337, Fl. Felicianus, and of one of the city's duumvirs.

2. On April 8, 344, the citizens of Paestum offered a new *tabula patronatus* to a certain Helpidius, not an *eques* but an *honestissimus vir*, who seems to have been a Christian. This we can judge from their address to him ("Helpidius, oh fortunate man, may God save you!") and from the qualities they ascribe to him, including tranquility, innocence, and humanity.[69] It would seem then that, in 344 at least, the people of Paestum were looking to a Christian notable to promote and defend their interests.[70]

3. On August 1, 347, Paestum's decurions recycled the first tablet in this dossier by inscribing on its reverse a new patronage agreement with a certain Aquilius Nestorius. There is a clear sense of edginess in this decree, which pleads with Nestorius to "favor both us and our *patria* in all things."[71]

4. On that same day, August 1, 347, the citizens of Paestum also assembled to offer a second *tabula* to Aquilius Nestorius and his entire household (*domus Aquili{ni} Nestori*) for its many and great constructions in their town.[72] The text goes on to record that on this occasion the citizens decreed to Nestorius the title *flamen* (imperial cult priest). This makes it more than likely that Nestorius was pagan, for as recently as 300 CE Christians had been forbidden from holding this overtly pagan civic office.[73] It is thus all the more striking that at the head of this fourth *tabula*, the people of Paestum have inscribed a large Christogram flanked by stars on either side and surrounded by a victory wreath (Fig. 46).

This striking incongruity—a chi-rho at the head of a document appointing an imperial cult priest—gets at the sorts of ambiguities we encounter in trying to assign frames of reference to Constantine's contemporaries in the reception and interpretation of his messages. As we saw in the introduction to this book, in many ways the chi-rho was a free-floating signifier. It was put out by Constantine's administration with the aim of attracting subjects into the emperor's reli-

FIGURE 46. Top register of a *tabula patronatus* of Paestum headed by chi-rho and stars flanked by doves. Drawing by D. Underwood, after Sabbatini Tumolesi, "Una nuova tabula patronatus da Paestum,"), figs. 1–2, reproduced with permission.

gious sphere, yet the readers who received it need not have interpreted it according to the dominant code in which it was issued and may even—as seems likely here—have refashioned it through negotiated readings to suit their own understandings. In other words, there is no reason that the pagans of Paestum who dedicated this *tabula patronatus* cannot have used a chi-rho to enhance the power—divine and worldly—of their overtly pagan *patronus*, Aquilius Nestorius.

What makes the dossier from Paestum particularly interesting is the rapidity and frequency with which the city's leadership assumed—and then discarded—patrons. Unlike Amiternum, which kept the same family of patrons over the course of four generations, Paestum named four patrons from three families in little over a single decade. Nor was this just any decade, for the years between 337 and 347 were punctuated by the first extant imperial decree openly forbidding sacrifice. *Cesset superstitio*, issued in 341 and discussed in more detail in Chapter 12, may explain Paestum's about-face: circa 344 it brusquely expunged any record of its trusted patron Gentianus and replaced him with the Christian Helpidius, yet by 347 it had switched back to a pagan in Aquilius Nestorius, whom it not only named as patron but also appointed priest of its imperial cult. Paestum thus navigated its way through the dangerous decade following Constantine's death by appointing a bewildering mix of patrons, each of whom it hoped would help it steer the stormy waters churned up by the empire's first Christian dynasty.[74]

This storm may indeed have made waves well beyond the territory of Paestum, a fact hinted at in the first of these *tabulae patronatus*. As mentioned, that document had been defaced with the erasure of Gentianus, but also with the obliteration of the names of one of the city's *duumvirs* and of the Consul Fl. Felicianus. Felicianus is of course the same figure we encountered earlier in this chapter who, as *Comes Orientis*, found himself under attack in 341 for his practice of pagan cult at Delphi. That dispute was resolved only when the Prefects Leontius, Placidus, and Titianus wrote granting Felicianus special permission to continue the conduct of his Delphic priesthood undisturbed. Among these three, Titianus stands out for having served alongside Felicianus as co-Consul in 337 and for having been, like Felicianus, a pagan priest.[75] Both men appear to have shared a concern for the deleterious effects of Constantine's religious policies, and in 350 Titianus actually took the side of the usurper Magnentius against Constantius II, whom he chided bitterly in an embassy to his court demanding Constantius's abdication and charging him and his father with having destroyed the cities.[76] Titianus and Felicianus were thus men convinced of the value of traditional religion and secure enough in their own status to stand up to imperial authority in defense of it. Whether the repercussions from Constantius's conflicts with Felicianus in 337 and again in 341 affected the city of Paestum when, circa 344, it chose to erase Gentianus's and Felicianus's names from its *tabula patronatus*, we can no longer say, but the possibility should at least be entertained.

The tiny city of Cillium (Kasserine/Al-Qasrayn), another polity in North African Byzacena, affords a narrow porthole onto another instance of a community that used a well-connected patron to pioneer the uncharted religious terrain of the Constantinian period.[77] In this instance, however, Cillium was more interested in support from a Christian rather than a pagan grandee. Much of what we know about the city's history comes from two epigraphs, both inscribed on its still standing monumental arch. The first records its receipt of the *insignia coloniae*—and thus full independence with Roman citizenship—in the late second or early third century.[78] The second reads: "In accordance with the clemency of the times and the divine virtue of our lords Constantine [[and Licinius]], unconquered and eternal Augusti, the ornaments of freedom and ancient insignia of city status have been restored with the aid of Ceionius Apronianus, Vir Clarissimus, patron of the city."[79] The text can be dated with some precision based on the fact that Licinius's name has been chiseled off and subsequently restored. This makes it all but certain that it was originally engraved during the period of Constantine's and Licinius's peaceful joint rule from summer 313 through summer 316, then erased in the period of open hostility from mid-316 to early 317, and then restored during the period of reconciliation lasting until 324.[80] Cillium's claim that the "ornaments of freedom and ancient insignia of city status have been restored" (*ornamenta liberta(tis) restituta et vetera civitatis insignia*) implies that, like Orcistus, it had seen its civic autonomy revoked, and that Constantine restored its independence in the years between 313 and 316.

Although we cannot say with certainty what provoked Cillium's loss of civic status, there is at least some indication that Christianity played a role in its restoration. Ceionius Apronianus, who as patron won back for the city its autonomy, is probably to be identified with the Apronianus known from the *Acta purgationis Felicis* as the lawyer who defended the Caecilianist bishop Felix of Abthugni against charges of being a traitor to the Christian cause (*traditor*) during his ecclesiastical trial at Carthage in 314/315.[81] The *Acta* portray Apronianus as an advocate heavily involved in promoting Catholic Christianity in the region. If Cillium's Apronianus is in fact the same, this tiny polity will have fixed on a powerful local champion of the church to promote its bid for the restoration of its civic status. This brings us, in other words, full circle to the situation described in the instances of Portus, Orcistus, and Maiouma. In a climate where Christian religious affiliation now factored in the assignment of civic privileges, it could pay rich dividends to enlist a patron well known for his public defense of the faith.

Allied in Promoting the Emperor

The cities on the Bay of Naples and inland from these on the Ager Campanus offer an excellent instance of how patronage played a role in helping navigate the complexities not just of political relationships with the emperor but also with one another. These cities formed a network of interlinking communities that sometimes squabbled but in general managed to work together quite well. Adding to the intricacy of the situation, their extraordinary fertility and wealth coupled with their proximity to Rome meant that the Campanian cities were locked in a constant state of rivalry with the queen of cities over control of their own resources. This was certainly true in 384 when Q. Aurelius Symmachus sent an official communiqué (*relatio*) to Emperor Valentinian II asking for help sorting through difficulties that had arisen with an intricate scheme for providing imperial grain to the cities on the Bay of Naples in recompense for their obligations to supply Rome with goods and services.[82] Tensions had arisen because Puteoli (Pozzuoli) had been ordered by Julian's Praetorian Prefect Mamertinus to pay its northerly neighbor Tarracina 5,700 *modii* from the grain it received through the emperor to make up for Tarracina's obligations to supply Rome with firewood and lime.[83] As the *relatio* reveals, Mamertinus's order had been drafted but never officially subscribed by the emperor before his death, so the Puteolani felt justified in refusing to honor it. With his *relatio*, Symmachus asks Valentinian to mediate. Beyond this specific case, the document reveals a network of compensatory arrangements for cities in the region that ultimately traced back to Constantine, who had set the whole scheme in motion by ordering the city of Rome to furnish Puteoli with 150,000 *modii* of grain annually from its own supply—an extraordinarily generous subvention.[84]

We have no firm idea when or precisely why Constantine created this lavish arrangement, but it is likely to have been later in his reign, after his relationship with Rome had taken a turn for the worse beginning in 326.[85] If so, this new privilege will have coincided with the dedication of an elaborate new monument in the forum of Puteoli to the Constantinian dynasty. Its remains consist of a single image of a horse along with two bases for equestrian statues of emperors.[86] The inscription on the first base clearly records a dedication to Constantine "Victori Aug(usto)," thus datable sometime after late 324, when Constantine assumed this title. The name of the Caesar on the second inscription has been erased, but is still just readable as that of Crispus, who was executed in 326. J. Bergemann has argued that the shape of the bases and their placement in a semicircular nymphaeum on the forum indicate that the original monument probably consisted of four equestrian statues[87]—to Constantine, Crispus, Constantine II, and Constantius II. This would fit well with the program of dynastic promotion so important in the latter part of Constantine's reign, and more specifically with the widely propagated dynastic image of the emperor and his Caesars as a four-horse chariot of rulers.[88] It seems likely that this costly and prominently displayed installation represented a thanks offering from the Puteolani to Constantine for the massive new grain allotment he had offered their city.

Their good fortune is unlikely to have been connected with any marked shift on their part toward a manifest adherence to Christianity. This can be surmised in no small part from the list of patrons they chose to cultivate. Sometime in the mid-330s Puteoli, along with neighboring Suessa Aurunca (near modern Caserta), established a patronage relationship with Q. Flavius Maesius Egnatius Lollianus Mavortius. This fact is advertised in five inscriptions from the former city and one from the latter.[89] Lollianus was a Roman senator from a well-established family who had caught the eye of the emperor early in his career. Constantine employed him in a variety of administrative posts and—of obvious interest to these two cities—as Consular Governor of Campania. His loyalty won him recognition as a *comes flavialis*, something both cities also took care to advertise, and both were eager to proclaim Lollianus's adherence to traditional religions as well, for on their inscriptions they prominently list his priestly office of *augur publicus populi romani quiritium*. Lollianus's attachment to paganism is independently attested in a Roman inscription he dedicated to Hercules in 342,[90] and we also know of his religious leanings from another of his clients, the literary adept Firmicus Maternus, who dedicated to Lollianus a polytheist treatise on the divine power of astrology.[91] Suessa Aurunca and Puteoli would thus have seen in Lollianus a patron well positioned to protect the ongoing practice of pagan religion. The importance of this issue to them is clear already in the inscriptions themselves. The dedications from Puteoli were made not by the city's council or decurions but by its neighborhoods and guilds. Of the five named, three had an overtly pagan religious profile: the Neighborhood of the Incense Dealers (*vicus turarius*), the Region of the Altar of Luculliana, and the College of the Decatrenses (a cult society devoted to the emperor as the "Thirteenth" Olympian deity).[92]

The Puteolans' pursuit of prominent pagans as supporters is further attested in an inscription of circa 340 in which they honored a new patron in the person of L. Aradius Valerius Proculus Populonius, brother of Q. Aradius Rufinus Valerius Proculus, whose patronage of the six cities of Byzacena was discussed above. As noted there, Populonius held priesthoods in three of the four most prominent colleges (*amplissima collegia*) in Rome and was priest of the imperial cult of Constantine's family (*pontifex flavialis*).[93] The Puteolans recorded all of these offices in their dedication alongside Populonius's political appointments. In 343 they selected yet another patron who fit the same profile, M. Maecius Memmius Furius Baburius Caecilianus Placidus. The inscription recording this fact lists its dedicatee's priestly offices as *pontifex maior, augur publicus*, and *quindecimvir sacris faciundis*.[94] Given the religious profile of all three patrons selected by the Puteolani and the readiness of the city and its cult centers to advertise the adherence of these grandees to traditional religion, it seems natural to conclude that Puteoli— and likely Suessa Aurunca as well—quite consciously sought patrons who shared a common adherence to traditional religion in the expectation of support for their civic, but also religious, interests.

This makes it all the more interesting that Constantine in fact offered special favors not just to Puteoli, but also to a broader spectrum of cities on the Bay of Naples, some of it aimed at the general promotion of urban welfare, but some targeted quite specifically at bolstering Christianity in the region. An inscription of 324 records Constantine's direct monetary subvention (*sua pecunia*) for the reconstruction of the *aquaeductus fontis Augustei*, which, as the stone reveals, fed the cities of Puteoli, Naples, Nola, Atella, Cumae, Acerrae, Baiae, and Misenum.[95] This same aqueduct is mentioned in the *Liber Pontificalis* alongside a notice that Constantine built a new forum in Naples and—of particular importance—paid for the construction of new churches at both Naples and Capua. His construction of the Neapolitan church is also recorded in the eighth-century *Gesta Episcoporum Neapolitanorum*.[96]

As was to be expected, these cities returned Constantine's favors in kind. The governor of Campania erected a statue to Constantine at Naples,[97] and the curial order and people of Naples dedicated two statues "to our most pious and venerable Lady Augusta Helena, mother of our Lord Victor and ever Augustus Constantine, grandmother of our lords the blessed Caesars."[98]

As with the equestrian statuary group in Puteoli, one finds once again the emphasis on dynasty, but one can also sense in the epithets "most pious and venerable" a hint at the empress's devotion to Christianity. Perhaps most interesting of all, John Lydus reports that Puteoli and Naples even teamed up to supply a "gift of thanks to Constantine" (*eis charin Kōnstantinou*) in the form of a set of magnificent columns used to line the Mesē leading up to Constantine's forum in his new eastern capital.[99] These cities, which were apparently taking rather different approaches to the religious changes going on around them, thus collaborated in a joint effort to support an emperor whose primary concern was always loyalty to his regime rather than strict adherence to his religion. Puteoli, which seems to have been striving to maintain its orientation toward traditional religions, and Naples, which was moving more rapidly in the direction of Christianization, both benefited from Constantine's generosity, and both displayed their gratitude with public shows of reverence for the emperor and his dynasty. Although we have no evidence what patrons Naples may have cultivated to help it foster this relationship, Puteoli, as we have seen, chose pagan mediators to work on its behalf. The success of both cities' efforts is clear to see in the material benefits both received.

Conclusion

Not all cities chose to align themselves with that version of Constantine cultivated by communities like Orcistus and Maiouma. We saw from the beginning that Constantine's public persona changed considerably over time, and the variety of "Constantines" he left in place along this path of development presented opportunities for alternative forms of engagement to the variety of communities that made up the empire. It is part and parcel of relations of governance that subject constituencies strive to modulate their interactions with the ruler to fit as comfortably as possible with their own desires and expectations. This was certainly the case with the cities examined in this chapter, for no two communities took precisely the same path in their approaches to Constantine, and no two communities arrived at precisely the same interpretation of their emperor.

Athens appealed to Constantine through its most prominent pagan families and offered him adoption into its native offices. These engagements won for the city not just the freedom to continue its traditions unmolested but also extraordinary favors, including an imperially guaranteed grain supply. Termessus, which may never have had direct contact with Constantine himself, folded him into its existing pantheon of local deities by equating him with their native solar deity, the All-Seeing Sun. In similar fashion, Sagalassus incorporated Constantine as deified ruler into its existing structures of the imperial cult. Delphi did much the same and even used its Constantinian connections to protect cultic practice at its shrine well into the 340s, when the central government became actively hostile toward the practice of sacrifice. Lepcis Magna dedicated a statue to Constantine's radiant divinity in terms that meshed well with the solar theism so prevalent in Constantinian propaganda in the 310s, although its efforts to sustain this message into the 320s strike us as nostalgic for a pagan Constantine who was, by this late date, receding from view. There was thus room in the imperial *oikoumene* for alternative Constantines depending on the viewpoint of the subject cities who encountered him. In fact, these were not only permitted but even encouraged— by a steady flow of words and images—to derive their own interpretations of imperial authority within the horizons of the acceptable as defined by imperial message makers.

Ultimately, Constantine's religious policy can best be characterized as experimental. He was forced by the constraints on his power to move carefully in enacting his Christian agenda and to work with those striving to assert their own agendas through principles of compromise and conciliation. For this reason, patrons took on particular importance in a world where access to imperial power, as also to divine truth, was always negotiated through intermediaries. As he and his administration exerted mounting pressures—incentives and punishments—on cities and their populations to convert, these communities selected patrons who would share their religious views in order to promote their interests before the imperial court. Whether the leadership of these cities favored pagan or Christian religion—and most surely had constituencies from both camps—they selected and honored powerful patrons like the pagan Lollianus, who supported neighborhood cults in Puteoli, or the Christian Apronianus, who helped Cillium obtain civic independence, in order to advance their cause before a court open to negotiation. Such intermediaries played an integral role in connecting the poles of power represented by the emperor and his people and in championing the interests of civic constituencies while channeling the authority of the emperor to the mutual benefit of both.

CHAPTER 12

Resisting Cities

Violence as Discourse

Religious violence has come into its own as a field of study. Recent work on the question in Late Antiquity has made great strides in detaching violence from the realm of the aberrant and resituating it into the range of the normal. Violence was not, in other words, a separate and distinct form of social discourse, or even less an anti-discourse. It was, instead, part and parcel of everyday social relations and should be studied alongside other forms of social practice in a continuum of relations of human interaction. This approach already informed the fine monographs of M. Gaddis and T. Sizgorich on religious violence between Christians and pagans and Christians and Muslims, respectively.[1] It has come into even sharper focus with the work of B. D. Shaw, which has shown that violence was used as a tool of communication between oppositional constituencies in North Africa as they struggled for self-assertion by taking sides in the Donatist controversy during the fifth century.[2]

The best recent scholarship on Constantine has laid emphasis on his generally tolerant attitude to non-Christians, at least as regards his reluctance to engage in direct religious coercion. In the aftermath of the Great Persecution and its aftershocks in the smaller-scale persecutions perpetrated by Licinius, violence against religious opponents had become naturalized as a way of policing the boundaries of the acceptable in religious dialogue. In taking the side of Christians following these open attacks against religious dissidents, Constantine faced a rising welter of support from some constituencies to turn the tables and persecute pagans and Jews. Nevertheless, as we saw in the previous chapter, by and large he maintained a spirit of engagement and forbearance. Moreover, in a number of documented instances, he even left open avenues for interaction and for interpretations of himself and his religious agenda that seemed entirely consonant with traditional pagan religious symbols and practices. All the same, as we shall see in what follows, at times Constantine did close off opportunities for peaceful dialogue by blatantly attacking pagan shrines and worshippers with violent force. This was true particularly of polytheist temples and cities that refused any entrée to Christianity and any harbor for Christian constituencies. Religious violence also occurred within some sectarian Christian communities in North Africa that refused obedience to the Carthaginian church as a result of the Donatist schism. This breakdown in positive engagement did not, however, end dialogue altogether. Instead it merely transferred it to the realm of resistance and at times violent conflict. Interestingly, as we shall see in what follows, in instances where Constantine went back on his broader policy of keeping the door open to peaceful negotiation, his enactment of violence reset the terms of engagement onto the plane of forceful interaction, where it then remained for decades and even centuries into the future. Once he began attacking religious resisters, he paved the way for ongoing forceful opposition by those whose behavior he had attempted to alter through coercion.

Tolerance and Intolerance

Constantine harbored a deep-seated distaste for blood sacrifice that grew increasingly pronounced over the course of his reign. This shows up in his *Oration to the Saints*, where he rails against pagans for "sacrificing irrational creatures," as well as in the letter he wrote to Shapur II, where he professed to "shun all abominable blood and foul ill-omened odors."[3] At some point in his reign, he refused to scale the Capitoline Hill in Rome and offer sacrifice in the course of a triumphal celebration, thus breaking with a millennium-long tradition and provoking the anger of the Roman people.[4] Eusebius even claims that, after Constantine gained control of the East in 324, he issued two laws (*nomoi*) in quick succession: the second, quoted in Chapter 9, ordered the construction or extension of churches. "The first restricted the pollutions of idolatry that had for a long time been practiced in every city and country district, so that no one should presume to set up cult objects, or practice divination or other occult arts, or even sacrifice at all."[5] The notice is quite specific and would seem to merit credence. Notwithstanding Eusebius's testimony, however, we have no law of Constantine extant in the *Theodosian Code* that bans sacrifice outright. We do possess a law of Constans dated to 341 that fumes: "Let superstition cease, let the insanity of sacrifices be abolished. For whoever should dare to celebrate sacrifices in contravention of the law of the divine Emperor my father and of this command of Our Clemency, let a fitting punishment and immediate sentence be passed against him."[6] The combination of the two sources would seem to speak for a Constantinian ban on sacrifice, and this is indeed how it has been taken by a number of scholars.[7]

On the other hand, in his letter to the eastern provincials, known to have been written in 324, Constantine again fulminates against the ills of paganism, but rounds off this hard-edged rhetoric with a decidedly conciliatory tone: "Let those in error, as well as the believers, gladly receive the benefit of peace and quiet. . . . Those who hold themselves back [i.e., from the truth of Christianity], let them keep if they wish their sanctuaries of falsehood."[8] Reinforcing this message of entente, Libanius claims in his *Oration on the Temples* that, while he was growing up in the 320s and 330s, Constantine had "made absolutely no alteration to the traditional forms of worship, but, though poverty reigned in the temples, one could see that all the rest of the ritual was fulfilled."[9] Libanius goes on to assert that it was only Constantius II who first issued laws against sacrifice, thus directly contradicting Eusebius's testimony. Libanius, it could be argued, had an agenda in choosing to portray Constantine as permissive, for his speech was designed to nudge Theodosius toward a similar tolerance. But Eusebius and for that matter Constans had agendas of their own, for both were also using Constantine as a rhetorical tool to bolster anti-pagan programs. This makes it difficult to know which authority to trust.[10]

The laws we do have in which Constantine set limits on pagan worship confirm what we read in the letter to the eastern provincials: he was more interested in controlling specific practices than in eliminating pagan ritual altogether.[11] A law of May 15, 319, issued "to the people" and thus intended for empire-wide distribution, forbids diviners and priests (*haruspices et sacerdotes*) from entering private homes to perform their rites, and a follow-up constitution posted by the Urban Prefect of Rome on February 1, 320, again forbids *haruspices* from entering private homes on pain of cremation.[12] Both laws are harsh, but both also uphold long-standing imperial legal tradition forbidding private divination, which, it was feared, could be used to the detriment of the emperor. More important, both explicitly permit the performance of such divinatory rites—which, in the instance of *haruspices*, almost certainly involved sacrifice—provided they were conducted in public shrines.[13] Indeed, when the imperial palace in Rome was struck by lightning in 320, Constantine explicitly allowed *haruspices* to interpret this sign by carrying out their traditional rites, provided these did not violate the ban on *haruspicina* in private homes.[14] This shows a considerable degree of tolerance toward pagan ritual, even when it entailed blood sacrifice and even the emperor's residence. Similarly, a law of May 318 forbade adepts in the magic arts from performing harmful curses or love spells, but explicitly permitted traditional spells used to remedy illnesses, speed the maturation of the vintage, or prevent hailstorms.[15] Again this law fits with long-standing imperial bans against maleficent magic while showing tolerance toward other forms of traditional worship.

With these constitutions we exhaust the storehouse of legal evidence for Constantine's regulation of pagan rites. Unfortunately, none traces to the final period of Constantine's rule, when Eusebius says he issued a general ban on sacrifice. Even so, this material already reflects a pattern of controlled tolerance that should not be discounted when evaluating Eusebius's notice. In every instance, Constantine's attitude is highly pragmatic, taking account of past legal precedent, but also of contemporary religious practice. This was an emperor uneasy with the idea that he might alienate any constituency, be they vintners, farmers, or priests—even *haruspices*. The same approach can be seen in the prayer Constantine issued for his pagan troops as recorded in Eusebius. These were not required to convert or even to attend Christian worship services on Sundays, but rather were issued a sort of nondenominational prayer to the "highest god," whom they were asked to address in unison in an open field once each week.[16] The soldiery was surely Constantine's most important constituency, and his willingness to meet them on their own terms is clear not just from this prayer but also from the records of a meeting between Constantine and his veterans at which the troops greeted him: "Constantine Augustus, may the gods preserve you for our benefit!"[17] Constantine appears to have been more than ready to tolerate such engagements even when they were structured on traditional terms, for whether or not they made him uneasy on a theological level, they were too much a part of Roman political traditions to be scorned or silenced.

Interestingly, this last exchange probably postdated Constantine's assumption of sole rule in 324. This would mean that it occurred after the turn in imperial policy noted by scholars, and especially T. Barnes, toward greater intolerance in the final dozen years of Constantine's reign.[18] This is indeed the period of the reputed ban on sacrifice. In the same context where Eusebius reports this ban, he also tells us that Constantine explicitly forbade imperial officials to sacrifice or worship idols. Here too, however, the policy was not draconian, for the church historian confirms that Constantine in no way forbade pagans from holding office, and his appointment of pagan officials is amply confirmed in the prosopographic record from late in Constantine's reign.[19] This is also the period during which Constantine sent officials to inventory and confiscate some temple treasures and even melted down pagan statues in gold and silver.[20] The hardening in Constantinian religious policy is thus impossible to deny and should not be overlooked. It did not, however, extinguish the pragmatic tolerance so evident in the above-cited laws from the middle years of his reign.

Nowhere can this be better observed than in the letter to the eastern provincials of 324, part of which was quoted above. The tenor of the letter is well summarized in its concluding paragraph: "Nevertheless, let each person do no harm to another through that which he has persuaded himself to undertake. Whatever one person has seen and understood, by this he ought to benefit his neighbor if it is possible, but if it is not, he should let it go. For it is one thing to undertake the contest for immortality willingly, but quite another to compel this through punishment."[21] As H. A. Drake has stressed, this extremely important manifesto not only set the tone for continued tolerance, it also constituted a legal pronouncement explicitly meant to nip what appears to have been a rising strain of agitation and even violence against pagans in the bud.[22]

Even in the years immediately following Constantine's death in 337, when imperial opposition to pagan practice became more pronounced and explicit bans on sacrifice are firmly attested,[23] this same pragmatic tolerance can still be witnessed. This was especially true when it came to the smooth conduct of civic politics and the maintenance of the imperial cult. A law of 342 issued by Constans to the Urban Prefect of Rome illustrates the situation well: "Although all superstition must be eradicated root and branch, nevertheless we wish that the structures of temples [aedes templorum] that are placed outside the city walls should remain intact and undefiled. For since many games, circus races, and contests [vel ludorum vel circensium vel agonum] take their starting points from some of these, it is best that they not be pulled down, in order that the annual celebration of the traditional entertainments [priscarum sollemnitas voluptatum] may be offered to the Roman people."[24] The language, and indeed the circumstances, bear a remarkable resemblance to that of the Hispellum rescript. Both show an awareness that the public spectacles associated with traditional pagan festivals represented an integral part of identity formation and group cohesion for the late antique city. Christian emperors like Constans and Constantine benefited from and were dependent upon the support generated through the practice of these collective celebrations. Depriving the cities of the venues, the spectacles, and even the rites associated with such celebrations was neither possible nor desirable in the early fourth century. At best, as both texts reveal, the emperor could hope to regulate them by stripping them of the one element he found most distasteful: sacrifice. In this context, it is my opinion—and given the contradictory evidence on the matter, opinion is all that can be ventured—Constantine likely did issue an edict against animal sacrifice late in 324, but one worded vaguely enough, constructed loosely enough, and enforced sporadically enough that it by no means put an immediate halt to the practice.

Strong-Arm Tactics

Constantine's willingness to accept advances from constituencies that were far from orthodox Christian (like the Hispellates or Athenians) and to permit the construction of his own self-image at the provincial level in ways that strike us as surprisingly pagan (as happened at Termessus or Lepcis Magna) should not lure us into assuming that his stance toward traditional religions was unwaveringly tolerant and welcoming. In certain cases, he quite unapologetically ordered the destruction of pagan shrines or monuments and even their replacement with Christian structures.

Nowhere was this more decisively undertaken than in Jerusalem. Eusebius is our sole contemporary source, but valuable though his testimony is, it must be used with caution.[25] Fortunately it has the advantage of preserving a letter of Constantine's to the bishop of Jerusalem, Macarius, that offers the emperor's own perspective on the process. By Eusebius's report, the site of Christ's passion (Golgotha) had been deliberately covered with a layer of earth and paving stone and then built upon by Roman emperors with a temple of Venus.[26] Reversing this defilement, Constantine had the temple destroyed and the layer of earth removed and carted away. Beneath it, Eusebius tells us, was discovered the cave in which Christ was entombed. In his letter to Macarius, Constantine terms the object discovered "the monument of his most holy Passion," which some have taken to be a reference to the discovery of the True Cross.[27] Our first direct references to this most prized of relics date to the 350s, but this does not preclude the possibility that the Cross was discovered earlier and may be referenced here.[28] If Constantine is in fact referring to what he thought was Christ's cross in this letter, Eusebius has certainly made no effort to draw attention to this in his literary frame.[29]

For our purposes a matter of greater import is the fact that, at least by Eusebius's reckoning, the destruction of the Venus shrine and the uncovering of Golgotha were carried out on Constantine's initiative, and that this preceded his decision to construct an elaborate church on the site of the Holy Sepulchre.[30] Constantine implies the same when he claims in his letter, "I have no greater care than how I may adorn with a splendid structure that sacred spot, which, under divine direction, I have disencumbered as it were of the heavy weight of foul idol worship."[31] This sequence is extremely important for two reasons: first, it indicates a willingness on the part of the emperor to destroy a pagan shrine prior to formulating firm plans for the reuse of the real estate it occupied; second, it shows that Constantine claimed he was operating not at the prompting of some petitioner but rather on his own initiative, or rather, driven by what he himself terms "divine direction."[32]

Even if the uncovering of Golgotha was originally Constantine's idea, his letter to Macarius gives the bishop considerable latitude to make crucial programmatic decisions about the construction of the church over the site. For these purposes, Constantine permits Macarius to receive imperially subsidized support in the form of labor and supplies from an agent of the Praetorian Prefect, Dracilianus, and from the governor of Palestine.[33] This was, as we have seen in Chapter 9, very much in keeping with Constantine's policy of promoting church construction by fostering cooperation between local ecclesiastical authorities and regional imperial officials. But while the emperor encourages Macarius to communicate with him directly on his decisions and demands regarding the new construction, there is no indication that the bishop initiated or conceived the project himself. On the contrary, as noted, Constantine takes credit for having destroyed the temple, and with his letter he seems intent on pulling Macarius into the project at a relatively advanced stage. It is unclear from Eusebius or the letter precisely what agents the emperor employed in his demolition activity, but it seems almost certain that military manpower was involved, whether to effect the destruction of the ancient temple or simply to stand guard while it occurred. Constantine thus appears to have been enacting his personal will in having this temple destroyed and its substructures excavated.

Not far from Jerusalem, Constantine also undertook the destruction of pagan cultic monuments at the holy site of Mamre (modern Rāmat el Khalīl). This was the place where three angels appeared to Abraham to announce the pregnancy of his wife Sarah and the future glory of his race (Gen. 14:13; 18:1–15). By the imperial period, however, it had become a place of ecumenical devotion that included idol worship and sacrifice.[34] The site, which had no urban infrastructure, had long played host to a summer trade fair (Hebrew *yarid*; Greek *panēgyris*) that attracted international participation along with devotion from Jews, Christians, and pagans in what must have been a heady mix of religious traditions.[35] For these purposes, it had been surrounded by a precinct wall, and the worshippers had built an altar for sacrifice, covered Abraham's sacred oak with fillets, lit lamps, and cast libations and other offerings into Abraham's holy well. Constantine, of course, saw this religious pluralism as an abomination against a locus he wished to reclaim exclusively for Christianity. This we know from Eusebius, who preserves a letter written by the emperor once again to Macarius of Jerusalem and other Palestinian prelates. It reports that the emperor's mother-in-law, Eutropia, had informed him of this state of affairs and that he had ordered his *comes* Acacius to burn all pagan idols, destroy the altar, forbid further sacrifices, and see to the construction of a Christian basilica.[36] Here again, archaeology would seem to confirm the texts, for fragments of votive statues were found under the Constantinian foundation.[37]

From this dossier alone, it is not entirely clear that these acts of religious violence were undertaken at Constantine's initial behest, for he was obviously responding to information communicated to him by his mother-in-law. Nevertheless, Eutropia's close connections with the imperial household raise the possibility that she was touring the Holy Land under imperial orders and trolling for opportunities to impose Christian religion onto the sacred landscape of Palestine. As with the previous letter to Macarius regarding the site of the Holy Sepulchre, this communiqué also invites petitions from fellow local bishops, who have been informed of the situation at Mamre precisely so that they can report any ongoing pagan worship there. Here again, we see a remarkably proactive Constantine enlisting bishops to police the religious frontiers of Palestine and flexing his muscles in the suppression of pagan shrines where these impinged on sites holy to the broader Christian community.

Constantine appears also to have taken a proactive role in the destruction of the temple on the slopes of Mount Lebanon at Aphaca (Nahr Ibrāhīm), near the source of the Adonis River between Heliopolis and Byblos.[38] Eusebius reports that the site was dedicated to "the hateful demon Aphrodite," whom local Semitic speakers would have worshipped as ʿAshtart. We know from other sources that the goddess's image depicted her in mourning for her lost lover Adonis and that she was revered in a grove that included a sacred pool used for divinatory purposes and a regular festival involving celestial phenomena.[39] The site is reputed to have promoted "sacred prostitution," reason enough for it to have become a target of religious violence from an emperor whose attitudes toward sexual promiscuity became ever harsher with the progress of his reign.[40] Eusebius states explicitly that "this was a grove and temple, not situated in the midst of any city, or in any public place."[41] The distinction is important and provides a point of contact with Mamre, which was also a natural retreat remote from any urban center. Moreover, a curious artifact, discovered in Palestine and now held in the University of Toronto Art Centre, links the two sites. It is a mold used to stamp tourist trinkets that features on one side the three angels of Genesis 18, seated at table and pointing to the Oak of Mamre, the well of Abraham, and the figures of Abraham and Sarah; on its other side the mold depicts the weeping goddess "Ourania," another name for Aphrodite of Aphaca (Figs. 47 and 48).[42] Precisely why these two cult images were displayed on the same object is not entirely clear, but their presence together indicates the object's creator saw at least some connection between the two sites and their cults. At a minimum, both were frequented by pilgrims from varied religious traditions who wished to collect efficacious mementos of their visits. Whether Constantine also believed there was a connection we can no longer know.

In contrast with Mamre, where we learn that the empress dowager Eutropia had reported on the intermingling of religious traditions to Constantine, Eusebius gives the impression that Constantine discovered the abominations at the site of Aphaca through his provident foresight and ordered its destruction on his own initiative using a military force.[43] Given that there is unlikely to have been a violent Christian constituency at or near a locale whose main architectural monument was its temple, Constantine seems to have been enacting his own program of violence against a regional religious center. Because, however, the site lacked an identity as an established polity, it was also an easy target whose destruction was unlikely to provoke local violence or the loss of tax revenues.

FIGURE 47. ΕΙΛΕΩΣ ΜΟΙ ΟΙ ΑΝΓΕΛΟΙ (May the angels pity me). Three angels at Mamre seated at table with the oak of Mamre to their right, the well above, and Abraham and Sarah in exergue. Two-sided mold, limestone, 13.8 cm diameter, Malcove Collection M82.271, Gift of Dr. Lillian Malcove to the University of Toronto, 1982. Courtesy of the University of Toronto Art Centre. Photo by Toni Hafkenscheid.

FIGURE 48. ΔΕΧΟΜΕ ΧΑΙΡΩΝ ΤΗΝ/ ΟΥΡΑΝΙΑΝ (I receive the heavenly goddess rejoicing). Weeping goddess with star-clad robe, headdress, and veil, enthroned, palm trees left and right. Two-sided mold, limestone, 13.8 cm diameter, Malcove Collection M82.271, gift of Dr. Lillian Malcove to the University of Toronto, 1982. Courtesy of the University of Toronto Art Centre. Photo by Toni Hafkenscheid.

Similarly unilateral action was at play in Constantine's destruction of the temple of Asclepius at Aegeae in Cilicia (modern Yumurtalık). This had been a prominent local shrine drawing worshippers from across the eastern Mediterranean who sought healing through nocturnal incubation. Once again Eusebius is our only contemporary source: "He did the right thing and, using the God that is truly zealous and a savior as his shield, he ordered this temple to be brought to the ground. With one command he flattened to the earth this marvel, so boasted about by the noble philosophers, and it was cast down by a military detachment, and with it the one who haunted it, not a spirit nor indeed a god, but a tricker of souls who had deceived people for so many years."[44] A passage in Zonaras confirms the destruction and indicates further that the columns of the temple were removed from the shrine and reconstructed into a Christian church nearby.[45] As with Aphaca, we hear once again of the use of the Roman military to enact violently Constantine's religious program. As such the incident stands in contrast with Eusebius's report on the relatively peaceful process of confiscations of bullion and statuary from temples elsewhere. It also gives no indication of the use of the petitioning process as a trigger, or even a cover, for the deployment of armed

force. By Eusebius's report, at least, the shrine was destroyed at Constantine's initiative, on Constantine's order, by Constantine's troops.[46] Moreover, as with the
rural site of Aphaca, Constantine is unlikely to have set upon the temple of
Asclepius at the behest of locals, for although the temple was located near the
neighboring port city at Aegeae, it exercised dominance over it.[47] Here too, then,
Constantine acted on his own initiative.

Much the same can be said of our last example of Constantinian strong-arm
tactics. Heliopolis-Baalbek was a city not far from Aphaca that had been founded
around a cult center devoted to the north Semitic sky god Baʿal, his consort
ʿAshtart, and son Aliyan. The local shrine there, dating as early as the second
millennium BCE, was architecturally developed by the Seleucids and was eventually built into a massive multi-temple complex by the Romans during the early
empire.[48] In typical fashion, the Romans chose to associate Baalbek's triad of
divinities with their own gods, in this instance Jupiter, Venus, and Mercury. Even
so, they continued to permit worship according to indigenous traditions into Late
Antiquity.[49] Local worship included some form of secret, apparently underground, sacrifice as well as temple prostitution, associated with ʿAshtart.[50] Both
practices were obviously sore spots for Constantine.

Baalbek was, as with other sites upon which Constantine visited his displeasure, exclusivist in its devotion to its traditional triad. During the Great Persecution, its citizens took great delight in torturing and then stoning Gelasinus, one of
the few Christians brazen enough to profess his religion openly in their city.[51] It is
thus extremely unlikely to have petitioned for a change to the status quo. Indeed,
Eusebius informs us regarding Constantine's interactions with Baalbek:

> But now a law [*nomos*] both new and moderate went out from the emperor
> commanding that none of the former customs should be ventured, and he
> also added written instructions [*engraphous didaskalias*] for them as if he
> had been appointed by God for the purpose of instructing all mankind in
> the laws of moderation. Wherefore he did not think it unworthy to preach
> to these people through a personal letter [*di'oikeiou prosomilein gramma-
> tos*], and he exhorted them to hasten toward knowledge of the Almighty.
> And thereupon he added deeds related to these words, for he laid the
> foundations for a massive house of worship to serve as a church among
> these same [*oikon euktērion ekklēsias megiston kai para toisde kataball-
> omenos*], so that a thing that has never been heard of in all of history came
> to pass for the first time, and the city of the superstitious was deemed
> worthy of priests and deacons of the church of God and a bishop conse-
> crated to the God of the universe was established over the people there.[52]

Eusebius speaks of two Constantinian documents: a law and an accompanying letter, the former of which forbade the continuation of "customary rites,"[53] while the latter justified this prohibition in decidedly Christian terms. The combination of dispositive law and explanatory epistle is of course reminiscent of the Orcistus dossier and is evidenced in other enactments of Constantine as well. The letter, apparently written very much in the spirit of the letter to the eastern provincials, "preached" the emperor's displeasure with Heliopolitan worship in a way that adds vividness to Constantine's famous claim to have considered himself "bishop of those outside."[54] He was, in other words, working proactively to impose his religion on a community that had expressed no interest in it and that apparently harbored no constituency willing to petition for help in replacing local religious practice with Christianity. Although Eusebius records no active destruction of existing pagan shrines,[55] Constantine's proactive moves there should still be placed among the examples of the strong-arm imposition of imperial will contrary to local requests or interests.

Strong Resistance

As might be expected, these efforts to subvert prevailing local customs met with resistance, which came in varying fashion and varying degrees—from open violence, to active protest, to mere passive continuation of prohibited ritual practices. An inscription from Epidauros, for example, confirms ongoing devotion to Asclepius of Aegeae in 355.[56] At Aegeae itself, Libanius records, laments against Constantine's violence promptly went up from the locals.[57] In two extant letters of 362, he claims to have received a copy of a speech composed by his friend Acacius praising Aegeae's shrine and "lamenting the war of the godless against the temple, its destruction, the fire, the altars overthrown."[58] Libanius also dispatched his brother to the temple to seek an oracle—to be obtained by incubation in the temple, in keeping with the custom—that might help cure him of his chronic headaches.[59] By this point, of course, Julian was in power, and symbolic forms of protest could give way to more active efforts to rebuild. We learn from Zonaras that, when Julian passed through Cilicia in winter 362/363, the priest of the ruined temple, Artemius, petitioned him and obtained an order commanding the local bishop to dismantle the church constructed from the temple's columns and use them to restore the original structure.[60] Moreover, the letter of Libanius quoted above indicates that Julian's homonymous uncle then pushed for the restoration of property taken from the temple with some urgency.[61] As was to be expected, this process was not completed in the lifetime of the apostate and was reversed after his death. Even so, pagans continued to resort to the tattered temple for healing. Libanius used it to obtain relief from debilitating headaches in the 370s,[62] and the *Life and Miracles of Thecla* indicates similar cultic activity there in the fifth century, although by this point the nearby church of Thecla had largely supplanted the temple as a local healing site and had even adopted its practice of ritual incubation.[63]

At Aphaca we have less detail, but both Zosimus and Sozomen indicate that some form of traditional worship continued at this mountain site into the fifth century.[64] Moreover, M. Frazer, who initially published the two-sided mold with the Angels of Mamre on one side and Ourania on the other (see Figs. 47 and 48), identifies a series of fifth- and sixth-century texts indicating that the "Grieving Goddess" was assimilated to the Virgin Mary in precisely this geographical context and at this time. For this reason, she has argued, the mold testifies to the ongoing vitality this cultic figure— albeit modified by the dominance of Christianity—deep into Late Antiquity.[65] We can add to this Sozomen's testimony on Mamre, which conveys much the same impression about what our mold-maker regarded to be a sister site. There it appears that Constantine's efforts to cordon off the site for Christian worship alone failed miserably in the polyethnic, multicultural world of the Palestinian desert:

> But at this place even up to today [*entautha . . . eiseti nun*] the locals, as well as Palestinians from further afield, and Phoenicians, and Arabs hold a splendid yearly festival in the summer. Many people rally together in order to buy and sell at the market [*panēgyrin*]. The festival is very popular, among Jews who boast of Abraham as patriarch, pagans [*hellēsi*], because of the visitation of the angels, and Christians, since the one who in due course revealed himself through the virgin in order to save the human race appeared to that pious man even then. They honor this place in a manner fitting to their religion, with some praying to the god of all, others calling upon the angels and pouring out libations of wine and sacrificing incense, or an ox, or goat, or sheep or rooster.[66]

The passage goes on to describe the care with which pilgrims prepared for the festival and the dignity and restraint with which they worshipped, lighting lamps around the well and casting offerings of wine, incense, myrrh, and honey into it "in pagan fashion" (*nomō hellēnikō*). If we can take Sozomen at his word that he is describing a situation contemporary to his world—and it bears repeating that he grew up just sixty kilometers from Mamre—his testimony indicates that Constantine's efforts to legislate away the ecumenical religious practices of the Christian, pagan, Jewish, and nomadic Arab pilgrims to Mamre had failed. Indeed, the large number of fourth- through sixth-century lamps found through excavation at Mamre along with the high number of fourth-century coins cast into the well would seem to confirm Sozomen's testimony.[67] The very uninhabited nature of Mamre that had made it vulnerable to attack by imperial forces and easy to colonize with a new Christian church also rendered it impossible to police when pilgrims from across the cultural spectrum of the Palestinian steppe showed up to worship in the manner appropriate to their own customs.

The situation was much more incendiary at Heliopolis-Baalbek. In his description of Constantine's imposition of Christianity there, Eusebius reports that the emperor "laid the foundations" of a church at the city but says nothing of whether the structure was brought to completion.[68] In fact, the archaeology of Baalbek shows that the city's first Christian basilica, placed in the courtyard of the temple of Jupiter Heliopolitanus, was not constructed until the reign of Theodosius I (379–395). This would seem to be consonant with John Malalas's report that Theodosius wreaked destruction on Heliopolis's temple.[69] Constantine had thus begun a process that was by no means finished before his death. Indeed, ongoing worship of Aphrodite at Heliopolis-Baalbek is well attested in the mid-fourth-century *Expositio Totius Mundi*.[70] Around the same time, the Heliopolitans had no compunction about exploiting Julian's tolerance of anti-Christian violence to murder the city's deacon Cyril for having attacked an altar during the reign of Constantius.[71] Under Julian, the Heliopolitans also flaunted Constantine's law against temple prostitution by publicly stripping a group of dedicated virgins in mockery, before brutally murdering them.[72] The Heliopolitans were surely emboldened by the fact that Julian had chosen as governor of Syria a denizen of their own city, Alexander, who was so excessive in his promotion of paganism that he was eventually prosecuted under Julian's successors.[73]

Nor did the city's strong pagan imprint disappear with the death of Julian, for Valens chose it as the place of exile for a group of recalcitrant Alexandrian ascetics precisely because "none of the inhabitants, who are all given over to idols, can endure so much as to hear the name of Christ."[74] Even Theodosius's imposition of a church within its sacred precinct appears to have had minimal effect on religious activity, for his own governor of Phoenicia in 382, the prominent young pagan Proculus, was praised in a verse inscription from nearby for leveling the road over the Lebanon Mountains to make access to the shrine easier and for making religious offerings of his own in Heliopolis according to local custom.[75] As late as the mid-fifth century, Rabbula of Edessa felt compelled to march on the precinct in an effort to destroy its idols but was nearly beaten to death by militant locals.[76] Indeed, the city's pagan majority seems to have continued to prevail deep into the sixth century, when John of Ephesus claims that the Heliopolitans were offering their daily sacrifices as the grand temple was struck by lightning in 555. Even as late as 579 Tiberius II and his officer Theophilus uncovered what they believed to be a massive conspiracy of crypto-pagans that took its starting point among the "wicked heathens of Baalbek."[77] The pagan majority was thus remarkably resilient in holding onto its traditional religion long after most eastern polities had converted. Set against this backdrop, Constantine's early efforts to ban ritual prostitution and impose a church upon the Heliopolitan cityscape take on new color.

Quid Pro Quo Reprisals
Between Pagans and Christians

By the close of Constantine's reign the conversion of traditionally pagan communities was still very much in process and was highly dependent on ongoing support from the emperor. At Aegeae and Heliopolis, Julian's brief reign provides a marvelous window into the contingent nature of this process and the tensions and resistance it fomented. Nor were these cities unique in serving as barometers of latent pagan tensions ready to explode on the accession to power of a co-religionist. At Gaza and Ascalon, both largely pagan cities of Palestine, Christian ascetics were martyred,[78] and at Sebaste and Scythopolis–Beth Shean, also majority pagan cities of Palestine, the relics of Christian saints were disinterred, defiled, and discarded.[79] The Phoenician town of Arethousa brutally tortured its bishop Mark for having destroyed their temple in the reign of Constantine and built over it with a church. We can no longer recover the details of this incident, but it became something of a cause célèbre as an example of the eye-for-an-eye reprisals that ensued from acts of violence against pagan monuments under Constantine.[80]

Meanwhile, Julian himself borrowed Constantine's tactic of rewarding those cities that uniformly professed Hellenic religion while letting others know he would punish them for their disobedience if they refused to countenance his religious dispensations. On his visit to Pessinus in 362, he learned that the city's renowned shrine to Cybēlē had been neglected by its inhabitants. In a letter to Arsacius, whom he appointed high priest of Galatia, he urged his correspondent to encourage the Pessinuntes to accept an offer of assistance but warned, "If they claim my patronage, the whole community must become suppliants of the Mother of the Gods."[81] Exclusive devotion to the emperor's religion thus came to matter as much to Julian as it had to Constantine.

By the same token, those cities that boasted exclusivist Christian communities were disadvantaged in their engagements with the Apostate, in stark contrast with their favored treatment under Constantine. As we saw in Chapter 6, Gaza used the petitioning process to regain political and religious control over its neighboring port Maiouma from Julian.[82] When Nisibis, on the eastern frontier, petitioned Julian for support against the Persians, who were on the point of invading, "he threatened not to assist them because they were wholly Christianized and would neither reopen their temples nor resort to the sacred places."[83] Mazaca-Caesarea in Cappadocia was also punished for its exclusivist Christian population and its destruction of the city's one remaining pagan temple shortly after Julian's accession. The emperor deprived it of its civic status as well as its imperial name, which it had obtained under Claudius Caesar. He also imposed a surtax on its Christian population and enrolled their clergy in the frontier army. Finally, Sozomen reports, "He ordered all possessions and money belonging to the churches of the city and suburbs of Caesarea to be sought out under torture and gathered together."[84] This netted him some three hundred pounds of gold, which he transferred into the imperial treasury. This was, as we have seen, a complete and deliberate reversal of Constantinian policy, which had for its part confiscated pagan treasuries to the imperial fisc and then used this reservoir to transfer wealth to Christian churches, and which had granted immunity to Christian clerics from enrollment in compulsory public services. Julian was turning Constantine's civic religious politics on its head in ways we have witnessed in Chapters 8 and 10, ways that are as illustrative of Constantine's own policies as of Julian's contrapuntal responses to them.

Conclusion

Power is always a dynamic relationship shared between ruler and ruled, a discourse between unequals, but a discourse nonetheless, that involves the reciprocal exchange of authority for recognition. Constantine was well aware of this reality and did his best to promote his new religious agenda within its parameters. In his legislation limiting pagan practice, he strayed very little from earlier imperial laws in forbidding private divination and maleficent magic while generally permitting signs to be taken and sacrifices made, at least down to the year 324. Beyond this we have contradictory indications about whether he issued a blanket ban on sacrifice. Even if such a decree there was, as seems likely, its enforcement was surely far from robust and by no means universal. This was first and foremost because of the emperor's acute awareness of the limitations of his own power, both to coerce belief and also to enforce his writ against inveterate resistance at the local level. It is with this as background that Constantine larded his letter to the eastern provincials with fiery anti-pagan rhetoric only to dampen the flames this surely stoked with demands that his subjects avoid religious violence.

There were, however, very real limits to Constantinian toleration beyond which he was ready to exert violence in the promotion of what he considered to be proper religion. In instances like Jerusalem and Mamre, where pagan monuments had encroached on spaces claimed as sacred by Christians, Constantine was swift and decisive in violently destroying traditional pagan holy places and turning them over to Christians. The motivations for other temple destructions are not always clear. We have no clear idea, for example, why Constantine singled out Asclepius's temple at Aegeae for destruction even though he left other temples intact, including those much more clearly implicated in inciting Christian persecutions like Didyma and Daphne. With Aphaca and Heliopolis, the presence of ritual prostitution appears to have played an important role, but the divergent fates of the two give a powerful indication of the limits of his ability to control local practice: the former, which had no developed civic apparatus, was simply obliterated, while the latter, which was a city in its own right, proved resistant to Constantine's efforts to construct a Christian church. If anything, these flagrant displays of power politics only strengthened local resistance, certainly at Heliopolis, which maintained its pagan character into the sixth century, but also at Aegeae and Aphaca, both of which witnessed continued cultic activity in the century following Constantine. With his temple destructions, Constantine of course started a trend that would continue to snowball throughout the course of the fourth and fifth centuries.[85] He was thus far from a shining model of religious toleration vis-à-vis pagan communities. Even so, toleration as stated explicitly in his letter to the eastern provincials and as practiced in his extant laws was generally the watchword, even as intolerance was generally rewarded only with further resistance.

CHAPTER 13

Opposing Christians
Donatists and Caecilianists

Resistant Christians in North Africa

Resistance to Constantine's religious agenda did not arise from pagans alone. Constantine had only barely announced his conversion publicly when he became aware of dissent in the Christian community of North Africa. Probably in 308, a controversy had broken out there over episcopal succession that would prove agonizingly long lived and disturbingly virulent.[1] This region, it must be remembered, had suffered more from the Great Persecution than any other in the West. Although our evidence indicates that only the first of Diocletian's four persecutory edicts—ordering the destruction of churches and the confiscation of scriptures and sacred vessels—was ever promulgated in North Africa, we have clear indications that sacrifice was also frequently demanded as a test of loyalty and that resisters were executed in considerable numbers between 303 and 304.[2]

These same texts confirm in explicit detail the degree to which the apparatus of civic and state governance was deployed in the process of prosecuting and executing North African Christians. In compliance with the imperial edict, curial officials conducted thorough inquests to identify suspected Christians and ferret out their property for confiscation and destruction; if the Christians resisted the order and refused to surrender sacred belongings, they were tried by civic officials and remanded to the court of the provincial governor in Carthage; there they were again tried and, if they continued to profess Christianity, executed.[3] The enforcement of the imperial order against the Christians was thus possible only with cooperation from the leadership classes of North African cities.

Although this pressure did not lead to the collapse of the Christian community, it created rifts in its membership when some—likely many—succumbed to pressures to hand over sacred vessels and scriptures in order to avoid arrest, loss of status, and even execution. Fellow Christians of a rigorist bent labeled these compromisers *traditores*, Latin for both "handers over" and "betrayers."[4] They questioned the faith of the accommodationists and argued that the taint of betrayal by any who were Christian clergy extended outward to those they had baptized, ordained, or consecrated. After all, could a bishop guilty of surrendering the scriptures for destruction baptize a catechumen or ordain another clergyman in any legitimate way? Rigorists and accommodationists alike agreed that any cleric proven to have turned over holy property should be deposed, but the rigorists went so far as to argue that those whom the *traditores* had baptized before their deposition should be rebaptized by a legitimate episcopal authority, and those they had consecrated were equally stained with the taint of betrayal and were thus unworthy of recognition. In other words, the rigorists believed that resistance to state persecution was definitional for Christian self-identity. True Christians were those who had stood up to the persecutors or who could claim direct descent—confessional and ritual rather than genetic—from these original martyrs and confessors.

The divisions this created in the African church came to a head after the bishop of Carthage, Mensurius, died in absentia and his deacon, Caecilianus, was hastily elected in his stead, probably in 308.[5] A shadow was cast over Caecilianus's election from the beginning, both because he was consecrated in the absence of the bishops of Numidia, who were normally charged with installing the Carthaginian prelate, and because his opponents also accused him of being a *traditor*, of having forcibly prevented faithful Christians from bringing aid to confessors in prison, and of having been consecrated by another alleged *traditor*, Felix, bishop of Abthugni.[6] Caecilianus's adversaries thus assembled a council of seventy bishops in Carthage (sometime between early 308 and early 311) that ordered his deposition and replacement by a *lector* named Maiorinus.[7] Thus was born a schism between two competing bishops of Carthage, each of whom immediately began rallying rival subordinates throughout the North African provinces to their respective sides.

In the years to come, the community of rigorists would be referred to as the Donatists, after Donatus of Casae Nigrae, who succeeded Maiorinus as bishop of Carthage in the course of 313.[8] Although modern scholarship preserves this collective appellation for convenience's sake, the rigorists referred to themselves as "the church of the pure" and "the church of the truth" because of their belief that their heritage had not been tainted by the stain of falsehood and betrayal.[9] Likewise, the Donatists foisted on their opponents the collective appellation Caecilianists, although they themselves preferred the name Catholics, affirming their understanding that they represented the universal, and more particularly, the Roman church.

The Church of the Martyrs

The Donatists gained widespread support from churches throughout North Africa and particularly in the western provinces of Numidia and Mauretania Caesariensis. Locale by locale, they challenged the Catholic leadership for the control of cities, villages, and farmsteads. Augustine, who spent much of his episcopal career combating the dissident church, indicates that the group emphasized its role as the "church of the martyrs" because of its belief that it alone carried on the hallowed tradition of sacred suffering.[10] We know of large numbers of martyr shrines connected with the parts of North Africa where the movement flourished and have several preserved martyr acts that were composed and transmitted by the Donatist community.[11] These textual and material constructions were then integrated into annual festivals commemorating the martyrs with ritualized recitations of their acts. The imbrication of text, shrine, and ceremony helped define and reinforce group identity around a cadre of heroes whose primary achievement consisted in unbending resistance to the coercive authority of the state.[12]

This message is clear, for example, in a Donatist hagiographical text known as the *Passion of the Martyrs of Abitina*.[13] The narrative lays heavy emphasis on the distinction between this small town's *traditor* bishop and those faithful martyrs who celebrated the mass "in defiance of the prohibition of the Emperors and Caesars" (*contra interdictum Imperatorum et Caesarum*).[14] When Anullinus—the proconsular governor of Africa during the Great Persecution and almost always the arch-persecutor in Donatist martyr narratives—is reported to have implored the confessors to spare their lives and abide by the imperial commands, these are said to have replied, "We are Christians. We cannot keep any law but the holy one of our Lord [*legem domini sanctam*], even if it means the spilling of our blood."[15] The text goes on to draw an equally bold line between authentic Christians and the imagined community of *traditores*— the true enemies—in a dramatic scene set shortly before the martyrs' execution. In it the unyielding confessors proclaim twice in quick succession: "If anyone should communicate with the *traditores*, he will have no part in the kingdom of heaven with us."[16] For the Donatist author of this text, then, the key to self-definition was unfailing adherence to the sect, uncompromising avoidance of communion with *traditores*, and an unflinching willingness to resist the state's laws if these impinged on right religion.

Defining Identity by Deploying the Imperial Legal Apparatus

Although the persecutions in Africa had ceased by 305, the Donatist schism came to a head only after pressures from the Roman state on the Christian community of North Africa had begun to subside. Already early in his reign, perhaps in 308,

Maxentius had called a formal halt to persecutions in his territories.[17] By 311 Galerius issued his Edict of Toleration, grudgingly granting Christians the right to exist, provided they caused no trouble to the commonweal.[18] Around the same time, Maxentius ordered the restoration of property confiscated from African Christians during the persecution, which occured at some point after he had regained the region from the usurper Domitius Alexander in 310, and probably only in summer 311.[19] Nevertheless, this process had clearly not reached completion before Constantine's defeat of Maxentius, for in the first extant letter of Constantine's from the immediate aftermath of the Battle of the Milvian Bridge, he ordered the Proconsul of Africa, Anullinus—not the infamous persecutor, but a relative who shared his name—to return confiscated property taken during the persecution to the churches in the cities of his province.[20] This letter, datable to late 312 or early 313, likely accompanied some sort of edict that granted both the restoration of property and the acknowledgment of Christianity as a *religio licita*. We find these same principles in the two copies of a letter sent by Licinius to eastern governors after his meeting with Constantine in Milan in early 313—the letter commonly referred to as the "Edict of Milan."[21]

In the same period, Constantine sent two further letters to North Africa: the first, directed once again to Anullinus, grants curial immunity to clergy of the Catholic church; the second, directed to Caecilianus, allows the bishop of Carthage to collect annual subsidies of three thousand folles from the imperial fisc for distribution to his congregation.[22] In both, it is clear that Constantine had been made aware of factional tensions among North African Christians, for in his second letter to Anullinus he specifies that "the Catholic church" eligible for the subsidies was to be defined as the collectivity led by Caecilianus—Constantine was thus aware that there were other claimants to episcopal authority in Carthage;[23] and in the letter to Caecilianus himself, Constantine mentions explicitly "some men who happen to be of unsettled mind and wish to turn the people of the holy Catholic church away with their shameful corruption."[24] The emperor had thus learned of the schism and already declared his favoritism for the Catholic cause.

Eager for a chance to air their side of the story, the rigorists lodged a petition for an imperial hearing. In a letter preserved by Augustine and dated precisely to April 15, 313, Anullinus reports to the emperor that Caecilianus's opponents had approached him with two petitions that he was forwarding to the emperor: one sealed in leather with a label attached, reading, "Petition [*libellus*] of the catholic church with charges [*crimina*] against Caecilianus, submitted by the party of Maiorinus," and the second an unsealed document attached to the first.[25] Numerous references in Augustine and the acts of the Council of Carthage of 411 reaffirm a point already clear from the title of the first petition: the rigorists were bringing formal charges (*crimina*) against the Carthaginian bishop, accusations of wrongdoing that, they felt, should be prosecuted in an imperial instance.[26] Of what precisely these consisted, we can no longer say. They may have been civil (wrongful possession or repossession of church property), criminal (lodging false accusations, fabrication of evidence, perhaps even physical abuse), or both.[27] Regardless, the rigorists had taken note that Constantine was now treating the church as a legally recognized entity and inviting it to enlist imperial officials for the restitution of its property, the enforcement of its rights, and the grant of imperial privileges. With their petitions, the Donatists were simply asking to move their ecclesiastical leadership dispute—with its attendant consequences on both the control of church property and the definition of church community—into the imperial courts.

For his part, Constantine was just as eager to bring the matter to a close without being pulled into the question. He therefore chose to sidestep the request for an imperial trial and called instead for a synod of bishops to decide the case in Rome under the leadership of Pope Miltiades.[28] He ordered three Gallic prelates, Reticius of Autun, Marinus of Arles, and Maternus of Cologne, to travel there and join Miltiades for a meeting, to which Miltiades then invited fifteen more bishops from Italy. The synod was convened on October 2, 313, at the *domus Faustae*, part of the imperial palace at the Lateran, near the site of the new episcopal church Constantine had initiated there the previous winter.[29] For all that he avoided direct involvement in the decision, Constantine had thus made it eminently clear that he and the imperial administration maintained an active interest in promoting the conduct of this church business. In the event, the council acquitted Caecilianus and may even have ordered the temporary detention of his accusers,[30] who by now had come under the leadership of Donatus, the party's champion for the next three decades. With this ecclesiastical decision, Constantine no doubt hoped the matter would be resolved.

Instead, once they reached Africa after this setback, the Donatists once again petitioned the emperor through his *vicarius Africae*, Aelafius, for a new inquest. They claimed their case had not been heard in its entirety before the presiding bishops had gone into a closed session to issue their judgment.[31] Furious with their persistence, Constantine nonetheless granted the request and ordered that a trial should be held in Gaul, at the city of Arles, beginning on August 1, 314.[32] This time, rather than entrust the organization of the hearing to a single bishop, the emperor assembled a much larger synod by sending out letters to numerous western prelates, ordering their attendance, and offering them permission to use the public posting system for travel to Gaul.[33] By constituting this ecclesiastical assembly, however, Constantine was himself able to sidestep for a second time the Donatists' request for an imperial audience.[34]

Once again, the Council of Arles found in favor of Caecilianus, but also issued a series of canons that included specific provisions regulating the practice of rebaptism, forbidding the repetition of ordinations performed by *traditores*, and punishing bringers of false accusations with excommunication.[35] In light of these findings, Constantine ordered that Donatist leaders—those who had come to the council, but also others who had remained in Africa—should be rounded up and sent to his court.[36] This we learn from a letter the emperor wrote to the Catholic bishops who had assembled at Arles reporting that, even after this second judgment, the Donatists had lodged yet another appeal in hopes that Constantine would at last hear the case.[37] Infuriated by their persistence, Constantine railed: "They demand judgment from me who am myself awaiting judgment from Christ. In fact, I say that if there is any truth in the matter, the judgment of priests ought to be treated as if the Lord himself had sat in judgment and passed sentence. . . . But these men abandon heavenly things to seek the things of this world. O the rabid shamelessness of their insanity! Just as happens with cases among the pagans, they interpose an appeal. . . . What should I do with these scofflaws, who refuse heavenly judgment but think they should demand my judgment instead?"[38]

We have already seen that by 318, and likely some years earlier, Constantine had granted bishops the right to try civil cases if one or both parties to a suit appealed for a shift of venue. We have also seen that Constantine initiated this new judicial instance in keeping with Christian traditions stretching back to Paul's First Epistle to the Corinthians (6:1–6) admonishing Christians to settle disputes among themselves rather than bringing them into the courts of pagans. Finally, we saw that the two extant laws attesting to this new *episcopale iudicium* confirm that bishops' judgments were to be considered equivalent to those of the emperor—*pro sanctis*—and thus ineligible for appeal.[39] These same principles clearly governed Constantine's conception of the Donatist appeals as represented in this quotation: neither were these dissidents justified in requesting a hearing in the imperial courts, nor were they justified in their persistent desire to overturn episcopal verdicts by appeal.

Ultimately, however, a state resolution is precisely what Constantine was forced into rendering. We have a number of documents from the period between the Council of Arles and 317 that confirm that not only did Constantine permit the Donatist detainees to return to their homes in April 315,[40] but he also granted their request for an inquest into the conduct of Caecilianus's consecrator, Felix of Abthugni. In the event, Felix was tried at Carthage in early 315 by the *proconsul Africae* Aelianus, but he too was acquitted.[41] Even this, however, did not put an end to the matter. A letter Constantine wrote to the Donatists later that same summer indicates he had contemplated sending a group of advisers to Africa to investigate the situation further, but decided instead to summon Caecilianus to

Italy for another hearing in Rome.[42] When this too fell through, Constantine sent yet another letter to the Vicar of Africa, Domitius Celsus, that responded to news of rioting there by issuing a threat that the emperor would soon come himself to resolve the dispute with force.[43] In the event, however, Constantine backed away from this bluster and instead brought Caecilianus and his Donatist accusers to northern Italy, where, at last, he heard their case personally at the imperial capital of Milan, probably in the summer of 316.[44]

Enforcing Judgments, Enacting Violence

Finally the Donatists had gotten the imperial audience they had persistently demanded, though, once again, they failed to win the favorable judgment they earnestly expected. The emperor found against them and was now obliged by the logic of the justice system to execute his decision. Thus, already in late 316, Constantine appears to have issued an edict ordering the Donatists to return to union with the Caecilianists and demanding that any ecclesiastical property in the Donatists' possession be confiscated to the fisc.[45] By early 317, he sent imperial troops to Africa to enforce his commands. In essence, these were enacting a possessory interdict against a dissident group now amply proven to have been in control of church property to which it had no valid claim. Nevertheless, to soften the blow, Constantine authorized his agents to offer schismatic clergy the same emoluments he was extending to Catholic clergy, provided they rejoined Caecilianus's church.[46]

For their part, the Donatists were unwilling to cede any ground. This was, as we have seen above, a movement born of resistance to the violent enforcement of imperial writ. The execution of Constantine's judgment against the Donatist rigorists thus offered an opportunity to enact once again their oppositional reading to imperial power, a reading that had been crucial to the formation of their group identity in the first place. Thus, when a cohort sent on the authority of the *Dux* Ursatius under the command of the Tribune Marcellinus attempted to evict a party of Donatist supporters from a church near Carthage in 317, a melee broke out during which Honoratus, bishop of Sicilibba, and a number of other congregants were killed.

The *Passio Donati*, our lone extant martyr narrative recounting this incident—and our only known evidence for the violent enforcement of Constantine's decree—portrays the scene in terms entirely consonant with those described in the acts of martyrs killed during the Great Persecution.[47] The emperor and his soldiers were like wolves in sheep's clothing (Matt 7:15; cf. John 10:10–13) who falsely claimed to represent God's people because they enjoyed good fortune in this world.[48] The truly faithful, the author assures his readers, were those who, like the Savior, were made to suffer in and by this world.[49] For this reason, when the Donatist faithful witnessed Constantine's troops surround their basilica outside Carthage, "not only were they not put to flight in fear of imminent death, instead they flocked all the more eagerly to the house of prayer out of a desire to suffer."[50]

This hagiographical representation of Donatist resistance can be taken as indicative of the attitude of the broader community: once the state had confirmed that it refused the Donatist party the recognition Constantine had promised to "Christians," they easily reverted to the model of resistance that had been for them a hallmark of community formation in the face of persecution. Furthermore, although Constantine took measures to minimize the chances for casualties in the enforcement of his judgment—by ordering the troops charged with confiscating Donatist churches to wield only clubs instead of swords[51]—and although he appears to have halted his efforts to enact the order of union shortly after this brief outburst, he had given the Donatists sufficient proof that the new Christian empire was little more than a perpetuator of the brutality of past regimes. In the eyes of the Donatists, state persecutions had never really ceased.[52] Having failed to see this, Constantine himself only made the situation worse with his efforts to coerce union. By applying the blunt instrument of state coercion to the fraught and fragile relations prevailing in post-persecution North Africa, Constantine thus shattered the delicate vessel of religious and civic union into a thousand sharp slivers.

Judgmentalism and Toleration

In many ways, Constantine's conflict with the Donatists resulted from his own mistaken assumptions about the totalizing power of Christian religion and the unimpeachable sacrality of its clergy. Blind faith in the power of God and his ministers led Constantine to believe in the real possibility of a unified and concordant church. This was, of course, an ideal that can be easily construed from biblical discourse and patristic writing, and it is one for which Constantine expresses a longing over and over again.[53] As the first Christian emperor, he was in a unique position to actuate this imagined harmony through the tools of governance. With his help as emperor, the church could reach a utopian state of perfect concord, or so he believed. From the start, however, he was confronted with a reality of infighting and factionalism that undermined these preconceptions. His anger and frustration at this turn of events is evident in his discourses with and about the Donatists, whom he blames for the controversy even as he charac-

terizes them as insane, stubborn, diseased, and possessed by the devil.[54] Reading
this prejudgment in his communiqués, the Donatists are sure to have been reaffirmed in their conviction that the new imperial leadership was just as wicked as
its predecessors, and just as adamantly to be resisted.

In some respects, however, the same preconceptions that led Constantine into
unrealistic paradigms of state-enforced church union also helped him find a way
forward that dampened—without extinguishing—further conflict, at least for the
remainder of his reign. When the Donatists lodged yet another petition in early
321 proclaiming that "they would never communicate with that scoundrel bishop
of his [that is, Caecilianus] and were prepared to continue to suffer whatever he
wished to do to them,"[55] Constantine relented with a letter to the vicar of Africa
revoking the exile of Donatist bishops.[56] At the same time he sent another reporting his relaxation of the order of union that was addressed "To all the bishops in
Africa and to the people [plebs] of the Catholic church."[57] Of itself this salutation
is noteworthy for interpellating the church into being as a unified and recogniz-
able political whole. The text grows even more remarkable as it continues, first
with a justification for the emperor's efforts to enforce concord, then with an
explanation of why the emperor had been unable to subdue this stubborn force of
wickedness, and finally with the concession that the mercy of the omnipotent
God (omnipotentis dei misericordia) alone could remedy the situation. This last
statement is followed by the imperial disposition:

> But while the heavenly medicine takes effect, our plans must be moder-
> ated, so that we cultivate long suffering [patientiam], and, whatever they
> attempt or do through their insolence in keeping with their habit of excess,
> we should tolerate everything with the virtue of tranquility [id totum tran-
> quillitatis virtute toleremus]. Let nothing be done out of revenge against
> any offense [iniuriae]; for it is the mark of a fool to take into his own hands
> the vengeance [vindicta] that we should reserve to God [Rom. 12:17–19],
> especially since our faith ought to trust that whatever is suffered by the
> outrages of this sort of people will count as martyrdom before God [mar-
> tyrii gratia apud deum esse valiturum].[58]

The entire passage is suffused with Christian discourse, a discourse that provides
Constantine with the rationale for his grant of toleration. The supreme representative of state authority has relinquished claims to the enforcement of justice even
against open violence and has remanded judgment of the offending Donatists to
the Christian god.[59] Turning the Donatist claims to superiority through martyrdom on their head, Constantine had thus invited the Catholic community to seek
dominance through the supreme act of submission.

It has become traditional to argue that this concession was reluctant and reflected above all Constantine's need to avoid open rioting in this vital but volatile region as he prepared for his second war with Licinius.[60] This interpretation ignores two important points. First, although Constantine's relations with Licinius did begin once again to deteriorate in early 321, open war was still some three years in the offing, making it far too early to excuse this relaxation of pressure on the Donatists as a simple act of realpolitik. Second, even after defeating Licinius in 324 and expressing an open desire to bring the North African conflict to a close in his letter to Alexander and Arius, Constantine maintained his policy of toleration until the end of his reign.[61] Thus, in 330 when the Donatist community in Cirta-Constantina—as we have seen, a city particularly beloved by Constantine—took over the church he had built for the Catholics there, he once again called for forbearance. In a letter sent to the Numidian bishops in 330, he promised to build the Catholics a new church and congratulated them for refraining from efforts to reclaim the previous structure out of vengeance (*vindicta*). Here again, his justification for this surprisingly conciliatory position was twofold. First, he argued, it was right for true Christian leaders to endure the insults inflicted on them by the Donatists with long suffering (*patientia*), a notion that recurs four times in the letter.[62] Second, he assures the Catholics, God's judgment will punish Donatist guilt much more severely than either emperor or clerics could.[63] To be sure, this is far from a call to love one's enemy in any unconditional sense, but the obvious intrusion of Christian ethics and theodicy into imperial political ideology helped Constantine rationalize a compromise position that allowed him to diffuse a potentially explosive situation and thereby maintain the peace in this crucial Numidian city.

The roots of this call for *patientia* toward wrongdoers and trust in divine judgment can be found in no less an ecclesiastical luminary than Lactantius. Here it should be recalled that Lactantius had affiliated himself with the court of Constantine as early as 310, when he probably first came to serve as tutor to Constantine's son Crispus.[64] Moreover, E. Digeser has shown that, by the time he composed his letter to the bishops of Arles in 314, Constantine shows clear familiarity with Lactantius's masterwork, the *Divine Institutes*, a book he rededicated to Constantine as early as the winter of 312/313.[65] It is thus reasonable to assume that it could have been this treatise that schooled Constantine in the principles of toleration he would apply to the Donatist cause.

The central argument of the *Divine Institutes* is that Christianity offers the only sure path to justice and that the truly just empire would be governed by its principles. In the fifth book, Lactantius goes on to discuss how a Christian ruler would never persecute his subjects for their religious beliefs but would instead endure wrongdoing with long suffering: "Religion must be defended not by killing but by dying, not with savagery but with *patientia*, not with crime but faith."[66] The notion of *patientia* as the core principle for properly safeguarding religion recurs eleven more times by the end of the fifth book, and it appears in other parts of the *Divine Institutes* as well.[67] Finally, Lactantius closes the book with reassurances that Christians need not fear that wrongs done to them will go unpunished, for, he assures them, God promises vengeance against those who wrong him.[68]

This is precisely the argument made by Constantine in his letters of 321 and 330. The emperor was thus reshaping Lactantius's Christian philosophy into political action in his dealings with the Donatists. To be sure, the military units Constantine sent to Africa to enforce his order of union in 316–317 had already overstepped the bounds of violence and thereby vitiated any claims he later made to have fostered an environment of purely peaceful interchange. All the same, Constantine's subsequent retreat from aggression and his generally tolerant attitude toward the rigorist sect, a group he actively distrusted and openly despised, was founded on well-articulated principles that allowed him to brook resistance with a remarkable degree of equanimity.

Ongoing Resistance in Christian North Africa

Nevertheless, with these opposing Christians, as indeed with oppositional pagan cities like Heliopolis-Baalbek, the close of Constantine's reign by no means brought an end to religious conflict. As happened in the pagan communities, Constantine's introduction of violence into the equation ultimately served to galvanize long-term opposition to imperial will. The result was a landscape pocked with regions, cities, neighborhoods, and even farmsteads that stood in opposition to one another and, many of them, to the emperor himself. Some notion of the degree of division can be had from the roll call taken at the Council of Carthage in 411, an event intended to put a final halt to the dispute. There 429 dioceses were represented, of which 198 shared both a Catholic and a Donatist bishop, 149 claimed only a Donatist, and 82 claimed only a Catholic. The exclusively Donatist communities thus outnumbered their Catholic counterparts by nearly two to one, making it clear that the entire region—and particularly the westerly territories of Numidia, Mauretania Sitifensis, and Mauretania Caesariensis—stood in principled opposition to the church of the emperors.[69] The power of the sovereign to compel religious compliance was thus patently circumscribed by the collective force of a determined opposition.

It is no surprise that tension and at times open violence continued long after Constantine's efforts to restore peace to the region. The next eruption of violence after his death in 337 occurred in the mid-340s when the *Comes Africae* Taurinus used armed force to put a halt to dissident efforts to prevail in property disputes using bands of "circumcellions"—itinerant farm workers employed as religious enforcers by the Donatists.[70] In 347 Constantine's youngest son Constans attempted to attract the dissidents back into union by sending agents under the leadership of two tribunes named Paulus and Macarius to distribute emoluments to African communities in the name of Catholic charity. This too provoked unrest in Numidia when the Donatist bishop of Bagaï, himself named Donatus, assembled a band of circumcellions and engaged in open fighting against imperial agents, which eventually resulted in the death of Donatus and many of his followers.[71] When the Proconsul of Africa subsequently posted an imperial edict ordering union in Carthage, a layman named Maximianus tore it down and was arrested and beaten. He and another dissident protestor named Isaac later died in prison, and their bodies were disposed of in the sea to prevent their veneration as martyrs.[72] And in Nova Petra, a bishop named Marculus was also beaten and eventually cast to his death from a cliff.[73] Such incidents became iconic in the imagination of the Donatists, for these martyrs were celebrated as heroes in text, shrine, and liturgy, and the "Persecution of Macarius" (*persecutio Macariana*) was reified as a canonical example of state violence against the "Church of Truth."[74]

Although violence remained relatively subdued throughout the remainder of the fourth century, the controversy rent region from region and city from city as Donatist or Catholic followers aligned themselves one against another in this symbolic, but at times fiercely bitter, battle for church authority. After the Donatists themselves split into rival factions in the 390s and then took the misstep of supporting—or at least seeking support from—the failed usurper Gildo (397–398), the Catholic leadership was able to turn up the heat on the dissidents by convincing the emperor Honorius (395–423) to issue edicts banning the Donatist church and confiscating its property.[75] A fearsome struggle ensued, and by the 430s the Donatist community had been seriously weakened by combined pressure from the imperial government and the Catholic hierarchy. Only the Vandal invasions were able to put a more decisive halt to the controversy, and even despite this huge sea-change in political leadership some Donatist communities continued to survive into the late sixth-century world of Gregory the Great.[76]

Conclusion

Donatist resisters, like their pagan counterparts discussed in the previous chapter, simultaneously provoked open violence from Constantine and demonstrated the very real limits of his authority. His inability to control this movement thwarted his efforts to impose religious uniformity on the cities of North Africa and set the stage for ongoing civic and religious conflict. Constantine's grant of official recognition to Christianity as a *religio licita* and his offer of fiscal and civic privileges to its leaders had invited the church to participate more fully in the structures and processes of government. It also presupposed a clearly identifiable church leadership and a fundamental union of community that had never been part of this mass movement and never would be.

When rigorist North African Christians began to assert counterclaims to authority over the church (or churches) of their cities and region, Constantine made every effort to deploy the tools of government to resolve the dispute, but also to transfer judgment over this fundamentally religious squabble to the community of bishops. Repeated requests from the Donatists for imperial judgment were pushed aside, with the result that a new form of judicial instance—the imperially sponsored church council—was invented. Ultimately, however, this did not quiet the protests, and Constantine was forced to concede to the Donatists' requests for an imperial trial. In the event he found against their community and began enforcing his judgment with the executive authority of the state. The violence that ensued was brief but decisive: it simultaneously convinced Constantine of the futility of state coercion against Christian dissenters and galvanized the Donatists in their opposition to the central government.

By the time Constantine relented in 321—after just five years of official sanctions and only a single attested instance of imperial violence—the damage had been done. He had offered the "church of the martyrs" the next episode in its ongoing narrative of suffering at the hands of an oppressive state. As the Donatists continued to fail to garner imperial support for their cause for the remainder of the fourth century, they gradually built on the enmity they encountered to maintain a separate and oppositional church for more than a century to come. In a world where church was fast becoming synonymous with polity, this meant that the movement also split North African cities into oppositional communities that remained locked in conflict. Thus even those of Constantine's subjects most likely to benefit from the claims to authority he offered them through his adoption of Christian religion could at times reject those claims and seek lasting confrontation instead.

In Habermasian terms, the Donatists were initially eager to redeem both of the claims to authority offered by their new emperor—his office as Augustus and his adherence to the Christian faith. Once Constantine ruled against them in court and attempted to enforce his decision with force, however, they retrenched and denied both of the sources of power he asserted: although Constantine was ruler of the secular world, this position held no sway in the spiritually contoured lifeworld they claimed to inhabit; and although Constantine professed Christianity on the surface, his faith was adulterated in ways that rendered it more noxious than the unbelief of pagans. In many ways, then, the Donatists proved to be even less receptive to Constantine's communicative actions than even traditional polytheists.

Only the passivity Constantine eventually came to practice and counsel to others could create the space necessary for a peaceful modus vivendi, even if it helped little in advancing dialogue between the two sides. His assumption that Christian leaders should endure mistreatment with long suffering (*patientia*) and that, in so doing, they would one day enjoy the reward of divine vengeance against their persecutors undergirded both the edict of toleration he issued regarding the Donatists in 321 and the order to the bishops of Cirta-Constantina to refrain from attacking their Donatist opponents in 330. In this sense as well, Constantine's dealings with oppositional Christian communities mirrored those with pagans, at least as expressed in the letter to the eastern provincials. Even if in both instances he at times allowed himself to be pulled into direct and open attacks on dissident communities, he generally exercised restraint in ways that reinforced his power without ever rendering it anything like supreme.

CHAPTER 14

Complex Cities
Antioch and Alexandria

Cultural and Religious Diversity
in the Metropoleis of the East

In numerous instances in Chapters 4 through 7, we have seen how Constantine was able to exploit interurban rivalries in order to impose aspects of his religious agenda at the local and regional levels. Orcistus and Nacoleia, Hispellum and Volsinii, Gaza and Maiouma offer just three particularly vivid examples of situations where he used relatively small and religiously homogeneous polities as wedges with which to drive pro-Christian policies into regions that were otherwise nearly seamless in their adherence to traditional religions. Urban politics was, however, often considerably more complicated than what we find in the small to mid-sized cities of Phrygia, Umbria, and southern Palestine. This was especially true in larger urban centers that, by virtue of their population size, were bound to have much more pluralistic ethnic and religious profiles. It was doubly so in eastern polities, where non-Roman religious traditions were more variegated and much more socially and ethnically pronounced.

Antioch and Alexandria both provide us with excellent cases in point of the complications posed by large eastern metropoleis and of the limitations Constantine confronted in his efforts to manage peer polity interactions in a way that would enhance his central authority. In both cities he was confronted with religiously diverse environments that were unlikely to yield rapidly to efforts to achieve universal conversion to Christianity. For that matter, the Christian communities in both cities were themselves divided, and the rival factions within each proved strongly resistant to compromise. This complex situation was then further complicated as leaders from other peer polities stepped in to mediate the situation, but also to promote their own claims to power. In this world, local leaders perceived the benefits of cultivating strategies of distinction as a means to enhance their power at the regional level and even to assert their opposition to central control. Thus the dialogic process of engagement between competing intra-urban civic factions, and the ongoing enactment of inter-urban peer polity rivalry, effectively fostered local autonomy from the imperial government and even resistance to the will of the emperor.

The Pagan Communities of Alexandria and Antioch

Alexandria and Antioch each played home to a bewildering variety of competing interest groups that struggled for power and supremacy both within and beyond their civic spaces. Both were home to as many as 200,000 inhabitants, each historically restive populations that had never been easy to control.[1] Both were religiously pluralistic, housing large pagan, Christian, and Jewish subcommunities, and these had traditions of interaction and rivalry that went far back in time and mirrored at the local level the inter-urban exchanges that had long characterized rival peer polities.[2] These competing religious communities—and the sectarian subgroups within them—generally coexisted peacefully, but they also maintained a strong sense of self-identity and with it a readiness to defend self-interests, even at the expense of civic harmony.

Both Antioch and Alexandria had thriving pagan populations when Constantine gained control of them in the 320s. In the reign of Maximinus Daia, both had asserted their claims to religious authority by sending embassies to Maximinus requesting permission to expel their local Christians.[3] Antioch had done so under the philosopher and decurion Theotecnus and, among other victims, saw to the execution of the outspoken and charismatic cleric Lucian on January 7, 312. Alexandria's Christian purge went all the way up to its bishop, Peter, who was beheaded on November 26, 311, the first known victim of Maximinus's renewed persecutions.[4] Both cities were duly rewarded for their aggressively pro-pagan posture when Maximinus granted them permission to resume the minting of civic coinages at their resident mints. Unsurprisingly, both chose to depict locally important deities on these new issues: Antioch minted its famous Tyche as well as Jupiter, while Alexandria minted Serapis and the holy Nile.[5]

Upon gaining control of both cities, Constantine seems to have made efforts to avoid similarly violent clashes. This does not mean, however, that he eschewed all efforts to rein in pagan control of civic religious mechanisms. In Alexandria, Eusebius tells us, he ordered the dissolution of the band of "effeminate priests" (likely eunuchs) who maintained the cult of the Nile, and Socrates reports that he also ordered Alexander, bishop of Alexandria, to confiscate the Nilometer—a sacred instrument used to measure the annual Nile flood—from the Temple of Serapis and transplant it to a Christian church.[6] This was obviously a bold move in a land that relied on the Nile flood for its livelihood—and its contribution to the grain supply of Rome and later Constantinople. In ordering it, Constantine was thus risking a cosmic confrontation with the pagan gods that might have cost him dearly in his secular domains. After all, in the early third century, Tertullian could write, "If the Nile fails to flood . . . a cry goes up from everyone: 'It's the fault of the Christians.'"[7] In the end, of course, this was a battle Constantine won, for the Nile flood arrived on schedule that year. This must have reinforced his sense of triumphalism, even while affirming in the minds of the Alexandrians the power of his Christian god. Yet the culture war was hardly over, for Julian defiantly restored the Nilometer to the Serapeum in 361,[8] and there it remained until the temple's destruction in 392, at which point it was still widely feared that the god would punish Egypt for this affront to his shrine.[9] Once again, Rufinus reports, these fears proved unfounded, leaving the Christians to assume their victory on the field of combat had been reenacted in the sphere of the divine.

Although the symbolic payoff of Constantine's gesture in permitting the removal of the Nilometer from the Serapeum was surely great, he does not appear to have pressed his suit against the pagan population of Alexandria any further than this. A ninth-century source does claim that Bishop Alexander (312–328) took over a temple to Kronos (perhaps the Egyptian Bes), melted down its bronze idol, and rededicated the structure as a church to the archangel Michael, but the absence of testimony in contemporary sources—especially Eusebius, who gleefully reports other temple destructions—makes this story suspicious.[10] On the face of it, Constantine seems unlikely to have permitted this sort of confrontation in so volatile an environment, for he was surely aware that such an assault would lead to open conflict.

Indeed, his successors learned the hard way the sorts of melees that could explode when Alexandria's Christians and pagans were permitted to clash openly.[11] Under Constantius II, the overseer of the mint Dracontius, the Count Diodorus, and the city's Arian bishop George made blatant and insulting attacks on traditional worshippers and their shrines. Once Julian came to power in 361 and executed Artemius, who as *Dux Aegypti* had tolerated these provocations, Alexandria's pagan community took justice into its own hands, murdered all three provocateurs, burned their bodies, and cast the ashes into the sea.[12] At the same time they also burned the great church of Alexandria known as the Caesareum.[13] Under Theodosius I, Alexandria witnessed open street warfare on an even grander scale that resulted in the complete destruction of the Serapeum in 392.[14] Similar riots would surely have ensued had Alexander attacked a prominent pagan shrine in the 320s, and these would surely be reported somewhere in our source record for the period. Rather than provoking or even just permitting this type of confrontation, Constantine seems to have favored toleration, and Alexandria remained quiescent under his rule. By setting a tone of peaceable relations, he not only avoided civil disturbance but also set the stage for the ongoing practice of pagan religion in Alexandria, which continued to fund an annual festival for the Holy Nile through the 380s and played home to an influential community of pagan intellectuals well into the fifth century.[15]

Our only source on Constantine's interactions with the pagan community in Antioch is a passage of Malalas that reports how he not only had a great octagonal church constructed in the city—a subject treated in Chapter 9—but he also had a temple of Hermes converted into a basilica (*basilikē*) and had a hospice (*xenōn*) built on the site of a bronze statue of Poseidon, which was melted down and refashioned in his own image.[16] Unfortunately, the passage is marred by errors and anachronisms, not least its assertion that Constantine visited Antioch personally, which he did not.[17] We know from instances discussed in Chapter 12 that Constantine did destroy and desacralize pagan monuments in a select number of cities, and from Chapter 8 that he confiscated sacred statues from many more cities for melting into bullion or transfer to Constantinople.[18] Malalas's report may not, therefore, be unreliable, but its palpable inaccuracies leave the matter open to debate. Even if the account has a basis in reality, it offers no clear proof that Constantine made a full frontal assault on the pagan community of Antioch. Malalas offers no hint that open conflict broke out, and Antioch's native son Libanius states explicitly in his *Oration on the Temples* that Constantine avoided attacking pagan cult.[19] Constantine's treatment of the pagans of this eastern megalopolis thus appears very much in line with his treatment of Alexandria's pagans. At most he forcefully appropriated sacred property, but he seems resolutely to have avoided open violence.

Antioch, Alexandria, and the Arian Controversy

Malalas's confusion over whether Constantine visited Antioch may be excusable on the grounds that the emperor did indeed have *plans* to travel to both Antioch and Alexandria in the aftermath of his victory over Licinius in late 324. In fact, his projected journey was so close to realization that it has left tantalizing traces in the sources. The mint of Antioch was ordered to issue coins heralding the "Arrival of our Augustus" (ADVENTVS AVGVSTI N[ostri]),[20] and from Egypt we have two papyri of early 325 outlining preparations for the emperor's impending visit.[21] Constantine also mentions his intended journey in a letter to Alexander, Bishop of Alexandria, and his recalcitrant presbyter Arius written in late 324 or early 325.

He writes because he had been informed of the dispute that had arisen between the two ecclesiastics over the nature of Christ's personhood, and he attributes his decision to *postpone* his eastward journey to their bickering:

> When I recently set foot in the city of Nicomedia, I had planned to hasten on to the East immediately. Although I was already eager to visit you and was in large part already in your presence, news of this affair tugged me back from my earlier undertaking, so that I would not be compelled to look with my own eyes on what I would scarce have considered possible to hear with my ears. Please open for me through your concord [*homonoia*] the road to the East which you have shut off through your bickering with one another, and permit me to look on you and all the other peoples with pleasure soon.[22]

It is difficult to know the degree to which the Arian controversy truly affected Constantine's decision to cancel his visit, for this seems a slender excuse on which to hang choices about the itinerary of the imperial court and army. He may have been making a virtue of necessity by cloaking other motives behind this patronizing veil of disappointment. On the other hand, he may just as well have been shielding himself from the embarrassment of having to wade into a messy and contentious situation, a controversy that his presence would only have exacerbated. In the instance of the Donatist affair, he had already struggled mightily to avoid entanglement in sectarian factionalism, and when he finally did render judgment and attempt to enforce it, the net result was open conflict and ultimately the need to back away from a controversy that was only exacerbated by his involvement. Here in 324, he may have been admitting the limitations of his authority by declining to carry through with his plans to visit the East.[23] Indeed, Eusebius reports in vague terms that tensions had reached such a boiling point in Alexandria that there was open rioting and even attacks on images of the emperor.[24] Rather than wade into this chaos, Constantine may have preferred to dangle the perquisites of an imperial journey before the Alexandrians as an incentive for them to solve their own problems before he would deign to grace them with his presence.[25]

The Arian controversy, which arose at some time between 318 and 321, pitted the priest Arius against his bishop over the question of Christ's relation to God the Father. The theological details of the matter can be studied elsewhere.[26] Of interest here is the way in which the dispute provided an arena within which intra- and inter-urban power dynamics were negotiated and renegotiated by ecclesiastics jockeying for position, and the way in which these same ecclesiastics used the emperor as a player whose authority they coveted but also questioned and at times challenged.[27] In fact, the sectarian squabbles—of which Arianism was but one—that plagued the Christian communities of eastern cities throughout the last dozen years of Constantine's reign offer an excellent test case of how peer polity interactions/rivalries of the sort outlined in Chapter 7 remained very much a part of the symbolic landscape of late antique cities. They also show well how local leaders could exploit long-standing traditions of interurban engagement and conflict in order to increase their power at the regional level and thereby place themselves in a position to respond to, shape, and at times oppose imperial policy.

From its beginning, the Arian controversy took on colors familiar from the long history of peer polity relations. Unwilling to accept his initial condemnation by Alexander, Arius traveled to Palestine, where he won support from a number of church leaders, including Eusebius, Bishop of Caesarea, and eventually to Bithynia, where the Bishop of Nicomedia, also named Eusebius, hosted a council that found his views to be orthodox. These and other bishops rallied to Arius's support against Alexander, insisting that the dissident priest be readmitted to communion in his home see. For his part Alexander circulated a letter warning fellow bishops from various cities against Arius's views and staunchly resisted external efforts to overturn decisions he had made for his own church community.[28] The growing intensity of this inter-urban bickering irritated Licinius, who was still eastern emperor at the time, so much that he forbade the convocation of further ecclesiastical councils in the final years of his reign.[29]

After gaining control of the East in 324, Constantine attempted swiftly to quash the Arian controversy by sending the letter quoted above to Alexander and Arius in which he chided both sides for "quarreling with each other about small and quite minute points."[30] It was hand delivered by the emperor's longtime ecclesiastical adviser, Ossius of Corduba, who had followed him to the East after his war with Licinius. Despite his imperially backed efforts to enforce concord between Arius and Alexander, Ossius's negotiations failed to produce a reconciliation. Nothing daunted, on his return journey to court, Ossius traveled through Antioch and there dealt with problems spilling over from Arius's visit to the region and the unrest this had provoked: after the death of their bishop Philogonius in late 323, the Antiochenes had transferred the pro-Arian Paulinus from Tyre to fill their see, but he expired shortly thereafter; in his stead, the anti-Arian Eustathius was transferred from Beroea.[31] Factional strife ensued, and Ossius organized a synod at Antioch in early 325 to put an end to the unrest. The meeting issued a creed that opposed subordinationist theology of the sort Arius propounded and provisionally excommunicated three bishops who refused to endorse it, including Eusebius of Caesarea.[32]

The Antiochene synod's decisions were to be reviewed at a council to be held in the late spring of 325 at Ancyra in central Anatolia.[33] This larger council was charged with making determinations on the Arian controversy as well as other pressing issues, especially the reckoning of the date of the Easter feast, which some calculated with reference to the Jewish Passover while others pointedly did not, and the reconciliation of the Alexandrian church hierarchy to the Melitians, a schismatic group that had already split from the establishment church in protest over its lenient treatment of lapsed Christians in 305/306.[34] We learn from another letter of the emperor that, early in 325, Constantine changed the venue for this upcoming council from Ancyra to Nicaea, a city that was easier to access from the sea coast and much closer to his residence in Nicomedia.[35] Despite his initial reluctance to be pulled into the controversy, then, Constantine was now edging toward direct involvement in the management of eastern ecclesiastical affairs.

In May of 325 the council assembled at Nicaea and Constantine was drawn inextricably into the fight. As many as three hundred bishops were present, all brought to the city and housed at imperial expense, and all feted in honor of Constantine's vicennalia, celebrated later that same summer.[36] We saw in Chapter 3 that, although Ossius of Corduba appears to have presided at the Council of Nicaea, Constantine attended and fancied himself responsible for the introduction of the term "homoousios" (one in being) to describe Christ's relationship to the Father.[37] More importantly, all extant ecclesiastical historians except Eusebius report that a number of bishops brought petitions outlining grievances against one another, but that Constantine chose to destroy them all without ever having read them.[38] He thus dispensed with the decorum of civic interchange by asserting the supremacy of his autocratic authority. This may have seemed a necessary and even logical response to the cacophony of voices he confronted, and it certainly represented a new direction relative to the one he took with the Donatists and their continuous stream of petitions to which the emperor furiously—in both senses of the word—responded. In the end, however, Constantine's power play at Nicaea served only to stoke the fires of the bitter and myriad rivalries.

At least in the moment, the Council achieved a consensus on the key issues it faced: Arius's views were declared heretical, and he was sent into exile; the question of Easter was resolved in favor of a non-Judaizing formula; and the Melitians were ordered into union with the bishop of Alexandria, who was himself required to readmit them. During the council, two Libyan bishops who had refused to sign the condemnation of Arius were exiled, and shortly afterward two more of Arius's strongest supporters, Eusebius of Nicomedia and Theognis of Nicaea, were also banished for having continued communication with Arian presbyters.[39] Consensus and unity were the watchwords as Constantine struggled to use his authority as emperor to enforce peace within the church and cooperation among its leaders. In his letter quoted above to Alexander and Arius, Constantine uses the rhetoric of concord (*homonoia*) as a rallying cry for an end to Christological dispute and the concomitant posturing that went with it, and in the years to come the same notion fairly resounds from extant Constantinian documents, where it recurs at least a dozen times.[40] It was Constantine's hope, therefore, that the display of imperial magnanimity and power he had shown at Nicaea would bring about a voluntary submission to his authority as each bishop subordinated himself to the greater good of harmony in compliance with the will of the emperor.

The Christian Community of Antioch

To the contrary, however, the bishops of the various eastern cities almost immediately made it clear that they would not cede control of the discourse to their sovereign. Much of their independent spirit was surely fostered in response to Constantine's conviction that bishops were his equals or even superiors in matters of faith. This we saw both in the third chapter of this book, where we explored the frequency with which Constantine humbled himself with the designation "fellow servant" in his addresses to bishops, as well as the thirteenth, where we witnessed his reluctance to pass judgment over ecclesiastics who were embroiled in the Donatist controversy. Bishops were, in Constantine's eyes, divinely ordained ministers whose counsels he was better qualified to facilitate than overturn. The refusal of eastern bishops to abide by Constantine's calls for concord also stemmed, however, from Constantine's own indecision on the matters decided by the Council of Nicaea. At some point in early 327 (or perhaps 328), having been persuaded to hear Arius's case and that of Eusebius of Nicomedia a second time, Constantine found both to be in compliance with the standards of orthodoxy and ordered their restitution to their dioceses.[41]

At around the same time, tensions had arisen in the Levant when the bishop of Antioch, Eustathius, whose appointment at Antioch had been reconfirmed by Ossius of Cordoba during his visit to the city in 325, began accusing Eusebius of Caesarea in neighboring Palestine of continuing to espouse Arian beliefs.[42] Eusebius of Caesarea fought fire with fire by accusing Eustathius of Sabellianism—failing to distinguish adequately the Father from the Son. Eusebius of Nicomedia, who was in the area touring Constantine's church-building program in Palestine, managed to pass through Antioch, attracted by an opportunity to retaliate against Eustathius for his earlier opposition to Arius and his allies. In the great tradition of peer polity embassies, Eusebius of Nicomedia moved with a large retinue of fellow bishops, including Eusebius of Caesarea, Patrophilus of Scythopolis, Aetius of Lydda, and Theodotus of Laodicea. Once in Antioch, probably in late 328, this group assembled a synod that issued a barrage of charges against Eustathius:

1. that he espoused Sabellian theology;
2. that he had behaved immorally by impregnating a young girl, who was produced at the hearing with babe in arms;
3. that he had insulted Constantine's mother Helena during her journey to the Holy Land.[43]

The details of the synod's proceedings as well as its chronology are sketchy in the source record, making it impossible to sort through the charges for their reliability. More important for our purposes is the intermingling of accusations of heresy, moral turpitude, and outright treason. This mix of theological, ethical, and criminal matters shows how bishops were exploring options for gaining the upper hand in this new variety of inter-urban power dispute. The shotgun approach adopted against Eustathius would quickly become the norm as controversies gained in frequency and intensity. Such barrages of accusations were already present, as we have seen, in the Donatist controversy, and their political importance should not be underestimated. After all, the emperor could rightfully recuse himself from deliberation over matters of theological concern, but civil and criminal delicts were squarely within his jurisdiction and could not, in the end, be sidestepped. For this reason, it was as often as not the finding of civil or criminal misbehavior that resulted in imperial action.

In the event, Eusebius of Nicomedia and his supporters succeeded in deposing Eustathius, and through ambassadors sent to Constantine's court at Nicomedia, they also secured an imperial hearing that eventually resulted in Eustathius's exile to Thrace.[44] This was surely facilitated by the troubles Eustathius himself had generated in his own city by violently banishing a number of his priests for their alleged Arian sympathies.[45] Indeed, there was a strong undercurrent of support for Arius's views in Antioch, particularly among those who rallied around the local ecclesiastical luminary cum martyr Lucian, executed in 312 under Maximinus Daia. Lucian's disciples numbered a large cadre of prominent figures who had sided with Arius,[46] and his devotees included even the empress Helena—which may explain why Eustathius insulted, or is alleged to have insulted, the queen mother.[47] Regardless, rather than diffusing the tensions in Antioch, the 328 synod's deposition of Eustathius served only to widen the rift between these factions, which quickly formed armed wings and began agitating for open combat.[48] The situation came to a head in no small part because the synod had decided that Eustathius's replacement as bishop should be none other than Eusebius of Caesarea, Eustathius's arch enemy. Sensing the potential for disaster, Eusebius declined the appointment, pleading as his excuse the Council of Nicaea's prohibition on the translation of sitting bishops from one see to another.[49]

Correspondence on the matter was sent to Constantine, who wrote a series of documents, three of which Eusebius has preserved in his *Life of Constantine*. Careful examination of these reveals the degree to which all parties involved—the council of bishops presiding over the trial, the people of Antioch, imperial officials, and even the emperor himself—followed procedural regulations established for civil processes in the conduct of this fundamentally ecclesiastical affair, very much the same behavior exhibited by the Donatists in North Africa. This can be seen by a closer examination of the material as it is presented in Eusebius:

- Eus. *V. Const.* 3.60.1–9 is a letter of Constantine directed to the people of Antioch, urging them to strive for concord (*homonoia*), warning them to set aside their riotous conduct, and chiding them for potentially provoking civil strife by depriving Caesarea of its prelate. Significantly, J. N. Dillon has noted that in this letter Constantine informs the Antiochenes of how he became aware of their desire to appoint Eusebius of Caesarea to their see through acclamations they had pronounced in Eusebius's favor, which had been reported to him in official reports (*hypomnēmata*).[50] Dillon goes on to argue that this must reflect compliance with a process outlined in a law of 331 whereby the *acclamationes* of provincials were to be reported directly to the emperor by his Praetorian Prefects or *comites* in order that he could evaluate the opinions of his subjects concerning the conduct of their governors.[51] Although the law Dillon references postdates the synod of Antioch by at least three years, there is good evidence that Constantine had already been experimenting with similar methods for accessing public opinion earlier in his reign, making it likely that this is an early attestation of this very process.[52]
- Eus. *V. Const.* 3.61.1–3 (cf. Soz. 2.19.3–4) is another letter of Constantine, written to Eusebius of Caesarea to congratulate him on his good judgment in refusing to accept the bishops' demand that he be transferred to the see of Antioch. The letter is couched very much in legal terms, although the law in question is that of god and the church.[53]
- Eus. *V. Const.* 3.62.1–3, a third letter of Constantine, easily the most interesting of the three, outlines in detail the procedural background to the production of the entire dossier. To understand this, we must examine the language of the document carefully. After its opening address, "To Theodotus, Theodorus, Narcissus, Aetius, Alpheius, and the other bishops who are at Antioch"—that is, the judicial body charged with adjudicating the case—Constantine continues:

I have read the transcripts [*ta graphenta*] from your judgment [*tēs humeteras suneseōs*],[54] and I have received the reasoned objection [*prothesin*] of Eusebius, your fellow priest, and in addition I have acknowledged all the reports [*ta pepragmena*], both the one in your letter [*tois humeterois grammasin*] and the one in that of Acacius and Strategius, the *clarissimi comites*. Having made the requisite decision [*diaskepsin*], I wrote to the people of Antioch what was pleasing to God and fitting for the church, and I ordered a copy of the letter [*antigraphon tēs epistolēs*] to be subjoined to this letter [*tois grammasi toutois*], in order that you might learn what I decided to write to the people after appeal was made [*proklētheis*] to me by reason of justice, because it is contained in your letter [*tois grammasin humōn*] that, according to the judgment and petition [*sunesin te kai boulēsin*] of the people and of your preference, Eusebius, the most holy bishop of the church of Caesarea, should be installed over the church of Antioch and should receive oversight over it. Yet the letter [*ta grammata*] of Eusebius, which appears best to safeguard the law of the church, relates the opposite judgment [*tēn enantian gnōmēn*], that he should in no way leave the church entrusted to him by God. Therefore I decree [*edoxen oun*] that his quite just objection [*prothesin*] should be safeguarded by all of you and made binding [*kyrian*] and that he should not be pulled away from his own church.

Constantine's letter clearly describes a legal appeal on the judgment rendered by the council of bishops at Antioch, lodged by none other than Eusebius himself. Of particular note is the fact that Constantine's judgment on the case was formulated on the basis of an entire dossier of documents, including:

1. The transcript of the council's original judgment (*ta graphenta tēs humeteras suneseōs),*
2. Eusebius's objection to it (*prothesis),*
3. A transcript of the proceedings (*ta pepragmena*) written up in a letter sent by the bishops (*tois humeterois grammasin*), and
4. A report transmitted in a letter from his counts Acacius and Strategius.

The type of dossier this letter outlines is prescribed in precisely these terms in several laws of Constantine governing appellate procedure preserved in the *Theodosian Code*. In fact, over the course of his reign, Constantine significantly reformed appellate procedure, above all by specifying the exact documents that must accompany any appeal to the emperor. These were:

1. A copy of the original judgment (*exemplum opinionis*),
2. A statement of the objections of the parties (*refutatoriis partium*),
3. A transcript of the proceedings (*acta*), and
4. The judges' own letter (*litteris*) reporting on the matter.[55]

What we have in this document (Eus. *V. Const.* 3.62) is thus a record of Constantine's decision on an appeal that has followed his new appellate procedure flawlessly. Insofar as there is any deviation, this arises because only bishops could sit in judgment over matters of theological concern, meaning that the state authorities (the *comites* Acacius and Strategius) forfeited the right to adjudicate, yet they clearly retained their role as overseers at the hearing and reporters to the emperor of its proceedings.

The most amazing thing about this dossier is, of course, the fact that Constantine, and the bishops, were adopting the forms and structures of the civil law system to deal with an ecclesiastical matter. By following both the requirement that Constantine's *comites* report the acclamations of the people of Antioch to the emperor and the requirement that appellate dossiers be composed of the four documents actually forwarded to the court, the parties to this ecclesiastical case were deliberately conforming to state mandates. On the one hand, this subordinated ecclesiastical governance to the legal superstructure of the empire. On the other, it also co-opted the power of the state to add strength and legitimacy to the actions of the bishops. Moreover, while Counts Acacius and Strategius were on hand at least in part to oversee and report the proceedings of this hearing to the emperor, it goes without saying that they were also present to maintain the peace in the face of imminent civic unrest.[56] This dispute over the episcopal succession at Antioch had thus boiled over into a civil law concern that demanded the intervention of the emperor and his officers, who proceeded naturally enough according to the norms of Roman law. But it was also a religious affair, to be solved to the satisfaction and for the satisfaction of god, in which the bishops and the emperor colluded in a brand-new marriage of Christian church and state.

Despite Constantine's best efforts, the dispute was by no means resolved with the close of the synod of Antioch. Ultimately, Eustathius was replaced with a certain Eulalius, who died within three months of his consecration. Eulalius was then succeeded by no fewer than four further bishops who were either short lived or promptly deposed, until 344, when the more durable Leontius—a disciple of Lucian who shared his subordinationist sympathies—gained the post.[57] Meanwhile, Eustathius's supporters never accepted his deposition and continued to congregate in their own conventicles. When Athanasius visited the city in 346, he felt compelled to plead with Constantius II to grant the "Eustathians" access to a church of their own.[58] Constantius would have been well acquainted with the controversy and the tensions it generated because he had been sent to reside in Antioch at some point in the mid-330s, primarily in response to escalating tensions with Persia, but surely also with an eye to maintaining civic order in this restive eastern capital.[59] The same dual purpose may also explain Constantine's creation of the *comes orientis*, an officer who performed both military and civilian functions from his base at Antioch.[60] Nevertheless, despite the regular presence of emperors and high-level imperial officials in the city through the 370s, the separatist Eustathians continue to be attested as late as the early 360s,[61] and schism continued to fester in the city until 414.[62]

This divisiveness put Antioch at a decided disadvantage in a world that was maintaining the traditions of peer polity interaction by transferring the arena for power struggles and self-assertion from city councils and pagan religious assemblies to episcopal sees and ecclesiastical jurisdiction. Antioch's authority in these inter-urban sparring matches was largely neutralized by its lack of a single strong bishop. Instead, the city became a locus for outside power plays by super-regional leaders who exploited its ataxia in order to boost their own power. Within this complex dynamic, the emperor was only one axis of authority, one with considerable influence, but by no means full control. In fact, in many ways Constantine was pulled willy-nilly into what had begun as a civic controversy but quickly exploded into a major regional conflict that rent the fabric of this eastern metropolis for nearly a century to come.

The Christian Community in Alexandria

The situation in Alexandria was even more complex. The deposition of Eusebius of Nicomedia in the wake of the Council of Nicaea had opened a bitter dispute between Eusebius and Alexander, the bishop of Alexandria.[63] After his return from exile in 327 or 328, Eusebius of Nicomedia assembled a large synod in Bithynia that, in the presence of the emperor, concluded that Arius should be sent back to Alexandria for reinstatement.[64] Confirming this decision, Constantine himself directed a letter to Alexander describing his own theological investigation of Arius (which had preceded the council) and demanding that the rehabilitated priest be restored to communion.[65] The situation may have been further complicated if, as the epitome of Philostorgius claims, the synod actually ordered the deposition of Alexander, who for his part refused to abide by any of these demands whatsoever, even despite their backing from the emperor.[66]

Before the situation could explode, Alexander died on April 27, 328. Two months later he was replaced by his gifted but mercurial presbyter Athanasius.[67] Philostorgius, once again, summarizes a letter sent by Constantine to the Alexandrians congratulating them on their choice, a gesture that points to the emperor's ongoing efforts to nudge local politics from behind.[68] This is all the more striking because Athanasius's election had been contested by the dissident Melitians, who upon Alexander's death had elected their own contender to the Alexandrian see. Constantine's letter was thus more than a congratulatory missive. It was an explicit endorsement for the candidate of the establishment church and an implicit warning to his rivals. In exchange for this favor, Constantine expected compliance with his demand for a reunion with the Melitians, for in another letter sent shortly after the election, he warns Athanasius, "If I learn that you have hindered or excluded any who claim to be admitted into communion with the church, I will immediately send someone who shall depose you by my command, and shall remove you from your place."[69] The emperor was thus playing quid pro quo politics. His endorsement of Athanasius came with the condition that the bishop effect a reconciliation with his dissident opponents.

Most of our evidence for the controversy that ensued comes from the pen of Athanasius. This has obviously affected scholarship in ways that should be made more explicit than they often are. Not only does Athanasius portray himself as innocent of all charges brought against him by his opponents, whom he brands as schemers and liars, but he is also intent on tarring the followers of Arius and the Melitians with a single brush, as if the two groups were entirely coterminous. Although both may well have been united in their opposition to Athanasius, his portrayal of both as a single, monolithic faction is at a minimum exaggerated, and may well be a figment of his imagination.[70] In the absence of independent testimony, it is difficult not to be suspicious that Athanasius's homology may represent a double-barreled strategy designed to frame the debate to the mutual disadvantage of the two groups that most vociferously opposed him while distracting attention away from real and pressing concerns over his own leadership.

For all that Athanasius was a staunch defender of Nicene doctrine and Alexandrian unity, he was also an unrepentant thug. Even if he managed to escape conviction on the accusations of assault brought against him at no less than three formal inquests—to be discussed below—we have solid indications of his penchant for the use of strong-arm tactics. The best piece of evidence for this comes from a papyrus dated May 335 that gives a detailed account of an unambiguously

violent incident against his Melitian opponents. It reports how Athanasius's supporters arranged for the detention and beating of adherents of Heraïscus, the
Melitian bishop of Alexandria, in order to prevent them from testifying in Athanasius's disfavor at the Council of Tyre, held in summer 335.[71] Athanasius was thus
a merciless enforcer of ecclesiastical conformity over his pastoral charges. Indeed,
his very ability to escape conviction for the unseemly use of raw violence hung in
no small part on his willingness to exert this same violence unflinchingly in order
to silence his opponents.

The rift between Athanasius and the dissidents grew into a gaping chasm in
330 when a delegation of Melitians, supported by Eusebius of Nicomedia, came to
Constantine to complain of Athanasius's repeated use of force against them. These
brought at least four charges:

1. that Athanasius was too young to hold office when he was first elected
   bishop;
2. that he had financially supported the *magister officiorum* Philumenus, who
   was implicated in a plot against Constantine;
3. that he had ordered a violent attack on a Melitian priest named Ischyras
   and, in the process, broken a chalice; and
4. that he had commandeered a consignment of linen tunics from the Egyp-
   tians as a sort of private tax assessment.[72]

To judge by these charges, Athanasius was running ecclesiastical affairs in Egypt
more in the manner of a mafia don than a good shepherd. Fearing the same, Constantine summoned the bishop to answer to these accusations in winter 331/332 at
a trial held in Constantinople.[73] There Athanasius was able to convince the
emperor of his version of events; he was acquitted and returned to Alexandria
with a letter from the emperor strongly supporting his innocence.[74]

Athanasius also returned armed with an imperial decree imposing *infamia/
atimia* on the Arians and a ranting letter ordering them into union and threatening them with fines if they refused.[75] As was to be expected, the willful bishop
took this vindication as encouragement to perpetuate the heavy-handed tactics
that had gotten him into trouble in the first place. Soon enough, then, the Melitians and Arians renewed their efforts to draw attention to Athanasius's ongoing
brutal behavior. By the spring of 334 they had gained enough traction that Constantine again summoned Athanasius to appear at a council, this time to be held
in Caesarea Maritima, on a further charge:

5. that he had ordered the torture and even the murder of a presbyter named
   Arsenius of Hypsele.[76]

Eusebius of Nicomedia was to preside over the synod as bishop, while Constantine's own half-brother, the Censor Dalmatius, was to oversee the proceedings. Here once again we see the commingling of civil and ecclesiastical jurisdiction, as well as the obvious practical concern of maintaining order in an environment where violence was more than a remote possibility. Predicting in advance a negative outcome, Athanasius flatly refused to attend this Caesarean synod. This display of insubordination indubitably rankled the emperor, but ultimately the synod was cancelled with no further consequence.[77] Perhaps around the same time, additional accusations surfaced:

6. that Athanasius had used similarly violent tactics against dissident opponents on a number of further occasions, and
7. that he had been embezzling annual imperial grain allotments granted to the widows and orphans of Alexandria and selling them for a profit.[78]

The sheer number and consistency of these charges—combined with the independent evidence of the London papyrus—show a distinctive pattern. Athanasius's methods for asserting power in his civic and provincial context seem to have included less pious persuasion than outright bribery, embezzlement, and racketeering. In the face of this, the emperor was hard pressed to exert control at the local level, for Athanasius had a lock hold both on the targeted use of force in his home region and on the free flow of information that might be deployed to convict him.

In light of the growing welter of accusations and of the fact that Athanasius had actually never answered to those meant to have been tried at Caesarea, yet another council was convened in the summer of 335 at Tyre. Here again, this was organized under the supervision of an imperial agent, the *comes* Flavius Dionysius, but this time Constantine was unwilling to brook defiance and commanded that Athanasius either arrive voluntarily or be brought by force.[79] Disputes arose immediately over the veracity of the charges, but an investigative party was dispatched to Egypt to gather evidence, and momentum began to gather for Athanasius's deposition.[80] Taking advantage of a break in the proceedings while the majority of bishops traveled to Jerusalem to dedicate the new church of the Holy Sepulchre, Athanasius managed to slip away from the harbor of Tyre on a raft.[81]

He made his way to Constantinople by late October 335 and there, in a scene justifiably famous for its sheer audacity, confronted Constantine as he was entering the city on horseback.[82] Despite the emperor's frustration with the situation, he permitted Athanasius one last chance at a defense before a group of six bishops who had followed him to the imperial capital as envoys from Tyre, including Eusebius of Nicomedia. Eusebius himself was well aware that this was likely his last chance to undermine his bitter rival, so he lodged the most grandiose accusation yet by charging:

> 8. that Athanasius had threatened to cut off Egypt's grain supply to Constantinople.

By now, of course, Constantine had wearied of Athanasius's obstinate refusal to abide by episcopal decisions in his disfavor, his adamant resistance to communion with his Arian opponents, and his violent engagements with Melitian dissidents, but this new charge amounted to no less than high treason and drove Constantine into a rage so heated that on November 7, 335, he at last exiled Athanasius to Gaul.[83] In the year and half to come, even despite urgent pleas on the part of Athanasius's Alexandrian supporters, Constantine refused to relax the order of exile for the remainder of his reign. To his mind, Athanasius was "an inciter of sedition who had been condemned by the judgment of the church."[84]

Constantine's gradually deepening involvement in the politics of the Alexandrian church in many ways had the opposite effect of what he had hoped. Far from creating unity and stability in the city and the region more broadly, his efforts to rein in the defiant authoritarianism of Athanasius and level the playing field for his opponents had accomplished very little. Even in the years of Athanasius's first exile between late 335 and Constantine's death in 337, Athanasius's supporters managed the city in his absence without ever turning jurisdiction over the church to either the dissidents or a successor. This is not to say, however, that Athanasius himself remained unchallenged in his see. Even though he secured his return to Egypt in September 337, the church of Alexandria remained fragmented through the last years of his career.[85] In 339, Athanasius was once again forced from Alexandria and replaced by Gregory, who was a staunch supporter of the compromise credal formula advocated by Constantius II. After Gregory's death in 345, Athanasius returned to the city once again but by 356 was once more deposed and forced into a third exile. At this point he was replaced by George, whose violent murder by an angry mob of pagans in 361 was described above. Although Athanasius returned to the city in 362, he would eventually suffer two more brief exiles before returning to Alexandria for the last time in 366 and continuing to live there until his death in 373. After this, the see of Alexandria erupted once again into open violence and was not restabilized until the 380s.[86] Imperial involvement in Alexandria's church politics thus did little to promote concord and even less to bring the church in this region under central control. The complexities of local politics were beyond the power of Constantine and his successors to dictate, leaving the imperial government no choice but to negotiate power relations with the biggest player on the civic scene, Athanasius.

Conclusion

When he took over governance of the eastern empire in 324, Constantine faced a new set of challenges that were posed by the workings of great metropoleis like Antioch and Alexandria, cities that were rivaled only by Rome in their size and social complexity. Unlike Rome, however, these eastern megalopoleis existed as part of a community of peer polities that had a millennium-long tradition of interacting with each other as structurally homologous and horizontally equal peers. The tradition of peer polity interaction affected not just the shared relationships among these cities, but also their interactions with the emperor, whose authority was respected, but who was also expected to behave within the parameters of legally and socially accepted norms predicated on centuries of previous engagement.

Constantine adapted well to this environment, particularly as regards his dealings with the traditional religious communities of Antioch and Alexandria. In both cities he seems to have been willing to pose symbolic challenges to the established religious order without threatening direct confrontation or open violence. Although we have no solid evidence for his interactions with the sizable Jewish communities of these cities, our sources for his dealings with their Christian groups is very rich indeed. In both instances, Constantine and his administration were drawn into ecclesiastical controversies over which the emperor rapidly lost control. His efforts to abide by the norms of civic engagement, coupled with power plays executed by the leaders of both cities as well as leaders from other, rival peer polities, created a spider's web of entanglements that pulled the emperor tighter with every effort he made to maneuver his way into a position of control. This situation showed the limits of his power and above all the limitations imposed by the intercommunicative nature of power relations.

Some would contend that the story that resulted was largely a matter of ecclesiastical rather than civic politics, but this distinction is artificial, on two levels. First, the bishops of eastern cities were every bit as interested in power politics as they were in doctrinal disputes. Athanasius was just as guilty of challenging the emperor's monopoly on tax collection, fiscal distributions, food supply, and above all violence as he was in debating the rightness of his faith. He and some other major players in eastern ecclesiastical controversies were thus every bit as much barons as they were bishops, for the bishop in general was fast becoming the central power broker in the late antique city—in no small part thanks to the powers, privileges, and perquisites granted him by Constantine. Second, insofar as doctrinal disputes truly mattered to the late antique mindset, and indeed they did, in many ways they simply constituted yet another arena of contention that took its place alongside more traditional fields of competition like wealth, status, euer-

getic display, and rhetorical or intellectual showmanship. Peer polity interaction/
rivalry thus simply absorbed Christian credal dispute as an additional arena
within which the new local leaders could vie for power and prestige. Much as
wrangling over titles like "first city in Asia" or "thrice neokoros" had exercised the
competitive spirit of cities and their leaders in the High Empire, the playing field
for civic competition in the late empire was laid out around the bounds of Christological formulations and liturgical orthopraxy.

In some ways, then, the Arian controversy and the doctrinal disputes that
succeeded it can be conceived of as inter-urban civic disputes that erupted into a
worldwide crisis of power. Had Athanasius and other bishops been willing to
abide by the emperor's requests to let concord trump their pursuit of dogmatic
aristeia, Constantine and his successors may have witnessed an increase in their
control over local polities as a result of their championing the universalizing
Christian cult. Instead, Constantine's grant of power to the bishops to engage in
ecclesiastical dispute on an equal or even superior footing with himself resulted
in a net increase in their authority at the civic level at the expense of the power of
the throne.[87]

When the magnificent chapel of Saint Sylvester was consecrated beside the church of the Santi Quattro Coronati in Rome in 1247, Pope Innocent IV was living in exile in Lyon because of fears he would be set upon by Frederick II, the Holy Roman Emperor. Innocent had excommunicated his rival just two years earlier for his refusal to cede territory and authority to the Roman see, and it was not until Frederick's death three years later that Innocent would be able to return to Rome in triumph to gaze on this masterpiece of trecento art. Its ornate fresco cycle depicts Sylvester's encounters with Constantine as recounted in the fifth- or sixth-century *Life of Sylvester* discussed in the introduction of this book. As we might expect, Pope Sylvester is depicted throughout as severe yet serene, supreme in the face of a sinful and submissive emperor. Constantine, by contrast, appears humble if not downright humiliated. He is nude and vulnerable as he receives the healing waters of baptism from Sylvester (Fig. 49) and spectacularly obsequious as he genuflects before the enthroned Pope to receive his crown. This was a Constantine perfectly suited to the needs of a papacy desperate to assert its supremacy over the secular ruler of Europe, a Constantine carefully groomed by a long succession of papal legend-makers intent on emphasizing the emperor's submissive favoritism for the church to the exclusion of all else.

No modern would contend that this thirteenth-century Constantine came at all close to the historical emperor of the fourth century CE. Nevertheless, the process this fresco cycle reflects—a process of creatively rereading and artfully misreading Constantine—began in the emperor's own lifetime and continues through to the present. As we have seen in the preceding discussion, there was never any one Constantine, for this emperor, like any other, was at once wrapped up in a process of becoming that left him open to constant change, and also surrounded by a sea of subjects whose own impressions buffeted him with varied and variable expectations, demands, and interpretations. To his ancient subjects as indeed to us moderns, Constantine was always multiform, a work in progress, a figure operating on the horizons between the known and the unknown, the expected and the unexpected. This was evident from the testimony of Constantine himself, which describes the changes he believed he underwent in his life-

FIGURE 49. Constantine being baptized by Pope Sylvester, fresco Santi Quattro Coronati, Rome, 1248 CE and following. The Art Archive at Art Resource, NY. Photo by Gianni Dagli Orti, reproduced with permission.

time, and from the shifts in nomenclature and appearance we can witness in his titles and portraiture over the thirty-one years of his reign. It is also evident in the quite varied reactions we find to Constantine from the message makers charged with creating and transmitting the public image of the emperor to his subjects. These offer varied emphases depending on the predilections and viewpoints of their creators, emphases that, unsurprisingly, are variously refracted according to circumstance and perspective.

Thus neither Constantine nor his contemporaries were able to define an essential and monolithic man behind the panegyrics and portraits, the legacies and legends left to us today. At the same time, however, these same panegyrists, artists, moneyers, and lawmakers tend to emphasize certain constants that recur throughout the reign: the power of light, the importance of victory, the prevalence of divine favor, and the significance of dynasty. The combination of these enduring constants with the gradual shift in emphases presented Constantine's subjects with a variegated palette on which to draw when they went about constructing their own images of the emperor. Faced with this same variability, we are well advised not to brush these conflicts and contrasts aside but rather to face them squarely and attempt to account for their complexity.

This does not mean that just any image of Constantine can or did emerge. The signs emanating from the emperor and his message makers are sufficiently circumscribed and the constants adequately repetitive to foreclose at least some avenues of interpretation. This can be seen most clearly from Constantine's communiqués with the one constituency for whom we have the most testimony: the community of Christians. Constantine's surviving exchanges with this group show signs of favoritism that were open and pronounced, so much so that we can say with some confidence that few of his subjects could have failed to notice the emperor's interest in this minority religion. Nevertheless, this pro-Christian message never drowned out competing signals from the emperor and his handlers that were clearly interpreted by non-Christians to mean that their emperor was receptive to them as well and even supportive of their interests and agendas.

Although the preceding study has focused primarily on religion, its investigation is very much based on the evidence and the structures of law. Indeed, it has attempted to show how the emperor used the tools of law and normative communication available to him by virtue of his office to effect changes in the landscape and culture of cities that would have profound effects on both religious and civic life for centuries—indeed millennia—to come. The laws Constantine issued, the legal pronouncements he made, created an empire—a sphere of rule—in which he reigned supreme, but only with the acknowledgment and complicity of his subjects. Knowing this reality, Constantine deployed the dialogic ontology of his rule, the dynamic basis of power, to best advantage by using it to move the empire from one place to the next in its development as a sphere of belief and religious practice.

Imperial power, like all political power, was inevitably constructed and mediated through language. An emperor ruled with words, both because his very office was invented from ideas of authority and symbols of power mediated by and reaffirmed through verbal expressions, and because his words possessed a special, purposive force that could compel action and create lived realities. The converse of this theorem of the linguistic construction of rule is that, for an emperor to have power, his subjects had to recognize it while accepting his claims to authority and following his commands. To guarantee that this occurred, emperors were compelled to obey a logic of governmentality that dictated the scope and nature of their powers and the grammar of the normative claims they could make.

This is epitomized in the Roman Empire in the process of petition and response, through which an emperor's subjects communicated their grievances, issued their claims, and brought forth demands to their ruler in a set form. They did so with the expectation that the emperor would follow prescribed protocols in his response and with the hope that he might see fit to support their cause.

Employing this age-old tool of communicative action, Constantine was able simultaneously to reaffirm his own claims to legitimate authority and to reshape and reconstruct the religious and ultimately political norms of his empire. By encouraging cities to enter new claims into their petitions, claims that emphasized their adherence to Christianity, and by promising the citizens of Christian polities rewards for making these claims, rewards in the form of civic independence, imperial emoluments, and at times a Constantinian name, Constantine was able to accelerate the process of religious change at the local level while reaffirming his own claims to operate as the source of political authority in the world.

Constantine also manipulated the traditional tools of civic finance to much the same effect. The emperor's vast estates served not only to fill his coffers with cash but also to act as a giant melting pot through which capital originally purposed for one objective could pass and be converted to another use. Where earlier emperors had confiscated the wealth of Christian churches and redistributed it to their subjects as a reward or simply a means to generate revenue, Constantine seems to have confiscated civic and temple properties and then redirected the proceeds from their liquidation or revenue generation to the benefit of the church. Here again, he was using the grammar of political action, in perfectly legitimate ways for his office, but ways that had profoundly revolutionary effects.

Drawing further on the wealth of his personal estates, Constantine also directed money to the construction of churches. Again falling back on the traditional tool of petition and response, he permitted bishops to tap into his *res privata* to create structures built to their own tastes and design that would become permanent features of the urban landscape. These lasting monuments served as local competitors to traditional temples for the religious devotion of civic communities. Simultaneously, Constantine granted bishops access to imperial subventions in the form of money and grain for redistribution to their clergy and even privileges of immunity from the compulsory public duties faced by those of the curial class. Here again, he used the well-tested tools of civic governance to radically alter the religious landscape and power dynamics at the local level. In the process, he favored a new class of civic power brokers, the bishops, vaulting them well beyond their old curial counterparts as local leaders and in so doing fundamentally changed the nature of civic governance for centuries to come.

Despite his fairly clear message of favoritism toward Christian communities, however, Constantine gave many cities both the signals and the space they needed to stop far short of fully accepting his alterations to their political and religious lifeworlds. In fact, many traditional cities dealt with Constantine using the same legal and communicative structures as their Christian counterparts, even as they succeeded in maintaining pagan religious practices with little interference from above. In their communications with the emperor, they chose to emphasize those versions of Constantine that were especially suited to their cause—the obsession with victory, the emphasis on dynasty, and above all the worship of the sun. Such cities could survive unscathed and even thrive in Constantine's empire provided they obeyed the relatively modest, and only sporadically enforced, regulations on sacrifice and divination imposed by the emperor. Some cities were not, however, willing to abide the emperor's restrictions on their civic and religious actions and paid the price with direct and open attacks by the emperor or his troops. This resistance showed the overwhelming power an emperor could bring to bear in attempting to demonstrate his claims to superiority, but also the very real limits of that power when even its application failed to achieve decisive results over the long term.

Such resisting cities also included communities dominated by schismatic and heretical Christians, who refused to abide by the decisions of Constantine and the bishops he appointed to judge their cases. At times these recalcitrant communities even invited imperial violence upon themselves by refusing to concede the legitimacy of the emperor's authority. Such oppositional engagements arose throughout the cities of North Africa and in the larger metropoleis of Alexandria and Antioch. In these places, more complex religious frameworks existed that involved long traditions of factional dispute and infighting. In these instances, instead of benefiting from the processes of communication he had managed so skillfully in the instance of smaller towns, Constantine was in some ways played the fool by local and regional ecclesiastical leaders. These leaders succeeded in manipulating the traditional process of petition and response to gain the upper hand against their local and regional rivals but also to forfend the full surrender of their own power to an emperor strongly desirous of keeping them under his control.

Understanding an emperor as complex as Constantine is thus first and foremost a matter of understanding that his exercise of power was an intersubjective process. Constantine is multiform in the ancient source record and remains polyvalent in all subsequent interpretations. The very nature of his position rendered him subject to competing interpretations, but this situation was further complicated by his own self-conscious representation of transformation over the course of his life and reign. Everyone had his or her own reaction to the radically new vision of emperorship Constantine presented, and the kaleidoscopic variety of Constantines that emerged continues to affect our understanding today. Beneath this chameleonic nature, however, lay a list of priorities at the top of which stood promotion of the Christian church. This comes out loud and clear in Constantine's abundant communications with the members of the Christian community, communications that also reveal the ways in which Constantine used the intersubjective process of rule to advance his agenda. Falling back on the traditional system of petition and response, Constantine primed the pump of imperial bene-faction and began to rain down favors on this new and increasingly exclusivist religion. While never foreclosing avenues for communication with dissidents—in both the Christian and non-Christian communities—he used instruments of government long available to emperors to move the process of conversion irre-trievably far down the road of history. In so doing, he was, to be sure, following a wave of conversion that affected many others just as profoundly as it affected him. Yet his uniquely powerful position as emperor and his unique skill at managing the operations of his office made Constantine into an epochal figure in the history of government and the history of the world.

SIGLA AND ABBREVIATIONS

∼

Abbreviations for late antique sources follow A. H. M. Jones, J. R. Martindale, and J. Morris, eds., *The Prosopography of the Later Roman Empire*, 3 vols. (Cambridge: Cambridge University Press, 1971–92). Abbreviations for classical authors follow Simon Hornblower and Antony Spawforth, eds., *The Oxford Classical Dictionary*, 4th ed. (Oxford: Oxford University Press, 2012). Abbreviations for epigraphic corpora follow François Bérard et al., *Guide de l'épigraphiste: Bibliographie choisie des épigraphies antiques et médiévales*, 3rd ed. (Paris: Éditions rue d'Ulm, 1986). Abbreviations for the titles of modern serials follow *The Database of Classical Bibliography*. The following abbreviations also appear:

Athan. *Ap. Const.*	Athanasius, *Apologia ad Constantium,* in H.-G. Opitz et al., eds., *Athanasius Werke*, II.1.8 (Berlin, 1934–).
Athan. *Apol. c. Arian*	Athanasius, *Apologia contra Arianos,* in H.-G. Opitz et al., eds., *Athanasius Werke*, II.1.5–6 (Berlin, 1934–).
Athan. *Festal Letter*	A. Camplani, ed., trans., comm., *Atanasio di Alessandria: Lettere festali* (Milan, 2003).
Athan. *Hist. Ar.*	Athanasius, *Historia Arianorum,* in H.-G. Opitz et al., eds., *Athanasius Werke*, II.1.7 (Berlin, 1934–).
Barrington Atlas	R. J. A. Talbert, ed., *Barrington Atlas of the Greek and Roman World* (Princeton, NJ, 2000).
BHG	F. Halkin, ed., *Bibliotheca hagiographica graeca*, 3 vols., Subsidia Hagiographica 8a (Brussels, 1957).
BHL	*Bibliotheca hagiographica latina antiquae et mediae aetatis*, 2 vols., with supplement, Subsidia Hagiographica 6 (Brussels, 1901–11), online at http://bhlms.fltr.ucl.ac.be/.
BMC	H. Mattingly et al., eds., *Coins of the Roman Empire in the British Museum,* 6 vols. (London, 1923).
Brennecke *Dokument*	Brennecke, H. C., U. Heil, A. Von Stockhausen, and A. Wintjes, eds., *Dokumente zur Geschichte des Arianischen Streites*, Athanasius Werke 3.1.3 (Berlin, 2007).

Can. Conspl.	Turner, C. H. "Canons Attributed to the Council of Constantinople, A.D. 381, Together with the Names of the Bishops, from Two Patmos MSS POB' POY," *JThS* 15 (1914): 161–78.
CCSL	*Corpus Christianorum Series Latina* (Turnhout, 1953–).
CLRE	R. Bagnall et al., *Consuls of the Later Roman Empire* (Atlanta, GA, 1987).
Conc. Elib.	*Concilii Eliberitani canones* in E. J. Jonkers, ed., *Acta et symbola conciliorum quae saeculo quarto habita sunt*, Textus Minores 19 (Brill, 1954), pp. 5–23.
CPL	E. Dekkers, ed., *Clavis Patrum Latinorum*, 3rd ed. (Steenbrugis, 1995).
CSEL	*Corpus Scriptorum Ecclesiasticorum Latinorum* (Vienna, 1866–).
DRB	R. I. Ireland, ed., *De rebus bellicis* (Leipzig, 1984).
Epit.	*Epitome de Caesaribus* in F. Pichlmayr, ed., *Sexti Aurelii Victoris Liber de Caesaribus* (Leipzig, 1961), pp. 131–76.
Eus. *DE*	I. A. Heikel, *Die Demonstratio Evangelica*, Eusebius Werke 6 (Berlin, 1913).
Eus. *LC*	Eusebius, *Laudatio Constantini* in I. A. Heikel, ed., Über *das Leben Constantins, Constantins Rede an die heilige Versammlung, Tricennatsrede an Constantin*, Eusebius Werke 1 (Leipzig, 1902), pp. 149–92.
Eus. *On.*	S. Timm, ed. and trans., *Das Onomastikon der biblischen Ortsnamen: Edition der syrischen Fassung mit griechischem Text, englischer und deutscher Übersetzung* (Berlin, 2005); cf. R. S. Notley and Z. Safrai, ed. and trans., *Onomasticon: The Place Names of Divine Scripture Including the Latin Edition of Jerome* (Leiden, 2005).
Eus. *Theophan.*	H. Gressmann and A. Laminski, eds., *Die Theophanie*, Eusebius Werke 3, 2nd ed. (Berlin, 1992).
Eus. *Triak.*	Eusebius, *Triakontaetērikos,* in I. A. Heikel, ed., Über *das Leben Constantins, Constantins Rede an die heilige Versammlung, Tricennatsrede an Constantin*, Eusebius Werke 1 (Leipzig, 1902), pp. 193–259.
Exp. Tot. Mundi	J. Rougé, ed., *Expositio totius mundi et gentium*, Sources Chrétiennes 124 (Paris, 1966).
Fest. Ind.	M. Albert, ed. and trans., *Histoire "Acéphale" et index syriaque des Lettres festales d'Athanase d'Alexandrie*, Sources Chrétiennes 317 (Paris, 1985).

Gel. Cyz. *HE*	G. C. Hansen, ed., *Anonyme Kirchengeschichte (Gelasius Cyzicenus, CPG 6034)*, GCS n.f. 9 (Berlin, 2002).
Guidi Vita	I. Guidi, "Un BIOS di Constantino," *RAL*, 5th ser. 16 (1907): 306–40, 637–60 (*BHG 364*).
Hier. Syn.	E. A. J. Honigmann, ed., *Le Synekdèmos d'Hiéroklès et l'opuscule géographique de Georges de Chypre*, Corpus Bruxellense Historiae Byzantinae 1 (Brussels, 1939).
Hilar. Pict. *Frg. Hist.*	A. Feder, ed., *S. Hilarii Pictaviensis Opera*, CSEL 65 (Vienna, 1916), pp. 53–177.
Itin. Burd.	*Itinerarium Burdigalense* in P. Geyer et al., eds., *Itineraria et alia geographica*, Corpus Christianorum Series Latina 175 (Turnhout, 1965), pp. 1–26.
Jul. *ELF*	J. Bidez and F. Cumont, eds., *Imp. Caesaris Flavii Claudii Iuliani Epistulae Leges Poemata Fragmenta Varia* (Paris, 1922).
Lat. Veron.	*Laterculus Veronensis* in O. Seeck, ed., *Notitia dignitatum, accedunt Notitia urbis Constantinopolitanae et laterculi prouinciarum* (Berlin, 1876), pp. 247–53.
Mansi	G. D. Mansi, ed., *Sacrorum conciliorum nova et amplissima collectio*, 53 vols. (Paris, 1901–27).
Mart. Theod.	*Martyrium Theodoti* in P. Franchi de' Cavalieri, ed., *I martirii di S. Teodoto e di S. Ariadne con un'appendice sul testo originale del martirio di S. Eleuterio*, Studi e testi 6 (Rome, 1901), pp. 61–87.
MGH.AA	*Monumenta Germaniae Historica. Auctores Antiquissimi*, 14 vols. (Berlin, 1877–1919).
Nil. Dox.	Nilus Doxapatrius, *Notitia patriarchatuum*, in G. Parthey, ed., *Hieroclis Synecdemus et Notitiae Graecae Episcoptuum accedunt Nili Doxapatrii Notitia Patriarchatuum* (Berlin, 1866), pp. 263–308.
Not. Episc.	*Notitiae Episcopatuum* in G. Parthey, ed., *Hieroclis Synecdemus et Notitiae Graecae Episcoptuum accedunt Nili Doxapatrii Notitia Patriarchatuum* (Berlin, 1866), pp. 53–261.
Not. Gall.	*Notitia Galliarum* in O. Seeck, ed., *Notitia dignitatum, accedunt notitia urbis Constantinopolitanae et laterculi prouinciarum* (Berlin, 1876), pp. 261–74.
Opitz *Urkunde*	H.-G. Opitz, ed., *Urkunden zur Geschichte des Arianischen Streites*, Athanasius Werke 3.1 (Berlin, 1934).

Optiz V. Const.   H.-G. Optiz. "Die *Vita Constantini* des Codex Angeli-cus 22," *Byzantion* 9 (1934): 535–93 (*BHG* 365).

Origo   *Origo Constantini* in J. Moreau, ed., *Excerpta Valesiana* (Leipzig, 1961), pp. 1–10.

Patr. Const.   *Patria Constantinoupoleos* in T. Preger, ed., *Scriptores Originum Constantinopolitanarum*, 2 vols. (Leipzig, 1901–07).

PCBE 1   A. Mandouze, ed., *Prosopographie Chrétienne du Bas-Empire*, vol. 1: *Prosopographie de l'Afrique Chréti-enne (202–533)* (Paris, 1982).

PCBE 4   L. Pietri and M. Heijmans, *Prosopographie Chretienne du Bas-Empire*, vol. 4: *Prosopographie de la Gaule Chrétienne (314–614)* (Paris, 2013).

RIC 6   C. H. V. Sutherland, *The Roman Imperial Coinage*, vol. 6: *From Diocletian's Reform (A.D. 294) to the Death of Maximinus (A.D. 313)* (London, 1967).

RIC 7   P. Bruun, *The Roman Imperial Coinage*, vol. 7: *Constan-tine and Licinius, A.D. 313–337* (London, 1966).

RIC 8   J. P. C. Kent, *The Roman Imperial Coinage*, vol. 8: *The Family of Constantine, A.D. 337–364* (London, 1981).

SCh   *Sources Chrétiennes* (Paris, 1942–).

Seeck *RG*   O. Seeck, *Regesten der Kaiser und Päpste für die Jahre 311 bis 476 n. Chr. Vorarbeit zu einer Prosopographie der christlichen Kaiserzeit* (Stuttgart, 1919).

TTH   *Translated Texts for Historians* (Liverpool, 1985–).

V. Luciani   *Vita Luciani* in J. Bidez and F. Winkelmann, eds., *Philostorgius Kirchengeschichte mit dem Leben des Lucian von Antiochien und den Fragmenten eines arianischen Historiographen*, 2nd ed. GCS (Berlin, 1972), pp. 184–201.

V. Rabbulae   *Vita Rabbulae Edesseni* in J. J. Overbeck and H. Taka-hashi, eds., *S. Ephraemi Syri, Rabulae episcopi Edesseni, Balaei, aliorumque opera selecta = Selected Works of St. Ephraem the Syrian, Rabbula, Bishop of Edessa, and Balai* (Piscataway, NJ, 2007), pp. 157–248.

NOTES

INTRODUCTION

1. On the history of the text, see esp. Pasquali; Barnes, "Panegyric, History and Hagiography"; Av. Cameron and Hall, *Eusebius*, pp. 1–53.

2. Av. Cameron, "Form and Meaning"; cf. Singh.

3. This brief survey does not cover some early witnesses to Constantine in the immediate aftermath of his reign, including Libanius, on whom see the contrasting opinions of Wiemer, "Libanius on Constantine"; and Malosse, but also Athanasius and Firmicus Maternus, on whom see Lenski, "Early Retrospectives."

4. Jul. *Caes.* 328D–329D. Bleckmann, "*Constantinus Tyrannus*," offers a fuller survey of negative depictions of Constantine in pagan sources.

5. Jul. *Or.* 7.22 (227D); *Caes.* 335B, 336A. Earlier in his life, Julian had praised Constantine's munificence; see Jul. *Or.* 1.6 (8A–B); cf. Aur. Vict. *Caes.* 40.15.

6. Jul. *Or.* 7.22 (228B); *Ep. ad Ath.* 270C–D; *Caes.* 336B. Amm. 21.10.8 claims Julian also criticized Constantine before the senate of Constantinople as "an innovator and disturber of ancient laws and of customs received of old." On this passage, see Lizzi Testa. If we can believe Sid. Ap. *Ep.* 5.8.2, Constantine came in for critique for his family murders already with a savage epigram penned by his Praetorian Prefect Ablabius.

7. Bastardy: Zos. 2.8.2, 9.2. Military shortcomings: Zos. 2.31.2, 34.1–2. Administrative reforms: Zos. 2.32.1–33.1, 38.2–4. Constantinople and *truphē*: Zos. 2.32.1, 38.1. See also Van Dam, *Remembering Constantine*, pp. 34–40; Al. Cameron, *Last Pagans*, pp. 654–58.

8. Zos. 2.7.1–2.29.5.

9. Zos. 2.29.2–4. See also Zosimus's critique of Constantine's murder of Licinius, 2.28.2. Philostorgius (2.4, 4a–b), who had access to Eunapius, is equally critical of Constantine's family murders.

10. On anti-Constantinianism, see Aiello, "Costantino 'eretico'"; cf. Bleckmann, "*Constantinus Tyrannus*."

11. Eutr. 10.2.2, 5.1, 6.1–3 (esp. *Licinius . . . se dedidit et contra religionem sacramenti Thessalonicae privatus occisus est*), 7.1, 8.1 (esp. *Multas leges rogavit, quasdam ex bono et aequo, plerasque superfluas, nonnullas severas*).

12. Jer. *Chron.* s.a. 306: *Constantinus ex concubina Helena procreatus*; s.a. 323: *Licinius Thessalonicae contra ius sacramenti privatus occiditur . . . Crispus, filius Constantini, et Licinius iunior, Constantiae Constantini sororis et Licinii filius, crudelissime interficiuntur*; s.a. 328: *Constantinus uxorem suam Faustam interficit*; s.a. 337: *Constantinus extremo vitae suae tempore ab Eusebio Nicomedensi episcopo baptizatus in Arrianum dogma declinat.* On the relationship between Eutropius and Jerome through the Kaisergeschichte, see Burgess, "Common Source";

cf. Burgess, "Date of the Kaisergeschichte." In the same tradition, see also *Epit.* 41.11–16, as well as the unrelated *DRB* 2.1 and Amm. 16.8.12.

13. Oros. 7.28.26.

14. Soz. 1.5.1–5, with Schoo, pp. 80–83; Bidez and Hansen, p. li, on Eunapius as the target of Sozomen's refutation. See also Evagr. *HE* 3.40–41 with Van Dam, *Remembering Constantine*, pp. 39–43, for a Christian critique of Zosimus.

15. Soz. 2.34.1–2.

16. *Actus beati Silvestri papae* (*CPL* 2235), for the text of which see De Leo. On the history of the legend, see Aiello, "Costantino, la lebbra, e il battesimo"; G. Fowden, "Last Days of Constantine"; Amerise, *Il battesimo di Costantino*; Liverani, "St. Peter's"; Lieu, "Constantine," pp. 298–301; Van Dam, *Remembering Constantine*, pp. 19–32.

17. For the text, see Pohlkamp; Fried, pp. 148–50. For translations, see Edwards, *Constantine and Christendom*, pp. 92–115; Fried, pp. 151–53. Fried attempts to re-date the document to the tenth century and to place it in a Frankish context, without, however, convincing. Miethke sidesteps the question of dating but offers an excellent catalog of the uses to which the legend has been put.

18. See also Berger, "Legitimation und Legenden," and Lieu, "Constantine," on the reception and use of Constantine in Byzantium, and especially the legendary lives of Constantine that begin to appear in the eighth century. The essays in Braschi and Di Salvo offer an interesting window into Slavic representations of Constantine.

19. For the text, see Bowersock, *On the Donation of Constantine*. For analysis, see Ginzburg, pp. 54–70.

20. Burckhardt. On the influence of Burckhardt's historiography, see Lenski, "Introduction"; Leppin. More on modern assessments of Constantine at Heinze and especially Schlange-Schöningen.

21. Seeck, *Geschichte des Untergangs*, vol. 1, pp. 42–188, esp. 56.

22. A. H. M. Jones, *Constantine and the Conversion*; MacMullen, *Constantine*. Piganiol, *L'empereur Constantin*, depicts a similarly impulsive but more deeply pious Constantine.

23. Grégoire, "La 'conversion' de Constantin"; "La vision de Constantin."

24. Bleicken. For a refutation of this viewpoint, which few still countenance, see Bringmann.

25. Baynes, *Constantine the Great*.

26. A. Alföldi, *Conversion of Constantine*; Calderone, *Costantino*; Barnes, *Constantine and Eusebius*. See also Dörries for an approach similar to Baynes's—that is, based primarily on documents attributable to Constantine himself.

27. See Barnes, *Dynasty, Religion and Power*, with earlier bibliography, and esp. Barnes, "From Toleration to Repression."

28. Elliott, *Christianity of Constantine*; Odahl, *Constantine and the Christian Empire*.

29. The following survey does not include the many multiauthored volumes and catalogs to have appeared on Constantine since 2000: Donati and Gentili; Hartley, Hawkes, Henig, and Mee; Demandt and Engemann; Schuller and Wolff; Ehling and Weber; Lenski, *Cambridge Companion*; Bonamente, Lenski, and Lizzi Testa.

30. Drake, *Constantine and the Bishops*.

31. Girardet, *Konstantinische Wende*; *Kaiser und sein Gott*.

32. Brandt.

33. Stephenson.

34. Veyne.

35. Marcone, *Costantino il Grande*; *Pagano e cristiano*.

36. Van Dam, *Roman Revolution*; *Remembering Constantine*.

37. Potter, *Constantine the Emperor*.

38. Harries, *Imperial Rome*, pp. 106–84; cf. "Constantine the Lawgiver."

39. Wallraff, *Christus Verus Sol*; *Sonnenkönig der Spätantike*.

40. Hermann-Otto. Cf. Stepper, pp. 194–97, for the tiny bit of evidence we have on Constantine's role as *pontifex maximus*, surely insufficient to support Hermann-Otto's thesis.

41. Schmitt.

42. Bardill.

43. A notable exception is the excellent book of Dillon, which focuses quite specifically on Constantinian legal procedure. Grubbs also focuses on laws, but is very much concerned with the presence or absence of religious motivations behind these.

44. De Man, p. xii.

45. Jauss, pp. 3–4.

46. S. Hall, "Encoding and Decoding"; cf. S. Hall, "Notes"; Morley. Kim shows the ongoing value of Hall's and Morley's interrelated schemes in contemporary interpretive environments.

47. On the meaning of the chi-rho, particularly its referentiality and interpretability as a Christian symbol, see the contrasting approaches of Singor; Girardet, *Kaiser und sein Gott*, pp. 54–62; Drake, *Constantine and the Bishops*, pp. 200–204; Bardill, pp. 159–202.

48. Lact. *Mort. Pers.* 44.5: *Fecit ut iussus est et transversa X littera, summo capite circumflexo, Christum in scutis notat.* For the date of the *De mortibus persecutorum*, see Barnes, "Lactantius and Constantine."

49. Bardill, pp. 160–78; Eus. *V. Const.* 1.28.1–31.3. See also Girardet, *Kaiser und sein Gott*, pp. 72–76. Hurtado, pp. 135–54, shows that the staurogram was in use already c. 200 CE as a scribal symbol for the cross of Christ's crucifixion.

50. *AE* 2000: 1799 and 1801; cf. Salama, "Les provinces d'Afrique," and see below pp. 69–71.

51. See below pp. 37–38.

52. Biscottini and Sena Chiesa, pp. 202–12, offer an excellent collection of the fourth- and fifth-century "chrismon," which appears at times in the form of a staurogram but more often as a Christogram. See also Abdy, "Appendix 2," which presents a convenient table of "Earliest Christian Symbols on Roman Coins" showing that the Christogram appears much earlier and more consistently than the staurogram.

53. See the contrasting interpretations of P. Bruun, "Christian Signs"; *Roman Imperial Coinage*, vol. 7, pp. 417–19, and De Caro Balbi.

54. See especially Wienand, *Der Kaiser als Sieger*, pp. 262–74.

55. Bardill, pp. 178–83, with earlier bibliography. See also Green and Ferguson for Celtic and Dacian parallels.

56. Rufin. *HE* 11.29 claims that Alexandrian pagans who were forced to convert in the late fourth century considered the cross to be a version of the ankh; cf. Thelamon, pp. 271–72. See also Soc. 5.17.7–11; Soz. 7.15.10 for similar interpretations.

57. Recent scholarship has grown increasingly aware of the importance of the authorial voice in the production of panegyrics in particular, see Nixon; Enenkel; Rees; Ronning. Similarly, recent studies of imperial law have revealed the central importance of bureaucrats in its composition and dissemination; cf. Honoré; Connolly, *Lives Behind the Laws*.

58. Habermas, *Theory of Communicative Action*, vols. 1–2. Much of Habermas's theory is clear already from essays presented in 1971 and conveniently published at Habermas, *Pragmatics of Social Interaction*. For a convenient précis of Habermas's theory, see C. Taylor, "Language and Society." An outstanding example of the application of the theory of communicative action to ancient history can be found at Ando, *Imperial Ideology*, esp. pp. 75–80.

59. Austin; Searle.

60. Noreña, esp. pp. 245–97, offers a fascinating analysis of the degree to which imperial communication resonated with subject communities.

61. See especially Habermas, *Theory of Communicative Action*, vol. 1, chapter 3, pp. 273–337.

62. See especially Habermas, *Theory of Communicative Action*, vol. 2, chapter 6, pp. 113–97.

63. On the Great Persecution, see especially Eus. *HE* 8.2.1–5, 8.6.6–10; *Mart. Pal.* proem. 2, 2.5–3.1, 4.8; and the studies of Rives, "Decree of Decius"; Bleckmann, "Zu den Motiven"; Moss, *Ancient Christian Martyrdom*; *Myth of Persecution*, and the still useful essays of De Ste. Croix.

64. Ma, *Antiochos III*. Other important studies in this arena include Boatwright; Dmitriev.

CHAPTER 1. CONSTANTINE DEVELOPS

1. Some modern accounts have also emphasized transformation, esp. Kraft, *Kaiser Konstantins religiöse Entwicklung*; Pietri, "Constantin en 324"; Rodgers, "Metamorphosis."

2. *Or. ad sanct.* 11.1–2, esp. ηὐξάμην δ' ἂν πάλαι τήνδε μοι τὴν ἀποκάλυψιν δεδωρῆσθαι, εἴ που μακάριος ὁ ἐκ νέων συσταθεὶς καὶ τῇ γνώσει τῶν θείων καὶ τῷ τῆς ἀρετῆς κάλλει κατευφρανθείς; cf. 21.4. The best edition of the *Oratio ad coetum sanctorum* remains Heikel, *Über das Leben*, pp. 151–273. For translations, see Maraval, *Eusèbe de Césarée*; *Constantin le Grand*; Edwards, *Constantine and Christendom*; and Girardet, *Rede an die Versammlung der Heiligen*, which, conveniently reprints Heikel's edition of the Greek.

3. Opt. App. 5 (*CSEL* 26: 208): *Fuerunt enim in me primitus quae iustitia carere videbantur nec ulla putabam videre supernam potentiam, quae intra secreta pectoris mei gererem.* The arguments of Rosen that Constantine's letter to the bishops of Arles is a forgery fail to convince, primarily because they are built on unfounded assumptions about the level of Constantine's commitment to Christianity in 314. On the document's authenticity, see esp. Odahl, "Constantine's Epistle."

4. Eus. *V. Const.* 1.28.1.

5. Lact. *Mort. Pers.* 44.5–9; Eus. *V. Const.* 1.28–30. It is interesting to note that Eus. *HE* 9.9.1–11, first composed circa 313/314, narrates the events of the Battle of the Milvian Bridge without reference to Constantine's conversion.

6. *Epit.* 41.16: *decem annis praestantissimus, duodecim sequentibus latro, decem novissimis pupillus ob profusiones immodicas nominatus.*

7. Eutr. 10.7.1: *Vir primo imperii tempore optimis principibus, ultimo mediis conparandus*; cf. Neri, *Medius Princeps*.

8. Jul. *Or.* 7.22 (228B); *Ep. ad Ath.* 270C–D; *Caes.* 336B; Zos. 2.29.2–4.

9. Grünewald.

10. For the portrait of Constantine and its transformation over time, see Harrison; Wright; R. R. R. Smith, "The Public Image of Licinius," pp. 185–87; Hannestad; Elsner, pp. 260–64; Gliwitzky.

11. For Constantine as Caesar, see Lact. *Mort. Pers.* 25.3–5; cf. *Pan. Lat.* 6[7].8.2; *CIL* 12: 5516 = 17.2:106, *CIL* 12: 5527 = 17.2:123; *ILS* 657, 682. Cf. Grünewald, pp. 14–16; Marcone, *Costantino il Grande*, pp. 15–30; *Pagano e cristiano*, pp. 1–63; Barnes, *Dynasty, Religion and Power*, p. 89.

12. E.g., *RIC* 6: Trier 716b, Ticinum 117, Aquileia 145, Roma 141.

13. On these titles, see Grünewald, pp. 16–20, 33–35. For an overview of the development of Constantine's titulature, see Grünewald, pp. 179–80.

14. *RIC* 6: Londinium 97, 111–12, 214–33, 263–68; Treveri 615, 627, 679–80, 745, 801–7, 835–43; Lugdunum 244–45, 270, 298–301, 305–6; Roma 284; Ostia 65, 67; Serdica 20. See Carlà and

Castello, *Questioni tardoantiche*, pp. 62–81, for Constantine's ongoing retention of tetrarchic elements in his coinage down to 312.

15. *Pan. Lat.* 7[6].6.1–2; cf. Jul. *Or.* 1.7D. More on Constantine's shrewd manipulation of a pro-tetrarchic stance in his earliest years at Warmington; Wienand, *Der Kaiser als Sieger*, pp. 91–142.

16. *Pan. Lat.* 7[6].1.1, 2.1, 3.2–3. It should be noted that, within the tetrarchic college, *Imperator* was itself used only of Augusti; cf. Creed, p. 91 n. 9.4.

17. *Pan. Lat.* 7[6].3.2–3, 13.3–4.

18. *Pan. Lat.* 7[6].2.5, 8.2.

19. *Pan. Lat.* 7[6].4.2; cf. *Pan. Lat.* 6[7].10.2–13.5. For an emphasis on Constantine's youthfulness, see *Pan. Lat.* 7[6].2.1, 3.2, 5.3, 13.2; cf. Lact. *Mort. Pers.* 29.5: *credit adulescens ut perito ac seni.* Ironically, Constantine was no longer young at his accession but must have been in his mid-thirties; cf. Lenski, "Reign of Constantine," p. 59 n. 1.

20. *Pan. Lat.* 7[6].14.1–2. For a penetrating analysis, see Nixon, "*Constantinus Oriens Imperator*," which highlights Constantine's subordination throughout the speech; cf. Wienand, *Der Kasier als Sieger*, pp. 115–19. Diocletian and Galerius manifested a similar relationship in 298 when Galerius conducted the war against Persia while Diocletian waited for him at Nisibis; Petr. Patr. fr. 14 (*FHG* 4: 184) with Barnes, *New Empire*, p. 55.

21. *RIC* 6: Lugdunum 246–48; cf. 249–50, which has the same type under the legend CONCORDIA PERPET DD NN.

22. Lact. *Mort. Pers.* 29.3–30.6.

23. *Pan. Lat.* 12[9].2.3–4: *quiescentibus cunctantibusque tunc imperii tui sociis primus invaderes*; 12[9].3.4; Eus. *V. Const.* 1.26.1: παρεχώρει μὲν τὰ πρῶτα τὴν ὑπὲρ αὐτῆς ἄμυναν τοῖς τῶν λοιπῶν κρατοῦσι μερῶν ἅτε δὴ χρόνῳ προάγουσιν; cf. *Pan. Lat.* 4[10].8.1–13.5; Aur. Vict. *Caes.* 40.16. On this theme, see Grünewald, pp. 73–77. The tetrarchs who attempted to suppress Maxentius included not just Severus and Galerius, as attested in the written sources, but also Licinius, a fact known only through the epigraphy; see Picozzi; cf. *Origo* 13.

24. Grünewald, pp. 16–17, 38–39; cf. Warmington, pp. 373–74. Contrast P. Bruun, "Portrait of a Conspirator," p. 8.

25. Lact. *Mort. Pers.* 32.5; cf. Barnes, *New Empire*, p. 6; *Dynasty, Religion and Power*, p. 89; Grünewald, pp. 22–23, 41; Stefan.

26. *CLRE*, pp. 309; Barnes, *New Empire*, p. 25.

27. *Pan. Lat.* 5[8].9.3: *imperator totius orbis*. The panegyrist of 313 also dedicates only scarce attention to Constantine's tetrarchic colleagues; cf. Nixon and Rodgers, p. 291.

28. *Pan. Lat.* 6[7].2.1–5, 21.3–7. More on Claudius below at 000. More on the vision of Apollo below at p. 49. This panegyric is well explicated at Wienand, *Der Kaiser als Sieger*, pp. 143–94

29. *RIC* 6: Londinium 79, 101, 141; Treviri 638, 802, 890; Lugdunum 213b, 302.

30. See, for example, the statue from the baths of Constantine in Rome, now in the entry of the Basilica of San Giovanni in Laterano, the recarved portraits on the arch of Constantine, or the numismatic portraits at *RIC* 7: Lyon 214, Trier 1, 8, 9, 13, 16, 21, 30, 35; Arles 6, 70, 100, 110; Rome 2, 33, 40, 45, 49, 52; Ticinum 28, 30–32, 42, 45, 50, 51; Aquileia 27, 35, 39. For an incisive discussion of the change in Constantine's portrait style beginning in 311, see P. Bruun, "Portrait of a Conspirator"; cf. M. R. Alföldi, *Constantinische Goldprägung*, pp. 57–69. For Trajanic allusions, see M. R. Alföldi, *Constantinische Goldprägung*, pp. 57–69. See also Bleckmann, "Costantino dopo la battaglia," pp. 202–7 and Wienand, *Der Kaiser als Sieger*, pp. 49 n. 119, 215–16 for multiple clear allusions to Trajanic types in Constantinian coinage.

31. Epigraphic testimonia are collected at Grünewald, pp. 54–56. The title first appears late in 310 but only becomes common by 315.

32. See below pp. 49–50.

33. Christodoulou, pp. 54–55.

34. Lact. *Mort. Pers.* 44.11: *Senatus Constantino virtutis gratia primi nominis titulus decrevit.* On the title MAXIMUS see Grünewald, pp. 86–92, 107–8, 118–19.

35. Lact. *Mort. Pers.* 43.4–6; *Pan. Lat.* 4[10].12.2; Zos. 2.14.1; *ILAlg.* 1: 3949; cf. Nixon and Rodgers, p. 300 n. 24. Numismatic evidence confirms that Maxentius exploited the death of his father for political purposes; *RIC* 6: Roma 243–44, 250–51. Maxentius's defense of his father was in part a reaction to the fact that Constantine subjected Maximianus to a *damnatio memoriae* in 311; cf. Lact. *Mort. Pers.* 42.1; Eus. *HE* 8.13.15. After Maxentius's death, Constantine then rehabilitated Maximianus and consecrated him as *divus*; cf. Barnes, "Lactantius and Constantine," p. 35; *Dynasty, Religion and Power*, pp. 72–74.

36. E.g., *CIL* 6: 1139 = *ILS* 694: *liberatori urbis . . . fundatori quietis*; *CIL* 14: 131 = *ILS* 687: *restitutori publicae libertatis, defensori urbis Romae, communis omnium salutis auctori*; *CIL* 8: 7006 = *ILS* 688: *q[u]i libertatem tenebris servitutis oppressam sua felici vi[ctoria nova] luce inluminavit*; *CIL* 2: 2721 = *ILS* 689: *reddita libertate triumfanti*; cf. *CIL* 8: 9042 = *ILS* 690; *CIL* 8: 7010 = *ILS* 691; *CIL* 9: 6060 = *CIL* 10: 6965 = *ILS* 693. Further testimonia at Grünewald, pp. 63–74.

37. *Pan. Lat.* 12[9].2.3, 3.4–7, 4.3–5; cf. Nixon and Rodgers, pp. 301–2 n. 28; Grünewald, pp. 64–65. The rhetoric of liberation persists as an important motif of Constantinian propaganda in subsequent years; *Or. ad sanct.* 25; *Pan. Lat.* 4[10].6.3–5, 31.1–2; Eus. *V. Const.* 1.37.1, 39.2; Eus. *HE* 9.9.2; cf. Lenski, "Constantine and Slavery."

38. *CTh* 15.14.3–4, dated to January 6, 313, at Seeck *RG* 64–65; *CTh* 5.8.1, dated to March 19, 314, at Seeck *RG* 162. Eus. *HE* 9.9.12 cites the letter to Maximinus in *oratio obliqua*.

39. Wickert, "Princeps," section VIIIB7b; Grünewald, pp. 64–71; Neri, "L'usurpatore come tiranno"; cf. Humphries, pp. 85–87.

40. Barnes, "Oppressor, Persecutor, Usurper."

41. *CIL* 6: 1139 = *ILS* 694. Also see now *AE* 2003: 2014: *[extinctori? ty]rannicae factionis*.

42. See Lenski, "Evoking," and "Senate and the Sun," with earlier bibliography.

43. *CIL* 10: 5061 = *ILS* 1217: *quod in correctura eius* (i.e., Cossinius Rufinus), *quae sevissimam tyrannidem incurrerat, nullam iniuriam sustinuerit.*

44. *Pan. Lat.* 4[10].4.4, 6.2, 7.4, 8.3, 30.1, 31.4, 32.3, 6, 33.4, 34.1, 4.

45. Eus. *HE* 9.9.11; cf. *V. Const.* 1.40.2. Eusebius alludes to the same statue already in his oration on the dedication of the church of Tyre, probably delivered in 314, *HE* 10.4.16, and in his *Tricennalian Oration* of 336, *Triak.* 9.8.

46. *Pan. Lat.* 12[9].4.4; Zos. 2.13.1; Aur. Vict. *Caes.* 40.24; *Chron. 354* (*MGH.AA* 9: 148).

47. For Maxentius's mistreatment of Senators, see Eus. *HE* 8.14.3; *V. Const.* 1.35.1; cf. Prud. *C. Symm.* 467–80. For his exile of the bishops Marcellus I and the rival claimants Eusebius and Heraclius, see Barnes, *Constantine and Eusebius*, pp. 38–39; Harries, *Imperial Rome*, p. 108.

48. Opt. 1.18.1; Eus. *HE* 8.14.1; Aug. *Brev. Coll.* 3.18[34] (*CSEL* 53: 84); *Contra partem Donati* 13.17 (*CSEL* 53: 113–14); *Gest. Coll. Carth.* cap. gest. 3.498–500 (*CCSL* 149A: 47); cf. Eus. *Mart. Pal.* 13.12–14. For analysis, see De Decker; Barnes, *Constantine and Eusebius*, pp. 37–39, 303–4; Maier, *Dossier*, vol. 1, p. 114 n. 21; Kriegbaum, "Religionspolitik," 22–34; Curran, *Pagan City*, pp. 63–65; Corcoran, *Empire of the Tetrarchs*, pp. 144–45; Donciu, pp. 142–54. On the date of Maxentius's toleration edict, see Kriegbaum, *Kirche der Traditoren*, pp. 143–48.

49. *Mort. Pers.* 1.3, 2. 6, 2.7, 3.1, 3.4, 6.3, 16.7, 31.5, 49.1.

50. *HE* 8.14.1, 3, 5–8, 16–17; 9.9.1–4, 8, 11–12. On the date, see Louth; Burgess, "Dates and Editions," pp. 498–502; cf. Neri, "Les éditions de l'*Histoire ecclésiastique*," pp. 151–83. A. P. Johnson, *Eusebius*, pp. 104–12, makes a spirited argument for a single edition completed in 324/325. The case is intriguing, but should be further developed in a more extensive study if it is to win wider acceptance.

51. *HE* 8.13.13, 14.7, 11–15; 9.1.1, 2.1, 4.2, 7.16, 8.2–3, 9.13, 9a.1, 10.6, 10.12, 11.2, 11.4, 11.7; cf. Grünewald, pp. 69, 98–99. See also the catalog of parallels between Maxentius and Maximinus as twin tyrants at Eus. *HE* 8.14.7–8, 11, 15; 9.1.1, 10.6–7, 11.2; 10.2.1, 4.10, 4.14, 4.35, 4.60, 8.2.

52. On Licinius's persecutions, which included everything from a prohibition on synods to forced exiles, enslavements, and even executions of Christians, see Eus. *HE* 10.8.10–18; *V. Const.* 1.52–56; 2.1–2; cf. *V. Const.* 2.3–5.

53. The first sign of an official break falls in 321 when Constantine and Licinius refuse to recognize one another's consuls; *CLRE*, pp. 176–77.

54. *CTh* 15.14.1–4. The first of these appears to date to December, 324, cf. Seeck, *RG*, pp. 99, 174.

55. Eus. *V. Const.* 2.46.1 (late 324); Const. *Ep. ad Nic.* 9–10 (Opitz *Urkunde* 27 p. 60 = Brennecke *Dokument* 31 p. 119: Nov./Dec. 325); *Conc. Nicaenum can.* 11 (Mansi 2: 689 = Jonkers 43). See also Opt. Porph. *Carm.* 14.4, 7.

56. *Or. ad Sanct.* 22.2. On the date of the *Oration to the Assembly of the Saints*, see Barnes, "Constantine's Speech," which builds on Bleckmann, "Ein Kaiser als Prediger"; cf. Maraval, *Eusèbe de Césarée*, pp. xxi–xxiv. Girardet, *Rede an die Versammlung der Heiligen*, pp. 30–40, attempts to locate the setting in Trier and the date to 314, but does not take account of the more convincing arguments of Bleckmann for Nicomedia.

57. On Licinius, see Eus. *HE* 10.4.14, 8.2, 9.2, 5, 9; *V. Const.* 1.49.2; 2.2.3, 4.2, 6.1, 11.2, 18.1, 19.1, 43.1; 3.3.2. On Maxentius, see *V. Const.* 1.5.1, 27.1, 27.3, 32.3, 33.1, 34.1, 35.1, 36.1–2, 37.1, 38.1, 38.5, 41.2–3. See also *Origo* 22; *Epit.* 41.8; Praxagoras fr. 1.5 (*FGH* 2B no. 219 p. 948); cf. Lib. *Or.* 59.21. Bonamente, "Per una cronologia," also emphasizes that Eusebius comes to portray Maxentius as a persecutor only in the *V. Const.* and not yet in the *HE*.

58. By the mid-fourth century, "tyrant" had become synonymous with "usurper"; cf. Neri, "L'usurpatore come tiranno."

59. *Pan. Lat.* 12[9].3.5: *monstrum illud*; 7.1: *turpissimo . . . prodigio* ; 14.2: *portentum illud*; 17.2: *tam deforme prodigium*; cf. 14.3: *stultum et nequam animal*; 18.1: *parricidam Urbis*. Here the panegyrist follows Cic. *Cat.* 2: 1.13: *monstro illo atque prodigio*.

60. *Pan. Lat.* 4[10].33.6–7: *dominatio feralis . . . illa monstrosa labes*.

61. Eus. *V. Const.* 1.49.1: δεινὸς γάρ τις θήρ; cf. 1.5.1.

62. Eus. *HE* 10.4.14: εἶτα δὲ δεινὰ συρίγματα καὶ τὰς ὀφιώδεις αὐτοῦ φωνὰς τοτὲ μὲν ἀσεβῶν τυράννων ἀπειλαῖς; *V. Const.* 2.1.2: οἷά τις ἢ σκολιὸς ὄφις περὶ ἑαυτὸν ἰλυσπώμενος; 2.46.2: τοῦ δράκοντος ἐκείνου; *Triak.* 9.8: ποῖ τὸ τῶν θεομάχων γιγάντων στῖφος καὶ τῶν δρακόντων τὰ συρίγματα.

63. For the rescript, see Eus. *V. Const.* 2.46.2; cf. Soc. 1.9.47; Gel. Cyz. *HE* 3.3.2; Theod. *HE* 1.15.2. For the image, see Eus. *V. Const.* 3.3.1–3; cf. Mango, *Brazen House*, pp. 22–24. See also Eus. *V. Const.* 2.1.2.

64. *RIC* 7: Constantinople 19, 26.

65. Attested at Jer. *Vir. ill.* 80; *Chron.* s.a. 317.

66. The influence of Lactantius on Constantinian thought is explored in Amarelli, pp. 113–33; Grubbs, pp. 30–36; Digeser, *Making of a Christian Empire*, pp. 56–63, 115–43. The question hangs very much on the dating of Lactantius's contact with Constantine and of the composition of his dedications to Constantine at *Div. Inst.* 1.1.13–16, 7.26.10b–g. I follow Barnes, *Dynasty, Religion and Power*, pp. 176–78 (cf. Barnes, "Lactantius and Constantine"; *Constantine and Eusebius*, pp. 13, 291) in assuming that Lactantius surrendered his position as a teacher of rhetoric by mid-305 and fled Nicomedia for the West. By around 310 he had received an appointment as tutor to Constantine's son Crispus but then returned to Nicomedia by early 313, where he was able to make a copy of the so-called Edict of Milan posted on June 13 (Lact. *Mort. Pers.* 48.1). Digeser, "Lactantius and Constantine's Letter to Arles"; *Making of a Christian Empire*,

pp. 134–35, would place the Constantinian dedications in the *Divine Institutes* in 310 and 313, respectively. The first date is surely incorrect, for in the first dedication, Lactantius addresses Constantine as *Imperator Maximus* (*Div. Inst.* 1.1.13), a title Constantine did not assume before 313, cf. above p.33. Digeser, "Lactantius and Constantine's Letter to Arles," pp. 44–48, attempts to argue this point away, without convincing. Digeser must be right, however, that Constantine had access to the *Div. Inst.* when he composed his letter to the Catholic bishops after the Council of Arles in 314 (Opt. *App.* 5). Moreover, I have argued in "Il valore dell'Editto di Milano" that Constantine had the *Div. Inst.* to hand when he composed the text underlying the letters of Licinius preserved in Lactantius and Eusebius and now known as the Edict of Milan in February 313. Therefore, the dedications almost certainly date to the winter of 312/313.

67. Eus. *HE* 10.9.6 alludes to the shift. For epigraphic attestations, see Chastagnol, "Gouverneur constantinien," pp. 544–46; Grünewald, pp. 134–38.

68. M. R. Alföldi, "Sol Comes-Münze"; cf. P. Bruun, "Disappearance of Sol." Using updated numismatic chronologies, Wienand, "Ein Abschied in Gold"; *Der Kaiser als Sieger*, pp. 296–319, points out that that Sol Invictus had in fact disappeared from the bronze coinage already by 318, but continued to be minted in gold—particularly multiples—down to 325. This has interesting implications for the sorts of audiences Constantine and his moneyers were speaking to with the religious messages on his coinage. Note that some other pagan deities persist on Constantinian coinage after 325; cf. A. Alföldi, "On the Foundation of Constantinople," pp. 12–14; Christodoulou, pp. 56–63; Vanderspoel and Mann; Carlà and Castello, *Questioni tardoantiche*, pp. 114–15; Ramskold and Lenski.

69. Salway.

70. *RIC* 7: Ticinum 36. The coins have traditionally been dated to 313/315 and assigned to the mint of Ticinum; cf. Kraft, "Silbermedallion"; M. R. Alföldi, *Constantinische Goldprägung*, pp. 38–41; Ntantalia, pp. 144–45; B. Overbeck, *Das Silbermedaillon*. Nevertheless, Bernardelli; and Carlà and Castello, *Questioni tardoantiche*, pp. 87–95, have argued for 326 as the date and Constantinople as the mint. To my mind, their arguments have been overturned at Bleckmann, "Costantino dopo la battaglia," pp. 196–200; cf. Wienand, *Der Kaiser als Sieger*, pp. 265–71.

71. *RIC* 7: Siscia 61 with P. Bruun, *Roman Imperial Coinage*, vol. 7, pp. 417–18. For discussion of Christian symbols in the coinage of Constantine, see P. Bruun, "Christian Signs"; *Roman Imperial Coinage*, vol. 7, pp. 417–19, and the slightly fuller catalog at De Caro Balbi; cf. Carlà and Castello, *Questioni tardoantiche*, pp. 101–3.

72. Eus. *V. Const.* 1.31.1 states explicitly that Constantine came to wear the chi-rho on his helmet.

73. Arguments and literature at Ramskold and Lenski.

74. *BHG* 365 p. 557 = Philostorgius, Anhang 5: 182; Joh. Mal. 13.8 (Dindorf, pp. 321–22 = Thurn, p. 247); cf. Bleckmann, "Die Vita BHG 365," p. 13.

75. This "heavenly gaze" portrait appears on a variety of coin types: *RIC* 7: Trier 497–99; Rome 273; Ticinum 179, 192–96; Sirmium 56; Thessalonica 131, 147–48, 167, 214–18; Heraclea 103–4; Constantinople 2, 5, 99, 128, 136; Nicomedia 70, 86–87, 103, 108, 110–12; Antioch 105, 107. M. R. Alföldi, *Constantinische Goldprägung*, pl. 11, offers an excellent visual catalog of the various types.

76. Eus. *V. Const.* 4.15.1–2. On Hellenistic precedents, see Leeb, pp. 57–60. Nicholson, "*Caelum Potius Intuemini*," treats this portrait type as a reflection of Lactantian aesthetics, and Girardet, *Kaiser und sein Gott*, pp. 57–59, adduces evidence from both Lactantius and from Constantinian documents that point toward Christian interpretations of the pose.

77. Eus. *V. Const.* 2.19.2; cf. *HE* 10.9.6.

78. Porena, pp. 339–579; Barnes, *Dynasty, Religion and Power*, pp. 153–63.

79. These documents are treated in detail at Pietri, "Constantin en 324." On the date of the first five, see Dörries, pp. 43–62. On the date of the *Oration to the Assembly of the Saints,* see above, p. 295, n. 56.

80. Eus. *V. Const.* 2.48.2–58.2, esp. 55.1–2. See also *Or. ad Sanct.* 25.2.

81. Eus. *V. Const.* 2.26.2; cf. 2.24.2–3, 25.1, 27.1–2, 42.1.

82. Eus. *V. Const.* 2.46.2, 65.1–66.2.

83. Eus. *V. Const.* 4.9.1, 11.2–13.1.

84. A theme also found in the letter to the eastern provincials, Eus. *V. Const.* 2.48.1, 58.1–2.

85. *Or. ad Sanct.* 24–25.

86. *Or. ad Sanct.* 22.1.

87. Bleckmann, "Ein Kaiser als Prediger," esp. pp. 189, 195–96.

88. Eus. *HE* 10.4.14–15, 8.2–3, 8–9, 9.1–5; *Triak.* 7.8–12, 9.8–19; Eus. *V. Const.* 1.49.2, 56.2, 58.1, 59.2, 2.27.1. See also *Chron. Pasch.* p. 524 (s.a. 324); *BHG* 365 p. 553 = Philostorgius Anhang 5: 178 ll. 14–16.

89. See, for example, the intaglio of Berlin (Staatliche Museen, Antikensammlung, Inv. 30931 = Donati and Gentili, cat. no. 31 = Demandt and Engemann, cat. no. I 9.29), or the colossal bronze head in the Palazzo dei Conservatori (Lenski, *Cambridge Companion,* fig. 15 = Donati and Gentili, p. 152 fig. 12 = Demandt and Engemann, p. 100 no. 8).

90. E.g., *RIC* 7: Constantinople 87, 101.

91. Grünewald, pp. 147–50.

92. Constantine was likely born in 272; cf. Barnes, *New Empire,* pp. 39–42; Lenski, "Reign of Constantine," p. 59.

93. Constantine II was born in 316, cf. *Epit.* 41.4; Zos. 2.20.2, with Barnes, *New Empire,* p. 44.

94. Barnes, "Victories of Constantine," p. 151; *Constantine and Eusebius,* p. 222; *New Empire,* p. 77.

95. *RIC* 7: Rome 298; Aur. Vict. *Caes.* 41.18; *Chron. Pasch.* 527 (s.a. 328), with Barnes, *Constantine and Eusebius,* p. 250.

96. Zos. 2.31.3–32.1, with Bleckmann, "Constantin und die Donaubarbaren." See also Joh. Lyd. *De mag.* 2.10 with 3.31.

97. The sources closest to the event and most accurate on militaria both make it clear that Constantine II shouldered the burden of combat (*Origo* 31: *Deinde adversum Gothos bellum suscepit et implorantibus Sarmatis auxilium tulit. Ita per Constantinum Caesarem centum prope milia fame et frigore extincta sunt;* Jul. *Or.* 1.9D: ὁ δὲ [Constantine II] τὴν πρὸς τοὺς Γέτας ἡμῖν εἰρήνην τοῖς ὅπλοις κρατήσας ἀσφαλῆ παρεσκεύασεν). On the former, see Aiello, *Pars Constantiniana,* p. 238. Remaining sources describe the war using impersonal constructions that do not assign agency to Constantine (*Cons. Const.* s.a. 332; Jer. *Chron.* s.a. 332; Eutr. 10.7.1; Festus 26; Aur. Vict. *Caes.* 41.13). Eus. *V. Const.* 4.5.1–2 does imply Constantine's active involvement, but in characteristically vague and fawning terms. *CIL* 3: 733 = *ILS* 820 and *RIC* 7: Rome 306 are not helpful in determining who actually fought. Barnes, "Victories of Constantine," pp. 150–53; *Constantine and Eusebius,* p. 250 believes Constantine conducted combat operations personally, but most others follow the sources indicating that it was his son, cf. König, pp. 173–74; Bleckmann, "Constantin und die Donaubarbaren," pp. 42–43; Tantillo, *La prima orazione,* p. 197. Constantine II would have been only fifteen at the time, young indeed, but no younger than Crispus when he was first entrusted with a Roman army. Cf. Barnes, *New Empire,* p. 83. For Constantine's presence at Marcianopolis, see *CTh* 3.5.4–5.

98. Aur. Vict. *Caes.* 41.11–12; *Origo* 35; Jer. *Chron.* s.a. 334; Polemius Silvius 1.63 (*MGH.AA* 9: 522); Theophan. a.m. 5825.

99. Eus. *V. Const.* 4.6.1; *Origo* 32; *Cons. Const.* s.a. 334; Jer. *Chron.* s.a. 334.

100. For sources and discussion, see Barnes, "Constantine and the Christians of Persia"; G. Fowden, "The Last Days," pp. 146–53; E. K. Fowden, "Constantine and the Peoples."

101. For Constantius's conduct of combat, see Lib. *Or.* 59.60, 72. For baptism in the Jordan, see Eus. *V. Const.* 4.62.2. The importance of piety for Constantine on this expedition is further indicated by his transport of a large tent in the shape of a church for use in daily prayer, Eus. *V. Const.* 4.57.1; cf. 2.12.1–2, 14.1–2.

102. Eus. *Triak.* 5.4. On the oration, see the translations and commentaries of Drake, *In Praise of Constantine*; and Maraval, *Eusèbe de Césarée*; cf. A. P. Johnson, *Eusebius*, pp. 146–55.

103. Drake, "What Eusebius Knew."

104. Eus. *V. Const.* 4.17.1, 22.1, 23.1–24.1, 29.1–5, 32.1–33.2, 61.1–3, 63.2; cf. *Triak.* 2.4–5; 9.9–10. See also *Triak.* 5.1–2, 9.11, where Constantine is said to have entrusted the care of his palace to Christian ministers and to have become a sort of spiritual guide for his own guardsmen. Girardet, "Christliche Priestertum Konstantins," explores the development of the idea of imperial priesthood.

105. Even Eusebius is aware of the significance of this novelty; *Triak.* 3.5. For Constantine's other rhetorical commissions to Eusebius, see *V. Const.* 4.33.1, 45.3–46.1.

106. Eus. *Triak.* 5.5.

107. During this period Constantine also initiated his correspondence with the Egyptian ascetic Antony, a fitting move for a ruler whose own lifestyle was coming to resemble more closely that of the holy man than the general. Rufin; *HE* 10.8; Soz. 1.13.1; 2.31.1–5; Athan. *V. Ant.* 81.

108. Eus. *V. Const.* 4.40.2, 43.1–45.3; Soc. 1.33.1; Soz. 2.26.1. The opening celebrations of Constantine's tricennalia began on July 25, 335, but the Church of the Holy Sepulchre was dedicated only on Sept. 13; cf. Brennecke *Dokument*, p. 129.

109. On the mausoleum, see Mango, "Constantine's Mausoleum"; M. J. Johnson, *Roman Imperial Mausoleum*, pp. 19–29. On the relics, see Burgess, "Passio S. Artemii"; cf. Leeb, pp. 93–120.

110. Eus. *V. Const.* 4.61.3; cf. 4.62.4. On Constantine's death, see Burgess, "Ἀχυρών."

111. Eus. *V. Const.* 4.61–64, esp. 62.3. Cf. Drake, *Constantine and the Bishops*, pp. 77–79.

CHAPTER 2. CONSTANTINIAN CONSTANTS

1. Tantillo, "Attributi solari," p. 56, is surely correct to describe Constantine as "una personalità ossessionata dall'opposizione tenebre/luce."

2. *Pan. Lat.* 7[6].1.1, with Nixon, *"Constantinus Oriens Imperator."* On *sol oriens,* see Berrens, pp. 178–84.

3. F. Kolb, *Diocletian*, pp. 88–114. Sol Invictus first appears on imperial coinage in 197; J. H. C. Williams, "Septimius Severus." This is not to deny that *Sol Invictus* continued to receive imperial attention under the tetrarchs; cf. Halsberghe, pp. 165–67; F. Kolb, *Diocletian*, pp. 15–16; Berrens, pp. 139–50.

4. The earliest images of Sol appear on coins with Constantinian obverses in 307/310 at London (*RIC* 6: Londinium 101–2, 113–15) and ca. 309 at Lugdunum (*RIC* 6: Lugdunum 307–11). See especially Wienand, *Der Kaiser als Sieger*, pp. 182–94.

5. *Pan. Lat.* 6[7].21.3–7; cf. Rodgers, "Constantine's Pagan Vision." See Müller-Rettig, pp. 339–50, on the site of Grand.

6. P. Weiss, "Die Vision," translated, with revisions and addenda, at P. Weiss, "The Vision." See also below pp. 69–72.

7. The literature on Constantine and Sol Invictus is voluminous. Good starting points include Bergmann, pp. 282–89; Wallraff, "Constantine's Devotion"; *Christus Verus Sol*, pp. 126–

43; Tantillo, "Attributi solari"; Berrens, pp. 146–69; Bardill, passim and especially pp. 89–109. For the introduction of Sol Invictus on Constantinian coinage, see Wienand, *Kaiser als Sieger,* pp. 184–88.

8. *RIC* 6: Ticinum 111; cf. Toynbee, p. 108 pl. 17: 11; M. R. Alföldi, *Constantinische Goldprägung,* pp. 40–42 no. 118 fig. 60; Bastien, 2:659. This extremely rare issue was of course meant for an exclusive audience, but the same message was broadcast much more widely via the SOLI INVICTO COMITI bronze type; cf. Berrens, p. 153.

9. See above pp. 38, 296 n. 68.

10. Sources and discussion at Bardill, pp. 28–36 and 151–58.

11. See especially Wallraff, *Christus Verus Sol.*

12. For this theme, so important in the 320s, see *Orat. ad Sanct.* 25.4; Eus. *HE* 10.8.19, 9.7; *V. Const.* 1.41.2, 43.3, 49.1, 59.2; 2.2.3, 19.1, 28.2, 42.1; *CIL* 8: 7006 = *ILS* 688; *CIL* 8: 7007. Cf. Tantillo, "Attributi solari," pp. 51–53.

13. Eus. *V. Const.* 2.57.1, 67.1, 71.4; 3.17.2, 60.9, 64.2; 4.9.1; cf. Eus. *V. Const.* 2.72.1; 3.64.2, 65.2.

14. Eus. *V. Const.* 2.71.4; 3.60.9; 4.9.1; Opt. *App.* 5, *App. 7* (*CSEL* 26: 208, 211); Opitz *Urkunde* 34.38, p. 74 = Brennecke *Dokument* 27.38, p. 114.

15. Our first firm evidence comes at *CJ* 3.12.2 (Mar. 3, 321): *Omnes iudices urbanaeque plebes et artium officia cunctarum venerabili die solis quiescant.* Nevertheless, Girardet, "Vom Sonnen-Tag zum Sonntag," has shown that this law assumes the existence of a previous law that can be dated to late 312 or early 313. See also *CTh* 2.8.1 (July 3, 321); Eus. *V. Const.* 4.17.1, 18.1–2, 23.1; *Triak.* 9.10; 17.14. *P.Oxy.* 54: 3759 ll. 37–40 (Oct. 2, 325) confirms that the Sunday legislation had an impact on legal proceedings almost immediately after Constantine gained control of the East. See also *CIL* 3: 4121 for an early attestation of the *dies solis* as holiday in Pannonia Superior.

16. *Pan. Lat.* 6[7].7.5: *repentinus tuus adventus inluxit, ut non advectus cursu publico sed divino quodam advolasse curriculo viderereis.* Cf. *Pan. Lat.* 7[6].14.3.

17. On the image of the sun on the arch, see Bardill, pp. 92–100; Lenski, "Sun and the Senate."

18. M. R. Alföldi, *Constantinische Goldprägung,* pp. 40–45; Toynbee, pp. 108–9; Lenski, *Cambridge Companion,* coin 4; Bardill, p. 93 fig. 75.

19. Eus. *Triak.* 3.4; cf. 5.4 and below p. 65.

20. Opt. Porf. *Carm.* 12.3–6, 15–19; 18.1–7, 25–27; cf. 8.1; 11.13; 14.2; 15.10, 14; 17.15; 19.2, 12, with A. Alföldi, *Conversion of Constantine,* p. 58; Wienand, *Der Kaiser als Sieger,* pp. 373–96; "Die Poesie des Bürgerkriegs."

21. Eus. *V. Const.* 3.10.3; Gel. Cyz. *HE* 2.7.28–31.38: δι' ἐμοῦ τοῦ αὐτοῦ θεράποντος ὁ θεὸς δεδουλωμένας ἐλευθεροῖ, καὶ εἰς ἐντελῆ αἰωνίου φωτὸς ἐξάξει λαμπρότητα. On the authenticity of the latter passage, see Maraval, *Constantin le Grand,* pp. xxvii–xxviii, with earlier bibliography.

22. Eus. *V. Const.* 4.22.1–2; cf. Pietri, pp. 84–85.

23. Eus. *V. Const.* 4.62.4–63.1. Cf. 1.43.3.

24. On the lion, see Praxagoras fr. 1.2 (*FGH* 2B no. 219 p. 948); cf. Lact. *Mort. Pers.* 24.4. On the Sarmatian, see *Origo* 3; Zon. 12.33. See also *Pan. Lat.* 6[7].3.3 and Eus. *V. Const.* 1.21.1. These episodes were surely exaggerated if not downright spurious, but they convey a profound sense of Constantine's self-image.

25. On the former, see *RIC* 6: 706 s.v. VIRTVS MILITVM. On the latter, see *RIC* 7: 740 s.v. GLORIA EXERCITVS. On the importance of victory and triumphalism in Constantine's self-presentation, see Wienand, *Der Kaiser als Sieger.*

26. Lact. *Mort. Pers.* 44.5–6; Eus. *V. Const.* 1.28.1–31.3.

27. See *RIC* 7: Ticinum 36; Siscia 61; cf. Eus. *V. Const.* 1.31.1, and see above pp. 9–10.

28. *RIC* 7: Constantinople 19, 26.

29. *RIC* 7: Siscia 207; Arles 394–99, with P. Bruun, "Christian Signs," pp. 21–22; cf. P. Bruun, "Early Christian Symbolism." For an image of the Siscia type, see M. R. Alföldi, *Constantinische*

Goldprägung, pl. 13: 204. De Caro Balbi, p. 153, also catalogs the chi-rho on standards in types from Trier and Siscia not listed in *RIC* 7.

30. See above pp. 34 and 294 n. 45.

31. E.g., *RIC* 7: Constantinople 65, pictured at P. Bruun, "Christian Signs," fig. 15a; *RIC* 7: Aquileia 126 with pl. 12. Cf. Girardet, *Kaiser und sein Gott*, pp. 52–54. More at Heim, pp. 37–105, which demonstrates well how the sacral idealization of victory was rapidly Christianized under Constantine.

32. *Pan. Lat.* 6[7].21.4: *vidisti enim, credo, Constantine, Apollinem tuum comitante Victoria coronas tibi laureas offerentem.*

33. See Lenski, "Sun and the Senate."

34. Bardill, p. 89 fig. 70.

35. *RIC* 7: Rome 301; cf. A. Alföldi, "On the Foundation of Constantinople"; Bardill, p. 253. Ntantalia, p. 254 Gruppe 3, raises the possibility these medallions were minted in Constantinople. See also the related silver type published at Wienand, *De Kaiser als Sieger*, p. 626 fig. 59.

36. *RIC* 7: Heraclea 99 pl. 17. For related images of Victoria on the reverses of Constantinian coinage, see Wienand, *Der Kaiser als Sieger*, p. 636 figs. 87, 88, 136, 137.

37. *Anth. Pl.* 282 with K. W. Wilkinson, "Palladas and the Foundation," pp. 185–89.

38. For Victoria qua pagan divinity, see, for example, Aug. *Civ. Dei* 4.16–17 and, of course, Symm. *Rel.* 3 passim.

39. *Pan. Lat.* 6[7].21.3–22.1. More on Constantine's conviction that he was graced with divine favor at Dörries, pp. 263–65; Bardill, passim, esp. pp. 81–109.

40. *Pan. Lat.* 12[9].2.4, 4.1–2, 5, 16.2. For the same assertion by Constantine himself in the same year, see Opt. *App.* 3 (*CSEL* 26: 206): *ex quibus forsitan commoveri possit summa divinitas non solum contra humanum genus sed etiam in me ipsum, cuius curae nutu suo caelesti terrena omnia moderanda commisit.*

41. *Pan. Lat.* 12[9].11.4.

42. *CIL* 6: 1139 = *ILS* 694; cf. Grünewald, pp. 63–86; L. Hall, "Cicero's *Instinctu Divino*"; Lenski, "Evoking."

43. This new type, with the legend SPQR OPTIMO PRINCIPI, was found in the still unpublished hoard of Misurata (Suk el Kedim), on which see http://www.misurata.unict.it.

44. *Pan. Lat.* 4[10].7.3–4, 12.1, 13.4–5, 14.1–6, 17.1.

45. Eus. *V. Const.* 1.28.2–30.1. In his oration on the Holy Sepulchre of 335, Eusebius speaks of a multitude of divinely inspired dreams witnessed by Constantine, *Triak.* 18.1–3.

46. Zon. 13.1.27–29 with B. Bleckmann, "Chronik des Johannes Zonaras," at pp. 351–52; Bleckmann, "Pagane Visionen." See also MacMullen, "Constantine and the Miraculous."

47. Eus. *V. Const.* 2.6.1.

48. Eus. *V. Const.* 2.12.2–14.2.

49. Eus. *Triak.* 2.1–5, 5.1, 4, characterizes Constantine as the "friend of God": ὁ δὲ τούτῳ φίλος αὐτῷ τῷ μονογενεῖ καὶ σωτῆρι λόγῳ; cf. Dörries, pp. 241–45; Calderone, "Teologia," pp. 238–39; Drake, *In Praise of Constantine*, p. 158; Neri, "Costantino e Licinio Theophiles."

50. Note that this letter is reported with rather different wording at Athan. *Apol. c. Arian.* 86. This collection of testimonia obviously undermines Van Dam, *Remembering Constantine*, pp. 74–81, which attempts to portray Eusebius as the inventor of the notion that Constantine was God's subordinate on earth.

51. Eus. *V. Const.* 2.28.2, esp. ὃς ἀπὸ τῆς πρὸς Βρεττανοῖς ἐκείνης θαλάσσης ἀρξάμενος καὶ τῶν μερῶν, ἔνθα δύεσθαι τὸν ἥλιον ἀνάγκη τινὶ τέτακται κρείττονι. This portion of the letter is also preserved at *P. Lond.* 3: 878 col. 2: 21–26; cf. A. Jones and Skeat.

52. Eus. *V. Const.* 4.9.1.

53. *AE* 1907: 47 = Beševliev, no. 190: τὸν τὰς ὅ[λας?]/ ἀναιμωτὶ νείκας ἀπ[ὸ τῆς]/ ἑσπέρας μέχρι τῆς ἕω ἀν[αιρ]ησάμενον. On this inscription, see the excellent study of Tantillo, "L'ideologia imperiale."

54. Petr. Patr. fr. 15 (*FHG* 4: 190). On the arch, see Lenski, "Sun and the Senate."

55. Eus. *V. Const.* 1.8.2–4; 4.50.1; cf. *V. Const.* 1.25.2; *HE* 10.9.6. Opt. Porph. *Carm.* 18.13–16 also alludes to the same trope, albeit in the abstruse language characteristic of his art.

56. Bardill, pp. 28–125, does a spectacular job of outlining the long tradition of ancient rulers who claimed to have had divine protectors, a tradition stretching from Alexander the Great through the tetrarchs. What Bardill does not demonstrate is the sense of personal connection between ruler and divine that is so palpable in the Constantinian documents cataloged in this chapter. This may be an accident of the source record, but I would argue rather that it was a peculiarity of Constantine's, who was the first ancient ruler—or at least the first Roman emperor—to present himself as a personal friend and unwavering agent of a single supreme divinity with whom he was in regular communication. On this question, Fears remains fundamental for its comprehensive collection of source material.

57. *Pan. Lat.* 7[6].3.2–5.1. See also 7[6].2.2, which emphasizes the potential for offspring and the extension of dynasty. On dynastic elements in this oration, see especially Wienand, *Der Kaiser als Sieger,* pp. 100–110.

58. *Pan. Lat.* 6[7].3.1–8.2 (a. 310); 5[8].4.4 (a. 311); cf. Rodgers, "Metamorphosis," pp. 235–37; Enenkel, pp. 107–11.

59. For the coins, see *RIC* 6: Londinium 110; Treviri 789–90, 809; Lugdunum 251, 264–69, 297; Ticinum 96–97; Aquileia 127. The relevant inscriptions are assembled at Grünewald, pp. 17–21.

60. *Pan. Lat.* 7[6].1.1, 2.1–2, 3.2, 6.2, 13.3. For the title M. AURELI VALERI MAXIMIANI AUGUSTI NEPOS, see Grünewald, pp. 32–33 and n. 119, to which add *AE* 2011: 709.

61. *Pan. Lat.* 6[7].2.2; cf. *Pan. Lat.* 5[8].2.5, 4.2, 4.4; *ILS* 699, 701, 702, 723, 725, 730, 732; *CIL* 12: 668 = *AE* 1952: 107; *AE* 1980: 576; Opt. Porf. *Carm.* 8.11–12, 14, 27–28; 10.28–32; Jul. *Or.* 1.6d; 3.51c; *Caes.* 336b; *Origo* 1; Eutr. 9.22; Jer. *Chron.* s.a. 290. The tradition has long been to assume that this dynastic link was pure invention; see Grünewald, pp. 46–50; Baldini, pp. 73–89; Enenkel, pp. 98–107; Wienand, *Der Kaiser als Sieger,* pp. 154–56, 381–82. Chausson, pp. 25–95, has made a valiant case that it is based in fact.

62. *RIC* 7: Trier 200–207; Arles 173–78; Aquileia 21–26; Rome 104–28, Siscia 41–46; Thessalonica 24–26; cf. Barnes, *Constantine and Eusebius,* p. 47; Grünewald, pp. 122–24; Enenkel, pp. 119–20. Note the recurrence of the same three ancestors in inscriptions honoring Constantine's sons, *CIL* 2: 4844 = *ILS* 730; *CIL* 2: 6209 = *ILS* 725; *CIL* 3: 3705 = *ILS* 732; *CIL* 3: 5207 = *ILS* 723.

63. This is not to deny that dynastic connections remained important to the tetrarchs. After all, Galerius married Valeria, daughter of Diocletian; Constantius Chlorus married Theodora, the daughter or stepdaughter of Maximianus; Maximinus Daia was the son of Galerius's sister; Maxentius married Valeria Maximilla, daughter of Galerius; and Constantine himself married Maximianus's daughter Fausta. More on the importance of dynasty under the Tetrarchy at Leadbetter, pp. 26–47; Barnes, *Dynasty, Religion and Power,* pp. 27–45. All this having been said, tetrarchic *public propaganda* did not emphasize dynasty to nearly the same degree as Constantine did in coins, inscriptions, and panegyrics.

64. *Pan. Lat.* 12[9].4.3–4; 24.4–25.3; cf. Eus. *V. Const.* 1.22.1. Constantine did not, of course, abandon claims to authority based on his ancestry in the years to come; cf. Eus. *V. Const.* 2.49.1; cf. 1.21.1–2, 24.1.

65. *PLRE* 1: Constantia 1. On the cognomen "Constantinus" for Licinius the younger, see Christol and Drew-Bear, "Documents latins," pp. 44–46.

66. *Origo* 14–15; cf. Lenski, "Reign of Constantine," p. 73; Barnes, *Dynasty, Religion and Power,* pp. 101–2.

67. *PLRE* 1: Fl. Claudius Constantinus 3; Fl. Iulius Crispus 4; Barnes, *New Empire,* pp. 7, 44–45, 73; Kienast, pp. 305–6, 310.

68. Eus. *V. Const.* 1.9.2, 21.2; 4.51.1–2, 63.3; *Triak.* 3.2; Lib. *Or.* 59.13, 48; Jul. *Or.* 1.7d, 19b–c, with Tantillo, "'Come un bene ereditario.'" See also the following milestones, *AE* 2009: 894 (Die): honoring Crispus as *patre avo maioribus imp(eratoribus) natus*; *AE* 2011: 393 (Villesse), honoring Constantine II and Constantius as *filis(sic) DN Constantini Maximi Victoris Augusti, nepotibus divi Consta(ntii).*

69. *Pan. Lat.* 4[10].4.1; cf. Rodgers, "The Metamorphosis," pp. 240–46.

70. *Laudes Domini* ll. 143–148 (Salzano, p. 42), esp. *exaequent utinam sua pignora patrem.*

71. *PLRE* 1: Fl. Iul. Constantius 8; Barnes, *New Empire,* pp. 8, 45; Kienast, p. 314; Grünewald, pp. 150–53.

72. Barnes, *New Empire,* p. 9; Grünewald, pp. 142–43; Kienast, pp. 304–5; Drijvers, p. 41–54; cf. *CIL* 10: 517 = *ILS* 708: *procreatrici d.n. Constantini . . . aviae . . . Caesarum*; *CIL* 6: 1134 = *ILS* 709: *genetrici d.n. Constantini . . . aviae . . . Caesarum.*

73. *RIC* 7: 724 s.v. FLAV MAX FAVSTA AVG and 725 s.v. FL HELENA AVGVSTA; cf. Carlà and Castello, *Questioni tardoantiche,* pp. 106–10.

74. *PLRE* 1: Fl. Iul. Constans 3; Barnes, *New Empire,* pp. 8, 45; Kienast, p. 312. On the significance of December 25 as both a Christian and pagan holy day, see Wallraff, *Christus Verus Sol,* pp. 174–95; Salzman, "Aurelian."

75. For medallions, see Toynbee, pp. 197–98.

76. Harlick; cf. Carlà and Castello, *Questioni tardoantiche,* pp. 131–43.

77. *PLRE* 1: Fl. Iulius Dalmatius 7; Kienast, p. 307, esp. *Origo* 35; *Epit.* 41.20. See also the medallion at *RIC* 7: Thessalonica 204, illustrated at Wienand, *Der Kaiser als Sieger,* p. 634 fig. 108, which features Dalmatius standing amidst the four Caesars before an enthroned Constantine.

78. So Barnes, "Praetorian Prefects," pp. 249–51; *Dynasty, Religion and Power,* pp. 158–68; cf. *New Empire,* pp. 134–39.

79. *PLRE* 1: Hannibalianus 2; Kienast, p. 308. For Constantia, see *PLRE* 1: Constantina 2, with Barnes, *Dynasty, Religion and Power,* pp. 150–52, on the spelling of her name. On the marriage, see Barnes, *Dynasty, Religion and Power,* p. 166.

80. *AE* 1981: 878 (Aïn Rchine: a. 331/332); *AE* 1925: 72 = *ILT* 814 (Tubernuc: a. 335/336); *AE* 1985: 823 (Antioch: a. 336). Zos. 2.32.2–33.1 and Joh. Lyd. *De mag.* 3.33 both assert that Constantine created regional prefectures, a point not to be dismissed as *post eventum* recreation in light of the epigraphic record. I follow Porena, pp. 398–562, both on the dating of these inscriptions and on Constantine's introduction of regional prefectures.

81. *PLRE* 1: Fl. Dalmatius 6 became Consul in 333 and was charged with the suppression of the revolt of Calocaerus in 334 and the oversight of the synod of Tyre that same year. *PLRE* 1: Iulius Constantius 7 was named Consul for 335 and given the title *Patricius* around the same time. See also Wiemer, "Libanios und Zosimus," pp. 475–77; "Libanius on Constantine," pp. 516–18, who shows that, despite having been forced into some form of exile earlier in Constantine's reign (Auson. *Prof.* 16.9–13; 17.9–12; Lib. *Or.* 14.29–30), both had been rehabilitated by 326 at the latest.

82. For sources and argument, see the magisterial article of Burgess, "Summer of Blood."

83. Eus. *Triak.* 3.4; cf. 2.5. On this passage, see Maraval, *Eusèbe de Césarée,* pp. 159–60; Tantillo, "Attributi solari," pp. 42–48.

84. See also the notion that Constantine was in a position to name each of his three sons at the beginning of each decade of his reign, a further sign of divine favor and cosmic order: Eus.

Triak. 1.3; 2.5–3.3; *V. Const.* 1.5.1; 4.40.1–2. Cf. Girardet, "Christliche Priestertum Konstantins," pp. 584–86.

CHAPTER 3. CONSTANTINE AND THE CHRISTIANS

1. *CTh* 16.8.3 (Dec. 11, 321: permitting Jews to be drafted into *curiae*); *CTh* 16.8.1 = *CJ* 1.9.3 (Oct. 18, 329: ordering the public cremation of any Jews who stone apostates from their religion and of anyone else who converts to Judaism); *CTh* 16.8.2, 4 (Nov. 29 and Dec. 1, 330: exempting members of the Jewish priestly class from personal and civic *munera*); *Sirm.* 4 = *CTh* 16.9.1 = 16.8.5 (Oct. 21, 335: prohibiting Jews from circumcising non-Jewish slaves and from harassing Jewish converts to Christianity). These reveal an interest in protecting the rights of Jews to practice their religion except where it impinged on the furtherance of Christianity. See more at Linder, pp. 120–44 nos. 7–10; cf. Applebaum, pp. 119–33.

2. For a cogent defense of the word "paganism" as the most neutral and appropriate way to characterize the collectivity of religions who were neither Christian nor Jew in Late Antiquity, see Al. Cameron, pp. 14–32.

3. Lact. *Mort. Pers.* 24.9: *Suscepto imperio Constantinus Augustus nihil egit prius quam Christianos cultui ac deo suo reddere. Haec fuit prima eius sanctio sanctae religionis restitutae.* Girardet, *Rede an die Versammlung der Heiligen,* p. 53 n. 237, would read *restituendae,* which would make more sense of the Latin. See also Lact. *Div. Inst.* 1.1.13.

4. For arguments against the validity of the text, see Moreau, vol. 2, pp. 343–44; Heck, *Die dualistischen Zusätze,* pp. 141–42. For support of Lactantius, see Barnes, "Lactantius and Constantine," pp. 44–46; *Constantine and Eusebius,* p. 28; *Dynasty, Religion and Power,* pp. 65–66.

5. *Or. ad Sanct.* 1.4–6, 15.4.

6. Hosius is first mentioned in Constantine's letter to Caecilianus of Carthage, datable to winter 312/313 (Eus. *HE* 10.6.2), but he is likely to have been among the advisers who helped Constantine interpret his vision earlier in 312 and perhaps as early as late 311, as described in Eus. *V. Const.* 1.32.1–3; cf. 42.1. See also Philost. *App.* 5: 182–83, and De Clercq, pp. 148–58.

7. Opt. 1.23.1–2; Eus. *HE* 10.5.19. On this relationship, see especially Eck; Girardet, *Kaiser und sein Gott,* p. 45, and below p. 250.

8. See above p. 37.

9. P. Weiss, "Die Vision"; "The Vision"; cf. above p. 49. Harris attempts to refute Weiss, without convincing: neither does he prove that the vision described in *Pan. Lat.* 6[7].21.3–4 occurred indoors rather than out (the Latin leaves either possibility open), nor does he prove that Constantine consciously manufactured (rather than unconsciously experienced) the dream described in Lactantius and Eusebius. To be sure, fabrication is a possibility, but this would change very little about the use to which the dream (or "dream") was put. Woods, "Postumus," has recently argued that the Gallic emperor Postumus may also have advertised a solar halo vision on his coinage.

10. Girardet, *Konstantinische Wende,* pp. 27–32; *Kaiser und sein Gott,* pp. 44–52; "Das Jahr 311" holds that Constantine had been convinced by Christian advisers while still in Trier that his vision of 310 had come from the Christian god by the time he undertook his war against Maxentius. He points out that *Pan. Lat.* 12[9].21.5 and Eutr. 10.4.3 indicate that this expedition began in the fall of 311 and thus dates the conversion earlier in this year.

11. Eus. *V. Const.* 1.28.1–32.3. Perhaps at the same meeting Constantine also told the stories reported in *V. Const.* 2.8.1–3 of the power of the labarum against the armies of Licinius.

12. Van Dam, *Remembering Constantine,* pp. 56–81.

13. Eus. *V. Const.* 2.55.1–2, esp. τὴν σὴν σφραγῖδα πανταχοῦ προβαλλόμενος καλλινίκου ἡγησάμην στρατοῦ. Constantine expresses the exact same notion in his letter to Shapur II of the same year; Eus. *V. Const.* 4.9.1: τοῦτον τὸν θεὸν πρεσβεύω, οὗ τὸ σημεῖον ὁ τῷ θεῷ ἀνακείμενός μου στρατὸς ὑπὲρ τῶν ὤμων φέρει. See also Eus. *V. Const.* 2.4.2: καὶ τό γε τοῦ σωτηρίου πάθους σύμβολον αὐτοῦ τε καὶ τοῦ παντὸς καθηγήσασθαι στρατοῦ; 2.6.2: τοῦ σωτηρίου τροπαίου προπομπεύοντος τῆς ἀμφ᾽ αὐτὸν φάλαγγος; 4.5.2: τῷ δ᾽ αὐτοῦ ἐπιθαρρῶν σωτῆρι τὸ νικητικὸν τρόπαιον καὶ τούτοις ἐπανατείνας.

14. Lact. *Mort. Pers.* 44.5–6. The attempt of Van Dam, *Remembering Constantine*, pp. 112–19, to explain this early witness away by claiming Lactantius was casting his own idiosyncratic interpretation on events does not convince.

15. On the dates of the editions of the *Ecclesiastical History*, see above p. 294 n. 50.

16. On Siscia, see above p. 38. On Crispus's shield, see *RIC 7*: Trier 372; Girardet, *Konstantinische Wende*, p. 78 with n. 137 and fig. 15; *Kaiser und sein Gott*, p. 65 fig. 12.

17. *AE* 2000: 1799 and 1801 with Salama, "Les provinces d'Afrique." Van Dam, *Remembering Constantine*, shows no awareness of this evidence.

18. Eus. *HE* 9.9.11; cf. *V. Const.* 1.40.2. Eusebius alludes to the same statue already in his oration on the dedication of the church of Tyre, probably delivered in 314, *HE* 10.3.16, and in his *Tricennalian Oration* of 336, *Triak.* 9.8.

19. See below chapters 9–10 and Lenski, "Reign of Constantine," pp. 71–72.

20. Eus. *HE* 10.5.1–14; Lact. *Mort. Pers.* 48.2–12. On this, see Lenski, "Il valore dell'Editto."

21. Eus. *HE* 9.9.12; Lact. *Mort. Pers.* 37.1.

22. See above p. 50.

23. *CJ* 1.13.1 (Jun. 8, 316); *CTh* 4.7.1 = *CJ* 1.13.2 (Apr. 18, 321); Soz. 1.8.6–7. On *manumissio in ecclesia*, see Lenski, "Constantine and Slavery," with earlier bibliography.

24. *CTh* 9.40.2 = *CJ* 9.47.17: *quo facies, quae ad similitudinem pulchritudinis caelestis est figurata, minime maculetur.* Cf. Rivière, pp. 353–54.

25. *CTh* 1.27.1; cf. *Sirm.* 1, and see below pp. 198–99.

26. Aur. Vict. *Caes.* 41.4–5; Soz. 1.8.12–13; cf. Ambrosiaster *Quaestiones* 115.67 (*CSEL* 50.341) with Barnes, *Constantine and Eusebius*, pp. 51, 312 n. 83; Rivière, pp. 358–61. Carlà and Castello, *Questioni tardoantiche*, pp. 161–69, make a valiant attempt to argue away this ancient evidence, mostly on the strength of the so-called *edictum de accusationibus*, a law long attributed to Constantine, which prescribes execution on the cross for slave *delatores*. They fall short, however, by failing to have noted that this law was actually issued by Galerius, as demonstrated by Corcoran, "Galerius' Jigsaw Puzzle." Cook offers a much broader range of evidence to prove that crucifixion was commonly regarded as illegal and generally avoided from Constantine onward.

27. *CTh* 16.2.4 = *CJ* 1.2.1 (Jul. 3, 321). There are also numerous other legislative measures—related to marriage and divorce, sexuality, infant exposure, and inheritance—for which Christian intent is not explicitly attested, but that can be argued to take their roots in Christian principles. For debates on this vexed question, see Grubbs; Humfress, "Civil Law and Social Life."

28. On coins, see above p. 38. On their small numbers, see P. Bruun, "Christian Signs."

29. Apart from the two inscriptions mentioned at p.9 and p. 291 n. 50, and another of Cuicul datable to 319, i.e., *AE* 1992: 1885 with Salama, "Le plus ancien chrisme," all remaining examples of the chi-rho from Africa date after 326; cf. Salama, "Anniversaires impériaux," p. 142 n. 14.

30. Opt. *App.* 5 (*CSEL* 26: 207–8). Maier, *Dossier*, vol. 1, p. 168 n. 5, notes that Opt. *App.* 5 constitutes the first appearance of Christ's name in an extant letter of Constantine's.

31. *Summus Deus*: Opt. *App.* 3 (*CSEL* 26: 206,13); 7 (*CSEL* 26: 211,28); 9 (*CSEL* 26: 213,1); 10 (*CSEL* 26: 213,31; 214,10, 34, 35; 215,16). ὁ μέγιστος θεός: Eus. *V. Const.* 2.37.2, 38.1, 59.1, 71.2, 71.4. See also *V. Const.* 2.51.1: τὸν ὕψιστον θεὸν; 4.19.1: τὸν δ᾽ ἐπὶ πάντων θεόν.

32. Firm. Mat. *Math.* 1.5.7, 10.14; 2.30.5; 5 pr. 3. See also Drake, "Firmicus Maternus"; Lenski, "Early Retrospectives."

33. On Constantine's divine inspiration, see *Pan. Lat.* 12[9].2.5, 3.3, 4.1. For these designations, see *Pan. Lat.* 12[9].2.4 (*quisnam deus*); 12[9].2.5, 16.2, 26.1 (*divina mens*); 12[9].4.1 (*divinum numen*); 12[9].13.2 (*ille mundi creator et dominus*); 12[9].26.1 (*summus rerum sator, cuius tot nomina sunt quot gentium linguas esse voluisti*). See also Rodgers, "Divine Insinuation," on the shift in language referring to the divine in Latin panegyrics after 312.

34. *Pan. Lat.* 4[10].7.3 (*rerum arbiter deus*); 4[10].7.4 (*illa vis, illa maiestas fandi ac nefandi discriminatrix*); 4[10].16.1 (*summa illa maiestas*); 4[10].19.2 (*benigna maiestas*); 4[10].16.2, 18.4, 26.1, 28.1 (*deus*).

35. On the monotheistic trend in late antique paganism, see Ando, "Pagan Apologetics," pp. 187–90; Athanassiadi and Frede; Mitchell and Van Nuffelen. It should be remembered that Lactantius also regularly uses *summus deus* to identify the Christian god: *Div. Inst.* 1.1.3, 1.13, 5.11, 5.19, 5.26, 6.4, 6.15, 7.6, 11.39, 11.52, 2.1.6, 8.7ad, 3.11.3, 4.4.6, 6.3, 6.5, 10.1, 12.16, 13.1, 13.17, 25.1, 29.12, 29.14, 5.1.6, 7.2.1, 2.36, 4.17, 4.19, 5.4, 9.11, 20.1, 24.1, 26.27ad; *Mort. Pers.* 1.7, 46.3. This does not detract from the argument that the name was generic enough to have appealed to all of Constantine's subjects, pagan, Jew, and Christian. It does, perhaps, speak to Lactantius's influence on Constantine's understanding of theology and cosmology; cf. above p. 37.

36. Eus. *V. Const.* 3.30.1, 4 (to Macarius of Jerusalem); 3.53.3 (to Macarius and the Palestinian bishops on Bethlehem); 4.36.1 (to Eusebius of Caesarea); *Or. ad Sanct.* 1.6, 5.1, 11.3–4, 7–8, 13, 16, 17.4–6, 18.1, 19.2, 8, 26.2.

37. Eus. *V. Const.* 3.2.2: τοιγάρτοι τὸν Χριστὸν τοῦ θεοῦ σὺν παρρησίᾳ τῇ πάσῃ πρεσβεύων εἰς πάντας διετέλει, μηδ<ὲν> ἐγκαλυπτόμενος τὴν σωτήριον ἐπηγορίαν, σεμνολογούμενος δ' ἐπὶ τῷ πράγματι.

38. Eus. *V. Const.* 4.20.1 with Wienand, *Der Kaiser als Sieger*, pp. 319–28.

39. See also Dörries, pp. 254–59; Maraval, *Constantin le Grand*, p. 176 n. 64.

40. Rom. 1:1; Tit. 1:1; cf. 2 Pet. 1:1; James 1:1; cf. D. B. Martin, *Slavery*.

41. LXX Ex. 14:3; 1 Num. 12:7–8; Deut. 34:5; Josh. 1:2; Heb. 3:5; Rev. 15:3.

42. Eus. *HE* 9.9.5–6; 10.8.19.

43. For Constantine and Moses, see Eus. *V. Const.* 1.12.1–2, 19.2, 38.2–39.1; 2.11.2; cf. Av. Cameron and Hall, *Eusebius*, pp. 192–93; Rapp, "Imperial Ideology." For Eusebius's own characterization of Constantine as the θεράπων τοῦ θεοῦ, see *V. Const.* 1.3.1, 1.5.2, 1.6.1 bis, 1.12.2, 1.47.2, 2.2.3, 4.14.1, 4.71.2; cf. *Triak.* 7.12.

44. Building on arguments first advanced by Baronius, Calderone, *Costantino*, pp. 292–93, and Barnes, *Constantine and Eusebius*, p. 58; *NE* p. 72 argue that Eus. *V. Const.* 1.44.1–2 and Opt. *App.* 4 (*CSEL* 26: 208,16) attest to Constantine's presence. Girardet, "Konstantin der Grosse und das Reichskonzil von Arles," however, makes a strong case against his presence and is followed by Av. Cameron and Hall, *Eusebius*, pp. 221.

45. Opitz *Urkunde* 20 p. 42 = Brennecke *Dokument* 22 p. 105; Brennecke *Dokument* 40 p. 133.

46. For Constantine's claims to attendance, see Eus. *V. Const.* 3.17.2; Opitz *Urkunde* 25.3 pp. 52–53 = Brennecke *Dokument* 29 p. 115; Opitz *Urkunde* 27.13 p. 61 = Brennecke *Dokument* 31.13 p. 119; Opitz *Urkunde* 32.2 p. 66 = Brennecke *Dokument* 37 p. 126. For the introduction of the term *homoousios*, see Opitz *Urkunde* 22 pp. 43–44 = Brennecke *Dokument* 24 p. 106. Philost. *HE* 1.7.7a claims that it was Ossius of Cordoba who devised the term.

47. For Nicomedia, see Eus. *V. Const.* 3.23.1; cf. Opitz *Urkunde* 31.5 p. 66 = Brennecke *Dokument* 36.5 p. 126, and Barnes, *Constantine and Eusebius*, p. 229–30; *New Empire*, p. 77. For the Council of Constantinople, see Hilar. Pict. *Frag. Hist.* A. IV 1.3.1–3 (*CSEL* 65: 50–51); cf. Soc. 1.36.7. Girardet, "Kaiser Konstantin der Grosse als Vorsitzender"; *Kaiser und sein Gott*, pp. 140–50,

argues that Constantine presided over these councils. Constantine was also present for the trials of Athanasius at Psamathia in winter 331/332 (Athan. *Apol. c. Ar.* 60.4, 65.4; *Festal Letter* 4.5; Soc. 1.27.10) and Constantinople in 335 (*Fest. Ind.* 8 [*SCh* 317: 000]; Athan. *Apol. c. Ar.* 87.1–2).

48. For the letter to Macarius, Eus. *V. Const.* 3.53 with Maraval, *Constantin le Grand,* p. 197. For the *Oration to the Assembly of the Saints,* see below p. 292 n. 2. See also Dörries, pp. 298–302, on Constantine's knowledge of scripture.

49. Opt. *App.* 5 (*CSEL* 26: 210): *Deus omnipotens perpetuam tribuat securitatem.* Eusebius renders this ἡ θειότης ὑμᾶς τοῦ μεγάλου θεοῦ διαφυλάξει πολλοῖς ἔτεσι, which appears at Eus. *HE* 10.5.20, 6.5; *V. Const.* 3.60.9, 61.3, 62.3.

50. Eus. *V. Const.* 1.44.1: οἷά τις κοινὸς ἐπίσκοπος ἐκ θεοῦ καθεσταμένος συνόδους τῶν τοῦ θεοῦ λειτουργῶν συνεκρότει.

51. Eus. *V. Const.* 4.24.1: ἀλλ᾽ ὑμεῖς μὲν τῶν εἴσω τῆς ἐκκλησίας, ἐγὼ δὲ τῶν ἐκτὸς ὑπὸ θεοῦ καθεσταμένος ἐπίσκοπος ἂν εἴην.

52. See especially Baynes, *Constantine the Great,* pp. 25–29; Calderone, *Costantino,* pp. xi–xlv; Straub; Girardet, "Christliche Priestertum Konstantins"; De Decker and Dupuis-Masay; Rapp, "Imperial Ideology"; Drake, *Constantine and the Bishops,* pp. 71, 227, 377, 389; Zecchini; Angelov.

53. 1 Cor. 5:12–13 (bis); Col. 4:5; 1 Thess. 4:12; 1 Tim. 3:7.

54. Al. Cameron, pp. 22–25. Al. Cameron and Long, pp. 35–37 cite numerous further examples of this usage in early Byzantine literature.

55. Eus. *V. Const.* 2.55.1–56.2.

56. Opitz *Urkunde* 27.7 p. 59 = Brennecke *Dokument* 31.7 pp. 118–19.

57. Opt. *App.* 3 (*CSEL* 26: 206).

58. Opt. *App.* 7 (*CSEL* 26: 211).

59. Eus. *V. Const.* 4.14.13: τούτους ἀγάπα ἁρμοδίως τῆς σεαυτοῦ φιλανθρωπίας· σαυτῷ τε γὰρ καὶ ἡμῖν ἀπερίγραπτον δώσεις διὰ τῆς πίστεως τὴν χάριν. On the letter, see Barnes, "Constantine and the Christians of Persia," pp. 128–32; Potter, *Roman Empire at Bay,* p. 447. Angelov should be used with caution.

60. Eus. *V. Const.* 4.56.1–57.1; *Origo* 35, with Barnes, "Constantine and the Christians of Persia"; cf. K. Smith.

61. Athan. *Apol. c. Ar.* 86.10–11. See also Soc. 1.34.9–10.

62. Rufin. *HE* 10.11; cf. Soc. 1.20.19–20; Soz. 2.7.12.

63. For sources and discussion, see Heather and Matthews, pp. 133–53, arguing for a date of 340. A date of 336 is supported by Barnes, "Consecration"; Schäferdiek. More at McLynn; Lenski, "Gothic Civil War."

64. Soc. 2.41.23.

65. See G. Fowden, *Empire to Commonwealth,* p. 91.

66. Eus. *HE* 10.7.1. See especially Baynes, *Constantine the Great,* pp. 11–16.

67. Opt. *App.* 3 (*CSEL* 26: 206): *ex quibus forsitan commoveri possit summa divnitas non solum contra humanum genus sed etiam in me ipsum.*

68. Opt. *App.* 5 (*CSEL* 26: 210): *ne ulterius sub tanta claritate dei nostri ea ab ipsis fiant, quae maximam iracundiam caelestis provdentiae possint incitare.*

69. Opt. *App.* 7 (*CSEL* 26: 212): *nam nequaquam me aliter maximum reatum effugere posse credo.*

70. Eus. *V. Const.* 2.65.2: εἰ κοινὴν ἅπασι τοῖς τοῦ θεοῦ θεράπουσιν ἐπ᾽εὐχαῖς ταῖς ἐμαῖς ὁμόνοιαν καταστήσαιμι, καὶ ἡ τῶν δημοσίων πραγμάτων χρεία σύνδρομον ταῖς ἁπάντων εὐσεβέσι γνώμαις τὴν μεταβολὴν καρπώσεται.

71. *Ep. ad Nic.* 13 (Opitz *Urkunde* 27 p. 61 = Brennecke *Dokument* 31 p. 119) and Eus. *V. Const.* 3.12.1–5.

72. On the date, see Barnes, "Exile and Recalls of Arius."

73. Opitz *Urkunde* 34.35 pp. 73–74 = Brennecke *Dokument* 27.35 p. 113.

74. Opitz *Urkunde* 34.42 pp. 74–75 = Brennecke *Dokument* 27.42 p. 114.

75. See below pp. 252–53.

76. See below pp. 234–39.

77. Opitz *Urkunde* 33 pp. 66–68 = Brennecke *Dokument* 33 p. 115; Soc. 1.9.30–1; Gel. Cyz. *HE* 2.36.1–2; cf. *CTh* 16.5.66.

78. Eus. *V. Const.* 3.64.1–65.3, esp. 3.64.2: ὦ τῆς μὲν ἀληθείας ἐχθροί, τῆς δὲ ζωῆς πολέμιοι καὶ ἀπωλείας σύμβουλοι. Note that his edict was limited to groups long recognized as heretical or schismatic by the mainstream church. It thus avoided the Donatists, Melitians, and Arians—that is, the groups whose demographic and ideological force was still great in the 320s and attempts at whose suppression would thus have been risky. For analysis and dating, see Norderval; Escribano Paño; cf. Minali, pp. 165–228.

79. On Eusebius, see Opitz *Urkunde* 27 pp. 58–62 = Brennecke *Dokument* 31 pp. 118–20. On Athanasius, see Lenski, "Early Retrospectives." See also his general threat to exile any who refused his invitation to attend the Synod of Tyre, Eus. *V. Const.* 4.42.4.

80. Opt. *App.* 5 (*CSEL* 26: 209): *meum iudicium postulant, qui ipse iudicium Christi expecto.* Constantine's bon mot is quoted at Opt. 1.23.1 and Aug. *Ep.* 43.13.

81. Opt. *App.* 9 (*CSEL* 26: 213), quoted below at p. 254.

82. Opt. *App.* 10 (*CSEL* 26: 214–15): *deus siquidem se omnium vindicem promisit. et ideo cum vindicta deo permittitur, acrius de inimicis supplicium sumitur.*

83. This notion also had a long history in Roman religion, see Scheid, p. 22. In Constantine's instance, however, it has a clear intellectual pedigree in Lact. *Div. Inst.*; see below pp. 255–56.

84. Eus. *V. Const.* 2.56.1: μηδεὶς τὸν ἕτερον παρενοχλείτω· ἕκαστος ὅπερ ἡ ψυχὴ βούλεται κατεχέτω, τούτῳ κατακεχρήσθω.

85. Eus. *V. Const.* 2.60.2.

86. On the Novatians, see *CTh* 1.16.2 (Sep. 25, 326); cf. Soc. 1.10.1–4; Soz. 2.32.1, 5; *Conc. Nic.* can. 8 (Mansi 2: 688–89 = Jonkers 42). On the Montanists of Phrygia, see Soz. 2.32.6.

87. On these events, see Soc. 1.14.1–7; Soz. 2.16.1–11, with Parvis, pp. 100–107; Barnes, "Exile and Recalls of Arius."

CHAPTER 4. APPROACHING CONSTANTINE

1. Millar, *Emperor*; *Greek Roman Empire*, pp. 192–234; cf. Errington, *Roman Imperial Policy.*

2. On petitions preserved in legal codes, see Corcoran, *Empire of the Tetrarchs*; Connolly, *Lives Behind the Laws.* For those on papyri, see Haensch, "Bearbeitungsweisen"; "Apokrimata und Authentica"; B. Kelly. See also the studies in Feissel and Gascou, *Pétition à Byzance*, for early Byzantine petitions.

3. Hauken, to which add *SEG* 53: 1517 from Saraycık (Tymion?); cf. Millar, *Emperor*, pp. 541–45. For Hellenistic parallels, see Ma, *Antiochos III*, pp. 179–242. For more on petitions from late antique cities, see Cecconi, *Governo imperiale*, pp. 87–96.

4. On the performative nature of inscribed communication, see Woolf; Ma, *Antiochos III*, pp. 211–12.

5. Corcoran, *Empire of the Tetrarchs*; Lenski, *Failure of Empire*, pp. 264–317; Schmidt-Hofner, *Reagieren und Gestalten.*

6. On dioceses, see Zuckerman; on regional prefectures, Porena.

7. See C. Kelly.

8. On the *Constitutio Antoniniana* and its consequences, see Ando, *Law, Language, and Empire.*

9. *Not. Dig.* Or. 19.6–11.

10. Connolly, *Lives Behind the Laws,* pp. 47–62.

11. On the interface between imperial and local law and the use of legal discourse to interpellate subject peoples into Roman structures of ideology and governmentality, see Ando, *Law, Language, and Empire.*

12. These qualities trace back to Hellenistic precedents; cf. Ma, *Antiochos III*, pp. 150–74; Schuler.

13. E.g., the inscription of Skaptopara at Hallof = Hauken, pp. 74–140, with English translation at Connolly, *Lives Behind the Laws,* pp. 167–73.

14. *Epit.* 41.14: *Commodissimus tamen rebus multis fuit: . . . legere ipse scribere meditari audire legationes et querimonias provinciarum.*

15. *CTh* 7.20.2, on which, see below p. 233. See also *CTh* 8.15.1, which preserves a hearing over a property transaction conducted before Constantine personally that may have begun with a petition.

16. Opt. *App.* 10.36b–37a (*CSEL* 26.215): *quam petitionem more instituti mei libenter amplexus sum.*

17. *Pan. Lat.* 4[10].38.4: *Omnia foris placida, domi prospera annonae ubertate, fructuum copia. Exornatae mirandum in modum ac prope de integro conditae civitates.* Similar rhetoric can be found at Dio Chrys. *Or.* 3.127.

18. *Pan. Lat.* 5[8]. For similar rhetoric, see *Pan. Lat.* 3[11].9.2–4.

19. Isid. *Orig.* 15.2.11: *vici et castella et pagi hi sunt, qui nulla dignitate civitatis ornantur, sed vulgari hominum conventu incoluntur et propter parvitatem sui maioribus civitatibus adtribuuntur.* On the acquisition of civic status and political freedom by cities, see Jacques, "*Municipia libera*"; Millar, *Emperor,* pp. 394–410; Mitchell, *Anatolia,* vol. 2, pp. 80–99.

20. *CIL* 3: 6866 = *ILS* 6090 = *MAMA* 4: 236 = *FIRA* 1: 92, and the more recent edition of Bru, Labarre, Özsaıt = *AE* 2009: 1474.

21. Bru, Labarre, and Özsaıt, pp. 200–204, suggest 297/305.

22. Lines 9–10: *ut per universum orbem nostrum civi/tatum honor ac numerus augeatur.*

23. Mitrev and Tarakov, whence *AE* 2002: 1293; cf. Lepelley, "Inscription d'Heraclea Sintica," whence *AE* 2004: 1331. For related grants, see *CIL* 2: 871 = 1423 = *ILS* 6092, in which Vespasian permits the construction of an *oppidum* at Sabora (modern Cerro de Sabora) to which he grants his name, and Feissel, "Rescrit de Justinien," which mentions the grant to Didyma of civic status under the name of Justinianopolis and independence from Miletus. See also Boatwright, pp. 36–56, for grants of civic status under Hadrian.

24. Mitrev; Lepelley, "Inscription d'Heraclea Sintica," pp. 224–25; Corcoran, "Galerius, Maximinus and the Titulature."

25. Lines 6–15: *etiamsi civitas vestra ante(h)ac minime iura civitatis/ habuisset tamen pro insito nobis erga rem publicam/ nostram studio et augendi favore novae provisi/onis ac benivol(enti) ae ornamentis et iure civitatis patri/am vestram nobilitare cuperemus. Unde cum/ etiam de praeterito eamdem Heracleotarum/ civitatem fuisse dicatis ac nunc postuletis/ beneficio nostro eidem tribui iura civita/tis libenter admodum petitionibus vestris/ opem ferimus.* Lepelley, "Inscription d'Heraclea Sintica," p. 221, supplies "patriam" at the end of line 11, which is gratuitous. He needs this substantive to render a translation suited to his argument that Heraclea had lost and then regained civic status. This is based, however, on unfounded assumptions that the situation at Heraclea Sintica parallels that at Orcistus, which lost then regained civic status. This is clearly

not the case, for at ll. 6–7 the Heraclea Sintica inscription states explicitly that the city *never* had civic status prior to this grant.

26. Lepelley, *Les cités de l'Afrique*, vol. 1, pp. 128–31; "Vers la fin de l'autonomie municipale." The *Constitutio Antoniniana* did not, however, extinguish the pursuit of these titles. See Gascou, "Politique municipale de Rome," pp. 310–12, which catalogs thirty-nine instances of cities in North Africa that obtained promotion to *municipium* or *colonia* after the death of Septimius Severus in 211 CE.

27. On the importance of municipal liberty after 212 CE, see Jacques, *Privilège de liberté*.

28. This new name for Perinthus is first attested at *Frag. Vat.* 284 (Oct. 13, 286). Perinthus won from the tetrarchs a mint, status as the capital of the province of Europa, and, eventually, charge over the diocese of Thracia; cf. Sayar, pp. 76–77. On Perinthus's claim to Heraclean origins, see sources at Sayar, pp. 91–92. See also the series of four inscribed statue bases at Perinthus dedicated to each of the tetrarchs from ἡ λαμπρὰ Ἡρακλεωτῶν πόλις at Sayar, pp. 198–200 nos. 14–17.

29. Eus. *Mart. Pal.* 4.8, 9.2; *HE* 9.2.1; Opt. 1.27; *App.* 1.5 (*CSEL* 26: 29, 188); *Passio Sancti Felicis Episcopi* 3.22 (*BHL* 2893 = Musurillo, p. 268 = Maier, *Dossier*, vol. 1, pp. 51, 54); *Passio Sanctorum Dativi, Saturnini presbyteri et aliorum* 2 (*BHL* 7492 = Maier, *Dossier*, vol. 1, pp. 62–63); *Passio Sanctarum Maximae, Secundae et Donatillae* 1 (*BHL* 5809 = Maier, *Dossier*, vol. 1, p. 96). This also explains why the responsibility for implementing the Edict of Toleration devolved to civic curators and magistrates, Eus. *HE* 9.1.6–7; cf. Lepelley, *Les cités de l'Afrique*, vol. 1, pp. 217–20, 333–43.

30. Lact. *Mort. Pers.* 36.1–2; cf. *CIL* 3: 7174 = *ILS* 663 for evidence of the alliance.

31. On Maximinus's religious policy more generally, see Lact. *Mort. Pers.* 36.1–37.6; Eus. *HE* 8.14.9; 9.1.1–2; 9.4.2–3; cf. Mitchell, "Maximinus and the Christians," pp. 112–13; Nicholson, "The 'Pagan Churches'"; Belayche, "La politique religieuse."

32. Eus. *HE* 9.9a.4–6.

33. Eus. *HE* 9.9a.6.

34. Eus. *HE* 9.2.1–3.1, 11.5–6; cf. Mitchell, "Maximinus and the Christians," p. 118. Pace Barnes, "Lactantius and Constantine," pp. 44–45; *Constantine and Eusebius*, p. 40, the letter of Constantine (Lact. *Mort. Pers.* 37.1; 44.10–12; Eus. *HE* 9.9.12, 9a.12) ordering Maximinus to relax the persecutions —and their consequent hiatus—must have postdated the Battle of the Milvian Bridge in late 312; cf. Baynes, "Two Notes," pp. 193–94; Calderone, *Costantino*, pp. 150–64; Creed, p. 115.

35. Eus. *HE* 9.11.6 with *Mart. Theod.* (*BHL* 1782 = Franchi de' Cavalieri) and Mitchell, "Life of Saint Theodotus," pp. 107–9. Eus. *HE* 8.14.9; 9.11.6 confirms that Maximinus appointed governors based on their willingness to implement his religious program; cf. Barnes, "Sossianus Hierocles," pp. 243–44.

36. Eus. *HE* 9.7.3–14.

37. *TAM* 2.3: 785 = *CIL* 3: 12132 = *OGIS* 569 = *IK* Arykanda 12; cf. Feissel, "Constitutions des tétrarques," p. 36 no. 10 with pp. 47–49.

38. Mitchell, "Maximinus and the Christians," p. 108 = *AE* 1988: 1046; *AE* 1995: 38; cf. Feissel, "Constitutions des tétrarques," pp. 47–49 no. 7.

39. *AE* 1988: 1046 ll. 4–8, trans. Mitchell, "Maximinus and the Christians," p. 108; cf. Eus. *HE* 9.7.12. The Colbasa inscription has been revised and republished as Horsley no. 338.

40. Eus. *HE* 9.9a.7–9: ταῖς κολακείαις καὶ ταῖς προτροπαῖς; cf. *Mart. Theod.* 8, 14, 26 (Franchi de' Cavalieri, pp. 66, 70, 77).

41. *Mart. Theod.*, esp. 10–12, 20–31 (Franchi de' Cavalieri, pp. 67–68, 73–80) with Mitchell, "Life of Saint Theodotus." For other martyrdoms, see Mitchell, "Maximinus and the Christians," p. 118.

42. Eus. *HE* 7.32.31; 9.6.2, with Telfer, who assembles fragments from a fourth-century account of the passion preserved in a Verona Latin codex; cf. Barnes, *New Empire*, p. 68.

43. *AE* 1988: 1046 ll. 4–5: *ita ut postolatis* [sic] . . . *iuxta petitionis vestrae*; ll. 8–9: *ut autem sciretis in quantum petitio ves/[tra nob]is esset accepta*; cf. Eus. *HE* 9.4.2, 7.1, 6, 12–13, 8.13, 9a.6; *IK* Arykanda 12 ll. 1–2, 10–11.

44. Lact. *Mort. Pers.* 36.3–4: *subornatis legationibus civitatum quae peterent, ne intra civitates suas Christianis conventicula extruere liceret, ut suasu coactus et impulsus facere videretur quod erat sponte facturus*; Eus. *HE* 9.2.1: εἶτα διά τινων πονηρῶν ἀνδρῶν αὐτὸς ἑαυτῷ καθ' ἡμῶν πρεσβεύεται, τοὺς Ἀντιοχέων πολίτας παρορμήσας ἐπὶ τὸ μηδαμῶς τινα Χριστιανῶν τὴν αὐτῶν οἰκεῖν ἐπιτρέπεσθαι πατρίδα.

45. Mitchell, "Maximinus and the Christians," p. 117; cf. Corcoran, *Empire of the Tetrarchs*, pp. 149–50.

46. *AE* 1988: 1046 ll. 10–15, trans. Mitchell, "Maximinus and the Christians," p. 108; cf. Eus. *HE* 9.4.3, 7.13–14, and see *HE* 9.2.1.

47. Lact. *Mort. Pers.* 23.1; 26.1–2; cf. *Pan. Lat.* 5[8].5.4–6 with Barnes, *New Empire*, pp. 227–32.

48. Mitchell, "Maximinus and the Christians," p. 122, with particular reference to Lact. *Mort. Pers.* 36.1 and *CTh* 13.10.21; cf. Barnes, *New Empire*, pp. 227–32.

49. Christol and Drew-Bear, "Antioche de Pisidie."

50. *MAMA* 1: 170 = *ILS* 9480 = Tabbernee, no. 69, with Christol and Drew-Bear, "Antioche de Pisidie," p. 71: "l'action politique de M. Valerius Diogenes apparaît, dans un certain crescendo, comme celle d'un païen convaincu et militant." Further epigraphic evidence of Maximinus's religious revival can be found at *IK* Stratonikeia 310 = *SIG*³ 900 (Panamara); cf. Lee, *Pagans and Christians*, pp. 78–79; Merkelbach and Stauber (Upper Tembris Valley).

51. Harl.

52. See above p. 94.

53. Van Heesch.

54. Soz. 5.3.4; cf. Lib. *Ep.* 18.129.

55. Important earlier studies of the Orcistus inscription include Mommsen, "Stadtrechtbriefe von Orkistos"; Chastagnol, "L'inscription Constantinienne"; Turpin, pp. 299–302; Grünewald, pp. 148–49; Jacques, "Les moulins d'Orcistus"; Millar, *Emperor*, p. 544; Feissel, "L'adnotatio de Constantin"; Van Dam, *Roman Revolution*, pp. 150–219.

56. Calder, *Monumenta Asiae Minoris Antiqua*, vol. 7.

57. Feissel, "L'adnotatio de Constantin," builds on an earlier suggestion by Turpin, pp. 300–302, and seconded by Corcoran, *Empire of the Tetrarchs*, pp. 331–32, that the opening text of the dossier is the *adnotatio* mentioned later in the first rescript rather than a separate letter of the Vicarius Ablabius. For a history of the inscription's publication, see Mommsen, "Stadtrechtbriefe von Orkistos"; Chastagnol, "L'inscription Constantinienne," pp. 381–84; Feissel, "L'adnotatio de Constantin," pp. 255–56.

58. At *CTh* 1.2.1 (a. 314), Constantine insists that his *adnotationes* be accepted only with an accompanying rescript; cf. *CJ* 9.16.4 (a. 290).

59. A. H. M. Jones, *Cities*, pp. 68–69; Mitchell, *Anatolia*, vol. 1, p. 183; F. Kolb, "Bemerkungen," pp. 336–38; Van Dam, *Roman Revolution*, p. 158. Chastagnol, "L'inscription Constantinienne," pp. 398–400, argues strongly for Orcistus's earlier claim to civic status.

60. *IGR* 4: 547 = *MAMA* 7: 304.

61. *MAMA* 1: 416.

62. Buckler.

63. Mitchell, *Anatolia*, vol. 1, pp. 181–83; F. Kolb, "Bemerkungen," p. 337; cf. Bru, Labarre, and Özsait, pp. 191–92.

64. In the rescript at Panel 1, ll. 16–20 (*vicum suum/ spatiis prioris aetatis oppidi splendore flor/uisse* etc.); at Panel 1, ll. 34–39 (*civitatis nomen amittat*); at Panel 1, ll. 43–44 (*ius antiquum nomenque civitatis*); twice in the disposition (Panel 1, l. 48–Panel 2, l. 1: *nominis et dignitatis/ reparation[em]*; Panel 2, ll. 4–6: *quae fuerant mut[ilata/ a]d integrum prisgi* [sic] *[honoris/re] duci sancimus*); twice also in the *adnotatio* that precedes the rescript (Panel 1, ll. 1–2 and 3–5); and once more in the original copy of the petition (Panel 2, ll. 23–25: *ex antiquis[s/im]is temporibus ab origine etiam/ [civ]itatis dignitatem obtinuit*).

65. These were standard features of the *narratio* of a city's petition; see Hauken, pp. 269–70.

66. See Chastagnol, "L'inscription Constantinienne," pp. 407–8; Jacques, "Les moulins d'Orcistus"; cf. Horden and Purcell, pp. 255–57. For archaeological evidence for watermills in Phrygia, see Ritti, Grewe, and Kessener.

67. See the famous description of standard civic attributes at Paus. 10.4.1. On this theme, see especially Chastagnol, "L'inscription Constantinienne," p. 402; Jacques, "Les moulins d'Orcistus"; F. Kolb, "Bemerkungen."

68. Panel 1, ll. 1–2: *nominis]/ et dignitatis reparationem*; Panel 1, l. 6: *expetito legum adque appellationis s[plendore]*; Panel 1, ll. 43–44: *ius antiquum nomenque/ civitatis*; Panel 1, l. 49–Panel 2, l. 1: *et nominis et dignitatis/ reparation[em]*; Panel 2, ll. 8–10: *expetito legum [ad/q]ue appellationis splen/[d]ore*; cf. Panel 3, ll. 12–14: *tributum non honore modo/ verum libertatis etiam privi/legium*.

69. Chastagnol, "L'inscription Constantinienne," pp. 409–11; Lane Fox, p. 587; Jacques, "Les moulins d'Orcistus," p. 436; Mitchell, *Anatolia*, vol. 2, pp. 60–62; F. Kolb, "Bemerkungen," pp. 333–34.

70. Van Dam, *Roman Revolution*, pp. 176–83. Even before Van Dam, more recent scholarship has tended to downplay the religious element in the Orcistus decree.

71. Eus. *V. Const.* 2.48.1–60.2.

72. *Passio Sanctorum Dativi, Saturnini presbyteri et aliorum* Praef.: *Qui religionis sanctissimae fide praeditus exsultat et gloriatur in Christo; 22: eos pollutis traditoribus iungens sub praetextu sanctissimae religionis* (*BHL* 7492 = Maier, *Dossier*, vol. 1, pp. 59.13; 90.1027). *Coll. Avell.* 13.8 (*CSEL* 35.56): *cum religionis sanctissimae disciplinam non cumulet· iteratio sed euertat.*

73. *Ep. ad Aelafium,* apud Opt. *App.* 3 (*CSEL* 26: 205,20): *dignus idem Caecilianus cultu sanctissimae religionis habeatur*; cf. *CSEL* 26: 305,17–18: *sanctissima observantia*; *CSEL* 26: 204,20: *super observantiam sanctissimae legis catholicae*. See the same usage in later sources: Aug. *De utilitate credendi* 7.17 (*CSEL* 25: 22); Cass. *Exp. Ps.* 106.7 (*CCSL* 98: 975); 128.4 (*CCSL* 98: 1183).

74. Opt. *App.* 5 (*CSEL* 26: 209): *si vel nunc mera fide voluerint obsequia sanctissimae legi deferre . . .* ; *CTh* 16.2.5 (a. 323): *qui sanctissimae legi serviunt*; see also Sirm. 1 (a. 333): *sacrosanctae religionis auctoritas*; Sirm. 4 (a. 336): *si quispiam . . . sanctis se cultibus mancipaverit et Christianus esse delegerit . . . sacrosanctae legis antistitem.*

75. Eus. *V. Const.* 3.17.2: ἑκάστου τῶν προσηκόντων τῇ ἁγιωτάτῃ θρησκείᾳ διάκρισις γένοιτο; *V. Const.* 4.9.1: τὴν ἁγιωτάτην θρησκείαν γνωρίζω; *HE* 10.5.22: τοῖς ἀνθρώποις τοῖς ἀλλοτρίας ἔχουσι τὰς ψυχὰς ἀπὸ τῆς ἁγιωτάτης θρησκείας ταύτης πρόφασιν χλεύης διδόναι; *HE* 10.6.1: τῆς ἐνθέσμου καὶ ἁγιωτάτης καθολικῆς θρησκείας. See also Eus. *V. Const.* 4.36.1: τῇ ἁγιωτάτῃ ἐκκλησίᾳ; *HE* 10.7.1: τὴν θρησκείαν, ἐν ᾗ ἡ κορυφαία τῆς ἁγιωτάτης ἐπουρανίου <δυνάμεως> αἰδὼς φυλάττεται; *HE* 10.5.21: περὶ τῆς θρησκείας τῆς ἁγίας; *HE* 10.7.2: τῇ ἁγίᾳ ταύτῃ θρησκείᾳ. See also Odahl, "Constantine's Epistle," pp. 284–88, on Constantine's religious terminology.

76. Opitz *Urkunde* 28.1 p. 63 = Brennecke *Dokument* 32 p. 120: τὴν ἁγιωτάτην . . . θρησκείαν.

77. Turpin.

78. See Connolly, *Lives Behind the Laws*.

79. Mathisen, esp. p. 32; cf. Corcoran, *Empire of the Tetrarchs*, pp. 57–58.

80. Panel 3, ll. 10–11: *indulgentiae nos/trae munere*; ll. 14–17: *Na/colensium iniuriam ultra in/dulgentiae nostrae beneficia/ perdurantem*; ll. 27–28: *indulgentiae concessae/ vobis*.

81. Rightly emphasized at Van Dam, *Roman Revolution*, pp. 154–55. This was not uncommon, for other inscribed—and paper—copies of imperial responses also put the emperor's *subscriptio* or *adnotatio* at the head; cf. Feissel, "Privilèges de Baitokaikè," pp. 22–26; Haensch, "Apokrimata und Authentica."

82. The road network described does not appear in extant itineraries, on which discrepancy see Chastagnol, "L'inscription Constantinienne," p. 403. On the history of civic foundations in this region, see Mitchell, *Anatolia*, vol. 2, pp. 86–88.

83. The reasons for this abrupt end are unclear. The stonecutter could easily have continued on the pillar's back side, which remained uninscribed, but for some reason chose not to. See Mommsen, "Stadtrechtbriefe von Orkistos," pp. 314–16, for speculation on the matter.

84. Hauken, pp. 280–81, lists examples.

85. Lenski, "Constantine and Slavery"; "Valore dell'Editto."

86. Panel 3, ll. 14–23, esp.: *pecuniam quam/ pro cultis ante solebatis in/ferre minime deinceps dependa/tis*; cf. ll. 28–30: *pecuniam deinceps pr[o]/ supra dicta specie expeti a vo/bis postularique prohibeb[it]*. Following Mommsen, "Stadtrechtbriefe von Orkistos," 319, F. Kolb, "Bemerkungen," pp. 330 and 339 n. 56, wishes to translate *"cultis"* with "für bebaute Äcker." This seems forced. For the proper meaning, see Chastagnol, "L'inscription Constantinienne," pp. 411–15.

87. See Chaniotis, pp. 160–68; Ma, *Antiochos III*, pp. 153–54, for Hellenistic examples. Dmitriev, pp. 291–309, carries the discussion down to the third century CE.

88. Byzantium/Perinthus: Cass. Dio 75.14.3; Hdn. 3.6.9. Antioch/Laodicea: Hdn. 3.3.3–5, 6.9; *Dig.* 50.15.1.3; Joh. Mal. 12.21 (Dindorf, p. 294 = Thurn, pp. 223–24); *SHA Sev.* 9.4; cf. Ziegler. The notice at *SHA Hadr.* 14.1 that Hadrian punished Antioch by splitting the province of Phoenice from Syria and thus reducing the number of cities it controlled as a metropolis is probably incorrect, but reflects an underlying awareness of the political purpose of this tactic.

89. Tigranocerta: Strabo 11.14.15 (532). Thouria: Paus. 4.31.1 with *BMC Peloponnesus*: xlv–xlvi and 119–20 Thuria nos. 4–7 with pl. 23.

90. Cyzicus: Tac. *Ann.* 4.36.2; Suet. *Tib.* 37.3; Dio Cass. 57.24.6. On Vespasian, see Levick, pp. 145–46 with references.

91. Reynolds, no. 25.

92. Maiouma: Soz. 5.3.6–7; cf. below pp. 132–33. Caesarea: Soz. 5.4.1–5, 11.8; Greg. Naz. *Or.* 4.92; 18.34; Theoph. a.m. 5835; cf. Fatti. See also Caudium, which lost its autonomy to Beneventum (*CIL* 9: 2165 = *ILS* 6488, with Chastagnol, "L'inscription Constantinienne," pp. 400–401), and Carcassonne, which lost its autonomy to Narbonne in the tetrarchic period (Gayraud, p. 323).

93. Chastagnol, "L'inscription Constantinienne," pp. 399–402.

94. Eus. *HE* 8.11.1. Cf. Lact. *Div. Inst.* 5.11.10: *Aliqui ad occidendum praecipites extiterunt, sicut unus in Phrygia, qui universum populum cum ipso pariter conventiculo concremavit.*

95. Ramsay, pp. 502–9, offers good reason for thinking the place in question was Eumeneia; cf. Mitchell, *Anatolia*, vol. 2, pp. 40–41. Chastagnol, "L'inscription Constantinienne," pp. 410–11, is surely wrong to believe it was Orcistus.

96. Tainia: Ephraem *Vita Abramii* in *AASS* Mart. 2: 3a pp. 932–37. Petra: Eus. *Comm. in Is.* 2.23 (42.9–10 = Ziegler, p. 273): Πέτρα δέ τίς ἐστι πόλις τῆς Παλαιστίνης δεισιδαιμόνων ἀνδρῶν καὶ πολλῇ τῇ πλάνῃ τῇ δαιμονικῇ βεβαπτισμένων. On Gaza, see below 131–35. On Heliopolis-Baalbek, see below pp. 242–43. See also the unnamed village in the region of Emesa described at Theod. *HR* 17.2 (*SCh* 257.36) as militant about its exclusive adherence to pagan cult.

97. Lib. *Or.* 18.129; Soz. 6.1.1.

98. Mitchell, *Anatolia*, vol. 2, pp. 40–41, 58–62. See also Gnoli and Thornton, pp. 157–62, on the cultural autonomy of Phrygian villages, and Thonemann, which describes the "cellular" organization of Phrygian society. For pre-Constantinian Christian epigraphy from Phrygia, which is remarkably abundant, see Chiricat.

99. *Pars paene mundi iam maior huic veritati adstipulatur, urbes integrae aut, si alquid suspectum videtur, contestatur de his etiam agrestis manus ignara figmenti*, reported at Ruf. *HE* 9.6.3, which adds a translation of Lucian's apology to his translation of Eusebius's original Greek, where this does not appear.

100. Price, *Rituals and Power,* pp. 53–77; Fishwick; Friesen; Frija. Gradel, pp. 261–371, argues for a crisis in the viability of imperial cult in the late third century, but this seems to me teleological and too reliant on traditional master narratives of broader crisis and decline in this period.

101. Cox and Cameron, *Monumenta Asiae Minoris Antiqua*, vol. 5, pp. xxii–xxv, xxxviii–lxiii; Haspels, vol. 1, pp. 196–99, 200–4, 349–52 nos. 132–38; Drew-Bear and Naour, "Divinités de Phrygie," pp. 1990–2004.

102. *IK* Stratonikeia 310 = *SIG*³ 900 (Panamara); cf. Van Dam, *Roman Revolution*, p. 168, with further references.

103. Drew-Bear, *Nouvelles inscriptions*, pp. 29–38; Gnoli and Thornton, pp. 157–59; Robert, *A travers l'Asie Mineure*, pp. 228–40; cf. Mitchell, *Anatolia*, vol. 2, pp. 60–61.

104. Cox and Cameron, *Monumenta Asiae Minoris Antiqua*, vol. 5, pp. xxxii–xxxiii; cf. "The inscriptions . . . bear eloquent witness to the vitality of paganism at Dorylaeum and Nacolea."

105. *CIL* 3: 350 = 13651a; cf. Christol and Drew-Bear, "Documents latins," pp. 53–55 no. 4. Note also that, even once it converted and despite its considerable size and regional importance, Nacoleia remained a suffragan of Synada into the seventh century (Belke and Mersich, pp. 345), another indication of its halting approach to Christianity.

106. On Julian's visit, see Amm. 22.9.5–8; Lib. *Or.* 12.17; 18.161. For the Oration, see Jul. *Or.* 8(5). For Callixeine, see Jul. *Ep.* 81; cf. *Ep.* 84.

CHAPTER 5. THE EXIGENCIES OF DIALOGUE

1. On Umbria and Umbro-Etruscan religion, see Bradley; Amann, *Die antiken Umbrer*, esp. pp. 327–403. See also Siniscalco on the rise of Christianity in Umbria, which only took off in the fifth century. Hispellum is not known to have had a bishop before the fifth century, although bishops are attested for neighboring Spoletium from the mid-fourth. On Etruria and Etruscan religion, see Aigner-Foresti, *Die Integration der Etrusker*; Jannot; De Grummond and Simon; De Grummond and Edlund-Berry; and, on late antique survivals, Matthews, "Continuity"; Sordi.

2. On Hispellum, see Sozi; Manconi, Camerieri, and Cruciani; Amann, "Das konstantinische 'Reskript von Hispellum'"; *Die antiken Umbrer*, pp. 116–17, 295; Sensi, "Sul luogo del ritrovamento"; "In margine al rescritto."

3. Plin. *HN* 3.113 on Hispellum's status as a *colonia*, and Plin. *Ep.* 8.8.6 on its control of the *fons Clitumni*; cf. *CIL* 11: 5266 for the remains of a possible honorary inscription to Augustus.

4. If we can take Symmachus (*Ep.* 1.49) at his word, multiple public sacrifices were performed to expiate a portent at Spoletium as late as 385 CE. It is unclear whether these were done at Rome or Spoletium. Regardless, the notice indicates ongoing strong connections between the pagan leadership of Rome and the region of Umbria.

5. For Constantine's distaste for sacrifice, see p. 231.

6. Mommsen, "Inschrift aus Hispellum." Other important studies include Piganiol, "Notes épigraphiques"; De Dominicis; Andreotti; Gascou, "Rescrit d'Hispellum"; Forni; Cecconi, *Governo imperiale,* pp. 87–97; "Rescritto di Spello"; Tabata; Sensi, "Sul luogo del ritrovamento"; "In margine al rescritto"; Coarelli; Amann, "Das konstantinische 'Reskript von Hispellum'"; Van Dam, *Roman Revolution,* pp. 23–129; Clauss, "Kein Aberglaube"; Girardet, "Verbot von 'Betrügerischen Machenschaften.'"

7. Tabata, pp. 371–86; Barnes, *Dynasty, Religion and Power,* pp. 20–23.

8. As already Mommsen, "Inschrift aus Hispellum," pp. 31–32; Dessau at *ILS* 705; De Dominicis, pp. 173–34; Andreotti, pp. 250–57; Gascou, "Rescrit d'Hispellum," pp. 617–23. It has also been noted that the absence of a date specifically contradicts Constantine's order that only rescripts with a date are to be considered valid (*CTh* 1.1.1), but Godefroy (1736–1743) 6: 6 has shown that Constantine's own chancery did not always follow this requirement.

9. De Dominicis, p. 174; Grünewald, pp. 152–53, 217; Van Dam, *Roman Revolution,* pp. 363–65.

10. Barnes, *Dynasty, Religion and Power,* pp. 20–23, with Andreotti, pp. 250–55, and Gascou, "Rescrit d'Hispellum," pp. 620–21. More on the date of the Caesars' promotion to Augusti at Burgess, "Summer of Blood," pp. 29–30.

11. Eus. *V. Const.* 4.67.3: ἐβασίλευε δὲ καὶ μετὰ θάνατον μόνος θνητῶν ὁ μακάριος, ἐπράττετό τε τὰ συνήθη ὡσανεὶ καὶ ζῶντος αὐτοῦ; cf. 4.68.2: ὡσανεὶ ζῶντος αὐτοῖς τοῦ μεγάλου βασιλέως.

12. Barnes, *Dynasty, Religion and Power,* p. 22.

13. This was already proven at Tabata, pp. 379–80. See also Galsterer-Kröll; Forni, pp. 402–4, and the evidence collected below in Chapters 6 and 7.

14. Girardet, "Das Verbot von 'Betrügerischen Machenschaften.'"

15. See, e.g., *CIL* 9: 329 = *ILS* 5557a = *AE* 1999: 511.

16. E.g., *CIL* 3: 14184,19; *CIL* 3: 3522 = 10384; *CIL* 3: 10052 = 15103; *CIL* 7: 4 = *RIB* 1: 98; *CIL* 13: 6562 = *AE* 1995: 1166; *AE* 1931: 86; *AE* 1931: 105; *AE* 1931: 107; *AE* 1955: 51; *AE* 1972: 677; *AE* 1994: 537; *AE* 1994: 637; *RIB* 1: 1912 = *AE* 1990: 665.

17. On the ceremony, see Eus. *V. Const.* 1.22.1–2, which has no obvious traces of pagan cult, combined with *Pan. Lat.* 7[6].14.3; 6[7].7.3, which do point to imperial cult ritual, a notion confirmed in the image on *RIC* 6: Trier 809. On the title *divus,* see Amici.

18. *CTh* 16.5.2. Tabata attempts to date the Hispellum rescript to 326 based on this coincidence, but this seems to stretch the evidence too far and is contradicted by the presence of the Caesar Constans in the heading.

19. Lines 16–17: *in{i}stituto consuetudinis priscae*; 33–34: *manente per Tuscia(m) ea consuetudine*; 55: *veteribus institutis.*

20. Coarelli. Various strands of this argument, which uses the Hispellum inscription to write a religious relationship between Tuscia and Umbria back into earlier periods of history, have been aired since Solari; cf. De Dominicis, pp. 176–77; Aigner-Foresti, "Regards sur Volsinii"; Bradley, pp. 123–24.

21. Sensi, "Sul luogo del ritrovamento," 468–69, had argued for a connection between the two sites through the archaic Etruscan goddess Nortia. The only evidence he adduces for worship of Nortia at Hispellum is *CIL* 11: 5334: . . . *epentin . . . / . . . ortiaes . . . / . . . ancil . . .* , which he wishes to read: *[R]epentin[a] [N]ortiaes ancil[la].* Even if this reading is accepted, it need not indicate a cult site to Nortia in Hispellum. Amann, "Reskript von Hispellum," pp. 6–9, 18–25, offers more detailed arguments against this and other readings of the Hispellum rescript as evidence for a religious bond between Etruria and Umbria.

22. Cecconi, "Rescritto di Spello," pp. 281–82; cf. Cecconi, *Governo imperiale,* pp. 97–100. Andreotti, p. 264, had already adduced evidence proving that *institutum consuetudinis priscae* need not refer to the distant past; cf. Amann, "Reskript von Hispellum," p. 9.

23. For evidence and discussion, see De Dominicis, pp. 173–76. Gascou, "Rescrit d'Hispellum," pp. 635–38, argues for a unification of the two regions under *iuridici* already in the second century, but his hypothesis is highly speculative.

24. *Lat. Ver.* 10.5; *Not. Dig.* Occ. 1.57; *CTh* 2.4.5; 12.1.72; *CIL* 6: 1702 = *ILS* 1251; *CIL* 11: 6958 = *ILS* 1252; Saquete, with Gascou, "Rescrit d'Hispellum," pp. 639–40, on the question of a *concilium Tusciae et Umbriae*.

25. Florence: *CTh* 9.1.8 with Cecconi, "Firenze tardoantica." Pistoia: Amm. 27.3.1, with *CTh* 2.1.5; 12.1.65.

26. Val. Max. 9.1; Zon. 8.7.4–8.

27. On this goddess in Late Antiquity, see *CIL* 6: 537 = 30787 = *ILS* 2944, with Matthews, "Continuity," pp. 490–91.

28. Liv. 4.23.5, 25.7–8, 61.2; 5.1.5, 17.6–10; 6.2.2.

29. Stopponi, "Notizie preliminari"; "Campo della Fiera." The ongoing progress of excavation at the site is being reported at http://www.campodellafiera.it.

30. Amann, *Die antiken Umbrer*, pp. 330–31 fig. 118 and 424 Spello/Hispellum n. 3.

31. Camerieri and Manconi, "Il 'Sacello' di Venere."

32. See especially Manconi, Camerieri, and Cruciani, pp. 381–92.

33. The Minerva and Venus temples are attested at *CIL* 11: 5263 and 5264. Jupiter worship is surmised from the third-/second-century inscription mentioned above; cf. Coarelli, pp. 45–48; Sensi, "Sul luogo del ritrovamento," pp. 465–71; Amann, "Reskript von Hispellum," p. 21.

34. Sensi, "Sul luogo del ritrovamento," pp. 472–73.

35. On the site of the inscription's discovery, see Sensi, "Sul luogo del ritrovamento."

36. Price, "Between Man and God," pp. 39–40, sees the Hispellum rescript as the final stage in a long process of exploration of the ambiguous status of the emperor between man and god.

37. Robert, *Les gladiateurs*, pp. 240, 270–75, 280–81; Price, *Rituals and Power*, pp. 89, 106–7; cf. 109, 140–43.

38. Volsinii, of course, also had a theater and amphitheater, the latter of which had dimensions quite similar to those of Hispellum's (56 × 40 m); see Thuillier, pp. 599–602.

39. Barnes, *Dynasty, Religion and Power*, p. 21, translates *aedem* as "house" rather than "temple," whether in ignorance of the fact that the Latin word means "house" only in the plural (*OLD* s.v. aedēs 1), or with the intent of masking implications that do not fit his agenda. Coarelli, p. 46, argues that the present-day church of San Fedele, whose earliest construction is late antique, was in fact originally the *aedis gentis Flaviae*; cf. Manconi, Camerieri, and Cruciani, pp. 387–88.

40. For imperial worship in Constantinople, see Bardill, pp. 151–58; cf. Ramskold and Lenski. For other cities, see below pp. 141–42, 212–14.

41. Lines 17–18: *per singulas annorum vi/ces*; 31: *anniversaria vice*; 51: *per vices temporis*.

42. Cecconi, *Governo imperiale*, pp. 91–95, with reference to *IKEph* 43 = *AE* 1906: 30b; cf. Sensi, "In margine al rescritto," pp. 366, 371.

43. These figures are derived from autopsy. More on the roadways at Gascou, "Rescrit d'Hispellum," pp. 641–45; Uggeri.

44. This was recognized already at Solari, p. 162; Amann, "Reskript von Hispellum," p. 13.

45. Tabata, pp. 387–90; Amann, "Reskript von Hispellum," pp. 11–14.

46. Cf. the law of Valentinian forbidding governors from ordering the transfer of games from one city to another to avoid perturbing those decurions who had funded them for the sake of their local prestige; *CTh* 15.5.1 (Apr. 25, 372).

47. Salzman, "Superstitio." Clauss, "Kein Aberglaube," had argued that, in the instance of the Hispellum rescript, *superstitio* applied only to black magic and *haruspicina* because, he believes, there was no Christian concept of paganism as *superstitio* before the late fourth century. Girardet, "Das Verbot von 'Betrügerischen Machenschaften,'" pp. 304–11, however, presents a crushing mountain of evidence that third- and early fourth-century Christian writers

regularly used the words *superstitio* as well as *contagio* to refer to pagan theology more generally and quite specifically to blood sacrifice.

48. *CTh* 9.16.1 (a. 320); 16.2.5 (a. 323); 16.10.2–3 (a. 341); cf. 16.10.17 (a. 399): *absque ullo sacrificio atque ulla superstitione damnabili exhiberi populo voluptates . . . decernimus.*

49. Tert. *Apol.* 22; Cyp. *De laps.* 35; *Ad Fortunatum* 11; *Ep.* 59.14; Firm. Mat. *De err.* 12.1, 20.7, 26.2. Cf. Andreotti, p. 279, and Gascou, "Rescrit d'Hispellum," pp. 651–52.

50. For laws banning sacrifice, see below pp. 231–33.

51. One wonders whether the prohibition on *contagiosa superstitio* also extended to the erection of imperial statues, which Eusebius claims Constantine forbade in pagan shrines in a law no longer extant; Eus. *V. Const.* 4.16.1.

52. Constantine's rescript does not regulate the conduct of the festival at Volsinii in any way. He did not, after all, wish to alienate this powerful city, which had honored his father with an inscription (*CIL* 11: 2697) and had erected a statue of Constantine himself in the early years of his reign (c. 315); see Giuliano.

53. Cecconi, *Governo imperiale,* pp. 88–97; "Rescritto di Spello"; Van Dam, *Roman Revolution,* p. 34: "In fact, religion, whether pagan cults or Christianity, was most likely not Constantine's primary concern in this rescript." Cf. De Dominicis, pp. 186–87; Andreotti, pp. 260–66. Against this view, see Amann, "Reskript von Hispellum," pp. 13–15.

54. Still in 366 CE the *Tusci et Umbri* dedicated a statue to their governor jointly; *CIL* 6: 1702 = *ILS* 1251. It should not go unremarked that a major function of provincial assemblies in the imperial period was the celebration of imperial cult festivals; see Rives, *Religion and Authority,* pp. 85–96, with bibliography.

55. Gascou, "Rescrit d'Hispellum," pp. 647–56; Tabata, pp. 386–401.

56. Price, "Between Man and God," p. 413; *Rituals and Power,* pp. 101–32; Rives, *Religion and Authority,* pp. 51–76; Van Nuffelen; cf. Friesen, pp. 114–41; Goddard, pp. 1047–79. See, for example, the testimony of Constantine's contemporary and adviser Lactantius, *Div. Inst.* 6.20.34: *nam ludorum celebrationes deorum festa sunt; siquidem ob natales eorum vel templorum novorum dedicationes sunt constituti.*

57. Lines 19–20: *sacerdotes creentur/ qui aput Vulsinios Tusciae civitate(m) <u>ludos /sc{h}(a) enicos et gladiatorum munus</u> exhibeant;* 30–33: *sacerdos quem anniversaria vice Umbria de/disset, <u>spectaculum tam sc(a)enicorum ludorum/ quam gladiatorii muneris</u> exhibere(t);* 34–37: *cre/ atus sacerdos aput Vulsinios ut solebat/ <u>editionum antedictarum spectacula</u> fre/quentare(t);* 48–52: *<u>editionum</u> in prae/dicta civitate exhibend<a>rum . . . <u>sollem/nitas editionum</u>;* 53: *ubi creati(s) e Tuscia <u>sacerdotibus</u>;* cf. 45–47: *ne <u>aedis</u> nostro nomini dedicata cuiusquam con/ tagios(a)e superstitionis fraudibus polluatur.*

58. *CIL* 11: 5283 = *ILS* 6623: *C(aio) Matrinio Aurellio/ C(ai) f(ilio) Antonino v(iro) p(erfectissimo)/ coronato Tusc(iae) et Umb(riae)/ pont(ifici) gentis Flaviae/ abundantissimi muneris sed et/ praecipuae laetitiae theatralis editori/ aedili quaestori duumviro/ iterum q(uin)q(uennali) i(ure) d(icundo) huius splendissimae/ coloniae curatori r(ei) p(ublicae) eiusdem/ colon(iae) et primo principali ob meritum/ benevolentiae eius erga se/ [ple]bs omnis urbana Flaviae/ Constantis patrono/ dignissimo.*

59. The early eighth-century *Ravennatis Anonymi Cosmographia* 4.33 (Schnetz, p. 71) records the fractured sentence: *Egubio q(uae) dicitur Interbio vel Constantiniana atque Iulia.* This may imply that Gubbio itself (forty kilometers from Hispellum) had taken the name Constantiniana or may record a distant memory of Hispellum's Constantinian name.

60. On the designation *coronatus* and its associations with imperial cult, see Fishwick, vol. 2, pp. 257–58, vol. 3, pp. 225–26. Ciotti et al., pp. 22, 24, indicates that a fragmentary inscription of Carsulae (San Gemini) also records the existence of a *coronatus* of the joint province of Tuscia et Umbria, but the text remains unpublished.

61. Rome is also attested as having a *Pontifex Flavialis* under Constantine (*CIL* 6: 1690 = *ILS* 1240 = *AE* 1976: 15; *CIL* 6: 1691; 1694) in the person of L. Aradius Valerius Proculus Populonius, who also served as Augur, Pontifex Maior, and Quindecemvir Sacris Faciundis; cf. Rüpke and Glock, no. 707.

62. The evidence on Constantine's legislation on gladiation is ambiguous. Eus. *V. Const.* 4.25.1 claims outright that Constantine forbade it; cf. Soc. 1.18.1; Soz. 1.8.6. There are two extant laws of relevance. *CTh* 9.18.1 = *CJ* 9.20.16 (a. 315) assumes the continuation of gladiatorial games (*ludum gladiatorium*), which it prescribes for the execution of kidnappers (*plagiarii*). With *CTh* 15.12.1 = *CJ* 11.44.1 (a. 325), the *CJ* version only forbids condemned criminals to be forced into gladiation, whereas the fuller version in the *CTh* implies that a more general ban was in effect. See also Callincus *V. Hypatii* 33.1 for Constantine's efforts to abolish the Olympic games of Chalcedon; cf. Rivière, pp. 354–58; Potter, "Constantine and the Gladiators."

63. Astonishingly, Barnes, *Dynasty, Religion and Power*, p. 23, ignores this long-known inscription and thus wrongly asserts that the mention of *editiones* in the disposition of the Hispellum rescript excluded the possibility of gladiatorial shows.

64. Aur. Vict. *Caes.* 40.28; *CTh* 12.1.21 (Aug. 4, 335); 12.5.2 (May 21, 337). This evidence is quoted and discussed below at pp. 141–42.

65. Lines 16: *adsereretis*; 22: *posceretis . . .* ; 37: *pr{a}ecationi {h}ac desiderio vestro*; 44: *ut desideratis*; 56–57: *vos qui ob praedictas causas/ nobis supplices extitistis*; 58: *postulastis*.

66. It would be interesting to know whether the establishment of this new cult site diminished or prolonged the survival of paganism in Hispellum. Certainly by the mid-fourth century, we have good evidence for the conversion of civic aristocrats at Volsinii; *CIL* 11: 7298 = *ILCV* 364; *CIL* 11: 2834 = *ILCV* 365.

CHAPTER 6. CONSTANTINE'S CITIES IN THE WEST

1. Marc. Diac. *V. Porph.* at Grégoire and Kugener, *Marc le Diacre*. For ongoing arguments about the authenticity of this text, see Belayche, "Pagan Festivals," p. 7 n. 12, with earlier bibliography, to which add Chuvin, at pp. 17–27, who presents a strong defense of the text, and Barnes, *Early Christian Hagiography*, pp. 260–83, who argues vociferously against, without mention of Chuvin. For Gaza as an *"urbs gentilium"* (Jer. *V. Hilar.* 8.5; cf. 11.7), see Belayche, *Iudaea-Palaestina*, pp. 232–51; "Pagan Festivals." On Gaza in Late Antiquity more broadly, see Glucker, pp. 43–51; Sivan, pp. 328–47. On religious conflict in Gaza, see Van Dam, "From Paganism to Christianity"; Hahn, *Gewalt*, pp. 191–222.

2. Eus. *HE* 8.13.5; *Mart. Pal.* 3.1, 8.4, 13.4–5.

3. Athan. *Apol. de fuga* 3.2; *Hist. Ar.* 5.2, Hil. Pict. *Fr. Hist.* 2.A.11, 13 (*CSEL* 65: 56–57), with Barnes, "Emperor and Bishops," pp. 59–60. Ephiphan. *Pan.* 68.5.8 claims that Melitius ordained clergy in Gaza when he passed through the town on his way toward penal slavery in the mines of Phaeno circa 312.

4. Marc. Diac. *V. Porph.* 20; cf. Soz. 5.9.9.

5. Marc. Diac. *V. Porph.* 19. For estimates of Gaza's population, see Broshi, p. 5.

6. Belayche, *Iudaea-Palaestina*, pp. 249–55; "Pagan Festivals," pp. 14–19, debunks the notion that there might have been a pagan "Maiouma" festival held at Palestinian Maiouma in this or any period. On the population size, see Broshi, p. 5.

7. Eus. *V. Const.* 4.38.1: Ἤδη μὲν οὖν ἐπὶ τοῦ Παλαιστινῶν ἔθνους ἡ Κωνστάντια τὴν σωτήριον ἐπιγραψαμένη θεοσέβειαν καὶ παρ' αὐτῷ θεῷ καὶ παρὰ βασιλεῖ τιμῆς κρείττονος ἠξιοῦτο, πόλις μὲν ἀποφανθεῖσα ὃ μὴ πρότερον ἦν, ἀμείψασα δὲ τὴν προσηγορίαν ἐπωνύμῳ κρείττονι θεοσεβοῦς ἀδελφῆς βασιλέως.

8. See also Soc. 1.18.13: ἐν Παλαιστίνῃ Κωνσταντίαν ἐπ' ὀνόματι τῆς ἑαυτοῦ ἀδελφῆς Κωνσταντίας.

9. Soz. 6.15.5–8.

10. Soz. 2.5.7–8, esp.: ἡνίκα δὴ τὸ ἐπίνειον τῆς Γαζαίων πόλεως, ὃ Μαϊουμᾶν προσαγορεύουσιν, εἰσάγαν δεισιδαιμονοῦν καὶ τὰ ἀρχαῖα πρὸ τούτου θαυμάζον εἰς Χριστιανισμὸν ἀθρόον πανδημεὶ μετέβαλεν. Georgius Cyprius *Descriptio* 1026 (Honigmann, p. 67) reports a Σάλτον Κωνσταντινιακῆς in Palaestina Prima. This name is confirmed in a fragment of the Beersheba edict (Alt, p. 12 no. 4), leading to speculation that this extra-urban territory may also have benefitted from Constantine's grant; cf. Di Segni, pp. 52–53.

11. Soz. 5.3.6–8.

12. Soz. 2.5.8: καὶ Κωνστάντιαν ἐπωνόμασε, τῷ τιμιωτάτῳ τῶν παίδων γεραίρων τὸν τόπον διὰ τὴν θρησκείαν.

13. Interestingly, Zacharias Scholasticus indicates that Maiouma was still termed "Constantina" in the late fifth century; cf. John of Beith-Aphthonia, *V. Severi Antiochensis* 137[221] (Kugener, p. 8).

14. Theodoret of Cyrrhus gives some indication of the degree to which fifth-century bishops of powerful cities continued to manipulate religious practice in the *kōmai* under their control. In *Ep.* 2.81 (*SCh* 92.196–98) he claims to have led back to orthodoxy eight villages of Marcionites, as well as one of Eunomians and another of Arians.

15. Soz. 5.3.9: πάντως που προσήκειν δοκιμάσασα τοὺς δι' εὐσέβειαν δικαίων πόλεως ἀξιωθέντας, διὰ δὲ κρίσιν Ἑλληνιστοῦ βασιλέως ἄλλως πράξαντας, ἐν ἱερωσύναις καὶ τάξει ἐκκλησιῶν μὴ χρῆναι ἀφαιρεῖσθαι τῶν δοθέντων γερῶν. In the sixth-century Madaba Map, we find the city designated as [Μαϊουμᾶς ἡ] καὶ Νεά[πο]λις, *IGLS* 21.2 Jord. no. 153–22.

16. Soz. 5.15.13–14.

17. Amb. *Ep.* 74(40).15 (*CSEL* 82.3: 63).

18. Greg. Naz. *Or.* 4.86; cf. Theod. *HE* 3.7.1; *Chron. Pasch.* p. 546 (s.a. 362); Theoph. a.m. 5853.

19. Soz. 5.9.1–13.

20. On Hilarion, see Soz. 5.10.1, 15.14–17, 6.16.5, and Jer. *V. Hilarionis* (*SCh* 508: 212–98).

21. Jer. *V. Hilar.* 11.3–13 (*SCh* 508: 242–44), esp. *clamor fit uulgi nimius, ita ut ethnici quoque ipsi concreparent: "Marnas uictus est a Christo."* On the nature of this festival, see Belayche, "Pagan Festivals," pp. 10–14; Z. Weiss, "Games and Spectacles."

22. Previous efforts to assemble a list of cities named after Constantine and his family can be found at Forni, pp. 402–4; Tabata, pp. 379–80; Van Dam, *Roman Revolution*, p. 113.

23. See Galsterer-Kröll for full details. See also Boatwright, pp. 104–5, for the specific instance of Hadrian, whose nomenclature was assumed by some twenty-four cities.

24. (1) Armorica/ Lugdunensis II = Cosedia – Constantia (Coutances): *Not. Dig.* Occ. 37.9: *Constantia*; 37.20: *Constantia*; 42.34: *Baiocas (Baiocasses) et Constantiae Lugdunensis secundae*; *Not. Gall.* 2.8: *Civitas Constantia*; cf. *Barrington Atlas*, Map 7, Aremorica, E2. (2) Raetia = Constantia (Konstanz): *Ravennatis Anonymi Cosmographia* 4.26 (Schnetz, p. 61); cf. *Barrington Atlas*, Map 19, Raetia, B2; Filtzinger, Planck, and Cämmerer, pp. 374–75. (3) Moesia II = Flaviana (Rasova): *Not. Dig.* Or. 39.3: *Flaviana*; 39.20: *Flaviana*; 41.3: *Flaviana*; 41.13: *Flaviana*; cf. *Barrington Atlas*, Map 22, Moesia Inferior, E4. (4) Valeria = Ulcisia Castra – Castra Constantia: *Not. Dig.* Occ. 33.13: *Constantia*; 33.34: *Constantiae*; see also *Not. Dig.* Occ. 33.45: *Equites Flavianenses, Ad Militare*; cf. *Barrington Atlas*, Map 20, Pannonia-Dalmatia, G2; Soproni, pp. 62–63. (5) Scythia Minor = Tomi – Constantia: Hier. Syn. 637.6 (Honigmann, p. 13): Κωνσταντιανά; *Not. Episc.* 3.542: ὁ Κωνσταντείας; *Not. Episc.* 10.634: ὁ Κωνσταντείας. (6) Arabia: Hier. Syn. 723.2 (Honigmann, p. 45): Κωνσταντία; *Not. Episc.* 1.1026: Κωνσταντίνη; *Can. Conspl.* sig. 38

(Turner, p. 168): Κωνσταντιανή. For (7–8) Mesopotamia = Amida-Constantina/Constantia and Antoninopolis-Tella-Constantina/Constantia, see n. 25. See also, in Britain, the province of Flavia Caesariensis: *Not. Dig.* Oc. 1.121: *Flaviae Caesariensis*; cf. *Lat. Veron.* 7.4: *Flaviae Caesariensis*; *Lat. Polem.* 11.4: *Flavia*.

25. Burgess, *Studies*, pp. 275–80, presents the evidence well and attempts a resolution that remains, nevertheless, inconclusive. To his sources, add *Can. Conspl. sig.* 44 (Turner, p. 168); Theodosius *De situ terrae Sanctae* 32 (*CCSL* 175: 125).

26. *Consult.* 9.4.

27. *CIL* 11: 6218 = 6219 = *ILS* 104 = 706.

28. *CIL* 9: 801: *Felici auspicio inposito Constantinianae nomine amore praeterea civi[3]/[3] vett[3] VSVCCI[.*

29. *Not. Episc.* 1.605; 3.463; 10.571; 13.421; Nil. Dox. 212.

30. *Pan. Lat.* 5[8], on which see Hostein, pp. 379–417. On the date and occasion, see Nixon and Rodgers, pp. 255–56.

31. *Pan. Lat.* 5[8].14.5: *Dabis enim veniam, amoris nostri contumeliam feres. Omnium sis licet dominus urbium, omnium nationum, nos tamen etiam nomen accepimus tuum: iam non antiquum Bibracte, quod hucusque dicta est Iulia Polia Florentia, sed Flavia est civitas Aeduorum.* The opening clearly falls back on the erotic literary topos of a wife unwilling to let her husband depart. For the development of Autun's name in the Roman period, see Rouche, pp. 58–59.

32. *Pan. Lat.* 5[8].1.1; 2.1; cf. Nixon and Rodgers, p. 264 n. 1.

33. *Pan. Lat.* 5[8].7.6–9.3; 14.3–4, esp. 7.6: *iam enim ad praedicanda remedia numinis tui ordine suo pervenit oratio*; 9.1: *Sponte nos ad numinis tui aditum vocare, sponte adfari, sponte quid opis desideraremus interrogare dignatus es.*

34. *Pan. Lat.* 5[8].2.5, 4.2–4.

35. *Pan. Lat.* 9[4].4.1, with Nixon and Rodgers, pp. 145–48, who point out that the speech's author, Eumenius, had served Constantius personally as *Magister Memoriae*. See also *Pan. Lat.* 8[5].21.2.

36. Opt. 1.23; Eus. *HE* 10.5.19 = Maier, *Dossier*, no. 16. Reticius was also present at the Council of Arles (Mansi 2: 476). See further Eck; Hostein, pp. 456–57.

37. For the most recent edition and commentary, see Salzano. On the date and authorship, see Salzano, pp. 13–22.

38. *Laudes Domini* ll. 143–48 (Salzano, p. 42).

39. Evidence for early Christianity at Autun is outlined at Hostein, pp. 453–60.

40. Interestingly, there is no evidence of Autun's Constantinian name in the signature lists of the Councils of Arles (a. 314) and Cologne (a. 346), where the city is called simply *civitas Augustudunensium* (*CCSL* 148: 14,41; 16,33; 20,30; 27,6). It is difficult to know what to make of *CIL* 13: 3255 = *ILS* 703 recording the completion of baths at Remi (Reims) using funds from Constantine that he claims to have donated to "his own city of the Remi" (*civitati suae Remorum*). We have no further evidence to indicate whether Reims was or was not given a Constantinian name.

41. *CTh* 11.30.5–6 with Barnes, *New Empire*, p. 73.

42. Zos. 2.20.2; *Epit.* 41.4, with Barnes, *New Empire*, pp. 43–44; Heijmans, *Arles*, pp. 45–46. Heijmans, "*Constantina Urbs*" offers a succinct summary of Constantine's involvement with Arles; cf. Loseby; Stephenson, p. 211; Esmonde Cleary, pp. 210–12.

43. Grünewald, pp. 36–37; cf. Heijmans, *Arles*, p. 44; "*Constantina Urbs*," 210; contrast Nixon and Rodgers, p. 185.

44. Grünewald, pp. 33–35; cf. Heijmans, *Arles*, pp. 51–52.

45. Von Gladiss. The arch was destroyed in 1689, but drawings preserve the inscription, *Imp(erator) Caes(ar) Fl(avio) Constantino P(io) F(elici) Aug(usto) Principi Opt(imo)/ Divi Constanti Aug(usti) F(ilio)*, which allows us to date the rededication to the early years of his reign.

46. *Not. Dig.* Occ. 11.43: *procurator monetae Arelatensis*; cf. 11.33: *praepositus thesaurorum Arelatensium*. On the date, see P. Bruun, *Roman Imperial Coinage*, vol. 7, p. 227.

47. *CIL* 12: 668 = *AE* 1952: 107 = *AE* 2004: 880.

48. Charron and Heijmans; Heijmans, *Arles*, pp. 239–43.

49. Heijmans, *Arles*, pp. 139–94; "Topographie"; cf. Esmonde Cleary, p. 211. Heijmans is wisely circumspect about connecting all late antique constructions at Arles to a Constantinian renaissance, as some previous scholars have done. Major structures are numerous, but few can be dated with precision.

50. Leo, *Ep.* 65 (*PL* 54: 882) = *Epistolae Arelatenses Genuinae* 12 (*MGH Epist.* 3: 19 ll. 12–14): *Haec in tantum a[d] gloriosissime memoriae Constantino peculiariter honorata est, ut ab eius vocabulo praeter proprium nomen, quo Arelas vocitatur, Constantina nomen accepit.* See also *Barrington Atlas*, Map 15, Arelate Massilia, D2: Theline/ Col. Arelate/ Constantina.

51. *Epistolae Arelatenses Genuinae,* 8 (*MGH Epist.* 3: 14 l. 12). Unaware of this source, Burgess, *Studies*, pp. 278–79, assumes the city was renamed Constantia in 353 (an assertion for which there is no evidence) and only revived the name Constantina in 450 to strengthen its appeal to Leo.

52. Hill, Kent, and Carson, *Late Roman Bronze Coinage*, p. 9; P. Bruun, *Roman Imperial Coinage*, vol. 7, p. 232.

53. P. Bruun, *Roman Imperial Coinage*, vol. 7, pp. 232, 268; cf. Pearce, *Roman Imperial Coinage*, vol. 9, pp. 57–60; Kent, *Roman Imperial Coinage*, vol. 8, pp. 197–98.

54. Constantine's presence at Trier in 328/329 is attested at *CTh* 1.4.2, 1.16.4, 7.20.5, and his campaigns in the region can be reconstructed from his victory titles, cf. Barnes, "Victories of Constantine," pp. 150–53; *New Empire,* pp. 77–78.

55. Charron and Heijmans.

56. Cyp. *Ep.* 68 passim (*CCSL* 3C: 461–68).

57. Opt. 3.23; Eus. *HE* 10.5.19 = Maier, *Dossier,* no. 17.

58. Opt. *App.* 4 (*CSEL* 26: 206,25); *Acta Concilii Arelatensis* praef., subscriptiones (*CCSL* 148: 4.1, 14.2, 85).

59. Odahl, "Constantinian Arles."

60. *AE* 1974: 418; cf. Rouquette. For more on the Christian sarcophagi of Arles and their connection with Constantine, see Stephenson, pp. 210–11.

61. *PLRE* 1: Ianuarinus 1 and 2; *CLRE*, pp. 190–91.

62. Aur. Vict. *Caes.* 40.28: *tum per Africam sacerdotium decretum Flaviae genti, Cirtaeque oppido, quod obsidione Alexandri conciderat, reposito exornatoque nomen Constantina inditum.* On this passage, see Aiello, "Costantino, Lucio Domizio Alessandro e Cirta." Aurelius Victor is surely to be trusted here, for he was himself a convinced pagan who had grown up in Roman North Africa; see Bird, p. vii–xi. Archaeological evidence for the ongoing maintenance of imperial cult structures in Africa during the fourth century is collected at Leone, pp. 108–18.

63. So also Lepelley, *Les cités de l'Afrique,* vol. 1, p. 344.

64. Khannousi and Mastino, whence *AE* 2003: 2014.

65. *AE* 2003: 2022 with Lepelley, "De la réaction païenne," pp. 274–75. This is, of course, the same Zenophilus who oversaw the trial of the Donatist bishop of Cirta, Silvanus, on charges of betrayal, theft, and simony; cf. Opt. *App.* 1 (*CSEL* 26: 185–88).

66. *CTh* 12.1.21 (Aug. 4, 335); 12.5.2 (May 21, 337); cf. De Giovanni, *Costantino e il mondo pagano,* pp. 135–36, which points out that these privileges continued down to 396, when *CTh* 16.10.14 eliminated them.

67. Opt. 1.14: *apud Cirtam civitatem, quia basilicae necdum fuerant restitutae*. On the nature of these structures, see Duval, *Chrétiens d'Afrique*, pp. 363–82. For an overview of Cirta in Late Antiquity, see Lepelley, *Les cités de l'Afrique*, vol. 2, pp. 383–89.

68. *Gesta apud Zenophilum* apud Opt. App. 1.17B (*CSEL* 26: 186). Cirta's pagan community remained strong into the 360s at least, when the governor of Numidia, Publilius Caeionius Caecina Albinus, restored a Mithraeum and another temple there; see *CIL* 8: 6975 = *ILAlg.* 2: 541; *CIL* 8: 19502 = *ILAlg.* 2: 618; cf. Lepelley, *Les cités de l'Afrique*, vol. 1, p. 348; vol. 2, pp. 385, 393.

69. See also Zos. 2.14.2–4. For questions about whether Domitius Alexander laid siege to or was besieged at Cirta, see Aiello, "Costantino, Lucio Domizio Alessandro e Cirta."

70. *CIL* 8: 7006 = *ILAlg.* 2: 582 = *ILS* 688: *q[u]i libertatem tenebris servitutis oppressam sua felici vi[ctoria(?)]/ [nova] luce inluminavit*; *CIL* 8: 7007 = *ILAlg.* 2: 583: *[qui libertatem tenebris] servitut[is op]pre[ssam sua]/[felici victoria nova luce inluminavit et re]vocavit*. The inscriptions are datable between 312/316 by Constantine's titulature, and the governor who dedicated them, Valerius Paulus, can be identified with the dedicant of *CIL* 8: 18905 = *ILAlg.* 2: 4673 = *AE* 1890: 21, which shows him to have been in office in 313; cf. *PLRE* 1: Val. Paulus 12; Grünewald, pp. 71–73.

71. Lenski, "Constantine and Slavery."

72. *Gesta apud Zenophilum* at Opt. *App.* 1.17A (*CSEL* 26: 185): *Victor dixit: patre decurione Constantiniensium*; cf. Opt. *App.* 1.22A (*CSEL* 26: 193): *Victor dixit: in basilica. Zenophilus v.c. consularis dixit: apud Constantinam?* The proceedings are dated to 320 at *App.* 1.17A (*CSEL* 26: 185). See also Galsterer-Kröll, p. 100.

73. *ILAlg.* 2: 533. For Crispus's victory over the Franks and its date, see Barnes, *New Empire*, p. 83. The name was hammered out—partially—after 326.

74. Opt. *App.* 10.36b–37a (*CSEL* 26: 215). On the date, see Maier, *Dossier*, p. 246.

75. *CIL* 8: 7037–38 = *ILAlg.* 2: 624A-B = *ILS* 5534. Interestingly, work on the basilica was brought to a close by Claudius Avitianus while he was serving as Vicar, which seems to imply ongoing financing from the imperial fisc.

76. *CTh* 12.1.29 = *CJ* 10.32.20: *Idem Augusti ordini civitatis Constantinae Cirtensium*. *CIL* 8: 7012 = *ILAlg.* 2: 589 = *ILS* 1235; *CIL* 8: 7015 = *ILAlg.* 2: 596; *CIL* 8: 7034 = *ILAlg.* 2: 619.

77. (1) *CIL* 8: 7010 = *ILAlg.* 2: 581 = *ILS* 691; (2) *CIL* 8: 7006 = *ILAlg.* 2: 582; (3) *CIL* 8: 7007 = *ILAlg.* 2: 583; (4) *CIL* 8: 7005 = *ILAlg.* 2: 584; (5) *CIL* 8: 7008 = *ILAlg.* 2: 585; (6) *CIL* 8: 7011 = *ILAlg.* 2: 587 = *ILS* 715; (7) *CIL* 8: 7012 = *ILAlg.* 2: 589 = *ILS* 1235; (8) *CIL* 8: 7013 = *ILAlg.* 2: 590 = *ILS* 1236; (9) *AE* 2005: 1695 = Benseddik.

78. *CIL* 8: 7012 = *ILAlg.* 2: 589 = *ILS* 1235: *ordo felicis/ coloniae Constanti/nae*; *CIL* 8: 7013 = *ILAlg.* 2: 590 = *ILS* 1236: *or/do coloniae Milevitanae in {f}o/ro Constantinae civitatis*. Both are dated 340/350 by the imperial college, and a date close to 343 is made likely by the governor they name, *PLRE* 1: Ceionius Italicus 3, known from the codes to have been in office in this year. See also *Not. Episc.* 1.666: Eparchia Noumidias: Κωνσταντίνη; cf. *Barrington Atlas*, Map 31, F4: Cirta-Constantina (Constantine).

79. *ILAlg.* 2: 595 with Lepelley, *Les cités de l'Afrique*, vol. 2, p. 388.

80. See especially *AE* 2005: 1695 = Benseddik, no. 1C; cf. Lepelley, *Les cités de l'Afrique*, vol. 2, p. 384; Duval, "Gouverneur de Numidie," p. 199.

81. For Cuicul, see *CIL* 8: 8324 = *ILS* 5535. For Tebessa (Theveste), see *AE* 1909: 223 = *AE* 1989: 784. For Cirta, see *ILAlg.* 2: 620.

82. For more on late antique Ostia, see Février; Rieger, pp. 35–37, 257–58; Steuernagel, pp. 110–19; Gering; Boin, *Ostia*. For Portus, see Keay, Millett, Paroli, and Strutt.

83. The temple has been identified only recently (and still tentatively) by Heinzelmann and Martin. C. Bruun, "*Aedes Castorum*," reinforces this theory.

84. *RIC* 6: Ostia no. 14–19, 34–38 AETERNITAS AVG N; cf. Albertson, pp. 123, 126–27. Ostia's close relationship with Maxentius is also attested by their dedication of a larger than life-size statue of him, whose head still remains in the Antiquarium of Ostia (inv. n. 70); cf. Donati and Gentili, pp. 207–8 no. 5.

85. Amm. 19.10.4: *apud Ostia in aede sacrificat Castorum.*

86. [Aethici] *Cosmographia* (Riese, *Geographi Latini Minores,* 83): *Tiber . . . insulam facit inter Portum Urbis et Ostiam civitatem ubi populus Romanus cum urbis praefecto vel consule Castorum celebrandorum causa egreditur sollemnitate iocunda,* with C. Bruun, "Aedes Castorum," pp. 118–21.

87. Gelas. *Ep. adv. Andromachum* 18 (*SCh* 65: 176): *Castores vestri certe, a quorum cultu desistere noluistis,* etc. See Chastagnol, "Restauration du temple d'Isis," pp. 140–42, for more on the worship of the Castores in Ostia.

88. For the Magna Mater dedication of Volusianus as Tauroboliatus, see *AE* 1945: 55a = *AE* 1955: 180; cf. Rieger, pp. 119, 167–68, 287; Boin, *Ostia,* pp. 183–88. For the temple of Isis, see *AE* 1961: 152 = *AE* 1968: 86 = Chastagnol, "Restauration du temple d'Isis." For the temple of Hercules, see *AE* 1948: 126–27; cf. Bloch; Steuernagel, p. 63. Boin, "A Hall for Hercules," rightly downplays Bloch's enthusiasm for a zealous pagan revival in the late fourth century, but stretches the evidence entirely out of shape in order to associate the Hercules inscription with a bath complex rather than a temple; cf. Boin, *Ostia,* pp. 133–36.

89. Mansi 2: 437 = Opt. 1.23: *Maximus ab Ostia.*

90. *Lib. Pont.* 34.28, 35.2(Duchesne, vol. 1, pp. 183, 202 = Geertman, p. 304).

91. Bauer and Heinzelmann, "Constantinian Bishop's Church"; Bauer, Heinzelmann, Martin, and Schaub, "Ostia"; cf. Boin, *Ostia,* pp. 159–61, 169–80.

92. On Gallicanus's endowment, see *Lib. Pont.* 34.29 (Duchesne, vol. 1, p. 184 = Geertman, pp. 304–5); *Acta Gallicani* 7 (*AASS Iun.* 7 [1867] 34). On the identification of Gallicanus the benefactor with *PLRE* 1: Ovinius Gallicanus 3, see Champlin. The funerary church at Pianabella, outside the walls, dates to the late fourth century; see Boin, *Ostia,* pp. 168–69.

93. Février; Brenk; Boin, *Ostia,* pp. 158–83.

94. Becatti; Steuernagel, pp. 111–12.

95. *Depositio Martyrum* (Valentini and Zucchetti, vol. 2, pp. 25–28): *Nonae Septembris: Aconti, in Porto, et Nonni et Herculani et Taurini; Idus Decembris: Ariston in Portum;* cf. Thylander, no. B 249. For the epigraphic attestations, see *CIL* 14: 1937–38 = Thylander, no. B 234–35: Zosima, Bonosa, Paula, Eutropius. For more on the martyrs of Portus, see Février, pp. 313–15; Meiggs, pp. 394–95, 518–31; Mazzoleni, p. 286.

96. Février, pp. 316–17; Paroli.

97. Jer. *Ep.* 66.11, 77.10 (*CSEL* 54: 661; 55: 47).

98. Mazzoleni.

99. *CIL* 14: 4449 = Thylander, no. B336 = *AE* 1926: 119; cf. *AE* 2007: 163: *Fide exercitatione{m}/ bonitati pollenti Lucio/ Crepereio Madaliano v(iro) c(larissimo)/ praef(ecto) ann(onae) cum iure gladii/ comiti flaviali corr(ectori) Flam(iniae)/ et Piceni leg(ato) pro praetore prov(inciae)/ Asiae leg(ato) prov(inciae) Africae consula(ri)/ aed(ium) sacrar(um) consul(ari) molium fari/ at(que?) purgaturae quaest(ori) candid(ato)/ praet(ori) consuli ob multa in se eius/ testimonia ordo et popu<l>us/ Fl(aviae) Constantinianae Portuens<i>s/ statuam public{a}e ponendam/ censuerunt.*

100. The road between Rome and Portus was also renamed the Via Flavia, probably when Portus was renamed; cf. Meiggs, pp. 160–61, 473, citing Thylander, no. A90.

101. Philost. *HE* 12.3: Ὁ δὲ θᾶττον καταλαμβάνει τὸν Πόρτον. μέγιστον δὴ οὗτος νεώριον Ῥώμης, λιμέσι τρισὶ περιγραφόμενον καὶ εἰς πόλεως μικρᾶς παρατεινόμενον μέγεθος; Cass. *Var.* 7.9.2 (*CCSL* 96: 270): *duo quippe Tiberini alvei meatus ornatissimas civitates tamquam duo lumina susceperunt;* *Lib. Pont.* 34.28 (Duchesne, vol. 1, p. 183 = Geertman, p. 304): *in civitate*

Hostia, iuxta Portum Urbis Romae; Proc. *Bella* 5.26.7–8: τὸ μὲν οὖν ἐν δεξιᾷ τοῦ ποταμοῦ μέρος . . . Πόρτον τε αὐτὴν τῷ λιμένι ὁμωνύμως καλοῦσιν· ἐν ἀριστερᾷ δὲ πρὸς τῇ ἑτέρᾳ τοῦ Τιβέριδος ἐς τὴν θάλασσαν ἐκβολῇ πόλις Ὀστία κεῖται; cf. Meiggs, pp. 85–89.

102. The Tabula Peutingeriana tells much the same story, depicting Portus in full detail alongside the diminutive "Hostia"; cf. Weber.

103. Chastagnol, *La préfecture urbaine*, p. 412.

104. Of the 159 inscriptions turned up with the name Crepereius in the *Epigraphische Datenbank Clauss-Slaby*, 81 are from North Africa: Numidia (n = 36), Africa Proconsularis (n = 27), or Mauretania Caesariensis (n = 18).

105. In addition to Praefectus Annonae, Madalianus's offices of Legatus Provinciae Africae and Consularis Molium Fari atque Purgaturae would have borne direct relevance to the grain supply. These same offices are also attested at *CIL* 6: 1151 = 31248 = *ILS* 707; *CIL* 8: 5348 = 17490 = *ILAlg.* 1: 271 = *ILS* 1228.

106. M. Overbeck, *Untersuchungen*, pp. 22, 2526, 38.

107. Chastagnol, *La préfecture urbaine*, p. 50.

108. *PLRE* 1: Lucius Crepereius Madalianus. On the late antique fate of suffect consuls, who were usually ex-imperial bureaucrats, now acting as essentially honorary civic officials of the city of Rome, see Vera, *Commento storico*, pp. 330–32; Sguaitamatti, pp. 52–54, 95–98, 161–69.

109. *CTh* 16.10.2: *Imp. Constantius a. ad Madalianum agentem vicem praefectorum praetorio.*

110. Chastagnol, *La préfecture urbaine*, pp. 52–53. On the temple confiscations, see below pp. 168–75.

111. It is striking that Ostia dedicated a massive statue base, large enough for an equestrian monument, near its Temple of Roma and Augustus to its patron (*pa]tronus splendidissim(a)e col(oniae) Ost(iensium)*), the *praefectus annonae* "Manilio Rus[ticiano]" under Maxentius. This is likely the same man who went on to serve as Maxentius's Praetorian Prefect, *CIL* 14: 34455 = *AE* 1972: 71; cf. *PLRE* 1: Manilius Rus(ticianus?) 2 and Manli(us) Rusticianus 3.

112. *Conc. Arel. Subscr.* (*CCSL* 148: 15 l. 83 = Mansi 2: 477): *Gregor(ius) episcopus, quo loco qui est in Portu Romae*; cf. *Leontius et Mercurius presbyteri ab Ostiis.*

113. *CTh* 13.5.4 (a. 324): *Portus Romae*; 14.22.1 (a. 364): *Portus Urbis Aeternae*; 14.15.2 (a. 366): *Portus Urbis Sacrae*; *Chron. 354*: *Portus Romanus*; Jer. *Ep.* 66.11.1 (*CSEL* 54: 661): *Portus Romanus*; [Aethici] *Cosmographia* (Riese, *Geographi Latini Minores*, 83): *Portum Urbis*; Cass. *Var.* 7.9 tit. (*CCSL* 96: 269): *Portus Urbis Romae*; 7.9.1: *Portu Romano*; Proc. *BG* 6.7.1, 12.29; 7.13.7, 15.1, 15.10, 18.4, 18.11: ὁ Ῥωμαίων λιμήν.

114. So also Dessau, *Corpus Inscriptionum Latinarum XIV*, p. 7; Wickert, *Corpus Inscriptionum Latinarum XIV, Supplementum*, p. 612; Chastagnol, *La préfecture urbaine*, pp. 53–54; cf. Meiggs, p. 88.

115. See above p. 140 and p. 320 n. 59.

116. *CIL* 14: 131 = *ILS* 687. The date can be derived from Constantine's designation as Valerius, which became uncommon after 315. On the *navicularii codicarii* stationed at Portus, see *CTh* 14.4.9 with Meiggs, p. 332. The inscription was brought to Rome from Ostia/Portus, but its original location is no longer known precisely.

117. Lenski, "Constantine and Slavery."

118. *IEAquil* 196 = *AE* 1996: 694 = *AE* 2001: 1008; cf. *AE* 2001: 1009, with Riess; Bratož, pp. 20–22. Aquileia had, of course, resisted, Constantine during his war with Maxentius in 312 and suffered siege as a consequence, *Pan. Lat.* 12[9].11.1–2; 4[10].27.1. Although these same passages confirm that Constantine forgave it this offense, it is interesting that so strategic a city with so powerful a Christian community did not receive more robust rewards from Constantine, especially since he visited Aquileia in 318 and 326. Cf. Seeck *RG* 166, 176; Barnes, *New Empire*, pp. 74, 77. More on Aquileia below at pp. 189–90.

119. For Rome, see *CIL* 6: 1750 = 31920 = *ILS* 5703; *CIL* 10: 1126; cf. Curran, *Pagan City*, pp. 85–86; Johnson, "Architecture," p. 281, fig. 33. For Trebula Balliensis, see *CIL* 10: 4559. Remis (Reims) received new baths early in Constantine's reign, although not under his name, but Constantine does refer to Reims as "his city" (*sua civitas*) in the dedicatory inscription; cf. *ILS* 703.

120. *Lib. Pont.* 34.31 (Duchesne, vol. 1, pp. 185–86 = Geertman, p. 306); cf. M. J. Johnson, "Constantinian Churches in Campania."

CHAPTER 7. CONSTANTINE'S CITIES IN THE EAST

1. Renfrew and Cherry, esp. chapters 1 and 3 by Renfrew and Snodgrass, respectively. More recently, see Robinson, pp. 207–16.

2. Ma, "Peer Polity Interaction."

3. See also Curty; C. P. Jones, *Kinship Diplomacy*.

4. Dmitriev, pp. 289–328; Gleason; cf. Ando, *Imperial Ideology*, pp. 80–130.

5. On the last especially, see Ma, "Fighting Poleis."

6. Dio Cass. 78.20.4, 22.3; 79.7.4; with Habicht, pp. 73–74.

7. See especially *Dig.* 50.15.1.2 (Ulpian): *Heliopolitana [colonia], quae a divo Severo per belli civilis occasionem Italicae coloniae rem publicam accepit.* Further evidence and arguments at Millar, "Roman *Coloniae*," pp. 32–37.

8. *CJ* 11.22.1: *Tyro nihil de iure suo derogetur.* For the date, see *PLRE* 2: Hormisdas. More on the pursuit of the title *mētropolis* by Tyre at Millar, *Emperor*, p. 409; cf. 432.

9. *ACOec.* II.1.3 [460–73] (Schwartz, pp. 101–14) with Millar, *Greek Roman Empire*, pp. 135–36.

10. Dio Chrys. *Or.* 38, esp. 21–24. Robert, "La titulature de Nicée," lays out in remarkable detail the complex history of this interurban bickering.

11. *ACOec.* II.1.3 [415–21] (Schwartz, pp. 56–62) with Lenski, *Failure of Empire*, p. 22 n. 52; Millar, *Greek Roman Empire*, p. 135.

12. *ACOec.* II.1.3 [418–19] (Schwartz, pp. 59–60), esp. Ὥσπερ Ταττάιος καὶ Δωρὶς ῥεγεῶνές εἰσιν ὑπὸ Νίκαιαν, οὕτως ἦν πρὸ τούτου καὶ Βασιλινούπολις ὑπὸ τὴν Νίκαιαν. βασιλεύς τις Ἰουλιανὸς ἢ οὐκ οἶδα τίς πρὸ αὐτοῦ, ἐποίησεν αὐτὴν πόλιν καὶ λαβὼν ἀπὸ Νικαίας πολιτευομένους κατέστησεν ἐκεῖ; cf. *PLRE* 1: Basilina. See also A. H. M. Jones, *Cities*, p. 166.

13. Amm. Marc. 22.9.3–4; cf. Lib. *Ep.* 35.2–3. Julian's presence in Nicomedia in 362 is attested at *CTh* 7.4.8. On the earthquake of 358, see Lenski, *Failure of Empire*, p. 386.

14. Lib. *Or.* 18.187–88 reports that Julian also adjudicated a dispute between two great cities of Syria (Laodicea and Apamea) over which merited the title *prōtē polis* and eventually selected Apamea because it was home to great pagan philosophers (i.e., Iamblichus and Sopater). On Sopater, see Woods, "Sopater of Apamea"; Digeser, *A Threat to Public Piety*, pp. 23–48 and 103–5.

15. Epiph. *Pan.* 30.4.1–12.9; cf. Thornton; Perkams.

16. Applebaum, pp. 60–63, with earlier bibliography. See Strack and Stemberger, pp. 99–105 on Tiberias as the home of the fourth- and fifth-century patriarch.

17. Epiph. *Pan.* 30.11.9–10.

18. Epiph. *Pan.* 30.12.1: Λαβὼν δὲ ὁ Ἰώσηπος τὰ γράμματα καὶ τὴν ἐξουσίαν μετὰ τοῦ ἀξιώματος ἐπὶ τὴν Τιβεριάδα ἧκεν, ἔχων καὶ ἐπιστολὰς ἀπὸ τῶν βασιλικῶν ἀναλίσκειν, ἀλλὰ καὶ αὐτὸς ὀψωνίοις παρὰ τοῦ βασιλέως τετιμημένος.

19. Sivan, pp. 158–75; Bar, pp. 281–83; Heyden.

20. Eus. *V. Const.* 4.39.1–2, esp. Ταὐτὸν δὲ καὶ ἕτεραι πλείους διεπράττοντο χῶραι, ὡς ἡ ἐπὶ τοῦ Φοινίκων ἔθνους αὐτοῦ βασιλέως ἐπώνυμος, ἧς οἱ πολῖται δυσεξαρίθμητα ξοάνων ἱδρύματα πυρὶ παραδόντες τὸν σωτήριον ἀντικατηλλάξαντο νόμον.

21. Soz. 2.5.8: ἐκ τοιαύτης δὲ αἰτίας καὶ Κωνσταντίναν τὴν παρὰ Φοίνιξιν ἔγνων ἐπιγράψασθαι τὴν τοῦ βασιλέως ἐπωνυμίαν.

22. Hier. *Syn.*. 716.5–7 (Honigmann, p. 41). Honigmann, p. 41, considers Antaradus and Constantina to be alternate names for the same city.

23. Theoph. a.m. 5838 (a. 345/346): καὶ πόλιν ἔκτισεν ἐν τῇ Φοινίκῃ, ἣν Κωνσταντίαν κέκληκεν, τὸ πρότερον καλουμένην Ἀντάραδον. Cf. Cedrenus p. 523 (Bekker); *Chron.* 724 (ed. and trans. Brooks and Chabot, *CSCO SS*, 3: 130 [text] = 4: 102 [trans.]); with Burgess, *Studies*, pp. 160 no. 42, 272.

24. *ACOec* II.5 [xxv] (Schwartz, p. 44.29). Devréesse, p. 196, shows that the city also continued to be called Antaradus.

25. Burgess, *Studies*, p. 272: "The *Continuatio* is the only source to preserve a record of this renaming and refoundation." See also Rey-Coquais, pp. 34–35, 141. Already A. H. M. Jones, *Cities*, pp. 268 and 458 n. 54, made the connection.

26. Rey-Coquais, pp. 53–90.

27. Polyb. 5.68.7; Diod. Sic. 33.5.1–6; Strabo 16.2.14 (754); cf. Rey-Coquais, pp. 123–29, 139–69.

28. *IGLS* 7: 4028, with commentary. Earlier editions at *CIL* 3: 184 (cf. *CIL* 3: p. 972) = *IGR* 3: 1020 = *OGIS* 262 (Greek only) = Abbott and Johnson, *Municipal Administration*, no. 147; cf. Millar, *Emperor*, pp. 454–45; Feissel, "Privilèges de Baitokaikè"; Dignas, pp. 74–84, 156–67.

29. See Dignas, pp. 158–59, with earlier bibliography.

30. Rey-Coquais, pp. 232–56.

31. On Zenodorus, see *Patrum Nicaenorum Nomina* 6:40 and 7:53 (Gelzer, Hilgenfeld, and Cuntz, pp. 72, 82). On Carterius, Athan. *Apol. de fuga* 3.2 (a. 357); *Hist. Ar.* 5.2 (a. 358); *Tomus ad Antiochenos* 11 (a. 361) and Theod. *HE* 2.15.8 indicate that Carterius was exiled in the aftermath of the Council of Antioch in 328 CE; cf. Barnes, "Emperor and Bishops," pp. 59–60; *Athanasius and Constantius,* p. 17 and n. 73; Parvis, pp. 109–10.

32. On Moses's translation of relics, see Chron. Pasch. p. 572 (s.a. 415). For ongoing assertion of independence, see Devréesse, pp. 196–97; Rey-Coquais, p. 141.

33. *ACOec* I.1.5 [151.16] (Schwartz, p. 123.28); cf. I.1.3 [90–91] (Schwartz, pp. 25, 27), which lists Musaios as bishop of Aradus with no mention of Antaradus.

34. For Paul of Aradus, see *ACOec.* II.1.1 (Schwartz, p. 59); II.1.2 (Schwartz, pp. 33, 72, 87, 133, 145); II.1.3 (Schwartz, p. 72). For Alexander of Antaradus, *ACOec.* II.1.2 (Schwartz, p. 41).

35. Flemming and Hoffmann, pp. 126–29 with 179 n. 127.20; cf. Schwartz, *Bischofslisten,* p. 47; Devréesse, pp. 55, 196.

36. For the name, see Joh. Mal. 12.48 (Dindorf, p. 313 = Thurn, p. 240); Epiph. *Pan.* 51.24.5.

37. Joh. Mal. 12.48 (Dindorf, p. 313 = Thurn, p. 240).

38. Theoph. a.m. 5824, 5834.

39. Aur. Vict. *Caes.* 41.11–12; Jer. *Chron.* s.a. 334; Theoph. a.m. 5825. Barnes, *Constantine and Eusebius,* p. 252, rather incautiously draws the various threads together. The revolt may also be related to a famine that struck the region; cf. Jer. *Chron.* s.a. 333.

40. So Mango and Scott, *Theophanes Confessor,* 48 n. 2, 61 n.d. At a minimum, we know Theophanes had access to good fourth-century sources; see Burgess and Kulikowski, *Mosaics of Time,* pp. 230–31.

41. Mitford, Nicolaou, Karageorghis, nos. 41–42. Compare Cypriot Paphos, rebuilt after an earthquake by Augustus and renamed Augusta; Dio 54.23.7–8.

42. Hier. *Syn.* 706.4 (Honigmann, p. 38); *Not. Episc.* 1.1051; Nil. Dox. 177, with G. Hill, *History of Cyprus,* p. 245; cf. Antoninus Placentinus *Itinerarium* 1 (*CCSL* 175: 129). Note that the name Iulia Constantia is attached to a number of the cities catalogued in Pliny's *Historia Naturalis*, written in the first century CE: 3.11 (Osset); 3.14 (Lacimurga); 5.2 (Zilis). Galsterer-Kröll,

pp. 57–61 and nos. 89, 115, 126, shows these supplementary names are attested nowhere else in the sources. See also Colonia Pia Flavia Constans Emerita Helvetiorum (Avenches), renamed under the first Flavian dynasty; cf. Galsterer-Kröll, no. 230.

43. Innocent, *Ep.* 24.2.3 (*PL* 20: 548–49).

44 *ACOec* I.7 [81] (Schwartz, pp. 119–20). For more on this document and the dispute, see Millar, *Greek Roman Empire*, pp. 20–21, 137–39.

45. On the last two, see Galsterer-Kröll, nos. 380 and 406.

46. Soz. 2.2.5: ἔχει δὲ αὐτῆς διηνεκοῦς μνήμης ἐνέχυρον ὁ μέλλων αἰὼν τὴν ἐπὶ Βιθυνίας πόλιν καὶ ἑτέραν παρὰ Παλαιστίνοις, ἀπ᾽ αὐτῆς λαβούσας τὴν προσηγορίαν. ταῦτα μὲν ἡμῖν ὧδε περὶ Ἑλένης εἰρήσθω.

47. *Barrington Atlas*, Map 69, Damascus-Caesarea, B4: Helenoupolis; Tsafrir, Di Segni, and Green, p. 142 s.v. Hellenoupolis.

48. Eus. *On.* 250 = Jer. *On.* 115 (Klostermann 78): Δαβειρά (Josh 10: 38), ἧς τὸν βασιλέα ἐπάταξεν Ἰησοῦς. ἢ γέγονε φυλῆς Δάν. καὶ νῦν ἐστιν ἑτέρα κώμη Ἰουδαίων ἐν τῷ ὄρει Θαβώρ, ἐν ὁρίοις Διοκαισαρείας.

49. Eus. *Mart. Pal.* 8.1–3, with supplement at Schwartz and Mommsen, *Eusebius*, vol. 2, p. 925 n. 4.

50. Miller, pp. 117–27. See also Sivan, pp. 317–28, on Diocaesarea-Sepphoris more broadly.

51. *Talmud J. Kila᾽im* 9 4.32b.

52. Z. Weiss, *Sepphoris Synagogue*, pp. 104–61, with 249–56.

53. Aur. Vict. *Caes.* 42.11: *et interea Iudaeorum seditio, qui patricium nefarie in regni speciem sustulerant, opressa*; cf. Jer. *Chron.* s.a. 352; Soc. 2.33.1–2; Soz. 4.7.5; Philost. *App.* 7: 6A–B; Cf. Theoph. a.m. 5843; Cedrenus p. 524 (Bekker). For analysis, see Schäfer.

54. Soc. 2.33.2: καὶ τὴν πόλιν αὐτῶν Διοκαισάρειαν εἰς ἔδαφος καθαιρεθῆναι ἐκέλευσεν; cf. Soz. 4.7.5. On the archaeology, see Strange, Longstaff, and Groh, p. 23.

55. The Talmudic sources are gathered at Avi-Yonah, pp. 180–81; cf. Geiger. For Peter's letter, see Theod. *HE* 4.22.35; cf. Pall. *Hist. Laus.* 46.3.

56. Z. Weiss and Netzer, "Sepphoris during the Byzantine Period." The city appears not to have had a Christian church until the early sixth century; Sivan, p. 325.

57. *Guidi Vita* 31 p. 646; cf. Beetham, p. 136. A visit by Helena may also explain why the Pamphylian city of Side erected no less than three statues in her honor; *IK Side* 47–48; *AE* 2006: 1504. We know nothing else of favors she may have granted the Sidetans.

58. Hier. *Syn.* 720.8 (Honigmann, p. 42). See also the acts of the Synod of Jerusalem in 536, *ACOec* III [133.28] (Schwartz, p. 188): Προκόπιος ἐλέει θεοῦ ἐπίσκοπος Ἑλενουπόλεως. Daburiyya continues to be a thriving town where systematic archaeology has not yet taken place. The only Christian church excavated there thus far appears to date to the early sixth century; cf. Saarisalo and Palva.

59. See especially Mango, "Empress Helena"; Mitchell, "Cities of Asia Minor," p. 52; cf. *Barrington Atlas*, Map 52, Byzantium, F3: Drepanon-Helenopolis.

60. Amm. 26.8.1: *Drepanum ante, nunc Helenopolim*; cf. Jer. *Chron.* s.a. 327: *Drepanam*; *Chron. Pasch.* p. 527: Δρέπανον; Soc. 1.18.13: Δρεπάνην. On the discrepancy between the neuter Drepanum and the feminine Drepana, see Burgess, *Studies*, p. 203. Joh. Mal. 13.12 (Dindorf, p. 323 = Thurn, p. 248) reports the original name as Souga.

61. Eus. *V. Const.* 4.61.1: κἄπειτα τῆς αὐτοῦ πόλεως ἐπὶ λουτρὰ θερμῶν ὑδάτων πρόεισιν, ἔνθεν τε τῆς αὐτοῦ μητρὸς ἐπὶ τὴν ἐπώνυμον ἀφικνεῖται πόλιν; Soc. 1.39.1; Soz. 2.2.5.

62. Philost. *HE* 2.12; cf. 2.12a = Opitz *V. Const.* 52.

63. Jer. *Chron.* s.a. 327; *Chron. Pasch.* p. 527; cf. *Chron. 724* (ed. and trans. Brooks and Chabot, *CSCO SS*, 3: 129 [text] = 4: 101 [trans.]); Theoph. a.m. 5818, with Burgess, *Studies*, pp. 153 no. 7 and 203–4.

64. Drijvers, pp. 73–76, and P. Bruun, *Roman Imperial Coinage*, vol. 7, pp. 72–73, argue that she died in 329. Proc. *Aed.* 5.2.1 is probably incorrect to assert that Helena was born in this city; cf. Mango, "Empress Helena," pp. 146–47; Drijvers, pp. 9–12, 16.

65. *V. Luciani* 20. This notice could be confirmed or denied only with further archaeological research.

66. Jer. *Chron.* s.a. 327: *Drepanam Bithyniae civitatem . . . instaurans*; Soc. 1.17.1: ἧς ἐπ᾽ ὀνόματι τὴν ποτε κώμην Δρεπάνην πόλιν ποιήσας ὁ βασιλεὺς Ἑλενόπολιν ἐπωνόμασεν; Joh. Mal. 13.12 (Dindorf, p. 323 = Thurn, p. 248): ἔκτισεν δὲ καὶ εἰς τὴν Βιθυνίαν τὴν πρῴην οὖσαν κώμην λεγομένην Σουγάν, δοὺς αὐτῇ καὶ δίκαιον πόλεως καὶ καλέσας αὐτὴν εἰς ὄνομα τῆς ἰδίας μητρὸς Ἑλενούπολιν; *V. Luciani* 20: τὴν τε πόλιν αὐτῆς συνῴκισεν; cf. Eus. *V. Const.* 4.61.1: πόλιν; Proc. *Aed.* 5.2.1–2: κώμης οὐκ ἀξιολόγου τὰ πρότερα οὔσης. ᾗπερ τὰ τροφεῖα Κωνσταντῖνος ἐκτίνων ὀνόματι μὲν καὶ ἀξιώματι πόλεως τὸ χωρίον δεδώρηται τοῦτο.

67. *Chron. Pasch.* p. 527: δωρησάμενος ἄχρι τοῦ νῦν ἕως φανερᾶς περιοχῆς πρὸ τῆς πόλεως εἰς τιμὴν τοῦ ἁγίου μάρτυρος Λουκιανοῦ ἀτέλειαν.

68. Robert, "Inscriptions de la région de Yalova."

69. Zuckerman.

70. Cedrenus 1 p. 517 (Bonn): καὶ Δρεπανᾶν τὸν ἐν Νικομηδείᾳ ἐπικτίσας εἰς τιμὴν Λουκιανοῦ τοῦ ἐκεῖσε μαρτυρήσαντος Ἑλενούπολιν διὰ τὴν μητέρα ἐκάλεσεν. A. H. M. Jones, *Cities*, pp. 165–66, also holds for Nicomedia.

71. On Nicomedia as the birthplace of the Great Persecution, see Eus. *HE* 8.5.1, 6.6; Lact. *Mort. Pers.* 12.1–5. On the renewed persecutions of 312, see above pp. 93–94.

72. Eus. *HE* 8.13.2; 9.6.3; Jer. *Vir. ill.* 77; *V. Luciani* 6, 9, 11, with Barnes, "Date of the Martyrdom of Lucian," on the date, Jan. 7, 312.

73. Opitz *Urkunde* 27.9–10 p. 60 = Brennecke *Dokument* 31.9–10 p. 119; cf. *Or. ad Sanct.* 22.1, with Bleckmann, "Ein Kaiser als Prediger."

74. On the church, see Eus. *V. Const.* 3.50.1; *LC* 9.14. On Eusebius of Nicomedia, see Parvis, pp. 40–41; Gwynn; Lenski, "Early Retrospectives," and below pp. 265–69. Eusebius was in fact a disciple of Lucian's and a promoter of his cult (Epiph. *Pan.* 69.5.2; cf. 43.1.1; 76.3.5), yet he obviously did not succeed in securing control of it under Constantine.

75. For Eusebius's deposition, which lasted down to 327 or 328, see below pp. 266–67. For accusations of conspiracy and the arrest of priests and deacons, see Const. *Ep. ad Nic.* 9–11 (Opitz *Urkunde* 27.9–10 p. 60 = Brennecke *Dokument* 31.9–10 p. 119 of December 325).

76. Eus. *V. Const.* 4.38.1.

CHAPTER 8. REDISTRIBUTING WEALTH

1. Dignas, pp. 13–35, outlines the—by no means systematic—theory behind this legal distinction, and 217–22 summarizes its—always imperfect—application under Roman rulers. See also Debord, pp. 127–62; Migeotte, pp. 20–25. A particularly good example of the despoiling of temples—which itself involved the confiscation of precious metal images—in the High Empire occurred under Nero in 66 CE; see Tac. *Ann.* 15.45.1–2. See also Hdn. 7.3.5–6 for confiscations of both civic and temple property by Maximinus Thrax that led to widespread unrest.

2. Eus. *V. Const.* 3.54.1–6, a passage Eusebius has largely copied from *LC* 8.2–4; cf. 9.5–6. This testimony forms the basis for Soc. 1.16.3 and Soz. 2.5.1–4. Far and away the best analysis of this issue is Bonamente, "Sulla confisca"; see also Metzler.

3. Eus. *V. Const.* 3.54.2–3; *LC* 8.4.

4. *Patr. Const.* 2.73 (1550ε: Preger 189); cf. Mitchell, "Cities of Asia Minor," p. 58. See Bassett, pp. 50–78, for further details on the provenance of confiscated objects.

5. Jer. *Chron.* s.a. 330: *dedicatur Constantinopolis omnium paene urbium nuditate*; cf. s.a. 331, cited below n. 22.

6. Jul. *Or.* 7 22 (228B): πατρῷα μὲν ἱερὰ κατεσκάπτετο παρὰ τῶν παίδων ὀλιγωρηθέντα πρότερον ὑπὸ τοῦ πατρὸς καὶ ἀποσυληθέντα τῶν ἀναθημάτων, ἃ ἐτέθειτο παρὰ πολλῶν μὲν καὶ ἄλλων, οὐχ ἥκιστα δὲ τῶν προπατόρων αὐτοῦ. Firmicus Maternus in his *De errore profanarum religionum* (completed c. 346) recommends in multiple places the melting down of idols for their precious metals; e.g., 28.5–6.

7. *AP* 9.528, with K. W. Wilkinson, "Palladas and the Age," pp. 52–56. Barnes, *Dynasty, Religion and Power*, pp. 128–30, has made rather too much of the heuristic value of Palladas's testimony and particularly its confirmation of a stanchly anti-pagan Constantine. The epigram in question does not constitute a new class of evidence for these confiscations but rather another testimony to an already well-documented event. Moreover, it actually confirms the testimony of Eusebius that bronze images were moved to Constantinople and not placed in the melting pot.

8. *DRB* 2.2: *Cum enim antiquitus aurum argentumque et lapidum pretiosorum magna vis in templis reposita ad publicum pervenisset, cunctorum dandi habendique cupiditates accendit.*

9. Lib. *Or.* 30.6: εἰς μὲν τὴν τῆς πόλεως περὶ ἣν ἐσπούδασε ποίησιν τοῖς ἱεροῖς ἐχρήσατο χρήμασι; 30.37: ἀλλὰ τίς οὕτω μεγάλην τῶν περὶ τὰ ἱερὰ χρήματα δέδωκε δίκην τὰ μὲν αὐτὸς αὐτὸν μετιών.

10. Lib. *Or.* 62.8: ὁ μὲν γὰρ ἐγύμνωσε τοῦ πλούτου τοὺς θεούς. For the date, see Norman, pp. 87–88.

11. Robert, "Deux Concours," pp. 11–17; Frantz, pp. 76–77.

12. Ruf. *HE* 11.22; Soz. 7.15; Soc. 5.16; Theod. *HE* 5.23, with Haas, pp. 161–63; Hahn, *Gewalt*, pp. 89–101; "Gewaltanwendung," pp. 242–45.

13. Jul. *Ep.* 79.

14. See esp. Caseau; cf. Deligiannakis. See more on the survival of pagan cult images through the fourth century at Watts, *Final Pagan Generation*.

15. Millar, *Emperor*, pp. 158–74.

16. Lact. *Mort. Pers.* 48.7–12; Eus. *HE* 10.5.9–11; cf. Eus. *V. Const.* 2.20.1–21.1; 2.35.1–36.1. Calderone, *Costantino*, pp. 135–204, is especially useful on the confiscation and return of church property in this period.

17. Eus. *V. Const.* 3.65.1, 3, esp. [ἅπαντα] τὰ τῆς δεισιδαιμονίας ὑμῶν συνέδρια, πάντων φημὶ τῶν αἱρετικῶν τοὺς εὐκτηρίους . . . ἀφαιρεθέντας ἀναντιρρήτως τῇ καθολικῇ ἐκκλησίᾳ χωρίς τινος ὑπερθέσεως παραδοθῆναι, τοὺς δὲ λοιποὺς τόπους τοῖς δημοσίοις προσκριθῆναι. The situation was somewhat different in the spring of 317 when Constantine attempted to displace Donatists from their basilicas in Carthage and turn these over to Catholics, for he appears never to have intended to confiscate the buildings. Sources and discussion at Maier, *Dossier*, vol. 1, pp. 198–211 no. 28; cf. Gaddis, pp. 54–55.

18. See below pp. 238–39.

19. Eun. *V. Soph.* 6.1.5: Κωνσταντῖνος γὰρ ἐβασίλευε, τά τε τῶν ἱερῶν ἐπιφανέστατα καταστρέφων καὶ τὰ τῶν χριστιανῶν ἀνεγείρων οἰκήματα.

20. Eus. *V. Const.* 3.1.5: οἱ μὲν ἐτίμων ἀναθήμασι τοὺς δαίμονας, ὁ δὲ ἀπεγύμνου τὴν πλάνην, τὴν ἄχρηστον τῶν ἀναθημάτων ὕλην τοῖς χρῆσθαι δυνατοῖς διηνεκῶς νέμων.

21. Theoph. a.m. 5822: Τούτῳ τῷ ἔτει ἐπέτεινε Κωνσταντῖνος ὁ εὐσεβὴς τὴν κατὰ τῶν εἰδώλων καὶ τῶν ναῶν αὐτῶν κατάλυσιν, καὶ κατὰ τόπους ἠφανίζοντο· καὶ αἱ πρόσοδοι αὐτῶν ταῖς ἐκκλησίαις τοῦ θεοῦ ἀπεδίδοντο.

22. Jer. *Chron.* s.a. 331: *edicto Constantini gentilium templa subversa sunt*; cf. Oros. 7.28.28 and Burgess, *Studies*, p. 155 no. 14.

23. Jerome's date is probably preferable.

24. Lib. *Or.* 30.38; cf. *Or.* 17.7; Amm. 22.4.3.

25. Lib. *Or.* 18.126; cf. Philost. *HE* 4c.

26. Lib. *Ep.* 724 (Antioch); 763 and 819 (Arabia); 1364 (Phoenicia).

27. Preserved at *Hist. Aceph.* 3: *iubebatur reddi idolis et neochoris et publice rationi quae praeteritis temporibus illis ablata sunt*; cf. Soz. 5.3.1, 5.5; Zon. 13.12.

28. Jul. *Ep.* 115 (424C–D); cf. Soz. 5.5.5.

29. Delmaire, *Largesses sacrées*, pp. 641–45, makes a strong case that he did. See also Sánchez, which reaches a similar conclusion but with a less careful reading of the sources.

30. *CTh* 10.10.24 (Nov. 6, 405): *Pro inclyti principis Constantini sanctione, quam nos etiam hac lege roboramus, in his possessionibus, quae velut de patrimoniali vel rei publicae aut templorum aut cuiuslibet huiusmodi tituli iure subtractae a nostra liberalitate poscuntur, cesset penitus delatorum nomen infestum omnesque se ab hac nefaria petitione retineant.* See also *CTh* 10.10.32 (May 13, 425).

31. Lib. *Or.* 30.6: ἀλλ᾽ ἦν μὲν ἐν τοῖς ἱεροῖς πενία.

32. *CTh* 10.1.8 (Feb. 4, 364): *Universa loca vel praedia, quae nunc in iure templorum sunt quaeque a diversis principibus vendita vel donata sunt retracta, ei patrimonio, quod privatum nostrum est, placuit adgregari.* The heading of this law assigns it to Valentinian and Valens, but its date seems secure and implies Jovian. *CTh* 5.13.3 (Dec. 23, 364): *Universa, quae ex patrimonio nostro per arbitrium divae memoriae Iuliani in possessionem sunt translata templorum, sollicitudine sinceritatis tuae cum omni iure ad rem privatam nostram redire mandamus.* See also Lib. *Or.* 7.10: οἱ δὲ καὶ τεμένη τε καὶ νεὼς κτήματα ἑαυτῶν ἐποιήσαντο.

33. Soz. 5.3.1–5; cf. Jul. *Ep.* 84A (429C–D); Joh. Chrys. *De S. Bab.* 14 (*PG* 50: 554); Philost. *HE* 7.4c and below p. 177.

34. On Gratian's law, see Amb. *Ep.* 18.16 with *CTh* 16.10.20.1 (a. 415); cf. *CTh* 10.3.4 = *CJ* 11.59.6 + 11.66.4; Symm. *Rel.* 3.11, 15. Still in 380, Symm. *Ep.* 1.68 confirms that the pontifical college in Rome managed an estate called Vaga; Marc. Diac. *V. Porph.* 46, 54, claims that the Marneion of Gaza controlled revenue-producing land in the early fifth century; *Sirm.* 12 = *CTh* 16.10.19 orders the confiscation of temple revenues in Rome in 407; and *CTh* 16.10.20 orders the confiscation of estates still under temple control in North Africa in 415. See also Metzler, pp. 30–31.

35. Bransbourg, "Fiscalité impériale," is built on the assumption that the emperor had long allowed cities to get away with turning over only a fraction of the *vectigalia* demanded of them and that the assumed confiscations in fact represented more stringent enforcement of more realistic demands. See also Bransbourg, "Julien, l'*immunitas Christi*." *CTh* 4.13.5 (July 14, 358) certainly does imply the appropriation of civic *vectigalia* under a previous emperor (*divalibus iussis*), but this is a different matter than the confiscation of civic estates.

36. Soz. 1.8.10: ἐκ δὲ τῆς οὔσης ὑποφόρου γῆς καθ᾽ ἑκάστην πόλιν ἐξελὼν τοῦ δημοσίου ῥητὸν τέλος ταῖς κατὰ τόπον ἐκκλησίαις καὶ κλήροις ἀπένειμε καὶ τὴν δωρεὰν κυρίαν εἰς τὸν ἅπαντα χρόνον εἶναι ἐνομοθέτησε. Cf. Soz. 5.5.2–3; Theod. *HE* 1.11.2, together with Delmaire, pp. 645–57.

37. *IKEph* 42 = *AE* 1906: 30 = *FIRA* 1: 108, with Lenski, *Failure of Empire*, p. 295.

38. For sources and discussion, see Lepelley, *Les cités de l'Afrique*, vol. 1, pp. 99–101; Wiemer, *Libanios und Julian*, pp. 104–5; Schmidt-Hofner, "Die städtische Finanzautonomie," pp. 215–16. On the history of civic patrimony in the classical and Hellenistic Greek city, see now Migeotte, pp. 125–74.

39. Schmidt-Hofner, "Die städtische Finanzautonomie," argues that the confiscations applied only to temple property in civic hands, but the language of the evidence does not support this.

40. Debord, pp. 68–70, 185–214; Dignas, pp. 139–55; cf. Migeottes, pp. 360–81. For a good late antique example, see *CIL* 8: 25520 = *ILS* 9358 (a. 286/93), recording the restoration of *aedes publicae* using *pecunia publica*.

41. Lepelley, *Les cités de l'Afrique*, vol. 1, p. 345, catalogs African inscriptions recording public work on temples in the fourth century and notes a sharp drop in numbers after the reign of Diocletian.

42. *CTh* 10.3.1 (a. 362): *Post alia: possessiones publicas civitatibus iubemus restitui ita, ut iustis aestimationibus locentur, quo cunctarum possit civitatium reparatio procurari*; cf. *CTh* 15.1.10 (a. 362). For further evidence on Julian's restoration of revenues to the cities, see Amm. 25.4.15: *vectigalia civitatibus restituta cum fundis absque his, quos velut iure vendidere praeteritae potestates*; Lib. *Ep.* 828 (a. 363): κελεύει δέ, ὡς ἴσμεν, ὁ βασιλεὺς τὰς μὲν πόλεις τὰ αὑτῶν κομίζεσθαι, τὰ δ' ἐκείνῳ δοθέντα μένειν; Theod. *HE* 1.11.3. See also *CJ* 11.70.1 (an undated law of Julian), which orders those who have built structures on *solo rei publicae* to pay rent.

43. Lib. *Or.* 13.45–46, with Wiemer, *Libanios und Julian*, pp. 101–7. Wiemer is right to point out that Libanius would have made much more of Julian's restoration had Constantine's confiscation been comprehensive. His—limited but religiously inflected—reaction in this passage fits perfectly, however, with the case for a circumscribed and symbolically charged confiscation of revenues, as presented here.

44. *AE* 1969–1970: 631: *templorum/ [re]stauratori cu/r[ia]rum et rei public/ae recreatori*.

45. Eun. *V. Soph.* 10.8.2 (493).

46. Soz. 6.3.4 with 5.4.2–3; Theod. *HE* 4.4.1.

47. *IKEph* 42 = *AE* 1906: 30 = *FIRA* 1: 108 (a. 370). On the earthquake in Asia, see Lenski, *Failure of Empire*, p. 387.

48. The quota is first attested at *CTh* 4.13.7 and 15.1.18, both dated to 374. See also *CTh* 5.14.35; 15.1.32–33; and Delmaire, *Largesses sacrées*, pp. 653–57, with further sources.

49. This may be related to Zosimus's (2.38.4) complaint that Constantine's policies created a gradual decline in civic revenues; cf. Jul. *Or.* 1.42d–43a.

50. Soz. 1.8.10, cited above at p. 173 n. 36. Cf. 5.5.2–3; 6.3.4. More on Constantine's subventions to the clergy at Wipszycka; Liebeschuetz, pp. 167–68.

51. Theod. *HE* 1.11.2–3; cf. 3.6.5; 4.4.1. On what follows, see especially Brown, *Poverty and Leadership,* pp. 26–27, 45–73; cf. *Through the Eye of a Needle*, which explains brilliantly the way that bishops became redistributors of wealth at the civic level.

52. Athan. *Apol. c. Ar.* 18.2, quoted below at p. 176; *Chron. Pasch.* p. 545; Theoph. a.m. 5824, which reports that the widows and orphans of Antioch were allotted 36,000 *modii*.

53. Eus. *V. Const.* 4.28.1; cf. 1.42.3–43.1; *HE* 10.2.2.

54. Eus. *HE* 10.6.1–5. The letter calls Ursus τὸν διασημότατον καθολικὸν τῆς Ἀφρικῆς and Heracleides τοῦ ἐπιτρόπου τῶν ἡμετέρων κτημάτων; cf. *PLRE* 1: Heraclides 2; Ursus 2.

55. The *follis* is a term much abused and misunderstood, but in this instance it surely indicates the unit of account whose value is known to have been 12,500 denarii in 300 CE from *P. Beatty Panop.* 2 ll. 301–4, cf. Skeat, p. 152; Hendy, pp. 339–40. Three thousand folles thus equaled 37,500,000 den. Wheat prices are difficult to index because of price inflation in the early fourth century, but we have four prices from papyri around 313 that list the following prices in drachms/artaba: (1) *P. Cair. Isid.* 11.50 (a. 311) = 1,333 dr./art.; (2) *P. NYU* 18 (a. 312/313) = 2,000 dr./art.; (3) *CPR* 8: 22 (a. 314) = 2,000 dr./art.; (4) *P. Princ. Roll* 157 (a. 315) = 3,000 dr./art., collected at Bagnall, *Currency and Inflation*, p. 29. These average out to 2,083.25 dr./art. At the standard ¼ dr./den. rate, this would mean an average of 520.8125 den./art.; thus Constantine's subvention would have purchased 72,002.88 artabas/year. One artaba equaled 38.8 liters (Bagnall, "Practical Help," p. 187), which would have weighed about 29.56 kilograms. Constantine's subvention could thus have purchased about 2,128,405 kilograms of wheat per year. The

average person's caloric needs can be met with a maximum of 800 grams of wheat per day or 292 kilograms per year; Garnsey, p. 229. This meant that Constantine's subvention to Carthage could have paid to feed as many as 7,289 people per year.

56. On imperial *beneficia* in earlier periods, see Millar, *Emperor*, pp. 420–34. On grain rations, see Carrié.

57. Athan. *Apol. c. Ar.* 18.2, on which see Wipszycka, p. 486; Haas, pp. 250–51. Cf. Soc. 2.17.1; Soz. 3.9.5.

58. Athan. *Hist. Ar.* 10.3, 31.2, 63.1; cf. *Apol. c. Ar.* 18.4.

59. Jul. *Ep.* 84a (429C–D); Joh. Chrys. *de S. Bab.* 76 (*PG* 50:554); *Philost. HE* 7.4; Soz. 5.3.1, 5.2; 6.3.4; Theod. *HE* 1.11.3; 3.6.5; 4.4.1; cf. Jul. *ELF* no. 42. On Julian's public funding of priesthoods, see Athanassiadi, *Julian and Hellenism*, pp. 184–86; Bradbury, "Julian's Pagan Revival," pp. 347–55. Both Constantine and Julian can be said to have followed Maximinus Daia, who attempted similar measures in Asia Minor: Lact. *Mort. Pers.* 36.4–5, with Nicholson, "The 'Pagan Churches'"; Belayche, "La politique religieuse."

60. Theod. *HE* 1.11.3; cf. 4.4.1; Soz. 5.5.3; 6.3.4. The continuation of these *salaria* into the mid-fifth century would seem to be attested by *CJ* 1.2.12 (a. 451). See Delmaire, *Largesses sacrées*, pp. 649–50.

61. It is difficult to evaluate the veracity of the claim at Just. *Nov.* 59 praef. (a. 537) that Constantine endowed the church of Constantinople with tribute revenues from 980 workshops in Constantinople for the maintenance of a burial society. Justinian claims that the endowment was extended under Anastasius, and with this law he himself reforms its management. This may represent a later rewriting of the history of this endowment, but it may also reflect yet another manifestation of Constantine's use of former imperial revenues to benefit urban populations through the intermediacy of the church.

62. *DRB* 2.2. On Constantine's gold revolution, see Carlà, *L'oro*, pp. 78–156.

CHAPTER 9. BUILDING CHURCHES

1. More on pre-Constantinian church structures at Krautheimer, *Early Christian and Byzantine Architecture*, pp. 23–37; Bowes, pp. 65–71; MacMullen, *Second Church*, passim.

2. Lact. *Mort. Pers.* 12.2–5; Eus. *HE* 8.2.4; *Mart. Pal.* praef. 1.

3. For permission to rebuild, see Lact. *Mort. Pers.* 34.4; Eus. *HE* 8.17.1, 9; *Theophania* 3.2. For Eusebius's speech, see Eus. *HE* 10.4.2–72, with Barnes, *Constantine and Eusebius*, pp. 162–63; Klein, pp. 86–90. Amerise, "Note sulla datazione del panegirico," proposes a date of 314 for the speech, but 315 seems more likely. On the structure, see MacMullen, *Second Church*, pp. 11–12.

4. More on Constantine's program of church construction at Krautheimer, *Three Christian Capitals*; "Ecclesiastical Building Policy"; Klein; Leeb, pp. 71–121; Diefenbach; M. J. Johnson, "Architecture of Empire."

5. Eus. *V. Const.* 2.45.1: ὁ δὲ τῶν εὐκτηρίων οἴκων τὰς οἰκοδομὰς ὑψοῦν αὔξειν τε εἰς πλάτος καὶ μῆκος τὰς ἐκκλησίας τοῦ θεοῦ διαγορεύων, ὡσανεὶ μελλόντων τῷ θεῷ σχεδὸν εἰπεῖν ἁπάντων ἀνθρώπων τοῦ λοιποῦ προσοικειοῦσθαι τῆς πολυθέου μανίας ἐκποδὼν ἠρμένης· cf. *V. Const.* 1.42.2: ναὶ μὴν καὶ ταῖς ἐκκλησίαις τοῦ θεοῦ πλουσίας τὰς παρ' ἑαυτοῦ παρεῖχεν ἐπικουρίας, ἐπαύξων μὲν καὶ εἰς ὕψος αἴρων τοὺς εὐκτηρίους οἴκους, πλείστοις δ' ἀναθήμασι τὰ σεμνὰ τῶν τῆς ἐκκλησίας καθηγιασμένων φαιδρύνων.

6. Eus. *LC* 9.12–13: τούτῳ τὸ πάντων ἀγαθῶν τέλος οἷόν τι χρέος βασιλεὺς ἀποδιδοὺς ἁπανταχοῦ γῆς στήλας ἐπινικίους ἱδρύετο, πλουσίᾳ καὶ βασιλικῇ χειρὶ νεώς τε καὶ τεμένη ἱερά τε προσευκτήρια συνίστασθαι τοῖς πᾶσι διακελευόμενος. ὑψοῦτο δὲ παραχρῆμα μέσαις αὐταῖς

ἐπαρχίαις τε καὶ πόλεσι βασιλικῆς μεγαλονοίας μεγαλουργήματα, ἐν ὀλίγῳ τε ταῦτα κατὰ πᾶν ἔθνος διέλαμπεν, ἀθέου τυραννίδος τὸν ἔλεγχον ἐφελκόμενα. Cf. *LC* 9.14–19; 11.5; 17.4–5.

7. Eus. *V. Const.* 2.46.3, esp. αἰτήσεις δὲ καὶ αὐτὸς καὶ διὰ σοῦ οἱ λοιποὶ τὰ ἀναγκαῖα παρά τε τῶν ἡγεμονευόντων καὶ τῆς ἐπαρχικῆς τάξεως. See also *V. Const.* 2.45.2; 3.29.1–2.

8. According to Jer. *Chron.* s.a. 336: *Eustathius Constantinopolitanus presbyter agnoscitur, cuius industria in Hierosolymis martyrium constructum est.* Jerome's notice would seem to be contradicted by Philost. *App.* 7: 13a = Theoph. a.m. 5828 (a. 335/336), which also mentions Eustathius as a presbyter in Constantinople but credits construction of the Martyrium in Jerusalem to one Zenobius, acting on Constantine's orders. It is difficult to reconcile these sources, although they do indicate some degree of—perhaps considerable—imperial involvement. This does not contradict the picture presented here. Macarius surely played a major role in dictating the terms of the commission—as Constantine's letter indicates—but received expert help with its design and implementation, which, like materials and manpower, was supplied by Constantine.

9. The date is uncertain but may well be after Constantine's death.

10. *Lib. Pont.* 34.9–15 (Duchesne, vol. 1, pp. 172–75 = Geertman, pp. 291–95); cf. Davis, *Book of the Pontiffs,* pp. 16–19. More on the Constantinian churches of Rome at Krautheimer, Corbett, and Frazer; Krautheimer, *Three Christian Capitals,* pp. 6–40; Brandenburg, *Roms Frühchristliche Basiliken*; Holloway, pp. 57–119; MacMullen, *Second Church,* pp. 76–89.

11. For the property over which the church was constructed, see Krautheimer, "Ecclesiastical Building," p. 530; Curran, *Pagan City,* pp. 93–96. For Pope Miltiades' use of the *Domus Faustae* in 313, see Opt. 1.23: *convenerunt in domum Faustae in Laterano.* For the architectural remains, see Scrinari, *Il Laterano Imperiale I*; *Il Laterano Imperiale II.* For the mural decoration, see McFadden.

12. Krautheimer, Corbett, and Frazer, vol. 5, p. 90; Krautheimer, *Three Christian Capitals,* pp. 15–20; Curran, *Pagan City,* pp. 94–95.

13. Bauer, *Das Bild der Stadt,* pp. 27–38; Davis, *Book of the Pontiffs,* pp. xxix–xxxvi. Vera, "Osservazioni economiche," points out that, although the list as currently edited dates after 383/384, most of the material on Constantinian churches reflects the situation at the end of Constantine's reign; cf. Maiuro. The skepticism of Logan, "Constantine, the *Liber Pontificalis,*" is largely unfounded.

14. For the Ostia church, see Bauer and Heinzelmann, "Constantinian Bishop's Church"; cf. Meiggs, pp. 264–65. For the via Ardeatina church, see Fiocchi Nicolai; Holloway, pp. 110–11.

15. See Barnes, *Dynasty, Religion and Power,* pp. 88–89, who seems unaware of Brandenburg, "Die Architektur"; cf. Diefenbach, pp. 72–73.

16. Bowersock, "Peter and Constantine"; Liverani, "La basilica costantiniana di S. Pietro"; "L'architettura costantiniana," 238–42; "Saint Peter's." More on the Constantinian structure at Krautheimer, Corbett, and Frazer, vol. 5, pp. 165–279. Westall has recently elaborated on Bowersock's argument in greater detail, but the argument still cannot explain away the evidence of the arch inscription at *ICUR* 2: 4092 = *ILCV* 1752.

17. Pietri, *Roma Christiana,* pp. 79–83, calculates the size of the estates based on their revenues. The number rises to 4,350 pounds if we accept the *Titulus Silvestri* as authentically Constantinian, which most do not.

18. *IK Ephesus* 42 = *AE* 1906: 30 = *FIRA* 1: 108 (a. 370) line 15; cf. Lenski, *Failure of Empire,* pp. 295–96.

19. Krautheimer, Corbett, and Frazer, vol. 2 pp. 1–151; Holloway, pp. 110–11.

20. For the cemetery of the *Equites singulares,* see Guyon, pp. 30–33. For the donation of Helena's estates, see *Lib. Pont.* 34.27 (Duchesne, vol. 1 p. 183 = Geertman, p. 303): *Fundum Larentum . . . possessio Augustae Helenae.* See also Rasch; Curran, *Pagan City,* pp. 99–102; Holloway, pp. 86–93. The church known as Hierusalem, built to house a relic of the True Cross, was also located on imperial property—in the Sessorian Palace; cf. Krautheimer, Corbett, and

Frazer, vol. 1, pp. 165–95; Blaauw. Krautheimer, "Ecclesiastical Building," pp. 534–35, also catalogs evidence from the *Liber Pontificalis* for connections between the landed endowments granted to these churches and former properties of the imperial *res privata*.

21. *Lib. Pont.* 34.16 (S. Pietro: Duchesne, vol. 1 p. 176 = Geertman, p. 295): *ex rogatu Silvestri episcopi*; 34.21 (S. Paul: Duchesne, vol. 1 pp. 178–79 = Geertman, pp. 298–99): *ex suggestione Silvestri episcopi*; 34.28 (Ostia: Duchesne, vol. 1 pp. 183–84 = Geertman, p. 304): *ex suggestione* [sic] *Silvestri episcopi*; 35.3 (Basilica Ardeatina: Duchesne, vol. 1 p. 202 = Geertman, p. 309): *ex huius [Marci] suggestione*. The notices on San Pietro and Ostia appear only in class E manuscripts; cf. Krautheimer, "Ecclesiastical Building," pp. 524–25.

22. *Lib. Pont.* 34.23 (S. Agnese: Duchesne, vol. 1 pp. 180–81 = Geertman, p. 300): *ex rogatu filiae suae*.

23. *ICUR* 8: 20752 = *ILCV* 1768 = *CLE* 301. Rasch and Arbeiter, *Mausoleum der Constantina in Rom*, pp. 6, 87, argue for a date between 337 and 351 based on what little we know about the movements of Constantina. This is by no means proven or even necessary, for Constantina was made Augusta already by her father (Philost. *HE* 2.22, 28) and would surely have accompanied him to Rome on his vicennalian visit in 326, when she might have initiated the construction; cf. *PLRE* 1: Constantina 2. See also Kleinbauer, pp. 131–38, which veers far from the written and epigraphic sources.

24. Krautheimer, "Ecclesiastical Building," pp. 522–23, 540–43, reaches the same conclusion. See also Liverani, "L'architettura costantiniana"; "I vescovi nell'edilizia pubblica" for the development of this process in Late Antiquity.

25. MacMullen, *Second Church*, pp. 117–41, offers an extensive, if not exhaustive, catalog of fourth-century churches, including those of Constantine.

26. Eus. *V. Const.* 3.50.1. On the church's destruction, see Lact. *Mort. Pers.* 12.5.

27. Eus. *V. Const.* 3.50.2; *LC* 9.15. The basilica was not dedicated until 341 or 342, under Constantius II: Jer. *Chron.* s.a. 342; Joh. Mal. 13.3–4, 18 (Dindorf, pp. 318–19, 326 = Thurn, pp. 244–45, 250); Theoph. a.m. 5833; *Chron. 724* (ed. and trans. Brooks and Chabot, *CSCO SS*, 3: 129 [text] = 4: 101 [trans.]); with Burgess, *Studies*, p. 158 no. 30. Kleinbauer, pp. 127–28, argues that Constantius II was responsible for the design of the church, but Jer. *Chron.* s.a. 327 reports that construction began in 327, and Eusebius *LC* 9.15 indicates that it was nearly complete already in 336 while Constantine was still alive. Joh. Mal. 13.18 (Dindorf, p. 326 = Thurn, p. 250) purports to record the building inscription, which indicates that design details were in fact left to the *cubicularius* Gorgonius. More likely the "Golden Octagon" represents yet another example of the implementation of architectural decisions taken at the local level. Further bibliography at MacMullen, *Second Church*, p. 118.

28. Sources at Downey, pp. 342–45, 358–59; Mayer and Allen, pp. 68–80. Discussion at Saliou. See also Leeb, pp. 76–82, on Constantine's tendency to collocate churches near the palace in imperial capitals.

29. Mladenova, Boiadzhiev, and Dinova-Ruseva, pp. 22–3; Ćurčić, p. 67.

30. For the imperial constructions in Trier, see Goethert and Kiessel, which emphasizes that many of these structures were only completed later in the fourth century.

31. Krautheimer, *Early Christian and Byzantine Architecture*, pp. 48–50; Heinen, pp. 103–17. On double churches, see Esmonde Cleary, pp. 157–59.

32. Athan. *Ap. Const.* 15.4 (Athanasius *Werke* 2.8: 290–91).

33. *ILCV* 1863 = *AE* 1986: 243: *Theodore feli[x]/ [a]diuvante deo/ omnipotente et/ poemnio caelitus tibi/ [tra]ditum[sic] omnia/ b{a}eate fecisti et/ gloriose dedicas/ ti*; cf. Iacumin, pp. 25–29; Steuernagel, pp. 143–44; Pelizzari, pp. 118–20; Bratož, pp. 20–27; Cuscito.

34. *Conc. Arel. Subscriptiones* (*CCSL* 148: 14 l.17 = Mansi 2: 476). Bratož, pp. 20–32, argues that, even if the inscription was posthumous, the Basilica Theodoriana is likely to have been of

Constantinian date given that it was already being replaced by the new—much larger basilica—in the early 340s. He would therefore venture a date of circa 320 for its construction.

35. On the structure, see Krautheimer, *Early Christian and Byzantine Architecture*, p. 43; Menis; Iacumin; Pelizzari, pp. 25–57.

36. Pelizzari, passim.

37. Note that this church is not listed in the *Liber Pontificalis*, although it is widely agreed to have been Constantinian; cf. Logan, "Constantine, the *Liber Pontificalis*," p. 40, with sources and bibliography.

38. Brandenburg, *Roms Frühchristliche Basiliken*, pp. 61–120; M. J. Johnson, "Architecture of Empire," pp. 288–89; Diefenbach, pp. 70–78. On the liturgical and hermeneutic function of these churches, often referred to in English as "deambulatory," see Yasin, pp. 157–61.

39. Eus. *V. Const.* 3.25.1–42.4; *LC* 11–19; cf. 9.16–18. More on Constantine's building program in Palestine at Leeb; J. E. Taylor, *Christians and the Holy Places*, pp. 110–12; Bloedhorn; Hunt, "Constantine and Jerusalem"; J. Wilkinson, *Egeria's Travels*, pp. 11–16; M. J. Johnson, "Architecture of Empire," pp. 293–95.

40. Eus. *V. Const.* 3.41.1–43.5, esp. 43.2–4; cf. 44.1. *Itin. Burd.* 594–95, 598–99 (*CCSL* 175: 17–18, 20) claims that all of the Constantinian churches in the Holy Land, including the Holy Sepulcher, Eleona, the Church of the Nativity, and the church at Mamre, were built *iussu Constantini*. This is clearly formulaic and should not be taken to supersede the circumstantial evidence of Eusebius that the original initiative for three of these four structures came from empresses; see Lenski, "Empresses."

41. Walker, pp. 171–98.

42. Eus. *V. Const.* 4.46.1; cf. *LC* 9.16; Soz. 2.26.3.

43. See Aleksova.

44. *CIL* 8: 9708 = *ILCV* 1821: *Pro(vinciae)/ CCLXXX et V XII Kal(endas)/ Dec(embres) eius basilicae/ fundamenta posita/ sunt et fa[. . .]ma/ pro(vinciae) CCLXX [. . .] in/ mente habeas [. . .]m/ servum dei [. . . i]n/ deo vivas.* On the architecture, see Krautheimer, *Early Christian and Byzantine Architecture*, pp. 43–44; Gui, Duval, and Caillet, pp. 11, 14. One could exclude *CIL* 8: 21517 = *ILCV* 2071, from discussion. It records the erection of a *memoria* at modern Mediouna in Algeria to a group of martyrs killed in fighting over the Donatist schism in 330 but clearly states that the parents of the victims were the dedicants.

45. Eus. *V. Const.* 2.45.1, quoted above at p. 180.

46. *In mente habeas [. . .]m/ servum dei.* The same church yielded another dedication (*CIL* 8: 9709 = *ILCV* 1105) to a certain Reparatus, a priest there commemorated in 475 CE. This has led to the false assumption that he was the church's chief dedicant.

47. Mitchell, "Cities of Asia Minor," p. 67; *History of the Later Roman Empire*, pp. 335–36.

48. Calder, *Monumenta Asiae Minoris Antiqua*, vol. 1, pp. xviii–xxii.

49. *MAMA* 1: 170 = *ILS* 9480 = Tabbernee, no. 69; cf. *MAMA* 1: 171. See *PLRE* 1: M. Iul. Eugenius 7; Rapp, *Holy Bishops*, pp. 203–7.

50. These included προῖκα, δία ἰδίαις δαπάναις, ἐκ τῶν ἰδίων; cf. the Latin *de sua pecunia, sumptibus suis.* See also McLean, p. 266. This is not to deny that bishops often did fund building projects from their own wealth; cf. Liebeschuetz, pp. 148–49.

51. Eus. *V. Const.* 3.31.3–32.1; cf. 3.53.2.

52. Note that here too, Julian attempted to put this process in reverse with *CTh* 15.1.3 (June 29, 362, with Seeck *RG* 93), which put temple construction ahead of all other building priorities in the cities of the province.

53. On the Romanization of city centers in the East through the coordination of civic buildings around *agorai*, see Gros. On *capitolia*, see now Quinn and Wilson, which demonstrates that, although common, these were by no means a universal feature of Roman cityscapes.

CHAPTER 10. EMPOWERING BISHOPS

1. On the rise of the bishop as the most powerful leader in the fourth-century urban environment, see the excellent work of Liebeschuetz, pp. 137–68; Rapp, *Holy Bishops*. For what follows, I have benefitted greatly from an advance reading of Lizzi Testa, "Costantino."

2. *Constitutiones Apostolorum* 2.45.1–46.1 (*SCh* 320: 284–86).

3. Cimma; Huck, "À propos de *CTh* 1, 27"; "La 'création' de l'*audientia episcopalis*"; Rapp, *Holy Bishops*, pp. 242–52; Delmaire and Rougé, *Lois religieuses*, vol. 2, pp. 541–46; Dillon, pp. 146–55.

4. Humfress, *Orthodoxy and the Courts*, pp. 153–73; "Bishops and Law Courts in Late Antiquity"; cf. Harries, *Imperial Rome*, pp. 161–62.

5. On the dating, a matter of dispute, Seeck *RG* 57 is most convincing.

6. On these issues, see Matthews, *Laying Down the Law*, passim, esp. pp. 55–120; cf. Sirks, pp. 79–86.

7. Dillon, pp. 153; see already Gaudemet, p. 241. On the *iudex vice Caesaris*, see Peachin.

8. On the authenticity of both laws, which have often been questioned, see Huck, "À propos de *CTh* 1, 27." On the authenticity of the *Sirmondian Constitutions*, see Huck, "Encore à propos des *Sirmondiennes*"; cf. Vessey.

9. *Sirm.* 1: *sicut edicti nostri forma declarat. . . . Hoc nos edicto salubri aliquando censuimus*; cf. *olim promulgatae legis ordinem. . . . Quidquid itaque de sententiis episcoporum clementia nostra censuerat et iam hac sumus lege conplexi.* Huck, "La 'création' de l'*audientia episcopalis*," pp. 302–4, agrees that *edictum* refers to a different law than *CTh* 1.27.1, but he would date it later than 318. This assumption is built largely on the patchy nature of *CTh* 1.27.1, but, as noted, we may have only a fragment of the original constitution. In the absence of further evidence, the issue cannot be resolved.

10. This remained the case in the future with bishops' judgments: *CTh* 1.27.2 (a. 408): *a quibus non licet provocare.*

11. *Sirm.* 1: *etiamsi alia pars refragatur.*

12. *Sirm.* 1: *apud vos, qui iudiciorum summam tenetis, et apud ceteros omnes iudices ad exsecutionem volumus pertinere.* Cf. *CTh* 1.27.2 (a. 408): *Per publicum quoque officium, ne sit cassa cognitio, definitioni exsecutio tribuatur.*

13. Sozomen (1.9.5), who was himself a lawyer and whose copy of the *Code* was—unlike ours—complete, reports on *audientia episcopalis* in precisely the same terms.

14. See esp. *Dig.* 4.8 with Roebuck and de Loynes de Fumichon, pp. 182–92; cf. Gagos and van Minnen; and Harries, *Law and Empire*, pp. 172–90.

15. Dillon, pp. 153–55, is right to argue that the motives for the creation of *episcopale iudicium* were connected to Constantine's larger efforts to render access to the courts cheaper and more manageable for the underprivileged; cf. Drake, *Constantine and the Bishops*, pp. 326–27; Huck, "La 'création' de l'*audientia episcopalis*," pp. 310–12, with special reference to *CTh* 1.16.7.

16. See Gaudemet, p. 233: "Trop vite et trop loin."

17. See Lamoreaux; Lenski, "Evidence for the *Audientia Episcopalis*."

18. For the argument that follows, see Harries, *Law and Empire*, pp. 196–203.

19. Jul. *Ep.* 114 (437A). Ironically, in some sense, Constantine had been anticipated in this policy by Maximinus Daia, for Maximinus's newly created civic high priests had been given juridical authority to arrest Christians who refused to sacrifice and turn them over to the magistrates; Lact. *Mort. Pers.* 36.4–5; cf. Eus. *HE* 8.14.8–9; 9.4.2–3 with Nicholson, "The 'Pagan Churches.'"

20. *Nov. Val.* 35 (a. 452). *CTh* 16.11.1 (a. 399) already implies severe limitations on episcopal jurisdiction; cf. Banfi, pp. 183–257.

21. See esp. *Sirm.* 1: *illud est enim veritatis auctoritate firmatum, illud incorruptum, quod a sacrosancto homine conscientia mentis illibatae protulerit.*

22. See especially Uhalde.

23. *CJ* 1.13.1. More on *manumissio in ecclesia* at Lenski, "Constantine and Slavery," with earlier bibliography, esp. Fabbrini.

24. *Iam dudum placuit, ut in ecclesia catholica libertatem domini suis famulis praestare possint, si sub adspectu plebis adsistentibus christianorum antistitibus id faciant.*

25. *CTh* 4.7.1 = *CJ* 1.13.2 (Apr. 18, 321).

26. Soz. 1.9.6–7. As noted above at n. 13, Sozomen had access to a full copy of the *Theodosian Code,* in contrast with the version now available to us, in which the relevant titles are fragmentary.

27. A. Kolb, *Transport*; Schmidt-Hofner, *Reagieren und Gestalten*, pp. 163–78.

28. *CTh* 10.5.1–5.

29. Eus. *HE* 10.5.23.

30. Opt. *App.* 3, 8 (*CSEL* 26: 205–6, 212).

31. Eus. *V. Const.* 3.6.1.

32. Eus. *V. Const.* 4.36.4, 43.2.

33. For Arius, see Soc. 1.25.8; cf. Opitz *Urkunde* 29 p. 63 = Brennecke *Dokument* 33 p. 120. For John Arkaph, see Athan. *Apol. c. Arian.* 70.2.

34. Amm. 21.16.18: *rei vehiculariae succideret nervos*; cf. Theod. *HE* 2.16.17. Julian's laws include *CTh* 8.5.12–16, esp. 8.5.12 (Feb. 22, 362): *Quoniam cursum publicum fatigavit quorundam inmoderata praesumptio et evectionum frequentia.* More on late fourth-century limitations at A. Kolb, *Transport,* pp. 87–92.

35. On the date, see Seeck *RG* 51. More on clerical immunity at Elliott, "Tax Exemptions"; Lepelley, *Les cités de l'Afrique,* vol. 1, pp. 279–86; De Giovanni, *Costantino e il mondo pagano,* pp. 60–66; Laniado, *Recherches,* pp. 49–51.

36. Eus. *HE* 10.7.2: διόπερ ἐκείνους . . . τὴν ἐξ αὐτῶν ὑπηρεσίαν τῇ ἁγίᾳ ταύτῃ θρησκείᾳ παρέχοντας, οὕσπερ κληρικοὺς ἐπονομάζειν εἰώθασιν, ἀπὸ πάντων ἅπαξ ἁπλῶς τῶν λειτουργιῶν βούλομαι ἀλειτουργήτους διαφυλαχθῆναι, ὅπως μὴ διά τινος πλάνης ἢ ἐξολισθήσεως ἱεροσύλου ἀπὸ τῆς θεραπείας τῆς τῇ θειότητι ὀφειλομένης ἀφέλκωνται, ἀλλὰ μᾶλλον ἄνευ τινὸς ἐνοχλήσεως τῷ ἰδίῳ νόμῳ ἐξυπηρετῶνται.

37. *CTh* 16.2.2 (Oct. 21, 313): *Qui divino cultui ministeria religionis impendunt, id est hi, qui clerici appellantur, ab omnibus omnino muneribus excusentur, ne sacrilego livore quorundam a divinis obsequiis avocentur.*

38. So already Godefroy, ad loc.; Seeck *RG* 51; Corcoran, *Empire of the Tetrarchs,* pp. 155–57, 162. On edicts as *epistulae*, see Corcoran, *Empire of the Tetrarchs,* pp. 198–203. This parallel gives further support against those who would impugn the credibility of documents preserved by Eusebius.

39. Girardet, *Konstantinische Wende*, p. 149, is right to counter those who charge that Constantine was simply extending the right long granted to imperial cult priests to Christian clergy. As he demonstrates, immunity was granted to priests of the imperial cult for brief tenures of office (usually one year) but to Christian clergy for life. On the tenure of priests of the imperial cult, see Frija, chapter 2.

40. This was part of a larger trend of exempting whole classes of privileged individuals from curial service, which was itself part of a larger trend toward the disappearance of curial governance altogether, on both of which see Liebeschuetz, pp. 104–36; Laniado, "From Municipal Councillors." Indeed, Constantine even granted limited immunities to benefit curial and provincial priests of the imperial cult (*flamines* and *sacerdotes*); cf. *CTh* 12.1.21 (Aug. 4, 335) and *CTh* 12.3.2 (May 21, 337) and above pp. 141–42. It is doubtful whether Constantine granted tax immunity to Catholic churches. This is nowhere explicitly attested but is implied at *CTh* 11.1.1 =

CJ 10.16.4, dated to June 17, 315, by the Theodosian compilers, but already Mommsen saw that it is more properly dated to 360; cf. Seeck *RG* 44, 207.

41. *Conc. Elib.* can. 2–4. On the date of the council, a matter of dispute, see Sotomayor.

42. *Conc. Elib.* can. 55: *Sacerdotes, qui tantum coronas portant nec sacrificant nec de suis sumptibus aliquid ad idola praestant, placuit post biennium accipere communionem.*

43. *Conc. Elib.* can. 56. Note also that the Council of Arles decreed that provincial governors (*praesides*) who were Christian were allowed to receive letters of communion for their province but were then to be observed by the bishop in that province and promptly excommunicated if they violated Christian precepts; *Conc. Arel.* can. 7 (*CCSL* 148: 6, 10 = Mansi 2: 471–72).

44. Similar concerns were at play in Constantine's grant of exemption to Jewish religious leaders. In the West, most Jews were required to serve, but "two or three each" per city were exempted, presumably rabbinical leaders, *CTh* 16.8.3 with Linder, pp. 120–24. In the East, "those devoted to synagogues," patriarchs, and "priests" (*presbyteris*, perhaps members of the Palestinian Sanhedrin) were exempted from curial service unless they came from families with prior curial obligations, in which case they were exempt only from *angariae* because "it was inappropriate that men of this sort be compelled to depart from the places in which they reside," *CTh* 16.8.2, 4, with Linder, pp. 134–38 no. 9 and Applebaum, pp. 126-32, citing earlier bibliography. Clearly Constantine's concern was that members of the Jewish rabbinical and priestly class not be required to violate their religious laws.

45. Chastagnol and Duval, "Survivances du culte impérial"; Lepelley, *Les cités de l'Afrique*, vol. 1, pp. 165–67, 293–303, 357–69; "De la réaction païenne"; Clover; Goddard, pp. 1049–79; Leone, pp. 87–95. *Symm. Ep.* 1.3.4 reports that the majority of councilors (*optimates*) in Beneventum were still pagan in 375.

46. *CTh* 16.2.5 (Dec. 25, 323).

47. Seeck *RG* 98–99, 173. For Licinius's forced enrollment of clergy in *curiae*, see Eus. *V. Const.* 2.20.2, 30.1.

48. This may also explain why Constantine was eager to free from curial duties Christians who had been forcibly enrolled into councils during the Great Persecution; Eus. *V. Const.* 2.20.2, 30.1.

49. Aug. *Ep.* 88.2 (*CSEL* 34: 408) = Maier, *Dossier*, vol. 1, p. 145 no. 14.

50. *CTh* 16.2.1; cf. Maier, *Dossier*, vol. 1, pp. 245–46 no. 32.

51. *CTh* 16.5.1 = *CJ* 1.5.1.

52. *CTh* 16.2.7 (Feb. 5, 330); Opt. *App.* 10.36b (*CSEL* 26: 215).

53. *CTh* 16.2.6.

54. *CTh* 16.2.3, with Seeck *RG* 179 on the date.

55. *CTh* 16.2.8–11, 13–16; cf. De Giovanni, *Chiesa e stato*, pp. 61–64; Rapp, *Holy Bishops*, pp. 282–89. Nevertheless, see also the restrictions imposed by Constantius II in 361 at *CTh* 12.1.49.

56. *CTh* 12.1.50 = 13.1.4 (Mar. 13, 363); Jul. *Ep.* 54; Philost *HE.* 7.4; Soz. 5.5.2; Theod. *HE* 3.6.5; cf. Lib. *Or.* 18.146–48; Amm. 25.4.21; cf. Laniado, *Recherches*, p. 12.

57. *CIL* 8: 2403 = 17824 = *ILS* 6122 col. 5: 13–24, with Chastagnol, *L'album Municipal*, pp. 37–39.

58. *CTh* 16.2.17–24. Note that restrictions and regulations continued to be added; cf. *CTh* 7.20.12 (a. 400); 12.1.59 (a. 364); 12.1.99 (a. 383); 12.1.104 (a. 383); 12.1.123 (a. 391); 12.1.163 (a. 399); 12.1.172 (a. 410); 14.3.11 (a. 364); 14.4.8 (a. 408).

59. According to Libanius, the council of Antioch went from six hundred members before the arrival of Constantine to just sixty under Theodosius I, Lib. *Or.* 2.33; 48.3; cf. 49.8; cf. Laniado, *Recherches*, pp. 3–26.

60. More on Julian's pro curial policies at Bonamente, "Le città"; Pack.

61. By the late fifth century, Zeno (474–491) could rule at *CJ* 1.2.25 that every *polis* was required to have its own bishop. The bishop had, in other words, become indispensable to civic identity.

CHAPTER 11. ENGAGING CITIES

1. For an excellent late fourth-century example, see the *Feriale Campanum* inscription of Capua from 387, *CIL* 10: 3792 = *ILS* 4918 with Trout.

2. Frantz, pp. 16–18; Watts, *City and School*, pp. 79–110.

3. Jul. *Or.* 1.7D–8D.

4. *FGH* 2B no. 219 = Phot. *Bibl.* 62; cf. Bleckmann, "Zwischen Panegyrik und Geschichts-schreibung."

5. R. B. E. Smith, "A Lost Historian."

6. *OGIS* 720–21 = *CIG* 4770 = *SEG* 37: 1650; cf. G. Fowden, "Nicagoras of Athens."

7. *IG* 4²: 428–31, with Clinton, p. 66. Nicagoras's family influence continued well into the fourth century; cf. Heath; Watts, *City and School*, p. 44.

8. It should be noted that Constantine may simply have been upholding or renewing a grant of annual grain subsidies extended to Athens from as early as the reign of Hadrian; Dio Cass. 69.16.2 with Boatwright, p. 92. On the other hand, he may also have been restoring or protecting Athens's grain supply in the wake of arrangements made to provision his new capital of Constantinople; see Tantillo, *La prima orazione*, pp. 187–89.

9. *IG* 2/3.5: 13269–72 = *AE* 2001: 1827–30 and *AE* 2001: 1831, with Sironen, pp. 257–64.

10. The primary duty of this officer was the regulation of the food supply, highlighting the quid pro quo relationship between this grant and Constantine's provision of grain; see Philostr. *V. Soph.* 1.23 (526). Constans later guaranteed the provision by granting Athens grain rations derived from the revenues of several Greek islands; Eun. *V. Soph.* 10.7.5-8 (492).

11. An early example of this comes in an inscription of Saepinum (Sepino) in southern Italy dated to 312 that honors Constantine as "born of the gods" (*dis genito*), *AE* 1984: 367. As Van Dam, *Roman Revolution*, pp. 250–51, points out, this was very much in keeping with rhetoric familiar from the tetrarchs. It can also be recovered from the public message-making of Aurelian, cf. Salzman, "Aurelian."

12. *SEG* 47: 1770 = *AE* 1997: 1493 = Waelkens and Poblome, pp. 310–13 no. 6.

13. On the term, see Friesen.

14. See Price, *Rituals and Power*; Friesen, pp. 142–68.

15. *TAM* 3.1: 45 = *AE* 2003: 1768 = *SEG* 53: 1612: Κωνσταντείνῳ Σεβ(αστῷ)/ Ἡλίῳ παντεπόπτῃ/ὁ δῆμος.

16. Tantillo, "Costantino e Helios," esp. 168–72, referencing *TAM* 3.1: 101, 132.

17. Aulock, *Sylloge*, vol. 12: no. 5355, pl. 117.

18. Eus. *LC* 3.4: ὁμοῦ τὴν σύμπασαν ὅσην ἥλιος ἐφορᾷ διϊππεύων, αὐτός τε τοῖς πᾶσιν ἐπιπαρὼν καὶ τὰ πάντα διασκοπούμενος.

19. *Or. ad Sanct.* 6.4: ἀεὶ παρεῖναι ἡμῖν τὸν ἐπόπτην τῶν πρασσομένων θεόν; 12.4: πρὸς τὸν πάντων ἐπόπτην ἔπαινος.

20. Eus. *V. Const.* 3.17.2: ἄχρις οὗ ἡ τῷ πάντων ἐφόρῳ θεῷ ἀρέσκουσα γνώμη πρὸς τὴν τῆς ἑνότητος συμφωνίαν εἰς φῶς προήχθη.

21. Athan. *Apol. c. Ar.* 86.7: μαρτυρεῖ μοι γὰρ ὁ πάντων ἔφορος θεός.

22. Weir, pp. 95–97; Laurence, pp. 161–63.

23. *SIG*³ 901 with important corrections at Bousquet. The written notice corresponds well with archaeological data indicating a major restoration at around this date; cf. Ginouvès.

24. Eus. *V. Const.* 2.50.1–51.2. Further references to these prophecies at Eus. *HE* 9.2.1–3.1; *Pr. Ev.* 4.2.10–11; Lact. *Mort. Pers.* 10.3–5, 11.7–8; *Div. Inst.* 4.27.4–5. Rehm, no. 306 = Fontenrose, *Delphic Oracle*, p. 425 no. D 34, is often cited as an epigraphic attestation of the oracle mentioned at Lact. *Mort. Pers.* 11.7–8, but it is too fragmentary to support this claim.

25. Thus Digeser, "Oracle of Apollo," building especially on Gelasius Caesariensis fr. 3 (cited from Hansen, *Theodoros Anagnostes*, p. 158); cf. Digeser, *Threat to Public Piety*, pp. 179–86. Her careful assessment supersedes previous, and indeed some subsequent, discussions— that is, Barnes, *Dynasty, Religion and Power*, p. 129. On the Didyma response, see sources and discussion at Fontenrose, *Didyma*, pp. 206–8 no. 33.

26. Eus. *HE* 9.11.5–6; *Pr. Ev.* 4.2.11.

27. Athanassiadi, "Fate of Oracles."

28. *Or. ad Sanct.* 18–19; *Ep. ad Arium* 18–19 (Opitz *Urkunde* 34 p. 71 = Brennecke *Dokument* 27 p. 112).

29. See above p. 49.

30. Eus. *V. Const.* 3.54.2; Zos. 2.31.1; Soc. 1.16.3; cf. Bassett, pp. 224–27 and nos. 141, 230–31.

31. See also the care taken over the statue of Theophanes of Mytilene, which was displayed in Constantinople's hippodrome with its original base proclaiming Theophanes a god, at Robert, "Théophane de Mytilène"; cf. Ma, "Traveling Statues."

32. On Delphi, see Athanassiadi, "Fate of Oracles," pp. 274–77; cf. Lenski, *Failure of Empire*, p. 217. On Didyma, see Fontenrose, *Didyma*, pp. 25, 227–28; Athanassiadi, "Fate of Oracles," p. 274, with special reference to Jul. *Ep.* 88 (451A) and 89B (298A), which indicate ongoing prophecy, albeit in defense of the shrine against threats; cf. Soz. 5.20.7. On Daphne, see Lieu, *Emperor Julian*, pp. 44–54.

33. On Didyma, see Soz. 5.20.7, with Parke, pp. 94–96; Athanassiadi, "Fate of Oracles," pp. 272–74. On Daphne, see the sources collected at Downey, p. 364; Lieu, *Emperor Julian*. This fact undermines the case at Lane Fox, pp. 671–72, that Constantine targeted Didyma and Aegeae for destruction because of the role both played in provoking the Great Persecution. Didyma, which did play such a role, was not targeted, while Aegeae, which is not known to have, was.

34. Athanassiadi, "Fate of Oracles," p. 276.

35. *CTh* 16.10.2. The date of the inscription can be derived from the prefectures of *PLRE* 1: Antonius Marcellinus 16 (PPO Italiae 340–341), Fl. Domitius Leontius 30 (PPO Orientis 340–344), and Fabius Titianus 6 (PPO Galliae 341–349). On the last, a firmly attested pagan, see below p. 224.

36. Joh. Mal. 13.4 (Dindorf, p. 318–19 = Thurn, p. 244–45), which wrongly asserts that Felicianus was Christian; cf. *PLRE* 1: Fl. Felicianus 5. Athanassiadi, "Fate of Oracles," p. 276, goes off the rails in asserting that Felicianus was a relative of Constantine.

37. Full sources at *CLRE*, pp. 208–9. These same sources (esp. *CIL* 10: 476 = *ILS* 6112) confirm that Felicianus later suffered *damnatio memoriae* for reasons we can no longer ascertain.

38. *FD* 3.4: 275 = *SIG*³ 903B and *SIG*³ 903A. See Vatin, pp. 229–30, on the date 232. Amandry, p. 733; Weir, p. 98. Amici offers a full catalog of epigraphic testimonia to Constantine's posthumous title *divus* in Latin inscriptions.

39. *IRT* 464 and 465: *Indulgentis/simo ac liber/tatis restitu/tori victori/osissimoque/ Imperatori*. Cf. Tantillo and Bigi, *Leptis Magna*, pp. 321–25 no. 5–6, with photographs.

40. *IRT* 468 = *AE* 1948: 40 = Tantillo and Bigi, *Leptis Magna*, no. 73, to Constantine I, Crispus, Constantine II, and Constantius II; *IRT* 467 = *AE* 1934: 172 = *AE* 1948: 37 = Tantillo and

Bigi, *Leptis Magna*, no. 71, to Constantine I; *IRT* 466 = Tantillo and Bigi, *Leptis Magna*, no. 2, to Constantius I or Constantine Caesar; *IRT* 469 = *AE* 1950: 207 = Tantillo and Bigi, *Leptis Magna*, no. 7, to Constantine II as Caesar.

41. Aur. Vict. *Caes.* 41.19–20; cf. *SHA Sev.* 18.3; *Alex.* 22.2 with Tantillo and Bigi, *Leptis Magna*, pp. 19–22. The elimination of the impost is confirmed archaeologically by the disappearance of Tripolitanian oil amphorae from the Roman market at precisely this time; cf. Revilla Castro, with earlier bibliography. On the building boom, see Pentiricci, pp. 120–43.

42. *PLRE* 1: Laenatius Romulus signo Romulius 4. Romulus also rebuilt the walls and the portico of the marketplace at Lepcis; *IRT* 468 = *AE* 1948: 40 = *AE* 1952: 73 = Tantillo and Bigi, *Leptis Magna*, no. 73.

43. *IRT* 467 = *AE* 1934: 172 = *AE* 1948: 37 = Tantillo and Bigi, *Leptis Magna*, no. 71, ll. 8–10: . . . *ad sempiternam memoriam statua[m]/ marmoream suo numine radiantem domino nostro/ Constantino maximo victori semper Aug(usto)*. See also *IRT* 771 = Tantillo and Bigi, *Leptis Magna*, no. 72, a fragment of a copy of the same inscription.

44. Tantillo, "L'impero della luce," esp. pp. 996–97 n. 20 and fig. 4, and the interesting discussion at 1015–22 of *CIL* 8: 7974 = *ILAlg.* 2: 25, a dedication to the *numen Costantini* at Rusicade on the base of a bust of Caracalla that was outfitted with similar holes on its forehead and was found in an underground mithraeum together with images of Mithras and Helios; cf. Salama, "Les provinces d'Afrique," p. 148.

45. See Tantillo, "L'impero della luce," pp. 997–1009 with *Pan. Lat.* 6[7].1.4–5: *tuo modo, Constantine, numini dicabo sermonem*; 2.1: *a primo igitur incipiam originis tuae numine*; 2.5: *nec possit Fortuna numini tuo imputare quod tuum est*; 22.2: *miraberis profecto illam quoque numinis tui sedem*. See also Opt. Porph. 11.14: *venerabile numen*; 13a.3 and 10; cf. 13b.3, 10: *salubre numen*; 13a.8–9, cf. 13b.8–9: *virtus vigore radians serena praestat/ sanctis videre superis remota mundi*. More on public dedications to the *numen* of Constantine at Moreno Resano, pp. 276–80, to which add *AE* 2003: 2014: *numini maiestatique eius semper de[votus]*. On the worship of the *numen Augustum* in imperial cult more broadly, see Gradel, pp. 234–50.

46. Chastagnol, "Gouverneur constantinien."

47. The collusion between Laenatius Romulus and the Lepcitani is further confirmed by a dedication the latter made to their governor "through the support of a most peaceful populace" (*IRT* 574 = *AE* 1948: 38: *suf(f)ragio quietissimi populi*). This phrase is pregnant with meaning in the charged atmosphere of the years around 324.

48. Harmand has been superseded by Krause, *Spätantike Patronatsformen*. Krause, "Das Spätantike Städtepatronat," offers a dataset for city patrons in Late Antiquity. This reveals that 37 out of the 106 (35 percent) datable instances cataloged between the late third and sixth centuries are Constantinian.

49. Nicols.

50. *SupIt* 9: 34 = *AE* 1937: 119 = *AE* 1992: 385. See also *PLRE* 1: C. Sallius Sophronius Pompeianus 9.

51. *SupIt* 9: 35 = *AE* 1937: 121 = *AE* 1984: 280a = *AE* 1992: 386. At lines 12–13, we learn he was also patron of Reate, Interamna, and Aveia.

52. *SupIt* 9: 34 ll. 11–12: *pronepos Salli(i) Procu/[li] pat(roni) fil(ius) Sal(ii) Proculi patroni patr(iae)*; cf. l. 15: *quod ex origine prisca genus eiusdem patronatus olim pro/cesseri{n}t*; *SupIt* 9: 35 ll. 5–7: *quanta sit b[enivo]/lentia... ge[neris]/ Salliorum patronatus patriae n(ostrae)*. On the question of the heredity of the status of patron, see Harmand, pp. 311–14; Chastagnol, *L'album Municipal*, pp. 23–24; Krause, "Das Spätantike Städtepatronat," p. 4.

53. *SupIt* 9: 34 ll. 24–26: *quarum dedicatio[[b]]ne biduum t(h)eatrum et dena iuve/naliorum spectaculis exs(h)ibuit*(sic) *sub [[u]] pr(a)esentia Cl(audi) Urani v(iri) p(erfectissimi) corr(ectoris) n(ostri) cives et or/dinem n(ostrum) {a} epulis ex suis viribus confrequentavit.*

54. *SupIt* 9: 35 ll. 3–4: *cum universi pagani seu vicani Forulani in [e]/pulo Aug(usteo?) fre-quentes obvenissent.*

55. On the fundamentally pagan nature of such celebrations in previous centuries, see Goddard, pp. 1042–45. For the votive of Atrius Arrenianus (and his brother), see *CIL* 9: 4349 = 5759.

56. *CTh* 15.12.1 (Oct. 1, 325); cf. Soc. 1.18.1 and above p. 128 and p. 317 n. 62.

57. *PLRE* 1: Q. Aradius Rufinus Valerius Proculus signo Populonius 12. All six were recovered in a single aristocratic *domus* on the Caelian in Rome in 1554.

58. *CIL* 6: 1687 = *ILS* 6111 (Hadrumetum); *CIL* 6: 1685 = *ILS* 6111a (Thaenae); *CIL* 6: 1686 = *CIL* 6: 6111c (Zama); *CIL* 6: 1689 (Mididi); *CIL* 6: 1684 (Municipium Chullitanum); *CIL* 6: 1688 = *ILS* 6111b (Civitas Faustianensis). More on these inscriptions at Lepelley, "La création de cités nouvelles."

59. *CIL* 6: 1686 = *ILS* 6111c. *CIL* 6: 1684 from Municipium Chullitanum also lists ten ambassadors, only one of whom styles himself *flamen perpetuus.* The remaining inscriptions do not list the names of their ambassadors. More on this embassy at Krause, "Das Spätantike Städtepatronat," pp. 53–54.

60. *CIL* 6: 1687 = *ILS* 6111 dates to March 13, 321; *CIL* 6: 1685 = *ILS* 6111a to April 9, 321; *CIL* 6: 1688 = *ILS* 6111b to May 22, 321; *CIL* 6: 1684 to August 29, 321; *CIL* 6: 1689 to October 5, 321. *CIL* 6: 1686 = *CIL* 6: 6111c, by contrast, dates to April 12, 322.

61. See below pp. 232–34.

62. *PLRE* 1: Aradius Rufinus 10; Chastagnol, *Fastes de la préfecture*, pp. 59–62; Lenski, "Evoking," p. 211.

63. *PLRE* 1: L. Aradius Valerius Proculus signo Populonius 11; Chastagnol, *Fastes de la préfecture*, pp. 96–102; Rüpke and Glock, no. 707.

64. *CIL* 6: 40776 = *AE* 1934: 158 = *AE* 1950: 174 = *AE* 1951: 102 = *AE* 1982: 11.

65. *CIL* 8: 14688–14689 = *ILS* 3937–38.

66. *CIL* 6: 1690 = *ILS* 1240 and *CIL* 6: 1691; cf. Rüpke and Glock, p. 543 no. 707.

67. *CIL* 8: 24521 = *AE* 1898: 8; cf. Lepelley, "De la réaction païenne," pp. 275–76.

68. *CIL* 10: 476 = *ILS* 6112 = Mello and Voza, vol. 1: 106, esp. *credimus/ eum et libenter suscipere et in om/nibus nos patriamque nostram fobere*(sic). Cf. *PLRE* 1: Aur. Gentianus 1.

69. *CIL* 10: 478 = *ILS* 6114 = Mello and Voza, vol. 1: 108: especially *Helpidi homo felix/ deus te servet . . . cuius tanta aequitas tranquilli/tas dignitas iustitia innocentia huma/nitas ex origine propagata monstra/tur.* See Krause, "Das Spätantike Städtepatronat," p. 25, for catalogs of virtues attributed to patrons, among which several of these stand out as peculiarly Christian.

70. So also Mello and Voza, vol. 1: 103, 175, who also point to a sense of desperation in the opening lines: *non aliunde* [sic] *aestimamus statum cibitatis* (sic)/ *altiorem cultioremque reddi nisi indus/trium virorum patrocinio fulciantur/ optimi cibes* (sic).

71. *CIL* 10: 477 = Mello and Voza, vol. 1: 107: *quam cum suscipere fu(e)rit dignatus spera/mus for(t)e quod et nos et patrianquae*(sic) *nos/tram in o(m)nibus fobeat* (sic).

72. *AE* 1990: 211 = Sabbatini Tumolesi.

73. See above 202–3.

74. Paestum's code switching should be set in the context of the well-grounded discussion of Rebillard, which demonstrates that Christian identity was not absolute but could be activated and deactivated to suit circumstances.

75. *ILS* 8983 confirms that Titianus was a Quindecemvir Sacris Faciundis; cf. Rüpke and Glock, no. 1603, which points out that Titianus was probably the maternal grandfather of Quintus Aurelius Symmachus.

76. Zos. 2.49.1: καὶ τὴν τῶν πόλεων ἀπώλειαν τῇ περὶ τὴν ἀρχὴν ἀναθεὶς ἐκμελείᾳ; cf. *PLRE* 1: Fabius Titianus 6.

77. On Cillium, see Lepelley, *Les cités de l'Afrique*, vol. 2, pp. 287–88. Recent fieldwork has demonstrated a flourish of economic activity around Kasserine in the fourth century; Hitchner.

78. *CIL* 8: 23207 confirms that Cillium was a municipium in the second century, and *CIL* 8: 2568 = 18055 l. 46 reveals that it had the name Flavia Cillium in this period. On Cillium's history, see also *CIL* 8: 211–16, with Les Flavii.

79. *CIL* 8: 210 = 11299 = *ILS* 5570 part 2: *clementia temporis et virtute/ divina d[[d]](ominorum) n[[n]](ostrorum) Constantini [[et Licini]] Inv(i)c(torum)/ semp(er) Aug(ustorum) ornamenta liberta(tis) restituta et vetera civi/tatis insignia curante Ceionio Aproniano c(larissimo) v(iro)/ patro(no) civitatis.*

80. As proposed by Mommsen ad loc. *CIL* 8: 210; accepted at *PLRE* 1: Ceionius Apronianus 5; Lepelley, *Les cités de l'Afrique*, vol. 2, pp. 287–88. The dating is further strengthened by use of the title *Invictus*, which gave way to *Victor* after 324, and by the absence of "Maximus" for Constantine, which became common on African inscriptions after 315; cf. Salama, "Anniversaires impériaux," p. 141.

81. Opt. *App.* 2.3, 6–8, 10 (*CSEL* 26: 197–204). *PLRE* 1: Apronianus 2 and Ceionius Apronianus 5 draws the connection between the two; cf. *PCBE* I Apronianus 1. On the *Acta*, see esp. Duval, *Chrétiens d'Afrique*, pp. 213–45.

82. Symm. *Rel.* 40. For interpretation, see Vera, *Commento storico*, pp. 296–305.

83. *CTh* 14.6.3 (a. 365) indicates that, by this time, according to long-established custom (*vetusto . . . more*), Tarracina's lime quota went to repair the lighthouse and other structures in Portus.

84. Symm. *Rel.* 40: *Puteolanis municipibus divus Constantinus centum quinquaginta milia modiorum in alimoniam civitatis indulsit.*

85. See especially Wiemer, "Libanios und Zosimus."

86. *AE* 1969/1970: 107–8, with modifications at *AE* 1983: 194. On the statues, see Bergemann, pp. 101–3 (P 48); 133–34 (E 40–41). On the inscriptions and their date, see Guadagno and Panciera; Camodeca, pp. 64–68.

87. Bergemann, p. 134.

88. On coins and medallions, see *RIC* 7: Nicomedia 164, 170; Toynbee, pl. 30: 7. On the image of the dynasty as quadriga, see above p. 65.

89. Suessa: *CIL* 10: 4752 = *ILS* 1223. Puteoli: *CIL* 10: 1695 = *ILS* 1224a; *CIL* 10: 1696 = *ILS* 1224; *ILS* 1224b; *CIL* 10: 1697= *ILS* 1226; *AE* 1977: 198. See also *CIL* 6: 1725 = *ILS* 1224, in Rome, but by the Puteolani; *PLRE* 1: Q. Flavius Maesius Egnatius Lollianus signo Mavortius 5; Chastagnol, *Fastes de la préfecture*, no. 45. The first inscription can be dated by its mention of *DD NN Aug et Caesarum*, that is, Constantine and his sons, and the lack of mention of Lollianus's position as *comes orientis*, held 330/336, and Proconsul Africae, held 334/337. The Puteoli inscriptions mention both offices but not Lollianus's Urban Prefecture of 342.

90. *CIL* 6: 30895 = *ILS* 3425.

91. Firm. Mat. *Math.* 1 pr. 1; 1.10.15; 2.29.20; 3 pr. 2; 4 pr. 3; 5 pr. 1; 7 pr. 2; 8.1.1–6; 8.33.1–4. Mommsen, "Firmicus Maternus," remains standard on the date. For more on Firmicus Maternus's relationship with Lollianus and Constantine, see Lenski, "Early Retrospectives."

92. *ILS* 1224b: *regio . . . vici turari. AE* 1977: 198: *regio arae Lucullianae. CIL* 10: 1696 = *ILS* 1224c: *colligeus* [sic] *decatressium*; *CIL* 10: 1697 = *ILS* 1226: *decatrenses cl/ientes.* On the Decatrenses, see Steuernagel, pp. 54–55, 172. Also listed are the *regio clivi vitrarii* and the *regio portae triumphalis.*

93. *CIL* 6: 1691.

94. *CIL* 10: 1700 = *ILS* 1231; cf. *PLRE* 1: M. Maecius Memmius Furius Baburius Caecilianus Placidus 2; Rüpke and Glock, no. 2323.

95. *AE* 1939: 151 with *PLRE* 1: M. Ceionius Iulianus signo Kamenius 26.

96. *Lib. Pont.* 34.31–32 (Geertman, p. 306): *Eodem tempore fecit Constantinus Augustus basilicam intra urbe Capua Apostolorum quae cognominavit Constantinianam. . . . Eodem tempore fecit Constantinus Augustus basilicam in civitatem Neapolim*; *Gesta Episcoporum Neapolitanorum* (*MGH.Scriptores Rerum Langobardarum,* 1: 404): *quique inter alias constructas ecclesias etiam in urbem Neapolim basilicam fecit, asserentibus multis, quod Sancta Restituta fuisset.* On these churches, see M. J. Johnson, "Constantinian Churches in Campania."

97. *CIL* 10: 1482; cf. *CIL* 10: 1245 at Nola.

98. *CIL* 10: 1484: *Piissimae ac venerabili/ dominae nostrae Hel{a}enae/ Augustae matri/ domini nostri victoris/ semper Aug(usti) Constantini et/ aviae dominorum nostrorum/ beatissimorum Caesarum/ ordo et populus Neapolitanus*; cf. *CIL* 10: 1483: *Piissimae ac clementissimae/ dominae nostrae etc.*

99. Joh. Lyd. *De mag.* 3.70.3 with Cavallaro.

CHAPTER 12. RESISTING CITIES

1. Sizgorich; Gaddis. See also Bryen for an excellent interpretation of violence as discourse in secular legal sources.

2. Shaw. See more on the Donatist controversy below at Chapter 13.

3. *Or. ad Sanct.* 16.1; Eus. *V. Const.* 4.10.1.

4. Zos. 2.29.5, with Paschoud; Wiemer, "Libanios und Zosimus"; cf. Lizzi Testa, "Alle origini."

5. Eus. *V. Const.* 2.45.1: Εἶθ᾽ ἑξῆς δύο κατὰ τὸ αὐτὸ ἐπέμποντο νόμοι, ὁ μὲν εἴργων τὰ μυσαρὰ τῆς κατὰ πόλεις καὶ χώρας τὸ παλαιὸν συντελουμένης εἰδωλολατρίας, ὡς μήτ᾽ ἐγέρσεις ξοάνων ποιεῖσθαι τολμᾶν, μήτε μαντείαις καὶ ταῖς ἄλλαις περιεργίαις ἐπιχειρεῖν, μήτε μὴν θύειν καθόλου μηδένα; cf. Eus. *V. Const.* 4.25.1, which reiterates 2.44.1–45.1.

6. *CTh* 16.10.2: *Cesset superstitio, sacrificiorum aboleatur insania. Nam quicumque contra legem divi principis parentis nostri et hanc nostrae mansuetudinis iussionem ausus fuerit sacrificia celebrare, competens in eum vindicta et praesens sententia exeratur.* See also *CTh* 16.10.4 (Dec. 1, 356), which lays down even stricter prohibitions on sacrifice and closes access to temples without, however, making reference to any similar law of Constantine's. Edwards, *Optatus,* p. 44 n. 55, points out that Opt. 2.15 (*CSEL* 26: 50: *sub imperatore christiano . . . nec paganis licebat exercere sacrilegia*) may confirm Constantine's abolition of pagan sacrifice, but, unfortunately, we cannot be certain that the *imperator* mentioned by Optatus was Constantine rather than Constans or Constantius II.

7. De Giovanni, *Chiesa e stato,* p. 139; *Costantino e il mondo pagano,* pp. 162–67; Barnes, *Constantine and Eusebius,* pp. 210–12; "Constantine's Prohibition"; "From Toleration to Repression," pp. 199–202; Delmaire and Rougé, *Lois religieuses,* vol. 1, p. 80.

8. Eus. *V. Const.* 2.56.1–2, esp. ὁμοίαν τοῖς πιστεύουσιν οἱ πλανώμενοι χαίροντες λαμβανέτωσαν εἰρήνης τε καὶ ἡσυχίας ἀπόλαυσιν . . . οἱ δ᾽ ἑαυτοὺς ἀφέλκοντες ἐχόντων βουλόμενοι τὰ τῆς ψευδολογίας τεμένη.

9. Lib. *Or.* 30.6: τῆς κατὰ νόμους δὲ θεραπείας ἐκίνησεν οὐδὲ ἕν, ἀλλ᾽ ἦν μὲν ἐν τοῖς ἱεροῖς πενία, παρῆν δὲ ὁρᾶν ἅπαντα τἄλλα πληρούμενα.

10. Drake, "Review of T. D. Barnes *Constantine and Eusebius.*" Errington, "Constantine and the Pagans," as well as Bradbury, "Constantine and the Problem" and "Julian's Pagan Revival" essay a middle ground, the former arguing that the ban was issued but promptly abrogated, the latter that it was issued but only haltingly enforced. More recent arguments at Sandwell; Delmaire and Rougé, *Lois religieuses,* vol. 1, p. 83; Belayche, "Realia versus Leges?"; Rives, "Between Orthopraxy."

11. On these laws, see especially Curran, "Constantine," with earlier bibliography.

12. *CTh* 9.16.2 (a. 319) and 1 (a. 320), with Seeck *RG* 169 on the dates.

13. For *haruspicium/haruspicina* and Etruscan religious practice, see Jannot, pp. 21–24. On the continuation of Etruscan religious practice in Late Antiquity, see Sordi.

14. *CTh* 16.10.1 (Dec. 17, 320), with Seeck *RG* 170 on the date.

15. *CTh* 9.16.3, with Seeck *RG* 166 on the date.

16. Eus. *V. Const.* 4.19.1–30.2; cf. Lact. *Mort. Pers.* 46.6 for a similar prayer used by Licinius's soldiery.

17. *CTh* 7.20.2: *Auguste Constantine, dii te nobis servent.* The Justinianic (*CJ* 12.46.1) compilers have changed this to "deus te servet." The date is a matter of dispute. The attempt by Barnes, *New Empire*, pp. 69 n. 102, 74, 76–77, to backdate to 307 has generally been rejected. Corcoran, *Empire of the Tetrarchs*, pp. 257–59, with earlier bibliography, prefers the transmitted date of 320. To my mind, Seeck *RG* 60 was correct to have argued that *CTh* 7.20.1 was the accompanying edict mentioned in 7.20.2, and that its mention of the battle of Adrianople in 324 calls for a date of March 1, 325, for the meeting with the veterans, and 326, for the posting of the edict and transcript at Beauvais. On this important document, see Connolly, "Constantine Answers the Veterans." Interestingly, the formula *di te servent* recurs no less than twenty-one times in acclamations "reported" in the late fourth-century *Historia Augusta*, *SHA Avid.* 13.1, 2; *Diad.* 1.6 (bis); *Alex.* 6.2, 9 (bis); 7.1 (ter); 8.3; 10.6, 7, 8; 11.2 (bis); 12.1; 56.9; *Tac.* 5.2; *Max.* 16.3; *Gord.* 8.4. In these contexts, it serves as a sort of mediated reading of imperial discourse, for it is used (generally by the senate) to "praise" the emperor even as it forces him to accept the polytheist cosmological assumptions of his "subjects."

18. Barnes, *Constantine and Eusebius*, pp. 208–12, 245–48; "From Toleration to Repression"; *Dynasty, Religion and Power*, pp. 107–43.

19. Eus. *V. Const.* 2.44.1. On the prosopography, see Von Haehling, pp. 513–21. Barnes, "Statistics," rightly critiques Von Haehling's method of counting, but does not disprove the fact that the majority of attested officeholders under Constantine were pagan. A ban on pagan officeholders was not enacted until 416; *CTh* 16.10.21.

20. See below pp. 168–70.

21. Eus. *V. Const.* 2.60.1–2; cf. 2.56.2. Much the same attitude is reflected in the "Edict of Milan" of 313; cf. Lact. *Mort. Pers.* 48.2: *haec inter cetera quae videbamus pluribus hominibus profutura, vel in primis ordinanda esse credidimus, quibus divinitatis reverentia continebatur, ut daremus et Christianis et omnibus liberam potestatem sequendi religionem quam quisque voluisset;* 48.6: *Quod cum isdem a nobis indultum esse pervideas, intelligit dicatio tua etiam aliis religionis suae vel observantiae potestatem similiter apertam et liberam pro quiete temporis nostri <esse> concessam, ut in colendo quod quisque delegerit, habeat liberam facultatem.*

22. Drake, *Constantine and the Bishops*, pp. 273–308. See also Kahlos, pp. 58–62; Schott, pp. 122–28.

23. *CTh* 16.10.2–6. The enforcement of these laws would appear to be confirmed by Julian's claim that, during his traverse of Asia Minor in 362, he found very few willing to sacrifice, and even these ignorant of what precisely to do, see Jul. *Ep.* 78.4 (375C).

24. *CTh* 16.10.3 (Nov. 1, 342). See the very similar provisions of *CTh* 16.10.17 (a. 399) and Van Nuffelen.

25. Eus. *V. Const.* 3.25.1–32.2; cf. *LC* 9.16–19. *Itin. Burd.* 594.2; 595.6; 598.7; 599.6 (*CCSL* 175: 17–20) is also contemporary but too slim to offer useful detail. See more at Lenski, "Empresses," with earlier bibliography, to which add Caseau, pp. 86–90; Belayche, *Iudaea-Palaestina*, pp. 142–54; Schott, pp. 128–35.

26. Eus. *V. Const.* 3.26.3: σκότιον Ἀφροδίτης ἀκολάστῳ δαίμονι μυχὸν οἰκοδομησάμενοι. Jer. *Ep.* 58.3 (*CSEL* 54: 531–32) claims that the site of Golgotha was home to an "image of Jupiter and a marble statue of Venus" (*simulacrum Iovis . . . statua ex marmore Veneris*) up to the reign

of Constantine; cf. Paul. Nol. *Ep.* 31.3 (*CSEL* 29: 270). Borgehammar, p. 108; Belayche, *Iudaea-Palaestina*, pp. 142–54, attempts to resolve this inconsistency.

27. Eus. *V. Const.* 3.30.1: τὸ γὰρ γνώρισμα τοῦ ἁγιωτάτου ἐκείνου πάθους. The case that this is a reference to the True Cross is made most eloquently by Drake, "Eusebius on the True Cross."

28. *CIL* 8: 9255 = *ILCV* 1822; Cyr. Hier. *Cat.* 10.19 (*PG* 33: 685–88). Borgehammar, pp. 105–22, lays out the case for an early discovery of the Cross, with earlier bibliography.

29. For possible reasons for this, see Rubin; Walker, pp. 72–92. More on the legend of the Cross at Hunt, *Holy Land Pilgrimage*, pp. 37–48; Heid; Borgehammar; Drijvers, pp. 79–180; Av. Cameron and Hall, *Eusebius*, pp. 273–91.

30. See esp. Eus. *V. Const.* 3.26.6: θεὸν τὸν αὐτοῦ συνεργὸν ἐπικαλεσάμενος καθαίρεσθαι προστάττει; 3.27.1: ἀλλὰ πάλιν βασιλεὺς . . . προστάττει . . . πάλιν δε . . . παρακελεύεται; 3.29.1: Τούτων δ' ὧδε πραχθέντων, αὐτίκα βασιλεὺς νόμων εὐσεβῶν διατάξεσι . . . οἶκον εὐκτήριον . . . ἐγκελεύεται . . . δείμασθαι.

31. Eus. *V. Const.* 3.30.4: ἄρα πάντων μοι μᾶλλον μέλει, ὅπως τὸν ἱερὸν ἐκεῖνον τόπον, ὃν θεοῦ προστάγματι [αἰσχίστης] εἰδώλου [προσθήκης] ὥσπερ τινὸς ἐπικειμένου βάρους ἐκούφισα, . . . οἰκοδομημάτων κάλλει κοσμήσωμεν.

32. See also Eus. *V. Const.* 3.25.1: ὑπ' αὐτοῦ τοῦ σωτῆρος ἀνακινηθεὶς τῷ πνεύματι. This claim should not be discounted, for although it represents a figment of Constantine's imagination, it fits perfectly with Constantinian rhetoric about divine inspiration more broadly (Mac-Mullen, "Constantine and the Miraculous"; Bleckmann, "Pagane Visionen").

33. Eus. *V. Const.* 3.31.1–32.2. See *PLRE* 1: Dracilianus.

34. Eus. *V. Const.* 3.51.1–53.3; *DE* 5.9.7; *On.* 76–77; Soc. 1.18.5–6; Soz. 2.4.1–8; cf. Julius Africanus, *Chronographiae*, fr. 30a (Wallraff, Roberto, and Pinggéra, p. 66). More on Mamre at Cline, *Ancient Angels*, pp. 106–18.

35. Belayche, *Iudaea-Palaestina*, pp. 96–104; Bar, pp. 284–85.

36. Eus. *V. Const.* 3.52.1–53.4; cf. *Itin. Burd.* 599 (*CCSL* 175: 20): *ibi basilica facta est iussu Constantini mirae pulchritudinis.* On Acacius, see *PLRE* 1: Acacius 4.

37. Mader, pp. 135–36.

38. Eus. *V. Const.* 3.55.1–5; *LC* 8.4–9; cf. Soc. 1.18.10; Soz. 2.5.5; 5.10.7. More on the site at Zos. 1.58.1–4; Lucian *Syr. D.* 9. A church was subsequently built over the site; Deichmann, pp. 108, 115 no. 4, Abb. 1.

39. Mac. *Sat.* 1.21.1–5; Lucian *Syr. D.* 8; Zos. 1.58.1.2; cf. Lightfoot, pp. 328–29.

40. The notion of "sacred prostitution" has been questioned by Budin. It is not within the scope of this study to reexamine the issue, but the arguments of Budin cry out for revision. On Constantine's sexual politics, see Grubbs, passim, esp. pp. 216–24.

41. Eus. *V. Const.* 3.55.2: ἄλσος δὲ τοῦτ' ἦν καὶ τέμενος, οὐκ ἐν μέσαις πόλεσιν οὐδ' ἐν ἀγοραῖς καὶ πλατείαις; cf. *LC* 8.4.

42. Frazer; Cline, "Two-Sided Mold."

43. Eus. *V. Const.* 3.55.5: χείρ τε στρατιωτικὴ τῇ τοῦ τόπου καθάρσει διηκονεῖτο; cf. *LC* 8.7.

44. Eus. *V. Const.* 3.56.1–3, esp. 2: ἐνὶ δὲ νεύματι κατὰ γῆς ἡπλοῦτο δεξιᾷ καταρριπτόμενον στρατιωτικῆ τὸ τῶν γενναίων φιλοσόφων βοώμενον θαῦμα καὶ ὁ τῇδε ἐνδομυχῶν οὐ δαίμων οὐδέ γε θεός. Cf. Eus. *LC* 8.4–9, as well as Soc. 1.18.11; Soz. 2.5.5; Theoph. a.m. 5816. On the shrine, see Hild and Hellenkemper, pp. 160–63; Lightfoot, pp. 328–31.

45. Zon. 13.12; cf. Deichmann, p. 129 no. 59.

46. Barnes, "From Toleration to Repression," p. 20; *Dynasty, Religion and Power*, p. 129, has speculated that Constantine's wrath may have been aroused by the city's association with Apollonius of Tyana, to whom Porphyry and the polemicist Sossianus Hierocles had mockingly compared Jesus. This is possible but by no means proven.

47. At a minimum, Aegeae had a Christian bishop—Tarcondimantus—who was present at the Council of Nicaea in 325, Philost. *HE* 1.8. We cannot know whether he played a role in provoking Constantine's attack on the temple of Asclepius.

48. Ragette, pp. 15–61; Hajjar, *Son culte et sa diffusion*; *Iconographie, Théologie, Culte*.

49. Indeed, the site boasts dedicatory bases to Diocletian and Galerius; *AE* 1939: 58 = *IGLS* 6: 2771 and 2772.

50. Eusebius describes temple prostitution there not just at *V. Const.* 3.58.1 but also at *Pr. Ev.* 4.16.22 and *Theoph.* 2.14; cf. Soc. 1.18.7; Soz. 1.8.6; 5.10.7; and perhaps *Exp. Tot. Mundi*, 30, with Hajjar, *Son culte et sa diffusion*, pp. 421–36. ʿAshtart/Atargatis was also worshipped at Hierapolis-Mabbug (Lightfoot, pp. 38–44), which Constantine actually honored with the status of metropolis of the newly formed province of Euphratesia, according to Joh. Mal. 13.3–4 (Dindorf, p. 318 = Thurn, p. 244). Mabbug was, of course, much quicker to Christianize in this period, which may explain Constantine's favoritism.

51. Joh. Mal. 12.50 (Dindorf, p. 314–15 = Thurn, p. 241–50); *Chron. Pasch.* p. 513; cf. Weisman.

52. Eus. *V. Const.* 3.58.2–3; cf. Soz. 1.18.7–9.

53. Soz. 5.10.7 also refers to this law: καὶ νόμῳ διεκώλυσε τὰς συνήθεις ἐπιτελεῖν πορνείας.

54. Eus. *V. Const.* 4.24.1, see above pp. 76–78.

55. Soz. 5.10.7 reports that Constantine destroyed Baalbek's temple of Aphrodite, but this is probably not to be credited; see Hajjar, *Son culte et sa diffusion*, pp. 461–62. To his arguments could be added the fact that Joh. Mal. 13.37 (Dindorf, p. 344 = Thurn, p. 266) and *Chron. Pasch.* p. 561 (s.a. 379) explicitly deny Constantine destroyed temples in Heliopolis-Baalbek. On the temple, see Ragette, pp. 52–61.

56. *IG* 4²: 438, with Robert, "De Cilicie à Messine," esp. 188–93.

57. Lib. *Or.* 30.39.

58. Lib. *Ep.* 695: τραγῳδῶν τὸν τῶν ἀθέων κατὰ τοῦ νεὼ πόλεμον, τὴν κατασκαφήν, τὸ πῦρ, τοὺς ὑβριζομένους βωμούς; cf. *Ep.* 1342. Libanius's friend Demetrius also composed two orations in honor of Asclepius at precisely this time, *Ep.* 727.2. See also Bradbury, *Selected Letters of Libanius*, pp. 184–86.

59. Lib. *Ep.* 706–8, 727.

60. Zon. 13.12. Banchich and Lane, p. 231 suggest a possible connection with Salmasian John of Antioch; Joh. Ant. fr. 268 (Roberto p. 452 = fr. 178.2 Müller). Julian's interest in the shrine is also attested at *C. Gal.* 200b.

61. Lib. *Ep.* 695.3, with Bradbury, *Selected Letters of Libanius*, p. 184 n. 15.

62. Lib. *Or.* 1.143; cf. *Ep.* 1483.

63. *VM Thecla* prol.; mir. 9; 39.

64. Zos. 1.58.1; Soz. 2.5.5, with Lightfoot, pp. 329–30.

65. Frazer, pp. 141–43. Cline, "Two-Sided Mold," p. 31, argues for an early to mid-fourth century date, but uses considerably fewer iconographic and textual reference points.

66. Soz. 2.4.2–3, esp. προσφόρως δὲ ταῖς θρησκείαις τιμῶσι τοῦτον τὸν χῶρον, οἱ μὲν εὐχόμενοι τῷ πάντων θεῷ, οἱ δὲ τοὺς ἀγγέλους ἐπικαλούμενοι καὶ οἶνον σπένδοντες καὶ λίβανον θύοντες ἢ βοῦν ἢ τράγον ἢ πρόβατον ἢ ἀλεκτρυόνα. On this passage and its implications, see E. K. Fowden, "Sharing Holy Places," pp. 125–29.

67. Mader, pp. 151–64.

68. But see Soz. 5.10.7: τότε πρῶτον παρ' αὐτοῖς ἐκκλησίαν ἐδείματο.

69. Ragette, pp. 68–71, with Joh. Mal. 13.37 (Dindorf, p. 344 = Thurn, p. 266); cf. *Chron. Pasch.* p. 561 (s.a. 379).

70. *Exp. Tot. Mundi* 30.

71. Theod. *HE* 3.7.2–4; cf. *Chron. Pasch.* pp. 546–47 (s.a. 362); Theoph. a.m. 5853.

72. Soz. 5.10.5–7, with Greg. Naz. *Or.* 4.86–87.

73. *PLRE* 1: Alexander 5; esp. Lib. *Ep.* 1256, 1294, 1351, 1361, 1411, 1456.

74. Theod. *HE* 4.22.21–2: ἔνθα τῶν ἐνοικούντων οὐδεὶς κἂν ἀκοῦσαι τὸ τοῦ Χριστοῦ ἀνέχεται ὄνομα· εἰδωλικοὶ γὰρ οἱ πάντες; cf. 4.22.26.

75. *SEG* 7: 195; cf. *PLRE* 1: Proculus 6.

76. *V. Rabulae* (J. J. Overbeck and Takahashi, pp. 169–70); cf. Gaddis, pp. 162–65.

77. For 555, see Nau, pp. 490–91. For 579, see Joh. Eph. *HE* 3.27; cf. Mich. Syr. 10.12. See *PLRE* 3: Theophilus 2.

78. Theod. *HE* 3.7.1; cf. Theoph. a.m. 5853. For pagan worship at Ascalon, see Belayche, *Iudaea-Palaestina*, pp. 222–27.

79. At Sebaste, relics of John the Baptist were defiled; Theod. *HE* 3.7.2; cf. Philost. *HE* 7.4. At Scythopolis, it was the relics of the city's former bishop Patrophilus (Theoph. a.m. 5835; *Chron. Pasch.* p. 546 [s.a. 362]). For Scythopolis's attachment to Hellenic religious traditions, see Belayche, *Iudaea-Palaestina*, pp. 258–67; Heyden, pp. 308–13. For its eager participation in the Great Persecution, see the brilliant article of Laniado and Porath, pp. 235–36.

80. Soz. 5.10.8–14; Theod. *HE* 3.6.6–10. Greg. Naz. *Or.* 4.88–91 places the temple destruction in the time of Constantius. The two source traditions could be reconciled if we assume it occurred when Constantius was Caesar in the East between 335 and 337. Gregory frequently refers to Mark as an old man (γέρων) at the time of his persecution. Lib. *Ep.* 819.6–7 reports the buzz the affair generated in the 360s.

81. Jul. *Ep.* 84 (432A): Πεῖθε τοίνυν αὐτούς, εἰ τῆς παρ' ἐμοῦ κηδεμονίας ἀντέχονται, πανδημεὶ τῆς Μητρὸς τῶν θεῶν ἱκέτας γενέσθαι. On Julian's visit, see Amm. 22.9.5–8; cf. Greg. Naz. *Or.* 5.40. See also above pp. 105–6.

82. See above pp. 132–33.

83. Soz. 5.3.5.

84. Soz. 5.4.1–5, 11.8; Greg. Naz. *Or.* 4.92; 18.34; Theoph. a.m. 5835. For Julian's personal dislike for the Cappadocians as intransigent Christians, see Jul. *Ep.* 78 (375c). On this incident, see Fatti.

85. Deichmann; G. Fowden, "Bishops and Temples"; De Giovanni, *Chiesa e stato*, pp. 131–32; Caseau; Nesselrath et al.; Bonamente, "Politica antipagana."

CHAPTER 13. OPPOSING CHRISTIANS

1. On the Donatist controversy, see Frend; Calderone, *Costantino*, pp. 230–96; Grasmück; Brisson, pp. 243–410; Tengström; Girardet, *Kaisergericht und Bischofsgericht*; Drake, *Constantine and the Bishops*, pp. 212–21; Shaw; Lenski, "Constantine and the Donatists"; cf. Tilley.

2. For the Great Persecution in general, see above pp. 14, 93–96, 162, 180. For the persecution in Africa, see Eus. *HE* 8.6.10; *Mart. Pal.* 13.12. For the duration of the African persecutions, see Vita-Evrard, pp. 308–13. Extant martyr accounts documenting those thought to have suffered in the North African persecution include (1) *Passio Sancti Felicis Episcopi* (of Thibiuca) martyred on July 15, 303 (*BHL* 2893 = Maier, *Dossier*, vol. 1, no. 3 = Musurillo, no. 20); (2) *Passio Sanctae Crispinae* (of Thagora) martyred on December 5, 303 (*BHL* 1989 = Maier, *Dossier*, vol. 1, no. 6 = Musurillo, no. 24, with Vita-Evrard, pp. 308–13, on the date); (3) *Passio Sanctorum Dativi, Saturnini presbyteri et aliorum* (also known as the Passion of the Martyrs of Abitina) martyred on Feb. 12, 304 (*BHL* 7492 = Maier, *Dossier*, vol. 1, no. 4); (4) *Passio Sanctarum Maximae, Secundae et Donatillae* (of Thuburbo) martyred on July 30, 304 (*BHL* 5809 = Maier, *Dossier*, vol. 1, no. 5). (5) *Acta Gallonii* (of Timida Regia) martyred on Dec. 31, 303(?) (Chiesa, "Testo agiografico africano"; cf. "Pellegrino martire"). See also the thirty-four martyrs recorded at Ammaedara (Haedra), *ILTun* 470B–D = Duval, *Loca sanctorum*, vol. 1, nos. 51–52; and the martyrs executed at Milev (in summer 303), *CIL* 8: 6700 = *ILCV* 2100.

3. For the involvement of civic officials, see Opt. *App.* 1 (Gesta apud Zenophilum) (*CSEL* 26: 186–88); Aug. *C. Cresc.* 3.27[30] (*CSEL* 52: 435–37); *Passio Felicis* 3.21–22 (Maier, *Dossier*, vol. 1, no. 3 pp. 53–54); *Passio Saturnini* 2–3 (Maier, *Dossier*, vol. 1, no. 3 pp. 63–64); *Passio Maximae, Secundae et Donatillae* 1 (Maier, *Dossier*, vol. 1, no. 5 pp. 95–96). For the role of the Proconsul, see *Passio Felicis* 2.8, 5.26–27, 29 (Maier, *Dossier*, vol. 1, no. 3 pp. 51, 54–55); *Passio Saturnini* 4 (Maier, *Dossier*, vol. 1, no. 4 pp. 64–66); *Passio Maximae, Secundae et Donatillae* 1 (Maier, *Dossier*, vol. 1, no. 5 pp. 95–96); *Passio Crispinae* 1–4 (Maier, *Dossier*, vol. 1, no. 6 pp. 107–12).

4. Shaw, pp. 66–106, with bibliography.

5. The date is disputed. I follow Kriegbaum, *Kirche der Traditoren*, pp. 130–49; cf. "Die Religionspolitik," pp. 22–34, which presents a strong case for 308. He is followed by Edwards, *Optatus*, p. 16 n. 69. Barnes, "Beginnings of Donatism," argues for 306 and is followed by Shaw, pp. 812–19. Monceaux, vol. 4, pp. 8–9, holds for 311 and is followed by Frend and Clancy, "When Did the Donatist Schism Begin," and Maier, *Dossier*, vol. 1, pp. 129–33.

6. Opt. *App.* 2 (*CSEL* 26: 197–204); cf. Opt. 1.27.1–6; cf. Maier, *Dossier*, vol. 1, pp. 128–34; Frend, *Donatist Church*, pp. 142–47; Girardet, *Kaisergericht und Bischofsgericht*, pp. 6–10.

7. Sources at Maier, *Dossier*, vol. 1, no. 10. Date at Kriegbaum, *Kirche der Traditoren*, pp. 135–43.

8. For Donatus, see *PCBE* 1: Donatus 5.

9. See Pelltari.

10. Aug. *Brev. Coll.* 3.4[4] (*CSEL* 53: 54); *C. part. Don.* 1.1, 23.29 (*CSEL* 53: 97–98, 140); cf. *Gest. Conl. Carth.* 3.116 (*CCSL* 149A: 208).

11. For shrines, see Duval, *Loca sanctorum*; cf. Yasin, pp. 240–50. For martyr acts, see Maier, *Dossier*, vol. 1, nos. 2–6, 28, 36–37; Dolbeau; Mastandrea; Chiesa, "Testo agiografico"; cf. Brown, *Cult of the Saints,* and see above n. 2.

12. Martyr veneration is not, of course, unique to the Donatists, but the Donatist community seems to have laid a particularly heavy emphasis on martyrdom as the hallmark of its self-construction; Shaw, pp. 598–629. On the use of martyrs for group identity construction, see Grig, pp. 34–58; Moss, *Myth of Persecution.*

13. Maier, *Dossier*, vol. 1, no. 4. The text we have dates to the early fifth century; cf. Dearn.

14. *Passio Saturnini* 5 (Maier, *Dossier*, vol. 1, no. 4 p. 65).

15. *Passio Saturnini* 13 (Maier, *Dossier*, vol. 1, no. 4 p. 76). See a similar emphasis on the polarities between resistance/obedience and imperial/divine law throughout the *Passio Crispinae* (Maier, *Dossier*, vol. 1, no. 6).

16. *Passio Saturnini* 21 (Maier, *Dossier*, vol. 1, no. 4 p. 86); cf. 19–20, 23 (Maier, *Dossier*, vol. 1, no. 4 pp. 84–86, 91).

17. For sources and date, see above pp. 34–35.

18. Eus. *HE* 8.17.1–5; Lact. *Mort. Pers.* 34.1–5.

19. Aug. *Brev. Coll.* 3.18[34] (*CSEL* 53: 84); *C. part. Don.* 13.17 (*CSEL* 53: 113–14); *Gest. Conl. Carth.* cap. gest. 3.498–500 (*CCSL* 149A: 47). All three sources indicate that the order was forwarded through Miltiades of Rome, who was consecrated on July 2, 311, *pace* Davis, "Pre-Constantinian Chronology," pp. 462–69, who attempts to correct the date transmitted at *Chron.* 354, episcopi Romani (*MGH.AA* 9: 76). Evidence that Maxentius restored Africa in 310 can be found in the massive output of coinage celebrating victory themes beginning in this year, Drost, pp. 150–59, 176–84.

20. Eus. *HE* 10.5.15–17. For the two Anullini, see *PLRE* 1: Anullinus 2; C. Annius Anullinus 3 and *PCBE* 1: Anulinus 1; Anulinus 2. The nomenclature of *PLRE* 1: Anullinus 2 has been supplemented by *AE* 2003: 2014, which calls him "C. Annius Ceionius Anullinas [*sic*]."

21. Eus. *HE* 10.5.2–14; Lact. *Mort. Pers.* 48.2–12; cf. Lenski, "Il valore dell'Editto."

22. Eus. *HE* 10.6.1–5, 7.1–2. On these documents, see above pp. 176 and 201–2.

23. Eus. *HE* 10.7.2: ἐν τῇ καθολικῇ ἐκκλησίᾳ, ᾗ Καικιλιανὸς ἐφέστηκεν.

24. Eus. *HE* 10.6.4–5: ἐπειδὴ ἐπυθόμην τινὰς μὴ καθεστώσης διανοίας τυγχάνοντας ἀνθρώπους τὸν λαὸν τῆς ἁγιωτάτης καὶ καθολικῆς ἐκκλησίας φαύλῃ τινὶ ὑπονοθεύσει βούλεσθαι διαστρέφειν.

25. Aug. *Ep.* 88.2 (*CSEL* 34: 408); cf. Aug. *Sermo Denis* 19.8 (Morin, vol. 1, pp. 106–7); *Gest. Conl. Carth.* 3.215–220 (*CCSL* 149A: 232–34). Girardet, "Petition der Donatisten," has argued convincingly that the letter reported at Opt. 1.22.1–2, which purports to be a Donatist petition to Constantine for a hearing by Gallic bishops, is a forgery.

26. E.g., Aug. *Ep.* 88 .2 (*CSEL* 34: 408): *libellus ecclesiae catholicae criminum Caeciliani traditus a parte Maiorini*; *Gest. Conl. Carth.*, cap. gest. 3.315 (*CCSL* 149A: 35–36): *chartas criminum eius.*

27. Girardet, "Petition der Donatisten," pp. 200–202, assembles nine citations from texts of Augustine confirming his understanding that the Donatists' original charges were criminal or civil and that they wished Constantine himself to grant them a hearing; cf. Girardet, *Kaisergericht und Bischofsgericht*, pp. 10–19; "Reichskonzil von Rom," pp. 105–7.

28. Eus. *HE* 10.5.18–20; cf. *Gest. Conl. Carth.*, cap. gest. 3.318 (*CCSL* 149A: 36); Aug. *Brev. Coll.* 3.12[24] (*CCSL* 149A: 289). On the Council of Rome, see Calderone, *Costantino*, pp. 180–81 and 231–49; Girardet, "Reichskonzil von Rom."

29. Opt. 1.23.1–2; Aug. *C. part. Don.* 33[56] (*CSEL* 53: 158); cf. Maier, *Dossier*, vol. 1, no. 17, with further references. On the Lateran church and the *domus Faustae*, see above pp. 182–83.

30. Opt. *App.* 3 (*CSEL* 26: 205): *ut istud post iudicium suum habitum Africam ipsos remeasse prohiberent.*

31. Opt. *App.* 3 (*CSEL* 26: 205): *respondendum aestimaverunt, omnis causa non fuisset audita, sed potius idem episcopi quodam loco se clausissent et prout ipsis aptum fuerat iudicassent*; Eus. *HE* 10.5.22: καὶ μὴ πρότερον ἁπάντων τῶν ὀφειλόντων ζητηθῆναι ἀκριβῶς ἐξετασθέντων πρὸς τὸ τὴν κρίσιν ἐξενέγκαι πάνυ ταχέως καὶ ὀξέως ἔσπευσαν; Aug. *Ep.* 88.3 (*CSEL* 34: 409): *non recte iudicatum neque omnem causam auditam esse conquesti sunt*; cf. *Ep.* 43.7[20] (*CSEL* 34: 101–2).

32. Opt. *App.* 3 (*CSEL* 26: 204–6).

33. Eus. *HE* 10.5.21.24; Opt. *App.* 3 (*CSEL* 26: 205–6), esp. *data evectione publica.*

34. Constantine does not seem to have attended the Council of Arles; see above pp. 76 and 305 n. 44.

35. Opt. *App.* 4 (*CSEL* 26: 206–8). On the canons, see *Concilium Arelatense a. 314* can. 9, 14–15 (*CCSL* 148: 6, 10, 12); cf. Maier, *Dossier*, vol. 1, no. 20. On the council, see Girardet, "Konstantin der Grosse und das Reichskonzil von Arles."

36. Opt. *App.* 5 (*CSEL* 26: 210): *ceterum direxi meos homines, qui eosdem infandos deceptores religionis protinus ad comitatum meum perducant, ut ibi degant, ibi sibi mortem peius pervideant.*

37. Opt. *App.* 5 (*CSEL* 26: 208–10); Opt. 1.25.2; Aug. *Ep.* 43.7[20] (*CSEL* 34: 101–2).

38. Opt. *App.* 5 (*CSEL* 26: 208–10): *meum iudicium postulant qui ipse iudicium Christi expecto. dico enim, ut se ueritas habet, sacerdotum iudicium ita debet haberi, ac si ipse dominus residens iudicet . . . perquirunt saecularia relinquentes caelestia. o rabida furoris audacia! sicut in causis gentilium fieri solet, appellationem interposuerunt . . . quid hi detractatores legis, qui renuentes caeleste iudicium meum putauerunt postulandum?*

39. *CTh* 1.27.1 (Jun. 23, 318); *Sirm.* 1 (May 5, 333); cf. above pp. 198–99.

40. For the Donatists' petitions to return, see Opt. 1.26.1; cf. Aug. *Brev. Coll.* 3.20[38] (*CCSL* 149A: 302). For Constantine's permission, see Opt. *App.* 8 (*CSEL* 26: 212).

41. The *acta* of the trial are recorded at Opt. *App.* 2 (*CSEL* 26: 197–204). See also Aug. *C. Cresc.* 3.70[81] (*CSEL* 52: 485–87); *C. part. Don.* 33[56] (*CSEL* 53: 158); *Ep.* 88.3–4 (*CSEL* 34: 409–11); Opt. 1.27.1–6. See Maier, *Dossier*, vol. 1, pp. 171–72, on the date.

42. Opt. *App.* 6 (*CSEL* 26: 210–11).

43. Opt. *App.* 7 (*CSEL* 26: 211–12).

44. Aug. *C. Cresc.* 3.71[82] (*CSEL* 52: 487); *C. part. Don.* 33[56] (*CSEL* 53: 158); Aug. *Ep.* 43.7[20] (*CSEL* 34: 101–2). Further references at Maier, *Dossier*, vol. 1, p. 197 n. 2.

45. The law itself is no longer extant, but Augustine's summary of it indicates fiscal confiscation, see Aug. *Ep.* 88.3 (*CSEL* 34: 409): *primus contra vestram partem legem consituit, ut loca congregationum vestrarum fisco vindicarentur*; *Ep.* 93.14 (*CSEL* 34: 458): *ille quippe imperator primus constituit in hac causa, ut res convictorum et unitati pervicaciter resistentium fisco vindicarentur*; cf. *Ep.* 105.9 (*CSEL* 34: 601); *C. Litt. Petil.* 2.92[205] (*CSEL* 52: 130). For the rhetoric of "*unitas*," see *Passio Donati* 3, 5 (Dolbeau, pp. 258, 260): *Christus, inquit, amator unitatis est; unitas igitur fiat*, and *Poterat igitur disciplinae salutaris eversor castitatem fidei unitatis vocabulo violare, id est unitatem ipsam sibi non Deo cogere.* Interestingly, in Constantine's extant law confiscating the property of heretics recorded at Eus. *V. Const.* 3.64–65, Constantine orders the transfer of their churches to Catholic clergy and fiscal confiscation only of their remaining property. One wonders if this was not also the principle followed in 316 but then elided in Augustine's summary of the law.

46. *Passio Donati* 2–3 (Dolbeau, p. 258): *non solum oblectans inani gloria miseros sed et regali amicitia muneribusque terrenis circumscribens avaros . . . mittit pecunias quibus vel fidem caperet vel professionem legis occasionem fecerit avaritiae.*

47. Dolbeau, cf. Maier, *Dossier*, vol. 1, no. 28. Dolbeau, p. 254, shows that the text describes the martyrdom of just one named cleric and an unspecified number of congregants in a single incident rather than a series of two or even three separate incidents.

48. *Passio Donati* 1 (Dolbeau, p. 257): *Proditione ergo luporum latentium sub vestitu ovium*; cf. 7 (Dolbeau, p. 261): *ministros diaboli.*

49. *Passio Donati* 7 (Dolbeau, p. 261): *quia nec alius ostendebatur Christi domini servus quam ille qui haec eadem patiebatur quae et ipse passus est dominus, etc.*

50. *Passio Donati* 6 (Dolbeau, p. 260): *non solum fugatus non est inmeninentis exitiosae mortis metu, quin potius ad orationis domum voto passionis animosius convolavit.*

51. *Passio Donati* 6 (Dolbeau, p. 260).

52. There may even have been "martyrs" in the riots that occurred in summer 315. This would seem to be the implication of Constantine's assertion at Opt. *App.* 7 (*CSEL* 26: 211–12): *cumque satis clareat neminem posse beatitudines martyris eo genere conquirere, quod alienum a veritate religionis et incogruum esse videatur.*

53. In the *De ecclesiae catholicae unitate* (*SCh* 500), Cyprian had already counseled unity as the underlying principle of church authority in the wake of dissension in the North African church following the persecution of Decius. On Constantine's longing for unity, see also Girardet, *Konstantinische Wende*, pp. 135–38; Kahlos, pp. 62–64.

54. See Opt. *App.* 3 (*CSEL* 26: 204): *uesano furore vanis criminationibus . . . ad ipsorum dedecus infamiamque . . . obnixe ac pertinaciter*; Opt. *App.* 5 (*CSEL* 26: 209): *malignitas diaboli . . . quibus ingenita est maxima durities animi . . . tanta vesania perseverat; vis malignitatis . . . perseverat*; Opt. *App.* 7 (*CSEL* 26: 211–12): *insania . . . errori se pravissimo dederunt . . . contra fas et religionem ipsam . . . insaniae suae obstinationisque temerariae*; Opt. *App.* 6 (*CSEL* 26: 210–11): *turbulentos satis et obstinato animo . . . nimia vestra obstinatione*; Opt. *App.* 10 (*CSEL* 26: 214–15): *insanus, perfidus, inreligiosus, profanus, deo contrarius . . . qui a diabolo possessi sunt . . . qui malo impiae mentis infecti sunt . . . impiis et sceleratis, sacrilegis et profanis, perfidis et inreligiosis et deo ingratis et ecclesiae inimicis.* More on this rhetoric at Girardet, *Konstantinische Wende*, pp. 140–41; Wienand, *Kaiser als Sieger*, pp. 404–11.

55. Aug. *Brev. Coll.* 3.20–22[38–40] (*CCSL* 149A: 302–3): *ibi dicunt nullo modo se communicaturos antistiti ipsius nebuloni paratosque esse perpeti quidquid eis facere voluissent.* Cf. Aug. *Ep.* 141.9 (*CSEL* 44: 243); *Gest. Conl. Carth.*, cap. gest. 3.543–7 (*CCSL* 149A: 50).

56. Aug. *C. part. Don.* 31[54], 33[56] (*CSEL* 53: 155, 158); *Ep.* 141.9 (*CSEL* 44: 242); *Gest. Conl. Carth.*, cap. gest. 3.548–50 (*CCSL* 149A: 50).

57. Opt. *App.* 9 (*CSEL* 26: 212–13): *Constantinus Augustus universis episcopis per Africam et plebi ecclesiae catholicae*; *Gest. Conl. Carth.*, cap. gest. 3.548 (*CCSL* 149A 50).

58. Opt. *App.* 9 (*CSEL* 26: 213).

59. The same rhetoric appeared in Constantine's letter to Verinus, Aug. *C. part. Don.* 33[56] (*CSEL* 53.158): *de illorum exilio soluto et eorum furore deo vindici dimittendo literas dedit*. See also Eus. *V. Const.* 1.45.1.

60. Frend, *Donatist Church*, p. 161; Maier, *Dossier*, vol. 1, p. 240; Wienand, *Der Kaiser als Sieger*, p. 410.

61. Eus. *V. Const.* 2.64–67.

62. Opt. *App.* 10 (*CSEL* 26: 214.34, 37; 215.16, 32). A paradigmatic case of the divisions that racked Cirta can be found in the Donatist bishop Petilianus, who had been born into a Catholic family but was kidnapped, baptized, and consecrated bishop by the Donatists; Aug. *C. lit. Petil.* 2.104[239] (*CSEL* 52: 155); *Sermo ad Caes. Pleb.* 8 (*CSEL* 53: 177).

63. Opt. *App.* 10 (*CSEL* 26: 214.32–215.10), esp. *deus siquidem se omnium vindicem promisit. et ideo cum vindicta deo permittitur, acrius de inimicis supplicium sumitur.*

64. Hier. *Vir. ill.* 80; *Chron. s.a.* 317–320. On the dating of Lactantius's career, see above pp. 37–38.

65. Digeser, "Lactantius and Constantine's Letter to Arles"; *Making of a Christian Empire*, pp. 169–71. On the date of the dedications, see Lenski, "Valore dell'Editto di Milano." Lactantius's thought was also central to Constantine's *Oration to the Saints*; see Girardet, *Rede an die Versammlung der Heiligen*, pp. 20–25.

66. Lact. *Div. Inst.* 5.19.22–24: *defendenda enim religio est non occidendo sed moriendo, non saevitia sed patientia, non scelere sed fide . . . recta igitur ratio est ut religionem patientia uel morte defendas*. See Digeser, *Making of a Christian Empire*, pp. 108–14, for analysis.

67. Lact. *Div. inst.* 5.20.12, 21.2, 21.7, 22.2, 22.3, 22.4, 22.5, 22.11, 22.12, 22.13, 23.23. On the importance of *patientia* as a Christian virtue, see also *Div. Inst.* 2.17.3, 4.18.1–19.11; 5.7.6, 13.11; 6.4.7–15, 17.7–23.32; 7.15.7–8, 27.3–11.

68. See especially Lact. *Div. Inst.* 5.23.3; cf. 2.17.1–5; 5.20.9–10; 7.21.1–8.

69. Shaw, pp. 807–810 app. A, with earlier literature.

70. Opt. 3.4.5–6. On the circumcellions, see Shaw, 630–74; cf. Lenski, "Harnessing Violence."

71. Opt. 3.4.8–12.

72. For the *Passio Isaac and Maximiani*, see Mastandrea, pp. 76–88; cf. Maier, *Dossier*, vol. 1, no. 36, with Shaw, pp. 173–78.

73. For the *Passio Marculi*, see Mastandrea, pp. 65–75; cf. Maier, *Dossier*, vol. 1, no. 37. For analysis, see Grig, pp. 54–58; Shaw, pp. 178–85. Aug. *Tract. in Joh.* 11.15 (*CCSL* 36: 120) claims Marculus jumped rather than being thrown. Marculus was commemorated in a chapel dedicated at the church of Ksar el Kelb (near Tebessa); cf. *AE* 1935: 121 with Cayrel, pp. 114–42; Duval, *Loca sanctorum*, vol. 1, no. 75; Grig, pp. 54–58.

74. Opt. 3.1.1, 12.2–6; *Gest. Conl. Carth.* 3.258 (*CCSL* 149A: 250); Aug. *C. lit. Pet.* 2.92[202]; 3.25[29] (*CSEL* 52: 125–26, 184–85).

75. *CTh* 16.5.37–38, 52; *CTh* 16.6.3–5.

76. Evidence at Maier, *Dossier*, vol. 2, pp. 207–400. Analysis at Conant, pp. 324–28.

CHAPTER 14. COMPLEX CITIES

1. On Alexandria's population, see Haas, pp. 45–47; Hahn, *Gewalt*, pp. 16–17. On Antioch's, see Downey, pp. 582–83; Hahn, *Gewalt*, pp. 125–26.

2. On Alexandria's ethnic and religious pluralism, see Alston, pp. 157–84; Kasher; Haas, passim; Hahn, *Gewalt*, pp. 21–120; Watts, *City and School*, pp. 143–68. On Antioch's, see Downey, passim, esp. pp. 586–87; Wilken; Hahn, *Gewalt*, pp. 121–90.

3. Eus. *HE* 9.1.3–2.1; Lact. *Mort. Pers.* 36.3 with Mitchell, "Maximinus and the Christians," p. 114; cf. above pp. 93–94.

4. See Bardy, pp. 61–81; Mitchell, "Maximinus and the Christians," p. 118; Barnes, "Date of the Martyrdom of Lucian," and above p. 162.

5. Van Heesch.

6. Eus. *V. Const.* 4.25.2–3; Soc. 1.18.1–3; cf. Soz. 1.8.5; 5.3.3 and Hermann. The confiscation had to have occurred before April 328, when Alexander died. The church in question is likely to have been that named after the patriarch Theonas.

7. Tert. *Ad nat.* 1.9 (*CCSL* 1: 23): *Si Tiberis redu<nda>uit, si Nilus non redundauit, si caelum stetit, si terra mouit, <si lues> <aes>tiua uastauit, si fames afflixit, statim omnium uox: christi<anorum meri>tum!*

8. Soz. 5.3.3; cf. Greg. Naz. *Or.* 5.32 (*PG* 35: 705B).

9. Ruf. *HE* 2.30 and below n. 14. Lib. *Or.* 30.35–36 makes it clear that, in the 380s, he continued to regard the elimination of the Nile cult as a threat to the flood and Egypt's grain supply. This helps explain why Christians simply adopted the ritual and iconographic elements of the Nile cult into their own worship, particularly through the figure of the archangel Michael; see Hermann, pp. 38–69; cf. Frankfurter, pp. 42–46.

10. Saʿid ibn al-Batrīq (Euthychius) *Chron.* 433–35 (*PG* 111: 1005); cf. Van Esbroeck, p. 1617.

11. For Alexandria's long history of public conflict and rioting, see Alston, pp. 219–35.

12. Amm. 22.11.2–12; Jul. *Ep.* 60 (379A–B); *Hist. Aceph.* 2.10 (*SCh* 317: 148); Soc. 3.2.1–3.25; Soz. 4.30.1–2; 5.7.2–9. See also *PLRE* 1: Diodorus 2; Dracontius 1; as well as Matthews, *Roman Empire*, pp. 442–44; Alston, p. 286; Hahn, *Gewalt*, pp. 60–74.

13. Epiph. *Pan.* 69.2.3.

14. Ruf. *HE* 2.22–30; Soc. 5.16.1–17.11; Soz. 7.15.2–10; Theod. *HE* 5.22.3–6; cf. Thelamon, pp. 245–79; Haas, pp. 161–69; Alston, p. 288; Hahn, *Gewalt*, pp. 85–97; Watts, *Riot in Alexandria*, pp. 191–96; *Final Pagan Generation*, pp. 1–5, 213–15.

15. Lib. *Or.* 30.35 confirms that the Nile rituals continued until 386 at least.

16. Joh. Mal. 13.3–4 (Dindorf, pp. 318–19 = Thurn, pp. 244–45). On the octagonal church, see above p. 188 fig. 36.

17. On the journey to Antioch, see below nn. 20–22. The passage is also incorrect to claim that "Felicianus" (presumably *PLRE* 1: Fl. Felicianus 5) was a Christian, an assertion disproven by the unpublished inscription translated at Athanassiadi, "Fate of Oracles," p. 276. It is also wrong to name Constantine's Praetorian Prefect said to have constructed the Basilica Rufinus. No PPO named Rufinus is attested under Constantine in extant fasti; cf. *PLRE* 1: 1048; Barnes, *New Empire*, pp. 131–32. By the same token, *PLRE* 1: Flavius Rufinus 18, the only attested Rufinus known to have served as PPO Orientis, is known to have constructed a basilica in Antioch, but only under Theodosius I, under whom he served from 392 to 395. The only other official named in the passage, "Plutarch," is otherwise unattested, but cannot have served as "governor of Antioch in Syria" (ἄρχοντα Ἀντιοχείας τῆς Συρίας)—as the passage suggests—for there was no such post; cf. *PLRE* 1: Plutarchus 2. On buildings in Malalas more generally, see Moffatt.

18. See above pp. 234–40 and pp. 170–71.

19. See above p. 232.

20. *RIC* 7: Antioch 48; cf. 39, 41 FELIX PROCESSVS COS VI AVG; 40, 46 FELIX PROCESSVS COS II. Following P. Bruun, *Roman Imperial Coinage*, vol. 7, pp. 77, 664, Barnes, *New Empire*, p. 76, and Lane Fox, pp. 638–39, accept a journey as far as Antioch in late 324, but Constantine's testimony at Eus. *V. Const.* 2.72.2–3, quoted below, seems decisive against this assumption.

21. *P. Oxy.* 1261; 1626.

22. Eus. *V. Const* 2.72.2–3; cf. 3.5.3 and Opitz *Urkunde* 25.9 p. 54 = Brennecke *Dokument* 29.9 p. 116. *V. Const.* 3.4.1 even indicates that the disturbances grew agitated enough that statues of the emperor were treated with insult (ταῖς βασιλέως τολμᾶν ἐνυβρίζειν εἰκόσιν).

23. On the Donatist controversy, see Chapter 13.

24. Eus. *V. Const.* 3.4.1.

25. Constantine continued to hold out the prospect of a visit to Egypt before the Alexandrians as a way to encourage the restoration of unity in the aftermath of the Council of Nicaea, Athan. *De decr. syn.* 38.9 (Opitz *Urkunde* 25.9 p. 54 = Brennecke *Dokument* 29 p. 116).

26. Hanson, *Search*; R. Williams, *Arius*; Roldanus, pp. 69–113; Parvis.

27. My approach is closely aligned with the outstanding work on heresy as a tool for articulating power dynamics done by MacMullen, *Voting About God*; Humfress, *Orthodoxy and the Courts*, pp. 217–68; and Galvão-Sobrinho.

28. See Hanson, *Search,* pp. 134–35, with sources, esp. Epiph. *Pan.* 69.1.1–5.3; Soc. 1.5–6; Soz. 1.15; Gel. Cyz. *HE* 2.3.3–21; Opitz *Urkunde* 1–5 pp. 1–12 = Brennecke *Dokument* 10, 15–16 pp. 86–87, 90–1. On this period in the controversy, Galvão-Sobrinho, pp. 35–77, is unparalleled for its insightful explanation of how both sides in the dispute, and particularly Arius, succeeded in mobilizing support.

29. Eus. *V. Const.* 1.51.1; cf. Barnes, *Constantine and Eusebius,* pp. 70–72; Corcoran, *Empire of the Tetrarchs,* p. 195.

30. Eus. *V. Const.* 2.64.1–72.3 (Opitz *Urkunde* 17 p. 32–35 = Brennecke *Dokument* 19 p. 99–101) at 71.1: ὑμῶν γὰρ ἐν ἀλλήλοις ὑπὲρ μικρῶν καὶ λίαν ἐλαχίστων φιλονεικούντων.

31. For the chronology, see Burgess, *Studies*, pp. 184–91.

32. Galvão-Sobrinho, pp. 74–75, 81–84. A letter from the synod was found in a Syriac version and first published by E. Schwartz in 1905. It is now most accessible at Opitz *Urkunde* 18 pp. 36–41 = Brennecke *Dokument* 20 pp. 102–4. See more on the document at Brennecke *Dokument*, pp. xxxiv–xxxvi.

33. Opitz *Urkunde* 18.15 p. 40 = Brennecke *Dokument* 20.15 p. 104 with Chadwick.

34. On the Melitians, see A. Martin, *Athanase d'Alexandrie*, pp. 217–98, 303–12, and the essays in Hauben.

35. The change of venue is reported at Opitz *Urkunde* 20 pp. 41–42 = Brennecke *Dokument* 22 p. 105; cf. Eus. *V. Const.* 3.6.1. For an imaginative effort to explain the change—with ample bibliography—see Logan, "Marcellus of Ancyra."

36. On the vicennalia, see Barnes, *New Empire*, p. 76. On the Council of Nicaea, see Hanson, *Search*, pp. 152–78; Drake, *Constantine and the Bishops*, pp. 250–57; Parvis, pp. 81–95; Galvão-Sobrinho, pp. 84–93.

37. For Ossius's presidency, see De Clercq, pp. 228–32; Hanson, *Search*, pp. 154–55. For Constantine's vaunted role, see above pp. 76 and 305 n. 46.

38. Soc. 1.8.18–19; Soz. 1.17.4; Theod. 1.11.4–6.

39. Philost. *HE* 1.10; Opitz *Urkunde* 23.5, 27.15–16, 28, 31.2 pp. 48, 62, 65 = Brennecke *Dokument* 25, 31, 32, 36 pp. 108, 120, 125; cf. Soz. 1.21.3–4.

40. Constantine's letter to Alexander and Arius (a. 324), Eus. *V. Const.* 2.66.1: ἐνίους ὑμῶν πρὸς τὴν τῶν πρὸς ἀλλήλους διχονοούντων ὁμόνοιαν βοηθοὺς ἀποστείλαιμι; 2.72.3: ἀνοίξατε δή μοι λοιπὸν ἐν τῇ καθ᾽ ὑμᾶς ὁμονοίᾳ τῆς ἑῴας τὴν ὁδόν; Constantine's speech to the Nicene assembly (a. 325), Gel. Cyz. *HE* 2.7.39: καταξιώσητε εἰς μίαν ὁμόνοιαν καὶ εἰρήνην τῆς καθολικῆς πίστεως βλέψαντες; Letter to the Antiochians (a. 328), Eus. *V. Const.* 3.60.1, 9: 1. Ὡς κεχαρισμένη γε τῇ τοῦ κόσμου συνέσει τε καὶ σοφίᾳ ἡ παρ᾽ ὑμῶν ὁμόνοια. . . . 9. ἐξ οὗ τὸν ῥύπον ἐκεῖνον ἀπωσάμενοι ἀντεισηνέγκατε ἤθει ἀγαθῷ τὴν ὁμόνοιαν; Letter to Alexander of Alexandria (a. 328), Gel. Cyz. *HE* 3.15.1 (Opitz *Urkunde* 32 p. 66 = Brennecke *Dokument* 37 p. 126): 3. ἐγώ

εἰμι ὁ ὑμέτερος συνθεράπων, ὃς πᾶσαν τὴν περὶ τῆς ἡ<μετέρας εἰρήνης> καὶ <u>ὁμονοίας</u> ἐπανήρημαι φροντίδα. . . . 4. τὰ μίση τῇ <u>ὁμονοίᾳ</u> νικήσητε ἄν. . . . 5. ἐπικουρήσατε οὖν, παρακαλῶ, τῇ <u>ὁμονοίᾳ</u>. . . . ποιήσατέ με ἀκοῦσαι ταῦτα, ἅπερ βούλομαι καὶ ἐπιθυμῶ, τὴν τῶν πάντων ὑμῶν εἰρήνην καὶ <u>ὁμόνοιαν</u>. Letter to the Alexandrians (a. 332), Athan. *Apol. c. Ar.* 62.6: παντὶ σθένει διώξατε τοὺς τὴν τῆς ἡμετέρας <u>ὁμονοίας</u> χάριν ἀφανίζειν ἐπιθυμοῦντας καὶ πρὸς τὸν θεὸν ἀπιδόντες ὑμᾶς αὐτοὺς ἀγαπᾶτε; Letter to John Arkaph, *Athan. Apol. c. Ar.* 70.2: ἔγνων γὰρ . . . σε, τῇ δὲ ἐκκλησίᾳ, ὡς προσῆκον ἦν, κεκοινωνηκέναι καὶ Ἀθανασίῳ τῷ αἰδεσιμωτάτῳ ἐπισκόπῳ ἐς τὰ μάλιστα εἰς <u>ὁμόνοιαν</u> ἐλθεῖν; Letter to the Synod of Tyre (a. 333), Eus. *V. Const.* 4.42.1: εἰς <u>ὁμόνοιαν</u> ἐπαναγαγεῖν τὰ διεστῶτα τῶν μελῶν. For related sentiments, see Constantine's Letter to the Alexandrians (a. 325), Athan. *De decr. syn.* 38 (Opitz *Urkunde* 25.9 p. 54 = Brennecke *Dokument* 29.9 p. 116): διὸ μηδεὶς ἀμφιβαλλέτω, μηδεὶς ὑπερτιθέσθω, ἀλλὰ προθύμως πάντες εἰς τὴν ἀληθεστάτην ὁδὸν ἐπάνιτε, ἵν᾽ ἐπειδὰν ὅσον οὐδέπω πρὸς ὑμᾶς ἀφίκωμαι, τὰς ὀφειλομένας τῷ παντεφόρῳ θεῷ μεθ᾽ ὑμῶν ὁμολογήσω χάριτας, ὅτι τὴν εἰλικρινῆ πίστιν ἐπιδείξας τὴν εὐκταίαν ἡμῖν ἀγάπην ἀποδέδωκεν. See also the penetration of this rhetoric into the ecclesiastical historians: Eus. *V. Const.* 4.41.4: σὺν <u>ὁμονοίᾳ</u> καὶ συμφωνίᾳ τῇ πάσῃ ἔχεσθαι τῶν προκειμένων διὰ γραφῆς οὕτως ἐχούσης ἐδήλου; Soz. 1.16.3: ἐκέλευσεν <u>ὁμονοεῖν</u>; 2.22.9: τοὺς ἐπιβουλεύοντας τῇ αὐτῶν <u>ὁμονοίᾳ</u> παντὶ σθένει διώκειν.

41. Soc. 1.14.1, 25.1–11; Soz. 2.16.2, 7; Philost. *HE* 2.7 with Opitz *Urkunde* 29–32 pp. 63–66 = Brennecke *Dokument* 33–34, 36–37 pp. 120–21, 126. On these events, see also Hanson, *Search*, pp. 175–78; Parvis, pp. 100–107. The chronology is a matter of ongoing dispute. For 328, see Barnes, "Exile and Recalls of Arius." For 327, see Galvão-Sobrinho, pp. 105–6, 165–71.

42. For what follows, see Eus. *V. Const.* 3.59.1–63.1; Theod. *HE* 1.20–21; Soc. 1.23–24; Soz. 2.18–19; Philost. *HE* 2.7, with Cavallera, pp. 33–49; Hanson, *Search*, pp. 208–17; Hahn, *Gewalt*, pp. 157–60. On the date of Eustathius's deposition, I follow Burgess, "Date of the Deposition," pace Hanson, "Fate of Eustathius." I follow Theodoret in assuming that Eusebius of Nicomedia led the synod, although Socrates and Sozomen imply it was Eusebius of Caesarea. Scholarly opinion is divided on the matter.

43. For Sabellianism, see Soc. 1.24.1–5. For impregnating the girl, Philost. *HE* 2.7; Theod. *HE* 1.20.5–8. For insulting Helena, Athan. *Hist. Ar.* 4.1.

44. Jer. *Vir. ill.* 85 places his exile in Trajanopolis; cf. Theod. *HE* 1.20.9; Philost. *HE* 2.7; Joh. Chrys. *In Eustathium* (*PG* 50: 602).

45. Athan. *Hist. Ar.* 4 with Hanson, *Search*, p. 209.

46. Philost. *HE* 1.8a; 2.3, 14; 3.15 catalogs eleven male disciples of Lucian, including Eusebius of Nicomedia (cf. Epiph. *Pan.* 69.5.2), Maris of Chalcedon, Theognis of Nicaea, and Leontius, who later became bishop of Antioch. The letter of Alexander of Alexandria transmitted at Theod. *HE* 1.4.4–61 charges at 36 that Arius himself was a disciple of Lucian (cf. Opitz *Urkunde* 14 p. 25 = Brennecke *Dokument* 36 p. 95). More on Lucian at Bardy; Downey, pp. 337–42.

47. Philost. *HE* 2.12, 12a, and pp. 161–62.

48. Eus. *V. Const.* 3.59.2, 60.8; Soc. 1.24.6; Soz. 2.19.2; cf. Opitz *Urkunde* 18.3 p. 37 = Brennecke *Dokument* 20.3 p. 102. On these disturbances, see Parvis, pp. 107–10.

49. *Conc. Nic.* can. 15 (Mansi 2: 673–76 = Jonkers 44–45).

50. Eus. *V. Const.* 3.60.3: ὁμολογῶ γὰρ ἀνεγνωκέναι τὰ ὑπομνήματα, ἐν οἷς λαμπραῖς {τ'} εὐφημίαις τε καὶ μαρτυρίαις, αἷς εἰς Εὐσέβιον εἰσηνέγκασθε ἐπίσκοπον ἤδη Καισαρέων ὄντα . . . ἑώρων ὑμᾶς ἐγκειμένως αὐτὸν σφετεριζομένους. On this passage, see Dillon, pp. 121–36, esp. 131–33.

51. *CTh* 1.16.6 (Nov. 1, 331). On the role of *acclamationes* in the later Roman Empire, see Roueché; Ando, *Imperial Ideology*, pp. 199–205; Wiemer, "Akklamationen." On the use of *acclamationes* in the context of religious dispute, see MacMullen, *Voting About God*, pp. 13–21 and passim; cf. Peterson, pp. 148–83.

52. See, for example, *CTh* 11.7.4 (a. 328) and *Frag. Vat.* 35.5.

53. Eus. *V. Const.* 3.62.1: τὸν κανόνα τῆς ἐκκλησιαστικῆς ἐπιστήμης εἰς ἀκρίβειαν φυλαχθέντα κατενόησα; 2: ἢ τάς τε ἐντολὰς τοῦ θεοῦ καὶ τὸν ἀποστολικὸν κανόνα καὶ <τὸν> τῆς ἐκκλησίας φυλάττειν ἔγνωκεν; 3: ὃ καὶ αὐτῷ τῷ θεῷ καὶ τῇ ἐκκλησίᾳ πρεπωδέστατον νομισθείη.

54. Σύνεσις, literally "union" and, by extension, "intelligence," is commonly used as an abstract designation for bishops in Eusebius's translation of Constantine's correspondence—e.g., Eus *V. Const.* 2.71.2; 4.36.2. The word can also mean a legal "decision, decree" (*LSJ* s.v. V.). It is unclear here which connotation is intended. My rendering of the word as "judgment" affords polyvalency along the same semantic vectors as the Greek. Note that the word is used in five instances in this letter, in at least one of which it almost certainly refers to the judgment of the bishops. It is also used three times in the document immediately preceding, Constantine's letter to Eusebius, Eus. *V. Const.* 3.61.1, 2, 3.

55. This list is most clearly prescribed at *CTh* 11.30.16 = *CJ* 7.62.19 (a. 331), but see also *CTh* 11.20.1 = *CJ* 7.61.1 (a. 312); *CTh* 11.30.5 = *CJ* 7.62.13 (a. 316); *CTh* 11.30.6 = *CJ* 1.21.2 (a. 316); *CTh* 11.30.8 (a. 319); *CTh* 11.30.14 (a. 327); *CTh* 11.30.11 = *CJ* 7.62.16 (a. 321). On Constantine's reforms to appellate procedure, see Pergami, pp. 85–119; Dillon, pp. 214–50.

56. For their presence, see Eus. *V. Const.* 3.62.1, cf. 3.59.3; Soc. 1.24.6; Soz. 2.19.2. See also *PLRE* 1: Acacius 4; Strategius Musonianus. Amm. 15.13.1–2 tells us that Strategius, a Christian, was a favorite of Constantine's and was nicknamed Musonianus by the emperor both for his linguistic acumen and for his ability to manage religious disputes.

57. Jer. *Chron.* s.a. 328 reports the succession as Eulalius, Eusebius, Euphronius, P/Flaccillus, Stephanus, Leontius. See also Soz. 3.20.4 and Theod. *HE* 21.1 for variant lists.

58. Soz. 3.20.4–8; Theod. *HE* 2.12.1–3; cf. 1.21.2.

59. Barnes, *New Empire,* p. 86; *Athanasius and Constantius,* p. 219.

60. The office is first attested at Joh. Mal. 13.4 (Dindorf, p. 319 = Thurn, p. 245), in the problematic passage discussed above at pp. 263 and 352 n. 17, which claims its first holder was *PLRE* 1: Felicianus 5. Other Constantinian *Comites Orientis* are also attested, including *PLRE* 1: Ianuarius 2 and Q. Flavius Maesius Egnatius Lollianus signo Mavortius 5.

61. Ruf. *HE* 1.31.

62. See Cavallera; Spoerl.

63. This has been questioned by Gwynn, who holds that the "Eusebians" are largely a construct of Athanasius's making. There seem to be enough cross-checks on Athanasius's report, however, that this is a difficult position to hold. The controversies attendant on the early years of the Arian controversy in Alexandria are covered most comprehensively at A. Martin, *Athanase d'Alexandrie,* pp. 341–89. See also Lenski, "Early Retrospectives," for intervening bibliography.

64. Soc. 1.23.3–5; Philost. *HE* 2.7, 7a; cf. Eus. *V. Const.* 3.23.1. The precise circumstances of this gathering are disputed, but see Parvis, pp. 97–105, for a reasoned assessment and bibliography.

65. Gel. Cyz. *HE* 3.15.1 (Opitz *Urkunde* 32 p. 66 = Brennecke *Dokument* 37 p. 126). For Arius's private interview with Constantine in late 327, see Soc. 1.25.1–11 (Opitz *Urkunde* 29 p. 63 = Brennecke *Dokument* 33 pp. 120–21).

66. Philost. *HE* 2.7, 7a.

67. *Fest. Ind.* pref. [330] (*SCh* 317: 226).

68. Philost. *HE* 2.11a.

69. Athan. *Apol. c. Arian.* 59.6: ἐὰν γὰρ γνῶ ὡς κεκώλυκάς τινας αὐτῶν τῆς ἐκκλησίας μεταποιουμένους ἢ ἀπείρξας τῆς εἰσόδου, ἀποστελῶ παραχρῆμα τὸν καὶ καθαιρήσοντά σε ἐξ ἐμῆς κελεύσεως καὶ τῶν τόπων μεταστήσοντα; cf. Brennecke *Dokument* 38 p. 127; Soc. 1.27.4; Soz. 2.22.5; Gel. Cyz. *HE* 3.14.14. As Brennecke *Dokument,* p. 127, points out, the date of this letter is uncertain, but it seems to fall early in Athanasius's episcopacy.

70. The same association is made at Epiphan. *Pan.* 68.6.1–6, but Epiphanius's version of events has clearly been influenced by Athanasius. Oddly, at *Pan.* 69.3.4, Epiphanius claims that it was Melitius who first denounced Arius to Alexander as a heretic.

71. *P. Lond.* 6: 1914 = *P. Jews* pp. 53–71; cf. A. Martin, *Athanase d'Alexandrie*, pp. 359–61; Galvão-Sobrinho, pp. 120–21.

72. Athan. *Apol. c. Arian.* 60.1–4; 63.1–5 with 65.1; Epiph. *Pan.* 68.7.5–9; Soc. 1.27.7–9; Soz. 2.22.7–8; Theod. *HE* 1.26.4; *Fest. Ind.* 3 (*SCh* 317: 228) with A. Martin, *Athanase d'Alexandrie*, pp. 348–51; Galvão-Sobrinho, pp. 173–74.

73. For Constantine's summons, see Athan. *Apol. c. Arian.* 60.3: ὁ δὲ βασιλεὺς γράφει καταγινώσκων μὲν Ἰσίωνος, κελεύων δὲ ἐμὲ ἀπαντῆσαι πρὸς αὐτόν. *Festal Letter* 4 (cf. *Fest. Ind.* 3 [*SCh* 317: 228]) confirms Athanasius's presence at the court under imperial orders on Apr. 2, 332. On the date of this letter, see Camplani, pp. 223–24; cf. Barnes, *Athanasius and Constantius*, pp. 188–89.

74. Athan. *Apol. c. Arian.* 61.1–62.7.

75. Opitz *Urkunde* 33–34 p. 66–75 with Galvão-Sobrinho, pp. 117–18.

76. Athan. *Apol. c. Arian.* 63.4; Epiph. *Pan.* 68.7.9. Although Athanasius's partisans were able to find Arsenius and produce him in person before the council of Tyre, his Melitian accusers continued to abide by the charge that Athanasius's bishop, Plousianus, had imprisoned Arsenius and tortured him; Soz. 2.25.11–12. More at Galvão-Sobrinho, pp. 172–73.

77. Athan. *Apol. c. Arian.* 65.1–5; Hilar. Pict. *Frg. Hist.* II.A.7 (*CSEL* 65: 54); cf. Soc. 1.27.19–21; Soz. 2.23.1, 25.1, 17; Theod. *HE* 1.28.2. For Dalmatius, see *PLRE* 1: Fl. Dalmatius 6. A similar situation had arisen in 315 when Constantine was forced to cancel a hearing against Caecilianus in Rome because the Carthaginian bishop refused to attend; see Opt. *App.* 6 (*CSEL* 26: 210–11); Aug. *Ep.* 43.7[20] (*CSEL* 34: 102).

78. On the charges of violence, see Soz. 2.25.2–12; cf. Galvão-Sobrinho, pp. 111–15. On the charge of grain embezzlement, see Athan. *Apol. c. Arian.* 18.2–3.

79. On the emperor's command ordering Athanasius to attend, see Athan. *Apol. c. Arian.* 71.3; cf. 72.1; Eus. *V. Const.* 4.42.4; Soc. 1.28.4. Athanasius's priest Macarius was actually brought to the council and detained there in chains; Athan. *Apol. c. Arian.* 71.2; Soc. 1.28.3.

80. On the Council of Tyre, see Athan. *Apol. c. Arian.* 71–81; Eus. *V. Const.* 4.41.1–42.5; Hilar. Pict. *Frg. Hist.* II.A.7 (*CSEL* 65: 54); Soc. 1.28.1–32.3; Soz. 2.25.2–20; Theod. *HE* 1.28.1–20.12 with A. Martin, *Athanase d'Alexandrie*, pp. 357–87; Parvis, pp. 123–27; Galvão-Sobrinho, pp. 120–23.

81. *Fest. Ind.* 8 (*SCh* 317: 232–34); Athan. *Apol. c. Arian.* 9.2; 82.1; *Ap. Const.* 1.3; cf. Soc. 1.31.4; Soz. 2.25.15–19; Theod. *HE* 1.30.11; Epiph. *Pan.* 68.9.4. Hilar. Pict. *Frg. Hist.* II.A.7 (*CSEL* 65: 54) is alone in indicating that Athanasius was present in Tyre to hear his sentence by the council. For the diversion of the bishops to Jerusalem for the dedication of the Holy Sepulchre, see Eus. *V. Const.* 4.43–44.

82. Athan. *Apol. c. Arian.* 86.6; cf. Soc. 1.34.5; Soz. 2.28.5; *Fest. Ind.* 8 (*SCh* 317: 232–34). On the exact chronology of this period, see Drake, "Athanasius' First Exile"; cf. *Constantine and the Bishops*, pp. 3–9, which paints the scene in lurid colors.

83. Athan. *Apol. c. Arian.* 9.3; 87.1–3; Soc. 1.35.2; Soz. 2.28.14, 31.2–3; *Fest. Ind.* 10 (*SCh* 317: 234); cf. Epiph. *Pan.* 68.9.1–6.

84. Soz. 2.31.2: ὡς στασιώδη καὶ ἐκκλησιαστικῇ καταδεδικασμένον κρίσει.

85. See Galvão-Sobrinho, pp. 171–72, for the ongoing resilience of the Arian community in Alexandria after 325.

86. See Barnes, *Athanasius and Constantius*; A. Martin, *Athanase d'Alexandrie*; cf. Lenski, *Failure of Empire*, pp. 235–38.

87. This argument is presented most eloquently in Drake, *Constantine and the Bishops*.

BIBLIOGRAPHY

Abbott, F. F., and A. C. Johnson. *Municipal Administration in the Roman Empire*. Princeton, NJ: Princeton University Press, 1926.

Abdy, R. "Appendix 2: Earliest Christian Symbols on Roman Coins." In *The Oxford Handbook of Greek and Roman Coinage*, ed. W. E. Metcalf, 662–66. Oxford: Oxford University Press, 2012.

Aiello, V. "Costantino, Lucio Domizio Alessandro e Cirta: Un caso di rielaborazione storiografica." In *L'Africa Romana: Atti del VI convegno di studio, Sassari, 16–18 dicembre 1988*, ed. A. Mastino, 179–96. Sassari: Gallizzi, 1989.

———. "Costantino 'eretico': Difesa della 'ortodossia' e anticostantinianesimo in età Teodosiana," *AARC* 10 (1991): 55–83.

———. "Costantino, la lebbra, e il battesimo di Silvestro." In *Costantino il Grande: dall'antichità all'umanesimo, Colloquio sul cristianesimo nel mondo antico, Macerata, 18–20 Dicembre 1990*, ed. G. Bonamente and F. Fusco, vol. 1, 17–58. Macerata, Italy: Università degli studi di Macerata, 1992.

———. *La Pars Costantiniana degli Excerpta Valesiana, introduzione, testo e commento storico*, 2nd ed. Messina: DICAM, 2014.

Aigner-Foresti, L., ed. *Die Integration der Etrusker und das Weiterwirken etruskischen Kulturgutes im republikanischen und Kaiserzeitlichen Rom*. Sitzungsberichte der Österreichischen Akademie der Wissenschaften, Philosophisch-Historische Klasse 658. Vienna: Verlag der Österreichischen Akademie der Wissenschaften, 1998.

———. "Regards sur Volsinii: Variations sur le thème de la survivance de la culture étrusque." In *Die Integration der Etrusker und das Weiterwirken etruskischen kulturgutes im republikanischen und kaiserzeitlichen Rom*, 421–34. Sitzungsberichte der Österreichischen Akademie der Wissenschaften, Philosophisch-Historische Klasse 658. Vienna: Verlag der Österreichischen Akademie der Wissenschaften, 1998.

Albertson, F. C. "Maxentian Hoards and the Mint at Ostia," *ANSMN* 30 (1985): 119–41.

Aleksova, B. "The Early Christian Basilicas at Stobi," *Corso di cultura sull'arte Ravennate e Bizantina* 33 (1986): 13–81.

Alföldi, A. "On the Foundation of Constantinople: A Few Notes," *JRS* 37 (1947): 10–16 + pls. I–IV.

———. *The Conversion of Constantine and Pagan Rome*. Oxford: Oxford University Press, 1948.

Alföldi, M. R. *Die Constantinische Goldprägung: Untersuchungen zu ihrer Bedeutung für Kaiserpolitik und Hofkunst*. Mainz: R. Habelt, 1963.

———. "Die Sol Comes-Münze vom Jahre 325: Neues zur Bekehrung Constantins." In *Mullus. Festschift Theodor Klauser*. Jahrbuch für Antike und Christentum Ergänzungsband 1, ed. K. Weitzmann, 10–16. Münster: Aschendorff, 1964. Reprinted in M. R. Alföldi, *Gloria Romanorum. Schriften zur Spätantike zum 75. Geburtstag der Verfasserin*. Stuttgart: Franz Steiner Verlag, 2001, no. 3.

Alston, R. *The City in Roman and Byzantine Egypt*. London: Routledge, 2002.

Alt, A. *Die griechischen Inschriften der Palaestina Tertia westlich der 'Araba*. Berlin: W. de Gruyter, 1921.

Amandry, P. "Chronique Delphique," *BCH* 105 (1981): 673–769.

Amann, P. "Das konstantinische 'Reskript von Hispellum' (*CIL* XI 5265) und seine Aussagekraft für die etrusko-umbrischen Beziehungen," *Tyche* 17 (2002): 1–27.

———. *Die antiken Umbrer zwischen Tiber und Apennin: Unter besonderer Berücksichtigung der Einflüsse aus Etrurien*. Vienna: Holzhausen, 2011.

Amarelli, F. *Vetustas-Innovatio: Un'antitesi apparente nella legislazione di Costantino*. Naples, Italy: E. Jovene, 1978.

Amerise, M. *Il battesimo di Costantino il Grande: Storia di una scomoda eredità*. Hermes Einzelschriften 95. Stuttgart: Franz Steiner Verlag, 2005.

———. "Note sulla datazione del panegirico per l'inaugurazione della basilica di Tiro (*HE* X, 4)," *Adamantius* 14 (2008): 229–34.

Amici, A. "*Divus Constantinus*: Le testimonianze epigrafiche," *RSA* 30 (2000): 187–216.

Ando, C. "Pagan Apologetics and Christian Intolerance in the Ages of Themistius and Augustine," *JECS* 4 (1996): 171–207.

———. *Imperial Ideology and Provincial Loyalty in the Roman Empire*. Berkeley: University of California Press, 2000.

———. *Law, Language, and Empire in the Roman Tradition*. Philadelphia: University of Pennsylvania Press, 2011.

Andreotti, R. "Contributo alla discussione del rescritto costantiniano di Hispellum." In *Problemi di storia e archeologia dell'Umbria: Atti del I convegno di studi umbri (Gubbio, 26–31 maggio 1963)*, 249–90. Perugia, Italy: Facoltà di lettere e filosofia dell'Università degli studi di Perugia, 1964.

Angelov, A. "Bishop over 'Those Outside': Imperial Diplomacy and the Boundaries of Constantine's Christianity." *GRBS* 54 (2014): 274–92.

Applebaum, A. *The Dynasty of the Jewish Patriarchs*. Texts and Studies in Ancient Judaism. Tübingen: Mohr Siebeck, 2013.

Athanassiadi, P. *Julian and Hellenism: An Intellectual Biography*. London: Routledge, 1981.

———. "The Fate of Oracles in Late Antiquity," *Deltion Christianikes Archaiologikes Etereias* 115 (1989–90): 271–78.

Athanassiadi, P., and M. Frede, eds. *Pagan Monotheism in Late Antiquity*. Oxford: Oxford University Press, 1999.

Aulock, H. von. *Sylloge Nummorum Graecorum Deutschland: Sammlung v. Aulock*. 18 vols. Berlin: Gebrüder Mann, 1957–1968.

Austin, J. L. *How to Do Things with Words*. Cambridge, MA: Harvard University Press, 1962.

Avi-Yonah, M. *The Jews of Palestine: A Political History from the Bar Kokhba War to the Arab Conquest*. Oxford: Blackwell, 1976.

Bagnall, R. S. *Currency and Inflation in Fourth Century Egypt*. BASP Supplement 5. Chico, CA: Scholars Press, 1985.

———. "Practical Help," in *Oxford Handbook of Papyrology*, ed. R. S. Bagnall, 179–96. Oxford: Oxford University Press, 2009.

Bagnall, R. S., A. Cameron, S. R. Schwartz, and K. A. Worp. *Consuls of the Later Roman Empire*. Atlanta: Scholars Press, 1987.

Baldini, A. "Claudio Gotico e Costantino in Aurelio Vittore ed *Epitome de caesaribus*." In *Costantino il Grande: Dall'antichità all'umanesimo, Colloquio sul cristianesimo nel mondo antico, Macerata, 18–20 dicembre 1990*, ed. G. Bonamente and F. Fusco, vol. 1, 73–89. Macerata, Italy: Università degli studi di Macerata, 1992.

Banchich, T., and E. Lane, eds. *The History of Zonaras: From Alexander Severus to the Death of Theodosius the Great*. London: Routledge, 2009.

Banfi, A. *Habent illi iudices suos: Studi sull'esclusività della giurisdizione ecclesiastica e sulle origini del privilegium fori in diritto romano e bizantino*. Milan: A. Giuffrè, 2005.

Bar, D. "Continuity and Change in the Cultic Topography of Late Antique Palestine." In *From Temple to Church: Destruction and Renewal of Local Cultic Topography in Late Antiquity*, ed. J. Hahn, 275–98. Leiden: Brill, 2008.

Bardill, J. *Constantine, Divine Emperor of the Christian Golden Age*. Cambridge: Cambridge University Press, 2012.

Bardy, G. *Recherches sur Saint Lucien d'Antioche et son école*. Paris: Beauchesne, 1936.

Barnes, T. D. "Lactantius and Constantine," *JRS* 63 (1973): 29–46.

——. "The Beginnings of Donatism," *JThS* n.s. 26 (1975): 13–22.

——. "The Victories of Constantine," *ZPE* 20 (1976): 149–55.

——. "Sossianus Hierocles and the Antecedents of the 'Great Persecution,'" *HSCPh* 80 (1976): 239–52.

——. "Emperor and Bishops, AD 324–44," *AJAH* 3 (1978): 53–75.

——. *Constantine and Eusebius*. Cambridge, MA: Harvard University Press, 1981.

——. *The New Empire of Diocletian and Constantine*. Cambridge, MA: Harvard University Press, 1982.

——. "Constantine's Prohibition of Pagan Sacrifice," *AJPh* 105 (1984): 69–72.

——. "Constantine and the Christians of Persia," *JRS* 75 (1985): 126–36.

——. "Panegyric, History and Hagiography in Eusebius' Life of Constantine." In *The Making of Orthodoxy: Essays in Honour of Henry Chadwick*, 94–123. Cambridge: Cambridge University Press, 1989.

——. "The Consecration of Ulfila," *JThS* n.s. 41 (1990): 541–45.

——. "Praetorian Prefects, 337–361," *ZPE* 94 (1992): 249–60.

——. *Athanasius and Constantius: Theology and Politics in the Constantinian Empire*. Cambridge, MA: Harvard University Press, 1993.

——. *From Eusebius to Augustine*. Aldershot, UK: Ashgate, 1994.

——. "Statistics and the Conversion of the Roman Aristocracy," *JRS* 85 (1995): 135–47.

——. "Oppressor, Persecutor, Usurper: The Meaning of 'Tyrannus' in the Fourth Century." In *Historiae Augustae Colloquium Barcinonense*, ed. G. Bonamente and M. Mayer, 55–65. Bari, Italy: Edipuglia, 1996.

——. "Constantine's Speech to the Assembly of the Saints: Place and Date of Delivery," *JThS* 52 (2001): 26–36.

——. "From Toleration to Repression: The Evolution of Constantine's Religious Policies," *SCI* 21 (2002): 189–207.

——. "The Date of the Martyrdom of Lucian of Antioch," *ZAC* 8 (2005): 350–53.

——. "The Exile and Recalls of Arius," *JThS* n.s. 60 (2009): 109–29.

——. *Early Christian Hagiography and Roman History*. Tübingen: Mohr Siebeck, 2010.

——. *Constantine: Dynasty, Religion and Power in the Later Roman Empire*. Chichester: Blackwell, 2011.

Bassett, S. G. *The Urban Image of Late Antique Constantinople*. Cambridge: Cambridge University Press, 2004.

Bastien, Pierre. *Le buste monétaire des empereurs romains*. Numismatique Romaine 19. Wetteren, Belgium: Editions numismatiques romaines, 1992.

Bauer, F. A. *Das Bild der Stadt Rom im Frühmittelalter: Papststiftungen im Spiegel des Liber Pontificalis von Gregor III. bis zu Leo III.* Palilia 14. Wiesbaden: Ludwig Reichert, 2004.

Bauer, F. A., and M. Heinzelmann. "The Constantinian Bishop's Church at Ostia: Preliminary Report on the 1998 Season," *JRA* 12 (1999): 342–53.

Bauer, F. A., M. Heinzelmann, A. Martin, and A. Schaub. "Ostia. Ein urbanistisches Forschungsprojekt in den unausgegrabenen Bereichen des Stadtgebiets. Vorbericht zur zweiten Grabungskampagne," *MDAI(R)* 107 (2000): 375–415.

Baynes, N. H. "Two Notes on the Great Persecution," *JRS* 18 (1924): 184–94.

———. *Constantine the Great and the Christian Church: The Raleigh Lecture on History.* Proceedings of the British Academy 15. London: H. Milford, 1929.

Becatti, G. *Case ostiensi del tardo impero.* Rome: Libreria dello stato, 1948.

Beetham, F., trans. "Constantine Byzantinus: The Anonymous Life of Constantine (BHG 364)." In *From Constantine to Julian: Pagan and Byzantine Views, A Source History*, ed. S. N. C. Lieu and D. Montserrat, 97–146. London: Routledge, 1996.

Belayche, N. *Iudaea-Palaestina: The Pagan Cults in Roman Palestine (Second to Fourth Century).* Tübingen: Mohr Siebeck, 2001.

———. "Pagan Festivals in Fourth-Century Gaza." In *Christian Gaza in Late Antiquity*, ed. B. Bitton-Ashkelony and A. Kofsky, 5–22. Leiden: Brill, 2004.

———. "Realia versus Leges? Les sacrifices de la religion d'état au IVe siècle." In *La cuisine et l'autel: Les sacrifices en questions dans les sociétés de la méditerranée ancienne*, ed. S. Georgoudi, R. Koch Piettre, and F. Schmidt, 343–70. Turnhout: Brepols, 2005.

———. "La politique religieuse 'païenne' de Maximin Daia: De l'historiographie à l'histoire." In *Politiche religiose nel mondo antico e tardoantico.* Munera 33, ed. G. A. Cecconi and C. Gabrielli, 235–59. Bari, Italy: Edipuglia, 2011.

Belke, K., and N. Mersich. *Phrygien und Pisidien.* Tabula Imperii Byzantini 7. Vienna: Verlag der Österreichischen Akademie der Wissenschaften, 1990.

Benoit, F. "L'inscription de la place du forum à Arles," *BSAF* 82 (1951): 227–40.

Benseddik, N. "Lueurs Cirtéenes," *ZPE* 153 (2005): 249–60.

Bergemann, J. *Römische Reiterstatuen: Ehrendenkmäler im öffentlichen Bereich.* Mainz: Philipp von Zabern, 1990.

Berger, A. "Legitimation und Legenden: Konstantin der Grosse und sein Bild in Byzanz." In *Konstantin der Grosse: Das Bild des Kaisers im Wandel der Zeiten*, ed. A. Goltz and H. Schlange-Schöningen, 5–21. Cologne: Böhlau Verlag, 2008.

Bergmann, M. *Die Strahlen der Herrscher: Theomorphes Herrscherbild und politische Symbolik im Hellenismus und in der römischen Kaiserzeit.* Mainz: Philipp von Zabern, 1998.

Bernardelli, A. "Il medaglione d'argento di Costantino con il cristogramma: Annotazioni sulla cronologia," *RIN* 8 (2007): 219–36.

Berrens, S. *Sonnenkult und Kaisertum von den Severern bis zu Constantin I. (193–337 N. Chr.).* Historia Einzelschriften 185. Stuttgart: Franz Steiner Verlag, 2004.

Beševliev, V. *Spätgriechische und Spätlateinische Inschriften aus Bulgarien.* Berlin: Akademie Verlag, 1964.

Bidez, J., and G. C. Hansen. *Sozomenus Kirchengeschichte*, 2nd ed. GCS n. F. 4. Berlin: Akademie Verlag, 1995.

Bird, H. W., trans. *Liber de Caesaribus of Sextus Aurelius Victor.* TTH 17. Liverpool: Liverpool University Press, 1994.

Biscottini, P., and G. Sena Chiesa. *Costantino 313 d. C. L'Editto di Milano e il tempo della tolleranza.* Milan: Electa, 2012.

Blaauw, S. de. "Jerusalem in Rome and the Cult of the Cross." In *Pratum Romanum: Richard Krautheimer zum 100. Geburtstag*, ed. R. L. Colella, 55–73. Wiesbaden: L. Reichert, 1997.

Bleckmann, B. "Die Chronik des Johannes Zonaras und eine Pagane Quelle zur Geschichte Konstantins," *Historia* 40 (1991): 341–65.

———. "Pagane Visionen Konstantins in der Chronik des Johannes Zonaras." In *Costantino il Grande: Dall'antichità all'umanesimo, Colloquio sul cristianesimo nel mondo antico, Macerata, 18–20 dicembre 1990*, ed. G. Bonamente and F. Fusco, vol. 1, 151–70. Macerata, Italy: Università degli studi di Macerata, 1992.

———. "Constantin und die Donaubarbaren. Ideologische Auseinandersetzungen um die Sieghaftigkeit Constantins," *JAC* 38 (1995): 38–66.

———. "Ein Kaiser als Prediger: Zur Datierung der konstantinischen 'Rede an die Versammlung der Heiligen,'" *Hermes* 125 (1997): 182–202.

———. "Zwischen Panegyrik und Geschichtsschreibung: Praxagoras und seine Vorgänger." In *Geschichtsschreibung und Politischer Wandel im 3. Jh. n. Chr*, ed. M. Zimmermann, 203–28. Stuttgart: Franz Steiner, 1999.

———. "Die Vita BHG 365 und die Rekonstruktion der verlorenen Kirchengeschichte Philostorgs," *JAC* 46 (2003): 7–16.

———. "Zu den Motiven der Christenverfolgung des Decius." In *Deleto paene imperio Romano. Transformationsprozesse des Römischen Reiches im 3. Jahrhundert und ihre Rezeption in der Neuzeit*, ed. K.-P. Johne, T. Gerhardt and U. Hartmann, 57–71. Stuttgart: Franz Steiner, 2006.

———. "*Constantinus Tyrannus*: Das negative Konstantinsbild in der paganen Historiographie und seine Nuancen." In *Private and Public Lies: The Discourse of Despotism and Deceit in the Graeco-Roman World*. Impact of Empire 11, ed. A. J. Turner, K. O. Chong-Gossard, and F. Vervaet, 343–54. Leiden: Brill, 2010.

———. "Costantino dopo la battaglia presso il Ponte Milvio: Note sul medaglione di *Ticininum*." In *Costantino il Grande: Alle radici dell'Europa. Atti del convegno internazionale di studio in occcasione del 1700° anniversario della Battaglia di Ponte Milvio e della conversione di Costantino*, ed. B. Ardura, 195–218. Rome: 2014.

Bleicken, J. *Constantin der Große und die Christen. Überlegungen zur Konstantinischen Wende*. Munich: Oldenbourg, 1992.

Bloch, H. "A New Document of the Last Pagan Revival in the West, 393–394 AD," *HThR* 38 (1945): 199–244.

Bloedhorn, H. "Die Eleona und das Imbomon in Jerusalem: Eine Doppelkirchenanlage auf dem Ölberg." In *Akten des XII. internationalen Kongresses für christliche Archaologie*, 568–71. JAC Ergänzungsband 20. Münster: Aschendorffsche Verlagsbuchhandlung, 1995.

Boatwright, M. T. *Hadrian and the Cities of the Roman Empire*. Princeton, NJ: Princeton University Press, 2000.

Boin, D. R. "A Hall for Hercules at Ostia and a Farewell to the Late Antique 'Pagan Revival,'" *AJA* 114 (2010): 253–66.

———. *Ostia in Late Antiquity*. Cambridge: Cambridge University Press, 2013.

Bonamente, G. "Le città nella politica di Giuliano l'Apostata," *AFLM* 16 (1983): 33–96.

———. "Sulla confisca dei beni mobili dei templi in epoca costantiniana." In *Costantino il Grande: Dall'antichità all'umanesimo, Colloquio sul cristianesimo nel mondo antico, Macerata, 18–20 dicembre 1990*, ed. G. Bonamente and Franca Fusco, vol. 1, 171–201. Macerata, Italy: Università degli Studi di Macerata, 1992.

———. "Politica antipaganae sorte dei templi da Costantino a Teodosio II." In *Trent'anni di studi sulla tarda antichità: bilanci e prospettive: atti del convegno internazionale, Napoli, 21–23 novembre 2007*, 25–59. Naples: M. D'Auria, 2009.

———. "Per una cronologia della conversione di Costantino." In *Costantino prima e dopo Costantino – Constantine Before and After Constantine*, ed. G. Bonamente, N. Lenski, and R. Lizzi Testa, 89–112. Bari, Italy: Edipuglia, 2012.

Bonamente, G., N. Lenski, and R. Lizzi Testa, eds. *Costantino prima e dopo Costantino – Constantine Before and After Constantine*. Munera 35. Bari, Italy: Edipuglia, 2012.

Borgehammar, S. *How the Holy Cross Was Found: From Event to Medieval Legend.* Bibliotheca Theologiae Practicae 47. Stockholm: Almqvist & Wiksell International, 1991.

Bousquet, J. "La donation de L. Gellius Menogenes à Delphes et les Thermes de l'Est," *BCH* 76 (1952): 653–60.

Bowersock, G. W. "Peter and Constantine." In *"Humana Sapit": Études d'antiquité tardive offertes à Lellia Cracco Ruggini,* ed. J.-M. Carrié and R. Lizzi Testa, 209–17. Bibliothèque de l'Antiquité Tardive 3. Turnhout, Belgium: Brepols, 2002.

———, trans. *On the Donation of Constantine.* I Tatti Renaissance Library 24. Cambridge, MA: Harvard University Press, 2007.

Bowes, K. D. *Private Worship, Public Values, and Religious Change in Late Antiquity.* Cambridge: Cambridge University Press, 2008.

Bradbury, S. "Constantine and the Problem of Anti-Pagan Legislation in the Fourth Century," *CPh* 89 (1994): 120–39.

———. "Julian's Pagan Revival and the Decline of Blood Sacrifice," *Phoenix* 49 (1995): 331–56.

———. *Selected Letters of Libanius: From the Age of Constantius and Julian.* TTH 41. Liverpool: Liverpool University Press, 2004.

Bradley, G. J. *Ancient Umbria: State, Culture, and Identity in Central Italy from the Iron Age to the Augustan Era.* Oxford: Oxford University Press, 2000.

Brandenburg, H. *Roms frühchristliche Basiliken des 4. Jahrhunderts.* Munich: Heyne, 1979.

———. "Die Architektur der Basilika San Paolo fuori le mura: Das Apostelgrab als Zentrum der Liturgie und des Märtyrerkultes," *MDAIR* 112 (2005/2006): 237–76.

Brandt, H. *Konstantin der Grosse: Der erste christliche Kaiser, Eine Biographie.* Munich: Beck, 2006.

Bransbourg, G. "Fiscalité impériale et finances municipales au IVe siècle," *AnTard* 16 (2008): 255–96.

———. "Julien, l'*immunitas Christi*, les dieux et les cités," *AnTard* 17 (2009): 151–58.

Braschi, F., and M. Di Salvo, eds. *La figura di Costantino imperatore e l'ideologia imperiale nella storia culturale, religiosa, civile dei paesi slavi.* Slavica Ambrosiana 4. Rome: Biblioteca Ambrosiana, 2013.

Bratož, R. "La Basilica di Aquileia nelle fonti letterarie dal IV al VII secolo." In *La Basilica di Aquileia: Storia, archeologia ed arte. Atti della XL settimana di studi aquileiesi (Aquileia 2009),* ed. G. Cuscito and T. Lehmann, 19–66. Trieste: Editreg, 2010.

Brenk, B. "La Christianisation d'Ostie." In *Ostie: Port et porte de la Rome antique,* ed. J.-P. Descoeudres, 262–71. Geneva: Georg Éditeur, 2001.

Brennecke, H. C., U. Heil, A. Von Stockhausen, and A. Wintjes, eds. *Dokumente zur Geschichte des Arianischen Streites.* Athanasius Werke III. 1. 3. Berlin: Walter de Gruyter, 2007.

Bringmann, K. "Die konstantinische Wende. Zum Verhältnis von politischer und religiöser Motivation," *HZ* 260 (1995): 21–47.

Brisson, J.-P. *Autonomisme et christianisme dans l'Afrique Romaine de Septime Sévère à l'invasion vandale.* Paris: Éditions de Boccard, 1958.

Broshi, M. "The Population of Western Palestine in the Roman-Byzantine Period," *BASOR* 236 (1979): 1–10.

Brown, P. *The Cult of the Saints: Its Rise and Function in Latin Christianity.* Chicago: University of Chicago Press, 1981.

———. *Poverty and Leadership in the Later Roman Empire.* Hanover, NH: University Press of New England, 2002.

———. *Through the Eye of a Needle: Wealth, the Fall of Rome, and the Making of Christianity in the West, 350–550 AD.* Princeton, NJ: Princeton University Press, 2012.

Bru, H., G. Labarre, and M. Özsaıt. "La constitution civique de Tymandos," *AnatAnt* 17 (2009): 187–207.

Bruun, C. "*Aedes Castorum, Ludi* und *Praedium Missale*: Drei Bemerkungen zur Topographie von Ostia-Portus und zum Ager Ostiensis," *Historia* 61 (2012): 115–26.

Bruun, P. "The Consecration Coins of Constantine the Great," *Arctos* 1 (1954): 19–31.

———. "The Disappearance of Sol from the Coins of Constantine," *Arctos* 2 (1958): 15–37. Reprinted in *Studies in Constantinian Numismatics: Papers from 1954 to 1988*, 37–48. Rome: Institutum Romanum Finlandiae, 1991.

———. "The Christian Signs on the Coins of Constantine," *Arctos* 3 (1962): 5–35. Reprinted in *Studies in Constantinian Numismatics: Papers from 1954 to 1988*, 53–70. Rome: Institutum Romanum Finlandiae, 1991.

———. "Early Christian Symbolism on Coins and Inscriptions." In *Atti del VI Congresso Internazionale di Archeologia Cristiana, Ravenna 1962*, 527–35. Studi di Antichità Cristiana 26. Rome: Tipografia nazionale di G. Bertero, 1965. Reprinted in *Studies in Constantinian Numismatics: Papers from 1954 to 1988*, 71–74. Rome: Institutum Romanum Finlandiae, 1991.

———. *The Roman Imperial Coinage*. Vol. 7, *Constantine and Licinius, AD 313–337*. London: Spink, 1966.

———. "Portrait of a Conspirator: Constantine's Break with the Tetrarchy," *Arctos* 10 (1976): 5–25. Reprinted in *Studies in Constantinian Numismatics: Papers from 1954 to 1988*, 107–18. Rome: Institutum Romanum Finlandiae, 1991.

Bryen, A. *Violence in Roman Egypt: A Study in Legal Interpretation*. Philadelphia: University of Pennsylvania Press, 2013.

Buckler, W. H. "A Charitable Foundation of AD 237," *JHS* 57 (1937): 1–10.

Budin, S. L. *The Myth of Sacred Prostitution in Antiquity*. Cambridge: Cambridge University Press, 2008.

Burckhardt, J. *Die Zeit Constantins des Großen*, 2nd ed. Leipzig: E. A. Seemann, 1880.

Burgess, R. W. "On the Date of the Kaisergeschichte," *CPh* 90 (1995): 111–28.

———. "The Dates and Editions of Eusebius' *Chronici Canones* and *Historia Ecclesiastica*," *JThS* n.s. 48 (1997): 471–504.

———. "Ἀχυρών or Προάστειον? The Location and Circumstances of Constantine's Death," *JThS* n.s. 50 (1999): 153–61.

———. *Studies in Eusebian and Post-Eusebian Chronography*. Historia Einzelschriften 135. Stuttgart: Franz Steiner Verlag, 1999.

———. "The Date of the Deposition of Eustathius of Antioch," *JThS* n.s. 51 (2000): 150–60.

———. "The *Passio S. Artemii*, Philostorgius, and the Dates of the Invention and Translation of the Relics of Sts. Andrew and Luke," *AnBoll* 121 (2003): 5–36.

———. "A Common Source for Jerome, Eutropius, Festus, Ammianus, and the *Epitome de Caesaribus* Between 358 and 378, Along with Further Thoughts on the Date and Nature of the Kaisergeschichte," *CPh* 100 (2005): 166–92.

———. "The Summer of Blood: The 'Great Massacre' of 337 and the Promotion of the Sons of Constantine," *DOP* 62 (2008): 5–51.

Burgess, R. W., and M. Kulikowski. *Mosaics of Time: The Latin Chronicle Traditions from the First Century BC to the Sixth Century AD*. Vol. 1, *A Historical Introduction to the Chronicle Genre from its Origins to the High Middle Ages*. Turnhout: Brepols, 2013.

Calder, W. M. "Studies in Early Christian Epigraphy," *JRS* 10 (1920): 42–59.

———. *Monumenta Asiae Minoris Antiqua*. Vol. 1. Manchester: Manchester University Press, 1928.

———. *Monumenta Asiae Minoris Antiqua*. Vol. 7, *Monuments from Eastern Phrygia*. Manchester: Manchester University Press, 1956.

Calderone, S. *Costantino e il cattolicesimo*. Florence: Le Monnier, 1962.

———. "Teologia, successione dinastica e *consecratio* in età costantiniana." In *Le culte des souverains dans l'empire romain*, ed. E. J. Bickerman and W. den Boer, 215–61. Vandœuvres-Genève: Fondation Hardt, 1973.

Camerieri, P. "Il catasto antico di Mevania: Primi studi sull'assetto territoriale della città romana." In *Invito al parco: Lungo i percorsi delle sue acque e della sua storia*, ed. M. R. Trabalza, and R. Colacicchi, 147–58. Foligno, Italy: Edizioni dell'Arquata, 2007.

Camerieri, P., and D. Manconi. "Il 'sacello' di Venere a Spello, dalla romanizzazione alla riorganizzazione del territorio: Spunti di ricerca," *Ostraca: Rivitsta di antichità* 21 (2012): 63–75.

Cameron, Al. *The Last Pagans of Rome*. Oxford: Oxford University Press, 2011.

Cameron, Al. and J. Long. *Barbarians and Politics at the Court of Arcadius*. Berkeley: University of California Press, 1993.

Cameron, Av. "Form and Meaning: The *Vita Constantini*." In *Greek Biography and Panegyric in Late Antiquity*, ed. T. Hägg and P. Rousseau, 72–88. Berkeley: University of California Press, 2000.

Cameron, Av., and S. G. Hall. *Eusebius Life of Constantine: Introduction, Translation, and Commentary*. Oxford: Oxford University Press, 1999.

Camodeca, G. "Puteoli," *Studi di Storia Antica* 4–5 (1980): 59–128.

Camplani, A. *Le lettere festali di Atanasio di Alessandria: Studio storico-critico*. Rome: C. M. I., 1989.

Carlà, F. *L'oro nella tarda antichità: Aspetti economici e sociali*. Turin: S. Zamorani, 2009.

Carlà, F., and M. G. Castello. *Questioni tardoantiche: Storia e mito della "Svolta Costantiniana."* Rome: Aracne, 2010.

Carrié, J.-M. "Les distributions alimentaires dans les cités de l'empire romain tardif," *MEFRA* 87 (1975): 995–1101.

Caseau, B. "ΠΟΛΕΜΕΙΝ ΛΙΘΟΙΣ: La déscralisation des espaces et des objets religieux païens durant l'antiquité tardive." In *Le sacré et son inscription dans l'espace à Byzance et en occident: Études comparées*, ed. M. Kaplan, 61–123. Paris: Publications de la Sorbonne, 2001.

Cavallaro, M. A. "A Proposito di Lyd. *De Mag*. III 70, p. 163 ll. 16–20W." *Helikon* 29–30 (1989–1990): 349–57.

Cavallera, F. *Le schisme d'Antioche (IVe–Ve siècle)*. Paris: A. Piccard, 1905.

Cayrel, P. "Une basilique Donatiste de la Numidie," *Mélanges d'Archéologie et d'Histoire* 51 (1934): 114–42.

Cecchelli, M. "S. Marco a Piazza Venezia: Una basilica romana del periodo costantiniano." In *Costantino il Grande: Dall'antichità all'umanesimo, Colloquio sul cristianesimo nel mondo antico, Macerata, 18–20 dicembre 1990*, ed. G. Bonamente and F. Fusco, vol. 1, 299–310. Macerata, Italy: Università degli studi di Macerata, 1992.

Cecconi, G. A. *Governo imperiale e élites dirigenti nell'Italia tardoantica: Problemi di storia politico-amministrativa (270–476 d. C.)*. Biblioteca di Athenaeum 24. Como, Italy: Edizioni New Press, 1994.

———. "Il rescritto di Spello: Prospettive recenti." In *Costantino prima e dopo Costantino – Constantine Before and After Constantine*, ed. G. Bonamente, N. Lenski, and R. Lizzi Testa, 273–92. Munera 35. Bari, Italy: Edipuglia, 2012.

———. "Firenze tardoantica: istituzioni e società." In *Archeologia a Firenze: Città e territorio, Atti del Workshop Firenze, 12–13 Aprile 2013*, edited by V. d'Aquino et al., 213–18. Oxford: Archaeopress.

Chadwick, H. "Ossius of Cordova and the Presidency of the Council of Antioch, 325," *JThS* n.s. 9 (1958): 292–304.

Champlin, E. "Saint Gallicanus (Consul 317)," *Phoenix* 36 (1982): 71–76.

Chaniotis, A. *Die Verträge zwischen kretischen Poleis in der hellenistischen Zeit.* Heidelberger Althistorische Beiträge und Epigraphische Studien 24. Stuttgart: Franz Steiner Verlag, 1996.

Charron, A., and M. Heijmans. "L'obelisque du Cirque d'Arles," *JRA* 14 (2001): 373–80.

Chastagnol, A. *La préfecture urbaine à Rome sous le bas-empire.* Publications de la Faculté des Lettres et Sciences Humaines d'Alger 34. Paris: Presses Universitaires de France, 1960.

———. *Les fastes de la préfecture de Rome au bas-empire.* Paris: Nouvelles Éditions latines, 1962.

———. "Un gouverneur constantinien de Tripolitaine: Laenatius Romulus, *Praeses* en 324–326," *Latomus* 25 (1966): 539–52.

———. "La restauration du temple d'Isis au Portus Romae sous le règne de Gratien." In *Hommages à Marcel Renard*, ed. Jacqueline Bibauw, vol. 2, 135–44. Collection Latomus 102. Brussels: Latomus, 1969.

———. *L'album Municipal de Timgad.* Bonn: Habelt, 1978.

———. "L'inscription Constantinienne d'Orcistus," *MEFRA* 93 (1981): 381–416.

Chastagnol, A., and N. Duval. "Les survivances du culte impérial dans l'Afrique du Nord à l'époque vandale." In *Mélanges d'histoire ancienne offerts à William Seston*, 87–118. Paris: E. de Boccard, 1974.

Chausson, F. *Stemmata Aurea: Constantin, Justine, Théodose: Revendications généalogiques et idéologie impériale au IVe siècle ap. J.-C.* Rome: L'Erma di Bretschneider, 2007.

Chiesa, P. "Un testo agiografico africano ad Aquileia: Gli *Acta* di Gallonio e dei martiri di *Timida Regia*," *AnBoll* 114 (1996): 241–68.

———. "Pellegrino martire *in Urbe Bollitana* e Pellegrino di Ancona," *AnBoll* 116 (1998): 25–56.

Chiricat, É. "The 'crypto-Christian' inscriptions of Phrygia." In *Roman Phrygia: Culture and Society*, ed. P. Thonemann, 198–214. Cambridge: Cambridge University Press, 2013.

Christodoulou, N. *The Figures of Ancient Gods on the Coinage of Constantine the Great (306–326 AD).* Athens: 1998.

Christol, M., and T. Drew-Bear. "Documents latins de Phrygie," *Tyche* 1 (1986): 41–87.

———. "Antioche de Pisidie capitale provinciale et l'oeuvre de M. Valerius Diogenes," *AnTard* 7 (1999): 39–71.

Chuvin, P. "Christianisation et résistance des cultes traditionnels." In *Hellénisme et Christianisme*, ed. M. Narcy and E. Rebillard, 15–34. Villeneuve-d'Ascq: Presses universitaires du Septentrion, 2004.

Cimma, M. R. *L'episcopalis audientia nelle costituzioni imperiali da Costantino a Giustiniano.* Turin: G. Giappichelli, 1989.

Ciotti, U., et al. *Sangemini e Carsulae.* Milan: Bestetti, 1976.

Clauss, M. "Kein Aberglaube in Hipsellum," *Klio* 93 (2011): 429–45.

Cline, R. *Ancient Angels: Conceptualizing Angeloi in the Roman Empire.* Leiden: Brill, 2011.

———. "A Two-Sided Mold and the Entrepreneurial Spirit of Pilgrimage Souvenir Production in Late Antique Syria-Palestine," *JLA* 7 (2014): 28–48.

Clinton, K. *The Sacred Officials of the Eleusinian Mysteries.* TAPS 64. 3. Philadelphia: American Philosophical Society, 1974.

Clover, F. M. "Emperor Worship in Vandal Africa." In *Romanitas—Christianitas*, ed. G. W. Wirth et al., 663–74. Berlin: Walter de Gruyter, 1982.

Coarelli, F. "Il rescritto di Spello e il santuario 'etnico' degli Umbri." In *Umbria Cristiana: dalla diffusione del culto al culto dei santi, secc. IV–X. Atti del XV congresso internazionale di studi sull'alto medioevo, Spoleto, 23–28 ottobre 2000*, 39–51. Spoleto: Centro italiano di studi sull'alto medioevo, 2001.

Conant, J. *Staying Roman: Conquest and Identity in Africa and the Mediterranean, 439–700.* Cambridge: Cambridge University Press, 2012.

Connolly, S. "Constantine Answers the Veterans." In *From the Tetrarchs to the Theodosians: Later Roman History and Culture, 284–450 CE.* YCS 34, ed. S. McGill, C. Sogno, and E. Watts, 93–114. Cambridge: Cambridge University Press, 2010.

———. *Lives Behind the Laws: The World of the Codex Hermogenianus.* Bloomington: Indiana University Press, 2010.

Cook, J. G. "Crucifixion in the West: From Constantine to Recceswinth," *ZAC* 16 (2012): 226–46.

Corcoran, S. *The Empire of the Tetrarchs: Imperial Pronouncements and Government, AD 284–324,* rev. ed. Oxford: Oxford University Press, 2000.

———. "Galerius, Maximinus and the Titulature of the Third Tetrarchy," *BICS* 49 (2006): 231–40.

———. "Galerius' Jigsaw Puzzle: The Caesariani Dossier," *AnTard* 15 (2007): 221–50.

Cox, C. W. M., and A. Cameron. *Monumenta Asiae Minoris Antiqua.* Vol. 5, *Monuments from Dorylaeum and Nacolea.* Manchester: University of Manchester Press, 1937.

Creed, J. L., ed. *Lactantius De Mortibus Persecutorum.* Oxford: Oxford University Press, 1984.

Ćurčić, S. *Architecture in the Balkans from Diocletian to Süleyman the Magnificent.* New Haven, CT: Yale University Press, 2010.

Curran, J. R. "Constantine and the Ancient Cults of Rome: The Legal Evidence," *G&R* 43 (1996): 68–80.

———. *Pagan City and Christian Capital: Rome in the Fourth Century.* Oxford: Oxford University Press, 2000.

Curty, O. *Les parentés légendaires entre les cités grècques: Catalogue raisonné des inscriptions contenant le terme syngeneia et analyse critique.* Hautes études du monde gréco-romain 20. Geneva: Droz, 1995.

Cuscito, G. "Aquileia, la svolta costantiniana e il polo episcopale." In *Costantino 313 d. C. L'Editto di Milano e il tempo della tolleranza,* ed. P. Biscottini and G. Sena Chiesa, 94–100. Milan: Electa, 2012.

Davis, R. "Pre-Constantinian Chronology: The Roman Bishopric from AD 258–314." *JThS* n. s. 48 (1997): 439–70.

———. trans. *The Book of Pontiffs (Liber Pontificalis): The Ancient Biographies of the First Ninety Roman Bishops to AD 715,* 3rd ed. TTH 6. Liverpool: Liverpool University Press, 2010.

Dearn, A. "The Abitinian Martyrs and the Outbreak of the Donatist Schism," *JEH* 55 (2004): 1–18.

Debord, P. *Aspects sociaux et économiques de la vie religieuse dans l'Anatolie gréco-romaine.* Leiden: Brill, 1982.

De Caro Balbi, S. "Comparsa di simboli cristiani sulle monete dell'impero in età Costantiniana," *AIIN* 16–17 (1969–1970): 143–71.

De Clercq, V. C. *Ossius of Cordova: A Contribution to the History of the Constantinian Period.* Washington, DC: Catholic University of America Press, 1954.

De Decker, D. "La politique religieuse de Maxence," *Byzantion* 38 (1968): 472–562.

De Decker, D., and G. Dupuis-Masay. "L'épiscopat de l'empereur Constantin," *Byzantion* 50 (1980): 118–57.

De Dominicis, M. "Il rescritto di Costantino agli Umbri (nuove osservazioni)," *Bollettino dell'Istituto di Diritto Romano* 65 (1962): 173–91.

De Giovanni, L. *Chiesa e stato nel Codice Teodosiano: Saggio sul libro XVI.* Naples: Tempi Moderni, 1980.

———. *Costantino e il mondo pagano: Studi di politica e legislazione,* 2nd ed. Naples: M. D'Auria, 1982.

De Grummond, N. T., and I. E. M. Edlund-Berry, eds. *The Archaeology of Sanctuaries and Ritual in Etruria.* JRA Supplement 81. Portsmouth, RI: Journal of Roman Archaeology, 2011.

De Grummond, N. T., and E. Simon, eds. *The Religion of the Etruscans*. Austin: University of Texas Press, 2006.

De Leo, P. *Il Constitutum Constantini, compilazione agiografica del sec. VIII: Note e documenti per una nuova lettura*. Reggio Calabria: Editori meridionali riuniti, 1974.

Deichmann, W. "Früchristliche Kirchen in antiken Heiligtümern," *JDAI* 54 (1939): 124–36.

Deligiannakis, G. "Religious Viewing of Sculptural Images of Gods in the World of Late Antiquity: From Dio Chrysostom to Damaskios," *JLA* 8 (2015): 168–94.

Delmaire, R. *Largesses sacrées et res privata: L'aerarium impérial et son administration du IVe au VIe siècle*. CEFR 121. Rome: École Française de Rome, 1989.

Delmaire, R., and J. Rougé, eds. *Les lois religieuses des empereurs romains de Constantin à Théodose II (312–438)*. Vol. 1, *Le Code Théodosien XVI*. SCh 497. Paris: Cerf, 2005.

———. *Les lois religieuses des empereurs romains de Constantin à Théodose II (312–438)*. Vol. 2, *Code Théodosien I–XV, Code Justinien, Constitutions Sirmondiennes*. SCh 531. Paris: Cerf, 2009.

De Man, P. "Introduction." In *Toward an Aesthetic of Reception*, ed. H. R. Jauss, trans. T. Bahti, vii–xxix. Minneapolis: University of Minnesota Press, 1982.

Demandt, A., and J. Engemann, eds. *Konstantin der Grosse: Ausstellungskatalog = Imperator Caesar Flavius Constantinus*. Trier, Germany: Konstantin-Ausstellungsgesellschaft, 2007.

Dessau, H., ed. *Corpus Inscriptionum Latinarum*. Vol. 14, *Inscriptiones Latii Veteris Latinae*. Berlin: Apud G. Reimerum, 1887.

De Ste. Croix, G. E. M. *Christian Persecution, Martyrdom, and Orthodoxy*, ed. M. Whitby and J. Streeter. Oxford: Oxford University Press, 2006.

Devréesse, R. *Le patriarcat d'Antioche, depuis la paix de l'église jusqu'à la conquête arabe*. Paris: J. Gabalda, 1945.

Diefenbach, S. "Kaiserkult und Totenkult: Konstantin und die christliche Sakraltopographie Roms." In *Konstantin der Grosse: Zwischen Sol und Christus*, ed. K. Ehling and G. Weber, 64–81. Darmstadt, Germany: Philipp von Zabern, 2011.

Digeser, E. D. "Lactantius and Constantine's Letter to Arles: Dating the *Divine Institutes*," *JECS* 2 (1994): 33–52.

———. *The Making of a Christian Empire: Lactantius and Rome*. Ithaca, NY: Cornell University Press, 2000.

———. "An Oracle of Apollo at Daphne and the Great Persecution," *CPh* 99 (2004): 57–77.

———. *A Threat to Public Piety: Christians, Platonists, and the Great Persecution*. Ithaca, NY: Cornell University Press, 2013.

Dignas, B. *Economy of the Sacred in Hellenistic and Roman Asia Minor*. Oxford: Oxford University Press, 2002.

Dillon, J. N. *The Justice of Constantine: Law, Communication, and Control*. Ann Arbor: University of Michigan Press, 2012.

Dindorf, L., ed. *Ioannis Malalae Chronographia*. Bonn: Weber, 1831.

Di Segni, L. "The Territory of Gaza: Notes of Historical Geography." In *Christian Gaza in Late Antiquity*, ed. B. Bitton-Ashkelony and A. Kofsky, 41–59. Leiden: Brill, 2004.

Dmitriev, S. *City Government in Hellenistic and Roman Asia Minor*. Oxford: Oxford University Press, 2005.

Dolbeau, F. "La 'Passio Sancti Donati' (BHL 2303b): Une tentative d'édition critique." In *Memoriam sanctorum venerantes. Miscellania in onore di Monsignor Victor Saxer*, 251–67. Vatican City: Pontificio Istituto di Archeologia Cristiana, 1992.

Donati, A., and G. Gentili, eds. *Costantino il Grande: La civiltà antica al bivio tra occidente e oriente*. Milan: Silvana, 2005.

Donciu, R. *L'empereur Maxence*. Munera 34. Bari, Italy: Edipuglia, 2012.

Dörries, H. *Das Selbstzeugnis Kaiser Konstantins.* Göttingen: Vandenhoeck & Ruprecht, 1954.

Downey, G. *A History of Antioch in Syria: From Seleucus to the Arab Conquest.* Princeton, NJ: Princeton University Press, 1961.

Drake, H. A. *In Praise of Constantine: A Historical Study and New Translation of Eusebius' Tricennial Orations.* Berkeley: University of California Press, 1975.

———. "Review of T. D. Barnes *Constantine and Eusebius* (1981)," *AJPh* 103 (1982): 462–66.

———. "Eusebius on the True Cross," *JEH* 36 (1985): 1–22.

———. "Athanasius' First Exile," *GRBS* 27 (1986): 193–204.

———. "What Eusebius Knew: The Genesis of the Vita Constantini," *CPh* 83 (1988): 20–38.

———. "Firmicus Maternus and the Politics of Conversion." In *Qui Miscuit Utile Dulci: Festschrift Essays for Paul Lachlan MacKendrick,* ed. G. Schmeling, 133–49. Wauconda, IL: Bolchazy-Carducci, 1998.

———. *Constantine and the Bishops: The Politics of Intolerance.* Baltimore: Johns Hopkins University Press, 2000.

Drew-Bear, T. *Nouvelles inscriptions de Phrygie.* Zutphen, The Netherlands: Centre nationale de la recherche scientifique, 1978.

Drew-Bear, T., and C. Naour. "Divinités de Phrygie," *ANRW* II.18.3 (1990): 1907–2044.

Drijvers, J. W. *Helena Augusta: The Mother of Constantine the Great and the Legend of Her Finding of the True Cross.* Leiden: Brill, 1992.

Drost, V. *Le Monnayage de Maxence (306–312 après J.-C.).* Zurich: Société Suisse de Numismatique, 2013.

Duchesne, L. *Le Liber pontificalis: Texte, introduction et commentaire,* 2nd ed. 3 vols. Paris: E. de Boccard, 1955–57.

Duval, Y. *Loca sanctorum Africae: Le culte des martyrs en Afrique du IVe au VIIe siècle.* 2 vols. CEFR 58. Rome: École Française de Rome, 1982.

———. "Le gouverneur de Numidie en sa capitale," *AnTard* 6 (1998): 193–207.

———. *Chrétiens d'Afrique à l'aube de la paix constantinienne: Les premiers échos de la grande persécution.* Collection des Études Augustiniennes 164. Paris: Institut d'études augustiniennes, 2000.

Eck, W. "Eine historische Zeitenwende: Kaiser Constantins Hinwendung zum Christentum und die gallischen Bischöfe." In *Konstantin der Grosse: Kaiser einer Epochenwende,* ed. F. Schuller and H. Wolff, 69–94. Munich: Kunstverlag Josef Fink, 2007.

Edwards, M., trans. *Optatus: Against the Donatists.* TTH 27. Liverpool: Liverpool University Press, 1997.

———, trans. *Constantine and Christendom: The Oration to the Saints, the Greek and Latin Accounts of the Discovery of the Cross, the Edict of Constantine to Pope Silvester.* TTH 39. Liverpool: Liverpool University Press, 2003.

Ehling, K., and G. Weber, eds. *Konstantin der Grosse: Zwischen Sol und Christus.* Darmstadt, Germany: Philipp von Zabern, 2011.

Elliott, T. G. "The Tax Exemptions Granted to Clerics," *Phoenix* 32 (1978): 326–36.

———. *The Christianity of Constantine the Great.* Bronx, NY: University of Scranton Press, 1996.

Elsner, J. "Perspectives in Art." In *The Cambridge Companion to the Age of Constantine,* ed. N. Lenski, 2nd ed., 255–77. Cambridge: Cambridge University Press, 2011.

Enenkel, K. "Panegyrische Geschictsmythologisierung und Propaganda: Zur Interpretation des Panegyricus Latinus VI," *Hermes* 128 (2000): 91–126.

Errington, R. M. "Constantine and the Pagans," *GRBS* 29 (1988): 309–18.

———. *Roman Imperial Policy from Julian to Theodosius.* Chapel Hill: University of North Carolina Press, 2006.

Escribano Paño, M. V. "Creación y límites del discurso heresiológico imperial: rectificaciones, nego-ciaciones y claudicaciones de Costantino." In *Inter cives necnon peregrinos: Essays in Honor of Boudewijn Sirks*, ed. J. Hallebeek et al., 181–97. Göttingen: Vandenhoek & Ruprecht, 2014.

Esmonde Cleary, S. *The Roman West, AD 200–500: An Archaeological Study*. Cambridge: Cambridge University Press, 2013.

Fabbrini, F. *La manumissio in ecclesia*. Milan: A. Giuffrè, 1965.

Fatti, F. *Giuliano a Cesarea: La politica ecclesiastica del principe apostata*. Rome: Herder, 2009.

Fears, J. R. *Princeps a diis electus: The Divine Election of the Emperor as a Political Concept at Rome*. PMAAR 26. Rome: American Academy in Rome, 1977.

Feissel, D. "Les privilèges de Baitokaikè: Remarques sur le rescrit de Valérien et le colophon du dossier," *Syria* 70 (1993): 13–26.

———. "Les constitutions des tétrarques connues par l'épigraphie: Inventaire et notes critiques," *AnTard* 3 (1995): 33–53.

———. "L'*adnotatio* de Constantin sur le droit de cité d'Orcistus en phrygie," *AnTard* 7 (1999): 255–67.

———. "Un rescrit de Justinien découvert à Didymes (1er Avril 533)," *Chiron* 34 (2004): 285–365.

Feissel, D., and J. Gascou, eds. *La Pétition à Byzance*. Paris: Association des amis du Centre d'histoire et civilisation de Byzance, 2004.

Février, P.-A. "Ostie et Porto à la fin de l'antiquité: Topographie religieuse et vie sociale," *MEFRA* 70 (1958): 295–330.

Filtzinger, P., D. Planck, and B. Cämmerer. *Die Römer in Baden-Württemberg*, 3rd ed. Stuttgart: K. Theiss, 1986.

Fiocchi Nicolai, V. "La nuova basilica circiforme della via Ardeatina," *Atti Della Pontificia Accademia Romana di Archeologia* 68 (1995–1996): 69–233.

———. *Strutture funerarie ed edifici di culto paleocristiana di Roma dal IV al VI secolo*. Vatican City: IGER, 2001.

Fishwick, D. *The Imperial Cult in the Latin West: Studies in the Ruler Cult of the Western Provinces of the Roman Empire*. 4 vols. Leiden: Brill, 1987–2005.

Flemming, J., ed., and G. Hoffmann, trans. *Akten der Ephesinischen Synode vom Jahre 449*. Abhandlungen der königlichen Gesellschaft der Wissenschaften zu Göttingen, Phil.-hist. Klasse, n. F. 15. Berlin: Weidmannsche Buchhandlung, 1917.

Fontenrose, J. E. *The Delphic Oracle: Its Responses and Operations, with a Catalogue of Responses*. Berkeley: University of California Press, 1978.

———. *Didyma: Apollo's Oracle, Cult, and Companions*. Berkeley: University of California Press, 1988.

Forni, G. "Flavia Constans Hispellum: Il Tempio ed il pontefice della gente Flavia Costantiniana," *AARC* 9 (1993): 401–6.

Fowden, E. K. "Sharing Holy Places," *Common Knowledge* 8 (2002): 124–46.

———. "Constantine and the Peoples of the Eastern Frontier." In *The Cambridge Companion to the Age of Constantine*, ed. N. Lenski, 2nd ed., 377–98. Cambridge: Cambridge University Press, 2011.

Fowden, G. "Bishops and Temples in the Eastern Roman Empire, AD 320–435," *JThS* 29 (1978): 53–78.

———. "Nicagoras of Athens and the Lateran Obelisk," *JHS* 107 (1987): 51–57.

———. *Empire to Commonwealth: Consequences of Monotheism in Late Antiquity*. Princeton: Princeton University Press, 1993.

———. "The Last Days of Constantine: Oppositional Versions and Their Influence," *JRS* 84 (1994): 146–70.

Franchi de' Cavalieri, P. *I martirii di S. Teodoto e di S. Ariadne con un'appendice sul testo originale del martirio di S. Eleuterio*. Studi e testi 6. Rome: Tipografia vaticana, 1901.

Frankfurter, D. *Religion in Roman Egypt: Assimilation and Resistance*. Princeton, NJ: Princeton University Press, 1998.

Frantz, A. *Athenian Agora*. Vol. 24, *Late Antiquity, A.D. 267–700*. Princeton, NJ: Princeton University Press, 1988.

Frazer, M. E. "A Syncretistic Pilgrim's Mould from Mamre (?)," *Gesta* 18 (1979): 137–45.

Frend, W. H. C. *The Donatist Church: A Movement of Protest in Roman North Africa*. Oxford: Oxford University Press, 1952.

Frend, W. H. C., and K. Clancy. "When Did the Donatist Schism Begin?" *JThS* n.s. 28 (1977): 104–9.

Fried, J. *Donation of Constantine and* Constitutum Constantini: *The Misinterpretation of a Fiction and Its Original Meaning*. Berlin: Walter de Gruyter, 2007.

Friesen, S. J. *Twice Neokoros: Ephesus, Asia and the Cult of the Flavian Imperial Family*. Leiden: Brill, 1993.

Frija, G. *Les Prêtres des empereurs: Le culte impérial civique dans la province romaine d'Asie*. Rennes: Presses universitaires de Rennes, 2012.

Gaddis, M. *There Is No Crime for Those Who Have Christ: Religious Violence in the Christian Roman Empire*. Berkeley: University of California Press, 2005.

Gagos, T., and P. van Minnen. *Settling a Dispute: Toward a Legal Anthropology of Late Antique Egypt*. Ann Arbor: University of Michigan Press, 1994.

Galsterer-Kröll, B. *Untersuchungen zu den Beinamen der Städte des Imperium Romanum*. Epigraphische Studien 9. Bonn: Rheinland-Verlag, 1972.

Galvão-Sobrinho, C. R. *Doctrine and Power: Theological Controversy and Christian Leadership in the Later Roman Empire*. Berkeley: University of California Press, 2013.

Garnsey, P. *Cities, Peasants, and Food in Classical Antiquity: Essays in Social and Economic History*. Cambridge: Cambridge University Press, 1998.

Gascou, J. "Le Rescrit d'Hispellum," *MEFRA* 79 (1967): 609–59.

———. "La politique municipale de Rome en Afrique du Nord II: Après la mort de Septime-Sévère," *ANRW* II.10.2 (1982): 230–320.

Gaudemet, J. *L'Église dans l'empire romain: IVᵉ–Vᵉ siècles*. Paris: Sirey, 1958.

Gayraud, M. *Narbonne antique: Des origines à la fin du IIIe siècle*. Paris: Diffusion de Boccard, 1981.

Geertman, H. "Documenti, redattori e la formazione del testo del *Liber Pontificalis*." In *Atti del colloquio internazionale Il Liber Pontificalis e la storia materiale, Roma, 21–22 febbraio 2002*. Mededelingen van het Nederlands Instituut te Rome 60–61, edited by H. Geertman, 266–312. Assen: Van Gorcum, 2003.

Geiger, J. "Ammianus Marcellinus and the Jewish Revolt Under Gallus: A Note," *LCM* 4 (1979): 77.

Gelzer, H., H. Hilgenfeld, and O. Cuntz, eds. *Patrum Nicaenorum Nomina, Latine, Graece Coptice Syriace Arabice Armeniace*. Leipzig: Teubner, 1898.

Gering, A. "Das Stadtzentrum von Ostia in der Spätantike: Vorbericht zu den Ausgrabungen 2008–2011," *MDAI(R)* 117 (2011): 409–509.

Ginouvès, R. "Thermes romains," *BCH* 79 (1955): 323–30.

Ginzburg, C. *History, Rhetoric, and Proof*. Hanover, NH: University Press of New England, 1999.

Girardet, K. M. *Kaisergericht und Bischofsgericht: Studien zu den Anfängen des Donatistenstreites (313–315) und zum Prozess des Athanasius von Alexandrien (328–346)*. Antiquitas 21. Bonn: R. Habelt, 1975.

——. "Das Christliche Priestertum Konstantins d. Gr. Ein Aspekt der Herrscheridee des Eusebius von Caesarea," *Chiron* 10 (1980): 569–92.

——. "Die Petition der Donatisten an Kaiser Konstantin (Frühjahr 313). Historische Voraussetzungen und Folgen," *Chiron* 19 (1989): 185–206. Reprinted in *Kaisertum, Religionspolitik und das Recht von Staat und Kirche in der Spätantike*, 1–26. Antiquitas 56. Bonn, 2009.

——. "Konstantin der Grosse und das Reichskonzil von Arles (314). Historisches Problem und methodologische Aspekte." In *Oecumenica et Patristica, Festschrift W. Schneemelcher*, ed. D. Papandreou, W. A. Bienert, and K. Schäferdiek, 151–74. Chambésy-Geneva: W. Kohlhammer, 1989. Reprinted in *Kaisertum, Religionspolitik und das Recht von Staat und Kirche in der Spätantike*, 43–72. Antiquitas 56. Bonn: Habelt, 2009.

——. "Das Reichskonzil von Rom (313): Urteil, Einspruch, Folgen," *Historia* 41 (1992): 104–16. Reprinted in *Kaisertum, Religionspolitik und das Recht von Staat und Kirche in der Spätantike*, 27–41. Antiquitas 56. Bonn: Habelt, 2009.

——. "Kaiser Konstantin der Grosse als Vorsitzender von Konzilien." In *Costantino il Grande: Dall'antichità all'umanesimo, Colloquio sul cristianesimo nel mondo antico, Macerata, 18–20 dicembre 1990*, ed. G. Bonamente and F. Fusco, vol. 1, 445–59. Macerata, Italy: Università degli studi di Macerata, 1992.

——. "Vom Sonnen-Tag zum Sonntag: Der Dies Solis in Gesetzgebung und Politik Konstantins d. Gr.," *ZAC* 11 (2007): 279–310.

——. *Die Konstantinische Wende: Voraussetzungen und Geistige Grundlagen der Religionspolitik Konstantins des Grossen*, 2nd ed. Darmstadt, Germany: Wissenschaftliche Buchgesellschaft, 2007.

——. *Kaisertum, Religionspolitik und das Recht von Staat und Kirche in der Spätantike*. Antiquitas 56. Bonn: Habelt, 2009.

——. *Der Kaiser und sein Gott: Das Christentum im Denken und in der Religionspolitik Konstantins des Grossen*. Berlin: Walter de Gruyter, 2010.

——. "Das Verbot von 'Betrügerischen Machenschaften' Beim Kaiserkult in Hispellum (*CIL* XI 5265 / *ILS* 705)," *ZPE* 182 (2012): 297–311.

——. "Das Jahr 311: Galerius, Konstantin und das Christentum." In *Costantino prima e dopo Costantino – Constantine Before and After Constantine*, ed. G. Bonamente, N. Lenski, and R. Lizzi Testa, 113–32. Munera 35. Bari, Italy: Edipuglia, 2012.

——, ed., trans., comm. *Konstantin. Rede an die Versammlung der Heiligen*. Fontes Christiani 55. Freiburg: Herder, 2013.

Giuliano, A. "Augustus—Constantinus," *Bolletino d'arte* 68–69 (1991): 3–10.

Gleason, M. "Greek Cities Under Roman Rule." In *A Companion to the Roman Empire*, ed. D. S. Potter, 228–49. Malden, MA: Wiley-Blackwell, 2006.

Gliwitzky, C. "Zwischen vergangener Grösse und glückbringender Zukunft." In *Konstantin der Grosse: Zwischen Sol und Christus*, ed. K. Ehling and G. Weber, 118–29. Darmstadt, Germany: Philipp von Zabern, 2011.

Glucker, C. A. M. *The City of Gaza in the Roman and Byzantine Periods*. BAR International Series 325. Oxford: British Archaeological Reports, 1987.

Gnoli, T., and J. Thornton. "Σῶζε Τὴν Κατοικίαν: Società e religione nella frigia romana. Note introduttive." In *Frigi e Frigio: Atti dello simposio internazionale, Roma, 16–17 Ottobre 1995*, ed. R. Gusmani, M. Salvini, and P. Vannicelli, 153–200. Rome: Consiglio nazionale delle ricerche, 1997.

Goddard, C. J. "Les formes festives de l'allégeance au prince en Italie centrale, sous le règne de Constantin: Un suicide religieux?" *MEFRA* 114 (2002): 1025–88.

Godefroy, J., ed. *Codex Theodosianus cum perpetuis commentariis Jacobi Gothofredi*. 6 vols. 1736–1743; repr. Hildesheim: Olms-Weidmann, 2000.

Goethert, K.-P., and M. Kiessel. "Trier—Residenz in der Spätantike." In *Konstantin der Grosse: Ausstellungskatalog = Imperator Caesar Flavius Constantinus*, ed. A. Demandt and J. Engemann, 304–12. Trier, Germany: Konstantin-Ausstellungsgesellschaft, 2007.

Gradel, I. *Emperor Worship and Roman Religion*. Oxford: Oxford University Press, 2002.

Grasmück, E. L. *Coercitio: Staat und Kirche im Donatistenstreit*. Bonner historische Forschungen 22. Bonn: L. Röhrscheid, 1964.

Green, M., and J. Ferguson. "Constantine, Sun-Symbols, and the Labarum," *Durham University Journal* 80 (1987): 9–17.

Grégoire, H. "La 'conversion' de Constantin," *Revue de l'Université de Bruxelles* 36 (1930): 231–72.

———. "La vision de Constantin 'liquidée.'" *Byzantion* 14 (1939): 341–51.

Grégoire, H., and M.-A. Kugener, eds. and trans. *Marc le Diacre: Vie de Porphyre évêque de Gaza*. Paris, 1930.

Grig, L. *Making Martyrs in Late Antiquity*. London: Duckworth, 2004.

Gros, P. "Les nouveaux espaces civiques du début de l'Empire en Asie Mineure: Les exemples d'Ephèse, Iasos et Aphrodisias." In *Aphrodisias Papers 3: The Setting and Quarries, Mythological and Other Sculptural Decoration, Architectural Development, Portico of Tiberius, and Tetrapylon*, ed. C. Roueché and R. R. R. Smith, 111–20. Ann Arbor: University of Michigan Press, 1996.

Grubbs, J. E. *Law and Family in Late Antiquity: The Emperor Constantine's Marriage Legislation*. Oxford: Oxford University Press, 1995.

Grünewald, Thomas. *Constantinus Maximus Augustus: Herrschaftspropaganda in der zeitgenössischen Überlieferung*. Stuttgart: Franz Steiner Verlag, 1990.

Guadagno, G., and S. Panciera. "Nuove testimonianze sul governo della Campania in età Costantiniana," *RAL* 25 (1970): 111–29.

Gui, I., N. Duval, and J.-P. Caillet. *Basiliques chrétiennes d'Afrique du Nord*. Paris: Institut d'études augustiniennes, 1992.

Guyon, J. *Le Cimetière aux Deux Lauriers: Recherches sur les catacombes romaines*. BEFAR 264. Rome: École française de Rome, 1987.

Gwynn, D. M. *The Eusebians: The Polemic of Athanasius of Alexandria and the Construction of the "Arian Controversy."* Oxford: Oxford University Press, 2007.

Haas, C. *Alexandria in Late Antiquity: Topography and Social Conflict*. Baltimore: Johns Hopkins University Press, 1997.

Habermas, J. *The Theory of Communicative Action*. Vol. 1, *Reason and the Rationalization of Society*, trans. T. McCarthy. Boston: Beacon Press, 1984.

———. *The Theory of Communicative Action*. Vol. 2, *Lifeworld and System: A Critique of Functionalist Reason*, trans. T. McCarthy. Boston: Beacon Press, 1987.

———. *On the Pragmatics of Social Interaction: Preliminary Studies in the Theory of Communicative Action*, trans. B. Fultner. Cambridge, MA: MIT Press, 2001.

Habicht, C. *Die Inschriften des Asklepieions*. Altertümer von Pergamon 8.3. Berlin: Walter de Gruyter, 1969.

Haensch, R. "Die Bearbeitungsweisen von Petitionen in der Provinz Aegyptus," *ZPE* 100 (1994): 487–546.

———. "Apokrimata und Authentica: Dokumente römischer Herrschaft in der Sicht der Untertanen." In *Herrschen und Verwalten: Der Alltag der Römischen Administration in der Hohen Kaiserzeit*, ed. J. Heinrichs and R. Haensch, 213–33. Kölner Historische Abhandlungen 46. Cologne: Böhlau, 2007.

Hahn, J. *Gewalt und Religiöser Konflikt: Studien zu den Auseinandersetzungen zwischen Christen, Heiden und Juden im Osten des römischen Reiches (von Konstantin bis Theodosius II)*. Klio Beihefte n. F. 8. Berlin: Akademie Verlag, 2004.

————. "Gewaltanwendung Ad Maiorem Gloriam Dei? Religiöse Intoleranz in der Spätantike." In *Für Religionsfreiheit, Recht und Toleranz*, ed. H.-G. Nesselrath et al., 151–75. Tübingen: Mohr Siebeck, 2011.

Hajjar, J. N. *La Triade d'Héliopolis-Baalbek: Son culte et sa diffusion à travers les textes littéraires et les documents iconographiques et épigraphiques*. Leiden: Brill, 1977.

————. *La Triade d'Héliopolis-Baalbek: Iconographie, théologie, culte et sanctuaires*. Montreal: Y. Hajjar, 1985.

Hall, L. "Cicero's *Instinctu Divino* and Constantine's *Instinctu Divinitatis*: The Evidence of the Arch of Constantine for the Senatorial View of the 'Vision' of Constantine," *JECS* 6 (1998): 647–71.

Hall, S. "Encoding and Decoding." In *Culture, Media, Language: Working Papers in Cultural Studies, 1972–79*, 128–38. London: Hutchison, 1973.

————. "Notes on Deconstructing the Popular." In *People's History and Socialist Theory*, ed. R. Samuel, 227–39. Amsterdam: Van Gennep, 1981.

Hallof, K. "Die Inschrift von Skaptopara: Neue Dokumente und Neue Lesungen," *Chiron* 24 (1994): 405–41.

Halsberghe, G. H. *The Cult of Sol Invictus*. Études préliminaires aux religions orientales dans l'Empire Romain 23. Leiden: Brill, 1972.

Hannestad, N. "Die Porträtskulptur zur Zeit Konstantins des Grossen." In *Konstantin der Grosse: Ausstellungskatalog = Imperator Caesar Flavius Constantinus*, ed. A. Demandt and J. Engemann, 96–116. Trier, Germany: Konstantin-Ausstellungsgesellschaft, 2007.

Hansen, G. C., ed. *Theodoros Anagnostes Kirchengeschichte*, 2nd ed. GCS 3. Berlin: Walter de Gruyter, 1995.

Hanson, R. P. C. "The Fate of Eustathius of Antioch," *ZKG* 95 (1984): 171–79.

————. *The Search for the Christian Doctrine of God: The Arian Controversy, 318–381*. Edinburgh: T. & T. Clark, 1988.

Harl, K. W. *Civic Coins and Civic Politics in the Roman East, A.D. 180–275*. Berkeley: University of California Press, 1987.

Harlick, R. M. "Anepigraphic Bronze Coins of Constantine and Family," *Celator* 21 (2007): 6–20.

Harmand, L. *Le patronat sur les collectivités publiques des origines au Bas-Empire*. Paris: Presses universitaires de France, 1957.

Harries, J. *Law and Empire in Late Antiquity*. Cambridge: Cambridge University Press, 1999.

————. "Constantine the Lawgiver." In *From the Tetrarchs to the Theodosians: Later Roman History and Culture, 284–450 CE*, ed. S. McGill, C. Sogno, and E. J. Watts, 73–92. YCS 34. Cambridge: Cambridge University Press, 2010.

————. *Imperial Rome, AD 284 to 363: The New Empire*. Edinburgh: University of Edinburgh Press, 2012.

Harris, W. V. "Constantine's Dream," *Klio* 87 (2005): 488–94.

Harrison, E. B. "The Constantinian Portrait," *DOP* 41 (1967): 81–96.

Hartley, E., J. Hawkes, M. Henig, and F. Mee. *Constantine the Great: York's Roman Emperor*. York: York Museums and Gallery Trust, 2006.

Haspels, C. H. E. *The Highlands of Phrygia: Sites and Monuments*. 2 vols. Princeton, NJ: Princeton University Press, 1971.

Hauben, H. *Studies on the Melitian Schism in Egypt (AD 306–335)*, ed. P. van Nuffelen. Farnham, UK: Ashgate, 2012.

Hauken, T. *Petition and Response: An Epigraphic Study of Petitions to Roman Emperors, 181–249*. Monographs from the Norwegian Institute at Athens 2. Bergen: Norwegian Institute at Athens, 1998.

Heath, M. "The Family of Minucianus?" *ZPE* 113 (1997): 66–70.

Heather, P. and J. Matthews. *The Goths in the Fourth Century*. TTH 11. Liverpool: Liverpool University Press, 1991.

Heck, E. *Die dualistischen Zusätze und die Kaiseranreden bei Lactantius*. Heidelberg: C. Winter, 1972.

———. "Constantin und Lactanz in Trier—Chronologisches," *Historia* 58 (2009): 118–30.

Heid, S. "Der Ursprung der Helenalegende im Pilgerbetrieb Jerusalems," *JAC* 32 (1989): 41–71.

Heijmans, M. "La topographie de la ville d'Arles durant l'antiquité tardive," *JRA* 12 (1999): 143–67.

———. *Arles durant l'antiquité tardive: De la duplex Arelas à l'Urbs Genesii*. CEFR 324. Rome: École Française de Rome, 2004.

———. "Constantina Urbs. Arles durant le IVᵉ siècle: Une autre résidence impériale?" In *Konstantin der Grosse: Geschichte, Archäologie, Rezeption. Internationales Kolloquium vom 10.–15. Oktober 2005 an der Universität Trier*, ed. A. Demandt and J. Engemann, 209–20. Schriftenreihe des Rheinischen Landesmuseums Trier 32. Trier, Germany: Rheinisches Landesmuseum, 2007.

Heikel, I. A. *Über das Leben Constantins, Constantins Rede an die heilige Versammlung, Trikennatsrede an Constantin*. Eusebius Werke 1. Leipzig: Akademie Verlag, 1902.

Heim, F. *La théologie de la victoire de Constantin à Théodose*. Théologie Historique 89. Paris: Beauchesne, 1992.

Heinen, H. *Frühchristliches Trier: Von den Anfängen bis zur Völkerwanderung*. Trier, Germany: Paulinus, 1996.

Heinze, T. *Konstantin der Grosse und das konstantinische Zeitalter in den Urteilen und Wegen der deutsch-italienischen Forschungsdiskussion*. Munich: H. Utz, 2005.

Heinzelmann, M., and A. Martin. "River Port, Navalia and Harbour Temple at Ostia: New Results of a DAI-AAR Project," *JRA* 15 (2002): 5–19.

Hendy, M. F. *Studies in the Byzantine Monetary Economy, c. 300–1450*. Cambridge: Cambridge University Press, 1985.

Hermann, A. "Der Nil und die Christen," *JAC* 2 (1959): 30–69.

Hermann-Otto, E. *Konstantin der Große*. Darmstadt, Germany: Primus Verlag, 2007.

Heyden, K. "Beth Shean/Scythopolis in Late Antiquity: Cult and Culture, Continuity and Change." In *One God—One Cult—One Nation: Archaeological and Biblical Perspectives*, ed. R. G. Kratz and H. Spieckermann, 301–37. Berlin: Walter de Gruyter, 2010.

Hild, F., and H. Hellenkemper. *Kilikien und Isaurien*. 2 vols. Tabula Imperii Byzantini 5. Vienna: Verlag der Österreichischen Akademie der Wissenschaften, 1990.

Hill, G. *A History of Cyprus*. Vol. 1, *To the Conquest by Richard Lion Heart*. Cambridge: Cambridge University Press, 1940.

Hill, P. V., J. P. C. Kent, and Carson, R. A. G. *Late Roman Bronze Coinage, A. D. 324–498*. London: Spink, 1960.

Hitchner, R. B. "The Kasserine Archaeological Survey, 1982–1986," *Antiquités Africaines* 24 (1988): 7–41.

Holloway, R. R. *Constantine and Rome*. New Haven, CT: Yale University Press, 2004.

Honigmann, E. A. J., ed. *Le Synekdèmos d'Hiéroklès et l'opuscule géographique de Georges de Chypre*. Corpus Bruxellense Historiae Byzantinae 1. Brussels: Éditions de l'Institut de philologie et d'histoire orientales et slaves, 1939.

Honoré, T. *Emperors and Lawyers*, 2nd ed. Oxford: Oxford University Press, 1984.

Horden, P., and N. Purcell. *The Corrupting Sea: A Study of Mediterranean History*. Malden, MA: Wiley-Blackwell, 2000.

Horsley, G. *The Greek and Latin Inscriptions in the Burdur Museum*. RECAM 5. London: British Institute at Ankara, 2007.

Hostein, A. *La cité et l'empereur: Les Éduens dans l'empire romain d'après* les Panégyriques Latins. Paris: Publications de la Sorbonne, 2012.

Huck, O. "À propos de *CTh* 1, 27, 1 et *CSirm* 1. Sur deux textes controverses relatifs à l'*episcopalis audientia* Constantinienne," *ZRG* 120 (2003): 78–105.

———. "Encore à propos des *Sirmondiennes*. Arguments présentés à l'appui de la thèse de l'authenticité en réponse à une mise en cause récente," *AnTard* 11 (2003): 181–96.

———. "La 'création' de l'*audientia episcopalis* par Constantin." In *Empire chrétien et église aux IVe et Ve siècles. Intégration ou "concordat." Le témoinage du Code Théodosien*, ed. J.-N. Guinot and F. Richard, 295–315. Paris: Cerf, 2008.

Humfress, C. *Orthodoxy and the Courts in Late Antiquity*. Oxford: Oxford University Press, 2007.

———. "Bishops and Law Courts in Late Antiquity: How (Not) to Make Sense of the Legal Evidence," *JECS* 19 (2011): 375–400.

———. "Civil Law and Social Life." In *The Cambridge Companion to the Age of Constantine*, ed. N. Lenski, 2nd ed., 205–25. Cambridge: Cambridge University Press, 2011.

Humphries, M. "From Usurper to Emperor? The Politics of Legitimation in the Age of Constantine," *JLA* 1 (2008): 82–100.

Hunt, E. D. *Holy Land Pilgrimage in the Later Roman Empire, AD 312–460*. Oxford: Oxford University Press, 1982.

———. "Constantine and Jerusalem," *JEH* 48 (1997): 405–24.

Hurtado, L. W. *The Earliest Christian Artifacts: Manuscripts and Christian Origins*. Grand Rapids, MI: Eerdmans, 2006.

Iacumin, R. *La Basilica di Aquileia*. Vol. 2, *Il mosaico dell'Aula Teodoriana*. Reana del Rojale, Italy: Chiandetti, 1993.

Jacques, F. *Le privilège de liberté: Politique impériale et autonomie municipale dans les cités de l'occident romain (161–244)*. CEFR 76. Rome: École Française de Rome, 1984.

———. "*Municipia libera* de l'Afrique Proconsulaire." In *Epigrafia: Actes du colloque international d'épigraphie latine en mémoire de Attilio Degrassi pour le centenaire de sa naissance: Rome, 27–28 mai 1988*, 583–606. CEFR 143. Rome: École Française de Rome, 1991.

———. "Les moulins d'Orcistus: Rhétorique et géographie au IVe s." In *Institutions, société et vie politique dans l'empire romain au IVe siècle ap. J.-C: Actes de la table ronde autour de l'œuvre d'André Chastagnol, Paris, 20–21 Janvier 1989*. CEFR 159, ed. M. Christol et al., 431–46 Rome: École Française de Rome, 1992.

Jannot, J.-R. *Religion in Ancient Etruria*. Madison: University of Wisconsin Press, 2005.

Jauss, H. R. *Toward an Aesthetic of Reception*. Trans. T. Bahti. 1970; repr. Minneapolis: University of Minnesota Press, 1982.

Johnson, A. C., P. Coleman-Norton, and F. C. Bourne. *Ancient Roman Statutes: A Translation, with Introduction, Commentary, Glossary, and Index*. Austin: University of Texas Press, 1961.

Johnson, A. P. *Eusebius*. London: I. B. Tauris, 2014.

Johnson, M. J. *The Roman Imperial Mausolem in Late Antiquity*. Cambridge: Cambridge University Press, 2009.

———. "Constantinian Churches in Campania: Texts and Contexts." In *The Apolline Project: Studies on Vesuvius' North Slope*, ed. R. Macfarlane and G. F. de Simone, 247–53. Naples: Università degli Studi Suor Orsola Benincasa, 2009.

———. "Architecture of Empire." In *The Cambridge Companion to the Age of Constantine*, ed. N. Lenski, 2nd ed., 278–97. Cambridge: Cambridge University Press, 2011.

Jones, A. H. M. *Constantine and the Conversion of Europe*. London: Hodder & Stoughton, 1949.

———. *The Cities of the Eastern Roman Provinces*, 2nd ed. Oxford: Clarendon Press, 1971.

Jones, A. H. M., and T. C. Skeat. "Notes on the Genuineness of the Constantinian Documents in Eusebius's Life of Constantine," *JEH* 5 (1954): 196–200.

Jones, C. P. *Kinship Diplomacy in the Ancient World*. Cambridge, MA: Harvard University Press, 1999.

Kahlos, M. *Forbearance and Compulsion: The Rhetoric of Religious Tolerance and Intolerance in Late Antiquity*. London: Duckworth, 2009.

Kasher, A. *The Jews in Hellenistic and Roman Egypt: The Struggle for Equal Rights*. Texte und Studien zum Antiken Judentum 7. Tübingen: Mohr-Siebeck, 1985.

Keay, S., M. Millett, L. Paroli, and S. Strutt. *Portus: An Archaeological Survey of the Port of Imperial Rome*. Archaeological Monographs of the British School at Rome 15. London: British School at Rome, 2005.

Kelly, B. *Petitions, Litigation and Social Control in Roman Egypt*. Oxford: Oxford University Press, 2011.

Kelly, C. *Ruling the Later Roman Empire*. Cambridge, MA: Harvard University Press, 2004.

Kent, J. P. C. *The Roman Imperial Coinage*. Vol. 8, *The Family of Constantine, AD 337–364*. London: Spink, 1981.

Khannousi, M., and A. Mastino. "Il culto imperiale a Thibaris ed a Thugga tra Diocleziano e Costantino," *Serta Antiqua et Medievalia* 6 (2003): 411–36.

Kienast, D. *Römische Kaisertabelle: Grundzüge einer römischen Kaiserchronologie*, 3rd ed. Darmstadt, Germany: Wissenschaftliche Buchgesellschaft, 2004.

Kim, S. "Rereading David Morely's The 'Nationwide' Audience," *Cultural Studies* 18 (2004): 84–108.

Klein, R. "Das Kirchenbauverständnis Constantins d. Gr. in Rom und in den Östlichen Provinzen." In *Das Antike Rom und der Osten: Festschrift für Klaus Parlasca zum 65. Geburtstag*, ed. C. Börker and M. Donderer, 77–101. Erlangen, Germany: Universitätsbund Erlangen-Nürnberg, 1990.

Kleinbauer, E. "Antioch, Jerusalem, and Rome: The Patronage of Emperor Constantius II and Architectural Invention," *Gesta* 45 (2006): 125–45.

Kolb, A. *Transport und Nachrichtentransfer im römischen Reich*. Klio Beihefte n. F. 2. Berlin: Akademie Verlag, 2000.

Kolb, F. *Diocletian und die erste Tetrarchie: Improvisation oder Experiment in der Organisation monarchischer Herrschaft?* Berlin: Walter de Gruyter, 1987.

———. "Bemerkungen zur urbanen Austattung von Städten im Western und im Osten des römischen Reiches anhand von Tacitus, *Agricola* 21 und der konstantinischen Inschrift von Orkistos," *Klio* 75 (1993): 321–41.

König, I. *Origo Constantini: Anonymus Valesianus*. Trierer Historische Forschungen 11. Trier, Germany: Verlag Trierer Historische Forschungen, 1987.

Kraft, H. "Das Silbermedaillon Constantins des Grossen mit dem Christusmonogramm auf dem Helm," *JNG* (1954): 151–78.

———. *Kaiser Konstantins religiöse Entwicklung*. Tübingen: Mohr, 1955.

Krause, J.-U. *Spätantike Patronatsformen im Westen des römischen Reiches*. Vestigia 38. Munich: C. H. Beck, 1987.

———. "Das Spätantike Städtepatronat," *Chiron* 17 (1987): 1–80.

Krautheimer, R. *Three Christian Capitals: Topography and Politics*. Berkeley: University of California Press, 1983.

———. *Early Christian and Byzantine Architecture*, ed. S. Ćurčić, 4th ed. New Haven, CT: Yale University Press, 1986.

———. "The Ecclesiastical Building Policy of Constantine." In *Costantino il Grande: Dall'antichità all'umanesimo, Colloquio sul cristianesimo nel mondo antico, Macerata, 18–20 dicembre*

1990, ed. G. Bonamente and F. Fusco, vol. 2, 509–52. Macerata, Italy: Università degli studi di Macerata, 1992.

Krautheimer, R., S. Corbett, and A. Frazer. *Corpus Basilicarum Christianarum Romae: The Early Christian Basilicas of Rome (IV–IX Cent.)*. 5 vols. Rome: Pontificio istituto di archeologia cristiana, 1937.

Kriegbaum, B. *Kirche der Traditoren oder Kirche der Märtyrer: Die Vorgeschichte des Donatismus*. Innsbruck: Tyrolia, 1986.

———. "Die Religionspolitik des Kaisers Maxentius," *Archivum Historiae Pontificiae* 30 (1992): 7–54.

Kugener, M.-A., ed. and trans. *Vie de Sévère*. Patrologia Orientalis II.3.8.7–115. Paris: Firmin-Didot, 1907.

Kuhnen, H.-P. *Das römische Trier*. Stuttgart: K. Theiss, 2001.

Lamoreaux, J. C. "Episcopal Courts in Late Antiquity," *JECS* 3 (1995): 143–67.

Lane Fox, R. *Pagans and Christians*. New York: Knopf, 1987.

Laniado, A. *Recherches sur les notables municipaux dans l'empire protobyzantin*. T&M Monographies 13. Paris: Association des amis du Centre d'histoire et civilisation de Byzance, 2002.

———. "From Municipal Councillors to 'Municipal Landowners': Some Remarks on the Evolution of Provincial Elites in Early Byzantium." In *Chlodwigs Welt: Organisation von Herrschaft um 500*, edited by M. Meier and S. Patzold, 545–66. Stuttgart: Franz Steiner Verlag, 2014.

Laniado, A., and P. Porath. "A Dedication to Galerius from Scythopolis: A Revised Reading," *ZPE* 98 (1993): 229–37.

Laurence, K. A. *Roman Infrastructural Changes to Greek Sanctuaries and Games: Panehellenism in the Roman Empire, Formations of New Identities*. Ph.D. Dissertation, University of Michigan, 2012.

Leadbetter, B. *Galerius and the Will of Diocletian*. London: Routledge, 2009.

Lee, A. D. *Pagans and Christians in Late Antiquity: A Sourcebook*. London: Routledge, 2000.

Leeb, R. *Konstantin und Christus: Die Verchristlichung der imperialen Repräsentation unter Konstantin dem Grossen als Spiegel seiner Kirchenpolitik und seines Selbstverständnisses als Christlicher Kaiser*. Berlin: Walter de Gruyter, 1992.

Lenski, N. "The Gothic Civil War and the Date of the Gothic Conversion," *GRBS* 36 (1995): 51–87.

———. "Evidence for the *Audientia Episcopalis* in the New Letters of Augustine." In *Law, Society, and Authority in Late Antiquity*, ed. R. W. Mathisen, 83–97. Oxford: Oxford University Press, 2001.

———. *Failure of Empire: Valens and the Roman State in the Fourth Century A.D.* Berkeley: University of California Press, 2002.

———. "Empresses in the Holy Land: The Making of a Christian Utopia in Late Antiquity." In *Travel, Communication, and Geography in Late Antiquity: Sacred and Profane*, ed. L. Ellis and F. Kidner, 113–24. Aldershot, UK: Ashgate, 2004.

———. "Introduction." In *Jacob Burckhardt: The Age of Constantine the Great*, trans. M. Hadas, xi–xix. London: Folio Society, 2007.

———. "Evoking the Pagan Past: *Instinctu Divinitatis* and Constantine's Capture of Rome," *JLA* 1 (2008): 204–57.

———. *The Cambridge Companion to the Age of Constantine*, rev. ed. Cambridge: Cambridge University Press, 2011.

———. "The Reign of Constantine." In *The Cambridge Companion to the Age of Constantine*, ed. N. Lenski, 2nd ed., 59–93. Cambridge: Cambridge University Press, 2011.

———. "Constantine and Slavery: *Libertas* and the Fusion of Roman and Christian Values," *AARC* 18 (2012): 235–60.

————. "Early Retrospectives on the Christian Constantine: Athanasius and Firmicus Maternus." In *Constantino prima e dopo Costantino – Constantine Before and After Constantine*, ed. G. Bonamente, N. Lenski, and R. Lizzi Testa, 465–80. Munera 35. Bari, Italy: Edipuglia, 2012.

————. "Harnessing Violence: Armed Force as Manpower in the Late Roman Countryside," *JLA* 6 (2013): 233–50.

————. "The Sun and the Senate: The Inspiration for the Arch of Constantine." In *Constantino il Grande: Alle radici dell'Europa. Atti del convegno internazionale di studio in occcasione del 1700° anniversario della battaglia di Ponte Milvio e della conversione di Costantino*, ed. B. Ardura, 153–94. Rome: Libreria Editrice Vaticana, 2014.

————. "Il valore dell'Editto di Milano." In *Costantino a Milano. L'editto e la sua storia (313–2013)*, ed. P. Moretti. Milan: Forthcoming.

————. "Constantine and the Donatists: Exploring the Limits of Religious Toleration." In *Religiöse Toleranz: Moderne Ideale im Spiegel antiker Realien*. Colloquium Rauricum 14, ed. M. Wallraff, 101–39. Berlin: Walter de Gruyter, 2015.

Leone, A. *The End of the Pagan City: Religion, Economy, and Urbanism in Late Antique North Africa*. Oxford: Oxford University Press, 2013.

Lepelley, C. *Les cités de l'Afrique romaine au bas-empire*. 2 vols. Paris: Études augustiniennes, 1979–81.

————. "La création de cités nouvelles en Afrique au Bas-Empire: Le cas de la *civitas Faustianensis*," In *L'Afrique, la Gaule, la Religion à l'époque romaine: Mélanges à la mémoire de Marcel le Glay*, ed. Y. Le Bohec, 288–99. Collection Latomus 226. Brussels: Latomus, 1994.

————. "Vers la fin de l'autonomie municipale: Le nivellement des status des cités de Gallien à Constantin," *AARC* 13 (2001): 455–72.

————. "Une inscription d'Heraclea Sintica (Macédoine) récemment découverte, rélévant un rescrit de l'empereur Galère restituant ses droits à la cité," *ZPE* 146 (2004): 221–31.

————. "De la réaction païenne à la sécularisation: Le témoinage d'inscriptions municipales romano-africaines tardives." In *Pagans and Christians in the Roman Empire: The Breaking of a Dialogue (IVth–VIth Century AD). Proceedings of the International Conference at the Monastery of Bose (October 2008)*, ed. P. Brown and R. Lizzi Testa, 273–89. Vienna: LIT Verlag, 2011.

Leppin, H. "Konstantin der Grosse und das Christentum bei Jacob Burckhardt." In *Konstantin der Grosse: Das Bild des Kaisers im Wandel der Zeiten*, ed. A. Goltz and H. Schlange-Schoningen, 263–76. Cologne: Böhlau Verlag, 2008.

Les Flavii. *Les Flavii de Cillium: Étude architecturale, épigraphique, historique et littéraire du Mausolée de Kasserine (CIL VIII, 211–216)*. Rome: Ecole française de Rome, 1993.

Levick, B. *Vespasian*. London: Routledge, 1999.

Lewis, N., and M. Reinhold, eds. *Roman Civilization: Selected Readings*, 3rd ed. Vol. 2. New York: Columbia University Press, 1990.

Liebeschuetz, J. H. W. G. *The Decline and Fall of the Roman City*. Oxford: Oxford University Press, 2001.

Lieu, S. N. C. *The Emperor Julian: Panegyric and Polemic*. TTH 1. Liverpool: Liverpool University Press, 1986.

————. "Constantine in Legendary Literature." In *The Cambridge Companion to the Age of Constantine*, ed. N. Lenski, 2nd ed., 298–321. Cambridge: Cambridge University Press, 2011.

Linder, A. *The Jews in Roman Imperial Legislation*. Detroit: Wayne State University Press, 1987.

Liverani, P. "La basilica costantiniana di S. Pietro in Vaticano." In *Petros Eni—Pietro è Qui: Catalogo della mostra: Città del Vaticano, Braccio Di Carlo Magno, 11 ottobre 2006–8 marzo 2007*, 141–47. Rome: Edindustria, 2006.

———. "L'architettura costantiniana, tra committenza imperiale e contributo delle élites locali." In *Konstantin der Grosse: Geschichte, Archäologie, Rezeption. Internationales Kolloquium vom 10.-15. Oktober 2005 an der Universität Trier*, ed. A. Demandt and J. Engemann, 235–44. Trier: Rheinisches Landesmuseum, 2006.

———. "Saint Peter's, Leo the Great and the Leprosy of Constantine," *PBSR* 76 (2008): 155–72.

———. "I vescovi nell'edilizia pubblica." In *Pagans and Christians in the Roman Empire: The Breaking of a Dialogue (IVth-VIth Century A.D.): Proceedings of the International Conference at the Monastery of Bose (October 2008)*, ed. P. Brown and R. Lizzi Testa, 529–39. Vienna: LIT Verlag, 2011.

Lizzi Testa, R. "Alle origini della tradizione pagana su Costantino e il senato romano (Amm. Marc. 21. 10. 8 e Zos. 2. 32. 1)." In *Transformations of Late Antiquity: Essays for Peter Brown*, ed. P. Rousseau and M. Papoutsakis, 85–127. Farnham, UK: Ashgate, 2009.

———. "Costantino tra fede, economia e politica: i privilegi ai sacerdoti cattolici e ai preti dei culti tradizionali." In *L'impero costantiniano e i luoghi sacri. Convegno internazionale (Roma, 2-3 dicembre 2013)*. Forthcoming.

Logan, A. H. B. "Marcellus of Ancyra and the Councils of 325: Antioch, Ancyra and Nicaea," *JThS* n.s. 43 (1992): 428–46.

———. "Constantine, the *Liber Pontificalis*, and the Christian Basilicas of Rome," *Studia Patristica* 50 (2010): 31–53.

Loseby, S. "Arles in Late Antiquity: *Gallula Roma Arelas* and *Urbs Genesii.*" In *Towns in Transition: Urban Evolution in Late Antiquity and the Early Middle Ages*, ed. N. Christie and S. Loseby, 45–70. Aldershot, UK: Ashgate, 1996.

Louth, A. "The Date of Eusebius' *Historia Ecclesiastica*," *JThS* n.s. 40 (1990): 111–23.

Lightfoot, J. L., ed. *Lucian: On the Syrian Goddess*. Oxford: Oxford University Press, 2003.

Ma, J. *Antiochos III and the Cities of Western Asia Minor*. Oxford: Oxford University Press, 1999.

———. "Fighting Poleis of the Hellenistic World." In *War and Violence in Ancient Greece*, ed. H. van Wees, 337–76. London: Duckworth, 2000.

———. "Peer Polity Interaction in the Hellenistic Age," *P&P* 180 (2003): 9–40.

———. "Traveling Statues, Traveling Bases? Ancient Statues in Constantinople," *ZPE* 180 (2012): 243–49.

MacMullen, R. "Constantine and the Miraculous," *GRBS* 9 (1968): 81–96.

———. *Constantine*. New York: Dial Press, 1969.

———. *Voting About God in Early Church Councils*. New Haven, CT: Yale University Press, 2006.

———. *The Second Church: Popular Christianity, AD 200-400*. Atlanta: Society of Biblical Literature, 2009.

Mader, E. *Mambre: Die Ergebnisse der Ausgrabungen im heiligen Bezirk Râmet el-Ḫalîl in Südpalästina, 1926-1928*. Freiburg: E. Wewel, 1957.

Maier, J. L. *Le dossier du Donatisme*. TU 134-135. Berlin: Akademie Verlag, 1987.

Maiuro, M. "Archivi, amminstrazione del patrimonio e proprietà imperiali nel *Liber pontificalis*: La redazione del *libellus* imperiale copiato nella *Vita Sylvestri*." In *Le proprietà imperiali nell'Italia romana: Economia, produzione, amministrazione, Atti del convegno, Ferrara-Voghiera, 3-4 giugno 2005*, ed. D. Pupillo, 235–58. Florence: Le Lettere, 2007.

Malosse, P.-L. "Libanius on Constantine Again," *CQ* 47 (1997): 519–24.

Manconi, D., P. Camerieri, and V. Cruciani. "Hispellum: Pianificazione urbana e territoriale." In *Assisi e gli Umbri nell'antichità: Atti del convengo internazionale, Assisi, 18-21 dicembre 1991*, ed. G. Bonamente and G. Coarelli, 375–92. Assisi: Società editrice Minerva, 1996.

Mango, C. A. *The Brazen House: A Study of the Vestibule of the Imperial Palace of Constantinople*. Copenhagen: I Kommission hos Munksgaard, 1959.

———. "Constantine's Mausoleum and the Translation of Relics," *BZ* 83 (1990): 51–62.

———. "The Empress Helena, Helenopolis, Pylae," *T&M* 12 (1994): 143–58 and Pl. I–VII.

Mango, C. A., and R. Scott, trans. *The Chronicle of Theophanes Confessor: Byzantine and Near Eastern History, AD 284–813*. Oxford: Oxford University Press, 1997.

Mansi, G. D. *Sacrorum conciliorum nova et amplissima collectio*, rev. ed. Paris: H. Welter, 1901.

Maraval, P. *Eusèbe de Césarée, la théologie politique de l'empire chrétien, louanges de Constantin (Triakontaétérikos)*. Paris: Cerf, 2001.

———. *Constantin le Grand: Lettres et discours*. Paris: Cerf, 2010.

Marcone, A. *Costantino il Grande*. Bari, Italy: Editori Laterza, 2000.

———. *Pagano e cristiano: Vita e mito di Costantino*. Rome: Editori Laterza, 2002.

Martin, A. *Athanase d'Alexandrie et l'église d'Egypte au IVᵉ siècle (328–373)*. CEFR 216. Rome: École Française de Rome, 1996.

Martin, D. B. *Slavery as Salvation: The Metaphor of Slavery in Pauline Christianity*. New Haven, CT: Yale University Press, 1990.

Mastandrea, P. "Passioni di martiri Donatisti (BHL 4473 e 5271)," *AnBoll* 113 (1995): 39–88.

Mathisen, R. W. "*Adnotatio* and *Petitio*: The Emperor's Favor and Special Exceptions in the Early Byzantine Empire." In *La pétition à Byzance*, ed. D. Feissel and J. Gascou, 23–32. Paris: Association des amis du Centre d'histoire et civilisation de Byzance, 2004.

Matthews, J. F. "Continuity in a Roman Family: The Rufii Festi of Volsinii," *Historia* 16 (1967): 484–509.

———. *The Roman Empire of Ammianus*. Baltimore: Johns Hopkins University Press, 1989.

———. *Laying Down the Law: A Study of the Theodosian Code*. New Haven, CT: Yale University Press, 2000.

Mayer, W., and P. Allen. *The Churches of Syrian Antioch (300–638 CE)*. Leuven: Peeters, 2012.

Mazzoleni, D. "Epigraphie chrétienne: Notes et observations." In *Ostia: Port et porte de la Rome antique*, ed. J.-P. Descoeudres, 283–88. Geneva: Musée d'art et d'histoire, 2001.

McFadden, S. "A Constantinian Image Program in Rome Rediscovered: The Late Antique Megalographia from the So-Called *Domus Faustae*," *MAAR* 58 (2013): 83–114.

McLean, B. H. *An Introduction to Greek Epigraphy of the Hellenistic and Roman Periods from Alexander the Great down to the Reign of Constantine (323 BC–AD 337)*. Ann Arbor: University of Michigan Press, 2002.

McLynn, N. "Little Wolf in the Big City: Ulfila and his Interpreters." In *Wolf Liebeschuetz Reflected: Essays presented by Colleagues, Friends and Pupils*, edited by J. Drinkwater and B. Salway, 125–35. BICS 91. London: Institute of Classical Studies, 2007.

Meiggs, R. *Roman Ostia*, 2nd ed. Oxford: Oxford University Press, 1973.

Mello, M., and G. Voza. *Le iscrizioni latine di Paestum*. 2 vols. Naples, 1968–69.

Menis, G. C. *Il complesso episcopale Teodoriano di Aquileia e il suo battistero*. Udine: Accademia di scienze lettere e arti di Udine, 1986.

Merkelbach, R., and J. Stauber. "'Unsterbliche' Kaiserpriester: Drei Dokumente der heidnischen Reaktion," *EA* 31 (1999): 157–65.

Metzler, D. "Ökonomische Aspekte des Religionswandels in der Spätantike: Die Enteignung der Heidnischen Tempel seit Konstantin," *Hephaistos* 3 (1981): 27–40.

Miethke, J. "Die 'Konstantinische Schenkung' in der mittelalterlichen Diskussion." In *Konstantin der Grosse: Das Bild des Kaisers im Wandel der Zeiten*, ed. A. Goltz and H. Schlange-Schoningen, 35–108. Cologne: Böhlau Verlag, 2008.

Migeotte, L. *Les finances des cités grecques aux périodes classique et hellénistique*. Paris: Belles lettres, 2014.

Millar, F. "The Roman *Coloniae* of the Near East: A Study of Cultural Relations." In *Roman Eastern Policy and Other Studies in Roman History: Proceedings of a Colloquium at Tvärminne,*

2–3 October 1987, ed. H. Solin and M. Kajava, 7–58. Commentationes Humanarum Litterarum 91. Helsinki: Finnish Society of Sciences and Letters, 1990.

———. *The Emperor in the Roman World (31 BC–AD 337),* rev. ed. Ithaca, NY: Cornell University Press, 1992.

———. *A Greek Roman Empire: Power and Belief Under Theodosius II (408–450).* Berkeley: University of California Press, 2006.

Miller, S. S. *Studies in the History and Traditions of Sepphoris.* Studies in Judaism in Late Antiquity 37. Leiden: Brill, 1984.

Minali, V. M. *Legislazione imperiale e manicheismo da Diocleziano a Costantino: Genesi di un'eresia.* Milan: Jovene Editore, 2013.

Mitchell, S. "The Life of Saint Theodotus of Ancyra," *AnatStud* 32 (1982): 93–114.

———. "Maximinus and the Christians in AD 312: A New Latin Inscription," *JRS* 78 (1988): 105–24.

———. *Anatolia: Land, Men, and Gods in Asia Minor.* 2 vols. Oxford: Oxford University Press, 1993.

———. "The Cities of Asia Minor in the Age of Constantine." In *Constantine: History, Historiography and Legend,* ed. S. N. C. Lieu and D. Montserrat, 52–73. London: Routledge, 1998.

———. *A History of the Later Roman Empire, AD 284–641: The Transformation of the Ancient World.* Malden, MA: Wiley-Blackwell, 2007.

Mitchell, S., and P. Van Nuffelen. *Monotheism Between Pagans and Christians in Late Antiquity.* Leuven: Peeters, 2010.

Mitford, T. B., I. Nicolaou, and V. Karageorghis. *The Greek and Latin Inscriptions from Salamis.* Nicosia: Department of Antiquities, Cyprus, 1974.

Mitrev, G. "Civitas Heracleotarum: Heraclea Sintica or the Ancient City at the Village of Rupite (Bulgaria)," *ZPE* 145 (2003): 263–72.

Mitrev, G., and T. Tarakov. "Civitas Heracleotarum: A New Epigraphic Inscription Indicating the Name of the Ancient City Near the Village of Rupite, Petrich Region" [in Bulgarian, English summary], *Archeologija* 43 (2002): 25–32.

Mladenova, M., S. Boiadzhiev, and V. Dinova-Ruseva. *Rannokhristiianski khram Sveta Sofiia.* Sofia: Universitetsko izd-vo "Sv. Kliment Okhridski," 1996.

Moffatt, A. "A Record of Public Buildings and Monuments." In *Studies in John Malalas,* ed. E. Jeffreys, B. Croke, and R. Scott, 87–110. Byzantina Australiensia 6. Sydney: Australian Association for Byzantine Studies, 1990.

Mommsen, T. "Inschrift aus Hispellum," *Epigraphische Analekten* 9 (1850): 199–238. Reprinted in *Gesammelte Schriften.* Vol. 8, 24–45. Berlin: Weidemann, 1905–13.

———. "Stadtrechtbriefe von Orkistos und Tymandos," *Hermes* 22 (1887): 309–22. Reprinted in *Gesammelte Schriften.* Vol. 5, 540–51. Berlin: Weidemann, 1905–13.

———. "Firmicus Maternus," *Hermes* 29 (1894): 468–72.

Monceaux, P. *Histoire littéraire de l'Afrique chrétienne depuis les origines jusqu'à l'invasion arabe.* 7 vols. Paris: E. Leroux, 1901–23.

Moreau, J., ed. *Lactance, De la mort des persécuteurs.* 2 vols. SCh 39. Paris: Cerf, 1954.

Moreno Resano, E. *Constantino y los cultos tradicionales.* Saragossa: Prensas Universitarias de Zaragoza, 2007.

Morin, G. *Sancti Augustini Sermones Post Mauros Reperti: Miscellanea Agostiniana.* 2 vols. Rome: Tipografia Poliglotta Vaticana, 1930.

Morley, D. *The "Nationwide" Audience: Structure and Decoding.* London: British Film Institute, 1980.

Moss, C. R. *Ancient Christian Martyrdom: Diverse Practices, Theologies, and Traditions.* New Haven, CT: Yale University Press, 2012.

———. *The Myth of Persecution: How Early Christians Invented a Story of Martyrdom.* New York: Harper One, 2013.

Müller-Rettig, B. *Der Panegyricus des Jahres 310 auf Konstantin den Grossen: Übersetzung und Historisch-philologischer Kommentar.* Stuttgart: Franz Steiner Verlag, 1990.

Musurillo, H. *The Acts of the Christian Martyrs.* Oxford: Oxford University Press, 1972.

Nau, F. "Analyse de la seconde partie inédite de l'histoire ecclésiastique de Jean d'Asie, Patriarche Jacobite de Constantinople († 585)," *Revue de l'Orient chrétien* 2 (1897): 455–93.

Neri, V. *Medius Princeps: Storia e immagine di Costantino nella storiografia latina pagana.* Bologna: CLUEB, 1992.

——. "L'usurpatore come tiranno nel lessico politico della tarda antichità." In *Usurpationen in der Spätantike*, ed. F. Paschoud and J. Szidat, 71–86. Stuttgart: Franz Steiner Verlag, 1997.

——. "Costantino e Licinio *Theophiles* ed il problema delle edizioni della *Historia Ecclesiastica* di Eusebio di Cesarea." In *Costantino prima e dopo Costantino – Constantine Before and After Constantine*, ed. G. Bonamente, N. Lenski, and R. Lizzi Testa, 381–404. Munera 35. Bari, Italy: Edipuglia, 2012.

——. "Les éditions de l'*Histoire ecclésiastique* (livres VIII–IX): Bilan critique et perspectives de la recherche." In *Eusèbe de Césarée, Histoire ecclésiastique: Commentaire, Tome I. Études d'introduction*, ed. S. Morlet and L. Perrone, 151–83. Paris: Belles Lettres, 2012.

Nesselrath, H.-G., et al., eds. *Für Religionsfreiheit, Recht und Toleranz: Libanios Rede für den Erhalt der heidnischen Tempel.* Tübingen: Mohr Siebeck, 2011.

Nicholson, O. "The 'Pagan Churches' of Maximinus Daia and Julian the Apostate," *JThS* n. s. 45 (1994): 1–10.

——. "*Caelum Potius Intuemini*: Lactantius and a Statue of Constantine," *Studia Patristica* 34 (2001): 177–96.

Nicols, J. "The Emperor and the Selection of the *Patronus Civitatis*: Two Examples," *Chiron* 8 (1978): 429–32.

Nixon, C. E. V. "*Constantinus Oriens Imperator*, Propaganda and Panegyric: On Reading Panegyric 7 (307)," *Historia* 42 (1993): 229–46.

Nixon, C. E. V., and B. S. Rodgers. *In Praise of Later Roman Emperors: The Panegyrici Latini, Introduction, Translation, and Historical Commentary.* Berkeley: University of California Press, 1994.

Norderval, Ø. "Kaiser Konstantins Edikt gegen die Häretiker und Schismatiker (*Vita Constantini* II. 64–65)," *Symbolae Osloenses* 70 (1995): 95–115.

Noreña, C. *Imperial Ideals in the Roman West: Representation, Circulation, Power.* Cambridge: Cambridge University Press, 2011.

Norman, A. F. *Antioch as a Centre of Hellenic Culture as Observed by Libanius.* TTH 34. Liverpool: Liverpool University Press, 2000.

Ntantalia, F. *Bronzemedaillons unter Konstantin dem Grossen und seinen Söhnen: Die Bildtypen der Constantinopolis und die Kaiserliche Medaillonprägung von 330–363 n. Chr.* Saarbrücker Studien zur Archäologie und Alten Geschichte 15. Saarbrücken, Germany: Saarbrücker Druckerei und Verlag, 2001.

Odahl, C. M. "Constantine's Epistle to the Bishops at the Council of Arles: A Defence of Imperial Authorship," *Journal of Religious History* 17 (1993): 274–89.

——. "Constantinian Arles and Its Christian Minters," *NECJ* 35 (2008): 3–20.

——. *Constantine and the Christian Empire*, 2nd ed. London: Routledge, 2010.

Opitz, H.-G. "Die *Vita Constantini* des *Codex Angelicus* 22." *Byzantion* 9 (1934): 535–93.

——, ed. *Urkunden zur Geschichte des Arianischen Streites.* Athanasius Werke 3.1. Berlin: Walter de Gruyter, 1934.

Overbeck, B. *Das Silbermedaillon aus der Münzstätte Ticinum: Ein erstes numismatisches Zeugnis zum Christentum Constantins I.* Milan: Centro culturale numismatico milanese, 2000.

Overbeck, M. *Untersuchungen zum afrikanischen Senatsadel in der Spätantike.* Frankfurter Althistorischen Studien 7. Kallmünz, Germany: Lassleben, 1973.

Overbeck, J.J. and H. Takahashi, eds. *S. Ephraemi Syri, Rabulae episcopi edesseni, Balaei, aliorumque opera selecta: Selected works of St. Ephraem the Syrian, Rabbula, bishop of Edessa, and Balai.* Piscataway, NJ: Gorgias Press, 2007.

Pack, E. *Städte und Steuern in der Politik Julians: Untersuchungen zu den Quellen eines Kaiserbildes.* Collection Latomus 194. Brussels: Latomus, 1986.

Parke, H. W. *The Oracles of Apollo in Asia Minor.* London: Croom Helm, 1985.

Paroli, L. "La Basilica Paleocristiana di Porto: Scavi 1997–1998," *MNIR* 58 (1999): 45–47.

Parvis, S. *Marcellus of Ancyra and the Lost Years of the Arian Controversy, 325–345.* Oxford: Oxford University Press, 2006.

Paschoud, F. "Zosime 2, 29 et la version païenne de la conversion de Constantin," *Historia* 20 (1971): 334–53.

Pasquali, G. "Die Composition der Vita Constantini des Eusebius," *Hermes* 45 (1910): 369–86.

Peachin, M. *Iudex Vice Caesaris: Deputy Emperors and the Administration of Justice During the Principate.* Heidelberger Althistorische Beiträge und Epigraphische Studien 21. Stuttgart: Franz Steiner Verlag, 1996.

Pearce, J. W. E. *The Roman Imperial Coinage.* Vol. 9, *Valentinian I—Theodosius I.* London: Spink, 1933.

Pelizzari, G. *Il Pastore ad Aquileia: La trascrizione musiva della catechesi catecumenale nella cattedrale di Teodoro.* San Daniele di Friuli, Italy: Glesie Furlane, 2008.

Pelltari, A. "Donatist Self-Identity and the Church of the Truth," *Augustinianum* 49 (2009): 359–69.

Pentiricci, M. "L'attività edilizia a Leptis Magna tra l'età tetrarchica e il V secolo: Una messa a punto." In *Leptis Magna: Una città e le sue iscrizioni in epoca tardoromana,* ed. I. Tantillo and F. Bigi, 97–171. Cassino, Italy: Università degli studi di Cassino, 2010.

Pergami, F. *L'appello nella legislazione del tardo impero.* Milan: A. Giuffrè, 2000.

Perkams, M. "Der Comes Josef und der frühe Kirchenbau in Galiläa," *JAC* 44 (2001): 23–32.

Peterson, E. *Eis Theos: Epigraphische, formgeschichtliche und religionsgeschichtliche Untersuchungen.* Göttingen: Vandenhoeck & Ruprecht, 1926.

Picozzi, V. "Una campagna di Licinio contro Massenzio nel 310 non attestata dalle fonti letterarie," *NAC* 5 (1976): 267–75.

Pietri, C. *Roma Christiana: Recherches sur l'église de Rome, son organisation, sa politique, son idéologie de Miltiade à Sixte III (311–440).* BEFR 224. Rome: École Française de Rome, 1976.

———. "Constantin en 324: Propagande et théologie impériales d'après les documents de la *Vita Constantini.*" In *Crise et redressement dans les provinces européennes de l'empire (milieu du IIIe-milieu du IVe siècle ap. J.-C.),* ed. E. Frézouls, 63–90. Strasbourg: AECR, 1983.

Piganiol, A. "Notes épigraphiques I. L'inscription d'Hispellum," *REA* 31 (1929): 139–41.

———. *L'empereur Constantin.* Paris: Rieder, 1932.

Pohlkamp, H. "*Privilegium Ecclesiae Romanae Pontifici Contulit:* Zur Vorgeschichte der Konstantinischen Schenkung." In *Fälschungen im Mittelalter: Internationaler Kongress der Monumenta Germaniae Historica, München, 16.–19. September 1986.* MGH Schriften 33, 413–90. Hanover: Hahnsche Buchhandlung, 1988.

Polara, G., ed. *Publilii Optatiani Porfyrii Carmina.* 2 vols. Turin: G. B. Paravia, 1973.

Porena, P. *Le origini della prefettura del pretorio tardoantica.* Rome: L'Erma di Bretschneider, 2003.

Potter, D. S. *The Roman Empire at Bay AD 180–395.* London: Routledge, 2004.

———. "Constantine and the Gladiators," *CQ* 60 (2010): 596–606.

————. *Constantine the Emperor*. Oxford: Oxford University Press, 2012.

Price, S. R. F. "Between Man and God: Sacrifice in the Roman Imperial Cult," *JRS* 70 (1980): 28–43.

————. *Rituals and Power: The Roman Imperial Cult in Asia Minor*. Cambridge: Cambridge University Press, 1984.

Quinn, J. C., and A. Wilson. "Capitolia," *JRS* 103 (2013): 117–73.

Ragette, F. *Baalbek*. London: Chatto and Windus, 1980.

Ramsay, W. M. *The Cities and Bishoprics of Phrygia*. Oxford: Clarendon, 1895.

Ramskold, L., and N. Lenski. "Constantinople's Dedication Medallions and the Maintenance of Civic Traditions," *NZ* 119 (2011): 31–58.

Rapp, C. "Imperial Ideology in the Making: Eusebius of Caesarea on Constantine as 'Bishop,'" *JThS* 49 (1998): 685–95.

————. *Holy Bishops in Late Antiquity: The Nature of Christian Leadership in an Age of Transition*. Berkeley: University of California Press, 2005.

Rasch, J. J. *Das Mausoleum der Kaiserin Helena in Rom und der "Tempio Della Tosse" in Tivoli*. Mainz: Philipp von Zabern, 1998.

Rasch, J. J., and A. Arbeiter. *Das Mausoleum der Constantina in Rom*. Mainz: Philipp von Zabern, 2007.

Rebillard, É. *Christians and Their Many Identities in Late Antiquity, North Africa, 200–450 CE*. Ithaca, NY: Cornell University Press, 2012.

Rees, R. *Layers of Loyalty in Latin Panegyric, AD 289–307*. Oxford: Oxford University Press, 2002.

Rehm, A., ed. *Didyma 2: Die Inschriften*. Berlin: Gebrüder Mann, 1958.

Renfrew, C., and D. Cherry, eds. *Peer Polity Interaction and Socio-Political Change*. Cambridge: Cambridge University Press, 1986.

Revilla Castro, V. "Les amphores africaines du IIe et IIIe siècles." In *In Africa et in Hispania. Etudes sur l'huile africaine*, ed. A. Mirabet and J. Remesal Rodríguez, 269–97. Barcelona: Publicacions i Edicions, Universitat de Barcelona, 2007.

Rey-Coquais, J.-P. *Arados et sa pérée aux époques grecque, romaine et byzantine*. Bibliothèque Archéologique et Historique 91. Paris: P. Geuthner, 1974.

Reynolds, J. *Aphrodisias and Rome: Documents from the Excavation of the Theater of Aphrodisias*. London: Society for the Promotion of Roman Studies, 1982.

Rieger, A.-K. *Heiligtümer in Ostia*. Munich: F. Pfeil, 2004.

Riese, A., ed., *Geographi latini minores*. Heilbronn: Henninger, 1878.

Riess, W. "Konstantin und seine Söhne in Aquileia," *ZPE* 135 (2001): 267–86.

Ritti, T., K. Grewe, and P. Kessener. "A Relief of a Water-Powered Stone Saw Mill on a Sarcophagus at Hierapolis and Its Implications," *JRA* 20 (2007): 139–63.

Rives, J. B. *Religion and Authority in Roman Carthage from Augustus to Constantine*. Oxford: Oxford University Press, 1995.

————. "The Decree of Decius and the Religion of Empire," *JRS* 89 (1999): 135–54.

————. "Between Orthopraxy and Orthodoxy: Constantine and Animal Sacrifice." In *Costantino prima e dopo Costantino – Constantine Before and After Constantine*, ed. G. Bonamente, N. Lenski, and R. Lizzi Testa, 153–64. Munera 35. Bari, Italy: Edipuglia, 2012.

Rivière, Y. "Constantin, le crime et le christianisme: Contribution à l'étude des lois et des moeurs de l'antiqué tardive," *AnTard* 20 (2002): 327–61.

Robert, L. *Les gladiateurs dans l'orient grec*. Amsterdam: A. M. Hakkert, 1940.

————. "Inscriptions de la région de Yalova en Bithynie," *Hellenica* 7 (1949): 30–44.

————. "Théophane de Mytilène à Constantinople," *CRAI* 113 (1969): 42–64.

————. "De Cilicie à Messine et à Plymouth avec deux inscriptions grecques errantes." In *Opera Minora Selecta: Épigraphie et antiquités grecques*. Vol. 7, 225–11. Amsterdam: A. M. Hakkert, 1969.

———. "Deux Concours Grecs à Rome," *CRAI* 114 (1970): 6–27.

———. "La titulature de Nicée et de Nicomédie: la gloire et la haine," *HSCPh* 81 (1977): 1–39.

_____. *A travers l'Asie Mineure: Poètes et prosateurs, monnaies grecques, voyageurs et géographie*. Paris: École française d'Athènes, 1980.

Robinson, E. W. *Democracy beyond Athens: Popular Government in Classical Greece*. Cambridge: Cambridge University Press, 2011.

Rodgers, B. S. "Constantine's Pagan Vision," *Byzantion* 50 (1980): 259–77.

———. "Divine Insinuation in the Panegyrici Latini," *Historia* 35 (1986): 69–104.

———. "The Metamorphosis of Constantine," *CQ* 39 (1989): 233–46.

Roebuck, D., and B. de Loynes de Fumichon. *Roman Arbitration*. Oxford: Holo Books, 2004.

Roldanus, J. *The Church in the Age of Constantine: The Theological Challenges*. London: Routledge, 2006.

Ronning, C. *Herrscherpanegyrik unter Trajan und Konstantin: Studien zur symbolischen Kommunikation in der Römischen Kaiserzeit*. Tübingen: Mohr Siebeck, 2007.

Rosen, K. *Constantin der Grosse, die Christen und der Donatistenstreit, 312–314. Eine Untersuchung zu Optatus von Mileve, Appendix V, und zum Verhältnis von Staat und Kirche im 4. Jahrhundert*. Paderborn, Germany: Ferdinand Schöningh, 2011.

Rouche, M. "Le changement de nom des chefs-lieux de cité en Gaul au Bas-Empire," *BSNAF*, ser. 9, vol. 4 (1968): 47–64.

Roueché, C. "Acclamations in the Later Roman Empire: New Evidence from Aphrodisias," *JRS* 74 (1984): 181–99.

Rouquette, J.-M. "Trois nouveaux sarcophages chrétiens de Trinquetaille (Arles)," *CRAI* (1974): 254–77.

Rubin, Z. "The Church of the Holy Sepulchre and the Conflict Between the Sees of Caesarea and Jerusalem," *Jerusalem Cathedra* 2 (1982): 79–105.

Rüpke, J., and A. Glock. *Fasti Sacerdotum: A Prosopography of Pagan, Jewish, and Christian Religious Officials in the City of Rome, 300 BC to AD 499*, rev. English ed. Oxford: Oxford University Press, 2008.

Saarisalo, A., and H. Palva. *A Byzantine Church at Kafr Kama*. Studia Orientalia 30.1. Helsinki: Societas Orientalis Fennica, 1964.

Sabbatini Tumolesi, P. "Una Nuova Tabula Patronatus da Paestum," *MGR* 15 (1990): 235–56.

Salama, P. "Le plus ancien chrisme officiel de l'Afrique romaine." In *Atti del VI congresso internazionale di archeologia cristiana, Ravenna 1962*, 537–43. Studi di Antichità Cristiana 26. Rome: Pontificio Istituto di archeologia cristiana, 1965.

———. "Anniversaires impériaux Constantino—Liciniens a Djemila." In *Institutions, société et vie politique dans l'empire romain au IVᵉ siècle ap. J.-C: Actes de la table ronde autour de l'œuvre d'André Chastagnol, Paris, 20–21 janvier 1989*. CEFR 159, ed. M. Christol et al., 137–59. Rome: École Française de Rome, 1992.

———. "Les provinces d'Afrique et les débuts du monogramme constantinien," *BSNAF* (1998): 137–59.

Saliou, C. "À propos de la Ταυριανὴ Πύλη: Remarques sur la localisation présumée de la grande église d'Antioche de Syrie," *Syria* 77 (2000): 217–26.

Salway, B. "Constantine Augoustos (not Sebastos)." In *Wolf Liebeschuetz Reflected: Essays Presented by Colleagues, Friends and Pupils*, ed. J. F. Drinkwater and B. Salway, 37–50. BICS 91. London: Institute of Classical Studies, 2007.

Salzano, A. *Laudes Domini: Introduzione, testo, traduzione e commento*. Naples: Arte Tipografica, 2000.

Salzman, M. R. "'*Superstitio*' in the Codex Theodosianus and the Persecution of Pagans," *VC* 41 (1987): 172–88.

————. "Aurelian and the Cult of the Unconquerable Sun: The Institutionalization of Christmas, Solar Worship and Imperial Cult," Forthcoming.

Sánchez, B. E. "Las disposiciones judiciales de Constantino y Juliano a propósito de las tierras de los templos paganos," *Gerion* 18 (2000): 407–23.

Sandwell, I. "Outlawing 'Magic' or Outlawing 'Religion'? Libanius and the *Theodosian Code* as Evidence for Legislation Against 'Pagan' Practices." In *The Spread of Christianity in the First Four Centuries: Essays in Explanation*, ed. William V. Harris, 88–123. Leiden: Brill, 2005.

Saquete, J. C. "Septimius Acindynus, *Corrector Tusciae et Umbriae*: Notes on a New Inscription from Augusta Emerita (Mérida, Spain)," *ZPE* 129 (2000): 281–86.

Sayar, M. H. *Perinthos-Herakleia (Marmara Ereğlisi) und Umgebung: Geschichte, Testimonien, griechische und lateinische Inschriften*. Denkschriften der Österreichische Akademie der Wissenschaften. Philosophisch-Historische Klasse 269.9. Vienna: Verlag der Österreichischen Akademie der Wissenschaften, 1998.

Schäfer, P. "Der Aufstand gegen Gallus Caesar." In *Tradition and Re-Interpretation in Jewish and Early Christian Literature: Essays in Honour of Jürgen C. H. Lebram*, edited by J. W. van Henten et al., 184–201. Leiden, Brill, 1986.

Schäferdiek, K. "Wulfila: vom Bischof von Gotien zum Gotenbischof," *ZKG* 90 (1979): 253–303.

Scheid, J. "Oral Tradition and Written Tradition in the Formation of Sacred Law in Rome." In *Religion and Law in Classical and Christian Rome*, ed. C. Ando and J. Rüpke, 14–33. Potsdamer Wissenschaftliche Beiträge 15. Stuttgart: Franz Steiner Verlag, 2006.

Schlange-Schöningen, H. "'Der Bösewicht im Räuberstaat': Grundzüge der neuzeitlichen Wirkungsgeschichte Konstantins des Grossen." In *Konstantin der Grosse: Das Bild des Kaisers im Wandel der Zeiten*, ed. A. Goltz and H. Schlange-Schoningen, 211–62. Cologne: Böhlau Verlag, 2008.

Schmidt-Hofner, S. "Die städtische Finanzautonomie im spätrömischen Reich." In *Staatlichkeit und Politisches Handeln in der Römischen Kaiserzeit*, ed. H.-U. Wiemer, 209–48. Berlin: Walter de Gruyter, 2006.

————. *Reagieren und Gestalten: Der Regierungsstil des spätrömischen Kaisers am Beispiel der Gesetzgebung Valentinians I*. Munich: C. H. Beck, 2008.

Schmitt, O. *Constantin der Grosse, 275–337: Leben und Herrschaft*. Stuttgart: Verlag W. Kohlhammer, 2007.

Schnetz, J. *Itineraria Romana*, vol. 2. Leipzig: Teubner, 1940.

Schoo, G. *Die Quellen des Kirchen Historikers Sozomenos*. Neue Studien zur Geschichte der Theologie und der Kirche 11. Berlin: Trowitzsch, 1911.

Schott, J. *Christianity, Empire, and the Making of Religion in Late Antiquity*. Philadelphia: University of Pennsylvania Press, 2011.

Schuler, C. "Kolonisten und Einheimische in einer Attalidischen Polisgründung," *ZPE* 128 (1999): 124–32.

Schuller, F., and H. Wolff, ed. *Konstantin der Grosse: Kaiser Einer Epochenwende*. Munich: Kunstverlag Josef Fink, 2007.

Schwartz, E. *Über die Bischofslisten der Synoden von Chalkedon, Nicaea und Konstantinopel*. Abhandlungen der Bayerischen Akademie der Wissenschaften, Philosophisch-historische Abteilung, n. F. 13. Munich: Verlag der Bayerischen Akademie der Wissenschaften, 1937.

————. "Die Dokumente des arianischen Streits bis 325." In *Gesammelte Schriften*. Vol. 3, 117–68. Berlin: Walter de Gruyter, 1959.

Schwartz, E., T. Mommsen, and F. Winkelmann. *Eusebius: Die Kirchengeschichte*, 2nd ed. 2 vols. GCS: Eusebius Werke 1–2. Leipzig: Akademie Verlag, 1999.

Scrinari, V. S. M. *Il Laterano Imperiale I: Dalle "aedes Laterani" alla "Domus Faustae*. Vatican City: Pontificio Istituto di Archeologia Cristiana, 1991.

———. *Il Laterano Imperiale II: Dagli "horti Domitiae" alla Cappella Cristiana*. Vatican City: Pontificio Istituto di Archeologia Cristiana, 1991.

Searle, J. R. *Speech Acts: An Essay in the Philosophy of Language*. Cambridge: Cambridge University Press, 1970.

Seeck, O. *Geschichte des Untergangs der antiken Welt*, 4th ed. 5 vols. Stuttgart: Metzler, 1920–1923.

———. *Regesten der Kaiser und Päpste für die Jahre 311 bis 476 n. Chr. Vorarbeit zu einer Prosopographie der christlichen Kaiserzeit*. Stuttgart: Metzler, 1919.

Sensi, L. "Sul luogo del ritrovamento del rescritto costantiniano di Spello," *AARC* 12 (1998): 457–77.

———. "In margine al rescritto costantiniano di Hispellum," *Annali della Fondazione per il Museo Claudio Faina* 6 (1999): 365–73.

Sguaitamatti, L. *Der spätantike Konsulat*. Fribourg: Academic Press, 2012.

Shaw, B. D. *Sacred Violence: African Christians and Sectarian Hatred in the Age of Augustine*. Cambridge: Cambridge University Press, 2011.

Singh, D. "Eusebius as Political Theologian: The Legend Continues," *HThR* 108 (2015): 129–54.

Singor, H. "The Labarum, Shield Blazons and Constantine's *Caeleste Signum*." In *The Representation and Perception of Roman Imperial Power*, ed. L. de Blois et al., 481–500. Amsterdam: J. C. Gieben, 2003.

Siniscalco, P. "Il cristianesimo dei primi secoli in Umbria: Tra occidente e oriente." In *Umbria cristiana: Dalla diffusione del culto al culto dei santi, secc. IV–X. Atti del XV congresso internazionale di studi sull'alto medioevo, Spoleto, 23–28 ottobre 2000*, 3–38. Spoleto, Italy, 2001.

Sirks, A. J. B. *The Theodosian Code: A Study*. Friedrichsdorf, Germany: Éditions Tortuga, 2007.

Sironen, E. "Lateinische Ehreninschriften für Constantin den Grossen und seine Nachfolger und andere Inscriften der Spätzeit aus Attika," *ZPE* 136 (2001): 257–66.

Sivan, H. *Palestine in Late Antiquity*. Oxford: Oxford University Press, 2008.

Sizgorich, T. *Violence and Belief in Late Antiquity: Militant Devotion in Christianity and Islam*. Philadelphia: University of Pennsylvania Press, 2009.

Skeat, T. C. *Papyri from Panopolis in the Chester Beatty Library*. Dublin: Hodges Figgis, 1964.

Smith, K. *The Martyrdom and History of Blessed Simeon Bar Sabbaᶜe*. Piscataway: Gorgias Press, 2014.

Smith, R. B. E. "A Lost Historian of Alexander 'Descended from Alexander' and Read by Julian? Praxagoras of Athens Reviewed in Light of Attic Epigraphy," *Historia* 56 (2007): 356–80.

Smith, R. R. R. "The Public Image of Licinius I: Portrait Sculpture and Imperial Ideology in the Early Fourth Century," *JRS* 87 (1997): 107–202.

Solari, A. "L'unione religiosa umbro-etrusca in un rescritto di Costantino," *Studi Etruschi* 13 (1940): 161–62.

Soproni, W. *Die letzten Jahrzehnte des pannonischen Limes*. Munich: Beck, 1985.

Sordi, M. "L'etrusca disciplina e l'impero romano cristiano." In *Da Costantino a Teodosio il Grande: Cultura, società, diritto. Atti del convegno internazionale, Napoli 26–28 aprile 2001*, ed. U. Criscuolo, 395–404. Naples: M. D'Auria, 2003.

Sotomayor, M. "Sobre la fecha del concilio." In *El Concilio de Elvira y su tiempo*, ed. M. Sotomayor and J. Fernández, 137–67. Granada: Ediciones Miguel Sánchez, 2005.

Sozi, G. *Spello: Guida Storico–Artistica*. Spello, Italy: Pro Spello, 1987.

Spoerl, K. M. "The Schism at Antioch since Cavallera." In *Arianism After Arius: Essays on the Development of the Fourth Century Trinitarian Conflicts*, ed. M. R. Barnes and D. H. Williams, 101–26. Edinburgh: T. & T. Clark, 1993.

Stefan, A. "Le titre de *filius augustorum* de Maximin et Constantin et la théologie de la tétrarchie." In *Prosopographie et histoire religieuse: Actes du colloque tenu en l'Université Paris*

XII- Val de Marne les 27 & 28 octobre 2000, ed. M.-F. Baslez and F. Prévot, 329–49. Paris: De Boccard, 2005.

Stepper, R. *Augustus et sacerdos: Untersuchungen zum römischen Kaiser als Priester*. Stuttgart: Franz Steiner Verlag, 2003.

Stephenson, P. *Constantine: Unconquered Emperor, Christian Victor*. London: Quercus, 2009.

Steuernagel, D. *Kult und Alltag in römischen Hafenstädten: Soziale Prozesse in archäologischer Perspektive*. Stuttgart: Franz Steiner Verlag, 2004.

Stopponi, S. "Notizie preliminari dello scavo di Campo della Fiera," *Annali della Fondazione per il Museo Claudio Faina* 14 (2007): 493–530.

———. "Campo della Fiera at Orvieto: New Discoveries." In *The Archaeology of Sanctuaries and Ritual in Etruria*, ed. N. T. De Grummond and I. Edlund-Berry, 16–44. JRA Suppl. 81. Portsmouth, RI: Journal of Roman Archaeology, 2011.

Strack, H. L. and G. Stemberger. *Introduction to the Talmud and Midrash*, trans. M. Bockmuehl. Edinburgh: T&T Clark, 1991.

Strange, J. F., T. R. W. Longstaff, and D. E. Groh. *Excavations at Sepphoris*. Vol. 1. Leiden: Brill, 2006.

Straub, J. "Constantine as Κοινὸς Ἐπίκοπος. Tradition and Innovation in the Representation of the First Christian Emperor's Majesty," *DOP* 21 (1967): 39–55.

Tabata, K. "The Date and Setting of the Constantinian Inscription of Hispellum," *SCO* 45 (1995): 369–410.

Tabbernee, W. *Montanist Inscriptions and Testimonia: Epigraphic Sources Illustrating the History of Montanism*. Macon, GA: Mercer University Press, 1997.

Talbert, R. J. A., ed. *Barrington Atlas of the Greek and Roman World*. Princeton, NJ: Princeton University Press, 2000.

Tantillo, I. *La prima orazione di Giuliano a Costanzo: Introduzione, traduzione e commento*. Rome: L'Erma di Bretschneider, 1997.

———. " 'Come un bene ereditario': Costantino e la retorica dell'impero-patrimonio," *AnTard* 6 (1998): 251–64.

———. "L'ideologia imperiale tra centro e periferie: a proposito di un 'elogio' di Costantino da Augusta Traiana in Tracia," *RFIC* 127 (1999): 73–95.

———. "Costantino e Helios Pantepoptês: la statua equestre di Termessos," *Epigraphica* 65 (2003): 159–84.

———. "L'impero della luce. Riflessioni su Costantino e il Sole," *MEFRA* 115 (2003): 985–1048.

———. "Attributi solari della figura imperiale in Eusebio di Cesarea," *MedAnt* 6 (2003): 41–59.

Tantillo, I., and F. Bigi, ed. *Leptis Magna: Una città e le sue iscrizioni in epoca tardoromana*. Cassino: Università degli studi di Cassino, 2010.

Taylor, C. "Language and Society." In *Communicative Action: Essays on Jürgen Habermas's The Theory of Communicative Action*, ed. A. Honneth and H. Joas, trans. J. Gaines and D. L. Jones. Cambridge: Polity Press, 1991.

Taylor, J. E. *Christians and the Holy Places: The Myth of Jewish-Christian Origins*. Oxford: Oxford University Press, 1993.

Telfer, W. "St. Peter of Alexandria and Arius," *AnBoll* 67 (1949): 117–30.

Tengström, E. *Donatisten und Katholiken: Soziale, wirtschaftliche und politische Aspekte einer nordafrikanischen Kirchenspaltung*. Stockholm: Almqvist & Wiksell, 1964.

Thelamon, F. *Païens et chrétiens au IVᵉ siècle: L'apport de l'"Histoire Ecclésiastique" de Rufin d'Aquilée*. Paris: Études Augustiniennes, 1981.

Thonemann, P. "Phrygia: An Anarchist History, 950 B.C.–A.D. 100." In *Roman Phrygia: Culture and Society*, ed. P. Thonemann, 1–40. Cambridge: Cambridge University Press, 2013.

Thornton, T. C. G. "The Stories of Joseph of Tiberias," *VC* 44 (1990): 54–63.

Thuillier, J.-P. "Les édifices de spectacle de Bolsena. Ludi et munera," *MEFRA* 99 (1987): 595–608.

Thurn, H., ed. *Chronographia*. CFHB 25. Berlin: Walter de Gruyter, 2000.

Thylander, H. *Inscriptions du port d'Ostie*. Lund: C. W. K. Gleerup, 1952.

Tilley, M. A. *The Bible in Christian North Africa: The Donatist World*. Minneapolis: Fortress Press, 1997.

Toynbee, J. M. C. *Roman Medallions*. Numismatic Studies 5. New York: American Numismatic Society, 1944.

Trout, D. E. "*Lex* and *Iussio*: The *Feriale Campanum* and Christianity in the Theodosian Age." In *Law, Society, and Authority in Late Antiquity*, ed. R. W. Mathisen, 162–78. Oxford: Oxford University Press, 2001.

Tsafrir, Y., L. Di Segni, and J. Green, eds. *Tabula Imperii Romani. Iudaea–Palaestina: Eretz Israel in the Hellenistic, Roman and Byzantine Periods*. Jerusalem: Israel Academy of Sciences and Humanities, 1994.

Turner, C. H. "Canons Attributed to the Council of Constantinople, AD 381, together with the Names of the Bishops, from Two Patmos MSS POB' POГ'," *JThS* 15 (1914): 161–78.

Turpin, W. "*Adnotatio* and Imperial Rescript in Roman Legal Procedure," *RIDA* 35 (1988): 285–307.

Uhalde, K. *Expectations of Justice in the Age of Augustine*. Philadelphia: University of Pennsylvania Press, 2007.

Uggeri, G. "L'organizzazione della viabilità in Umbria." In *Umbria Cristiana: Dalla diffusione del culto al culto dei santi, secc. IV–X. Atti del XV congresso internazionale di studi sull'alto medioevo, Spoleto, 23–28 ottobre 2000*, 89–115. Spoleto, Italy: Centro italiano di studi sull'alto Medioevo, 2001.

Valentini, R., and G. Zucchetti, eds. *Codice topografico della città di Roma*. Vol. 2. Rome: Tipografia del Senato, 1942.

Van Dam, R. "From Paganism to Christianity in Late Antique Gaza," *Viator* 16 (1985): 1–20.

———. *The Roman Revolution of Constantine*. New York: Cambridge University Press, 2007.

———. *Rome and Constantinople: Rewriting Roman History During Late Antiquity*. Waco, TX: Baylor University Press, 2010.

———. *Remembering Constantine at the Milvian Bridge*. New York: Cambridge University Press, 2011.

Vanderspoel, J., and M. L. Mann. "The Empress Fausta as Romano-Celtic Dea Nutrix," *NC* 162 (2002): 350–55.

Van Esbroeck, M. "Michael the Archangel, Saint." In *The Coptic Encyclopedia*, 5 (1991): 1615–20.

Van Heesch, J. "The Last Civic Coinages and the Religious Policy of Maximinus Daia (AD 312)," *NC* 153 (1993): 65–75 and pl. XI.

Van Nuffelen, P. "Zur Rezeption des Kaiserkultes in der Spatantike," *AncSoc* 32 (2002): 263–82.

Vatin, C. "Les empereurs du IVe siècle à Delphes," *BCH* 86 (1962): 229–41.

Vera, D. *Commento storico alle* Relationes *di Quinto Aurelio Simmaco*. Pisa: Giardini editori e stampatori, 1981.

———. "Osservazioni economiche sulla *Vita Sylvestri* del Liber Pontificalis." In *Consuetudinis Amor: Fragments d'histoire romaine (II–VI siècles) offerts à Jean-Pierre Callu*, ed. F. Chausson and E. Wolff, 419–30. Saggi di Storia Antica 19. Rome: L'Erma di Bretschneider, 2003.

Vessey, M. "The Origins of the *Collectio Sirmondiana*: A New Look at the Evidence." In *The Theodosian Code: Studies in the Imperial Law of Late Antiquity*, ed. J. Harries and I. Wood, 188–99. Ithaca, NY: Cornell University Press, 1993.

Veyne, P. *When Our World Became Christian, 312–394*, trans. J. Lloyd. Cambridge: Polity, 2010.

Vita-Evrard, G. "Une inscription errante et l'"extra-territorialité" de Théveste au IVe siècle," *AfrRom* 6 (1989): 293–313.

Von Gladiss, A. "Der 'Arc du Rhône' von Arles," *MDAI(R)* 79 (1972): 17–87.

Von Haehling, R. *Die Religionszugehörigkeit der hohen Amtsträger des römischen Reiches seit Constantins I: Alleinherrschaft bis zum Ende der Theodosianischen Dynastie (324–450 bzw. 455 n. Chr.)*. Bonn: Habelt, 1978.

Waelkens, M., and J. Poblome, eds. *Sagalassos IV: Report on the Survey and Excavation Campaigns of 1994 and 1995*. Acta Archaeologica Lovaniensia Monographiae 9. Leuven: Leuven University Press, 1997.

Walker, P. W. L. *Holy City, Holy Places? Christian Attitudes to Jerusalem and the Holy Land in the Fourth Century*. Oxford: Oxford University Press, 1990.

Wallraff, M. "Constantine's Devotion to the Sun After 324," *Studia Patristica* 34 (2001): 256–69.

———. *Christus Verus Sol: Sonnenverehrung und Christentum in der Spätantike*. JAC Ergängungsband 32. Münster, Germany: Aschendorffsche Verlagsbuchhandlung, 2001.

———. *Sonnenkönig der Spätantike: Die Religionspolitik Konstantins des Grossen*. Freiburg: Herder, 2013.

Wallraff, M., U. Roberto, and K. Pinggéra, eds. *Sextus Julius Africanus. Chronographiae: The Extant Fragments*. GCS n. F. 15. Berlin: Walter de Gruyter, 2007.

Warmington, B. H. "Aspects of Constantinian Propaganda in the Panegyrici Latini," *TAPhA* 104 (1974): 371–84.

Watts, E. J. *City and School in Late Antique Athens and Alexandria*. Berkeley: University of California Press, 2006.

———. *Riot in Alexandria: Tradition and Group Dynamics in Late Antique Pagan and Christian Communities*. Berkeley: University of California Press, 2010.

———. *The Final Pagan Generation*. Berkeley: University of California Press, 2015.

Weber, E., ed. *Tabula Peutingeriana: Codex Vindobonensis 324 vollständige Faksimile-Ausgabe im Originalformat*. Graz: Akademischer Druck- und Verlagsanstalt, 1976.

Weir, R. *Roman Delphi and Its Pythian Games*. Oxford: J. and E. Hedges, 2004.

Weisman, W. "Gelasinos von Heliopolis, ein Shauspieler-Märtyrer," *AB* 93 (1975): 39–66.

Weiss, P. "Die Vision Constantins." In *Colloquium aus Anlass des 80: Geburtstages von Alfred Heuss*, ed. J. Bleicken, 143–69. Frankfurter althistorische Studien 13. Kallmünz, Germany: M. Lassleben, 1993.

———. "The Vision of Constantine," trans. A. R. Birley, *JRA* 16 (2003): 237–59.

Weiss, Z. "Games and Spectacles in Ancient Gaza: Performances for the Masses Held in Buildings Now Lost." In *Christian Gaza in Late Antiquity*, ed. B. Bitton-Ashkelony and A. Kofsky, 23–39. Leiden: Brill, 2004.

———. *The Sepphoris Synagogue: Deciphering an Ancient Message Through Its Archaeological and Socio-Historical Context*. Jerusalem: Israel Exploration Society, 2005.

Weiss, Z., and E. Netzer. "Sepphoris During the Byzantine Period." In *Sepphoris in Galilee: Crosscurrents of Culture*, ed. R. M. Nagy et al. Raleigh: North Carolina Museum of Art, 1996.

Westall, R. "Constantius II and the Basilica of St. Peter in the Vatican," *Historia* 64 (2015): 205–42.

Wickert, L., ed. *Corpus Inscriptionum Latinarum*. Vol. 14 suppl., *Incriptiones Latii Veteris Latinae. Supplementum Ostiense*. Berlin: Walter de Gruyter, 1930.

———. "Princeps," *RE* 22 (1954): 2119–27.

Wiemer, H.-U. "Libanios und Zosimus über den Rom-Besuch Konstantins I. Im Jahre 326," *Historia* 43 (1994): 469–94.

———. "Libanius on Constantine," *CQ* 44 (1994): 511–24.

―――. *Libanios und Julian: Studien zum Verhältnis von Rhetorik und Politik im vierten Jahrhundert n. Chr.* Vestigia 46. Munich: Beck, 1995.

―――. "Akklamationen im spätrömischen Reich," *Archiv für Kulturgeschichte* 86 (2004): 27–73.

Wienand, J. "Ein Abschied in Gold." In *Konstantin der Grosse: Zwischen Sol und Christus*, ed. K. Ehling and G. Weber, 53–61. Darmstadt, Germany: Philipp von Zabern, 2011.

―――. *Der Kaiser als Sieger: Metamorphosen triumphaler Herrschaft unter Constantin I.* Klio Beihefte 19. Berlin: Akademie Verlag, 2012.

―――. "Die Poesie des Bürgerkriegs: Das Constantinische *Aureum Saeculum* in den *Carmina* Optatians." In *Costantino prima e dopo Costantino – Constantine Before and After Constantine*, ed. G. Bonamente, N. Lenski, and R. Lizzi Testa, 419–44. Munera 35. Bari, Italy: Edipuglia, 2012.

Wilken, R. L. *John Chrysostom and the Jews: Rhetoric and Reality in the Late Fourth Century.* Berkeley: University of California Press, 1983.

Wilkinson, J. *Egeria's Travels: Newly Translated, with Supporting Documents and Notes.* 3rd ed. Warminster: Aris and Phillips, 1999.

Wilkinson, K. W. "Palladas and the Age of Constantine," *JRS* 99 (2009): 36–60.

―――. "Palladas and the Foundation of Constantinople," *JRS* 100 (2010): 179–94.

Williams, J. H. C. "Septimius Severus and Sol, Carausius and Oceanus: Two New Roman Acquisitions at the British Museum," *NC* 159 (1999): 307–13.

Williams, R. *Arius: Heresy and Tradition.* Grand Rapids, MI: W. B. Eerdmans, 2002.

Wipszycka, E. "La sovvenzione Costantiniana in favore del clero," *RAL*, ser. 9, vol. 8 (1997): 483–88.

Woods, D. "Sopater of Apamea: A Convert at the Court of Constantine?" *Studia Patristica* 39 (2006): 139–43.

―――. "Postumus and the Three Suns: Neglected Numismatic Evidence for a Solar Halo," *NC* 172 (2012): 85–92 and pl. 6.

Woolf, G. "Monumental Writing and the Expansion of Roman Society in the Early Empire," *JRS* 86 (1996): 22–39.

Wright, D. "The True Face of Constantine," *DOP* 41 (1987): 493–507.

Yasin, A. M. *Saints and Church Spaces in the Late Antique Mediterranean: Architecture, Cult, and Community.* Cambridge: Cambridge University Press, 2009.

Zecchini, G. "Costantino Episcopus Paganorum?" In *Costantino prima e dopo Costantino – Constantine Before and After Constantine*, ed. G. Bonamente, N. Lenski, and R. Lizzi Testa, 145–51. Munera 35. Bari, Italy: Edipuglia, 2012.

Ziegler, R. "Antiochia, Laodicea und Sidon in der Politik der Severer," *Chiron* 8 (1978): 493–514.

Zuckerman, C. "Sur la Liste de Vérone et la province de Grande Arménie, la division de l'empire et la date de création des diocèses." In *Mélanges Gilbert Dagron*, ed. V. Déroche, 617–37. T&M 14. Paris: Association des amis du Centre d'histoire et civilisation de Byzance, 2002.

INDEX

ACKNOWLEDGMENTS

This book came into being as a series of essays formulated to grapple with the problem of the interactions between Constantine and his subjects. I first embarked on the topic after delivering a lecture under the title "Constantine and the Cities" at the conference hosted by Guy Halsall at York University on the occasion of the 1,700th anniversary of Constantine's accession to power in 2006. A revised version was later offered at Princeton at a conference organized by Helmut Reimitz and Jamie Kreiner in honor of Peter Brown. I thank the organizers of both events for providing me with both an impetus and a venue to explore this subject.

Constantine and the Cities grew up alongside a series of other research projects with which it has had to vie for my attention. These include a book on late Roman slavery and another, directly related to this study, *Constantine's Capitals*. The latter, nearly complete, should serve as a pendant to this study, examining as it does the abundant evidence for Rome and Constantinople as subjects to and influences on Constantine. All three projects benefited greatly from a series of fellowships I received in 2009 from the John Simon Guggenheim Foundation, the American Council of Learned Societies, and Dumbarton Oaks. I am deeply grateful to all three institutions for the support they have provided me. Without it I could never have completed this work, much of which has been sandwiched between two terms as department chair. I am also grateful to the University of Colorado, Boulder, for supporting a sabbatical, taken in conjunction with these fellowships, that freed me from teaching and service obligations long enough to write. Colorado's Graduate Committee on the Arts and Humanities also provided me with funding to travel in central Italy and Rome collecting photographs and data for my research and its Arts and Sciences Fund for the Humanities offered funding to pay for photographs and permissions.

My thoughts on Constantine have developed in communication with fellow scholars and students, all of whom have taught me much. Among the many researchers who discussed the topic with me and shared their own work, I should like to single out with particular gratitude the late Enzo Aiello, Giorgio Bonamente, Peter Brown, Andrew Cain, Giovanni Cecconi, Simon Corcoran, Sible De Blaauw, Hal Drake, Jan Willem Drijvers, Rita Lizzi Testa, Alessandro Maranesi, Ralph

Mathisen, Dirk Rohmann, Irfan Shahid, Ignazio Tantillo, Martin Wallraff, Ed Watts, John Weisweiler, Johannes Wienand, Kevin Wilkinson, and Giuseppe Zecchini. Klaus-Martin Girardet has been especially generous with advice and materials, all of the highest quality. Equally important are my students present and past, whose own ideas and questions have presented me with both inspiration and insight. Special thanks in this group are due to Amy Coles, Aaron Johnson, Richard Payne, and above all Andrew Clay, whose valuable efforts as research assistant and editor played a major role in the completion of this book. Cristiana Sogno deserves special thanks for having painstakingly edited a version of the first section in her native language, at a point when I was considering publishing that material as an article. I thank Clifford Ando both for inviting me to submit to his Empire and After series and for offering a careful reading of my manuscript. So too I thank the readers for the University of Pennsylvania Press, Michael Kulikowski and David Potter, who indulgingly revealed their identities to me. Their comments and advice spared me several errors and helped me rethink the final structure of the monograph. Also worthy of thanks are my editors, Jerry Singerman, Noreen O'Connor-Abel, and Joyce Ippolito, whose patience with an overburdened author has been tempered with just the right amount of pressure.

More than anyone I must thank my family. My wife, and colleague, Alison Orlebeke, provided me with the initial inspiration for this book and much advice on its composition. My children, Paul, Helen, and Chloe, have demonstrated exemplary patience with both me and Constantine over the past decade. Paul, a young man of great intelligence and potential, deserves special thanks for drawing all of the digital maps and some of the graphics for this book. I have learned much from all of them and been leavened by their love and support.